DOCUMENTS ON
INTERNATIONAL AFFAIRS
1952

DOCUMENTS ON INTERNATIONAL AFFAIRS

1952

SELECTED AND EDITED
BY
DENISE FOLLIOT

Issued under the auspices of the
Royal Institute of International Affairs

OXFORD UNIVERSITY PRESS

LONDON   NEW YORK   TORONTO

1955

Oxford University Press, Amen House, London E.C. 4

GLASGOW NEW YORK TORONTO MELBOURNE WELLINGTON
BOMBAY CALCUTTA MADRAS KARACHI CAPE TOWN IBADAN

Geoffrey Cumberlege, Publisher to the University

———

PRINTED IN GREAT BRITAIN

CONTENTS

I. THE WESTERN ALLIANCE

1. Nato and Mutual Security

II. GERMANY AND THE EUROPEAN DEFENCE COMMUNITY

CONTENTS

III. THE U.S.S.R.

A. STATE AND PARTY

B. THE MOSCOW ECONOMIC CONFERENCE

B. ISRAEL

C. PERSIA

1. AMERICAN AID

2. PERSIAN OIL

V. THE FAR EAST

A. KOREAN NEGOTIATIONS

ABBREVIATIONS

Documents (R.I.I.A.) for 1951	Royal Institute of International Affairs: *Documents on Foreign Affairs 1951* (London, Oxford University Press for R.I.I.A., 1954)
E.D.C.	European Defence Community
G.A.T.T.	General Agreement on Tariffs and Trade
G.D.R.	German Democratic Republic
NATO	North Atlantic Treaty Organization
O.E.E.C.	Organization for European Economic Co-operation
O.N.U.	Organisation des Nations Unies
O.T.A.N.	Organisation du Traité de l'Atlantique Nord
R.I.D.A.	Rural and Industrial Development Authority
SHAPE	Supreme Headquarters of the Allied Powers in Europe
T.C.C.	Temporary Council Committee of North Atlantic Council

NOTE

British Parliamentary Debates (Hansard) are cited in the form suggested in the bound volumes of the Official Reports, preceded by the date (if not given above in the text) and followed by the column number, e.g.

(for the House of Commons)

12 February 1951, H.C. Deb. 5th ser. vol. 484, coll. 42–51;

(for the House of Lords)

8 March 1950, H.L. Deb. 5th ser. vol. 166, coll. 142–3.

Symbols of United Nations documents are composed of capital letters combined with figures, e.g. A/1938. Mention of such a symbol indicates a reference to a United Nations document. Unless otherwise stated references to United Nations Debates and supplements are always to the Official Records.

Authorization has been obtained for all excerpts quoted or translated from unofficial sources, and full reference to the book, the author, editor or translator, and the publisher has been given in a footnote in each case under the first mention of the work.

Where not taken from printed sources the translations have been made by members of the staff of Chatham House.

PART I

THE WESTERN ALLIANCE

1. NATO and Mutual Security

(i) COMMUNIQUÉ ON THE AGREEMENT REACHED BETWEEN PRESIDENT TRUMAN AND THE BRITISH PRIME MINISTER, MR. WINSTON CHURCHILL, ON THE APPOINTMENT OF A SUPREME COMMANDER FOR THE ATLANTIC, WASHINGTON, 18 JANUARY 1952[1]

The President and the Prime Minister with their advisers have had several discussions relating to the arrangements about the Atlantic Command recommended by NATO and accepted by the late Government of the United Kingdom. As a result of their discussions they agreed that His Majesty's Government and the United States Government would recommend to NATO certain alterations in the arrangements designed to extend the United Kingdom home command to the 100 fathom line. They also agreed on the desirability of certain changes which would provide greater flexibility for the control of operations in the Eastern Atlantic. These changes however do not go the full way to meet the Prime Minister's objections to the original arrangements. Nevertheless the Prime Minister, while not withdrawing his objections, expressed readiness to allow the appointment of a Supreme Commander to go forward in order that a command structure may be created and enabled to proceed with the necessary planning in the Atlantic area. He reserved the right to bring forward modifications for the consideration of NATO, if he so desired, at a later stage.

(ii) OFFICIAL SUMMARY OF THE TEMPORARY COUNCIL COMMITTEE'S REPORT TO THE NORTH ATLANTIC COUNCIL ON THE BUILDING UP OF DEFENCE FORCES IN THE NORTH ATLANTIC TREATY AREA, 24 FEBRUARY 1952[2]

1. The North Atlantic Council yesterday adopted the plan of action of its Temporary Council Committee. The approval of the Council resolution on the Temporary Council Committee report brought to a successful conclusion the work of the Temporary Council Committee, established by the Council at its meeting at Ottawa on September 19, 1951.[3]

---

[1] U.S.A.: *Department of State Bulletin* (Washington, U.S.G.P.O.), 28 January 1952, p. 116. For the Anglo-American conversations see further below, pp. 39 seqq.

[2] *Department of State Bulletin*, 10 March 1952, pp. 368–70.

[3] *Documents* (R.I.I.A.) for 1951, pp. 58–60.

2. By its resolution on the TCC report, the North Atlantic Council agreed on specific policies and plans for building NATO defensive strength during the present year. NATO nations agreed to provide approximately 50 divisions in appropriate conditions of combat readiness and 4,000 operational aircraft in Western Europe as well as strong naval forces. It further provided a definite program for taking measures this year necessary to increase the defensive power of NATO in following years. This defensive force does not include the contributions of Greece and Turkey.

There was general agreement that this increase in defensive power will constitute an important increased deterrent against aggression. While not covered specifically by the Council action at Lisbon, it was recognized that Allied strategic air power is already a powerful deterrent to aggression and in the event of attack would be a most valuable addition to the defense of Western Europe.

3. The primary task of the TCC was to develop a plan of action reconciling the issues arising from the requirements of a militarily acceptable defense plan and the politico-economic capabilities of the member countries. Through the work of a screening and costing staff under the direction of General McNarney, it considered ways and means of building balanced effective defensive forces at minimum cost. At the same time it made a careful appraisal of the politico-economic capabilities of each NATO country and of the economic problems which will have to be dealt with in order to develop those capabilities.

4. The Council resolution, derived from the TCC report, lays the emphasis on defense which is prompt, effective and practicable. This requires (a) action for the earliest build-up of balanced collective forces, (b) policies designed to maintain and strengthen the economic and social structure of each country and (c) appropriate organizational arrangements.

(1) The threat which the member countries of NATO now face clearly requires that they promptly build up their effective forces. The various elements of this build-up should be kept in balance so as to make possible at all times the maximum combat-ready forces as an effective deterrent against aggression.

(A) The Council resolution stated measures essential to the achievement of the planned build-up of NATO defensive strength in this and following years. These measures emphasized:

    (1) Economy in the use of resources for defense,

    (2) The elimination of less essential defense activities,

    (3) Adoption of detailed measures developed by TCC for improving the combat efficiency of national forces,

    (4) A further development of NATO-wide equipment supply planning,

(5) Initiation of a system of NATO priority recommendations to assist in the allocation of equipment by nations,

(6) An increased efficiency through improved organizational arrangements.

On these and other points, specific recommendations have been agreed to by NATO governments, and instructions for action given with provisions for NATO follow-up.

(B) The directives defining the duties and responsibilities of General Eisenhower and of the military committee's standing group have been revised to reflect added responsibilities.

(C) The TCC plan of action included the assumption that Germany will in subsequent years contribute forces through the European Defense Community to the defense of Europe.

(2) Adequate defensive strength can be created and maintained only if the economic and social foundation in each country remains sound and healthy. The Council made a number of recommendations for strengthening the economies of the participating countries, involving national and cooperative action. The Council recommended that all NATO governments should take all practicable measures

(A) To encourage general economic expansion;

(B) To increase production of scarce raw materials and to control their use as necessary to conserve supplies and insure defense requirements are met;

(C) To prevent inflation by adoption of necessary sound fiscal, financial, and monetary policies;

(D) To facilitate labor mobility among NATO countries and to alleviate manpower shortages in defense industries;

(E) To adopt measures to improve the equitable distribution of the internal burden of defense in the NATO countries;

(F) To maintain essential imports through a satisfactory solution of balance of payments problems, in particular by increasing the dollar earnings of European countries.

(3) NATO activities are shifting in emphasis from the planning to the operational stage. The machinery and methods of operation of NATO must be adjusted to this new situation. In particular, the TCC recommended methods to develop and keep up to date a NATO-wide defense program which is balanced, feasible and economical. On this basis, there is a need for continual planning and follow-up by NATO agencies, based on annual reviews of the TCC type, by the permanent NATO, to provide a firm program for the immediately ensuing year and provisional guidance for longer-term actions.

The Council recognized the existence of a number of military, economic and political problems which the member countries face in implementing fully its recommended program for 1952. The Council agreed that urgent and sustained action on these problems is of vital importance to the achievement of NATO security objectives, and urged that the governments and the NATO agencies undertake without delay the specific actions required.

The Council resolution recognizes that the risk of aggression will continue. It also recognizes that there is a great urgency for increased defensive power in the North Atlantic Treaty area on a truly operational basis, and that governments individually and collectively should devote their best efforts to this end.

5. The Council invited the Governments of Greece and Turkey to consider with appropriate NATO bodies the applicability of the findings and recommendations of the TCC to Greece and Turkey. It opened the way for the participation of Greece and Turkey on a full and equal basis in the annual review to be undertaken beginning next summer.

(iii) COMMUNIQUÉ AND DECLARATION OF AIMS ISSUED AFTER THE NINTH SESSION OF THE NORTH ATLANTIC COUNCIL, LISBON, 25 FEBRUARY 1952[1]

The ninth session of the North Atlantic Council was held in Lisbon from February 20 to February 25, 1952, under the chairmanship of the Honorable Lester B. Pearson, Canadian Secretary of State for External Affairs.

On February 18, the kingdom of Greece and the republic of Turkey acceded to the treaty, and representatives of their respective Governments attended throughout the session. In all, thirty-five Ministers of fourteen countries took part in the discussions of the council.

(2) The Council made further progress in dealing with current and long-range problems of the Atlantic community. The decisions taken and the agreements reached by the Council are the practical result of projects initiated at earlier sessions and reflect the continuing work of the treaty agencies. They represent the united efforts of member Governments to safeguard the peace, stability and well-being of the North Atlantic community through the strengthening of their collective defense.

(3) The Council took note of a report of the Paris conference on the European Defense Community and a report by the occupying powers on the proposed contractual arrangements with the German Federal Republic.[2] The Council found that the principles underlying the treaty to establish the European Defense Community conformed to the interests of the parties to the North Atlantic Treaty. It also agreed on the principles which should govern the relationship between the proposed community and the North Atlantic Treaty Organization. The North Atlantic Council agreed to propose to its members and to the European Defense Community

---

[1] *Department of State Bulletin*, 10 March 1952, pp. 367–8.
[2] See below, pp. 68 seqq.

reciprocal security undertakings between the members of the two organizations. Such undertakings would require ratification in accordance with the constitutional process of the states involved. All these decisions are inspired by the conviction that the North Atlantic Treaty Organization and the European Defense Community have a common objective, to strengthen the defense of the Atlantic area, and that the development of the European Defense Community should be carried forward in this spirit. Therefore, the Council considered that the obligations and relationships between the communities should be based on the concept of two closely related organizations, one working, so far as this objective is concerned, within the framework of, and reinforcing the other.

(4) The Council took detailed and comprehensive action based on the recommendations of the Temporary Council Committee. The decisions taken by the Council provided for the earliest building-up of balanced collective forces to meet the requirements of external security within the capabilities of member countries. Agreement was reached on the specific defensive strength to be built this year, and on a definite program of measures to be taken this year to increase defensive strength in following years. A number of important steps were agreed to be taken by the treaty organization and by member governments to accomplish this building-up with a more efficient use of resources. Policies designed to maintain and strengthen the economies and social stability of member countries were agreed and recommended to governments.

(5) Agreement was reached on the financing of a further portion of the infrastructure program, for airfields, communications and headquarters.

(6) The terms of reference of the Standing Group and of the Supreme Commander, Allied Powers in Europe, were revised to reflect added responsibilities, notably for equipment priorities and planning for the logistical support of the military forces.

The Council agreed that the ground and air forces of Greece and Turkey assigned to NATO will operate under the over-all command of SACEUR [Supreme Allied Commander Europe] through Commander in Chief, Southern Europe. The naval forces of Greece and Turkey will remain for the present under their national Chiefs of Staff, operating in close coordination with all other naval forces in the Mediterranean. The Standing Group was directed to continue its study of command of naval forces in the Mediterranean area and their coordination with land and air forces and to submit a definitive report to the Council at its next meeting.

(7) The Council also took action to adapt the Treaty Organization to the needs arising from the development of its activities from the planning to the operational stage. The North Atlantic Council, while continuing to hold periodic ministerial meetings, will henceforth function in permanent

session through the appointment of permanent representatives. The Council decided to appoint a Secretary General, who will head a unified international secretariat designed to assist the Council in the fulfilment of the increasing responsibilities. All civilian activities of the organization will be concentrated in the geographical area where are situated other international agencies whose work is closely related to that of the Treaty Organization and with which close administrative connection is essential to efficiency. These are presently situated in the vicinity of Paris. When these changes become effective, the Council will assume the functions hitherto performed by the Council Deputies, the Defense Production Board, and the Financial and Economic Board.

(8) The Council adopted a report of the Atlantic Community Committee, established at its Ottawa meeting. This report emphasized the importance of economic cooperation, the expansion and liberalization of trade, and the possibility of working out closer cooperative arrangements with other bodies, particularly the OEEC [Organization for European Economic Cooperation]. In approving the analysis of the problem of the movement of labor between member countries in the report of the Atlantic Community Committee, the Council acknowledged the importance of this problem and endorsed the resolution of the Temporary Council Committee on this subject. It was agreed that the permanent North Atlantic Treaty Organization should keep this problem under continuous review, and make recommendations for the elimination, by the most effective utilization of manpower resources, of general or specific manpower shortages which hinder defense production. As cooperation in the field covered by the five-power Atlantic Community Committee is of direct and common concern to each member of the Council, it was decided that the future work in this sphere should be transferred to the Council.

(9) The Council issued a declaration reaffirming the aims of the North Atlantic Treaty Organization as the promotion of peace through defensive strength and enduring progress.

The Declaration of Aims

In the course of their discussions in Lisbon the members of the North Atlantic Council reviewed the aims of their association.

They wish once more to emphasize that this association was forged as a shield against aggression. Its first aim is peace, and the armed strength which is being built up by the united efforts of the member nations will be used only for the defense of their countries and the security of their peoples.

The plan for the build-up of defense forces for the North Atlantic Treaty area laid down by the TCC has been adopted at the present session of the Council in the belief that defensive strength will prove the best deterrent to aggression.

The Council has learned with approval of the main provisions of the plan worked out between five of its members (France, Italy, Belgium, the Netherlands, Luxembourg) and the German Federal Republic for a European Defense Community.

The establishment of this community will help to promote the closer association of the Western European countries and to strengthen the defense of the North Atlantic area.

The North Atlantic Treaty Organization, respecting the principles on which the community is founded, will support and cooperate with its institutions.

The arrangements to govern the relationships between the two organizations which have been approved at Lisbon will insure that in pursuit of the common objective, the defense of the North Atlantic Treaty area, the E.D.C. will reinforce and work within the framework of NATO.

The partnership between the nations of the North Atlantic Treaty is not for defense alone but of enduring progress. The members of the Council look forward to the time when the main energies of their association can be less concentrated on defense and more fully devoted to cooperation in other fields, for the well-being of their peoples and for the advancement of human progress.

Then, as now, the North Atlantic Treaty Organization will have to play its part, and to this end it has been agreed in Lisbon to strengthen its structure so that it may become a still more effective association of like-minded nations determined to maintain in peace the unity of purpose and effort achieved in the face of present dangers, and to express itself by continuous collaboration on common problems.

The understanding and sense of fellowship which the members wish to see develop between their countries cannot be achieved by governmental action alone. All citizens can play their part in the work of uniting the peoples in one Atlantic community which will afford, in ever increasing measure, the benefits of peace, freedom and prosperity.

(iv) EXTRACTS FROM PRESIDENT TRUMAN'S RECOMMENDATIONS TO CONGRESS FOR THE MUTUAL SECURITY PROGRAMME, 6 MARCH 1952[1]

I recommend that the Congress authorize the continuance of the Mutual Security Program for the fiscal year ending June 30, 1953. Such action is essential to advance our program for world peace and to protect the security of the United States.

The Mutual Security Program provides equipment, supplies, and tech-

[1] *Department of State Bulletin*, 17 March 1952, pp. 403–11.

nical cooperation to enable friendly countries to carry out military and economic programs that will bring very great returns in increasing their security and our own. In such case, the countries concerned are driving to accomplish objectives which will bring closer to full realization our mutual goals of freedom and peace under the great principles of the Charter of the United Nations. Without some resources from us to add to their own, these objectives cannot be accomplished.

My support for this program rests on four propositions:

First, the plain fact is that we cannot achieve lasting security for ourselves except in association with other nations.

Second, the funds provided by the United States under the Mutual Security Program are essential to the success of the common efforts we are making with other free nations for peace.

Third, the funds thus invested by the United States will yield far larger returns, in terms of our own security, than if the same amount were used for our own defense establishment.

Fourth, the cost of the Mutual Security Program, together with the much larger costs of our military services and other defense measures, are well within our economic capacity.

I do not need to review here the tragic circumstances which have compelled this Nation to undertake massive programs for national defense and for mutual security. Most of us fully understand today the grimness of the threat which Soviet aggression carries for the survival of civilization.

Neither do I need to dwell upon the fact that all our military preparations are defensive preparations. We are seeking to create strength in the world sufficient to prevent aggression. We do not contemplate expenditures in the magnitude or of the character necessary to launch aggression. These facts underline the statement which cannot be too often repeated: Our objective is peace, not war.

The point I do want to emphasize, for there still appear to be some people who do not recognize it, is that to achieve peace we must work together with other nations.

Some people would have us withdraw to our own shores and gamble our national safety on air and naval power. A glance at some of the vital materials that go into air and naval power illustrates how self-defeating this would be. Four-fifths or more of the manganese, the tin, and the chrome in a United States destroyer or jet fighter comes from outside the western hemisphere. Should we turn our back on the rest of the world, these and other precious resources, so vital to our own security, would not only be lost to us, but in all probability would be added to the military strength of the Soviet empire.

Without our friends abroad, the threat of aggression would move close to our own shores. Without their armed forces, the bases on their soil, and the raw materials from their mines and forests, our military power would be gravely hampered in its defense of the United States, and our whole economy would be seriously weakened. Our support and assistance for other nations, therefore, are not in the nature of charity. These are not hand-outs which we can carelessly offer or withdraw without regard to the effect on our own safety. The problems of American survival would be multiplied to an incalculable extent if we had to face the Soviet threat without the support and assistance of other nations.

The Mutual Security Program is justified not only by these hard strategic and military realities. It is, in addition, the only course which fulfils our position as a world leader in the battle for freedom and the rights of man. That is the reason so many nations freely join with us in a common faith in democracy and a common desire for peace. These nations are our friends, and not our satellites. As friends, they contribute to the shared wisdom and faith of the free world—a wisdom and faith on which no single nation can claim a monopoly. We must accordingly take care to treat them as friends. We must not act as though we wished to degrade them to the rank of satellites by exacting a rigid and humiliating subservience which no free nation could with dignity accept. We will never be defeated as long as we truly stand for a free partnership of free peoples. The unconquerable power of the free world lies in the fact that loyalties are not concerned.

The concrete requirements of American security compel us to a policy of international cooperation. But it would be, I believe, a misrepresentation of the American people to suppose that self-interest—even wise and enlightened self-interest—is the only cause for our concern with the outside world. As a nation, we have been dedicated through our history to the belief that responsible men deserve a democratic government and a free society. This belief is the essence of our way of life. We would betray our innermost convictions if today we were to flee the cause of the free peoples. If through inaction we desert the cause of democracy, the democratic hope may be exterminated in broad areas of this earth. If we rise to our historic traditions, we can add powerful momentum to the democratic counter-offensive which inspires in the people of the world a sense of their own destiny as free men—and which will in the end burst the bonds of tyranny everywhere on earth.

The pursuit of mutual security through mutual strength is thus the keystone of the broad foreign policy which the United States and other free nations have adopted as the surest road to lasting peace.

The American people have steadfastly supported this foreign policy since the Second World War. Its pattern today is sharp and clear. If I were to make a brief definition of our policy, I would call it the policy of peace through collective strength. We are joined with other countries in the patient and systematic building in the free world of enough military strength to deter external Communist aggression, and of economic and political and moral strength to remove internal threats of Communist subversion and point the way toward democratic progress.

I wish to emphasize very strongly that all these forms of strength are necessary if we are to achieve freedom and peace. The plain and inescapable fact is that they are indivisible. Neither military strength nor economic strength nor political strength nor moral strength can do the job alone.

Military strength is the first necessity, for without a shield against aggression the free world would be helpless before the enemy. Military strength must be built, and we must help build it, in Europe and in other critical areas of the world. But military strength is not just a matter of delivering arms to our allies. It is also a matter of defense support to enable our allies to do more to expand and equip their own defense forces.

And even arms and defense support together do not provide a full answer to the Soviet threat; to believe that they do is dangerously to misunderstand the nature of the foe. The gun is but one weapon in the Soviet arsenal of aggression. If we ignored the necessity for building moral and political and economic strength, we would expose ourselves to the danger of Communist gains which could be at least as damaging as outright aggression. Since the Soviet Union does not rely exclusively on military attack, we would be foolish indeed to rely exclusively on military defense.

The funds required under the Mutual Security Program fall into two broad categories.

The first of these, which is by far the larger, is for assistance in building up the military strength of friendly nations. This aid is of two types: (1) direct military aid, primarily in the form of military equipment and components thereof, and (2) defense support—primarily in the form of raw materials, commodities, and machinery—to enable other countries to sustain and increase their military efforts where that type of support produces greater returns in military strength than would an equal amount of direct military aid. The bulk of the direct military aid and of the defense support will go to strengthen the defenses of the free nations in Europe. Amounts for direct military aid and defense support make up about 90 percent of the total funds recommended for the Mutual Security Program for the fiscal year 1953.

The second broad category is for economic and technical assistance, primarily for the underdeveloped areas of the world, where economic progress is the first essential in the battle for freedom. Some of these funds will in fact also support defense efforts in certain countries in Southeast Asia, where Communist aggression is an immediate menace. Amounts recommended for economic and technical assistance are about 10 percent of the total.

The distribution of the amounts recommended is shown in more detail in the following table:

Mutual Security Program, 1953
(In millions)

	Direct military	Defense support	Economic and technical	Admin- istration	Area totals
Europe	4,070	1,819[1]	..	..	5,889
Near East and Africa . .	606	..	196	..	802
Asia and the Pacific . .	611	..	408[2]	..	1,019
American Republics . .	62	..	22	..	84
Multilateral Technical Assistance, Migration, and Relief Package Freight	..	..	30	..	30
Administration . . .	..	..	..	75	75
Total	5,350[3]	1,819	656	75	7,900[3]

[1] Includes economic assistance for Austria.
[2] Includes assistance to support military efforts in Southeast Asia and the Pacific.
[3] Columns do not add to totals because of rounding.

EUROPE

Today, the problem of achieving security and strength in free Europe, in my judgment, is on the way to solution. The last 5 years have recorded remarkable gains as a result of actions we have taken under our policy of peace through collective strength—first in Greece and Turkey; then, in 1948, through the European Recovery Program, and since 1949 through the growing defensive power of the North Atlantic Treaty Organization. The American contribution did not of itself create these gains; but it did supply the essential margin without which the Europeans could not have fought their way out of their post-war slough of despond.

Five years ago, many European nations were on the verge of economic or political collapse. A divided and despairing continent—next to our own, the most productive and industrially powerful in the world—lay open for Soviet conquest.

How different the picture is today. Europe has made immense advances—in economic output, in military strength, in political self-confidence, in progress toward unity. Today, the Soviet Union knows that it cannot achieve its purposes in Europe, so long as the policy of collective strength continues.

Europe still has far to go. Economic health and vitality in Europe require a series of specific actions—varying from country to country—

to raise industrial and agricultural productivity, to knock down trade barriers and exchange restrictions, and to encourage the vigorous forces of competition in European and world markets. They require further progress toward the democratic goals of a fair distribution of income, strong and free trade unions, fair and effective tax systems, and programs of land reform.

Above all, we in the United States do not believe that Western Europe can achieve its full strength without accelerated progress toward unity. Only this unity can release the great potential energy of free Europe. We will continue in every way we can to encourage its attainment.

The difficulties are very great. It is only candid to report that progress in this direction has not always been as fast as we hoped. Yet, in many respects the progress has been most impressive. . . .

In the coming fiscal year, European military expenditures will be considerably more than twice as large as they were in the year preceding the Communist aggression in Korea. Production of military matériel in Western Europe has multiplied about four times in that period. The European nations have lengthened the training periods under their compulsory military service programs and have substantially enlarged and improved their armed forces. The pace of the military build-ups has given many millions of Europeans new confidence in their capacity to resist aggression.

This is an impressive record of progress. Of course, the record is far from perfect—especially in view of the urgency of the threat posed by aggressive Soviet imperialism. We can find many specific weaknesses and shortcomings to criticize—and some people in our country fasten their attention so exclusively on such things as to advocate that the defense of Europe be abandoned. I do not wish to minimize the shortcomings, but the fundamental question to ask is: 'Are we moving at a substantial rate in the right direction? Is real progress being made?' The answer is obvious. So is the conclusion to be drawn. The record abundantly warrants confidence in our European allies, and our continued steadfast support for them.

Two weeks ago, at Lisbon, the member nations took the most far reaching strides in European defense since the adoption of the North Atlantic Treaty itself in 1949. The North Atlantic Council at Lisbon endorsed the specific means through which the forces of the European Defense Community—including German contingents—will be organized and tied into General Eisenhower's command. After months of planning by the special committee under the chairmanship of Mr. Harriman, the Council made specific and concrete decisions providing for the more rapid build-up of forces and for the provision of the necessary equipment and construction to support them.

By the end of this calendar year, General Eisenhower's command is expected to have at its disposal a formidable force—including some 50 army divisions, about half of them on active duty, and some 4,000 military planes—and a sound base for further build-up in 1953 and 1954. These forces, joined by those of Greece and Turkey, will bring within measurable distance the time when even the most foolhardy man in the Kremlin will not dare risk open attack.

In order to equip the forces being raised by our allies under the Lisbon agreements, we as well as they must step up our efforts. There have been delays in our own production and delivery of arms. And combat requirements for Korea have, of course, received top priority for deliveries from our current output. I am assured that production is now being accelerated substantially, and I have consequently directed that deliveries to the North Atlantic Treaty defense forces be greatly speeded up.

The rearmament effort has also created problems in Europe. The European economy, after its extraordinary comeback in the years of the European Recovery Program, has now been subjected to new and severe pressures. The Marshall Plan was designed to help restore minimum economic health, not to produce a surplus capable of creating military forces adequate for European defense. Today, not only has rearmament imposed a heavy direct burden, but the global consequences of rearmament—including rises in the prices both of raw materials generally and of finished goods from the United States—have drastically upset the European balance of payments. Substantial and sustained efforts will be necessary to meet these problems, even with our help.

However, the European countries have a sizable capacity to increase their armed forces, to construct military bases and facilities, and to produce military equipment and supplies—if we provide the crucial margin of raw materials and other support for their defense efforts. If we provide this margin of resources, the European countries will be able to produce far more military equipment than they otherwise could, and to maintain far larger armed forces than would otherwise be possible. Our defense support will allow them to use plants, machinery, materials, and manpower which exist in Europe, but which otherwise could not be devoted to defense purposes. For this reason, our defense support is an extremely economical way to achieve military strength for our mutual security. The funds included in the Mutual Security Program for defense support will yield, according to the best estimates, more than twice as much military strength in Europe as would the same funds spent for the direct transfer of military equipment from the United States.

Accordingly, the Mutual Security Program for Europe is planned so that the United States will provide both weapons and defense support. The form of assistance—whether military equipment or assistance in financing imports of raw materials and other items where required to make possible the necessary level of European defense efforts—has been decided in each case on the basis of which form produces the most results in defensive strength at the least cost.

In addition to the funds for the North Atlantic Treaty countries and Western Germany, limited amounts are included in the Mutual Security Program for Yugoslavia, whose defiance of the Soviet Union is giving heart to untold millions behind the Iron Curtain; for Austria, where continued economic assistance is necessary to maintain economic stability in the face of occupation of part of the country by Soviet forces; and for facilitating emigration from Europe under international arrangements. We expect soon to complete arrangements with Spain which will assist in the defense of the Mediterranean area; our part in these arrangements will be carried forward with funds already made available by the Congress. . . .

The Near East and Africa

The Near East presents a sharp challenge to American statesmanship. The countries of these areas are of vital importance to the security of the free world, but the problems of achieving constructive and orderly development are extremely difficult.

Living standards are generally very low. Transportation and land tenure systems are often archaic. Political and religious controversies simmer throughout the region. Nationalism is sometimes misdirected into fanatical outbursts which ignore the benefits to be gained from international cooperation. The Communists are doing their best to stir up confusion and trouble.

Most of these problems can only be solved by the people of these countries finding ways to make solid progress in developing economic strength and effective free institutions. But we can and must help them.

We can help dig wells for irrigation and clean water in Iran and Iraq. We can help set up farm credit institutions and agricultural extension services in Lebanon and Liberia. We can help build roads and establish public health services in Israel. We can help build up school and hospital services in countries throughout the area. For projects of this type, I recommend economic and technical assistance in this area (including help for the Arab refugees) of 196 million dollars.

Military assistance for nations in this area is recommended in the amount of 606 million dollars. Most of these funds are for Greece and Turkey, whose military assistance programs are carried under the heading of the Near East; defense support funds for those countries are included with those for Europe.

To help in maintaining security in the Near East, the United States has joined with Turkey, France, Great Britain, and three Commonwealth countries in proposing the establishment of a Middle East Command.[1] We hope this Command will become the center of cooperative efforts by all countries concerned for the defense of the region as a whole from outside aggression.

Asia and the Pacific

Much of Asia at this moment is under Communist attack. The free nations are holding the line against aggression in Korea and Indochina, and are battling Communist-inspired disorders in Burma, Malaya, and the Philippines. The loss of any of these countries would mean the loss of freedom for millions of people, the loss of vital raw materials, the loss of points of critical strategic importance to the free world.

The Mutual Security Program for this area includes military assistance in the amount of 611 million dollars, and economic and technical assistance of 408 million dollars, some of which will contribute directly to the defense programs of certain countries of Southeast Asia.

Of our military assistance, a large part will go to Indochina where the troops of the French Union and of the Associated States are battling valiantly against the Communist-led forces, and another large part will go to continue to help prepare the Chinese armies on Formosa to resist Communist aggression. The rest will go to the Philippines and Thailand, to help build forces strong enough to insure internal security.

As in the Near East and Africa, however, security in Asia is far more than a military problem. Our military assistance is essential to check the encroachments of Communist imperialism. But the long-run promise of stability and progress lies, not alone in arms, but in the provision of sufficient economic and technical support to enable the peoples of Asia to conquer their old, deep-seated and agonizing economic problems and to share in the benefits of an expanding world economy.

In India, for example, the key to economic progress lies in boosting food production. This is the only way to remove the constant threat of famine and ease the desperate struggle for a daily livelihood. It is the only way of freeing funds now spent to import food, so they can be used instead for productive investment in developing natural resources, transportation, and industry.

The whole future of India as a free nation may well lie in her ability to raise her food production and do it quickly.

We must support India's own efforts to get this done. The Indian Government has already set in motion a plan under which, in a very few years, she will be able to grow the food needed by her people, and will have established a sound basis for further economic development. It is a good plan, practical and definite. India itself is financing most of it.

[1] *Documents* (R.I.I.A.) for 1951, p. 425.

And we are greatly stepping up our aid for this plan with confidence that the sums we spend will bring concrete results.

This is an example of how our aid can produce large-scale results by supporting the efforts of the people of the Asian countries. In the same way, we are helping to expand irrigation in Pakistan, to eliminate malaria in Thailand, to increase rice yields in Burma.

It is vital that this work be carried forward rapidly. For in this region, there is still time to set in motion programs which will tap the energies of the people and give them solid hope for advancement under governments determined to resist Communist expansion. We must not let this opportunity go by default. Let it never be said of the American people that our eyes are focused only on what might have been—that we grow concerned about the countries of Asia only after they have been lost to the enemy. The bold and wise investment of American funds in this region in the next few years can make a vital difference to the future of freedom.

Special note should be taken of the contribution that the new, free Japan can make to the growth of economic strength in Asia. A growing trade partnership of Japan with Southeast and South Asia can benefit everyone concerned. Such a partnership in free Asia can result in a self-supporting, expanding regional economy, free of permanent dependence on United States economic aid, and free from the danger of satellite slavery under the Soviet orbit. . . .

The major national security programs I am recommending for the fiscal year 1953, including the Mutual Security Program, total about 64 billion dollars. This request raises once again the question whether the American nation can afford so much money for national security. This is a serious question. It requires a serious answer.

Certainly the total security program—of which the Mutual Security Program is a relatively small part—is by any standard a large one. It has resulted in some unavoidable economic dislocations and inflationary pressures. Yet, the burden has been carried with remarkably little strain.

The fundamental reason for this is that our national production has been expanding rapidly, and will continue to rise. Security expenditure, measured in 1951 prices, rose about 18 billion dollars from 1950 to 1951; but the increase in our national output was even larger—totaling about 26 billion dollars. During the next 2 years, we can continue to raise output by not less than 5 percent annually, increasing the gross national product (at 1951 prices) to about 340–345 billion dollars in 1952, and to about 355–360 billion in 1953, compared with 327 billion in 1951 and 301 billion in 1950. If output rises at this rate, we will have increased our total annual production about one-fifth in 3 years. Even with the immense diversion to security purposes, production should be high enough, by the beginning of 1953, to permit total civilian consumption and capital investment at least 50 percent higher than during World War II.

There will certainly be cutbacks in some things. Yet, even if automobile production should drop to around 4 million units this year, it must be remembered that this is only slightly less than the average production of 1948 and 1949. If housing should dip below one million units, it must be remembered that we have succeeded in producing more than one million units per year in only 3 years of our history. And as we expand our output of vital materials such as steel and aluminium, we can again increase the output of such civilian items.

All in all, our present security expenditures are clearly within our economic capacity. And as our basic productive strength continues to increase in the years ahead, we should be able to carry more easily the substantial security costs which may continue to be necessary.

Let us consider for a moment the costs of possible alternatives to our present policy.

The alternative of premeditated and deliberate war is one which no democratic or God-fearing people can for a moment entertain. Even if we were insane enough to consider it, however, it would obviously entail expenditures immensely greater than our present ones, not to speak of the terrible waste and destruction of human life, property, and natural resources.

Another alternative—of contracting our commitments and retreating to the Western Hemisphere—has a momentary seductiveness, because it would seem to relieve us of the contributions we are now making to collective defense. But, in fact, if we followed the policy of retreat, we would have to try to replace the contributions to our security which now come from the cooperation of our allies. We could not replace some of those contributions at any cost; others only at very high cost, not just in money, resources, and military manpower, but in the precious political and economic freedoms we are mobilizing to defend.

The policy of retreat would deprive us of armed forces which, if called upon to fight for the defense of their own countries, would at the same time be fighting for the defense of ours. It would deprive us of essential raw materials. It would impose upon us a much higher level of mobilization than we have today. It would require a stringent and comprehensive system of allocation and rationing in order to husband our smaller resources. It would require us to become a garrison state, and to impose upon ourselves a system of centralized regimentation unlike anything we have ever known.

In the end, when the enemy, encouraged by our retreat, began to organize the rest of the world against us, we would face the prospect of bloody battle—and on our own shores. The ultimate costs of such a policy would be incalculable. Its adoption would be a mandate for national suicide.

I am asking the Congress for 7·9 billion dollars for the Mutual Security Program—an amount which will bring returns no other policy could hope to produce so economically. . . .

I would not counsel the Congress to spend one dollar more than is necessary to support our policy of peace. But there is no economy more false than that which is summed up in the tragic phrase, 'too little and too late'. Such a policy risks the loss of our investment as well as our objective. It would be foolish and dangerous to withhold a dollar now at the risk of expending, not just many times as many dollars, but human lives as well, a few years later.

The question is frequently—and properly—asked: How long are we going to have to continue this type of program? I cannot—no one can— give an answer in terms of a specific month and year. But I can say that one of the central purposes in everything we are doing under the Mutual Security Program is to build strength which will eliminate the need for assistance from the United States.

This is not a program for carrying the rest of the world on our backs. This is a program for getting the other free nations on their own feet, so they can move ahead without special help from us or anyone else.

As the Mutual Security Program moves ahead—as larger military forces become equipped and trained, as economic strength continues to increase —we can expect the costs to the United States to decline. This is not only our own desire; it is also the natural hope and objective of the people of other countries. Free people do not relish dependence on other nations. They wish to achieve as rapidly as possible the economic health and vigor which will enable them to sustain their own programs of defense and economic progress. The Mutual Security Program will hasten the day when this will become possible.

History has thrust a fearful responsibility upon the United States. Today, the survival of freedom and civilization on this earth may depend on the initiative and decisions taken in our own Nation's capital. The free peoples look to us for leadership. Leadership implies more than a recognition of the problem. It implies also a capacity to work out a joint solution with our partners, and to stay with it till the end; it implies resolution and fortitude. We have shown that we understand the threat. But some are doubtful whether we will stay the course until we achieve peace in a free world.

I am not in doubt. I know that we shall succeed. It is perhaps true that our history has been characterized by impatience, by a passion for quick results. It is equally true, however, that it has also been characterized by perseverance and determination—the perseverance of the pioneer, making his steadfast way into the unknown West; the determination of the farmer and worker, transforming a savage wilderness into the strongest and most productive nation known to history. Perseverance and determination, steadfastness and dependability—it was these qualities, and not recklessness or imprudence, which built America. It is our obligation to turn these qualities outward. We must show the world that we can meet any crisis, and that temporary frustration will not drive us to panicky aggression or to ignominious retreat. This is the challenge of free world leadership.

In the last analysis, our leadership must stand or fall on the moral power behind it. No nation, of course, can undertake policies which are not squarely and solidly based on national self-interest. But world leadership in these perilous times calls for policies which, while springing from self-interest, transcend it—policies which serve as a bridge between our own national objectives and the needs and aspirations of other free people.

I deeply believe that the Mutual Security Program is an expression of a new spirit in the world—a spirit based on faith in democracy and human decency, and looking to a new collaboration among nations and peoples. It expresses the deep reality of our friendship for other peoples—the sincerity of our determination to join with them in building a world where freedom, justice, and security will exist for all.

HARRY S. TRUMAN.

THE WHITE HOUSE,
March 6, 1952.

(v) LETTER FROM THE UNITED STATES SECRETARY OF STATE, MR. DEAN ACHESON, TO SENATOR BURNET R. MAYBANK, CHAIRMAN OF THE SENATE BANKING AND CURRENCY COMMITTEE, EXPRESSING THE DEPARTMENT OF STATE'S OPPOSITION TO THE PROPOSED RENEWAL OF SECTION 104 OF THE DEFENSE PRODUCTION ACT OF 1951,[1] 10 MARCH 1952[2]

In view of the fact that your Committee is now considering a bill to extend the Defense Production Act, it occurred to me that it might be useful to review the developments with regard to Section 104 of the Act which have taken place since the fall of 1951, when last the Department had an opportunity to testify on the subject. These developments have a particular bearing on your Committee's consideration of S.2645 as proposed to be amended by Senator Ives, which would extend the terminal date of Section 104 from June 30, 1952, to June 30, 1954.

As you know, the Department of State was concerned from the very

[1] Public Law 96, 82nd Congress. This was the so-called cheese amendment.
[2] *Department of State Bulletin*, 31 March 1952, pp. 517–19.

beginning over the effects which Section 104 was bound to have on the ability of friendly foreign countries to earn the dollars they need to put themselves on a self-supporting basis.   It was foreseen that these restrictions would prevent them from earning considerable sums, running into millions of dollars, and that they would be profoundly discouraged by this particular experience in any further efforts to build up their export industries.   As we saw the problem then, we were simply putting these countries in a position in which they would need even more financial help to carry their share of the defense burden.   We felt also that, in the end, the measures were bound to hurt our own exports of agricultural products as the affected countries acquired fewer dollars with which to buy our products.

We felt even greater concern at the broader implications of these restrictions.   Section 104 requires the United States to take action contrary to the basic provisions of agreements under the Trade Agreements Act to which the United States is a party, and to take action contrary to the objectives of the Mutual Security Act.   Apart from the immediate effects of the particular measure, inconsistencies of this sort tend to undermine the basis on which our position of leadership rests, by raising fundamental doubts in the minds of the other countries of the free world as to our sense of responsibility and the nature of our goals.

The damage which these restrictions have done is aggravated by the fact that the provisions involved embody principles on which the United States has always put great store.   These principles are aimed at developing the kind of trading system among the friendly countries of the world in which businessmen could buy and sell their goods with a minimum of governmental interference in their activities.   This attitude towards quotas and other governmental restrictions on trade is essential if private enterprise is to maintain its place in the conduct of international trade.

It is against that general background that we have appraised the developments in the international field since last summer which have occurred as a result of Section 104.   These developments have convinced me that the Department's original estimate of the effect of Section 104 on other countries, if it erred at all, erred in the direction of understatement.   It is clear now that Canada and Western Europe have been profoundly disturbed by the implications of these restrictions.   It is not so much the immediate dollar loss involved in these restrictions which concerns them, though that is serious enough for some of them.   Much more important is the uncertainty which these measures have created, uncertainty as to the direction in which the United States proposes to move in the field of trade policy.   Our friends in Europe and elsewhere, whether they produce cheese or not, have begun to wonder whether the imposition of these restrictions means that the United States proposes to revert to a policy of raising trade barriers, even though the policy may weaken the collective economic strength of the free world.

This deep concern on the part of Canada and Western Europe has been evident in a number of ways. Last October, at Geneva, nine Contracting Parties of the General Agreement on Tariffs and Trade formally protested against our restrictions under Section 104, charging [that] this Government was acting inconsistently with its trade-agreement undertakings. The countries filing the complaint were the Netherlands, Italy, Denmark, New Zealand, Norway, Australia, France, Canada, and Finland. The filing of a complaint of this sort is not done lightly; it is a fairly important political step on the part of any government. In this case, the Contracting Parties concluded that our action was in fact inconsistent with the General Agreement. They went on to counsel the countries affected to withhold any offsetting actions on their part for the time being until it was clearer what steps the United States Government might take to rectify the situation.

There have been at least two developments since that meeting which are worth noting. The Dutch Government has announced that it is consulting with its partners in the Benelux Union, Belgium and Luxembourg, on increasing its duties against American goods, a step which it may eventually be compelled to take because of the reduction in the amount of dollars it has available to buy dollar goods. Meanwhile, the Italian Government has filed a long and carefully drafted memorandum with the Department describing the cumulative effect of recent United States import measures upon the Italian economy.[1]

I should like to quote two paragraphs from the Italian memorandum, since it sets out succinctly the nature of the concern which other countries have felt as a result of our cheese restrictions.

Finally, there are the political and psychological effects to be considered. These can hardly be overestimated. What is at stake is the vast store of good will and gratitude which exists in Italy and other friendly countries as a result of the generous post-war American aid, and of Marshall Plan aid in particular. For, most segments of Italian public opinion are altogether at a loss to understand how the vast amount of help poured into Italy during the past three years, with the express purpose of restoring the stability of both the domestic and the international economy of the nation, can be reconciled with the recent restrictions that have hit vital sectors of the Italian economy. The very fact that these restrictions are but incidental and almost trivial within the over-all context of U.S. policies, is bound to intensify their adverse impact. This is because they appear to involve the mistaken idea that, while American policies are liberal and indeed generous at their over-all level, they acquire an altogether different connotation as soon as the protection of special interests is concerned.

This implication, no matter how unwarranted, plays directly into the hands of that vocal minority of opinion which is swayed by communist propaganda

[1] For the full text of the memorandum see *Department of State Bulletin*, 28 April 1952, pp. 661–6.

in Europe. As it is known, the communists noisily press their line that the
Marshall Plan and other aid programs are not really meant to bring about the
economic emancipation of Western Europe but to perpetuate their dependence
on American bounty, and that American aid programs are calculated to find
additional outlets for domestic production, while barring the door to foreign
products. The result is that a state of confusion and doubt is generated in the
minds of some people—which is sedulously exploited by the communist minority
for its own ends—despite the constant emphasis of the Italian Government on
the true facts.

Italy's sensitivity to the possibilities which these cheese restrictions have
created for communist propaganda is due in part to the fact that Southern
Italy has been particularly hard hit by the restrictions. As you know,
the widespread poverty and unemployment in Southern Italy have created
a fertile ground for communist agitators. Before Section 104 was enacted,
one of the bright spots in the economy of Southern Italy was a growing
export trade in cheese. Pecorino, romano, and other pungent cheeses of
the area were coming to the United States in growing volume, giving
employment to Southern Italy, and giving dollars to the Italian economy.
Shortly after Section 104 put a halt to this development, we received
reports out of Southern Italy that agents of the Soviet Government were
ostentatiously making bids for various agricultural products of the same
area, with obvious propaganda effect.

Of course, in any balanced appraisal of the desirability of Section 104,
one has to take into account not only its effect upon our foreign policy
objectives, but also upon our domestic agriculture. On this score, representatives of the Department of Agriculture have repeatedly stated
their considered judgment that the measure hurts rather than helps
American agriculture. They have also stated it as their conclusion that
Section 104 is unnecessary for the protection of domestic agriculture, and,
in the end, is bound to do it real injury. This Department is in agreement
with these conclusions. Other provisions of the law, such as Section 22
of the Agricultural Adjustment Act, and the escape clauses of the Trade
Agreements Act, provide the means whereby American agriculture can
be protected in any individual cases of injury. Moreover, American
agriculture relies heavily upon foreign markets for the sale of its products.
In 1950, for example, American farmers sold 2·9 billion dollars of their
products overseas, to foreign consumers they never saw and often never
knew were their customers. On the other hand, American imports of
agricultural products of the type we grow at home amounted to about
1·8 billion dollars. Even some of the products that Section 104 aims at
protecting have regularly been on an export basis. In 1950, we sold the
world 87 million dollars of dairy products and imported only 34 million
dollars worth of such products.

In his own protection, the American farmer must live in a world in which nations stand ready to receive the products of one another and in which nations are willing and have the financial means to buy the products of one another. So far as international trade is concerned, this is the surest protection that can be provided the American farmer.

In sum, therefore, it appears to this Department that our major foreign policy objectives and our interest in the protection of the American farmer alike require that the terminal date of Section 104 should not be extended.

(vi) CABLE FROM SENATOR TOM CONNALLY, CHAIRMAN OF THE UNITED STATES SENATE COMMITTEE ON FOREIGN RELATIONS, TO GENERAL DWIGHT D. EISENHOWER, SUPREME ALLIED COMMANDER EUROPE, REQUESTING HIS VIEWS ON THE EFFECT OF POSSIBLE CUTS IN MUTUAL SECURITY FUNDS, 5 MAY 1952[1]

Senate debate on mutual-security legislation starts today. As you know, Foreign Relations Committee, without objection, has reported bill making $1,000,000,000 over-all cut in President's request, including reduction title I, military aid, from $4,145,000,000 to approximately $3,620,000,000 and reduction in title I, defense support, from approximately $1,819,000,000 to approximately $1,589,000,000. Some Members of Senate urging deeper cuts. In view of these facts would appreciate having your attitude particularly concerning effect further substantial reduction would have on development of necessary military build-up in Western Europe and on security of United States. I, of course, and all members of committee eager to keep cost of program as low as possible without impairing our structure for collective defense so painfully built up under North Atlantic Treaty. Believe Senate would attach great weight to your views with respect to probable effect proposed cuts would have on ability of our European allies to meet Lisbon goals and continue military build-up at desired rates after 1952. If you feel such cuts would materially retard necessary European military build-up, would appreciate your views on resulting effect on United States military security in light of your evaluation of Soviet aggressive threat.

TOM CONNALLY
Chairman, Senate Committee on
Foreign Relations.

(vii) GENERAL EISENHOWER'S REPLY DEPLORING THE POSSIBILITY OF SUBSTANTIAL REDUCTIONS IN THE MUTUAL SECURITY PROGRAMME, 5 MAY 1952[2]

In response to your request, I furnish the following statement of views concerning the foreign assistance program as it applies to my command.

[1] *Department of State Bulletin*, 26 May 1952, p. 840. [2] Ibid. 26 May 1952, pp. 840-1.

You asked particularly for my views as to the amount proposed and the effects of possible cuts below that amount. This reply is essentially a summary of the conclusions presented to your committee by General Gruenther in March.

First, please permit me to draw attention to the fact that over the past several years I have publicly insisted on the importance of America's solvency to her own security. I am keenly aware that Congress has the onerous responsibility of weighing and balancing the obvious risks of attack against the equally obvious risks of ruinous spending.

As you know, my own headquarters does not compute the specific money figures for the various elements of the program, but we do recommend the composition of the military forces required and the essentials of expansion programs for developing collective security. In order to answer your request I must therefore make certain assumptions which cover matters outside my direct cognizance but which I nevertheless have every reason to believe are factual in their application to the program as actually prepared and submitted to the Congress.

Specifically, these assumptions are:

A. That the financial computations have been carefully and competently made on the basis of our military requirements.

B. That strong efforts are being made to do this on an austerity basis, both as to design and quantity.

C. That we are passing through what must be regarded as an emergency period. The free world and particularly the United States could not afford, indefinitely, to provide the sums for military purposes that are now being allocated. As quickly as a satisfactory defensive posture has been established in our vital areas we must pass to a maintenance condition in which each cooperating nation will be largely responsible for its own forces.

D. That the Mutual Security Program as proposed to the American Congress has been adjusted to provide for maximum effort on the part of co-operating nations.

Proceeding from these assumptions, it is apparent that any cut in the program would inevitably tend to curtail or retard the build-up of forces. Manifestly, in calculations of this scope and magnitude, moderate-sized cuts can be absorbed without critical damage. But substantial reductions in end-item aid would slow up the formation and impair the readiness of units.

Reductions in defense support would have a peculiarly adverse effect, since available production facilities in Europe could not be put to use for lack of a critical fraction of their raw materials and other requirements. This would mean, of course, that nationals depending upon receipt of scheduled end items or materials could not make maximum use of available manpower, manufacturing facilities, and training installations.

While we here are not in position to compute in detail the effects of specific fund reductions, it is quite clear that in terms of impact on our military programs, an aggregate reduction of the order of a billion dollars would be heavily and seriously felt. Any cut materially greater than this would create such difficulties that a drastic revision of the whole program might well be indicated and might therefore endanger the proposed military build-up now visualized, and which I consider essential in the interest of United States security.

I believe the American approach must always be to weigh these questions in terms of the effects upon the security of the United States. At a time of such heavy costs as the United States is incurring it is more essential than ever that each dollar be made to count to the maximum. It is my understanding that our Mutual Security Program was adopted because of a conviction that there is no acceptable alternative. The development of collective security through cooperation is obviously more efficient and less costly than for any one country to attempt to achieve it alone.

There can be little question but that our policy of aiding free nations in their own defense has been producing a gradually improving stability on the international scene. The situation is better than a year ago and the outlook for peace has improved markedly since the initial decision by the Congress more than two years ago to embark on a large-scale military-assistance program.

The degree of this progress is perhaps best reflected in the redoubled efforts now being exerted by the Iron Curtain world to weaken unity in the West and to block further constructive steps such as those relating to the European defense force and the integration of Germany into the Western European complex.

In the SHAPE annual report submitted about a month ago,[1] we reviewed progress achieved in the European region well into 1952. If we are to achieve comparable and greater progress here during the remainder of this year and in 1953, it is manifest that unflagging joint efforts are required, and that the programs of aid in military end items and defense support must be buttressed by sufficient appropriations to enable the recommended build-up to go forward.

My final observation is that America, in partnership with others, is participating in a program that has the ultimate aim of security and peace. Attainment of this goal remains necessary regardless of the exact speed of progress in any one fiscal year period.

My own belief is that this purpose will become more expensive if it is unnecessarily postponed, dragged out, and delayed. It seems to me to be in America's interest to attain as quickly as possible a satisfactory posture

[1] *Annual Report to the Standing Group, North Atlantic Treaty Organization, from General of the Army Dwight D. Eisenhower, Supreme Allied Commander, Europe* (Paris, SHAPE, 1952).

of defense in the free world so as to relieve us of the necessity of further build-up and place us substantially on a maintenance basis.

The foregoing statement is for such use, public or private, as you may deem desirable.

DWIGHT D. EISENHOWER.

(viii) JOINT STATEMENT ISSUED BY THE UNITED STATES EMBASSY AND THE MUTUAL SECURITY AGENCY IN PARIS REGARDING UNITED STATES AID TO FRANCE AND THE FRENCH GOVERNMENT'S REQUEST FOR ADDITIONAL OFF-SHORE CONTRACTS, 9 MAY 1952[1]

L'engagement pris par les États-Unis en novembre dernier de mettre 600 millions de dollars à la disposition de la France avait été pris afin d'aider le gouvernement français à réaliser un effort militaire conforme au programme de l'O.T.A.N.[2] Cet effort devait notamment comporter une accélération de la construction de bases et d'autres installations militaires, des mesures destinées à faciliter la passation des commandes 'off-shore' et toutes mesures destinées à consolider l'économie française.

Il avait en effet été reconnu que la situation financière de la France exigeait la mise au point d'un programme d'importation soigneusement adapté aux ressources en dollars qui seraient disponibles pour couvrir ces besoins.

Sur la somme globale de 600 millions de dollars, 270 millions ont été fournis sous forme d'aide économique et 30 millions sous forme d'achats aux États-Unis d'équipement militaire dont les forces françaises d'Indochine avaient un besoin urgent.

On estime, d'autre part, que le montant des dépenses effectuées par les forces américaines pour la construction de bases et pour l'entretien de troupes en France s'élèvera approximativement à 100 millions de dollars pour l'année fiscale se terminant le 30 juin 1952.

Les négociations actuellement en cours portent donc sur le solde de 200 millions de dollars. Sur cette somme, 20 millions seront prélevés pour l'achat d'équipement militaire américain à destination de l'Indochine. Le reste, soit 180 millions, sera affecté aux commandes 'off-shore' passées en France pour du matériel militaire qui sera mis à la disposition du gouvernement français, notamment pour faciliter la poursuite des opérations en Indochine.

Le programme des commandes 'off-shore' entre dans le cadre des accords conclus à Lisbonne aux termes desquels les représentants français se sont engagés à exécuter, au cours de l'année 1952, un programme militaire entraînant une dépense de 1.400 milliards de francs, chiffre dépassant

---

[1] *Combat*, 10–11 May 1952.
[2] Organisation du Traité de l'Atlantique Nord = NATO.

celui proposé par le Comité des 'Sages'. Cette somme de 1.400 milliards de francs comprend la contrepartie en francs des:

270 millions de dollars accordés au titre de l'aide économique.

30 millions de dollars d'équipement militaire déjà acheté aux États-Unis, 200 millions de dollars prévus pour des commandes 'off-shore' à venir.

Indépendamment de la somme de 600 millions de dollars sur laquelle le gouvernement des États-Unis avait donné des assurances en novembre dernier, le gouvernement français vient de demander aux États-Unis de passer en France de nouvelles commandes 'off-shore' de matériel militaire d'environ 170 milliards de francs au cours des trois prochaines années. Du côté français, on déclarait en effet que sans cela la production française serait sérieusement ralentie et qu'un certain nombre de contrats importants devraient être annulés.

Les autorités américaines n'ont encore pris aucune décision sur ce point, mais se sont déclarées disposées à prendre la demande française en considération. Les fonds qui seraient éventuellement attribués au financement de commandes 'off-shore' ne pourraient provenir que de fonds existant déjà ou de crédits susceptibles d'être votés ultérieurement par le Congrès en application de la loi de sécurité mutuelle de 1951.

(ix) Extracts from a statement by President Truman regarding the Mutual Security provisions of the Supplemental Appropriation Act of 1953,[1] 15 July 1952[2]

I have today signed H.R.8370, the Supplemental Appropriation Act of 1953. This is an omnibus measure, appropriating funds for a great many agencies.

In a number of ways, this act falls so far short of what is required in the national interest that I feel I cannot let it go without comment. Fortunately, some of the most drastic and unwise slashes proposed were averted by the Congress before the act was finally passed. I have been particularly gratified by the determined stand of many Members of the Congress in the days before adjournment, which saved the vital expansion of our atomic energy facilities from disastrous curtailment.

Nevertheless, the act contains a number of appropriation cuts which will seriously hamper our total defense effort. In particular, I am deeply concerned by the slashes in funds for civil defense, for anti-inflation controls, and for our Mutual Security Program. . . .

As for the Mutual Security Program, the Congress has cut almost 25 percent from the program which I recommended last February.[3]

[1] Public Law 547, 82nd Congress.
[2] *Department of State Bulletin*, 4 August 1952, pp. 199–200.
[3] The amount recommended by the President was $7,900 million; the final amount

The passage of the mutual security legislation and the appropriations for it included in this act are a reaffirmation of one of the cardinal points of our foreign policy—the achievement of peace through helping to build the collective strength of the free world to resist aggression from without and subversion from within. I am gratified that the Congress had the wisdom to reject many of the crippling amendments which were proposed by those who sought to clothe their all-out opposition to this program with devious and specious devices to destroy it. Nevertheless, it is clear that the amount of this appropriation is inadequate and was arrived at in an effort to present the American people in an election year with the illusion of economy rather than with the reality of an adequate collective defense.

Slashes in funds have been particularly severe in the programs for Europe and for the Indian subcontinent.

Our contributions toward building up the forces of our North Atlantic Treaty partners are but a small portion of the contributions made by our allies, but ours is a critical portion. By virtue of the cuts made by the Congress in the military equipment program and in defense support, the European forces will have less equipment and consequently less fire power and less air cover. As a result, our own forces in Europe become both more vulnerable and less effective in the defense tasks they might be called on to perform. I think the American people should clearly understand that every dollar which has been cut from the amount requested represents a loss of much more than a dollar's worth of strength for the free world.

There has been an equally short-sighted reduction in funds available for the Point Four Program in the new nations of South Asia, including India, Pakistan, Burma, and Indonesia. The original program recommended for this area amounted to 178 million dollars. The amount finally appropriated was slightly over 67 million dollars, or a slash of more than 60 percent. Similar slashes were made in our contribution for technical assistance through the United Nations.

This is an exceedingly dangerous thing for the Congress to have done. Take India for example. India, the largest democratic nation in all Asia, is now engaged in a tremendous effort of her own to build up her economy and living standards—to show that democratic government and democratic methods can succeed in curing the poverty, the hunger, and the misery that afflicts so much of Asia. Every dollar of the aid recommended was to back up the concrete and constructive efforts that the Indians themselves are making. Upon these efforts may well depend the whole future course of freedom and democracy on the continent of Asia.

The cut for these Asian countries is even more cruel because it comes at

appropriated by the Congress was $6,001,947,750. For text of the President's message, see above, p. 7.

a time when they are facing severe economic strain—when even Pakistan, normally a country of grain surplus, is facing a grain shortage. The American people should carefully note the strange fact that prominent among the proponents of this cut were some of the very individuals who have shouted loudest that we are not doing enough in Asia.

The cuts in our Mutual Security Program have allegedly been made in the name of economy. To me, this is the falsest kind of economy. I am convinced that such cuts will in the long run cost us much more. I am equally convinced that the Congress itself will eventually recognize the necessity of making additional funds available during this fiscal year to meet the needs of this program.

(x) Extracts from a speech in the House of Commons by Mr. Churchill on the progress of the British defence programme, 30 July 1952[1]

The Chancellor of the Exchequer spoke yesterday mainly about the civil economy. It falls to me to speak more at length about defence. One of our greatest problems in the hard discussions which we have had has been that of finding means by which, despite our economic difficulties, we can still maintain a defence effort in accordance with our duties and our needs. We shall not weaken in our resolve to do our utmost in the defence of the free democracies. We reaffirm our determination to stand fast with the Commonwealth, with the United States and our other Allies, in resisting the encroachments of Communism. In particular, in the West, we are resolved to stand shoulder to shoulder with the United States and our Allies in Europe in resisting any aggression.

But there can be no assurance of lasting military strength without a firm economic foundation, and no defence programme can stand without the economic resources to carry it through. The defence programmes must be kept within the limits of our economic strength. The right hon. Gentleman the Member for Leeds, South (Mr Gaitskell) seemed to suggest that no review or revision of our armament scheme could be undertaken by us except in conjunction with all the other Allied Powers.

I trust indeed that we shall continue to set an example to the European States, and no doubt when the meetings of N.A.T.O. take place in the autumn we shall all discuss together our common affairs and how we have got on. But to suggest, as the right hon. Gentleman did, that we have no right to make necessary or even beneficial changes in our own military organisation and expenditure without a general meeting of all the N.A.T.O. Powers would be an abrogation of our rights and an alteration of our ordinary practice such as I have not hitherto seen in peace or war.

Let me now look back a little. Two years ago, after the outbreak of the

[1] H.C. Deb. 5th ser. vol. 504, coll. 1495–1501.

war in Korea, the Socialist Government, with praiseworthy zeal but little study, announced a re-armament programme of £3,600 million to cover both new equipment and the maintenance of the Forces, spread over three years. Five months later, for reasons which were not made clear at the time, they raised this figure to £4,700 million. Now, by the decline in the purchasing power of the pound, it would be about £5,400 million.

The original £4,700 million at the old prices was divided by the late Government in their three-year plan as follows: 1951, £1,250 million; 1952, £1,531 million; 1953, £1,694 million, making a total for the three years of £4,475 million, to which they added £225 million for civil defence and stock-piling, thus making up the total of £4,700 million.

I pointed out, however, in December that it would not be possible to complete so vast a scheme in the period prescribed. There are the inevitable time-lags which may be put, in the first two years, at between 10 per cent, and 20 per cent. In the first year, 1951, actual expenditure amounted to only £1,132 million as compared with the programme figure of £1,250 million. In the current year, 1952, we expect, though this is nothing more than a very speculative estimate, to spend £1,462 million against the forecast of £1,531 million made by our predecessors. I thought that the House might like to have these figures in their minds.

Nevertheless, had we not made a considerable slowing down of the programme to which we had been committed, spreading it into the fourth year, the total bill for these three years would have been far above £4,700 million. Actually, on our present decisions and calculations, we and our predecessors, allowing for the price increase, which has been continuous, will have spent in the three years a sum not far short of the £4,700 million originally proposed.

But, through the time-lag and increased costs, there will be a short-fall in the results achieved in the first three years. Our resources are not expanding at the rate we need to enable us to recover in any period which can be foreseen the position which we held before the war. As a contribution to the immense new burden of the re-armament plan, we are receiving in this year, 1952, about £175 million from the United States; but this is quite different from the £400 million or £500 million a year enjoyed by the late Government before the arms programme was begun, in loans or gifts from the United States and, to a lesser extent, from Canada and the Commonwealth. It must never be forgotten that this foreign aid, on which the Socialist Government lived for its whole tenure of power, virtually made good the loss of foreign investments that we suffered at the beginning of the war. Now we are facing the increased burden without having either the one or the other. Now we are striving to repay the American loan with interest. . . .

The original programme was conceived by the late Government in the mood of the crisis which came upon them when the Korean war began. Many of the resources and much of the equipment in hand at the end of the war had been improvidently dispersed or destroyed. Virtually no new equipment had been provided. For five years the Forces had lived on vanishing war stocks, and there was a heavy lee-way to make up.

Re-armament was such a violent reversal of the policy previously pursued that many errors in the programme were inevitable. Since we assumed office nine months ago, we have made a comprehensive review of defence policy and strategy, and we are now engaged in reshaping the original programme so as to bring it into accord with the results of our new assessment of the position.

There are two requirements to be met. First, we have to take account of the ceaseless technical developments which affect our preparations for a world war, should such a disaster come upon us. In the two years that have passed since the original programme was launched, some weapons, on which immense sums were to be spent, have become obsolescent, and new types and devices of a greatly improved character have come into view. These technical advances have resulted in changes in military tactics, and, in turn, changes of emphasis as between the various sectors of the defence production programme.

Immense strides have been made by the United States, not only in their stock-pile of atomic weapons, but in the power of atomic weapons, and in the range and accuracy of their delivery. All this is reinforced by the advent of new aircraft which profoundly affect the tactics of air warfare, and anti-air defence. Remarkable progress has also been made in our own development of guided missiles, or guided rockets, as was mentioned by the Minister of Supply the other day. On the other hand, the development, such as it may be, of the atomic weapon by Russia is a factor which, though unknowable, we must increasingly bear in mind.

At sea, we have to be prepared to meet new and faster types of U-boat and novel methods of mining. All these developments change the picture of the likely course and character of a future war, and many consequential changes are enforced upon the scale and pattern of weapons and equipment required.

We must not think of a possible third world war in terms of the first, or even the second, of these vast human catastrophes. The days of prolonged artillery bombardment, of immense and almost stationary armies, had vanished before the Second World War came. The expenditure on ammunition in the future may be far less than in the Second World War, and merely to proceed on the previous conventional lines would be to squander our military treasure and our strength.

These developments have affected the views of our military experts on the character and course of any future struggle, and this process of change continues, and even accelerates, with the remorseless march of the science of human destruction.

The second requirement we may have to meet is the continuance of armed peace or cold war, as forecast by the right hon. Gentleman the Member for Lewisham, South (Mr H. Morrison), for a prolonged period. The technical developments which I have just mentioned will not help us much in that. It is by more conventional armaments, mainly, in fact, by the infantry soldier serving in so many parts of the world, that we have to make our current contribution towards security against Communist encroachment.

The need to maintain this kind of military strength in peace must be balanced against the other need to ensure that, if war comes, we shall be able to meet the first intense phase with all its new inventions. I do not doubt that, if the party opposite had continued in power, they would also have been impelled by these developments to review and recast their original scheme, which we supported.

To sum up this part of the argument, I would say that, allowing for the time-lag on the one hand, and the increase of costs on the other, we shall in four years have spent more on re-equipment than was proposed by the late Government for three. But the improvements in types of weapons will have enabled many practical economies and reductions to be made in the original programme with a positive increase in war power. Had that original programme been allowed to continue in its expanding course after the third year, the expenditure would have risen enormously beyond our power to bear. . . .

So far I have been dwelling on finance. Money, however, is not the only limiting factor in re-armament. Steel and its companion products impose absolute limits, alike on our solvency and on our security. We are importing more than a million tons of steel and pig iron this year, and prospects of an improvement in our outlook next year are not unfavourable. Perhaps that is an under-statement. I hope so. If so, the under-statement may be set against any errors in the opposite direction which I may be considered to make.

The problem is how exactly the steel available after domestic needs are met should be allocated between defence services and exports, for without a sufficiency of exports, as the House knows and as I have so often said, a collapse of our economic and financial life would overwhelm us. It cannot be dogmatically stated that defence should have absolute priority over exports, or *vice versa*. Our supply of steel and various other metals is limited, and it would be equally foolish for the Government to lay it down that either armaments or exports should have an unlimited call on them at the expense of the other. Demands on these materials by those engaged in manufacturing goods for exports have to be carefully weighed one at a time—weighed carefully against our individual defence requirements—and we hope and believe that we can, with patience, strike a balance which will build up our defences without endangering our solvency.

(xi) EXTRACTS FROM A SPEECH BY THE FRENCH MINISTER FOR DEFENCE, M. RENÉ PLEVEN, REGARDING FRANCE'S REQUIREMENTS FOR DEFENCE CONSTRUCTION, LORIENT, 5 AUGUST 1952[1]

La France a le cœur bien placé. Elle n'a jamais éprouvé et n'éprouvera jamais aucune gêne à exprimer à haute voix sa gratitude envers ceux qui ont aidé à sa libération, puis à son relèvement, et contribuent aujourd'hui généreusement à la reconstitution de ses forces armées. Elle n'en est que plus à l'aise pour regretter que certains éditorialistes de Washington, heureusement fort peu nombreux, risquent, par leur présentation tendancieuse des demandes françaises de commandes 'off shore', de donner à une discussion délicate, un tour qu'elle ne doit pas avoir.

Si ces éditorialistes avaient visité Lorient ou Brest après leur libération, s'ils avaient additionné le total des milliards que la France a consommé et consomme pour relever ses ruines, tout en assurant en Indochine la protection d'une aire immense du continent asiatique, s'ils s'étaient donné la peine d'étudier les effectifs que nous entretenons aussi bien en Europe qu'en Afrique, s'ils avaient observé le niveau des soldes perçues par notre personnel militaire . . . ces messieurs ne commettraient pas l'injustice d'attribuer nos demandes à un souci de ménager nos efforts.

Les demandes françaises, comme celles d'autres pays, s'inscrivent dans un programme de défense commune et d'aide mutuelle où chaque nation fait sa part et où la France, à Lisbonne, sur le plan financier a spontanément accepté de fournir plus que ne suggéraient les experts internationaux.

Les hommes responsables de la politique américaine le savent bien. Nous sommes persuadés qu'après un examen plus approfondi du problème posé à l'occasion des commandes 'off shore' ils reconnaîtront que le point de vue que nous défendons n'est point inspiré par un étroit particularisme ou un nationalisme mal compris, mais par le souci de réaliser au plus tôt les objectifs que nous avons fixés en commun dans le but d'assurer la sécurité de l'Europe et de protéger la paix.

Les difficultés présentes sont à mon avis bien moins le signe d'un désaccord fondamental entre la France et les États-Unis, qu'elles ne marquent la nécessité d'une révision profonde des méthodes employées au sein de l'organisation atlantique pour assurer les moyens financiers exigés par la réalisation sans à-coup des objectifs arrêtés en commun.

La crise actuelle peut être une crise salubre d'où pourra sortir un

[1] *Le Monde,* 6 August 1952.

meilleur fonctionnement du pacte atlantique si les uns et les autres nous nous mettons en face des problèmes dans un esprit de bonne foi, de bonne volonté et de confiance mutuelle, sans vaine récrimination.

Il y a longtemps que devant le Parlement, et aussi devant d'autres instances, nous avons souligné qu'un programme de réarmement ne peut pas être établi à l'année. Tant que les programmes d'achats 'off shore', comme d'ailleurs tous les autres, seront conduits sur une base annuelle, ils ne pourront permettre une politique cohérente, et nous risquerons à tout moment le renouvellement de difficultés analogues à celles d'aujourd'hui.

Sur le plan international comme sur le plan national il faut, pour prendre une expression budgétaire française, des autorisations de programmes tout autant que des crédits de paiement.

Quant à nous, je le répète encore, nous ne défendons pas un intérêt particulier. Nous défendons une cause commune. Celle de la sécurité et de la paix, aussi essentielle aux États-Unis, au Canada, au Benelux, à la Grande-Bretagne qu'à la France. La réduction des objectifs militaires n'est pas une solution acceptable pour les peuples d'Europe les plus immédiatement menacés en cas d'agression.

Nous avons pris au sérieux l'effort de réarmement parce que nous avons pris au sérieux la menace d'agression. L'étalement des programmes en termes militaires signifie qu'on étale aussi la durée du risque et la période d'insécurité.

La France n'est pas prête à accepter cela légèrement.

L'intérêt commun ne peut pas être que le fonctionnement du pacte atlantique conduise à une situation où, parce que certains sont engagés dans des luttes lointaines soutenues dans ce même intérêt commun et sont appelés en même temps par leur position géographique à fournir le gros des forces terrestres, ils doivent renoncer à garder sur leur sol une industrie d'armement ou être contraints de réduire leur potentiel industriel de telle manière qu'en fait le gros des livraisons d'armes, d'avions ou de matériels, devrait parvenir, en supposant que cela soit possible, d'un ou de deux pays seulement de la coalition.

L'Europe ne pourrait être longtemps défendue exclusivement avec des armes importées. Outre que cette politique serait pour nous inacceptable, elle serait dangereuse du point de vue militaire, elle aboutirait enfin à ce que l'aide américaine, sous forme de livraison de matériel, ne puisse jamais cesser.

Le problème est à prendre de haut et d'ensemble. Il doit l'être devant le Conseil atlantique, sans d'ailleurs que cessent les conversations bilatérales entre les États-Unis et la France.

Mais je peux dire dès aujourd'hui que nous n'accepterons pas de mettre nos ouvriers en chômage.

(xii) Statement to the House of Commons by Mr. Churchill on the Government's decision to modify the defence production programme, 4 December 1952[1]

The House is already aware, from statements which the Chancellor of the Exchequer and I made in the debate on the economic position last July, that during the past months the Government have been engaged upon a thorough review of the defence programme in all its aspects. This review, which is still in progress, must of course take fully into account the results of the Ministerial meeting of the North Atlantic Council to be held in 10 days' time.

Our conclusions will be fully set out in the Defence White Paper for 1953, which, in accordance with previous practice, will be issued in February. However, certain decisions have been made affecting the defence production programme which must be put into effect now if they are to produce the results desired. I have therefore thought it right to inform the House at this stage of the broad effect of these decisions.

We made it clear at the Lisbon meeting of the Atlantic Council that our ability to carry out our programme in full, and to make our contribution to the forces of the North Atlantic Treaty Organisation, depended on the solving of our financial and economic problems and especially the balance of payments problem. This was well understood and accepted by our Allies.

In spite of the successful measures which the Government have taken to strengthen our financial position, these problems are not yet solved, and this is—I will not say a decisive—but at any rate an important factor in determining the magnitude of our defence effort. It must be remembered that our effort has to provide not only for the defence of these islands and for our contribution to common defence within N.A.T.O., but also for our world-wide commitments where we are heavily extended.

The defence budget for this year which was presented in a White Paper last February, amounted to £1,462 million, of which something under £600 million was for production. To this must be added certain supplementary estimates to which the Chancellor recently referred.

If the three-year rearmament programme drawn up by the late Government had been carried through in full, expenditure on defence at the end-1951 prices would have been in the present financial year over £1,650 million, and would have risen in 1953 to more than £1,800 million. Within these totals, expenditure on production would have been over £725 million this year and over £850 million next year. Moreover, much of this increased burden would have fallen on the engineering industry, on which we depend so much for the vitally needed expansion of our export trade.

[1] H.C. Deb. 5th ser. vol. 508, coll. 1775-7.

In the light of these considerations, the Government have come to the conclusion that we must prevent any substantial rise above this year's high level of expenditure on defence production.

Some curtailment must therefore now be made. This will to some extent involve the cancellation or modification of contracts already placed. The firms concerned will be fully informed of these changes by the production Departments.

The reductions will so far as possible be brought about by spreading deliveries of equipment over a longer period. The effect will be to prevent further increases in the amount of labour and materials used for defence production rather than to reduce the total of these resources now devoted to this purpose. It will, however, not be possible to solve the problem entirely by spreading deliveries forward into future months or years.

This applies in particular to aircraft. We shall somewhat reduce the production of types now in service, but we shall continue to press forward as rapidly as possible with the introduction of the newer and still more advanced types. Moreover, in view of the progress which has taken place in the medium bomber, we are able to curtail to some extent earlier plans for re-equipment with light bombers.

The changes which we are making will not have any serious effect on industry as a whole, but they may well cause local difficulties. Happily these difficulties are being partially alleviated by the orders we are receiving for defence equipment from our N.A.T.O. Allies, the Commonwealth and other friendly countries. These will not only contribute to the security of the free world, but will also help to maintain the war potential of British industry and help the balance of our exports.

I should like those firms, large and small, who have given such ready help by taking on re-armament work when they already had full order books, to know how much Her Majesty's Government valued their co-operation, and to understand with what regret we shall now have to ask them to adjust their plans. I am sure that they will not be deterred by any disappointment of this kind from continuing to do their utmost, whether as employers or workers, to provide the Fighting Services with the equipment they need.

These decisions have been taken in the knowledge that it is on a satisfactory development of our economic position, and particularly our balance of payments, that the maintenance of our future defence effort must depend. The decisions, of course, in no way imply any weakening in Her Majesty's Government's resolve to carry through a defence programme which will enable this country to defend itself, to fulfil its obligations overseas, and to take its full share, militarily and industrially, in the common effort of the North Atlantic Treaty Organisation.

(xiii) Communiqué issued after the Tenth Session of the North Atlantic Council, Paris, 18 December 1952[1]

The Ministerial Meeting of the North Atlantic Council ended in Paris today. The Chairman was Mr. Ole Bjørn Kraft, Foreign Minister of Denmark. It was attended by thirty-two Ministers of Foreign Affairs, Finance, Economics and Defence.

2. The Council received a progress report by the Secretary-General, which outlined the structure of the International Secretariat. It described the work accomplished in the last eight months by the Council, meeting regularly through the Permanent Representatives, and the development of close working relations between NATO's civilian and military authorities. It also dealt with the constructive work of the Council's Committee on civil defence, and of those concerned with non-military aspects of the Treaty covered by Article 2, such as over-population and social, cultural and informational matters.

3. After taking note of Lord Ismay's report, the Council adopted a resolution (see Annex E)[2] periodically to review the Organisation's work under Article 2 of the Treaty.

4. In parallel with the Secretary-General's report, the Council considered a progress report prepared by the Military Committee. This report showed a great advance in the training and effectiveness of the various national forces assigned to the Supreme Commanders. Combined land, air and sea manœuvres had shown a marked improvement in co-operation between units as well as at the staff level. The report also showed a substantial advance in the standardisation of international military procedures, notably in signals.

5. The Council approved proposals from the Military Committee for the establishment of a Mediterranean Command, so completing the European Command structure for the defence of the North Atlantic Area. Admiral Lord Mountbatten has been appointed.

6. The Council considered the Strategic Guidance submitted to them by the Military Committee, which took account of the accession of Greece and Turkey to NATO. In approving it the Council reaffirmed their determination to defend all the territories of the North Atlantic Treaty area.

7. The Council also had the benefit of statements from the Supreme Allied Commander Europe, and the Supreme Allied Commander Atlantic. General Ridgway paid tribute to the high quality of the forces under his

---

[1] Great Britain: Foreign Office: *Report of the North Atlantic Council Meeting, Paris, 15–18 December 1952* (Cmd. 8732) (London, H.M.S.O., 1953), pp. 9–11.
[2] Ibid. p. 9. Not printed here.

command but emphasised that only by a continuing increase in the forces assigned to him would he be able to carry out his responsibilities. Consequently, there could be no relaxation: on the contrary every effort must be made to increase NATO armed strength as rapidly as possible. Admiral McCormick spoke in similar vein.

8. Against this background the Council then considered the first report on the Annual Review for 1952. They noted with satisfaction that the increase in forces agreed to at Lisbon had been substantially achieved by the end of 1952, and that it was planned to make further individual and collective efforts in 1953 to increase, improve and strengthen the forces now in being. At the same time they recognised that strong defence requires a healthy economy.

9. For the future, the Council directed that more emphasis should be given to increasing the effectiveness of the forces of the alliance and the units necessary for their support rather than to the provision of greater numbers, to the extent that resources were not available for both tasks. The Council noted the progress being made in the co-ordination of production of defence equipment and directed that further study be given to this and to further standardisation in this field. The Council also welcomed the assistance given to European production by United States offshore procurement contracts.

10. Agreement was reached on the financing of a further portion of the Infrastructure programme for airfields, communications and jet fuel supplies, to the amount of approximately £80 million.

11. During the past eight months, the Council have regularly exchanged views and information on political problems affecting their common interests. At this meeting the Council paid particular attention to the struggle in Indo-China, to the European Defence Community Treaty, and to the situation in Eastern Germany. They noted in particular that, despite the Soviet Union's repeated declarations favouring a German peace treaty and German unification, no reply had been received to the proposals of the United Kingdom, France and the United States sent three months ago. The Council also received a progress report upon the work of the Interim Commission of the European Defence Community. The Council adopted resolutions (see Annexes C and D) on Indo-China and the European Defence Community.[1]

12. It was agreed that the next Ministerial Meeting of the Council should be held as early as possible in the spring of 1953, when its first task will be to consider the final report on the Annual Review for 1952.

13. In the course of the present Meeting, the Council considered the

[1] See below, pp. 502 and 205.

present situation of the Atlantic Community and its prospects for the future.   In the North Atlantic Treaty Organisation, fourteen sovereign states have developed a degree of voluntary co-operation without precedent in history.   By combining their resources and their knowledge, by sharing the material burden of defence, by the constant practice of mutual consultation and mutual assistance, member states have already increased their common strength, understanding and unity.

14. Member Governments are more than ever convinced that the course they have chosen is the best way of protecting their free society from direct or indirect Communist attempts to overwhelm it.   Such improvement as has taken place in the general international situation can be attributed to the efforts which Member Governments have made in increasing their collective strength since the foundation of the alliance.   If there were any relaxation in these efforts, there would be a corresponding increase in the dangers to which they are exposed.   The increasingly successful co-operation of the fourteen Member Governments is a clear proof that the avowed intentions of the Soviet Government to sow dissension in the free world will not succeed.

15. The Council re-affirmed the purpose of their alliance as being for defence, for peace, and for security, and their resolve to extend the scope of their joint action, and collectively to preserve their common heritage of freedom.   The Council welcomed the sense of unity which is steadily growing among the peoples of the Atlantic Community.

2. Anglo-American Conversations

(i) Communiqué issued after the talks between President Truman and Mr. Churchill, Washington, 9 January 1952[1]

The President and the Prime Minister held four meetings at the White House on January 7 and 8, 1952.   The Prime Minister was accompanied by the Foreign Secretary, Mr. Anthony Eden, by the Secretary of State for Commonwealth Relations, Lord Ismay, and by the Paymaster-General, Lord Cherwell.   The President's advisers included the Secretaries of State, Treasury, Defense, Mr. Charles E. Wilson, and Mr. W. Averell Harriman.   The visit of Mr. Churchill and his colleagues also afforded opportunities for a number of informal meetings.

At the end of the talks the President and the Prime Minister issued the following announcement:

During the last two days we have been able to talk over, on an intimate and personal basis, the problems of this critical time.   Our discussions

[1] *Department of State Bulletin*, 21 January 1952, pp. 83–84.

have been conducted in mutual friendship, respect and confidence. Each of our Governments has thereby gained a better understanding of the thoughts and aims of the other.

The free countries of the world are resolved to unite their strength and purpose to ensure peace and security. We affirm the determination of our Governments and peoples to further this resolve, in accordance with the purposes and principles of the United Nations Charter. The strong ties which unite our two countries are a massive contribution to the building of the strength of the free world.

Under arrangements made for the common defense, the United States has the use of certain bases in the United Kingdom. We reaffirm the understanding that the use of these bases in an emergency would be a matter for joint decision by His Majesty's Government and the United States Government in the light of the circumstances prevailing at the time.

We share the hope and the determination that war, with all its modern weapons, shall not again be visited on mankind. We will remain in close consultation on the developments which might increase danger to the maintenance of world peace.

We do not believe that war is inevitable. This is the basis of our policies. We are willing at any time to explore all reasonable means of resolving the issues which now threaten the peace of the world.

The United States Government is in full accord with the views expressed in the joint statement issued in Paris on December 18, 1951, at the conclusion of the Anglo-French discussions.[1] Our two Governments will continue to give their full support to the efforts now being made to establish a European Defense Community, and will lend all assistance in their power in bringing it to fruition. We believe that this is the best means of bringing a democratic Germany as a full and equal partner into a purely defensive organization for European security. The defense of the free world will be strengthened and solidified by the creation of a European Defense Community as an element in a constantly developing Atlantic Community.

Our Governments are resolved to promote the stability, peaceful development, and prosperity of the countries of the Middle East. We have found a complete identity of aims between us in this part of the world, and the two Secretaries of State will continue to work out together agreed policies to give effect to this aim. We think it essential for the furtherance of our common purposes that an Allied Middle East Command should be set up as soon as possible.

As regards Egypt, we are confident that the Four Power approach offers the best prospect of relieving the present tension.

We both hope that the initiative taken by the International Bank for

[1] *Documents* (R.I.I.A.) for 1951, p. 141.

Reconstruction and Development will lead to a solution of the Iranian oil problem acceptable to all the interests concerned.

We have discussed the many grave problems affecting our two countries in the Far East. A broad harmony of view has emerged from these discussions; for we recognize that the over-riding need to counter the Communist threat in that area transcends such divergencies as there are in our policies toward China. We will continue to give full support for United Nations measures against aggression in Korea until peace and security are restored there. We are glad that the Chiefs of Staff of the United States, the United Kingdom, and France will be meeting in the next few days to consider specific measures to strengthen the security of Southeast Asia.

We have considered how our two countries could best help one another in the supply of scarce materials important to their defense programs and their economic stability. The need of the United Kingdom for additional supplies of steel from the United States, and the need of the United States for supplies of other materials, including aluminium and tin, were examined. Good progress was made. The discussions will be continued and we hope that agreement may be announced shortly.[1]

We have reviewed the question of standardization of rifles and ammunition in the North Atlantic Treaty Organization. Neither country thinks it wise at this critical time to take the momentous step of changing its rifle. In the interest of economy, both in time and money, we have agreed that the United States and the United Kingdom will continue to rely upon rifles and ammunition now in stock and currently being produced. In the interest, however, of eventual standardization, we have also agreed that both countries will produce their new rifles and ammunition only on an experimental scale while a common effort is made to devise a rifle and ammunition suitable for future standardization.

The question of the Atlantic Command is still under discussion.[2]

Throughout our talks we have been impressed by the need to strengthen the North Atlantic Treaty Organization by every means within our power and in full accord with our fellow members. We are resolved to build an Atlantic community, not only for immediate defense, but for enduring progress.

(ii) EXTRACTS FROM A SPEECH BY THE BRITISH FOREIGN SECRETARY, MR. ANTHONY EDEN, COLUMBIA UNIVERSITY, NEW YORK, 11 JANUARY 1952[3]

... Let us make no mistake. The Communist assault on free and democratic thought is more formidable than was its Fascist counterpart of

---

[1] An agreement was announced on 18 January: *Agreement between the Governments of the United States and of the United Kingdom on Mutual Assistance in steel, aluminium and tin, Washington, 18th January 1952* (Cmd. 8464) (London, H.M.S.O., 1952).

[2] See above, p. 1.   [3] *New York Times*, 12 January 1952.

yesterday. Taking advantage of every contradiction and weakness in western society, communism nearly absorbed a western Europe confused by the aftermath of war. That no doubt is what the Communists hoped for. But they failed. Moral resistance began to stiffen in the west. Thanks to American generosity in Marshall Aid, lifeblood flowed again, and the economies of the western nations began to revive.

But side by side with this policy of penetration, the Communists have not hesitated to use the threat of force. We know the story only too well— Greece, Czechoslovakia, Korea. The Soviets never disarmed, and they rearmed their satellites in defiance of the terms of the peace treaties. Overwhelming force in the Communist camp has been used to intimidate or overthrow the weaker and more exposed of the struggling democratic states. To all this there could only be one answer. We had to look to our physical defenses. We had to re-arm: to oppose positions of strength to the use of force, wherever it might appear. The free democracies have rejected dictatorial doctrines on their merits. They must not be imposed by force of arms. To allow this would be to betray our heritage.

We seek to establish a more even balance of force between the East and West. But this does not stand alone in our endeavor. We must not for a moment forget that other challenge—the unceasing attempt to undermine the economic life and the morale of our people. This is the heart of the matter, and the Communists know it. I would put it to you like this. The purpose of our armed strength is to provide a dike behind which the practice of freedom may grow and flourish. We know for certain that, provided the dike holds, freedom will triumph over fear. That is the most that material force can ever do—or should ever attempt to do—in a conflict of ideas. It is not in our minds to use the new strength which we are building up for any other purpose than that. We must never cease to make it clear that this is our objective.

Already there must be serious doubts in the minds of any aggressor who might be tempted to dare a direct trial of strength. But there are parts of the world where it is not clear beyond doubt that open or concealed aggression will lead to such an issue between East and West. That is dangerous for us all. We can afford no breach in the dike at any point.

But apart from communism, we are confronted with another problem. The sentiment of nationalism is usually good. When it is genuine we all respect and wish to encourage it. But this same sentiment can also find expression in an unbridled frenzy, which is none the less formidable to deal with because it is often a cloak for domestic failure. Where standards of life are falling when they should be rising, the temptation is strong to divert attention from home politics and foster anti-foreign hatreds. It is not often resisted. This is conspicuously true in the Middle East.

Let me make it clear where my country stands in that area of the world.

We have no imperialist ambitions. We neither added, nor sought to add, one square inch to our territories as a result of the war in which we played a not unworthy part. We are not seeking selfish ends. Our policy in Egypt today bears this out. The Suez Canal is an international waterway, whose free passage is of world concern. We do not guard the canal for ourselves alone. The approach which we have recently made to Egypt is a joint one with the United States, France and Turkey.[1] It offers Egypt a full and equal partnership with us all. We seek in effect a joint arrangement to ensure the freedom of this international highway and the security of the Middle East as a whole.

In Persia, too, we are looking for a reconciliation between genuine national aspirations and the wider needs of the free nations. We want to see the great oil industry which we founded there working once again, bringing prosperity to the Persian people and adding to the resources of the world's economy. There is nothing greedy about that. We have not, so far, been able to obtain any practical proposals from the Persian Government on which we could negotiate a settlement.[2] But now the International Bank is making an approach which we sincerely hope will lead to constructive negotiation. We ourselves accept the general principles which the bank have worked out, and we believe that they are fair.

Let me repeat, our main purpose in all these Middle Eastern problems is to make them a matter of joint endeavor with you and with all others who will work with us to build a sense of confidence and security. I have been encouraged to find in these last few days how closely our thoughts and policies are aligned with yours in this great enterprise. Throughout the Middle East there is other work to do; the standards of life and the prospects for the future present startling contrasts. Some have gained new wealth from oil, while others still balance a precarious budget. You on a large scale, we on a more limited one within our present resources, are giving active financial and material help to these Middle Eastern lands today. And in what we are doing we shall work together. . . .

The American and British peoples should each understand the strong points in the other's national character. If you drive a nation to adopt procedures which run counter to its instincts, you weaken and may destroy the motive force of its action. This is not something you would wish to do, or any of us would wish to do, to an ally on whose effective cooperation we depend.

You will realize that I am speaking of the frequent suggestions that the United Kingdom should join a Federation on the Continent of Europe. This is something which we know, in our bones, we cannot do. We know that if we were to attempt it, we should relax the springs of our action in

[1] *Documents* (R.I.I.A.) for 1951, p. 425.
[2] See below, p. 338, for negotiations with Persia later in the year.

the Western Democratic cause and in the Atlantic Association which is the expression of that cause. For Britain's story and her interests lie far beyond the Continent of Europe. Our thoughts move across the seas to the many communities in which our people play their part, in every corner of the world. That is our life: without it we should be no more than some millions of people living on an island off the coast of Europe.

But does this mean that we are turning our backs on Europe?

Certainly not.

I would remind you of a few facts. Apart from the bitter struggle which we are waging in Malaya and our contribution to the United Nations forces in Korea, apart from the substantial force which we have to keep in the Middle East in the interests of common defense, we have the largest armored force on the Continent of Europe of any of the Atlantic powers. And we have undertaken to keep it there, as well as our other forces, as long as they are required in the interests of North Atlantic defense.

Is this abandoning Europe?

We have played a leading part in the economy of Europe. We have promised our full support to all European efforts to achieve greater unity. Our position on all this is well understood by our European friends. When the Prime Minister and I were in Paris, shortly before we came to the United States, we had talks with the French Government on these matters and the statement which we issued jointly then showed how thoroughly we are agreed.[1] I do not think there should be any more misunderstanding.

I therefore claim that we should be judged by our effective actions. I have heard it suggested that further military aid from the United States should be made conditional upon quicker progress toward political and economic unity. This is surely illogical. The test for material aid in building up a joint defense should be the effective use of the resources which each partner commands. By this standard, the formidable British rearmament program is the measure of our contribution.

I have spoken about Europe, the Middle East and the Atlantic.

What of the Far East?

In that vast area the threat of Communist advance and infiltration confronts us at many points. In Korea a direct aggression has been halted and hurled back by the action of the United Nations, in which by far the largest part has been courageously borne by your country. I bring to you the tribute of the British people—our admiration and our sympathy for the sacrifices which it has involved. We are proud to have a Commonwealth force fighting alongside yours in this great enterprise. Each one of us is in debt to those thousands of young men who have risked and given up their lives in this cause. All good men now hope that the fighting in

[1] *Documents* (R.I.I.A.) for 1951, p. 141.

Korea can be brought to an end with an armistice, and that a political settlement in Korea will follow, which will give effect to the principles which the United Nations has fought to uphold.[1]

But even this would not give us a Far Eastern settlement.

In Indo-China the French have been fighting a defensive battle with utmost difficulty—at heavy cost and with a severe drain on their resources. Today we salute the memory of their great soldier-statesman General de Lattre. In Malaya, we, for our part, have been waging a long and bitter struggle against guerrilla forces. These positions must be held. It should be understood that the intervention by force by Chinese Communists in South-East Asia—even if they were called volunteers —would create a situation no less menacing than that which the United Nations met and faced in Korea. In any such event the United Nations should be equally solid to resist it.

The world is in grievous trouble. It is divided into two camps. The war or the threat of war weighs directly or indirectly on all peoples. I do not consider that the risks of a world war are greater today than they were a year or two years ago. In fact I believe the reverse. But it is essential that we should understand the realities and be patient in seeking solutions of the issues which divide the nations.

I believe that the Russian Communist empire shares with other states and nations the desire for survival. I do not believe that the Soviet leaders are eager to face the utter chaos and destruction which would result from a full-scale conflict with the West. They are on the whole careful and calculating in the risks they take. It is part of their dogma that the home of the revolution must not be needlessly endangered.

Therefore, we have grounds to expect that so long as our own position is clear, and so long as we are plainly capable of punishing an aggression, there will be no major war. We have reason to hope that it will eventually be possible to establish, not all at once, but agreement by agreement, a basis for existence free from the constant fear of war. This may well be something less than true peace and understanding—for Soviet methods and doctrine offer little prospect of that—but it would be far better than the present atmosphere in which we live. We might then advance through a period of lessening tension. During this phase the West would continue firmly and patiently with its present policy to restore equilibrium of force; seek to conclude local and limited settlements of outstanding issues; avoid provocation; and work toward a general agreement to live and let live, based on mutually recognized positions of strength. Thus the world might move forward toward stability and settled relations.

A program of this kind explains and justifies the sacrifices which we are now called upon to make. It gives us a prospect for our future and the

---

[1] See below, p. 427, for the progress of the truce talks.

future of our children. It places our rearmament effort in its true per-
spective. It answers the doubts and fears of those who tell us that to
rearm on the present scale must lead in the end to war. We do not accept
this fatalism.

Here, then, is what we can do.

First, to build up sufficient strength to deter aggression and to prevent
the intimidation of free and democratic peoples.

Secondly, not to overstrain ourselves and our economies so that we give
victory to communism through the back door.

Thirdly, as we grow strong, and when we are strong, to remember and
make plain to all the strictly defensive and protective purpose of our
armed strength.

And, finally, to seek, by negotiation from strength, settlements of disputes and lasting peace.

We believe that this is the way out. We believe that our gathering
strength can and must be used for peace. The United States and the
British Commonwealth, keeping these purposes always in their minds, and
remaining at all costs united to pursue them, can lead the world into a
peaceful future by tolerance, understanding and restraint.

(iii) SPEECH BY MR. CHURCHILL TO THE UNITED STATES CONGRESS, WASHINGTON, 17 JANUARY 1952[1]

MR. PRESIDENT, MR. SPEAKER, MEMBERS OF THE CONGRESS:—

This is the third time it has been my fortune to address the Congress of
the United States upon our joint affairs.

I am honoured indeed by these experiences, which I believe are unique
for one who is not an American citizen. It is also of great value to me,
on again becoming the head of His Majesty's Government, to come over
here and take counsel with many trusted friends and comrades of former
anxious days.

There is a lot for us to talk about together so that we can understand
each other's difficulties, feelings and thought, and do our best for the
common cause. Let us therefore survey the scene this afternoon with cool
eyes, undimmed by hate or passion, guided by righteous inspiration and
not uncheered by hope.

I have not come here to ask you for money to make life more com-
fortable or easier for us in Britain. Our standards of life are our own
business, and we can only keep our self-respect and independence by
looking after them ourselves. During the war we bore our share of the
burden and fought from first to last unconquered and for a while alone,

---

[1] Great Britain: Prime Minister: *Mr. Churchill's Speech to the Congress of the United States o
America, January 17th, 1952* (Cmd. 8468) (London, H.M.S.O., 1952).

to the utmost limit of our resources. Your majestic obliteration of all you gave us under Lend-Lease will never be forgotten by this generation of Britons or by history.

After the war, unwisely as I contended, and certainly contrary to American advice, we accepted as normal debts nearly four thousand million pounds sterling of claims by countries we had protected from invasion, or had otherwise aided, instead of making counter-claims which would at least have reduced the bill to reasonable proportions. The thousand million loan we borrowed from you in 1946, and which we are now repaying, was spent, not on ourselves, but mainly in helping others. In all, since the war, as the late Government affirmed, we have lent or given to European or Asiatic countries £1,300 million in the form of unrequited exports. This, added to the cost of turning over our industry from war to peace, and rebuilding homes shattered by bombardment, was more than we could manage without an undue strain upon our life energies, from which we shall require both time and self-discipline to recover.

Why do I say all this? Not to compare our financial resources with yours, for we are but a third your numbers, and much less than a third your wealth. Not to claim praise or rewards but to convince you of our native and enduring strength, and that our true position is not to be judged by the present state of the dollar exchange or by sterling area finance. Our production is half as great again as it was before the war. Our exports are up by two-thirds. Recovery, while being retarded, has been continuous, and we are determined that it shall go on.

As I said at Fulton in Missouri six years ago, under the auspices of President Truman:—

> 'Let no man underrate the abiding power of the British Commonwealth and Empire. Do not suppose that we shall not come through these dark years of privation as we came through the glorious years of agony, or that half a century from now you will not see 70 or 80 millions of Britons spread about the world and united in defence of our traditions, our way of life, and of the world causes which you and we espouse. If the population of the English-speaking Commonwealths be added to that of the United States with all that such co-operation implies, in the air, on the sea, and all over the globe, and in science, industry, and moral force, there will be no quivering precarious balance of power to offer its temptation to ambition or adventure.'

I am very glad to be able to say the same to you here to-day.

It is upon this basis of recovery, in spite of burdens, that the formidable problem of the new rearmament has fallen upon us. It is the policy of the United States to help forward in many countries the process of rearmament.

In this, we who contribute ourselves two-thirds as much as the rest of Europe put together require your aid if we are to realise in good time the very high level of military strength which the Labour Government boldly aimed at, and to which they committed us. It is for you to judge to what extent United States interests are involved. Whether you aid us much or little we shall continue to do our utmost in the common cause. But, Members of the Congress, our contribution will perforce be limited by our own physical resources, and thus the combined strength of our two countries and also of the free world will be somewhat less than it might be. That is why I have come here to ask not for gold but for steel, not for favours but equipment. And that is why many of our requests have been so well and generously met.

At this point I will venture, if I may, to make a digression. After a lot of experience I have learned that it is not a good thing to dabble in the internal politics of another country. It is hard enough to understand one's own. But I will tell you something about our British politics all the same. In our island we indulge, from time to time, in having elections. I believe you sometimes have them over here. We have had a couple in 20 months, which is quite a lot and quite enough for the time being. We now look forward to a steady period of administration, in accordance with the mandate we have received. Like you we tend to work on the two-Party system. The difference between parties on our side of the Atlantic and perhaps elsewhere—between British parties—are often less than they appear to outsiders.

In modern Britain the dispute is between a form of Socialism which has hitherto respected political liberty, on the one hand, and on the other, free enterprise, regulated by law and custom. These two systems of thought, whose differences, I assure you, give plenty of room for argument between political opponents, fortunately overlap quite a lot in practice. Our complicated society would be deeply injured if we did not practise and develop what is called in the United States the bi-partisan habit of mind which divides, so far as possible, what is done to make a party win and bear in their turn the responsibility of office and what is done to make the nation live and serve high causes. I hope here, Members of Congress, you will allow me to pay a tribute to the late Senator Vandenberg. I had the honour to meet him on several occasions. His final message in these anxious years gave the feeling that in this period of United States leadership and responsibility all the great Americans should work together for all the things that matter most. That at least is the spirit which we shall try to maintain among British leaders in our own country. That was the spirit that enabled us to survive the perils of the late war.

But now let me return to my theme of the many changes that have taken place since I was last here. There is a jocular saying, 'To improve is to change. To be perfect is to have changed often'. I have used that once or twice in my long career. If that were true, everyone ought to be getting on very well. The changes that have happened since I last spoke to Congress are indeed astounding. It is indeed hard to believe we are living in the same world.

Former allies have become foes. Former foes have become allies. Conquered countries have been liberated. Liberated nations have been enslaved by Communism. Russia, eight years ago our brave ally, has cast away the admiration and good will her soldiers had gained for her by their valiant defence of their own country. It is not the fault of the Western powers if an immense gulf has opened between us. It took a long succession of deliberate and unceasing words and acts of hostility to convince our peoples, as they are now convinced, that they have another tremendous danger to face and that they are now confronted with a new form of tyranny and aggression as dangerous and as hateful as that which we overthrew. When I visited Washington during the war I used to be told that China would be one of the Big Four Powers among the nations, and most friendly to the United States. I was always a bit sceptical and I think it is now generally admitted that this hopeful dream has not yet come true. But I am by no means sure that China will remain for generations in the Communist grip.

The Chinese said of themselves several thousand years ago, 'China is a sea that salts all the waters that flow into it'. There is another Chinese saying about their country which is much more modern. It dates only from the Fourth Century. This is the saying, 'The tail of China is large, and will not be wagged'. I like that one.

The British democracy approves the principle of movable party heads and unwaggable national tails. It is due to the working of these important forces that I have the honour to be addressing you at this moment. You have rightly been resolute, Members of the Congress, in confronting Chinese Communist aggression. We take our stand at your side. We are grateful to the United States for bearing nine-tenths or more of the burden in Korea, which the United Nations have morally assumed. I am very glad that whatever diplomatic divergencies there may be from time to time about procedure you do not allow the Chinese anti-communists on Formosa to be invaded and massacred from the mainland. We welcome your patience in the armistice negotiations and our two countries are agreed that, if the truce we seek is reached only to be broken our response will be prompt, resolute and effective. What I have learnt over here convinces me that British and United States policy in the Far East will be marked by increasing harmony.

I can assure you that our British hearts go out in sympathy to the families of the hundred thousand Americans who have given their lives or shed their blood in Korea. We also suffer these pangs for the loss of our own men there and not only there but in other parts of Asia as well under attack by the same enemy.

Whatever course events in Korea may take in the near future—and prophecy would be difficult—much too difficult for me to embark upon it—I am sure our soldiers and your soldiers have not made their sacrifice in vain. The cause of world law has found strong and invaluable defence, and the foundations of the world instrument for preserving peace, justice and freedom among the nations have been deepened and strengthened. They stand now not on paper but on rock. Moreover, the action which President Truman took in your name, and with your full support in his stroke against aggression in Korea, has produced consequences far beyond Korea, consequences which may well affect the destiny of mankind.

The vast process of American rearmament in which the British Commonwealth and Empire and the growing power of United Europe will play their part to the utmost of their strength—has already altered the balance of the world and may well, if we all persevere steadfastly and loyally together, avert the danger of a third World War, or the horror of defeat and subjugation should one come upon us.

Mr. President and Mr. Speaker, I hope the mourning families throughout the Great Republic will find some comfort and some pride in these thoughts.

Another extraordinary change has taken place in the Far East since I last addressed you. Peace has been made with Japan. There indeed I congratulate you upon the policy which, in wise and skilful hands, has brought the Japanese nation from the woe and shame of defeat in their wicked war back to that association with the Western democracies, upon which the revival of their traditions, dignity and happiness can alone be regained and the stability of the Far East assured.

In the anxious and confused expanses of Southeast Asia there is another sphere where our aims and interests and those of the French, who are fighting bravely at heavy cost to their strength in Europe, may find a fertile field for agreement on policy. I feel sure that the conversations we have had between our two Foreign Secretaries, Mr. Eden and Mr. Acheson, men whose names and experience are outstanding throughout the world, will help to place the problems of Southeast Asia in their right setting. It would not be helpful to the common cause—for our evils all spring from one centre—if an effective truce in Korea led only to a transference of Communist aggression to these other fields. Our problems will not be solved unless they are steadily viewed and acted upon in their integrity as a whole.

In the Middle East enormous changes have also taken place since I was last in power in my own country. When the war ended, the Western nations were respected and predominant throughout these ancient lands, and there were quite a lot of people who had a good word to say about Great Britain. Today it is a sombre and confusing scene. Yet there is still some sunshine as well as shadow.

From the days of the Balfour Declaration I have desired that the Jews should have a national home. I rejoice to pay my tribute here to the achievements of those who have founded the Israelite State, who have defended themselves with tenacity, and who offer asylum to great numbers of Jewish refugees. I hope that with their aid, they may convert deserts into gardens. But if they are to enjoy peace and prosperity, they must strive to renew and preserve their friendly relations with the Arab world without which widespread misery might swallow all.

Britain's power to influence the fortunes of the Middle East and guard it from aggression is far less today now that we have laid aside our imperial responsibility for India and its armies.

It is no longer for us alone to bear the whole burden of maintaining the freedom of the famous waterway of the Suez Canal. That has become an international rather than a national responsibility. I welcomed the statesmanlike conception of a four-power approach to Egypt announced by the late British Government, in which Britain, the United States, France and Turkey may share with Egypt in the protection of the world interests involved, among which Egypt's own interests are paramount. Such a policy is urgent. Britain is maintaining over 50,000 troops in the Suez Canal Zone, who again might be well employed elsewhere, not for national vainglory or self-seeking advantage, but in the common interests of all nations. We do not seek to be the masters of Egypt. We are there only as the servants and guardians of the commerce of the world.

It would enormously aid us in our task if even token forces of the other partners in the Four Power proposal were stationed in the Canal Zone as a symbol of the unity of purpose which inspires us. And I believe it no exaggeration to state that such token forces would probably bring into harmony all that movement by which the Four Power policy may be made to play a decisive part by peaceful measures, and bring to an end the wide disorders of the Middle East in which, let me assure you, there lurk dangers not less great than those which the United States have stemmed in Korea.

Now I come to Europe where the greatest of all our problems and dangers lie. I have long worked for the cause of United Europe and even of a United States of Europe, which would enable that continent, the source of so much of our culture, ancient and modern, and the parent of the New World, to resume and revive its former splendours. It is my sure hope and conviction that European unity will be achieved and that it will not ultimately be limited only to the countries at present composing Western Europe.

I said at Zurich in 1946 that France should take Germany by the hand and lead her back into the family of nations, and thus end the thousand-years quarrel which has torn Europe to pieces and finally plunged the whole world twice over into slaughter and havoc. Real and rapid progress is being made towards European unity, and it is the duty and the policy of both Great Britain and her Commonwealth and of the United States to do our utmost all of us to help and speed it.

As a forerunner of United Europe there is the European army, which could never achieve its necessary strength without the inclusion of Germany. If this necessary and urgent object is being achieved by the fusion of the forces of the continental nations outside what I have called in former times 'The Iron Curtain', that great operation deserves our fullest support.

But, Members of the Congress, fusion is not the only way in which the defence of Western Europe can be built. The system of a grand alliance such as has been created by the North Atlantic Treaty Organisation is no bar to the fusion of as many of its members as wish for this closer unity, and the United States, British and Canadian troops will stand, indeed are already standing, shoulder to shoulder with their European comrades in defence of the civilisation and freedom of the West. We stand together under General Eisenhower to defend the common cause from violent aggression. What matters most is not the form of fusion or melding (a word I learned over here), but the numbers of divisions and of armoured divisions, and the power of the Air Forces and their weapons available for unified action under the Supreme Commander. We in Britain have denuded our island of military formations to an extent I have never seen before, and I cannot accept the slightest reproach from any quarter that we are not doing our full duty, because the British Commonwealth of Nations, spread all over the world, is not prepared to become a state or group of states in any continental federal system on either side of the Atlantic.

The sooner strong enough forces can be assembled in Europe under united command, the more effective will be the deterrents against a third world war; the sooner also will our sense of security and the fact of our security be seen to reside in valiant, resolute and well-armed manhood, rather than in the awful secrets which science has wrested from nature. These are at present, it must be recognised, the supreme deterrent against a third world war and the most effective guarantee of victory in it.

If I may say this, Members of the Congress, above all things, therefore, not to let go of the atomic weapon until you are sure, and more than sure, that other means of preserving peace are in your hands.

It is my belief that by accumulating deterrents of all kinds, against aggression, we shall in fact ward off the fearful catastrophe, the fears of which darken the life and mar the progress of all the peoples of the globe. We must persevere steadfastly and faithfully in the task to which under United States leadership we have solemnly bound ourselves. Any weakening of our purpose, any disruption of our organisation, would bring about the very evils which we all dread, from which we should all suffer and from which many of us would perish.

We must not lose patience and we must not lose hope. It may be that presently a new mood will reign behind the Iron Curtain. If so it will be easy for them to show it. But the democracies must be on their guard against being deceived by a false dawn. We seek or covet no one's territory. We plan no forestalling war. We trust and pray that all will come right.

Even during these years of what is called the Cold War, material production in every land is continually improving through the use of new machinery and better organisation and the advance of peaceful science. But the great bound forward in progress and prosperity for which mankind is longing, cannot come till the shadow of war has passed away.

There are, however, historic compensations for the stresses which we suffer in the Cold War. Under the pressure and menace of Communist aggression, the fraternal association of the United States with Britain and the British Commonwealth and the new unity growing up in Europe, nowhere more hopeful than between France and Germany, all these harmonies are being brought forward perhaps by several generations in the destiny of the world. If this proves true—and it has certainly proved true up to date—the architects in the Kremlin may be found to have built a different and a far better world structure than what they planned.

Members of the Congress, I have dwelt today repeatedly upon many of the changes that have happened throughout the world since you last invited me to address you here, and I am sure you will agree that it is hardly possible to recognise the scene or believe it can truly have come to pass.

But there is one thing that is exactly the same as when I was here last. Britain and the United States are working together, and working for the same high cause. Bismarck once said that the supreme fact of the nineteenth century was that Britain and the United States spoke the same language. Let us make sure that the supreme fact of the twentieth century is that they tread the same path.

(iv) EXTRACTS FROM A STATEMENT TO THE HOUSE OF COMMONS BY MR. CHURCHILL ON HIS VISIT TO THE U.S.A., 30 JANUARY 1952[1]

I was led to cross the Atlantic by my conviction that, in view of all that is going on in all continents, it was important for His Majesty's new Government to establish intimate and easy relations and understandings

[1] H.C. Deb. 5th ser. vol. 495, coll. 195–204.

with the President and the governing authorities of the United States.
I also thought it important to try to give the impression to the American
people that we rejoice in their effort to defend the cause of world freedom
against Communist aggression and penetration and that we will aid them
in this purpose, which is also ours, with all our strength and goodwill.

My hon. Friend the Member for Morecambe and Lonsdale (Sir I.
Fraser) asked me a Question on the Order Paper today about the Joint
Atlantic Command.[1] I remain unconvinced of the need for the appointment of a Supreme Commander and I think that the method adopted in
the last war afforded the most practical foundation for maintaining the
traffic across the Atlantic in time of war. I was, however, confronted
with the agreements which had been made and announced during the
term of the late Government and with the fact that these agreements could
not be altered except by discussions in the North Atlantic Treaty Organisation. I felt it would be very unfortunate if a protracted argument arose
between us and the United States in this wide audience, and I have therefore been forced to accept in principle the situation as it was left to me.

The House will be aware, however, from the communiqué which was
issued after my last meeting with President Truman on 18th January that
I was able in my discussions in Washington to introduce into the Atlantic
Command proposals certain alterations which will provide great flexibility
in the Command of the whole Atlantic sphere and will also ensure that
there is the fullest co-operation between the Commanders-in-Chief of the
Eastern Atlantic and the Home Station, both of whom will be British
officers. The Commander-in-Chief of the Home Station will be directly
responsible to the Admiralty for the safe arrival and dispatch of the con-
voys upon which our survival and the survival of any armies in Europe
which the United States may have sent necessarily depend.

As an example of the greater degree of flexibility achieved in our dis-
cussions, I may say that it has been arranged that the new Supreme
Commander will send instructions to his area commanders which will
enable them to support adjoining commands in operations throughout the
Atlantic and in British home waters without constant reference to himself.
Further, His Majesty's Government, with the full agreement of the United
States, are putting forward to the North Atlantic Treaty Organisation an
amendment to the existing command boundaries so as to extend our Home
Command to the westward as far as the one-hundred-fathom line. The
right hon. Gentleman will remember that I mentioned that to him at the
beginning of this controversy many months ago. The one-hundred-
fathom line has many advantages; among others, it broadly corresponds
to the limits within which moored mining is profitable and was a very well-
known feature in all our affairs in the war.

[1] See above, p. 1.

I can also state, subject to these amendments, that His Majesty's Government are prepared in the interests of N.A.T.O. unity, to agree to the appointment within that organisation of an American Supreme Commander and a British Deputy Supreme Commander. The choice of the officer whose name has been announced today, Admiral McCormick, is one which should ensure the highest confidence among all members of the Atlantic Organisation.

I now come to the question of the war in Korea, the prolongation of the truce negotiations there, with the possibility of their break-down or breach after a settlement had been made, and the attitude we should adopt in that event towards the Chinese Communists whom we have recognised, but who have not entered into relations with us. As we all know on both sides of the House, we can recognise many people of whose conduct we do not entirely approve.

In discussing these matters, we must first of all bear in mind always, I think, the fact that the contribution by Britain and the British Commonwealth to the war in Korea is less than one-tenth of the forces employed; and while our losses, for which we grieve, have amounted in killed, wounded and missing, to nearly 3,000, similar American losses are over 105,000, or 35 or 40 times as great. So there should be no party differences on the reasons why we are in this war. It was entered upon by the late Government with our full support, and it is authorised and sustained by the United Nations.

I was most anxious therefore, that we should make the United States Government feel that we meant to be their good comrades at the council board, as our Commonwealth Division and Naval and Air Forces have proved themselves to be in the field of action.

The House is aware that for six months negotiations for a truce have been going on between the United States and the Chinese Communist Government. We do not know whether the negotiations—[Hon. Members: 'The United Nations']—what did I say?—[Hon. Members: 'The United States']—between the United States on behalf of the United Nations—[Hon. Members: 'Hear, hear']—we have a lot of things to quarrel about and we need not add to them—between the United Nations and the United States and the Chinese Government will be spun out indefinitely or whether a conclusion will be reached, or whether, after that conclusion has been reached, the Chinese Communists will break their engagement and take any advantages which might be open to them. Neither do we know whether a truce in Korea might not be reached only as a means of transferring Communist strength to the frontiers of French Indo-China or Malaya. This important aspect must be borne in mind.

The whole hypothetical question of what should be done, should a truce be made only to be broken, had been discussed before we left for America between the United Kingdom and the United States and the other Governments who have fighting forces in the field. It was agreed that clearly a very serious situation would arise in such an event as a breach of the truce; and various contingencies had been examined without any definite or formal commitments being entered into.

No change was made in the situation while we were in the United States. In fact, the matter did not figure to any large extent in our discussions. I do not feel it would be an advantage to go into the details of the discussions which took place before we left upon our voyage, those discussions about what we should do, or should not do, in the event, first of a truce being reached, and secondly of it being broken. It is not wise, when a war is going on, to tell everything always to everybody, including the enemy. I suppose I may call them the enemy—they are shooting our soldiers—but including, shall we say, the other side. I think they may sometimes be left with something to guess about.

I thought it better, therefore, when I was invited to address the American Congress—which I regarded as a very great honour for this House, one in which the Leader of the Opposition has also shared—to speak in general terms of the action we should take in the event of a breach of the truce, and I used the words, 'prompt, resolute and effective'. I do not believe they were bad words to use. Certainly, if one is dealing in general terms, they are better than 'tardy, timid and fatuous.' I certainly did not mean to suggest that the words, 'prompt, resolute and effective' represented any new designs or decisions arrived at during our visit. . . .

I will now turn to some of the larger issues which are in the background of all thought upon the Korean campaign. At the outset, 18 months ago, I was personally disquieted by seeing, as I told the House at the time, the attention and resources of the United States being diverted from the main danger in Europe to this far-distant peninsula in the China Seas. But we must recognise that the United Nations have gained authority by the fact that unprovoked aggression has been met by armed force, and that the rule of law which we seek to establish has not lacked either will-power or resources.

This is of extreme importance. The ruin of the League of Nations, out of which so many disasters came, was because this will-power was lacking. It is also a fact that the stimulus of the fighting in Korea has developed to a degree otherwise impossible the re-armament of the free world, and, above all, of the United States. As I said to Congress, 'the balance of the world has been altered' by the decision of President Truman, with the approval of the United Nations, to make this bold American stroke against aggression, in support of which we have all followed.

At the same time, when the main dangers are so much nearer home, we do not want to see ourselves tied down or entangled in a war in Korea—

still less in a war in China. That would indeed, as General Bradley so forcibly said, 'be the wrong war, in the wrong place, at the wrong time'....

I do not think we have gained security during this long period of haggling and wrangling which has gone on at Panmunjom. Apart from anything else, the Chinese Communist Government, whose troops were being slaughtered at the rate of about 40 to 1 by the United Nations Forces, and who had a terrible mass of wounded and invalids flung back upon them far beyond their resources to handle, have, since the Soviet suggestion of a cease-fire and truce negotiations, re-established what is called their 'face'. That, I believe, is a technical term, a term of art which has great vogue in China, and they have since been bargaining all this time on equal terms with the representatives of the United Nations.

We still hope that an agreement will be reached. We still hope that, being reached, it will be kept. I think we have secured a better chance for the reaching of an agreement by making it plain that the United States and Britain are working together in true comradeship, and that in the event of a treacherous renewal of the war they will together take 'prompt, resolute and effective action'.

We have improved the chances of a settlement and limited the risks of a spread by making this declaration instead of giving the impression that we were disunited and taking small points off one another. I am sure that the way to play into the hands of those who direct the Communist menace from the centre would be to magnify differences between Britain and the United States and that nothing would be more likely than that to lead to renewal on a larger scale of the local war in Korea.

My own thoughts are never long absent from the European front and I was, therefore, very glad to have the opportunity in Washington of making it clear that the English-speaking world are acting together in true loyalty and unity and are resolved to bring the local events in the Far East into their proper relationship to our predominating danger in Europe.

Apart from the turmoil in the Far East and in South-East Asia, there are the troubles in the Middle East and Egypt. I have never had the feeling that we should make a bargain with the United States that if we worked smoothly with them in the Far East they should do the same for us in the Middle East. I think this should not be the subject of a bargain. Both cases should be dealt with on their merits, and both cases are pretty strong when looked at on their merits. It is certain that if Britain and the United States are known to be acting together, the difficulties will by that very fact be substantially reduced and the possibilities of peaceful arrangements will be greatly strengthened.

It is certain also that the main interest of the Communist oligarchy in the Kremlin is to provoke or at least to suggest divergencies between us.

That, I think, should not be overlooked even in our debates in this House. On the other hand, the fact of simultaneous or concerted action between us and the United States becoming apparent will be beneficial to both of us and even more beneficial to the free world as a whole.

No more hopeful course has yet been suggested for the Middle East than the approach to all its problems in the spirit of the Four Power proposals. This was the policy of the late Government, for which they deserve the fullest credit, and we have given it immediate, cordial, sustained and determined support. Now that we no longer have available the former Imperial armies which existed in India, the burden of maintaining the control and security of the international waterway of the Suez Canal is one which must be more widely shared.

It is upon an international basis that the most hopeful solution of our Middle Eastern difficulties will be reached, and I trust that all the Powers concerned will play their part, working together and sharing the burden and responsibilities for the peace and security of the Middle East. It may be some time before that is achieved, but that should clearly be our aim and goal.

(v) STATEMENT ISSUED BY MR. CLEMENT ATTLEE, LEADER OF THE PARLIA-MENTARY LABOUR PARTY, REGARDING COMMITMENTS ON THE FAR EAST ENTERED INTO BETWEEN THE BRITISH AND UNITED STATES GOVERNMENTS DURING THE LABOUR GOVERNMENT'S TENURE OF OFFICE, 28 FEBRUARY 1952[1]

As there is some misapprehension as to the attitude of the Labour Government in regard to the Korean war, owing to the disclosure by the Prime Minister of the substance of one of a series of confidential communications on the military operations in Korea exchanged between the Governments of the United Kingdom and the United States,[2] I am setting out the facts.

There had been pressure in certain American quarters for the extension of the war in the Far East by various operations including a naval blockade of the mainland, military operations against China, and the bombing of Manchurian cities. The two Governments were opposed to such a policy. From time to time questions arose as to the conduct of the operations in the Korean theatre of war and these were the subject of correspondence. Among them was the question of what action should be taken in the event of heavy air attacks being launched against the forces of the United Nations by aircraft from bases on the far side of the Yalu River.

It was represented that where attacks of this kind took place it was unreasonable that the General Officer Commanding should be precluded

[1] *Manchester Guardian*, 29 February 1952.
[2] See 26 February 1952, H.C. Deb. 5th ser. vol. 496, col. 969.

from attacking these airfields. The Labour Government agreed with this point of view and the Government of the United States were informed that in these circumstances, after consultation with His Majesty's Government or, if time did not allow, with the British liaison officers on the spot, the General Officer Commanding should be permitted to attack those airfields from which the attacks were being launched.

It is obvious that there was here no departure from the general policy of confining operations to the Korean theatre of war.

3. The Commonwealth in Council

(i) Statement issued after the Conference of Commonwealth Finance Ministers, London, 21 January 1952[1]

We recognise that the sterling area is faced with a very serious crisis which, if it is not effectively dealt with, will have far-reaching consequences. The crisis has arisen because the sterling area as a whole is spending more than it is earning, with the result that its gold and dollar reserves have been falling at a rapid rate.

We are confident that this situation can be set right, and that the steps which will be taken will give to sterling the strength it must have to continue as a widely used international currency.

We are convinced that this cannot be attained by negative and restrictive methods alone, or merely by the imposition of cuts on imports from certain parts of the world. The present difficulties of the sterling area, while partly due to short-term factors, also reflect continuing underlying problems. These problems must and can be solved.

For this reason we are strongly of the opinion that measures taken to stop the drain upon reserves must form part of a long-term policy designed to restore and maintain the full strength of sterling.

It is quite clear that the only way to prevent recurrent drains on the central gold reserves is for every country in the area strenuously to endeavour to live within the means which are, or can be, available to it. The sterling area as a whole must succeed in this endeavour.

The urgency of the immediate situation, and the present level of the gold reserves, require that the sterling area as a whole should be in balance with the rest of the world at latest in respect of the second half of 1952. It is imperative that this should include at least a balance with the dollar area within the same period.

During the course of our discussions the Finance Ministers and representatives of the Commonwealth countries in the sterling area agreed to bring urgently to the attention of their Governments the critical nature

[1] *Financial Times*, 22 January 1952.

of the present situation and the need for immediate corrective action. In this connection they will put before their Governments certain definite proposals calculated in the aggregate to ensure that the sterling area as a whole will be in balance with the rest of the world in respect of the second half of 1952.

Proposals to the same end will be recommended by the Secretary of State for the Colonies to the Governments of the territories with which he is concerned.

It was also agreed that, where any country in the sterling area was likely to be in overall deficit, corrective measures should be taken as soon as possible, in order to relieve the current pressure on the resources of the area.

The methods by which members will contribute to these ends are within the discretion of each country concerned and will vary according to their individual circumstances. The first, and most important, step is to ensure that the internal economy is sound and that all possible measures are taken to combat inflation. This is not only essential for an improvement in the balance of payments but it will also help to keep down the cost of living.

Another important requirement is to increase exports and earning power. In some cases long-term borrowing from outside the sterling area may be practicable. Finally, so far as other methods do not fully achieve the desired results, it will be necessary, as a temporary measure, to reduce imports.

It was agreed that, while emergency measures to stop the immediate drain upon the gold reserves were necessary and inevitable, they could only be palliatives. A lasting solution of the sterling area's problems must be found in order to prevent the recurrence of crises, to make sterling strong and to establish the economies of member countries on a sound and stable basis.

These aims can best be achieved when the world-wide trade of the sterling area is on a substantially higher level than at present, when sterling is freely convertible into all the main currencies of the world and its position need no longer be supported by restrictions on imports.

When this state of affairs has been reached the countries of the sterling area will have freer access to the output of North America and other important regions and to adequate resources of external capital for development.

It is accordingly necessary that for some years to come the sterling area should be in surplus with the rest of the world (including a surplus with the dollar area), and that, after taking account of available sterling assets and long-term investment from abroad, all member countries should balance their external accounts.

To do this in the face of the need for national security and higher standards of living clearly requires the maximum possible expansion of earning power. By the development of their productive power members of the sterling area will not only strengthen their own economies but will also help to meet the inevitably growing world demand for food, raw materials and other essential goods.

Such development will require the investment of substantial financial resources, and it is clear that, after taking account of whatever they themselves can provide, it will be necessary for many member countries to obtain those resources from overseas.

For some time to come the Commonwealth will not be able to meet its growing needs entirely from its own resources, and developing countries will therefore need to rely in varying degrees on investment from outside the sterling area. We are agreed that such investment is to be welcomed, and that all necessary steps should be taken to encourage it.

We feel that the production of essential raw materials within the sterling area would be greatly encouraged by regularity in purchases of such materials by countries outside the area, as this would contribute materially to the long-term stability of the area and indeed of the free world as a whole.

We are also agreed that an examination should be made as quickly as possible of the opportunities for an early increase in the productive power of member countries and of the possibilities of matching available financial and technical resources with the enterprises most likely to achieve that purpose.

This examination should take account not only of the general development requirements of member countries and of their need for capital equipment, but also of the possibilities of increasing their production of food, raw materials, and other essential goods.

We have made arrangements for such an examination to begin forthwith.

While steps are thus being taken to overcome the immediate problems of the sterling area and to accelerate its development, we agree that its recovery will not be complete until the conditions have been created in which sterling can become and remain convertible.

Accordingly it is our definite objective to make sterling convertible and to keep it so. We intend to work towards that goal by progressive steps aimed at creating the conditions under which convertibility can be reached and maintained.

It is primarily the responsibility of the members of the sterling area themselves to create these conditions (including the achievement of adequate gold reserves); but they cannot be completely realised without the active co-operation of other countries, notably those countries which are consistently in surplus with the rest of the world.

We have arranged for an investigation of the steps which should be taken along the road to convertibility to begin forthwith.

We reaffirm the need for frequent and comprehensive consultation between Governments within the Commonwealth on the problems of the sterling area. In particular, steps will be taken within the next few months and from time to time to review progress on the measures now being taken and proposed.

(ii) COMMUNIQUÉ ISSUED AT THE END OF THE CONFERENCE OF COMMONWEALTH PRIME MINISTERS, LONDON, 11 DECEMBER 1952[1]

1. The Commonwealth Economic Conference, which ended today, was convened with the aim of concerting measures for increasing the economic strength of the Commonwealth countries, including the colonial territories, and creating conditions in which their peoples can play their part in securing prosperity and contentment for themselves and for the world.

2. In recent years the sterling area has been faced with recurrent economic crises which have forced its members to take emergency measures of trade and exchange restriction. These measures were necessary but they have inevitably tended to frustrate the long-term economic expansion on which our hopes and opportunities for the future are founded.

This was recognized at the January meeting of the Commonwealth Finance Ministers. The measures taken in accordance with the conclusions of that meeting have, however, enabled the present conference to decide that a more positive policy can now be adopted both by the Commonwealth countries themselves and in concert with other friendly countries, to promote the expansion of world production and trade.

3. The conference agreed that Commonwealth countries would work together to achieve certain broad common objectives. They have no intention of seeking the creation of a discriminatory economic *bloc*; rather their object is, by strengthening themselves, to benefit the world economy generally.

Accordingly, the following principles were agreed upon as governing the approach to the whole range of subjects under discussion:

(*a*) Internal economic policies designed to curb inflation and rises in the cost of living should be steadily followed.

(*b*) Sound economic development should be encouraged with the object of increasing productive strength and competitive power, providing employment, and raising the standards of life.

(*c*) A multilateral trade and payment system should be extended over the widest possible area.

[1] *The Times*, 12 December 1952.

4. The application of these principles will require individual action by Commonwealth Governments, cooperation among them, and international action with other trading nations and existing international organizations.

5. All Commonwealth Governments have agreed to persevere in their efforts to curb inflation. Inflationary conditions frustrate the progress of sound development, both by increasing its cost and by destroying the savings necessary to finance it. Moreover, they damage the external balance by stimulating excessive imports and by diverting to internal use goods which would otherwise be available for export.

6. An adequate and stable external balance must be a first objective for all Governments. Failure to achieve this means repeated crises, a continuously rising cost of living, a constant threat to employment and failure to develop resources effectively.

The conference welcomed the improvement which had taken place in the balance of payments both of the individual sterling area countries and of the sterling area as a whole, following upon the conclusions reached by Commonwealth Finance Ministers at their meeting in January, 1952. It noted with satisfaction that the sterling area would achieve balance with the rest of the world in the second half of this year.

It was agreed, however, that this achievement, while reassuring, was only the first step towards a stable balance for the sterling area. Policies were agreed upon for 1953 which, it is hoped, will lead to further improvement in the reserves during that year. Nevertheless, while there has been steady improvement, the level of the reserves is as yet too low to warrant any substantial relaxation of the restrictions on imports from outside the sterling area.

7. The conference considered the extensive restrictions which some countries of the sterling Commonwealth have needed to impose upon imports from the United Kingsom and other Commonwealth sources. There was agreement that restrictions imposed because of balance of payments problems should be relaxed as the external financial position of countries improved. In considering the whole problem the Governments concerned would have clearly in mind the difficulties which the restrictions have raised for the export industries affected.

8. The economic and social objectives of the Commonwealth countries, individually and in association, depend upon their ability to produce and supply under competitive conditions an expanding flow of exports. There was therefore general agreement in the conference on the vital need to expand the earning power of all sterling countries.

9. DEVELOPMENT POLICY.—Throughout the Commonwealth there is wide

scope for expanding the production of the essential supplies which the whole world needs—food and agricultural products, minerals, and engineering products—and improving the means for transporting them. This development of the basic essentials has on occasion been impeded by other development of a less sound and permanent kind, which have over-taxed the countries' resources and have failed to contribute to the building of economic strength.

The conference agreed that in sterling area countries development should be concentrated on projects which directly or indirectly contribute to the improvement of the area's balance of payments with the rest of the world. Such projects should strengthen the economy of the countries concerned and increase their competitive power in world markets and so, by improving their balance of payments, bring increasing prosperity to their peoples.

In some countries of the area, however, development plans have been or are being made to provide for some basic improvement in the standards of living, which is a necessary foundation for further economic develop-ment. Some social investment is also urgently needed in the more de-veloped countries, certain of which have rapidly increasing populations. The conference recognized the need in such cases for these types of investment.

10. To enable development to go forward a sufficient flow of savings must be provided in the countries undertaking the development, and also in other countries which are ready to invest their savings there.

The amount of savings which will be available from external sources will at best be small in relation to the size of the development programmes of countries of the sterling Commonwealth, and it is therefore essential that these countries should themselves adopt policies which increase the flow of savings—although this is inevitably a slow process for countries with low incomes and little margin above the basic needs for existence. The process of development will itself increase income and increase the flow of savings.

11. The United Kingdom is the traditional source of external capital for Commonwealth investment, and has special responsibilities in the colonial territories. The United Kingdom Government are determined that the flow of capital from London for sound development throughout the Com-monwealth shall be maintained and increased.

This will only be possible if the United Kingdom can sustain the neces-sary level of internal savings, and can achieve a surplus on oversea account additional to that required to meet its heavy existing commitments.

12. The United Kingdom Government have, however, undertaken to make a special effort to provide additional capital for Commonwealth

development by facilitating the financing of schemes in other Commonwealth countries which will contribute to the improvement of the sterling area's balance of payments.

The conference took note that the United Kingdom Government would wish, before making any of this additional finance available for Commonwealth development, to be sure that the country concerned was itself devoting an adequate part of its resources to investment designed to improve the sterling area's balance of payments, and was ready to make a sufficient contribution towards the particular scheme in question, to ensure that both countries had an interest in seeing that it was carried through as efficiently and economically as possible.

13. The conference welcomed the proposal by a group of important financial, industrial, and commercial concerns in the United Kingdom to form a company to further development in other countries of the Commonwealth and the Colonial Empire. It was pleased to note that an announcement by this group is being issued today.

The conference also welcomed a statement by the United Kingdom representatives that the United Kingdom Government intend to discuss with the International Bank for Reconstruction and Development arrangements to give effect to their decision to make sterling available for lending by the bank for projects designed to improve the sterling area's balance of payments.

14. The conference recognized the important contribution which investors outside the sterling area, particularly in the United States, can make to economic development in the sterling area and agreed that every effort should be made to create conditions which would encourage such investment. It further agreed that all sterling area Governments should strive to attain this by reducing such obstacles as controls over the movements of capital across the exchanges.

The United Kingdom Government have reviewed the right which is now enjoyed by residents outside the sterling area who have invested capital in approved projects in the United Kingdom and Colonial Empire since January 1, 1950, to transfer their capital across the exchanges. At present this right only extends to the sterling equivalent of the initial investment. The United Kingdom Government informed the conference that they have decided that henceforth it shall extend also to capital profits.

15. COMMODITY POLICY.—The conference recognized that there was no one universal remedy for the problem of instability of prices for primary commodities. Each commodity must be considered on its merits, in the light of the conditions prevailing at the time; and the circumstances must determine what form of arrangements would be appropriate. The conference agreed that violent fluctuations and an uneconomic level of prices for

primary commodities were against the interests of consumers as well as producers.

All Commonwealth Governments are therefore ready to cooperate in considering, commodity by commodity, international schemes designed to ensure stability of demand and prices at an economic level. They also recognize the need for an agreed procedure for calling together the Governments concerned to consider emergency action in the event of rapidly developing conditions of surplus or shortage of commodities entering into international trade.

16. IMPERIAL PREFERENCE.—There was general recognition at the conference of the value of existing preferences.

On the initiative of the United Kingdom a discussion took place on a proposal that all Commonwealth countries should join in seeking release from the 'no new preference' rule in the General Agreement on Tariffs and Trade (G.A.T.T.) and this United Kingdom proposal was supported by the representatives of some countries. The representatives of other countries felt that such an approach would not advance the agreed objective of restoring multilateral world trade and the conference was therefore unable to support it.

All Commonwealth Governments agreed, however, to cooperate with the United Kingdom Government in an approach to the other contracting parties to the G.A.T.T. to meet particular difficulties arising on the United Kingdom tariff.

The object would be to enable the United Kingdom, consistently with the basic provisions of G.A.T.T., to continue the duty-free entry for Commonwealth goods notwithstanding any increases that might from time to time become necessary in duties designed to protect domestic industry and agriculture in the United Kingdom. The Commonwealth Governments also agreed to consider sympathetically certain special tariff problems affecting the colonies.

17. Resolute action in accordance with the conclusions recorded above will in itself do much to strengthen the economies of the sterling Commonwealth countries. But this is not enough. Action in a wider sphere is also necessary. The conference therefore agreed to seek the cooperation of other countries in a plan to create the conditions for expanding world production and trade.

The aim is to secure international agreement on the adoption of policies, by creditor and debtor countries, which will restore balance in the world economy on the lines of 'Trade not Aid' and will, by progressive stages and within reasonable time, create an effective multilateral trade and payments system covering the widest possible area.

18. TRADE.—The plan envisages positive international action for the pro-

gressive removal, as circumstances permit, of import restrictions imposed for the purpose of bringing a country's external accounts into balance. Action will be required by both creditor and debtor countries. The rate of progress in removing discrimination will depend upon the advance towards equilibrium between the United States and the rest of the world.

19. The sterling Commonwealth countries will not all be able to remove restrictions at the same time. In particular, the representatives of some countries have emphasized that they must continue to use their exchange resources in the manner which enables them to carry out their planned development programmes most effectively, and that they are likely to continue to need import restrictions for this purpose.

20. FINANCE.—The conference agreed that it is important, not only for the United Kingdom and the sterling area but also for the world, that sterling should resume its full role as a medium of world trade and exchange. An integral part of any effective multilateral system is the restoration of the convertibility of sterling, but it can only be reached by progressive stages. The achievement of convertibility will depend fundamentally upon three conditions:—

(a) The continuing success of the action by sterling Commonwealth countries themselves, as outlined above;

(b) the prospect that trading nations will adopt trade policies which are conducive to the expansion of world trade;

(c) the availability of adequate financial support, through the International Monetary Fund or otherwise.

21. PROCEDURE.—It is proposed to seek acceptance of this plan by the Governments of the United States and of European countries, whose co-operation is essential, and to work as far as possible through existing international institutions dealing with finance and trade.

22. The timing of the successive stages of this plan cannot be decided at present. This can only be judged as the necessary conditions are satisfactorily fulfilled.

23. CONCLUSION.—The conference is happy to be able to present this account of the confident understanding which exists between members of the Commonwealth and the wide measure of agreement which they have been able to achieve over the whole range of economic policy. The aims of their cooperation are entirely consistent with their close ties with the United States and the members of the Organization for European Economic Cooperation.

The Commonwealth countries look outward to similar cooperation with other countries, not inward to a closed association. It is their common purpose, by their own efforts and together with others, to increase world trade for the mutual benefit of all peoples.

PART II

GERMANY AND THE EUROPEAN DEFENCE COMMUNITY

1. Before Signature of the Treaties

(i) DRAFT ELECTORAL LAW FOR THE CONDUCT OF ALL-GERMAN ELECTIONS, PRESENTED TO THE VOLKSKAMMER OF THE GERMAN DEMOCRATIC REPUBLIC ON 9 JANUARY 1952[1]

Preamble

Since it is the desire of all patriotic Germans to end the unhappy division of Germany, agreement between the representatives of east and west Germany is essential. Together we must solve the vital problems of restoring the unity of Germany, of guaranteeing a quiet and peaceful life to our people and of giving to other nations the assurance that their peaceful avocations shall never again be endangered by German aggression.

The basic principle of such a state must be—By the people, for the people, with the people.

This purely German task cannot and must not be entrusted to foreigners. Representatives of east and west Germany must therefore meet immediately in an All-German Council in order to satisfy the demand for free elections for a constituent German National Assembly now being made in all parts of our fatherland. The national electoral law of 6 March 1924 is suggested as a basis for such an election. It will be the task of the All-German Council to reach agreement on the preparation and carrying out of this election. By this means our people will safeguard their right to govern their own country and to choose the form of government under which they wish to live. The question of international control of the election will be discussed by the All-German Council.

A Central Election Committee composed of members from east and west Germany will be set up by the All-German Council to prepare and carry out free, universal, equal, direct and secret elections for a German National Assembly.

To facilitate the execution of these basic principles, the government of the German Democratic Republic publishes the following draft of an electoral law, which would be laid before the All-German Council of the representatives of east and west Germany.

---

[1] Translated from *Europa Archiv*, 20 March 1952, pp. 4787–91. For the west German law approved on 6 February see ibid. pp. 4791–2, and *Documents* (R.I.I.A.) for 1951, p. 283 (text of draft law).

I. *Principles*

1. (1) Political freedom will be guaranteed to all citizens during the preparation and carrying out of the election.

(2) All democratic parties, organizations and associations have the same freedom of action. They have the right to nominate candidates for the National Assembly and complete freedom in the conduct of the election campaign.

2. The right to express opinions verbally, in writing, in print, in pictures or in any other way, shall be guaranteed throughout Germany.

3. No person may be imprisoned or prosecuted on account of political opinions nor suffer any discrimination in his employment or position. No person may discriminate against him if he makes use of this right.

4. Political freedom and personal freedom shall be guaranteed to every candidate for the National Assembly. He shall be given leave of absence for the period of the election. A candidate shall not be imprisoned, put under provisional arrest, legally or officially prosecuted, dismissed from his position or his employment, or otherwise called to account.

5. Unimpeded freedom of action shall be guaranteed to every candidate in all provinces of Germany and in Greater Berlin.

6. All limitations on passenger traffic inside Germany, including Greater Berlin, shall end at least three months before the election.

7. (1) Public meetings held by the parties, organizations and associations whose electoral lists of candidates have been duly presented and by the candidates for the National Assembly themselves, are permitted unconditionally. They do not require prior notification and shall have official protection.

(2) The right to participation, in the proposals and demonstrations arising at these meetings, whether by speech or by any other method of expressing opinion, shall be guaranteed.

8. The right of the parties, organizations and associations whose electoral lists of candidates have been duly presented, and of the candidates themselves, to express and disseminate their opinions verbally, in writing, in print, in pictures or by any other means throughout Germany, shall be guaranteed.

II. *Voting rights and eligibility for election*

9. (1) The members of the German National Assembly shall be elected in free, universal, equal, direct and secret elections by all German men and women over eighteen years of age, according to the principles of proportional representation.

(2) Every voter has one vote.

10. All persons who have completed their eighteenth year on the day of the poll are eligible to vote. Any person entitled to vote and who has

completed his or her twenty-first year on the day of the poll, is eligible to stand as a candidate.

11. Not entitled to vote are those persons who

(1) are under protection or under provisional guardianship or under care and maintenance on account of mental infirmity,

(2) have lost their civic rights through a valid legal sentence. Persons confined in a mental home or lunatic asylum on account of mental illness or mental weakness, persons detained in prison or awaiting trial and persons taken in custody on account of a judicial order are not permitted to vote.

12. Only such persons may vote whose names appear on a list or register of voters or who hold a voting certificate.

13. A member of the Assembly loses his seat

(1) by renunciation,

(2) by subsequent loss of eligibility,

(3) if the poll is declared invalid or any other cause for rejection arises during the scrutiny of the poll,

(4) through a subsequent change in the result of the poll.

Renunciation must be submitted to the Central Election Committee in writing. It cannot be recalled.

III. *Preparation for the Election*

14. (1) The date of the election for the National Assembly shall be decided by the All-German Council. It must take place either on a Sunday or a public holiday.

(2) This decision of the All-German Council shall be announced in the form of a law by the authorities in east and west Germany at least three months before the day of the election.

15. (1) The All-German Council shall form a Central Election Committee to organize the preparation and carrying out of the election and the preliminary scrutiny and confirmation of the result of the poll.

(2) The Central Election Committee shall select the bodies necessary for the performance of the tasks entrusted to it.

16. The Central Election Committee shall consist of representatives of the parties, organizations and associations in existence in Germany at the time when this electoral law comes into force. It will be increased by representatives of such parties, organizations and associations as are admitted to stand for election to the National Assembly after the publication of this electoral law.

17. Every province shall constitute an Electoral District. Greater Berlin shall constitute one unified Electoral District. Every Electoral District shall be divided into voting districts which shall correspond as far as possible with existing communities. Large communities may be

divided into several voting districts. Small communities or parts of communities may be combined with neighbouring communities or parts of communities to form one voting district.

18. An Election Committee shall be formed for every Electoral District and every voting district, composed of representatives of those parties, organizations and associations eligible for the election.

The Election Committee shall select an executive committee for the election, composed of a controller, his deputy and a secretary.

19. A list or register of all voters resident in the district shall be made in every voting district.

20. The following persons shall receive a voting certificate—

I. Voters whose names appear on a list or register of voters, but who
(1) are compelled for urgent reasons to be absent from their voting district on the day and during the period of the poll;
(2) have moved their residence to another voting district after the conclusion of the period during which objections to the electoral register can be lodged (para. 21);
(3) are impeded in their movements by bodily malady or infirmity and would, by means of a voting certificate, be enabled to select a more convenient place to cast their votes.

II. Voters whose names do not appear on any list or register of voters, or have been crossed off such lists or registers, but who
(1) can prove that they have missed the period during which objections could be lodged (para. 21) through no fault of their own;
(2) have not been included in or have been deleted from the list or register on account of a suspension of voting rights, the grounds for the validity of which ceased to exist after the conclusion of the period during which objections could be lodged;
(3) have been living abroad and have returned to their own country after the conclusion of the period during which objections could be lodged.

21. The lists or registers of voters shall be open to inspection by the public. The local authorities shall announce the time and place where they may be inspected and shall at the same time announce during what period and where objections may be lodged against such lists or registers of voters.

22. Voters may only cast their votes in the voting district in whose list or register of voters their names are included. Holders of voting certificates may cast their votes in whatever voting district they wish.

23. Political parties, organizations and associations of voters may present lists of candidates for the election. They have the right to draw up joint lists of candidates. Several lists of candidates may be combined together.

24. Lists of candidates for an Electoral District, and declarations of combinations of lists of candidates must be handed in to the District Electoral Committee at least seventeen days before polling day.

25. (1) The lists of candidates must be signed by at least 500 voters in the Electoral District. The names of the candidates must appear in recognizable sequence. Only such persons may appear on the list of candidates as have declared their willingness to do so. This declaration may be handed in together with the list of candidates.

(2) The signature of twenty voters will suffice in place of 500 in the case of a list of candidates presented by a party, organization or association already in existence in Germany at the time when this law comes into force.

26. The parties, organizations and associations admitted to stand for the election may declare that surplus votes gained by them in district elections shall be counted towards a central list of candidates (Pooling Agreement).

27. (1) Central lists of candidates may be handed in to the Central Election Committee and this must be done at least fourteen days before polling day. They must be signed by at least 500 voters. The signatures of 20 voters instead of 500 will be sufficient for lists presented by parties, organizations or associations already in existence in Germany at the time when this law comes into force.

(2) The names of the candidates must appear in recognizable sequence. Only such persons may appear on the lists of candidates as have declared their willingness to do so. This declaration may be handed in to the Central Election Committee together with the list of candidates.

(3) Nomination in a central list of candidates does not exclude nomination in a district list, as long as both nominations are made on behalf of the same party, organization or association or a declaration of combination has been presented.

28. The Central Election Committee shall publish the central lists of candidates, as they are admitted in a continuous numerical order. Publication shall take place at least 11 days before polling day.

29. The District Electoral Committee shall publish the district lists of candidates, and declarations of combination of lists, together with the central lists of candidates with which such district lists have been combined.

30. (1) The voting papers and envelopes shall be the same for all voters and no mark shall be made upon them which would reveal the identity of the voter.

(2) The voting papers shall be officially prepared for the electoral district by the provincial government, in such a way that all admitted district lists of candidates, together with the name of the party, organization or association concerned and the names of the candidates, appear on them.

In Greater Berlin the voting papers shall be prepared in the same manner by the Electoral Committee of Greater Berlin.

IV. *Polling and scrutiny of the election result*

31. A secret ballot shall be guaranteed.

32. Polling and scrutiny of the election result shall be public.

33. Polling shall be upon voting papers in officially stamped envelopes. Persons who are absent can neither be represented by proxies nor take part in the polling in any other way.

34. The marking of the ballot papers by voters shall take place in a part of the polling booth where they cannot be overlooked by other persons. The voter will place his ballot paper in an envelope in the ballot box in front of the election committee.

35. No departure from these rules will be permitted. Any contravention will render the entire poll of the voting district invalid.

36. The votes shall be publicly counted by the Election Committee composed of representatives of the parties, organizations and associations.

37. In the scrutiny of the election result the Election Committee shall establish how many valid votes have been cast and how many of these are given to each list of candidates.

38. (1) Seats in the National Assembly shall be allotted to each list of candidates in the proportion of one seat for every 60,000 votes cast for that list in the Electoral District.

(2) Votes numerically insufficient for the allotment of one, or one more, seat to a district list (surplus votes), shall be passed on for counting to the Central Election Committee.

39. The Central Election Committee shall count the surplus votes from the electoral districts on behalf of the central lists of candidates. For every 60,000 votes gained in this way, one, or one more, seat shall be allotted. Should there still be a remainder of at least 30,000 votes, this remainder shall be regarded as equivalent to 60,000 votes.

40. Seats shall be allotted to candidates according to the sequence in which they appear on the lists of candidates.

41. (1) If a list of candidates contains the names of fewer candidates than the seats allotted to it, then the District Electoral Committee shall require the appropriate party, organization or association to nominate the appropriate number of candidates. The District Electoral Committee shall be informed of the nominations not more than three days after the request has been received.

(2) A similar procedure will be observed in the case of central lists of candidates.

42. (1) If a member refuses his election, or if a member withdraws, his place shall be taken by the next candidate named on the list.

(2) If no further candidate is available, the procedure outlined in para. 41 shall be used.

43. (1) If the poll of an entire Electoral District is declared invalid by the Central Election Committee, then the Central Election Committee shall allot all the surplus votes again on the basis of the result of a repetition of the poll.

(2) If as a result of this, more seats are allotted to a central list of candidates or combined list of candidates, a corresponding number of new seats shall be filled in accordance with the procedure laid down in paras. 38–40. If any list of candidates should receive fewer seats than before, the Central Election Committee shall declare a corresponding number of seats vacated.

44. (1) If the poll has not been carried out according to rule only in single voting districts, the District Electoral Committee may resolve that the poll be taken again (repetition of the poll). The repetition of the poll is to be held on the third Sunday or holiday following the decision of the District Electoral Committee for a repetition of the poll.

(2) The same lists of candidates and the same lists or registers of voters shall be used in a repetition of the poll as were used on the main polling day.

V. *Final Decisions*

45. (1) The National Assembly shall meet in Berlin not more than 30 days after the election.

(2) Members of the National Assembly are guaranteed personal freedom and protection from prosecution.

46. The electoral law accepted by the All-German Council shall be proclaimed as law by the authorities in east and west Germany at least 3 months before polling day.

47. The Central Election Committee shall announce the result of the election. The results shall be published in the official gazettes of east and west Germany.

48. The National Assembly shall be summoned by the Central Election Committee. Time and place of the meeting shall be announced immediately by the authorities in east and west Germany. The members of the National Assembly shall be informed of their election and of the time and place of the meeting by the Central Election Committee as quickly as possible.

(ii) Communiqué issued by the conference of six Foreign Ministers on the European army, Paris, 28 January 1952[1]

Les ministres des affaires étrangères d'Allemagne, de Belgique, de France, d'Italie, du Luxembourg et des Pays-Bas se sont réunis à Paris les

---

[1] *Le Monde*, 29 January 1952.

26 et 27 janvier afin d'étudier les questions qui leur avaient été soumises à la conférence des experts chargés de l'élaboration d'un projet de traité et de l'organisation de la communauté européenne de défense.

Sur tous les points qui figuraient à l'ordre du jour de cette conférence des décisions ont été prises *ad referendum*. Elles sont soumises par les ministres à l'examen de leurs gouvernements. Une nouvelle réunion des ministres pourrait être tenue si cela apparaissait nécessaire.

Les ministres recommanderont à leurs gouvernements les propositions suivantes:

1. L'autorité collégiale exécutive de la communauté portera le nom de 'commissariat de la communauté européenne de défense'.

2. Ce commissariat comprendra neuf membres, nommés pour six ans et choisis pour leur compétence générale parmi les nationaux des États participants, les règles de nomination et de renouvellement seront analogues à celles qui ont été adoptées pour la communauté du charbon et de l'acier;

3. Il a été précisé que l'organisation des institutions de la communauté (conseil des ministres, assemblée, commissariat, cour de justice) restera en vigueur dans sa forme actuelle jusqu'à l'établissement aussi proche que possible d'une structure fédérale ou confédérale de l'Europe;

4. L'assemblée de la communauté de défense sera la même que celle prévue pour le traité de la communauté du charbon et de l'acier. Les ministres ont en effet le souci de ne pas multiplier indûment le nombre des institutions communes. Toutefois il a été décidé que les trois pays de la communauté qui fourniront la contribution la plus élevée, c'est-à-dire la France, l'Allemagne et l'Italie, désigneront chacun trois délégués supplémentaires à cette assemblée pour les délibérations de la communauté européenne de défense. La composition de l'assemblée pourrait être révisée au cas où la conférence, dont la réunion a été décidée pour la constitution d'une structure fédérale ou confédérale européenne, n'aurait pas abouti dans le délai d'un an après sa convocation;

5. Les règles de vote au conseil des ministres de la communauté ont été déterminées;

6. La cour de justice de la communauté de défense sera la même que celle de la communauté du charbon et de l'acier;

7. Il a été décidé qu'il n'y avait pas lieu de fixer le siège des institutions de la communauté de défense avant la signature du traité;

8. Les ministres ont procédé à un très complet échange de vues sur le problème de la mise en harmonie des engagements qui seront souscrits dans le traité à conclure avec ceux contenus dans le traité de l'Atlantique nord, ainsi que sur la question des rapports à établir entre la future communauté européenne de défense et l'organisation du traité de l'Atlantique nord. A cette occasion le secrétaire d'État aux affaires étrangères de la

République fédérale allemande a précisé l'attitude de principe de son gouvernement, et a exposé que l'inclusion de l'Allemagne dans la communauté de défense, dont l'élaboration est actuellement en cours, ne pourrait être interprétée comme une renonciation de sa part à une association ultérieure au traité de l'Atlantique nord. Après avoir précisé de nombreuses questions relatives à ces divers problèmes les ministres ont décidé que l'étude en serait continuée les prochains jours, tant par les experts que par les gouvernements eux-mêmes, compte tenu, comme il avait été prévu à Rome par le Conseil de l'Atlantique nord,[1] des travaux que les organismes compétents du pacte atlantique poursuivent pour leur part sur le même sujet;

9. La question de la durée du traité et celle des pouvoirs budgétaires de l'assemblée ont été examinées par les ministres, qui ont donné aux experts des directives pour leur mise au point.

Enfin les ministres ont pris connaissance de l'état des travaux de la conférence des experts qui ont été présentés par son président. Ils ont constaté les progrès accomplis et les accords de principe intervenus en ce qui concerne notamment les problèmes du budget commun, du programme commun d'armement et d'équipement, les questions relatives aux relations entre le commissariat, le conseil des ministres et l'assemblée, et les principaux problèmes de caractère militaire.

Les ministres ont considéré que sur ces points essentiels on peut envisager qu'une entente finale interviendra dans un proche avenir. Ils se sont félicités de l'esprit qui a présidé à ces discussions. Chaque délégation y a participé avec la volonté de constituer rapidement l'institution nouvelle et l'espoir que la communauté européenne de défense sera un élément capital pour le maintien de la paix et la création d'une Europe véritablement unie.

(iii) Resolutions on the European Defence Community, the Saar, and the future of Germany, adopted by the Bundestag of the Federal German Republic on 8 February 1952[2]

I

The German Bundestag, by an overwhelming majority on July 26, 1950, expressed its readiness to conclude a European Federal Pact and to create a supra-national European Federal Authority. We renew our resolve to see Europe united in a federation of all free European peoples extending equal rights to and imposing equal obligations upon its members.

In view of the world situation, the developing European Community

---

[1] *Documents* (R.I.I.A.) for 1951, pp. 61–62.

[2] Office of the U.S. High Commissioner for Germany: *Tenth Quarterly Report on Germany, January 1 1952–March 31 1952*, Appendix I, pp. 83–85.

cannot evade the duty of defending, in cooperation with the other nations of the free world, the basic rights of freedom and democracy. It must be the exclusive aim of these common efforts to ensure peace and to ward off any threat to this peace. Germany will cooperate as an equal partner in this task, conscious that there can be no neutrality toward the foes of liberty. In peace and liberty we want to reunite the whole of Germany.

II

The Bundestag shares the opinion of the Federal Government that, as long as the Federal Republic is not yet a member of NATO, agreements must be made in order to ensure for the Federal Republic those rights which correspond to the conception of the European Defense Community as a voluntary association of partners with equal rights.

III

The exchange of letters between the Federal Chancellor and the French Minister of Foreign Affairs, in which the French Government gave assurances to the effect that the political fate of the Saar would be decided only by the peace treaty, had been attached to the 'Treaty establishing a European Coal and Steel Community', signed in Paris on April 18, 1951, and had been made an integral part of this instrument.[1] The German Bundestag regrets to note that the following measures conflict with this assurance:

The appointment of a French Ambassador in the Saar, and the French intention, which became known at the same time, to attach Saar representatives to the French Foreign Missions.

The French interest in being supplied with coal and steel from the Saar has already been satisfied by the European Coal and Steel Community. Therefore, the Bundestag firmly opposes the attempt by the French Government to anticipate the decision on the political fate of the German Saar population before conclusion of a peace treaty. Above all, the Bundestag expects the Federal Government to do all in its power in order that the population of the Saar may at last recover their political liberties in accordance with the Charter of the United Nations.

IV

The Bundestag requests the Federal Government to insist during the negotiations on the assessment of a German financial defense contribution that the same criteria be used with regard to the Federal Republic's financial capacity as are applied to the other nations of the Western Defense Community. The German special burdens must be adequately

---

[1] *Documents* (R.I.I.A.) for 1951, p. 242.

taken into account. The social and economic order, being the best protection against Bolshevism, must not be undermined. The present German tax burden is the heaviest of any European country. An attempt to further increase taxation would certainly achieve the opposite of the desired result: output and productivity would decrease and thereby jeopardize a German defense contribution.

V

The Bundestag considers it necessary that all those Germans be released who have either been convicted on charges of war crimes by Allied courts or who are still detained without sentence, except where individuals are to be called to account for crimes in the traditional meaning of the word. An impartial review of the individual cases must take place without delay.

VI

1. The Occupation regime must terminate. The only task left for the Allied troops remaining in Germany is to contribute to the common defense of Europe and of the free world. Their legal status must be adjusted to this task and must be kept within the framework of international practice in comparable situations. Any functions exceeding this framework are incompatible with the principle of equal rights and duties.

2. The sovereignty of the Federal Republic over domestic and foreign affairs may only be curtailed, if at all, to the extent and as long as the peculiar present international position of Germany, especially the division of Germany and the exposed position of Berlin, require such restrictions in the interest of Germany.

3. The maintenance and 'perpetuation' (*Versteinerung*) of parts of existing Occupation legislation and of Allied rights of intervention are not compatible with the foregoing, except for technical liquidation measures. The Federal Republic must recover its full legislative sovereignty and must, in principle, be able to decide freely which legislation and measures enacted during the Occupation should remain in force.

4. It would also be incompatible with this principle if the contractual agreements should in any way render the position of the Federal Republic more difficult in regard to a future peace treaty.

5. It is incompatible with the spirit of free and equal partnership on which the Defense Community of the nations of Europe and of the free world must be built, to have any one-sided discriminatory restrictions on industrial production and on research. Control agencies similar to those under Occupation regime, such as the Military Security Board, must be dissolved and terminate their functions.

6. There can be only one overall German defense contribution in military as well as in financial respect. Labor Groups (*Dienstgruppen*) in

the service of the Allied armed forces are therefore to be dissolved in due time. The global amount of the German financial defense contribution must be assessed in accordance with the economic capacity of the Federal Republic, with appropriate consideration for the particular burdens arising from the care for nine million expellees. Out of this global amount must come the contribution to the European Defense Community and the financial assistance to Berlin; expenditure for the troops stationed in the territory of the Federal Republic must be charged against the contribution to the European Defense Community.

7. All disputes arising from the contractual relations of the Federal Republic with the Three Powers, and particularly from the stationing of Allied forces in the Federal territory, must be settled by impartial arbitration tribunals established on a basis of parity. Provision for revision must be made in all contracts.

8. The Federal Government is requested
   to strive for the earliest possible establishment in Berlin of a system of legislation which is in conformity and consistent with that of the Federal Republic,
   to strengthen the self-government of Berlin,
   and
   to ensure that in the meantime the City of Berlin and the Berlin population be represented abroad by the agencies of the Federal Republic.

(iv) Letter from the east German Prime Minister, Herr Otto Grotewohl, to the four occupying Powers requesting the early conclusion of a peace treaty with Germany, 13 February 1952[1]

At a moment exceedingly grave for Germany, the Government of the German Democratic Republic, in great anxiety over the future of the German people, turns to the Government of the Union of Soviet Socialist Republics, the United States of America, the United Kingdom of Great Britain and Northern Ireland, and the Republic of France with the request that they hasten the conclusion of a peace treaty with Germany.

Although nearly seven years have passed since the capitulation of Hitler's Germany, Germany thus far still has no peace treaty to which it is entitled. Germany is split and the German nation at present has no possibility of reconstructing its own, unified, independent, peace-loving and democratic state.

The Allied Powers assured the German people in the Decisions of the Potsdam Conference of a peace treaty and of the restoration of Germany's

---

[1] Office of the U.S. High Commissioner for Germany: *Tenth Quarterly Report on Germany, January 1, 1952–March 31, 1952*, Annex V, pp. 94–95. The three western Powers did not reply. For the Russian reply see below, p. 85.

unity, and they showed the German nation that it had the opportunity to take, in future, a dignified place among the family of peace-loving nations of the world.

The German nation is fully cognizant of its guilt ensuing from Hitler's war; it does not, however, feel that it is being treated justly.

The German nation is imbued with the wish and the will for peace, for its political and economic unity. It wants to live in peaceful alliance with the nations of the world and, through the reconstruction of its peacetime economy, it wants to achieve an improvement in its living conditions. The German nation does not wish to be dragged into any international complications or conflicts which are connected with the striving of aggressive forces to exploit the absence of a peace treaty and the division of Germany to unleash a new world war.

The peace treaty with Germany is imperative for the German people in eliminating the division of Germany and in creating a unified, independent, democratic, and peace-loving state.

The peace treaty would make the peaceful development of the German state possible and would, in accord with the national interests of the German people, preserve and ensure the peace of Europe.

The peace treaty with Germany is necessary to prevent the danger of a rebirth of German militarism and new attempts at aggression on its part.

The peace treaty would enable the German people to place its full strength at the service of peaceful reconstruction.

The peace treaty would also ensure the early restoration of normal relations between Germany and other states and would place the German nation in an equal position with all peace-loving nations of the world.

The Government of the German Democratic Republic declares that it will take a firm and resolute stand for the realization of the above-named principles. It will fight resolutely any attempt to revive German militarism that threatens to involve Germany in a new world war. This world war would imply for the German people a murderous war of brother against brother among Germans themselves and the destruction of Germany.

The Government of the German Democratic Republic expects that the Government of the United States of America will consider the request to hasten the conclusion of a peace treaty with Germany and will comply with it. The Government of the German Democratic Republic is expressing the hope that the Allied Powers will adopt a positive decision that will end the present abnormal conditions in Germany.

An analogous letter has been sent to the Governments of the Union of Soviet Socialist Republics, the United Kingdom of Great Britain and Northern Ireland, and the Republic of France.

(v) Resolution on a European Defence Force and German participation in the Defence Community adopted by the French National Assembly on 19 February 1952[1]

L'Assemblée nationale:

Consciente de la nécessité de ne rien négliger dans l'effort de défense collective imposé au monde libre,

Affirme la volonté de la France de contribuer de toute son énergie à l'édification d'une Europe politiquement et économiquement unie.

Et approuve l'idée d'intégrer les forces nationales des pays d'Europe dans une armée européenne.

Elle souligne que cette volonté de renforcer la puissance des peuples libres — susceptible d'entraîner sous réserve des garanties indispensables une participation allemande à la communauté européenne de défense — n'est rendue nécessaire que par la persistance de la méfiance internationale.

Convaincue de la nécessité de tout faire pour atténuer cette méfiance et de tout mettre en œuvre pour maintenir et consolider la paix en même temps que se renforcent les peuples libres,

Persuadée que l'organisation de la défense commune ne saurait en aucune manière contredire les efforts simultanément entrepris pour assurer un désarmement général et contrôlé,

Approuve l'appel solennel adressé par le président du conseil en vue de mener à bonne fin les travaux de la commission du désarmement de l'O.N.U. et d'aboutir à un règlement pacifique des problèmes qui divisent actuellement les nations du monde.

Précise qu'aucun recrutement de contingents d'origine allemande ne saurait avoir lieu avant la ratification du traité par les parlements.

L'Assemblée nationale accepte que soit accordé à l'Allemagne un traitement non discriminatoire dans les organisations intégrées, rappelle que les accords contractuels qui seront substitués au régime d'occupation lorsque la communauté européenne de défense sera entrée en vigueur devront comporter les garanties nécessaires en ce qui concerne les fabrications d'armement, la police et la répartition des charges financières et rappelle qu'en aucun cas l'admission de l'Allemagne à la communauté européenne de défense n'est liée à son entrée dans l'organisation atlantique.

Étant rappelé qu'il ne saurait être dérogé à la règle selon laquelle un État ne peut être invité à cette organisation sans décision préalable des parlements et que, d'autre part, l'organisation étant de caractère exclusivement défensif, ne doit réunir que des États n'ayant pas de revendications territoriales,

Elle recommande au Gouvernement

a) De veiller à ce que la rédaction du traité précise que la communauté

[1] *Journal Officiel, Débats*, 17 February 1952, p. 726.

européenne de défense ait pour objet exclusif d'assurer une défense plus efficace du territoire des États membres de la communauté européenne et une répartition équitable des charges qui tiennent compte en particulier de l'étendue des sacrifices que la France consent en Indochine pour la défense du monde libre;

b) De réaliser les conditions économiques de base que nécessite la construction d'une force militaire européenne;

c) De demander aux gouvernements britannique et américain de garantir, en cas de rupture ou de violation du traité par une nation membre, les engagements pris envers la communauté européenne de défense, cette garantie étant matérialisée par le maintien aussi longtemps qu'il apparaît nécessaire de forces américaines et britanniques suffisantes sur le continent européen;

d) Que des contingents français disponibles en Europe et mis à la disposition de la communauté européenne de défense soient à tout moment au moins égaux à ceux de tout autre membre de la communauté, qu'un rapport de forces acceptable et constant soit ainsi assuré au sein de l'armée européenne qui n'excède pas pour la France ses possibilités tant dans le domaine financier qu'en matière d'effectifs;

e) Que l'intégration des contingents nationaux s'effectue à l'échelon le plus bas possible et de manière à éviter tout danger de reconstitution par l'adjonction aux unités de base de services de même nationalité, de forces nationales autonomes;

f) Que le Gouvernement prenne les initiatives nécessaires pour qu'aussitôt que possible le texte du traité instituant la communauté européenne de défense soit soumis pour avis à l'Assemblée consultative du Conseil de l'Europe;

g) De prévoir dans les protocoles annexes du traité, la mise en place progressive des unités, au fur et à mesure que pourra matériellement être établie l'organisation commune.

Elle demande que tout soit mis en œuvre pour assurer:

1. La subordination de l'armée européenne à un pouvoir politique supranational à compétence limitée, mais réelle, responsable devant des représentants des assemblées ou des peuples européens et invite le Gouvernement à prendre dans ce sens toutes initiatives nécessaires;

2. La stricte limitation et l'énumération précise des cas où peut jouer la règle d'unanimité ainsi que l'établissement d'un budget commun voté par l'Assemblée et non soumis à un droit de veto.

Elle maintient son opposition à la reconstitution d'une armée nationale et d'un état-major allemands.

Elle invite le Gouvernement à renouveler tous ses efforts avec volonté profonde d'aboutir, en vue d'obtenir la participation dans la communauté européenne de défense d'autres nations démocratiques et, notamment, de la Grande-Bretagne; cette solution constituant une garantie qui répond pleinement aux soucis exprimés par l'Assemblée nationale, comporterait naturellement l'étude et la mise au point des institutions et des modalités les plus susceptibles d'en assurer la réussite,

Et repoussant toute addition, passe à l'ordre du jour.

(vi) COMMUNIQUÉ ISSUED AFTER TALKS BETWEEN MR. EDEN, MR. ACHESON AND M. SCHUMAN REGARDING THE ESTABLISHMENT OF A EUROPEAN DEFENCE COMMUNITY, LONDON, 19 FEBRUARY 1952[1]

During their meetings at the Foreign Office on the 17th, 18th, and 19th of February, the Foreign Ministers of the United Kingdom, the United States and France considered a number of questions which were subsequently discussed with the German Federal Chancellor. They also examined the relationship to be established between the European defense community and the North Atlantic Treaty Organization.

The Foreign Ministers of the United Kingdom and the United States declared their abiding interest in the establishment and integrity of the European defense community and, in association with the Foreign Minister of France, studied means by which their governments could support and co-operate with the community. These subjects will be matters of continuing consultation between the three ministers and between their governments in order to find appropriate means of giving the community the desired co-operation and support.

The Foreign Ministers of the United Kingdom and the United States recalled the decision of their governments to maintain armed forces in Europe which, in association with the European defense forces, will contribute their fair share in joint defense of the North Atlantic area.

(vii) COMMUNIQUÉ ISSUED AFTER THE TALKS BETWEEN MR. EDEN, MR. ACHESON, M. SCHUMAN AND DR. ADENAUER ON THE EUROPEAN DEFENCE COMMUNITY AND ON THE GERMAN CONTRIBUTION TO WESTERN DEFENCE, LONDON, 19 FEBRUARY 1952[2]

The Foreign Ministers of the United States, France and the United Kingdom and the Chancellor of the German Federal Republic met for discussions in the Foreign Office on the 18th and 19th of February. They reviewed the position reached in the parallel negotiations in Paris and in Bonn, now approaching a successful conclusion, for the establishment of the European defense community and for the creation of a new relationship between the three Western powers and the Federal Republic of Germany based on a series of freely negotiated conventions.

---

[1] *Department of State Bulletin*, 3 March 1952, p. 325.
[2] Ibid., pp. 325-6.

The Foreign Ministers and the Chancellor are well pleased with the results of their work. They reached agreement on outstanding issues arising from the negotiations in Bonn. The question of Germany's financial contribution to European defense is dealt with below.

On the difficult problem concerning the future regulation and distribution in the interests of Western defense of arms production in the states of the European defense community they have reached certain conclusions and provided for a series of meetings which they are confident will produce speedy results.

They reached agreement on methods for dealing with the question of war criminals now detained in the Federal Republic.

They reviewed the report made by the Executive Bureau of the Temporary Council Committee of the North Atlantic Treaty Organization on the financial contribution of the Federal Republic to Western defense. The ministers agreed that this report, which reached them on the 16th of February, should be published tonight.[1] There is every prospect that an agreed decision on the total financial contribution of the Federal Republic to defense will be reached by the end of the current week.

Negotiations on other matters arising out of this report, including the distribution of the Federal Republic's contribution, will proceed at once in Bonn between representatives of the German Federal Republic and of the three powers.

The four ministers welcome the progress made towards the conclusion of the treaty for the establishment of the European defense community which will provide a solid foundation for the agreements to be concluded between the three Western powers and the Federal Republic of Germany. This treaty and the agreements will constitute a single structure designed to bring about the association of the Federal Republic with the free world and to solidify the defense of Western Europe.

The four ministers discussed the relationship between the European defense community and the North Atlantic Treaty Organization and agreed on certain recommendations which will be made by the three foreign ministers to the NATO Council for settling this question.

It will be the concern of the four governments, together with the other interested governments, to ensure the preservation and the progressive strengthening of the European defense community which, as a part of the wider Atlantic community, creates a partnership for peace.

The four ministers are agreed that continuing efforts should be made to accomplish the unification of Germany through democratic and peaceful means.

The four ministers are convinced that their meeting has removed the obstacles which have hitherto delayed the conclusion of the negotiations and has thus marked a decisive advance in the cause of peace.

[1] *Department of State Bulletin*, 17 March 1952, pp. 423–6.

(viii) Reply from the U.S.S.R. to the east German note of 13 February requesting the early conclusion of a peace treaty with Germany, 20 February 1952[1]

The Soviet Government confirms having received the note regarding the question of hastening the conclusion of a peace treaty with Germany, which the Government of the German Democratic Republic has communicated to the Governments of the Soviet Union, the United States of America, Great Britain and France.

The Soviet Government shares the view which the Government of the German Democratic Republic has set forth in its note.   It is likewise of the opinion that such a situation—namely, that Germany is still without a peace treaty after almost seven years since the end of the war and that the German state remains divided—is absolutely abnormal.

The Government of the U.S.S.R. is of the opinion that it is necessary forthwith to conclude a peace treaty with Germany, in accordance with the Potsdam decisions and with the participation of Germany.   It is convinced that this agrees with the interests of all peace-loving nations of Europe.

Realizing that the conclusion of a peace treaty with Germany is of the greatest significance for the consolidation of peace in Europe, the Soviet Government for its part will do everything possible to hasten the conclusion of a peace treaty with Germany as well as the restoration of the unity of the German state.

The Soviet Government expects that the other Great Powers which exercise control functions in Germany will also take corresponding steps.

(ix) Note from the U.S.S.R. to the three western Powers containing proposals for a treaty of peace with Germany, 10 March 1952[2]

The Soviet Government considers it necessary to direct the attention of the Government of the United States of America to the fact that although about seven years have passed since the end of the war in Europe a peace treaty with Germany is not yet concluded.

With the aim of eliminating such an abnormal situation the Soviet Government, supporting the communication of the Government of the German Democratic Republic to the Four Powers requesting that conclusion of a peace treaty with Germany be expedited, on its part addresses itself to the Government of the United States and also to the Governments

[1] Office of the U.S. High Commissioner for Germany: *Tenth Quarterly Report on Germany, January 1, 1952–March 31, 1952*, Annex V, pp. 95–96.
[2] *Department of State Bulletin*, 7 April 1952, pp. 531–2.

of Great Britain and France with the proposal to urgently discuss the question of a peace treaty with Germany with a view to preparing in the nearest future an agreed draft peace treaty and present it for examination by an appropriate international conference with the participation of all interested governments. It is understood that such a peace treaty must be worked out with the direct participation of Germany in the form of an all-German Government. From this it follows that the U.S.S.R., U.S.A., England, and France, who are fulfilling control functions in Germany, must also consider the question of conditions favoring the earliest formation of an all-German Government expressing the will of the German people.

With the aim of facilitating the preparation of a draft peace treaty the Soviet Government on its part proposes for the consideration of the Governments of the U.S.A., Great Britain and France the attached draft as a basis of a peace treaty with Germany.

In proposing consideration of this draft the Soviet Government at the same time expresses its readiness also to consider other possible proposals on this question.

The Government of the U.S.S.R. expects to receive the reply of the Government of the U.S.A. to the mentioned proposal at the earliest possible time.

Similar notes have also been sent by the Soviet Government to the Governments of Great Britain and France.

ENCLOSURE

Draft of Soviet Government of Peace Treaty with Germany

Almost seven years have passed since the end of the war with Germany but Germany still does not have a peace treaty, finds itself divided, continues to remain in an unequal situation as regards other governments. It is necessary to end such an abnormal situation. This responds to the aspirations of all peace loving peoples. It is impossible to assure a just status to the legal national interests of the German people without the earliest conclusion of a peace treaty with Germany.

Conclusion of a peace treaty with Germany has an important significance for the strengthening of peace in Europe. A peace treaty with Germany will permit final decision of questions which have arisen as a consequence of the second world war. The European states which have suffered from German aggression, particularly the neighbors of Germany, have a vital interest in the solution of these questions. Conclusion of a peace treaty with Germany will aid improvement of the international situation as a whole and at the same time aid the establishment of a lasting peace.

The necessity of hastening the conclusion of a peace treaty with Germany is required by the fact that the danger of re-establishment of German militarism which has twice unleashed world wars has not been eliminated in as much as appropriate provisions of the Potsdam conference still remain unfulfilled. A peace treaty with Germany must guarantee elimination of the possibility of a rebirth of German militarism and German aggression.

Conclusion of the peace treaty with Germany will establish for the German people permanent conditions of peace, will aid the development of Germany as a unified democratic and peace-loving government in accordance with the Potsdam provisions and will assure to the German people the possibility of peaceful cooperation with other peoples.

As a result of this, the Governments of the Soviet Union, the United States of America, Great Britain and France have decided urgently to set about working out a peace treaty with Germany.

The Governments of the Union of Soviet Socialist Republics, United States of America, Great Britain and France consider that preparations of the peace treaty should be accomplished with the participation of Germany in the form of an all-German Government and that the peace treaty with Germany should be formed on the following basis:

Basis of Peace Treaty with Germany

Participants

Great Britain, the Soviet Union, the United States of America, France, Poland, Czechoslovakia, Belgium, Holland and other governments which participated with their armed forces in the war against Germany.

Political Provisions

(1) Germany is re-established as a unified state, thereby an end is put to the division of Germany and a unified Germany has a possibility of development as an independent democratic peace-loving state.

(2) All armed forces of the occupying powers must be withdrawn from Germany not later than one year from the date of entry into force of the peace treaty. Simultaneously all foreign military bases on the territory of Germany must be liquidated.

(3) Democratic rights must be guaranteed to the German people to the end that all persons under German jurisdiction without regard to race, sex, language or religion enjoy the rights of man and basic freedoms including freedom of speech, press, religious persuasion, political conviction and assembly.

(4) Free activity of democratic parties and organizations must be guaranteed in Germany with the right of freedom to decide their own internal affairs, to conduct meetings and assembly, to enjoy freedom of press and publication.

(5) The existence of organizations inimical to democracy and to the maintenance of peace must not be permitted on the territory of Germany.

(6) Civil and political rights equal to all other German citizens for participation in the building of peace-loving democratic Germany must be made available to all former members of the German army, including officers and generals, all former Nazis, excluding those who are serving court sentences for commission of crimes.

(7) Germany obligates itself not to enter into any kind of coalition or military alliance directed against any power which took part with its armed forces in the war against Germany.

Territory

The territory of Germany is defined by the borders established by the provisions of the Potsdam Conference of the Great Powers.

Economic Provisions

No kind of limitations are imposed on Germany as to development of its peaceful economy, which must contribute to the growth of the welfare of the German people.

Likewise, Germany will have no kind of limitation as regards trade with other countries, navigation and access to world markets.

Military Provisions

(1) Germany will be permitted to have its own national armed forces (land, air, and sea) which are necessary for the defense of the country.

(2) Germany is permitted to produce war materials and equipment, the quantity and type of which must not exceed the limitations required for the armed forces established for Germany by the peace treaty.

Germany and the United Nations Organization

The governments concluding a peace treaty with Germany will support the application of Germany for acceptance as a member of the United Nations Organization.

(x) EXTRACT FROM A SPEECH BY THE FEDERAL CHANCELLOR, DR. KONRAD ADENAUER, ON THE RUSSIAN NOTE OF 10 MARCH, SIEGEN, 16 MARCH 1952[1]

The aim of German policy, today as yesterday, is that the west should become strong enough to be able to conduct reasonable conversations with the Soviet Union. We are firmly convinced—and the latest note from Soviet Russia is only another proof of this—that if we continue in this path

---

[1] Translated from *Relazioni Internazionali* (Milan, Istituto per gli Studi di Politica Internazionale), 22 March 1952, p. 314.

the moment will not be too distant when Soviet Russia will declare itself ready for reasonable negotiations.   The Russian note regarding the conclusion of a peace treaty with Germany already marks a distinct progress, for we should not let slip any possibility of reaching a peaceful agreement and a new order in Europe.   On the other hand delay in the construction of European defence and European union should not, at any cost, be permitted.   Such a delay would, in all probability, mean the end of the efforts, which are of vital importance, for the unification of the west.

How does Soviet Russia conceive of a single government for the whole of Germany?   According to German opinion a common German government can be set up only after free and secret elections.   How should the problem of the German territories beyond the Oder–Neisse line be solved? The answer to this question would explain many things.   German national rearmament, as foreseen in the Soviet note, is not possible, given the continued technical progress in armaments.   Since 1945 there has been such progress made in military science that with its own financial and material resources alone Germany is not in a position to maintain national rearmament.   In this respect this part of the Soviet note is only 'a scrap of paper'.   Moreover it is not suitable for the Federal government to reply immediately to the Soviet note, in view of the fact that the note is addressed to the western Powers.   I think that the German side should put forward its point of view.   This should naturally be done with all due moderation.

(xi) United States reply to the Russian note of 10 March, 25 March 1952[1]

The United States Government, in consultation with the Governments of the United Kingdom and France, has given the most careful consideration to the Soviet Government's note of March 10, 1952, which proposed the conclusion of a peace treaty with Germany.   They have also consulted the Government of the German Federal Republic and the representatives of Berlin.

The conclusion of a just and lasting peace treaty which would end the division of Germany has always been and remains an essential objective of the United States Government.   As the Soviet Government itself recognizes, the conclusion of such a treaty requires the formation of an all-German Government, expressing the will of the German people.   Such a Government can only be set up on the basis of free elections in the Federal Republic, the Soviet zone of occupation and Berlin.   Such elections can only be held in circumstances which safeguard the national and individual liberties of the German people. In order to ascertain whether this first essential condition exists, the General Assembly of the United

[1] *Department of State Bulletin*, 7 April 1952, pp. 530–1.

Nations has appointed a Commission to carry out a simultaneous investigation in the Federal Republic, the Soviet zone and Berlin.[1] The Commission of Investigation has been assured of the necessary facilities in the Federal Republic and in Western Berlin. The United States Government would be glad to learn that such facilities will also be afforded in the Soviet zone and in Eastern Berlin, to enable the Commission to carry out its task.

The Soviet Government's proposals do not indicate what the international position of an all-German Government would be before the conclusion of a peace treaty. The United States Government considers that the all-German Government should be free both before and after the conclusion of a peace treaty to enter into associations compatible with the principles and purposes of the United Nations.

In putting forward its proposal for a German peace treaty, the Soviet Government expressed its readiness also to discuss other proposals. The United States Government has taken due note of this statement. In its view, it will not be possible to engage in detailed discussion of a peace treaty until conditions have been created for free elections and until a free all-German Government which could participate in such discussion has been formed. There are several fundamental questions which would also have to be resolved.

For example, the United States Government notes that the Soviet Government makes the statement that the territory of Germany is determined by frontiers laid down by the decisions of the Potsdam conference. The United States Government would recall that in fact no definitive German frontiers were laid down by the Potsdam decisions, which clearly provided that the final determination of territorial questions must await the peace settlement.

The United States Government also observes that the Soviet Government now considers that the peace treaty should provide for the formation of German national land, air, and sea forces, while at the same time imposing limitations on Germany's freedom to enter into association with other countries. The United States Government considers that such provisions would be a step backwards and might jeopardize the emergence in Europe of a new era in which international relations would be based on cooperation and not on rivalry and distrust. Being convinced of the need of a policy of European unity, the United States Government is giving its full support to plans designed to secure the participation of Germany in a purely defensive European community which will preserve freedom, prevent aggression, and preclude the revival of militarism. The United States Government believes that the proposal of the Soviet Government for the formation of German national forces is inconsistent with the achievement

[1] *Documents* (R.I.I.A.) for 1951, p. 287.

of this objective. The United States Government remains convinced that this policy of European unity cannot threaten the interests of any country and represents the true path of peace.

(xii) RESOLUTION ON FOREIGN POLICY ADOPTED BY THE BUNDESTAG ON
3 APRIL 1952[1]

The Bundestag, in conformity with the Federal government's declaration of 27 September 1951, reaffirms that the reunification of Germany within a free and united Europe is the principal object of Germany policy.

In the exchange of notes between the Soviet Union and the three western Powers on 10 and 25 March 1952 the Bundestag sees an important contribution towards the clarification of the premises essential for the attainment of this objective and a renewed opportunity for the efforts of the Federal government towards reconstituting a single state on a democratic basis which should include all Germany.

The Bundestag asks the Federal government to approach the occupying Powers again with a view to the holding of free elections for a National Assembly for the whole of Germany on the basis of the draft electoral law approved by the Bundestag on 6 February 1952,[2] and under international guarantees, in order that freedom of decision in internal and external politics may be assured to the organs of state created by such elections.

The Bundestag expresses the hope that negotiations will continue between the Federal government and the western occupying Powers for the abolition of the Occupation Statute and for a security pact and that the results of these negotiations will be submitted to the Bundestag.

The Federal government is requested to present to the Bundestag an exposal of all the appropriate facts to support the German point of view in the international negotiations for the reunification of Germany and the conclusion of a treaty of peace.

(xiii) FURTHER NOTE FROM THE U.S.S.R. TO THE THREE WESTERN POWERS
REGARDING A PEACE TREATY FOR GERMANY AND ALL-GERMAN ELECTIONS,
9 APRIL 1952[3]

In connection with the note of the Government of the United States of America of March 25, the Soviet Government considers it necessary to state the following:

In its note of March 10 the Soviet Government suggested to the Government of the United States of America and also to the Governments of

---

[1] Translated from *Relazioni Internazionali*, 12 April 1952, p. 394.

[2] See *Documents* (R.I.I.A.) for 1951, p. 283, for the original draft law, and for the draft law as approved on 6 February 1952 see *Europa Archiv*, 20 March 1952, pp. 4791–2. For the east German electoral law see above, p. 68.

[3] *Department of State Bulletin*, 26 May 1952, pp. 819–20.

Great Britain and France without delay to discuss the question of the peace treaty with Germany in order that an agreed draft of a peace treaty would be prepared at the earliest time. With the aim of facilitating the preparation of a peace treaty the Soviet Government presented a draft of bases of a peace treaty with Germany, expressing agreement also to discuss any other suggestion.

The Soviet Government suggested in this connection that the peace treaty be worked out with the immediate participation of Germany in the form of an all-German Government. In the note of March 10 it was foreseen also that the U.S.S.R., U.S.A., England, and France, fulfilling occupation functions in Germany, should review questions of conditions favourable to the earliest formation of an all-German Government expressing the will of the German people.

Introducing its suggestion regarding the question of the peace treaty with Germany and the formation of an all-German Government, the Soviet Government proceeded from the fact that the decision to state basic questions has great significance for strengthening peace in Europe and responds to the requirements of just relationship to lawful national interests of the German people.

The urgency of the conclusion of the peace treaty with Germany creates the necessity that the Governments of the U.S.S.R., U.S.A., England, and France take immediate measures for the unification of Germany and the formation of an all-German Government.

In this connection the Soviet Government considers it necessary that the Governments of the U.S.S.R., U.S.A., England, and France without delay discuss the question of conducting free all-German elections as was suggested earlier. Recognition on the part of the Governments of the U.S.S.R., U.S.A., England, and France of the necessity of conducting free all-German elections will create the full possibility of conducting such elections in the nearest future.

As regards the suggestion in connection with the future free all-German elections, regarding checking by the U.N. commission of the existence of conditions for such elections, this suggestion is in contradiction with the U.N. Charter which, in accordance with article CVII, excludes interference by the U.N. in German affairs. Such check could be carried out by a commission formed by the Four Powers fulfilling occupation functions in Germany.

The Government of the U.S.A. has had opportunity to acquaint itself with the draft of bases of a peace treaty with Germany set forth by the Soviet Government. The Government of the U.S.A. did not express agreement to enter into discussion of this draft and does not propose its own draft of a peace treaty.

Meanwhile the Government of the U.S.A. introduced a series of objections to the specific points of the Soviet draft of bases of the peace treaty with Germany which involved further exchange of notes between the Governments and delay of decision of questions in dispute which could have been avoided by direct discussion between the powers. Inasmuch, however, as in the note to the U.S.A. of March 25 such questions are presented, the Soviet Government considers it necessary to dwell on these questions.

In the Soviet draft of the bases of a peace treaty with Germany it is said:

Germany obligates itself not to enter any kind of coalition or military alliances directed against any power which has taken part with armed forces in the war against Germany.

The Soviet Government suggests that such proposal is in accord with the interests of the powers fulfilling occupational functions in Germany and of neighboring powers, and, in equal measure, with the interests of Germany itself as a peace-loving and democratic government. In such suggestion there is no inadmissible limitation of the sovereign rights of the German Government. But this suggestion also excludes the inclusion of Germany in any one or other group of powers directed against any kind of peace-loving state.

In the Soviet draft regarding the peace treaty with Germany it said:

Germany will be permitted its own national armed forces (land, air and sea), necessary for the defense of the country.

As is known, the Soviet Government introduced similar suggestions also regarding the draft peace treaty with Japan.[1] Such suggestion is in accord with the principle of national sovereignty and equal rights between governments. It is impossible to imagine such a position whereby Japan would have the right of its national armed forces designed for the defense of the country but Germany would be deprived of this right and would be placed in a worse position. There cannot be any doubt that in the interest of peace, as in the interest of the German nation, it will be much better to create such armed forces than to create in West Germany hireling troops of revanchistes headed by Fascist-Hitlerite generals ready to engulf Europe in a third world war.

Regarding German frontiers, the Soviet Government considers quite sufficient and definitive the provisions in this matter of the Potsdam Conference which were accepted by the Government of the U.S.A. as well as the Governments of U.S.S.R. and Great Britain with which France associated itself.

The Soviet Government proposes anew to the Government of the U.S.A. to enter, together with the Governments of England and France, into discussion of the peace treaty with Germany and also the question of the

[1] *Documents* (R.I.A.A.) for 1951, pp. 579–605.

unification of Germany and the creation of an all-German Government. The Soviet Government does not see the basis for delays to the decision of these questions.

It is just now that the question is being decided whether Germany will be re-established as a united, independent, peace-loving state entering into the family of peace-loving peoples of Europe or whether the division of Germany, and connected with it the threat of war in Europe, will remain.

The Soviet Government is simultaneously sending similar notes to the Governments of England and France.

(xiv) Letter from Dr. Kurt Schumacher, leader of the Social Democrat Party, to Dr. Adenauer regarding the Russian note of 9 April, 22 April 1952[1]

Although the conduct of the Federal government and its parties during the debate in the Bundestag on 3 April did not encourage the renewal by letter of proposals for a common stand to be taken by the government and the opposition on the question of the reunification of Germany, I should like to repeat once more, on behalf of the Social Democrat Party, how urgent is the need to put forward the concrete German requests in connexion with the exchange of notes between the four occupying Powers. This is all the more urgent from the fact that it is not known whether, within a not too remote period, another opportunity may be given for attaining the reunification of Germany by peaceful and democratic means.

The governments of the western Powers are at present working on the text of a reply to the Soviet communication of 9 April. In my opinion the common German opinion should be put before the three western Powers, namely, that there should be no failure to make clear if the Soviet note offers a real possibility of attaining the reunification of Germany in freedom. To establish this negotiations between the four Powers should develop as soon as possible. If it should turn out that even on the basis of the last note of the Soviet government there is no possibility of guaranteeing, by agreement between the four Powers, the existence of the necessary conditions for conducting free elections in the four zones and in Berlin, then at least it will be clear that the Federal Republic has spared no effort in making use of the opportunity offered to it to reunite Germany and contribute to the pacification of Europe.

The Soviet note of 9 April offers a possibility of ascertaining, through negotiations between the four Powers, if agreement could now be reached in order, among other things, to guarantee the existence of the indispensable conditions for the holding of free elections in the four zones and in

[1] Translated from *Relazioni Internazionali*, 3 May 1952, p. 450.

Berlin. On the German side the draft electoral law presented by the Bundestag on 6 February should be given as the German contribution. As regards the necessary international control for guaranteeing the existence of the same conditions in the four zones and in Berlin, several alternatives should be presented from the German side for discussion. These alternatives would be: (a) the four Powers take advantage of the good offices of the United Nations for the international control of the elections; (b) the four Powers agree to create a commission consisting of representatives of neutral states charged with exercising international control over the elections; or (c) the four Powers wish to exercise control themselves, given a guarantee that none of the four Powers can oppose or favour a particular German party. It does not matter so much which alternatives for international control are finally chosen, but rather that only those alternatives are acceptable which assure free elections, under equal conditions, in all parts of Germany.

The Soviet note of 9 April offers the possibility of conducting an inquiry for verifying the existence of the conditions necessary for free elections by a commission to consist of the four occupying Powers. In fact this proposal is a concession from the former attitude of the Soviet government which has hitherto entirely opposed a direct inquiry to establish the existence of the indispensable conditions for conducting free elections. In my opinion advantage should be taken of this offer to carry out such an inquiry. Inspection of the Soviet prisons could, for example, be insisted on once such a commission was formed.

I do not consider that these proposals exhaust all the possibilities of drawing positive profit from the proposals contained in the Soviet note of 9 April. At present I am concerned only with underlining the way in which the Federal Republic should react to these proposals and try to influence the reply of the three western occupying Powers. The representatives of the Social Democrat Party are always at the disposal of the government for the discussion of such questions.

(xv) Resolution on the Saar presented by the Social Democrat Party and defeated in the Bundestag on 23 April 1952[1]

1. The Saar territory is by international law a German territory.
2. Its present situation has been brought about without any legal basis and in contradiction to the principles of democracy and self-determination.
3. Only the entire German people has the right to dispose of German territory.

[1] Translated from *Deutscher Bundestag, 205. Sitzung*, 23 April 1952, p. 8830.

4. Fruitful co-operation between the peoples of Europe can be founded only on the respect for the rights and freedoms of others.

5. The Bundestag will not agree to any solution which contradicts these principles.

(xvi) Resolution on the Saar adopted by the Bundestag on 23 April 1952[1]

(1) The Saar territory is by international law a German territory.

(2) Present conditions in the Saar have been brought about without any legal basis and in contradiction to the democratic principles of self-determination.

(3) German territory cannot legally be disposed of without German consent.

(4) Through the unification of Europe we seek to transcend national frontiers in a reciprocal regard for justice and freedom.

(xvii) United States reply to the Russian note of 9 April, 13 May 1952[2]

1. In reply to the Soviet Government's note of the 9th of April, the United States Government wishes to make the following observations in regard to the unity of Germany, the election of a free all-German government and the conclusion of a peace treaty with that government. It remains the policy of the United States Government to achieve these objectives on terms that will insure unity with freedom and peace with security.

2. It is ready to begin negotiations with the Soviet Government on these issues; and it desires to do so just as soon as it is clearly apparent that it is also the intention of the Soviet Government to avoid the fruitless negotiations of the past. The United States Government and the Governments of the United Kingdom, France and the Soviet Union must therefore first reach a clear understanding upon the scope of the negotiations and upon the fundamental problems to be examined. Proper preparation is essential to success and to avoid long delays. The Soviet Government's note of the 9th of April throws little new light on what it considers should be the means of insuring the success of any such negotiations.

3. In its latest note the Soviet Government now stipulates that Germany must not be included 'into one or another grouping of powers directed against any peace-loving state'. Germany's proposed membership in the

---

[1] Translated from *Deutscher Bundestag, 205. Sitzung,* 23 April 1952, p. 8843.

[2] *Department of State Bulletin,* 26 May 1952, pp. 817–19. Identical notes were sent by France and the United Kingdom.

United Nations should surely make any such provision unnecessary. In any case the United States Government could not accept any provisions forbidding Germany to enter into association with other states which one of the signatories of the peace treaty might arbitrarily choose to regard as 'directed against any peace-loving state'. It cannot admit that Germany should be denied the basic right of a free and equal nation to associate itself with other nations for peaceful purposes. It must assume that the Soviet Government likewise cannot object to Germany's right to enter into defensive agreements.

4. In its note of March 25, the United States Government pointed out that it is giving full support to the efforts which the free states of Western Europe, including the German Federal Republic, are making to bring into being a peaceful European community and thus to begin a new era in which international relations will be based on cooperation and not on rivalry and distrust. The United States Government welcomes the development of such a European community in which Germany will participate. Germany is divided because Europe is divided. This policy of European unity cannot threaten the interests of the Soviet Union or of any country whose policy is devoted to the maintenance of peace. The United States Government will, therefore, not be deflected from its support of this policy. It is more than ever convinced that it represents the true path of peace.

5. The United States Government has no responsibility for the failure to extend this cooperation beyond its present limits. It remains ready to examine with sincerity and good will any practical and precise suggestions designed to reduce tension and to heal existing divisions.

6. A German peace treaty can be worked out only if there is an all-German government formed as a result of free elections and able to participate in full freedom in the discussions of such a treaty. It is, therefore, not possible to hold discussions now about the provisions of a German peace treaty. The United States Government has already made known its views on some of the Soviet Government's proposals, especially its erroneous interpretation of the territorial provisions of the Potsdam protocol and its intention to confine Germany in a position of permanent isolation from Western Europe while obliging her to seek to provide for her defense solely through her own national armed forces. The Soviet proposals would mean permanent shackles upon Germany's rights of international association and a permanent state of tension and insecurity in the center of Europe.

7. The all-German government resulting from free election must itself be free. Such freedom is essential both before and after a peace treaty has been negotiated. It must be able to maintain its genuinely representative character; to assume its responsibilities as the government of

a reunited Germany and to play its full part in the discussion of the peace treaty. This question of freedom is, therefore, inseparable from the problem of elections. The Soviet Government has still failed to give any indication of its views on this subject. The United States Government must ask specifically whether the Soviet Government considers that an all-German government, resulting from free elections, would be under four-power control until after the conclusion of a peace treaty or whether they agree that it should have the necessary freedom of action and powers of government.

8. The United States Government is happy to note that the Soviet Government now agrees in principle that there should be free elections throughout Germany. Such free elections can, however, only be held if the necessary conditions exist in all parts of Germany and will be maintained not only on the day of voting, and prior to it, but also thereafter. An essential first step is, therefore, to insure such conditions. Otherwise, no progress can be made. In recent years the eastern part of Germany has evolved in a direction increasingly divergent from the main path of German progress. This is a principal reason why an impartial inquiry is needed before elections can take place.

9. The Soviet Government does not agree, however, that the international commission set up by the General Assembly of the United Nations should carry out such an inquiry throughout Germany. It bases this refusal on its interpretation of Article 107 of the United Nations Charter. But this reads as follows: 'Nothing in the present Charter shall invalidate or preclude action, in relation to any state which during the Second World War has been an enemy of any signatory to the present Charter, taken or authorized as a result of that war by the Governments having responsibility for such action.' These words clearly do not preclude the United Nations from considering these aspects of German affairs. This interpretation was upheld by the United Nations General Assembly by an overwhelming majority. However, even under the Soviet Government's erroneous interpretation of the Charter there is nothing to prevent the Four Powers from availing themselves of the United Nations Commission in order to determine the conditions in which genuinely free elections could be held throughout Germany.

10. The Soviet Government suggests instead that responsibility for the inquiry could be entrusted to a commission formed by the four occupying powers. Before the United States Government could feel assured that this suggestion would result in an impartial inquiry it would need to know what would be the composition and functions of such a body. A commission composed solely of members with direct responsibilities in Germany would be both judge and party. Experience during the period of four-power control of Germany suggests that it would not be able to reach

useful decisions. Thus the elections would be greatly delayed. Nor can the United States Government overlook the fact that the appointment of a four-power commission might be interpreted as a step towards the re-establishment of four-power control in Germany. This would be a retrograde move, out of keeping with constitutional developments in the Federal Republic.

11. For these reasons the United States Government maintains its preference for the United Nations Commission. It is already in being, its functions have been laid down and it can take action without delay. Nevertheless, the United States Government is ready to examine every possibility of determining whether conditions of freedom exist throughout Germany for the holding of genuinely free elections. The United States Government in agreement with the United Kingdom and French Governments and after consultation with the German Federal Government and the German authorities in Berlin, accordingly makes the following proposals:

(i) An impartial commission should immediately determine whether there exist in the Soviet Zone of Germany, as well as in the German Federal Republic and in all sectors of Berlin, the conditions necessary for the holding of free elections and, if not, should recommend for consideration by the Four Powers exercising responsibilities in Germany what step should be taken to create such conditions. The Four Powers should give the necessary facilities for the investigation of such a commission in the German Federal Republic, in the Soviet Zone, and in all sectors of Berlin. The three Western Powers and the German Federal Government have already stated their willingness to do so.

(ii) The Four Powers should utilize for this purpose the United Nations Commission which is already available. This seems the quickest and most practical course.

(iii) Despite its strong preference for the procedure under (ii) above, the United States Government is ready to consider any other practical and precise proposals for an impartial commission of investigation which the Soviet Government may wish to put forward, on the one condition that they are likely to promote the early holding of free elections throughout Germany.

(iv) As soon as the report of such an impartial commission is available, representatives of the United States, United Kingdom, French and Soviet Governments would meet to consider it, with a view to reaching agreement on:

(A) The early holding of free elections throughout Germany, including the creation where necessary of the appropriate conditions; and

(B) The assurances to be given by the Four Powers that the all-German government, formed as the result of these free elections, will have the necessary freedom of action during the period before the peace treaty comes into effect.

(xviii) Note from the U.S.S.R. to the U.S.A. accusing the western Powers of trying to avoid the conclusion of a peace treaty with Germany and further urging direct negotiations between the four Powers, 24 May 1952[1]

In connection with the note of the Government of the United States of America of May 13 of this year, the Soviet Government finds it necessary to state the following:

1. Concerning the urgency of a decision of the German question and the delaying by the Western Powers of the exchange of written communications on this question:

In its note of March 10, 1952, the Soviet Government proposed to the Governments of the United States of America, Great Britain, and France that they examine together the question of the conclusion of a treaty of peace with Germany and of the establishment of an all-German Government. In order to facilitate and expedite preparation of a treaty of peace with Germany the Soviet Government put forward its draft of this treaty, expressing at the same time its readiness to consider other possible proposals on this question. The Soviet Government considers it necessary to solve this question immediately, being guided by the interests of the strengthening of peace in Europe and the necessity of satisfying the legitimate national demands of the German people.

Inasmuch as there was advanced in the reply of the Government of the United States of America of March 25 in connection with the question concerning the formation of an all-German Government a proposal for the study of conditions existing for the conduct of general elections in Germany, the Soviet Government in its note of April 9 agreed with this proposal, insisting, however, that the study in question should be conducted, not by a commission of the United Nations Organization, which is not competent to deal with the question of the making of peace with Germany, but an impartial commission of the Four Powers exercising the occupational function in Germany. At the same time, the Soviet Government once again proposed to the Government of the United States of America and likewise to the Governments of Great Britain and France that the consideration of a treaty of peace with Germany should no longer be postponed and likewise the question of unification of Germany and the creation of an all-German Government.

Notwithstanding the fact that the Soviet Government accepted the proposal of the Government of the U.S.A. for verification of the presence

[1] *Department of State Bulletin*, 21 July 1952, pp. 93–96.

of conditions for conducting in Germany free general elections and the proposal of the Soviet Government for appointment of a commission for conducting this verification by agreement between the Four Powers guaranteeing the objectivity and impartiality of the commission in question, the decision on the question concerning the peace treaty with Germany and the unification of Germany as demonstrated by the note of the Government of the United States of America of May 13 is again postponed for an indefinite period. It is evident from this note that the Government of the U.S.A. is also unwilling to agree that the Four Powers proceed to the examination of these questions without further delays.

In view of this the Government of the U.S.A. in its note of May 13 advanced a whole series of new preliminary conditions which it had not advanced in its note of March 25 and about which it now proposes to negotiate by means of a continuation of the exchange of notes before proceeding to direct negotiations. Thus, in its note of May 13 the Government of the U.S.A. proposes before the beginning of direct negotiations that agreement be reached 'concerning the framework of negotiations and concerning the basic problems to be taken under consideration' and likewise to continue the written exchange of communications concerning the composition of and functions of the commission for verification of the conditions in Germany for general elections, etc.

All these facts make evident that the Government of the U.S.A. is continuing to delay the conclusion of a treaty of peace with Germany, a decision on the question of unification, and also the establishment of an all-German Government. Only this could explain the fact that in its note of May 13 the Government of the U.S.A. introduced a whole new series of questions for the prolongation of the exchange of notes which, apart from this, has already dragged on for several months, instead of the Four Powers proceeding to direct negotiations and beginning the joint consideration of a peace treaty with Germany and with all the related questions.

In these circumstances the opinion cannot fail to be strengthened in Germany as well as beyond its borders that the Government of the U.S.A. in reality is not aiming at the conclusion of a peace treaty with Germany and putting an end to the division of Germany. But without the conclusion of a peace treaty and the unification of Germany a fully equal German Government cannot be restored, a German Government both independent and in full possession of rights and expressing the genuine will of the entire German people.

2. Regarding separate agreements of the Western Powers with Western Germany and their attempts to avoid conclusion of a peace treaty with Germany:

The Soviet Government considers it necessary to direct special attention to the fact that, simultaneously with the extended exchange of notes, the Government of the U.S.A., together with the Governments of Great Britain and France, is conducting separate negotiations with the Bonn Government of Western Germany regarding the conclusion of the so-called 'general' contract. Actually this is in no way a 'general' contract but a separate treaty which is falsely called 'general' in order to deceive the people. Thus the Potsdam Agreement by which the responsibility for the preparation of a peace treaty with Germany was placed upon the Four Powers—the United States of America, Great Britain, France, and the U.S.S.R.—was flagrantly violated.

Despite the secret character of the negotiations carried on with the Bonn Government and despite the fact that the full text of this separate agreement until now has not been published, from the information which has appeared in the press the contents of this separate treaty have become known already. From these facts it is evident that the peace treaty prepared by the Governments of the U.S.A., Great Britain, and France with West Germany in no way has as its aim the extension of freedom and independence of Western Germany. Together with formal abrogation of the Occupation Statute, this treaty preserves the regime of factual military occupation, keeping West Germany in a dependent and subservient status with regard to the Governments of the U.S.A. and of Great Britain and France.

In addition, by means of the conclusion of this separate treaty with West Germany, the Governments of the U.S.A., Great Britain, and France legalize the re-establishment of the German Army headed by Hitlerite generals, which means that they open the way to the re-establishment of aggressive West German militarism. Actually this treaty is an open military alliance of the U.S.A., Great Britain, and France with the help of West Germany by means of which the German people are drawn by the Bonn Government into preparations of a new war.

Moreover, the Governments of the U.S.A., Great Britain, and France achieve the inclusion of West Germany into the group of powers created by them under the name of 'European Defence Community': France, West Germany, Italy, Belgium, Holland, and Luxembourg. This self-styled 'European community' is supposed to become an integral part of the North Atlantic bloc and the great and so-called 'European army' into which should go the presently created German armed forces in West Germany. It is quite obvious that the aim of the creation of a 'European community' and 'European army' is not only to legalize the remilitarization of West Germany, as is taking place, in fact, but also to include West Germany in the aggressive North Atlantic bloc.

It is known to all that in recent times the Government of the U.S.A. has attempted to hasten by all means the conclusion of a separate treaty with West Germany as well as the inclusion of West Germany into the 'European community'. Likewise it attempts not only definitively to separate from but to oppose one portion of Germany to the other. This means that the Government of the U.S.A. is interested not in the unification of Germany and not in a peace treaty with Germany but, by means of the new separate agreement, more strongly than before to tie Western Germany and the Western German army now created with the North Atlantic bloc of powers, which is incompatible with the possibilities of a peaceful development in Europe.

All this shows that at the present time an agreement is taking place between right-wing revanchist circles of Western Germany and the North Atlantic group of powers. This agreement can be based only on the support of the revanchist aspirations of the Bonn Government of Adenauer, which is preparing to unleash a new war in Europe. The restoration now of a West German army under the leadership of Fascist Hitlerite generals can only serve the aggressive aims of the German revanchists. On the other hand, the inclusion of West Germany in the so-called European army, and consequently in the army of the North Atlantic bloc, even more underlines the aggressive character of the whole North Atlantic group.

In the light of these facts, no one can believe that the presently created 'European community' and 'European army' can represent 'a path to peace' as is stated in the American note of May 13. The real meaning of the agreement of the North Atlantic bloc with the government of Adenauer can comprise only the further strengthening of the aggressive character of the North Atlantic group of powers presently striving for the direct union with the German revanchists who represent the most aggressive circles in Europe.

The conclusion with the Bonn Government of West Germany of agreements such as the above-mentioned separate treaty or agreement regarding the 'European community' places upon this part of Germany new obligations strengthening its dependence on the Occupying Powers and creating new difficulties for unification with the Eastern part of Germany which is not tied by such obligations and is developing in conditions favorable to national unification of Germany into a unified independent democratic and peace-loving state. The desire of the Government of the U.S.A. to conclude as soon as possible the above-mentioned separate agreement with West Germany at the same time that negotiations regarding a peace treaty and unification of Germany again and again are postponed means that it intends by means of the above-mentioned separate agreement to confront the German people with a *fait accompli*: The German people will be confronted with the fact of the remilitarization of West Germany and the retention of Occupation troops in West Germany. And there will presently arise insurmountable obstacles in the path of the conclusion of a peace treaty and the unification of Germany.

However, it is not possible on the one hand to make statements about recognition of the necessity of a peace treaty and the unification of Germany and on the other to do everything to make difficult and to impede the conclusion of a peace treaty with Germany and the restoration of a unified German state. This leads to the undermining of any kind of confidence toward the dual policy of such powers and places the German people in the necessity of seeking its own way to a peace treaty and national unification of Germany.

3. Proposal of the Soviet Government: Despite the presence of disagreement regarding the peace treaty with Germany and also the unification of Germany and the formation of an all-German Government, the Soviet Government again proposes to the Government of the U.S.A. and also to the Governments of Great Britain and France to enter into joint discussion of these questions and not to permit extended delay in this matter.

Continued review of these questions by means of further exchange of notes cannot produce the results which might be achieved by direct negotiations and can only make achievement of agreement more difficult. Meanwhile, further delay of decision of the question of a peace treaty and unification of Germany cannot fail to arouse legitimate dissatisfaction of the German people, even overlooking the fact that delay in this matter is contradictory to the interests of the establishment of normal and permanent relations between Germany and neighboring states as well as the interests of strengthening of general peace.

The Soviet Government proceeds on the principle that in working out a peace treaty with Germany the Government of the U.S.S.R. as well as the Governments of the U.S.A., Great Britain, and France will be guided by the provisions of the Potsdam Agreement, particularly in the question of the boundaries of Germany as was mentioned by the Soviet Government in its note of April 9.

As regards the all-German Government and its powers, it is understood that this Government also must be guided by the Potsdam provisions and also, after conclusion of the peace treaty, by the provision of the peace treaty which serves the establishment of a permanent peace in Europe. In this connection, the Soviet Government continues to consider it the inalienable right of the German people to have its own national armed forces necessary for the defense of the country without which it is impossible to decide the question of the powers of the all-German Government in a just and proper fashion.

Proposing to enter into direct negotiations urgently regarding a peace treaty with Germany and the formation of an all-German Government, the Soviet Government proceeds also from the fact that no separate agreement of one or another part of Germany with governments of other states can impose any kind of obligations and that the all-German Government which will have signed the peace treaty will possess all the rights which the governments of other independent sovereign states possess.

2. The Contractual Agreements and the European Defence Treaty

(i) CONVENTION ON RELATIONS BETWEEN THE THREE POWERS AND THE FEDERAL REPUBLIC OF GERMANY, BONN, 26 MAY 1952[1]

The United States of America, the United Kingdom of Great Britain and Northern Ireland and the French Republic, of the one part, and the Federal Republic of Germany, of the other part:

WHEREAS a peaceful and prosperous European community of nations firmly bound to the other free nations of the world through dedication to the principles of the Charter of the United Nations can be attained only through united support and defence of the common freedom and the common heritage;

WHEREAS it is the common aim of the Signatory States to integrate the Federal Republic on a basis of equality within the European Community, itself included in a developing Atlantic Community;

WHEREAS the achievement of a fully free and unified Germany through peaceful means and of a freely negotiated peace settlement, though prevented for the present by measures beyond their control, remains a fundamental and common goal of the Signatory States;

WHEREAS the retention of the Occupation Statute with its powers of intervention in the domestic affairs of the Federal Republic is inconsistent with the purpose of integrating the Federal Republic within the European Community;

WHEREAS the United States of America, the United Kingdom of Great Britain and Northern Ireland and the French Republic (hereinafter referred to as 'the Three Powers') are therefore determined to retain only those special rights of which the retention is necessary, in the common interest of the Signatory States, having regard to the special international situation in Germany;

WHEREAS the Federal Republic has developed free and responsible political institutions and is determined to maintain the liberal-democratic federal constitution which guarantees human rights and is enshrined in its Basic Law;

[1] Great Britain: Foreign Office: *Memorandum on Relations between the Three Powers and the Federal Republic of Germany, 26th May, 1952* (Cmd. 8563) (London, H.M.S.O., 1952).

WHEREAS the Three Powers and the Federal Republic recognise that both the new relationship to be established between them by the present Convention and its related Conventions and the Treaties for the creation of an integrated European community, in particular the Treaty on the Establishment of the European Community for Coal and Steel[1] and the Treaty on the Establishment of the European Defence Community,[2] are essential steps to the achievement of their common aim for a unified Germany integrated within the European Community;

HAVE entered into the following Convention setting forth the basis for their new relationship:

ARTICLE 1

1. The Federal Republic shall have full authority over its internal and external affairs, except as provided in the present Convention.

2. The Three Powers will revoke the Occupation Statute and abolish the Allied High Commission and the Offices of the *Land* Commissioners upon the entry into force of the present Convention and the Conventions listed in Article 8 (hereinafter referred to as 'the related Conventions').

3. The Three Powers will thenceforth conduct their relations with the Federal Republic through Ambassadors who will act jointly in matters the Three Powers consider of common concern under the present Convention and the related Conventions.

ARTICLE 2

1. The Three Powers retain, in view of the international situation, the rights, heretofore exercised or held by them, relating to (*a*) the stationing of armed forces in Germany, and the protection of their security, (*b*) Berlin, and (*c*) Germany as a whole, including the unification of Germany and a peace settlement.

2. The Federal Republic, on its part, will refrain from any action prejudicial to these rights and will co-operate with the Three Powers to facilitate their exercise.

ARTICLE 3

1. The Federal Republic agrees to conduct its policy in accordance with the principles set forth in the Charter of the United Nations and with the aims defined in the Statute of the Council of Europe.

2. The Federal Republic affirms its intention to associate itself fully with the community of free nations through membership in international organizations contributing to the common aims of the free world. The Three Powers will support applications for such membership by the Federal Republic at appropriate times.

[1] *Documents* (R.I.I.A.) for 1951, p. 173.   [2] See below, p. 116.

3. In their negotiations with States with which the Federal Republic maintains no relations, the Three Powers will consult with the Federal Republic in respect of matters directly involving its political interests.

4. At the request of the Federal Government, the Three Powers will arrange to represent the interests of the Federal Republic in relations with other States and in certain international organizations or conferences, whenever the Federal Republic is not in a position to do so itself.

ARTICLE 4

1. The mission of the armed forces stationed by the Three Powers in the Federal territory will be the defence of the free world, of which the Federal Republic and Berlin form part.

2. The Three Powers will consult with the Federal Republic, in so far as the military situation permits, regarding the stationing of such armed forces in the Federal territory. The Federal Republic will co-operate fully, in accordance with the present Convention and the related Conventions, in facilitating the tasks of such armed forces.

3. The Three Powers will obtain the consent of the Federal Republic before bringing into the Federal territory, as part of their forces, contingents of the armed forces of any nation not now providing such contingents. Such contingents may nevertheless be brought into the Federal territory without the consent of the Federal Republic in the event of external attack or imminent threat of such attack but, after the elimination of the danger, may only remain there with its consent.

4. The Federal Republic will participate in the European Defence Community in order to contribute to the common defence of the free world.

ARTICLE 5

1. In the exercise of their right to protect the security of the armed forces stationed in the Federal territory, the Three Powers will conform to the provisions of the following paragraphs of this Article.

2. In case the Federal Republic and the European Defence Community are unable to deal with a situation which is created by an attack on the Federal Republic or Berlin, subversion of the liberal democratic basic order, a serious disturbance of public order or a grave threat of any of these events, and which in the opinion of the Three Powers endangers the security of their forces, the Three Powers may, after consultation to the fullest extent possible with the Federal Government, proclaim a state of emergency in the whole or any part of the Federal Republic.

3. Upon the proclamation of a state of emergency, the Three Powers may take such measures as are necessary to maintain or restore order and to ensure the security of the forces.

4. The proclamation will specify the area to which it applies. The state of emergency will not be maintained any longer than necessary to deal with the emergency.

5. The Three Powers shall consult the Federal Government to the fullest extent possible while the state of emergency continues. They will utilise to the greatest possible extent the assistance of the Federal Government and the competent German authorities.

6. If the Three Powers do not terminate a state of emergency within thirty days after a request by the Federal Government to do so, the Federal Government may submit a request to the Council of the North Atlantic Treaty Organization to examine the situation and consider whether the state of emergency should be terminated. If the Council concludes that continuance of the state of emergency is no longer justified, the Three Powers will restore the normal situation as promptly as possible.

7. Independently of a state of emergency, any military commander may, if his forces are imminently menaced, take such immediate action appropriate for their protection (including the use of armed force) as is requisite to remove the danger.

8. In all other respects, the protection of the security of these forces is governed by the provisions of the Convention on the Rights and Obligations of Foreign Forces and their Members in the Federal Republic of Germany referred to in Article 8 of the present Convention.

ARTICLE 6

1. The Three Powers will consult with the Federal Republic in regard to the exercise of their rights relating to Berlin.

2. The Federal Republic, on its part, will co-operate with the Three Powers in order to facilitate the discharge of their responsibilities with regard to Berlin. The Federal Republic will continue its aid to the political, cultural, economic and financial reconstruction of Berlin and, in particular, will grant it such aid as is set out in the annexed Declaration of the Federal Republic (Annex A to the present Convention).[1]

ARTICLE 7

1. The Three Powers and the Federal Republic are agreed that an essential aim of their common policy is a peace settlement for the whole of Germany, freely negotiated between Germany and her former enemies, which should lay the foundation for a lasting peace. They further agree that the final determination of the boundaries of Germany must await such a settlement.

[1] Not printed here.

2. Pending the peace settlement, the Three Powers and the Federal Republic will co-operate to achieve, by peaceful means, their common aim of a unified Germany enjoying a liberal-democratic constitution, like that of the Federal Republic, and integrated within the European Community.

3. In the event of the unification of Germany, the Three Powers will, subject to such adjustments as may be agreed, extend to a unified Germany the rights which the Federal Republic has under the present Convention and the related Conventions and will for their part agree that the rights under the treaties for the formation of an integrated European Community should be similarly extended, upon the assumption by such a unified Germany of the obligations of the Federal Republic toward the Three Powers or to any of them under those conventions and treaties. Except by common consent of all the Signatory States, the Federal Republic will not conclude any agreement or enter into any arrangements which would impair the rights of the Three Powers under those conventions or treaties or lessen the obligations of the Federal Republic thereunder.

4. The Three Powers will consult with the Federal Republic on all other matters involving the exercise of their rights relating to Germany as a whole.

ARTICLE 8

1. The Three Powers and the Federal Republic have concluded the following related Conventions which will enter into force simultaneously with the present Convention:

Convention on the Rights and Obligations of Foreign Forces and their
    Members in the Federal Republic of Germany;
Finance Convention;
Convention on the Settlement of Matters Arising out of the War and
    the Occupation.

2. During the transitional period provided for in paragraph 4 of Article 6 of Chapter One of the Convention on the Settlement of Matters Arising out of the War and the Occupation, the rights of the Three Powers referred to in that paragraph shall be deemed to be included within the exception set forth in paragraph 1 of Article 1 of the present Convention.

ARTICLE 9

1. There is hereby established an Arbitration Tribunal which shall function in accordance with the provisions of the annexed Charter (Annex B to the present Convention).[1]

---

[1] Not printed here.

2. The Arbitration Tribunal shall have exclusive jurisdiction over all disputes arising between the Three Powers and the Federal Republic under the provisions of the present Convention or the annexed Charter or any of the related Conventions which the parties are not able to settle by negotiation, except as otherwise provided by paragraph 3 of this Article or in the annexed Charter or in the related Conventions.

3. Any dispute involving the rights of the Three Powers referred to in Article 2, or action taken thereunder, or involving the provisions of paragraphs 1 to 7 inclusive of Article 5, shall not be subject to the jurisdiction of the Arbitration Tribunal or of any other tribunal or court.

ARTICLE 10

The Three Powers and the Federal Republic will review the terms of the present Convention and the related Conventions

(*a*) upon the request of any one of them, in the event of the unification of Germany or the creation of a European federation; or

(*b*) upon the occurrence of any other event which all of the Signatory States recognise to be of a similarly fundamental character.

Thereupon, they will, by mutual agreement, modify the present Convention and the related Conventions to the extent made necessary or advisable by the fundamental change in the situation.

ARTICLE 11

1. The present Convention and the related Conventions shall be ratified or approved by the Signatory States in accordance with their respective constitutional procedures. The instruments of ratification shall be deposited by the Signatory States with the Government of the Federal Republic of Germany.

2. The present Convention shall enter into force immediately upon

(*a*) the deposit by all the Signatory States of instruments of ratification of the present Convention and of all the Conventions listed in Article 8; and

(*b*) the entry into force of the Treaty on the Establishment of the European Defence Community.

3. The present Convention and the related Conventions shall be deposited in the Archives of the Government of the Federal Republic of Germany, which will furnish each Signatory State with certified copies thereof and notify each such State of the date of the entry into force of the present Convention and the related Conventions.

IN FAITH WHEREOF the undersigned representatives duly authorised thereto by their respective Governments have signed the present Convention.

Done at Bonn this 26th day of May, 1952, in three texts, in the English, French and German languages, all being equally authentic.

For the Government of the United States of America:

DEAN ACHESON.

For the Government of the United Kingdom of Great Britain and Northern Ireland:

ANTHONY EDEN.

For the Government of the French Republic:

SCHUMAN.

For the Government of the Federal Republic of Germany:

ADENAUER.

(ii) SUMMARY OF RELATED CONVENTIONS TOGETHER WITH THEIR ANNEXES, BONN, 26 MAY 1952[1]

A.—A CONVENTION ON THE RIGHTS AND OBLIGATIONS OF FOREIGN FORCES AND THEIR MEMBERS IN THE FEDERAL REPUBLIC OF GERMANY.

This Convention is intended to lay down the conditions under which foreign forces will be stationed in Germany for the defence of the Federal Republic. It deals with such matters as the legal status of members of the forces and their dependants, their co-operation with the German authorities and their security and logistical support. It is accompanied by Annexes dealing with certain resultant amendments to German criminal law and with the allocation of radio frequencies.

B.—A FINANCE CONVENTION.

This Convention is intended to ensure that the Federal Republic of Germany will make a continuing contribution to Western defence comparable to that made by the other principal Western countries, to provide that a part of this contribution shall be used to assist in meeting the costs of Allied forces stationed in Germany and to lay down the arrangements under which this support will be provided. An Annex provides for the settlement of damage claims against United Kingdom forces.

C.—A CONVENTION ON THE SETTLEMENT OF MATTERS ARISING OUT OF THE WAR AND THE OCCUPATION.

This Convention consists of twelve chapters dealing with the following matters:—

 1. General Provisions, such as the validity of rights and obligations

---

[1] Cmd. 8563. For the full text of the Related Conventions see Great Britain: Foreign Office: *Conventions between the Governments of the United States of America, the United Kingdom of Great Britain and Northern Ireland and the French Republic of the one part and the Federal Republic of Germany of the other part with accompanying instruments, Bonn, 26th May, 1952* (Cmd. 8571) (London, H.M.S.O., 1952).

created by acts of the Occupation Authorities or under international agreements; the general principles applicable to Occupation legislation; non-discrimination against persons who have co-operated with the Allies; the future handling of war criminals and other matters.

2. The Deconcentration and Decartelisation of German Industry.
3. Internal Restitution; the return of identifiable property of Nazi victims, together with a Charter for a Supreme Restitution Court.
4. Compensation for the Victims of Nazi Persecution.
5. External Restitution; the return of property looted from German-occupied territories with provisions for the establishment of a Federal Administrative Agency.
6. Reparation.
7. Displaced Persons and Refugees.
8. Claims against Germany; embodying transitional provisions related to the settlement of the German external debt.
9. Certain Claims against Foreign Nations and Nationals; their suspension until a final settlement and the transfer to the Federal Government of the assets and liabilities of the Joint Export–Import Agency.
10. Foreign Interests in Germany, together with provisions for the establishment of a Federal Administrative Agency.
11. Facilities for the Embassies and Consulates of the Three Powers in the Federal Republic of Germany.
12. Civil Aviation.

To this Convention is annexed the Charter of the Arbitral Commission on Property Rights and Interests in Germany. This Commission will decide disputes arising out of Chapters V and X of the Convention.

(iii) SUMMARY OF OTHER DOCUMENTS SIGNED AT BONN, 26 MAY 1952[1]

A. A letter from the Allied High Commissioners on behalf of their Governments to the Federal Chancellor regarding the right in respect of Germany as a whole reserved to the Three Powers by Article 2, paragraph 1 (c), of the Convention on Relations.
B. A letter from the Allied High Commissioners on behalf of their Governments to the Federal Chancellor regarding relationships between the Federal Republic and Berlin.
C. A letter from the Foreign Ministers of the Three Powers to the Federal Chancellor concerning the future consideration of the time of entry into effect of certain provisions contained in the Conventions.
D. An exchange of letters between the Foreign Ministers of the Three Powers and the Federal Chancellor, specifying certain Control Council

[1] Cmd. 8563. For the text of these documents see Cmd. 8571.

legislation which is not to be deprived of effect after the ratification of the Convention and related Conventions.

E. An exchange of letters between the Allied High Commissioners on behalf of their Governments and the Federal Chancellor, specifying those treaties and agreements, made on behalf of one or more of the three Western Zones during the Occupation, under which the Federal Republic will assume obligations after the ratification of the Convention and related Conventions and expressing a reservation with regard to the Saar.

F. An exchange of letters between the Foreign Ministers of the Three Powers and the Federal Chancellor concerning the tax immunity of Successor Organizations and Trust Corporations.

G. Letters from the Federal Chancellor to the Allied High Commissioners concerning pre-war contractual relationships.

H. A letter from the Federal Chancellor to the Allied High Commissioners for the information of their Governments on the application in the territory of the Federal Republic of Germany of Article 44 of the International Telecommunications Convention.

There was also signed on 26th May a special agreement on taxation of the forces and their members, which pertains to the Convention on the Rights and Obligations of Foreign Forces and their Members in the Federal Republic of Germany but which is not a part of the complex of the Conventions. It was accompanied by a letter from the Federal Chancellor to the Foreign Ministers of the Three Powers referring to Article 3 of that agreement.[1]

(iv) DECLARATION ON BERLIN ISSUED BY THE THREE WESTERN COMMANDERS IN BERLIN, 26 MAY 1952[2]

Taking into consideration the new relations established between France, the United Kingdom of Great Britain and Northern Ireland, the United States of America, and the Federal Republic of Germany and
    wishing to grant the Berlin authorities the maximum liberty compatible with the special situation of Berlin,
    the Allied *Kommandatura* makes this declaration:

I

Berlin shall exercise all its rights, powers and responsibilities set forth

---

[1] Great Britain: Foreign Office: *Agreement between the Governments of the United States of America, the United Kingdom of Great Britain and Northern Ireland and the French Republic of the one part and the Federal Republic of Germany of the other part on the Tax Treatment of the Forces and their Members, Bonn, 26th May 1952* (Cmd. 8569) (London, H.M.S.O., 1952).

[2] Great Britain: Foreign Office: *Memorandum on the Principles Governing the Relationship between the Allied Kommandatura and Greater Berlin, 26th May, 1952* (Cmd. 8564) (London, H.M.S.O., 1952).

in its Constitution as adopted in 1950 subject only to the reservations made by the Allied *Kommandatura* on 29th August, 1950, and to the provisions hereinafter.

II

The Allied authorities retain the right to take, if they deem it necessary, such measures as may be required to fulfil their international obligations, to ensure public order and to maintain the status and security of Berlin and its economy, trade and communications.

III

The Allied authorities will normally exercise powers only in the following fields:—

(a) Security, interests and immunities of the Allied Forces, including their representatives, dependants and non-German employees. German employees of the Allied Forces enjoy immunity from German jurisdiction only in matters arising out of or in the course of performance of duties or services with the Allied Forces;

(b) Disarmament and demilitarisation, including related fields of scientific research, civil aviation, and prohibitions and restrictions on industry in relation to the foregoing;

(c) Relations of Berlin with authorities abroad. However, the Allied *Kommandatura* will permit the Berlin authorities to assure the representation abroad of the interests of Berlin and of its inhabitants by suitable arrangements;

(d) Satisfaction of occupation costs. These costs will be fixed after consultation with the appropriate German authorities and at the lowest level consistent with maintaining the security of Berlin and of the Allied Forces located there;

(e) Authority over the Berlin police to the extent necessary to ensure the security of Berlin.

IV

The Allied *Kommandatura* will not, subject to Articles I and II of this Declaration, raise any objection to the adoption by Berlin under an appropriate procedure authorised by the Allied *Kommandatura* of the same legislation as that of the Federal Republic, in particular regarding currency, credit and foreign exchange, nationality, passports, emigration and immigration, extradition, the unification of the customs and trade area, trade and navigation agreements, freedom of movement of goods, and foreign trade and payments arrangements.

V

In the following fields:—

(a) restitution, reparations, decartelisation, deconcentration, foreign interests in Berlin, claims against Berlin or its inhabitants,

(b) displaced persons and the admission of refugees,

(c) control of the care and treatment in German prisons of persons charged before or sentenced by Allied courts or tribunals; over the carrying out of sentences imposed on them and over questions of amnesty, pardon or release in relation to them,

the Allied authorities will in future only intervene to an extent consistent with, or if the Berlin authorities act inconsistently with, the principles which form the basis of the new relations between France, the United Kingdom and the United States on the one part and the Federal Republic of Germany on the other, or with the Allied legislation in force in Berlin.

VI

All legislation of the Allied authorities will remain in force until repealed, amended or deprived of effect.

The Allied authorities will repeal, amend or deprive of effect any legislation which they deem no longer appropriate in the light of this declaration.

Legislation of the Allied authorities may also be repealed or amended by Berlin legislation: but such repeal or amendment shall require the approval of the Allied authorities before coming into force.

VII

Berlin legislation shall come into force in accordance with the provisions of the Berlin Constitution. In case of inconsistency with Allied legislation, or with other measures of the Allied authorities, or with the rights of the Allied authorities under this declaration, Berlin legislation will be subject to repeal or annulment by the Allied *Kommandatura*.

VIII

In order to enable them to fulfil their obligations under this declaration, the Allied authorities shall have the right to request and obtain such information and statistics as they deem necessary.

IX

The Allied *Kommandatura* will modify the provisions of this declaration as the situation in Berlin permits.

X

Upon the effective date of this declaration the State of Principles

Governing the Relationship Between the Allied *Kommandatura* and Greater Berlin of 14th May, 1949, as modified by the First Instrument of Revision, dated 7th March, 1951,[1] will be repealed.

(v) THE EUROPEAN DEFENCE TREATY, PARIS, 27 MAY 1952
(a) *Treaty setting up a European Defence Community*[2]

Le Président de la République Fédérale d'Allemagne, Sa Majesté le Roi des Belges, le Président de la République Française, le Président de la République Italienne, Son Altesse Royale la Grande Duchesse de Luxembourg, Sa Majesté la Reine des Pays-Bas,

Résolus à contribuer, en coopération avec les autres nations libres, et dans l'esprit de la Charte des Nations Unies, au maintien de la paix, notamment en assurant contre toute agression la défense de l'Europe occidentale, en étroite liaison avec les organismes ayant le même objet;

Considérant que l'intégration aussi complète que possible, dans la mesure compatible avec les nécessités militaires, des éléments humains et matériels que leurs forces de défense rassemblent au sein d'une organisation européenne supranationale est le moyen le plus propre à permettre d'atteindre ce but avec toute la rapidité et l'efficacité nécessaires;

Certains que cette intégration aboutira à l'emploi le plus rationnel et le plus économique des ressources de leurs pays, en particulier grâce à l'établissement d'un budget commun et de programmes d'armement communs;

Décidés à assurer ainsi le développement de leur force militaire sans qu'il soit porté atteinte au progrès social;

Soucieux de sauvegarder les valeurs spirituelles et morales que sont le patrimoine commun de leurs peuples et convaincus qu'au sein de la force commune, constituée sans discrimination entre les États participants, les patriotismes nationaux, loin de s'affaiblir, ne pourront que se consolider et s'harmoniser dans un cadre élargi;

Conscients de franchir ainsi une étape nouvelle et essentielle dans la voie de la formation d'une Europe unie;

Ont décidé de créer une Communauté Européenne de Défense et ont désigné à cet effet comme plénipotentiaires:

. . . .

Le Président de la République Fédérale d'Allemagne,

M. le Docteur Konrad Adenauer, Chancelier, ministre des Affaires étrangères;

---

[1] See *Documents* (R.I.I.A.) for 1951, pp. 116–17.
[2] France: Ministère des Affaires Étrangères: *La Documentation Française*: *Traité instituant la Communauté européenne de défense et Documents annexes* (Paris, August 1952), pp. 5–29.

Sa Majesté le Roi des Belges,
M. Paul van Zeeland, ministre des Affaires étrangères;
Le Président de la République Française,
M. Robert Schuman, ministre des Affaires étrangères;
Le Président de la République Italienne,
M. De Gasperi, ministre des Affaires étrangères;
Son Altesse Royale la Grande-Duchesse de Luxembourg,
M. Bech, ministre des Affaires étrangères;
Sa Majesté la Reine des Pays-Bas,
M. Stikker, ministre des Affaires étrangères;

Lesquels, après avoir échangé leurs pleins pouvoirs reconnus en bonne et due forme, sont convenus des dispositions qui suivent.

TITRE PREMIER

PRINCIPES FONDAMENTAUX

CHAPITRE PREMIER

DE LA COMMUNAUTÉ EUROPÉENNE DE DÉFENSE

Article premier

Par le présent Traité les Hautes Parties Contractantes instituent entre Elles une COMMUNAUTÉ EUROPÉENNE DE DÉFENSE, de caractère supranational, comportant des institutions communes, des Forces armées communes et un budget commun.

Article 2

§ 1. La Communauté a des objectifs exclusivement défensifs.

§ 2. En conséquence, dans les conditions prévues au présent Traité, elle assure contre toute agression la sécurité des États membres, en participant à la défense occidentale dans le cadre du Traité de l'Atlantique Nord et en réalisant l'intégration des forces de défense des États membres et l'emploi rationnel et économique de leurs ressources.

§ 3. Toute agression armée dirigée contre l'un quelconque des États membres en Europe ou contre les Forces européennes de défense sera considérée comme une attaque dirigée contre tous les États membres.

Les États membres et les Forces européennes de défense porteront à l'État ou aux Forces ainsi attaqués aide et assistance par tous les moyens en leur pouvoir, militaires et autres.

Article 3

§ 1. La Communauté emploie les méthodes les moins onéreuses et les plus efficaces. Elle ne recourt à des interventions que dans la mesure nécessaire à l'accomplissement de sa mission et en respectant les libertés publiques et les droits fondamentaux des individus. Elle veille à ce que les intérêts propres des États membres soient pris en considération dans toute la mesure compatible avec ses intérêts essentiels.

§ 2. Pour permettre à la Communauté d'atteindre ses buts, les États membres mettent à sa disposition des contributions appropriées, fixées selon les dispositions des articles 87 et 94 ci-après.

Article 4

La Communauté poursuit son action en collaboration avec les nations libres et avec toute organisation qui se propose les mêmes buts qu'elle-même.

Article 5

La Communauté coopère étroitement avec l'Organisation du Traité de l'Atlantique Nord.

Article 6

Le présent Traité ne comporte aucune discrimination entre les États membres.

Article 7

La Communauté a la personnalité juridique.

Dans les relations internationales, la Communauté jouit de la capacité juridique nécessaire pour exercer ses fonctions et atteindre ses buts.

Dans chacun des États membres, la Communauté jouit de la capacité juridique la plus large reconnue aux personnes morales nationales; elle peut, notamment, acquérir et aliéner des biens immobiliers et mobiliers et ester en justice.

La Communauté est représentée par ses institutions, chacune dans le cadre de ses attributions.

Article 8

§ 1. Les institutions de la Communauté sont:

— Un Conseil de Ministres, ci-après dénommé: le Conseil,
— une Assemblée commune, ci-après dénommée: l'Assemblée,
— un Commissariat de la Communauté, ci-après dénommé: le Commissariat,
— une Cour de Justice, ci-après dénommée: la Cour.

§ 2. Sans préjudice des dispositions de l'article 126 ci-après, l'organisation de ces institutions, telle qu'elle est fixée par le présent Traité, demeurera en vigueur jusqu'à son remplacement par une organisation nouvelle résultant de l'établissement de la structure fédérale ou confédérale visée à l'article 38 ci-après.

CHAPITRE II

Des Forces européennes de défense

Article 9

Les Forces armées de la Communauté, ci-après dénommées « Forces européennes de défense », sont composées de contingents mis à la disposition de la Communauté par les États membres, en vue de leur fusion dans les conditions prévues au présent Traité.

Aucun État membre ne recrutera ou n'entretiendra de forces armées nationales en dehors de celles qui sont prévues à l'article 10 ci-après.

Article 10

§ 1. Les États membres peuvent recruter et entretenir des forces armées nationales destinées à être employées dans les territoires non européens à l'égard desquels ils assument des responsabilités de défense, ainsi que les unités stationnées dans leur pays d'origine et nécessaires à la maintenance de ces forces et à l'exécution des relèves.

§ 2. Les États membres peuvent également recruter et entretenir des forces armées nationales répondant aux missions internationales qu'ils ont assumées, à Berlin, en Autriche ou en vertu de décisions des Nations Unies. A l'issue de ces missions, ces troupes seront soit dissoutes, soit mises à la disposition de la Communauté. Des relèves peuvent être exécutées, avec l'accord du Commandant Suprême compétent relevant de l'Organisation du Traité de l'Atlantique Nord, par échange avec des unités composées de contingents originaires des États membres intéressés et appartenant aux Forces européennes de défense.

§ 3. Les éléments destinés, dans chaque État membre, à assurer la garde personnelle du Chef de l'État demeurent nationaux.

§ 4. Les États membres peuvent disposer de Forces navales nationales, d'une part pour la garde des territoires non européens à l'égard desquels ils assument les responsabilités de défense visées au paragraphe 1 du présent article et pour la protection des communications avec et entre ces territoires, et, d'autre part, pour remplir les obligations qui découlent pour eux des missions internationales visées au paragraphe 2 du présent article ainsi que d'accords conclus dans le cadre du Traité de l'Atlantique Nord antérieurement à l'entrée en vigueur du présent Traité.

§ 5. Le volume total des forces armées nationales visées au présent article, y compris les unités de maintenance, ne doit pas être d'une ampleur telle qu'elle compromette la participation de chaque État membre aux Forces européennes de défense, déterminée par un accord entre les gouvernements des États membres.

Les États membres ont la faculté de procéder à des échanges individuels de personnel entre les contingents qu'ils mettent à la disposition des

Forces européennes de défense et les forces qui n'en font pas partie, sans qu'il doive en résulter une diminution des Forces européennes de défense.

Article 11

Des forces de police et de gendarmerie, exclusivement préposées au maintien de l'ordre intérieur, peuvent être recrutées et entretenues au sein des États membres.

Le caractère national de ces forces n'est pas affecté par le présent Traité.

Le volume et la nature desdites forces existant sur les territoires des États membres doivent être tels qu'elles ne dépassent pas les limites de leur mission.

Article 12

§ 1. Dans le cas de troubles ou de menaces de troubles sur le territoire d'un État membre en Europe, la fraction des contingents fournis par cet État aux Forces européennes de défense nécessaire pour faire face à cette situation est, sur sa demande, et le Conseil informé, mise à sa disposition par le Commissariat.

Les conditions d'emploi de ces éléments sont déterminées par la réglementation en vigueur sur le territoire de l'État membre demandeur.

§ 2. Dans le cas de sinistre ou de calamité nécessitant un secours immédiat, les éléments des Forces européennes de défense, quelle que soit leur origine, en état d'intervenir utilement, doivent prêter leur concours.

Article 13

Dans le cas d'une crise grave affectant un territoire non européen à l'égard duquel un État membre assume des responsabilités de défense, la fraction des contingents fournis par cet État aux Forces européennes de défense nécessaire pour faire face à la crise est, sur sa demande, et avec l'accord du Commandant Suprême compétent relevant de l'Organisation du Traité de l'Atlantique Nord, mise à sa disposition par le Commissariat, le Conseil informé. Les contingents ainsi détachés cessent de relever de la Communauté jusqu'au moment où ils sont remis à sa disposition, dès que leur emploi n'est plus nécessaire pour faire face à la crise.

Les implications militaires, économiques et financières du retrait ci-dessus prévu sont, dans chaque cas, examinées et réglées par le Commissariat, avec l'avis conforme du Conseil statuant à la majorité des deux tiers.

Article 14

Dans les cas où une mission internationale à accomplir en dehors du territoire défini à l'article 120, § 1, est confiée à un État membre, la fraction des contingents fournie par cet État aux Forces européennes de défense nécessaire pour remplir cette mission est, sur sa demande et avec l'accord du Commandant Suprême compétent relevant de l'Organisation du Traité de l'Atlantique Nord, mise à sa disposition par le Commissariat, sur avis conforme du Conseil statuant à la majorité des deux tiers. Les contingents ainsi détachés cessent de relever de la Communauté jusqu'au moment où ils sont remis à sa disposition dès que leur emploi n'est plus nécessaire pour remplir la mission susvisée.

En pareil cas les dispositions de l'alinéa 2 de l'article 13 ci-dessus sont applicables.

Article 15

§ 1. Les Forces européennes de Défense sont constituées de personnels recrutés par conscription et de personnels de métier ou servant à long terme par engagements volontaires.

§ 2. Elles sont intégrées selon les dispositions organiques des articles 68, 69 et 70 ci-après.

Elles portent un uniforme commun.

Elles sont organisées selon les types définis au Protocole militaire. Cette organisation peut être modifiée par le Conseil statuant à l'unanimité.

§ 3. Les contingents destinés à composer les Unités sont fournis par les États membres suivant un plan de constitution arrêté par accord entre les Gouvernements. Ce plan est susceptible de révision dans les conditions prévues à l'article 44 ci-après.

Article 16

La défense intérieure des territoires des États membres contre les attaques de toute nature ayant des buts militaires, provoquées ou effectuées par un ennemi extérieur, est assurée par des formations homogènes de statut européen, spécialisées pour chaque État membre dans la mission de défense de son territoire, et relevant pour leur emploi des autorités prévues à l'article 18 ci-après.

Article 17

La protection civile est assurée par chacun des États membres.

Article 18

§ 1. Le Commandant Suprême compétent relevant de l'Organisation du Traité de l'Atlantique Nord est habilité, sous réserve du cas visé au paragraphe 3 du présent article, à s'assurer que les Forces européennes de défense sont organisées, équipées, instruites et préparées à l'emploi de façon satisfaisante.

Dès qu'elles sont en état d'être employées, et sous réserve du même cas, elles sont affectées au Commandant Suprême compétent relevant de l'Organisation du Traité de l'Atlantique Nord, qui exerce à leur égard les pouvoirs et responsabilités qu'il détient en vertu de ses attributions, et, en particulier, soumet à la Communauté ses besoins en ce qui concerne l'articulation et le déploiement des Forces; les plans correspondants sont exécutés dans les conditions prévues à l'article 77 ci-après.

Les Forces européennes de défense reçoivent des directives techniques des organismes appropriés de l'Organisation du Traité de l'Atlantique Nord, dans le cadre de la compétence militaire de ces derniers.

§ 2. En temps de guerre, le Commandant Suprême compétent relevant de l'Organisation du Traité de l'Atlantique Nord exerce, à l'égard des Forces visées ci-dessus, les pleins pouvoirs et responsabilités de Commandant Suprême que lui confèrent ses attributions.

§ 3. Dans le cas des Unités des Forces européennes de défense affectées à la défense intérieure et à la protection maritime rapprochée des territoires des États membres, la détermination des autorités dont elles relèvent pour le commandement et l'emploi résulte soit des conventions conclues dans le cadre du Traité de l'Atlantique Nord, soit des accords entre l'Organisation du Traité de l'Atlantique Nord et la Communauté.

§ 4. Si le Traité de l'Atlantique Nord cesse d'être en vigueur avant le présent Traité, il appartiendra aux États membres de déterminer, d'un commun accord, l'autorité à laquelle seront confiés le commandement et l'emploi des Forces européennes de défense.

TITRE II

DES INSTITUTIONS DE LA COMMUNAUTÉ

CHAPITRE PREMIER
Le Commissariat

Article 19

En vue de remplir des tâches qui lui incombent en vertu du présent Traité et dans les conditions prévues par celui-ci, le Commissariat est investi de pouvoirs d'action et de contrôle.

Article 19 *bis*

Le Commissariat entre en fonctions dès la nomination de ses membres.

Article 20

§ 1. Le Commissariat est composé de neuf membres nommés pour six ans et choisis en raison de leur compétence générale.

Seuls des nationaux des États membres peuvent être membres du Commissariat. Celui-ci ne peut comprendre plus de deux membres ayant la nationalité d'un même État.

Les membres sortants peuvent être nommés de nouveau.

Le nombre des membres du Commissariat peut être réduit par décision du Conseil statuant à l'unanimité.

§ 2. Dans l'accomplissement de leurs devoirs, les membres du Commissariat ne sollicitent ni n'acceptent d'instructions d'aucun Gouvernement. Ils s'abstiennent de tout acte incompatible avec le caractère supranational de leurs fonctions.

Chaque État membre s'engage à respecter ce caractère supranational et à ne pas chercher à influencer les membres du Commissariat dans l'exécution de leur tâche.

Les membres du Commissariat ne peuvent, pendant la durée de leurs fonctions, exercer aucune autre activité professionnelle.

Pendant une durée de trois années à partir de la cessation desdites fonctions, aucun ancien membre du Commissariat ne peut exercer une activité professionnelle que la Cour, saisie par lui ou par le Conseil, jugerait, en raison de sa connexité avec ces fonctions, incompatible avec les obligations découlant de celles-ci. En cas d'infraction à cette disposition, la Cour peut prononcer la déchéance du droit à pension de l'intéressé.

Article 21

§ 1. Les membres du Commissariat sont nommés d'un commun accord par les Gouvernements des États membres.

§ 2. Les membres nommés pour la première fois après l'entrée en vigueur du présent Traité demeurent en fonctions pendant une période de trois ans à dater de leur nomination.

Au cas où, pendant cette première période, une vacance se produit pour l'une des causes prévues à l'article 22 ci-après, cette vacance est comblée dans les conditions prévues au paragraphe 1 du présent article.

La même procédure s'applique au renouvellement général rendu nécessaire en cas d'application de l'article 36, § 2 ci-après.

§ 3. A l'expiration de la période initiale de trois ans, un renouvellement général a lieu.

§ 4. Le renouvellement partiel des membres du Commissariat a lieu ensuite par tiers tous les deux ans.

Aussitôt après le renouvellement général prévu au paragraphe 3 du présent article, il sera procédé par le Conseil à un tirage au sort pour désigner les membres dont le mandat viendra à expiration respectivement à la fin de la première et de la deuxième période de deux ans.

§ 5. Au cas où les membres du Commissariat abandonnent leurs fonctions par application de l'article 36, § 2 ci-après, les dispositions des paragraphes 3 et 4 du présent article sont applicables.

Article 22

En dehors des renouvellements réguliers, les fonctions des membres du

Commissariat prennent fin individuellement par décès ou démission volontaire ou d'office.

L'intéressé est remplacé, pour la durée du mandat restant à courir, dans les conditions prévues à l'article 21 ci-dessus. Il n'y a pas lieu à remplacement si la durée du mandat restant à courir est inférieure à trois mois.

Article 23

Tout membre du Commissariat, s'il ne remplit plus les conditions nécessaires à l'exercice de ses fonctions ou s'il a commis une faute grave, peut être déclaré démissionnaire d'office par la Cour, à la requête du Conseil ou du Commissariat.

En pareil cas, le Conseil, statuant à l'unanimité, peut, à titre provisoire, le suspendre de ses fonctions et pourvoir à son remplacement jusqu'au moment où la Cour se sera prononcée.

Article 24

§ 1. Les délibérations du Commissariat sont acquises à la majorité des membres présents. En cas de partage égal des voix, celle du Président est prépondérante. Toutefois, aucune délibération n'est acquise si elle n'a recueilli au moins quatre voix.

§ 2. Le règlement intérieur fixe le quorum. Celui-ci doit être au moins de cinq.

§ 3. Le Conseil, s'il décide, dans les conditions prévues à l'article 20, § 1, de réduire le nombre des membres du Commissariat, apporte, dans les mêmes conditions, aux chiffres fixés aux deux paragraphes précédents, les adaptations nécessaires.

Article 25

§ 1. Les Gouvernements des États membres nomment d'un commun accord le Président du Commissariat parmi les membres de celui-ci.

Le Président est désigné pour quatre ans. Son mandat peut être renouvelé. Il prend fin dans les mêmes conditions que celui des membres du Commissariat.

§ 2. Le Président est exclu de toute opération de tirage au sort qui pourrait avoir pour effet d'abréger la durée de son mandat de Président par la perte de qualité de membre du Commissariat.

Lorsque le Président est choisi parmi les membres déjà en fonctions du Commissariat, la durée de son mandat de membre du Commissariat est prorogée jusqu'à l'expiration de la durée de son mandat de Président.

§ 3. Sauf dans le cas d'un renouvellement général, la désignation est faite après consultation des membres du Commissariat.

Article 25 bis

Pour la première fois, le mandat du Président expire à la fin d'une période de trois ans.

Article 26

§ 1. Le Commissariat établit un règlement général d'organisation, qui détermine notamment:

a. sur la base du principe de la collégialité, les catégories de décisions qui devront être prises collectivement par le Commissariat et celles qui pourront être déléguées à des membres du Commissariat agissant individuellement selon leurs compétences respectives;

b. une répartition des tâches du Commissariat qui tienne compte de la nécessité d'une structure stable, tout en ménageant la possibilité des adaptations que l'expérience ferait apparaître nécessaires; cette répartition ne correspondra pas obligatoirement au nombre des membres du Commissariat.

§ 2. Dans le cadre de ce règlement:

a. le Commissariat détermine les attributions respectives de ses membres;

b. le Président:

— coordonne l'exercice de ces attributions;

— assure l'exécution des déliberations;

— est chargé de l'administration des services.

Dans les cas et les conditions prévus à l'article 123 ci-après, le Président peut être temporairement investi de pouvoirs spéciaux.

Article 27

Pour exercer ses pouvoirs, le Commissariat prend des décisions, formule des recommandations et émet des avis.

Les décisions sont obligatoires en tous leurs éléments.

Les recommandations comportent obligation quant aux buts qu'elles assignent, mais laissent à ceux à qui elles sont adressées le choix des moyens propres à atteindre ces buts.

Les avis ne lient pas.

Lorsque le Commissariat est habilité à prendre une décision, il peut se borner à formuler une recommandation.

Article 28

Toutes les décisions et recommandations, tous les avis du Commissariat sont publiés ou notifiés selon les modalités établies par le Conseil.

Les décisions, recommandations ou avis du Commissariat destinés au Gouvernement d'un État membre sont adressés à l'autorité désignée à cet effet par ledit État.

Article 29

Le Commissariat fait rapport au Conseil à intervalles périodiques.

Il fournit au Conseil les renseignements qui lui sont demandés par celui-ci et procède aux études dont il est chargé par lui.

Le Commissariat et le Conseil procèdent à des échanges d'informations et à des consultations réciproques.

Article 30

Le Commissariat dispose du personnel civil et militaire nécessaire pour lui permettre d'assurer toutes les tâches qui lui sont dévolues par le présent Traité.

Les Services qu'il constitue à cette fin, tant civils que militaires, dépendent de lui au même titre et sur le même plan.

Article 31

§ 1. Les grades supérieurs à ceux de Commandant d'Unité de base de nationalité homogène sont conférés par décision du Commissariat, sur avis conforme du Conseil statuant à l'unanimité.

§ 2. A titre provisoire les grades, dans les Unités de nationalité homogène des Forces européennes de défense, et tous autres grades, sont conférés, au choix de chaque État membre :

— soit par les autorités nationales appropriées, sur proposition du Commissariat ;

— soit par le Commissariat, sur proposition des échelons hiérarchiques intéressés, après consultation d'autorités nationales.

§ 3. a. Les emplois de Commandant d'Unité de base, d'officier général ayant autorité sur des éléments de différentes nationalités, et certains postes élevés du Commissariat déterminés par le Conseil, sont conférés par le Commissariat, sur avis conforme du Conseil statuant à l'unanimité.

b. Tous les autres emplois militaires sont conférés par décisions du Commissariat, compte tenu des propositions des échelons hiérarchiques intéressés.

§ 4. En ce qui concerne les emplois civils, les chefs de service directement responsables envers le Commissariat sont nommés par celui-ci, sur avis conforme du Conseil statuant à l'unanimité.

Article 32

Le Commissariat assure toutes liaisons utiles avec les États membres, avec les États tiers et, d'une manière générale, avec toutes organisations internationales dont le concours s'avérerait nécessaire pour atteindre les buts du présent Traité.

CHAPITRE II

L'ASSEMBLÉE

Article 33

§ 1. L'Assemblée de la Communauté européenne de défense est l'Assemblée prévue aux articles 20 et 21 du Traité du 18 avril 1951 instituant la Communauté européenne du charbon et de l'acier,[1] complétée, en ce qui concerne respectivement la République Fédérale d'Allemagne, la France et l'Italie, par trois délégués, qui sont élus dans les mêmes conditions et pour la même durée que les autres délégués et dont le premier mandat prend fin à la même date que celui de ces derniers.

L'Assemblée ainsi complétée exerce les compétences qui lui sont conférées par le présent Traité. Si elle le juge nécessaire, elle peut élire son Président et son bureau et arrêter son règlement intérieur.

§ 2. Si la Conférence visée au paragraphe 2 de l'article 38 ci-après n'est pas parvenue à un accord dans un délai d'un an à dater sa convocation, il sera, sans attendre la fin de ses travaux, procédé, du commun accord des États membres, à une revision des dispositions du paragraphe 1 du présent article.

Article 34

L'Assemblée tient une session annuelle. Elle se réunit de plein droit le dernier mardi d'octobre. La durée de cette session ne peut excéder un mois.

L'Assemblée peut être convoquée en session extraordinaire à la demande du Commissariat, du Conseil, du Président de l'Assemblée ou de la majorité de ses membres ou, dans le cas visé à l'article 46 ci-après, à la demande d'un État membre.

Article 34 bis

L'Assemblée se réunit un mois après la date d'entrée en fonctions du Commissariat sur convocation de celui-ci. Les dispositions de l'article 34 relatives à la durée de la session ordinaire de l'Assemblée ne s'appliquent pas à sa première session.

L'Assemblée peut, dès sa réunion, exercer les attributions qui lui sont dévolues par le présent Traité, à l'exception du vote de la motion de censure prévue à l'article 36, § 2 ci-après, qui ne pourra intervenir qu'à partir de l'expiration d'un délai d'un an à compter de la date d'entrée en fonctions du Commissariat.

Article 35

Les membres du Commissariat peuvent assister à toutes les séances de l'Assemblée. Le Président ou les membres du Commissariat désignés par

---

[1] *Documents* (R.I.I.A.) for 1951, pp. 180–1.

ce dernier sont entendus sur leur demande. Le Commissariat répond, oralement ou par écrit, aux questions qui lui sont posées par l'Assemblée ou par ses membres.

Les membres du Conseil peuvent également assister à toutes les séances et sont entendus sur leur demande.

Article 36

§ 1. Le Commissariat présente chaque année à l'Assemblée, un mois avant l'ouverture de la session ordinaire, un rapport général sur son activité. L'Assemblée discute ce rapport, peut formuler des observations, exprimer des vœux et des suggestions.

§ 2. L'Assemblée, si elle est saisie d'une motion de censure sur la gestion du Commissariat, ne peut se prononcer sur ladite motion que trois jours au moins après son dépôt et par scrutin public.

Si la motion de censure est adoptée à une majorité des deux tiers des voix exprimées et à la majorité des membres qui composent l'Assemblée, les membres du Commissariat doivent abandonner collectivement leurs fonctions. Ils continuent à expédier les affaires courantes jusqu'à ce qu'il ait été pourvu à leur remplacement, dans les conditions prévues à l'article 21 ci-dessus.

Article 37

Le règlement intérieur de l'Assemblée est arrêté à la majorité des membres qui la composent.

Les actes de l'Assemblée sont publiés dans les cas et les conditions fixés par elle.

Article 38

§ 1. Dans le délai prévu au deuxième paragraphe du présent article, l'Assemblée étudie:

a. la constitution d'une Assemblée de la Communauté européenne de défense, élue sur une base démocratique;

b. les pouvoirs qui seraient dévolus à une telle Assemblée;

c. les modifications qui devraient éventuellement être apportées aux dispositions du présent Traité relatives aux autres institutions de la Communauté, notamment en vue de sauvegarder une représentation appropriée des États.

Dans ses études, l'Assemblée s'inspirera notamment des principes suivants:

— l'organisation de caractère définitif qui se substituera à la présente organisation provisoire devra être conçue de manière à pouvoir constituer un des éléments d'une structure fédérale ou confédérale ultérieure, fondée sur le principe de la séparation des pouvoirs et comportant, en particulier, un système représentatif bicaméral;

— l'Assemblée étudiera également les problèmes résultant de la co-existence de différents organismes de coopération européenne déjà créés ou qui viendraient à l'être, afin d'en assurer la coordination dans le cadre de la structure fédérale ou confédérale.

§ 2. Les propositions de l'Assemblée seront soumises au Conseil dans un délai de six mois à dater de l'entrée en fonctions de l'Assemblée. Avec l'avis du Conseil, ces propositions seront ensuite transmises par le Président de l'Assemblée aux Gouvernements des États membres, qui, dans un délai de trois mois à compter de la date à laquelle ils en auront été saisis, convoqueront une Conférence chargée d'examiner lesdites propositions.

CHAPITRE III
Le Conseil

Article 39

§ 1. Le Conseil a pour mission générale d'harmoniser l'action du Commissariat et la politique des Gouvernements des États membres.

§ 2. Le Conseil peut formuler, dans le cadre du présent Traité, des directives pour l'action du Commissariat.

Ces directives sont formulées à l'unanimité.

En ce qui concerne les matières qui n'ont pas donné lieu, de la part du Conseil, à des directives, le Commissariat peut agir, en vue d'assurer la réalisation des objets fixés par le présent Traité, dans les conditions prévues par celui-ci.

§ 3. Conformément aux dispositions du présent Traité, le Conseil:

a. prend des décisions;

b. émet les avis conformes que le Commissariat est tenu d'obtenir avant de prendre une décision ou de formuler une recommandation.

§ 4. Sauf dispositions contraires du présent Traité, les décisions du Conseil sont prises et ses avis émis à la majorité simple.

§ 5. Lorsque le Conseil est consulté par le Commissariat, il délibère sans procéder nécessairement à un vote. Les procès-verbaux des délibérations sont transmis au Commissariat.

Article 40

Le Conseil est formé par les représentants des États membres.

Chaque État membre y délègue un membre de son Gouvernement, qui peut se faire représenter par un Suppléant.

Le Conseil est organisé de manière à pouvoir exercer ses fonctions à tout instant. A cet effet, chaque État membre doit avoir en tout temps un représentant en mesure de participer, sans délai, aux délibérations du Conseil.

La présidence est exercée, à tour de rôle, par chaque membre du Conseil, pour une durée de trois mois, suivant l'ordre alphabétique des États membres.

Article 41

Le Conseil se réunit aussi souvent qu'il est nécessaire et au moins tous les trois mois. Il est réuni sur convocation de son Président, à l'initiative de celui-ci ou à celle d'un de ses membres ou du Commissariat.

Article 41 *bis*

Le Conseil se réunit dès l'entrée en vigueur du présent Traité.

Article 42

En cas de vote, chaque membre du Conseil peut recevoir délégation d'un seul des autres membres.

Article 43

§ 1. Dans les cas où le présent Traité requiert un avis conforme ou une décision du Conseil à la majorité simple, l'avis ou la décision sont acquis s'ils recueillent:
— soit les voix de la majorité absolue des représentants des États membres;
— soit, en cas de partage égal des voix, celles des représentants d'États membres mettant ensemble à la disposition de la Communauté au moins les deux tiers du total des contributions des États membres.

§ 2. Dans les cas où le présent Traité requiert un avis conforme ou une décision du Conseil à une majorité qualifiée, l'avis ou la décision sont acquis:
— soit à la majorité ainsi déterminée, si cette majorité comprend les voix des représentants d'États membres mettant ensemble à la disposition de la Communauté au moins les deux tiers du total des contributions des États membres;
— soit s'ils recueillent les voix des représentants de cinq États membres.

§ 3. Dans les cas où le présent Traité requiert un avis conforme ou une décision du Conseil à l'unanimité, l'avis ou la décision sont acquis s'ils recueillent les voix de tous les membres présents ou représentés au Conseil, les abstentions ne faisant pas obstacle à l'adoption de l'avis ou de la décision.

§ 4. Dans les paragraphes 1 et 2 du présent article, le mot « contributions » s'entend de la moyenne entre le pourcentage des contributions financières effectivement versées pendant l'exercice antérieur et le pourcentage des effectifs composant les Forces européennes de défense au premier jour du semestre en cours.

Article 43 bis

§ 1. Pour l'application du paragraphe 4 de l'article 43 ci-dessus et jusqu'à la date fixée pour l'exécution du plan de mise sur pied du premier échelon de forces, la moyenne, visée audit paragraphe, des contributions fournies par les États membres est évaluée forfaitairement comme suit:

Allemagne	3
Belgique	2
France	3
Italie	3
Luxembourg	1
Pays-Bas	2

§ 2. Pour la période de transition définie au paragraphe précédent, le montant des contributions requises à l'article 43 § 1, ci-dessus sera réputé acquis s'il atteint $9/14^e$ au moins de la valeur globale des contributions forfaitaires des États membres.

Article 44

Les textes définissant ou modifiant les statuts des personnels, l'organisation générale, le recrutement, les effectifs et l'encadrement des forces, ainsi que les modifications au plan de constitution des forces européennes de défense sont arrêtés par le Conseil statuant à l'unanimité, sur proposition, soit d'un membre du Conseil, soit du Commissariat, et mis en vigueur par ce dernier.

Article 45

Le Conseil fixe les traitements, indemnités et pensions du Président et des membres du Commissariat.

Article 46

Le Conseil, statuant à la majorité des deux tiers, peut, à l'initiative d'un de ses membres, inviter le Commissariat à prendre toute mesure entrant dans les limites de sa compétence.

Si le Commissariat ne défère pas à cette invitation, le Conseil, ou un État membre, peut saisir l'Assemblée, en vue de l'application éventuelle de l'article 36, § 2, ci-dessus.

Article 47

§ 1. Le Conseil décide s'il y a lieu de demander une réunion commune du Conseil de l'Organisation du Traité de l'Atlantique Nord et du Conseil de la Communauté.

§ 2. Les délibérations prises à l'unanimité au cours des réunions communes des deux Conseils lient les institutions de la Communauté.

Article 48

La décision du Conseil prévue au paragraphe 4 du Protocole relatif aux relations entre l'Organisation du Traité de l'Atlantique Nord et la Communauté européenne de défense[1] est prise à l'unanimité.

Article 49

Les procès-verbaux des délibérations du Conseil sont communiqués aux États membres et au Commissariat.

Article 50

Le Conseil arrête son règlement intérieur.

CHAPITRE IV
LA COUR

Article 51

La Cour assure le respect du droit dans l'interprétation et l'application du présent Traité et des règlements d'exécution.

Article 52

La Cour est la Cour de justice de la Communauté européenne du charbon et de l'acier.[2]

Article 53

Pour l'accomplissement de sa mission, et dans les cas et les conditions fixés au Protocole juridictionnel et au Statut juridictionnel prévus à l'article 67, la Cour est assistée par une organisation juridictionnelle comprenant notamment des tribunaux de caractère européen.

Article 54

§ 1. La Cour est compétente pour se prononcer sur les recours en annulation pour incompétence, violation des formes substantielles, violation du présent Traité ou de toute règle de droit relative à son application, ou détournement de pouvoir, formés contre les décisions ou recommandations du Commissariat par un des États membres, par le Conseil, ou par l'Assemblée.

§ 2. Les recours doivent être formés dans le délai d'un mois, à compter soit de la publication, soit de la notification de la décision ou de la recommandation.

§ 3. En cas d'annulation, la Cour renvoie l'affaire devant le Commissariat

---

[1] See below, p. 163.   [2] *Documents* (R.I.I.A.) for 1951, pp. 184–7.

qui est tenu de prendre les mesures que comporte l'exécution de la décision d'annulation.

Article 55

§ 1. Dans le cas où le Commissariat, tenu, par une disposition du présent Traité ou des règlements d'exécution, de prendre une décision ou de formuler une recommandation, ne se conforme pas à cette obligation, il appartient aux États membres ou au Conseil de saisir le Commissariat.

Il en est de même dans le cas où le Commissariat, habilité par une disposition du présent Traité ou des règlements d'exécution à prendre une décision ou à formuler une recommandation, s'en abstient et où cette abstention constitue un détournement de pouvoir.

§ 2. Si, à l'expiration d'un délai de deux mois, le Commissariat n'a pris aucune décision ou formulé aucune recommandation, un recours peut être formé devant la Cour, dans un délai d'un mois, contre la décision implicite de refus qui est réputée résulter de ce silence.

Article 56

§ 1. Lorsqu'un État membre estime que, dans un cas déterminé, une action ou un défaut d'action du Commissariat est de nature à provoquer, en ce qui le concerne, des troubles fondamentaux et persistants, il peut saisir le Commissariat.

Celui-ci, après consultation du Conseil, reconnaît, s'il y a lieu, l'existence d'une telle situation et décide des mesures à prendre, dans les conditions prévues au présent Traité, pour mettre fin à cette situation tout en sauvegardant les intérêts essentiels de la Communauté. Il est tenu de statuer dans un délai de deux semaines.

§ 2. Lorsque la Cour est saisie d'un recours fondé sur les dispositions du présent article contre cette décision ou contre la décision explicite ou implicite refusant de reconnaître l'existence de la situation ci-dessus visée, il lui appartient d'en apprécier le bien-fondé et de prendre, à titre provisoire, toutes les mesures nécessaires.

§ 3. En cas d'annulation, le Commissariat est tenu de décider, dans le cadre de l'arrêt de la Cour, des mesures à prendre aux fins prévues au premier paragraphe, deuxième alinéa, du présent article.

Article 57

§ 1. La Cour est compétente pour se prononcer sur les recours en annulation pour incompétence, violation des formes substantielles, violation du présent Traité ou de toute règle de droit relative à son application, ou détournement de pouvoir, formés contre les délibérations du Conseil par un des États membres, par le Commissariat ou par l'Assemblée.

§ 2. La requête doit être formée dans le délai d'un mois à dater de la communication de la délibération du Conseil aux États membres ou au Commissariat.

Article 58

§ 1. La Cour peut annuler, à la requête d'un des États membres ou du Commissariat, les délibérations de l'Assemblée.

Seuls les moyens tirés de l'incompétence ou de la violation des formes substantielles peuvent être invoqués à l'appui d'un tel recours.

§ 2. La requête doit être formée dans le délai d'un mois à compter de la publication de la délibération de l'Assemblée.

Article 59

Les recours formés devant la Cour n'ont pas d'effet suspensif.

Toutefois, la Cour peut, si elle estime que les circonstances l'exigent, ordonner le sursis à l'exécution de la décision ou de la recommandation attaquée.

Elle peut prescrire toutes autres mesures provisoires nécessaires.

Article 60

La Cour est compétente, dans les cas et les conditions fixés au Protocole juridictionnel[1] et au Statut juridictionnel prévu à l'article 67, pour statuer sur les litiges relatifs à la responsabilité civile de la Communauté ainsi qu'aux statuts de ses agents.

Article 61

La Cour est compétente pour statuer en matière pénale, dans les cas et les conditions fixés au Protocole juridictionnel et au Statut juridictionnel prévu à l'article 67.

Article 61 *bis*

Jusqu'à la mise en vigueur d'une législation pénale militaire commune, des dispositions transitoires sont prévues par le Protocole juridictionnel.

Article 62

Sans préjudice des dispositions du Statut juridictionnel prévu à l'article 67, la Cour est seule compétente pour statuer, à titre préjudiciel, sur la validité des décisions ou recommandations du Commissariat et des délibérations du Conseil, dans le cas où un litige porté devant un tribunal national mettrait en cause cette validité.

---

[1] Not printed here. See *Traité instituant la Communauté européenne de défense et Documents annexes*, pp. 38–42.

Article 63

La Cour est compétente, dans les cas et les conditions fixés par son Statut, pour statuer en vertu d'une clause compromissoire contenue dans un contrat de droit public ou de droit privé passé par la Communauté ou pour son compte.

Article 64

La Cour est compétente pour statuer dans tout autre cas prévu par une disposition additionnelle du présent Traité.

Elle peut également statuer dans tous les cas en connexité avec l'objet du présent Traité où la législation d'un État membre lui attribue compétence.

Article 65

§ 1. Tout différend entre les États membres au sujet de l'application du présent Traité, qui n'aurait pu être réglé par une autre voie, pourra être soumis à la Cour, soit en vertu d'une requête commune des États parties au litige, soit à la requête d'un d'entre eux.

§ 2. La Cour est également compétente pour statuer sur tout différend entre États membres en connexité avec l'objet du présent Traité, si ce différend lui est soumis en vertu d'un compromis.

Article 66

Les arrêts de la Cour ont force exécutoire sur le territoire des États membres.

L'exécution forcée sur le territoire des États membres est poursuivie suivant les voies de droit en vigueur dans chacun de ces États; notamment l'exécution ne peut être poursuivie à l'égard d'un État membre que dans la mesure et par les voies admises par la législation de cet État.

Cette exécution a lieu après qu'a été apposée, sans autre contrôle que celui de la vérification de l'authenticité de ces arrêts, la formule exécutoire usitée dans l'État sur le territoire duquel l'arrêt doit être exécuté. Il est pourvu à cette formalité à la diligence d'un ministre désigné à cet effet par chacun des gouvernements.

Article 67

L'application des dispositions du présent chapitre et du Protocole juridictionnel sera fixé par un Statut juridictionnel, établi par voie d'une convention entre les États membres et apportant notamment les adaptations nécessaires à cet effet au Statut de la Cour annexé au Traité instituant la Communauté européenne du Charbon et de l'Acier.

DISPOSITIONS MILITAIRES

CHAPITRE PREMIER

Organisation et administration des Forces européennes de défense

Article 68

§ 1. Les Unités de base où devra se combiner l'action des différentes armes constituant l'Armée de Terre sont formées d'éléments de la même nationalité d'origine. Ces Unités de base sont aussi légères que le permet le principe d'efficacité. Elles sont déchargées au maximum des fonctions logistiques et dépendent, pour leur vie et leur entretien, d'échelons supérieurs intégrés.

§ 2. Les Corps d'Armée sont formés d'Unités de base de différentes nationalités d'origine, sauf dans des cas exceptionnels résultant de nécessités tactiques ou d'organisation et déterminés par le Commissariat sur proposition du Commandant suprême compétent relevant de l'Organisation du Traité de l'Atlantique Nord et avec l'avis conforme du Conseil statuant à l'unanimité. Leurs unités de soutien tactique, ainsi que les formations de support logistique, sont de type intégré; ces dernières unités élémentaires, de l'ordre du régiment ou du bataillon, restent homogènes et leur répartition entre nationalités se fait selon la proportion qui existe entre les Unités de base. Le Commandement et l'État-Major des Corps d'Armée sont intégrés; cette intégration est effectuée de la manière la plus propre à assurer l'efficacité de leur emploi.

§ 3. Les Unités de base et leurs soutiens et supports peuvent occasionnellement être introduits dans les Corps d'Armée relevant de l'Organisation du Traité de l'Atlantique Nord et, réciproquement, des divisions relevant de l'Organisation du Traité de l'Atlantique Nord peuvent l'être dans des Corps d'Armée européens.

Les échelons de Commandement des Forces relevant de l'Organisation du Traité de l'Atlantique Nord auxquels sont organiquement rattachées les unités européennes intègrent des éléments provenant de ces Unités et réciproquement.

Article 69

§ 1. Sont constituées d'éléments de la même nationalité d'origine les Unités de base de l'Armée de l'Air dont chacune est dotée d'un matériel de combat homogène correspondant à une mission élémentaire déterminée.

Ces Unités de base sont déchargées au maximum des fonctions logistiques et dépendent, pour leur mise en œuvre et leur entretien, d'échelons supérieurs intégrés.

§ 2. Un certain nombre d'Unités de base d'origines nationales différentes sont groupées sous les ordres d'échelons supérieurs de type intégré, sauf dans des cas exceptionnels résultant de nécessités tactiques ou d'organisation et déterminés par le Commissariat sur proposition du Commandant suprême compétent relevant de l'Organisation du Traité de l'Atlantique Nord et avec l'avis conforme du Conseil statuant à l'unanimité. Les formations de support logistique sont de type intégré, les unités élémentaires des services restant de composition nationale homogène et leur répartition entre nationalités se faisant selon la proportion qui existe entre les Unités de base.

§ 3. Des Unités de base européennes ainsi que leurs unités de support peuvent être introduites sous des Commandements relevant de l'Organisation du Traité de l'Atlantique Nord et, réciproquement, des Unités de base relevant de l'Organisation du Traité de l'Atlantique Nord peuvent l'être sous des Commandements européens.

Les échelons de Commandement relevant de l'Organisation du Traité de l'Atlantique Nord auxquels sont organiquement rattachées des Unités européennes intègrent des éléments européens et réciproquement.

Article 70

§ 1. Les Forces navales européennes comprennent les formations qui sont liées à la protection maritime rapprochée des territoires européens des États membres, et qui sont fixées par des accords entre les Gouvernements.

§ 2. Les contingents des Forces navales européennes constituent des groupements de nationalité homogène et de statut européen, répondant à une même mission tactique.

§ 3. Ces groupements, en totalité ou en partie, peuvent occasionnellement être incorporés à des formations relevant de l'Organisation du Traité de l'Atlantique Nord, dont les commandements intègrent dès lors des éléments fournis par eux.

Article 71

Le Commissariat établit les plans d'organisation des forces, sur avis conforme du Conseil statuant à l'unanimité. Il en assure l'exécution.

Article 72

§ 1. Les personnels recrutés par conscription pour servir dans les Forces européennes de défense accompliront le même temps de service actif.

§ 2. L'uniformisation sera réalisée aussi rapidement que possible, sur proposition du Commissariat, par décision du Conseil statuant à l'unanimité.

Article 73

§ 1. Le recrutement des Forces européennes de défense dans chaque État membre est réglé par les lois dudit État dans le cadre des dispositions de principe communes définies par le Protocole militaire.[1]

§ 2. Le Commissariat suit les opérations de recrutement effectuées par les États membres en conformité des dispositions du présent Traité et, en vue d'assurer cette conformité, adresse, le cas échéant, les recommandations aux États membres.

§ 3. A partir de la date déterminée d'un commun accord par les Gouvernements des États membres, le Commissariat procédera au recrutement selon les règles définies par ledit accord, dans le cadre des dispositions de principe communes fixées par le Protocole militaire.

Article 74

§ 1. Le Commissariat procède à l'instruction et à la mise en condition des Forces européennes de défense suivant une doctrine commune et des méthodes uniformes. En particulier, il dirige les écoles de la Communauté.

§ 2. A la demande d'un État membre, il est tenu compte, dans l'application des principes définis au paragraphe 1 du présent article, de la situation particulière résultant pour cet État de l'existence, en vertu de la Constitution, de plusieurs langues officielles.

Article 75

Les plans de mobilisation des Forces européennes de défense sont préparés par le Commissariat, en consultation avec les Gouvernements des États membres.

Sans préjudice de l'organisation définitive visée à l'article 38 ci-dessus, la décision de procéder à la mobilisation relève des États membres; l'exécution des mesures de mobilisation est partagée entre la Communauté et les États membres, dans les conditions définies par des accords entre le Commissariat et lesdits États.

Article 76

Le Commissariat procède aux inspections et contrôles indispensables.

Article 77

§ 1. Le Commissariat détermine l'implantation territoriale des Forces européennes de défense dans le cadre des recommandations du Commandant Suprême compétent relevant de l'Organisation du Traité de l'Atlantique Nord. En cas de divergences de vues qui n'auraient pu être aplanies

---

[1] Not printed here. See *Traité instituant la Communauté européenne de défense et Documents annexes*, pp. 30–37.

avec ce dernier, il ne peut s'écarter de ces recommandations qu'avec l'approbation du Conseil statuant à l'unanimité.

Dans le cadre des décisions générales visées à l'alinéa 1 du présent article, le Commissariat prend les décisions d'exécution, après consultation avec l'État dans lequel les troupes seront stationnées.

§ 2. Dans le cas de divergences de vues sur des points essentiels, l'État intéressé peut saisir le Conseil. Cet État doit se conformer à l'avis du Commissariat si le Conseil, statuant à la majorité des deux tiers, se prononce en faveur de cet avis.

La faculté dont les États membres peuvent se prévaloir, en vertu de l'article 56 ci-dessus, n'est pas affectée par les dispositions qui précèdent.

Article 78

Le Commissariat administre les personnels et les matériels conformément aux dispositions du présent Traité.

Il veille à une répartition visant à assurer l'homogénéité en armement et équipement des unités composant les Forces européennes de défense.

Article 78 bis

§ 1. Dès son entrée en fonctions, le Commissariat:

— établit les plans de constitution et d'équipement du premier échelon des Forces d'après les dispositions adoptées d'un commun accord par les Gouvernements des États membres, et dans le cadre des plans de l'Organisation du Traité de l'Atlantique Nord;

— détermine et organise les concours à demander aux États parties au Traité de l'Atlantique Nord, en vue de l'instruction des contingents;

— établit une réglementation provisoire sommaire sur les points essentiels.

§ 2. Dès son entrée en fonctions, le Commissariat entreprend la constitution des unités du premier échelon des forces.

§ 3. Dès l'entrée en vigueur du présent Traité, les unités déjà existantes et les contingents à recruter par les États membres pour compléter ce premier échelon relèvent de la Communauté et sont placés sous l'autorité du Commissariat, qui exerce à leur égard les pouvoirs prévus au présent Traité, dans les conditions définies par le Protocole militaire.

§ 4. Le Commissariat soumet dans les plus brefs délais au Conseil les plans et textes visés au paragraphe 1 du présent article.

Le Conseil arrête:

— à l'unanimité, le plan de constitution du premier échelon des Forces;

— à la majorité des deux tiers, les autres textes.

Les textes sont mis en vigueur par le Commissariat dès qu'ils ont été arrêtés par le Conseil.

Article 79

Un Règlement unique de discipline générale militaire applicable aux membres des Forces européennes de défense sera établi par accord entre les Gouvernements des États membres et ratifié selon les règles constitutionnelles de chacun de ces États.

CHAPITRE II

STATUT DES FORCES EUROPÉENNES DE DÉFENSE

Article 80

§ 1. Dans l'exercice de la compétence qui lui est conféré, par le présent Traité, et sans préjudice des droits et obligations des États membres:

la Communauté a, en ce qui concerne les Forces européennes de défense et leurs membres, les mêmes droits et obligations que les États en ce qui concerne leurs Forces nationales et les membres de ces Forces, d'après le droit coutumier des gens;

la Communauté est tenue au respect des règles de droit conventionnel de la guerre qui obligent un ou plusieurs États membres.

§ 2. En conséquence, les Forces européennes de défense et leurs membres jouissent, au point de vue du droit des gens, du même traitement que les Forces nationales des États et leurs membres.

Article 81

§ 1. La Communauté veille à ce que les Forces européennes de défense et leurs membres conforment leur conduite aux règles du droit des gens. Elle assure la répression de toute violation éventuelle de ces règles qui viendrait à être commise par lesdites Forces ou leurs membres.

§ 2. La Communauté prend, dans le cadre de sa compétence, les mesures de répression pénale et toutes autres mesures appropriées au cas où une telle violation serait commise par les Forces d'États tiers ou leurs membres.

En outre, les États membres prennent, de leur côté, dans le cadre de leur compétence, les mesures de répression pénale et toutes autres mesures appropriées contre toute violation des règles du droit des gens commise envers les Forces européennes de défense ou leurs membres.

Article 82

Le Statut des Forces européennes de défense est fixé par une convention particulière.[1]

---

[1] See *Traité instituant la Communauté européenne de défense et Documents annexes*, pp. 54–61.

TITRE IV
DISPOSITIONS FINANCIÈRES
Article 83

La gestion financière de la Communauté est assurée selon les dispositions du présent Traité, du Protocole financier[1] ou du Règlement financier.

Afin de veiller au respect de ces dispositions, il est créé un Contrôleur financier et une Commission des Comptes, dont les attributions sont définies aux articles ci-après.

Article 84

Le Contrôleur financier est indépendant du Commissariat et responsable envers le Conseil. Il est désigné par le Conseil statuant à l'unanimité. La durée de son mandat est de cinq années. Ce mandat est renouvelable.

Article 85

La Commission des Comptes est une autorité collégiale indépendante qui comprend des nationaux de chacun des États membres.

Le Conseil, statuant à l'unanimité, fixe le nombre des membres de cette Commission et procède, à la majorité des deux tiers, à leur désignation ainsi qu'à celle du Président. Le mandat des membres de la Commission des Comptes est de cinq années. Ce mandat est renouvelable.

Article 86

Dès l'entrée en vigueur du présent Traité, toutes les recettes et toutes les dépenses de la Communauté sont inscrites dans un budget commun annuel.

La durée de l'exercice financier est fixée à un an et son point de départ au premier janvier, cette date pouvant être modifiée par décision du Conseil.

Article 87

§ 1. Le Commissariat prépare, en consultation avec les Gouvernements des États membres et en tenant compte notamment des dispositions de l'article 71, le budget de la Communauté. Le projet de plan commun d'armement, d'équipement, d'approvisionnement et d'infrastructure est joint en annexe à ce projet de budget.

Les recettes et dépenses propres à chaque institution de la Communauté font l'objet de sections spéciales, au sein du budget général.

§ 2. Le Conseil est saisi de ce projet trois mois au moins avant le commencement de l'exercice.

Le Conseil, dans un délai d'un mois, décide:

[1] Ibid. pp. 44–48.

a. à l'unanimité, du volume total du budget en crédits de payement et en crédits d'engagement, et du montant de la contribution de chaque État membre, déterminée conformément à l'article 94 ci-après, contribution dont il incombe au Gouvernement de chaque État membre d'assurer l'inscription au budget dudit État selon les règles constitutionnelles de celui-ci;

b. à la majorité des deux tiers, de la répartition des dépenses.

Les dispositions *a* et *b* du présent paragraphe ne sont pas applicables aux recettes et dépenses résultant d'un accord relatif à une aide extérieure prévu à l'article 99 ci-après, ni à celles qui ne font que transiter par le budget commun, ainsi qu'il est prévu au Protocole financier.

§ 3. Le budget commun ainsi approuvé par le Conseil est transmis à l'Assemblée, qui se prononce au plus tard deux semaines avant le début de l'exercice.

L'Assemblée peut proposer des modifications supprimant, réduisant, augmentant ou créant des recettes ou des dépenses. Ces propositions ne peuvent avoir pour effet d'augmenter le montant total des dépenses du projet établi par le Conseil.

L'Assemblée peut proposer le rejet de la totalité du budget, à la majorité des deux tiers des voix exprimées et à la majorité des membres composant l'Assemblée.

§ 4. Dans tous les cas visés au paragraphe précédent, le Commissariat ou un État membre peut, dans les quinze jours du vote, saisir le Conseil en vue d'une deuxième lecture dans un délai de deux semaines. Les propositions de l'Assemblée sont adoptées si le Conseil ainsi saisi les approuve à la majorité des deux tiers. Si le Conseil n'est pas saisi dans ce délai de quinze jours, les propositions sont considérées comme adoptées par lui.

Article 87 *bis*

§ 1. Par dérogation à l'article 87 ci-dessus, la procédure budgétaire relative à l'exercice qui correspond à la période qui s'écoule entre l'entrée en vigueur du présent Traité et la fin de l'année civile relève du seul Conseil.

En dépenses, ce budget devra être établi en tenant compte, dans toute la mesure du possible, des programmes militaires et financiers de tous les États membres pour la mise sur pied des Unités devant constituer les Forces européennes de défense.

§ 2. Pour l'exécution de ce budget, le Commissariat déléguera aux services nationaux appropriés le soin d'exécuter pour son compte les dépenses intéressant les Forces européennes de défense, dans la mesure où ses propres services ne lui permettraient pas d'accomplir ces tâches.

§ 3. En attendant l'approbation de ce budget, et pour lui permettre de faire face à ses premières dépenses, la Communauté recevra des États membres des avances imputées ultérieurement sur les contributions. Les dépenses réglées sur ces avances seront réintégrées dans le budget.

§ 4. Le budget de l'exercice qui suivra l'exercice défini au paragraphe 1 du présent article sera préparé, arrêté et exécuté selon les dispositions du présent Traité. Toutefois:

a. Les contributions des États membres au budget de cet exercice seront établies selon la procédure adoptée par l'Organisation du Traité de l'Atlantique Nord, à l'exclusion de toute autre méthode de répartition;

b. A la demande de tout État membre qui estimerait que le budget commun ainsi établi ne correspond pas aux intentions manifestées par son Gouvernement ou son Parlement, quant à l'exécution de ses engagements à l'égard du Traité de l'Atlantique Nord, ou aux moyens utilisés pour réaliser ces engagements, la Communauté devra soumettre, pour avis, le budget ainsi arrêté, aux autorités compétentes de cette Organisation.

Article 88

§ 1. Si, au début de l'exercice, le budget n'a pas encore été approuvé définitivement, la Communauté est habilitée à pourvoir à ses dépenses par tranches mensuelles égales au douzième des crédits du budget de l'année écoulée. Ce pouvoir prend fin à l'expiration d'un délai de trois mois à dater du début de l'exercice. La dépense ne peut excéder le quart des dépenses de l'année écoulée.

Dans le cas visé à l'alinéa précédent, les États membres doivent consentir à la Communauté des avances, sur la base des contributions inscrites au budget de l'exercice précédent. Ces avances sont imputables sur leurs contributions.

Si, à l'expiration du délai prévu à l'alinéa premier du présent paragraphe, le budget n'est pas devenue définitif, le budget fixé par le Conseil entre en vigueur, à condition que l'Assemblée ait disposé d'un délai d'au moins deux semaines pour l'examiner.

§ 2. En cas de nécessité, le Commissariat peut soumettre, en cours d'exercice, un projet de budget supplémentaire, qui sera approuvé de la même manière que le budget normal, les délais étant réduits de moitié.

Article 89

§ 1. Le budget se subdivise en sections, chapitres et articles. Il est établi en montants bruts, et contient toutes les recettes et toutes les dépenses de la Communauté.

Il comporte notamment les dépenses annuelles nécessaires à l'exécution de programmes communs d'armement, d'équipement, d'approvisionnement et d'infrastructure intéressant plusieurs exercices.

§ 2. Le budget est établi en une monnaie de compte commune choisie par le Conseil statuant à la majorité des deux tiers.

Le rapport entre la monnaie de compte et la monnaie nationale résulte du taux de change officiel notifié par chaque État à la Communauté.

Article 90

§ 1. Le Commissariat peut procéder à des virements de crédits entre les postes relevant de sa gestion, dans la limite des autorisations générales ou particulières qui lui sont données, soit dans le budget lui-même, soit par décision du Conseil statuant à la majorité des deux tiers, soit par le Règlement financier. Ces virements nécessitent l'accord du Contrôleur financier lorsqu'ils sont exécutés en vertu d'autorisations générales.

§ 2. Dans les mêmes conditions, des possibilités de virement analogues sont données aux autres institutions de la Communauté, par les postes dont elles assurent la gestion.

Article 91

L'exécution du budget est assurée par le Commissariat et par les autres institutions de la Communauté, selon les dispositions du Protocole financier.

Dans l'établissement et l'exécution du budget, les institutions de la Communauté doivent assurer le respect des engagements pris par les États membres à l'égard de l'Organisation du Traité de l'Atlantique Nord. Les contrats passés par les États membres avec des tiers, antérieurement à l'entrée en vigueur du présent Traité, doivent être exécutés, à moins qu'ils ne puissent, avec l'accord du Gouvernement qui a signé le contrat, être modifiés dans l'intérêt de la Communauté.

Article 92

L'exécution du budget est suivie par le Contrôleur financier.

Toutes décisions du Commissariat comportant un engagement de dépenses sont soumises au visa du Contrôleur financier, qui vérifie la régularité budgétaire de la dépense et sa conformité avec les dispositions du Règlement financier.

Sans préjudice des dispositions des articles 54 et 57 ci-dessus, le Commissariat peut passer outre au refus de visa du Contrôleur financier, en adressant par écrit à ce dernier une réquisition spéciale pour la dépense. Après avoir reçu cette réquisition, le Contrôleur financier doit en rendre compte immédiatement au Conseil, qui se saisit de l'affaire dans les moindres délais.

Le Contrôleur financier adresse tous les trois mois au Conseil, qui le communique à l'Assemblée, un rapport sur l'exécution du budget. Ce rapport doit contenir toutes observations utiles sur la gestion financière du Commissariat.

Le Contrôleur financier donne son avis sur les projets de budget. Cet avis est communiqué au Commissariat. Il est joint par le Conseil au projet soumis à l'Assemblée.

Article 93

Les recettes de la Communauté comprennent:

a. les contributions versées par les États membres;

b. les recettes propres à la Communauté;

c. les sommes que la Communauté peut recevoir en vertu des articles 7 ci-dessus et 99 ci-après.

La Communauté dispose également de prestations en nature reçues en vertu des mêmes articles.

Article 94

Dès l'entrée en vigueur du présent Traité, les contributions des États membres sont arrêtées par le Conseil selon la procédure adoptée par l'Organisation du Traité de l'Atlantique Nord.

Le Conseil recherchera une méthode propre de détermination des contributions qui, notamment en fonction des possibilités financières, économiques et sociales des États membres, assurera une répartition équitable des charges. Cette méthode devra être approuvée par le Conseil statuant à l'unanimité et sera mise en application dès le premier exercice suivant cette approbation.

A défaut d'accord sur une telle méthode, les contributions continueront à être arrêtées selon la procédure adoptée par l'Organisation du Traité de l'Atlantique Nord.

Article 95

§ 1. Les contributions, établies conformément aux articles précédents, sont payables en monnaie nationale, par douzièmes, au premier jour de chaque mois. Le Conseil, statuant à l'unanimité, peut accepter qu'un État règle sa contribution dans une monnaie autre que sa monnaie nationale.

§ 2. En cas de modification des taux de change, les sommes restant dues sur les contributions font l'objet d'un ajustement sur la base du nouveau taux. Toutefois, l'État débiteur envers la Communauté des sommes correspondant à cet ajustement, peut demander que le montant en soit limité au seul préjudice subi par la Communauté, du fait de la modification du taux de change. Cette limitation est arrêtée par le Conseil statuant à l'unanimité.

Les États membres conservent la charge intégrale des dépenses complémentaires que pourrait entraîner, pour les contrats souscrits par la Communauté, l'application des dispositions prises par un État en faveur des titulaires de contrats à l'occasion d'une réforme monétaire.

§ 3. Si, en cours d'exécution du budget, le pouvoir d'achat de la monnaie d'un État membre se trouve sensiblement diminué par rapport aux pouvoirs d'achat des monnaies des autres États membres, sans qu'il y ait une modification officielle du taux de change de cette monnaie, le Conseil, à la demande du Commissariat ou d'un État membre, examinera les possibilités de compenser le préjudice causé à la Communauté du fait d'une telle situation.

Article 96

La Communauté, lors de l'établissement et de l'exécution du budget, s'efforce de limiter les règlements entre les États membres, ou entre ceux-ci et les pays tiers, qui pourraient affecter la stabilité économique et monétaire des États membres.

Le Règlement financier précisera les modalités selon lesquelles ces règlements seront exécutés.

Si, du fait de l'exécution du budget, la stabilité économique et monétaire d'un État membre vient à être compromise, le Commissariat, sur demande de cet État et en accord avec les Gouvernements intéressés, prend les mesures de redressement nécessaires. Si un accord sur ces mesures ne peut intervenir, le Conseil, à la demande du Commissariat ou d'un État membre, se saisit de la question et prend les dispositions nécessaires, dans les conditions prévues au présent Traité.

Les États membres s'engagent à assouplir, au profit de la Communauté, les restrictions apportées par leur législation des changes aux règlements internationaux.

Article 97

§ 1. La vérification des comptes est effectuée par la Commission des Comptes selon des modalités qui seront fixées par le Règlement financier.

La Commission des Comptes vérifie, sur la base des pièces justificatives, la régularité des opérations et la bonne utilisation des crédits ouverts au budget de la Communauté. Elle peut demander, pour son activité de vérification, l'assistance des institutions de vérification des États membres.

§ 2. Le rapport sur le résultat de la vérification des comptes doit être présenté au Conseil, qui le transmet à l'Assemblée, au plus tard six mois après l'expiration de l'exercice financier.

Sur la base de ce rapport, la Commission des Comptes soumet au Conseil une proposition sur la décharge à donner à chaque institution en ce qui concerne sa gestion financière pour la période considérée. Le Conseil prend position à l'égard de cette proposition et la présente à l'Assemblée, qui statue.

La décharge est considérée comme donnée si l'Assemblée ne l'a pas refusée aux deux tiers des voix exprimées et à la majorité des membres qui la composent.

Article 98

Les Gouvernements des États membres peuvent demander au Contrôleur financier et à la Commission des Comptes communication des documents justificatifs dont ils disposent pour remplir leur mission.

Article 99

Le Commissariat traite des questions relatives à l'aide extérieure en matériels ou en finances, fournie à la Communauté.

Tout accord relatif à une aide extérieure fournie à la Communauté est soumis à l'avis conforme du Conseil, sans préjudice des dispositions particulières du Protocole financier relatives à l'aide extérieure.

La Communauté peut, sur avis conforme du Conseil statuant à l'unanimité, accorder une aide à des États tiers, pour atteindre les fins définies à l'article 2 ci-dessus.

L'aide extérieure en matériels destinée aux Forces européennes de défense que la Communauté ou les États membres peuvent recevoir est administrée par le Commissariat.

Le Conseil, statuant à la majorité des deux tiers, est habilité à adresser au Commissariat des directives générales, afin d'assurer que l'action de celui-ci, en ce qui concerne l'aide extérieure, ne porte pas atteinte à la stabilité économique, financière et sociale d'un ou plusieurs États membres.

Article 100

Les conditions de rémunération des personnels militaires et civils de la Communauté, ainsi que leurs droits à pension, sont fixés par un Protocole annexé au présent Traité.[1]

TITRE V

DISPOSITIONS ÉCONOMIQUES

Article 101

Le Commissariat prépare, en consultation avec les Gouvernements des États membres, les programmes communs d'armement, d'équipement, d'approvisionnement et d'infrastructure des Forces européennes de défense et assure, en conformité de l'article 91 ci-dessus, l'exécution de ces programmes.

[1] *Traité instituant la Communauté européenne de défense et Documents annexes*, pp. 49–50.

Article 102

§ 1. Dans la préparation et l'exécution des programmes, le Commissariat doit:

a. utiliser au mieux les aptitudes techniques et économiques de chacun des États membres et éviter de provoquer des troubles graves dans l'économie de chacun d'entre eux:

b. tenir compte du montant des contributions à fournir par les États membres et respecter les règles définies par le présent Traité en matière de transfert monétaire;

c. En collaboration avec les organismes appropriés de l'Organisation du Traité de l'Atlantique Nord, simplifier et standardiser les armements et les équipements, les approvisionnements et l'infrastructure autant et aussi rapidement que possible.

§ 2. Le Conseil peut adresser au Commissariat des directives générales dans le cadre des principes énoncés ci-dessus. Ces directives sont données à la majorité des deux tiers.

Article 103

§ 1. Les dépenses nécessaires à l'exécution des programmes sont reprises dans le budget qui comporte, en annexe, un état indicatif de la répartition géographique de l'exécution des différentes catégories de programmes. L'approbation du budget vaut approbation de ces programmes.

§ 2. Le Commissariat peut établir des programmes s'étendant sur une période de plusieurs années. Il porte ces programmes à la connaissance du Conseil et demande à celui-ci de donner une approbation de principe à ceux d'entre eux qui comportent des engagements financiers s'étendant sur plusieurs années. Cette approbation est acquise à la majorité des deux tiers.

Article 104

§ 1. Le Commissariat assure l'exécution des programmes en consultation avec le Conseil et les Gouvernements des États membres.

§ 2. Le Commissariat assure la passation des marchés, la surveillance de l'exécution, la recette et le règlement des travaux et des fournitures.

Le Commissariat comporte des services civils, décentralisés de telle sorte qu'il soit en mesure de faire appel aux ressources de chaque État membre dans les conditions les plus avantageuses pour la Communauté.

§ 3. La passation des marchés doit se faire après appel à la concurrence la plus étendue possible, sauf exceptions justifiées par le secret militaire, les conditions techniques et l'urgence définies par le règlement prévu au paragraphe 4 ci-dessous. Les marchés sont conclus après adjudication publique ou restreinte, ou sans adjudication (de gré à gré), avec des entrepreneurs capables d'assurer les prestations, et qui ne sont pas exclus dans leur pays des adjudications publiques. L'exclusion fondée sur la nationalité n'est pas retenue en ce qui concerne les ressortissants des États membres.

Dans le cadre des dispositions de l'article 102 ci-dessus, les commandes doivent être attribuées aux offres les plus avantageuses.

§ 4. Les conditions de procédure relatives à la passation des marchés, à la surveillance de l'exécution, à la recette et au règlement des travaux et des fournitures sont fixées par voie de règlements. Ces règlements sont soumis par le Commissariat à l'avis conforme du Conseil, qui statue à la majorité des deux tiers. Ils peuvent être amendés selon la même procédure.

§ 5. Les marchés supérieurs à certains montants sont soumis avant décision par le Commissariat à l'avis d'une Commission des marchés, comprenant des nationaux de chacun des États membres.

S'il passe outre à l'avis de la Commission des marchés compétente, le Commissariat doit présenter un rapport motivé au Conseil.

Les conditions d'application du présent paragraphe sont fixées par voie de règlement. Ce règlement est soumis par le Commissariat à l'avis conforme du Conseil, qui statue à la majorité des deux tiers. Il peut être amendé selon la même procédure.

§ 6. En ce qui concerne les litiges relatifs aux contrats passés entre la Communauté et des tiers résidant sur le territoire de l'un des États membres, le caractère administratif ou judiciaire de la juridiction compétente, la compétence *ratione materiae* et *ratione loci* de celle-ci, ainsi que la loi applicable sont déterminés:

a. en matière immobilière, par le lieu de la situation de l'immeuble;

b. en toute autre matière, par le lieu de résidence du fournisseur.

Il peut être dérogé à ces règles par accord entre les parties, sauf en ce qui concerne le caractère administratif ou judiciaire de la juridiction compétente et la compétence *ratione materiae*.

Le Commissariat ne recourt normalement à de tels accords que dans des cas particuliers ou pour saisir une juridiction dépendant de la Communauté.

§ 7. Si le Commissariat constate, dans l'exécution des programmes, que des interventions d'ordre public ou des accords ou des pratiques concertées entre entreprises tendent à fausser ou à restreindre gravement le jeu normal de la concurrence, il saisit le Conseil, qui statue à l'unanimité sur les mesures destinées à porter remède à une telle situation.

Le Conseil peut être saisi dans les mêmes conditions par un État membre.

Article 104 *bis*

Les règlements prévus aux paragraphes 4 et 5 de l'article 104 ci-dessus doivent être soumis à l'approbation du Conseil dans un délai maximum de six mois à dater de l'entrée en vigueur du présent Traité.

En attendant la promulgation de ces règlements, le Commissariat assure la passation des marchés conformément aux dispositions législatives ou réglementaires en vigueur dans les États membres.

Article 105

Si le Commissariat constate que l'exécution de tout ou partie d'un programme se heurte à des difficultés telles qu'il ne peut être exécuté, par exemple par suite d'une insuffisance dans l'approvisionnement en matières premières, d'un manque d'équipement ou de capacités installées, ou de prix anormalement élevés, ou que son exécution ne peut être assurée dans les délais requis, il doit saisir le Conseil et chercher avec lui les moyens propres à éliminer ces difficultés.

Le Conseil, statuant à l'unanimité, décide, en consultation avec le Commissariat, des mesures à prendre.

A défaut d'une décision unanime du Conseil sur les mesures visées à l'alinéa précédent, le Commissariat, après consultation des gouvernements intéressés, leur adresse des recommandations afin d'assurer le placement et l'exécution des commandes dans les délais prévus au programme et à des prix qui ne soient pas anormalement élevés, en tenant compte de la nécessité de répartir aussi équitablement que possible les charges en résultant entre les économies des États membres. Le Conseil peut, à la majorité des deux tiers, adresser au Commissariat des directives générales relatives à l'établissement de telles recommandations.

Un État membre recevant une telle recommandation peut, dans un délai de dix jours, saisir le Conseil qui statue.

Article 106

Le Commissariat prépare un programme commun de recherche scientifique et technique dans le domaine militaire, ainsi que les modalités d'exécution de ce programme. Celui-ci est soumis à l'approbation du Conseil dans les mêmes conditions que les programmes communs d'armement, d'équipement, d'approvisionnement et d'infrastructure des Forces européennes de défense.

Le Commissariat assure l'exécution du programme commun de recherche.

Article 107

§ 1. La production de matériel de guerre, l'importation et l'exportation de matériel de guerre en provenance ou à destination des pays tiers, les mesures intéressant directement les installations destinées à la production de matériel de guerre, ainsi que la fabrication de prototypes et la recherche technique concernant le matériel de guerre sont interdites, sauf autorisations résultant de l'application du paragraphe 3 ci-dessous.

Le présent article s'applique dans le respect des règles du Droit des gens relatives à l'interdiction de l'emploi de certains moyens de guerre.

§ 2. Les catégories de matériel de guerre faisant l'objet des interdictions visées au paragraphe 1 ci-dessus sont définies dans l'annexe I jointe au présent article.

Cette annexe peut être amendée sur avis conforme du Conseil statuant à la majorité des deux tiers, à l'initiative soit du Commissariat, soit d'un membre du Conseil.

§ 3. Le Commissariat définit par voie de règlement les règles de procédure pour l'application du présent article et pour la délivrance d'autorisations de production, d'importation, d'exportation et de mesures intéressant directement les installations destinées à la production de matériel de guerre, ainsi que de fabrication de prototypes et de recherches techniques concernant le matériel de guerre.

§ 4. Pour la délivrance des autorisations par le Commissariat, les dispositions suivantes sont applicables:

a. Le Commissariat ne doit pas accorder d'autorisation en ce qui concerne les rubriques de l'annexe II jointe au présent article dans les régions stratégiquement exposées, sauf décision du Conseil statuant à l'unanimité;

b. Le Commissariat ne délivre d'autorisations relatives à la construction de poudreries nouvelles à des fins militaires qu'à l'intérieur d'un territoire défini par accord entre les Gouvernements des États membres. Il doit assortir de telles autorisations de la désignation d'un contrôleur surveillant en permanence le respect par l'établissement en cause des dispositions du présent article.

La même procédure s'applique aux engins guidés à courte portée pour la défense anti-aérienne définis au paragraphe IV (*d*) de l'Annexe II;

c. En ce qui concerne l'exportation, le Commissariat accorde les autorisations s'il estime qu'elles sont compatibles avec les besoins, la sécurité intérieure et les engagements internationaux éventuels de la Communauté;

d. En ce qui concerne la fabrication de prototypes et la recherche technique concernant le matériel de guerre, les autorisations sont accordées, à moins que le Commissariat n'estime que ces fabrications et ces recherches risquent de porter préjudice à la sécurité intérieure de la Communauté et sauf autres directives du Conseil formulées dans les conditions prévues à l'article 39, § 2;

e. Le Commissariat délivre des autorisations générales pour la production, l'importation et l'exportation de matériel de guerre nécessaire aux Forces des États membres ne faisant pas partie des Forces européennes de défense et aux forces des États associés à l'égard desquels les États membres assument des responsabilités de défense. Il établit simultanément un contrôle assurant que les bénéficiaires de ces licences n'y recourent pas au delà de leurs besoins;

f. Le Commissariat délivre des autorisations générales intéressant les produits figurant à l'Annexe I, destinés à des fins civiles, et établit simultanément un contrôle assurant que les bénéficiaires de ces licences n'y recourent qu'à ces fins.

§ 5. Les règlements prévus au paragraphe 3 ci-dessus sont arrêtés par le Commissariat sur avis conforme du Conseil statuant à la majorité des deux tiers. Ils peuvent être amendés sur avis conforme du Conseil statuant à la majorité des deux tiers, à l'initiative soit du Commissariat, soit d'un membre du Conseil.

§ 6. A la requête du Commissariat, la Cour peut, dans les conditions fixées par le Statut juridictionnel prévu à l'article 67, prononcer contre les personnes ou les entreprises qui contreviendraient aux dispositions du présent article:

— pour ce qui concerne la production, l'importation et l'exportation du matériel de guerre, des amendes et des astreintes dont le montant ne peut excéder cinquante fois la valeur des produits en cause, ce montant maximum pouvant être, dans les cas particulièrement graves ou de récidive, soit doublé, soit porté à l'équivalent en monnaie nationale de un million d'unités de compte;

— pour ce qui concerne la recherche technique, la fabrication de prototypes et les mesures tendant directement à la production de matériel de guerre, des amendes d'un montant maximum correspondant à l'équivalent en monnaie nationale de 100.000 unités de compte, ce montant pouvant être porté à l'équivalent en monnaie nationale de un million d'unités de compte dans les cas particulièrement graves ou de récidive.

Annexe I à l'Article 107

1. *Armes de guerre.*

 a. Armes à feu portatives, à l'exception des armes de chasse et des armes de calibre inférieur à 7 mm.
 b. Mitrailleuses.
 c. Armes anti-chars.
 d. Pièces d'artillerie et mortiers.
 e. Armes anti-aériennes (D.C.A.).
 f. Appareils émetteurs de brouillard, de gaz et de flammes.

2. *Munitions et fusées de toutes sortes à usage militaire.*

 a. Munitions pour armes de guerre définies au paragraphe 1, ci-dessus, et grenades.
 b. Engins auto-propulsés.

   c. Torpilles de toutes sortes.

   d. Mines de toutes sortes.

   e. Bombes de toutes sortes.

3. *Poudres, explosifs y compris les substances essentiellement utilisables pour la propulsion par fusées, à usages militaires.*

   Seront exemptés les produits à usages principalement civils et notamment :

   Compositions pyrotechniques;

   Explosifs d'amorçage :

     Fulminate de mercure;

     Azoture de plomb;

     Trinitrorésorcinate de plomb (Styphnate);

     Tétrazène;

     Explosifs chloratés;

     Explosifs nitratés au dinitrotoluène ou à la dinitronaphtaline;

     Eau oxygénée à concentration inférieure à 60 %;

     Nitrocellulose;

     Poudres noires;

     Acide nitrique à concentration inférieure à 99 %;

     Hydrate d'hydrazine à concentration inférieure à 30 %.

4. *Matériel blindé.*

   a. Chars de combat.

   b. Véhicules blindés.

   c. Trains blindés.

5. *Navires de guerre de tous types.*

6. *Avions militaires de tous types.*

7. *Armes atomiques.*

8. *Armes biologiques.*[1]   } Suivant les définitions données à l'annexe II ci-dessous.

9. *Armes chimiques.*[1]

10. *Pièces constitutives ne pouvant être utilisées qu'à la construction de l'un des objets énumérés dans les groupes 1, 2, 4, 5, 6 ci-dessus.*[2]

11. *Machines ne pouvant être utilisées que pour la fabrication de l'un des objets énumérés dans les groupes 1, 2, 4, 5, 6 ci-dessus.*[2]

Annexe II à l'Article 107

La présente annexe est considérée comme comprenant les armes définies aux paragraphes I à VI ci-après et les moyens de production spécialement

---

[1] Le Commissariat peut exempter des autorisations requises les substances chimiques et biologiques dont l'usage est principalement civil. S'il estime ne pouvoir accorder ces exemptions, le contrôle exercé par lui porte uniquement sur les emplois.

[2] La fabrication de prototypes et la recherche technique intéressant les matériels visés aux groupes 10 et 11 ci-dessus ne tombent pas sous le coup des dispositions de l'article 107.

conçus pour la production de ces armes. Toutefois, les dispositions des paragraphes II à VI de cette annexe sont considérées comme excluant tout dispositif ou partie constituante, appareil, moyen de production, produit et organisme utilisé pour des besoins civils ou servant à la recherche scientifique, médicale et industrielle dans les domaines de la science fondamentale et de la science appliquée.

I. *Arme atomique*

a. L'arme atomique est définie comme toute arme qui contient, ou est conçue pour contenir ou utiliser, un combustible nucléaire ou des isotopes radio-actifs et qui, par explosion ou autre transformation nucléaire non contrôlée ou par radio-activité du combustible nucléaire ou des isotopes radio-actifs, est capable de destruction massive, dommages généralisés ou empoisonnements massifs.

b. Est en outre considérée comme arme atomique toute pièce, tout dispositif, toute partie constituante ou toute substance, spécialement conçu ou essentiel pour une arme définie au paragraphe *a.*

c. Toute quantité de combustible nucléaire produite au cours d'une année quelconque en quantité supérieure à 500 grammes sera considérée comme substance spécialement conçue ou d'utilité essentielle pour des armes atomiques.

d. Sont compris dans le terme « combustible nucléaire » tel qu'il est utilisé dans la précédente définition, le plutonium, l'uranium 233, l'uranium 235 (y compris l'uranium 235 contenu dans l'uranium enrichi à plus de 2,1 p. 100 en poids d'uranium 235) et toute autre substance capable de libérer des quantités appréciables d'énergie atomique par fission nucléaire ou par fusion ou par une autre réaction nucléaire de la substance. Les substances ci-dessus doivent être considérées comme combustible nucléaire, quel que soit l'état chimique ou physique sous lequel elles se trouvent.

II. *Arme chimique*

a. L'arme chimique est définie comme tout équipement ou appareil spécialement conçu pour l'utilisation à des fins militaires des propriétés asphyxiantes, toxiques, irritantes, paralysantes, régulatrices de croissance, anti-lubrifiantes ou catalytiques d'une substance chimique quelconque.

b. Sous réserve des dispositions du paragraphe *c*, les produits chimiques ayant de telles propriétés et susceptibles d'être utilisés dans les équipements ou appareils mentionnés dans le paragraphe *a* sont considérés comme compris dans cette définition.

c. Les appareils et les quantités de produits chimiques mentionnés dans les paragraphes *a* et *b* qui n'excèdent pas les besoins civils du temps de paix sont considérés comme exclus de cette définition.

III. *Arme biologique*

a. L'arme biologique est définie comme tout équipement ou appareil spécialement conçu pour utiliser à des fins militaires des insectes nuisibles ou d'autres organismes vivants ou morts ou leurs produits toxiques.

b. Sous réserve des dispositions du paragraphe *c*, les insectes, organismes et leurs produits toxiques, de nature et en quantité telle qu'ils puissent être utilisés dans les équipements ou appareils mentionnés dans le paragraphe *a*, sont considérés comme compris dans cette définition.

c. Les équipements, les appareils et les quantités d'insectes, organismes et leurs produits toxiques mentionnés dans les paragraphes *a* et *b* qui n'excèdent pas les besoins civils du temps de paix sont considérés comme exclus de cette définition.

IV. *Engins à longue portée, engins guidés et mines à influence*

a. Sous réserve des dispositions du paragraphe *d*, les engins à longue portée et les engins guidés sont définis comme des engins tels que leur vitesse ou leur direction de marche puisse être influencée après le moment du lancement par un dispositif ou mécanisme placé à l'intérieur ou à l'extérieur de l'engin, y compris les armes du type V mises au point au cours de la dernière guerre et leurs modifications ultérieures.   La combustion est considérée comme un mécanisme qui peut influencer la vitesse.

b. Sous réserve des dispositions du paragraphe *d*, les mines à influence sont définies comme des mines navales dont l'explosion peut être déclanchée automatiquement par des influences qui émanent seulement de sources extérieures, y compris les mines à influence mises au point au cours de la récente guerre, et leurs modifications ultérieures.

c. Les pièces, dispositifs ou parties constituantes spécialement conçus pour être employés dans ou avec les armes mentionnées dans les paragraphes *a* et *b* sont considérés comme inclus dans cette définition.

d. Sont considérés comme exclus de cette définition les fusées de proximité et les engins guidés à courte portée pour la défense anti-aérienne répondant aux caractéristiques maxima suivantes:
— longueur, 2 mètres;
— diamètre, 30 centimètres;
— vitesse, 660 mètres-seconde;
— portée, 32 kilomètres;
— poids de l'ogive et de la charge explosive, 22,5 kilogrammes.

V. *Navires de guerre autres que les petits bâtiments défensifs*

Par navires de guerre autres que les petits bâtiments défensifs, il faut entendre:

a. les navires de guerre d'un déplacement supérieur à 1.500 tonnes;

b. les sous-marins;

c. les navires de guerre propulsés autrement que par des machines à vapeur, par les moteurs Diesel ou à essence, par les turbines à gaz ou les moteurs à réaction.

VI. *Aéronefs militaires*

Sont compris sous ce terme, les aéronefs militaires et les parties constituantes suivantes:

a. cellules: armatures de section centrale, armatures d'ailes, longerons;

b. moteurs à réaction: rotors de turbo-compresseurs, disques de turbines, brûleurs, rotors de compresseurs à écoulement axial;

c. moteurs à pistons: blocs cylindres, rotors de turbo-compresseurs.

Article 107 *bis*

Les règlements prévus au paragraphe 3 de l'article 107 ci-dessus, seront soumis au Conseil dans un délai de trois mois à dater de l'entrée en vigueur du présent Traité.   Entre temps, le Commissariat accordera les autorisations appropriées.

Article 108

§ 1. Sans préjudice des dispositions de l'art. 114 ci-après, le Commissariat peut, pour ce qui concerne les matériels de guerre définis dans les annexes à l'article 107 ci-dessus, demander directement aux entreprises en cause les informations nécessaires à l'accomplissement de sa mission, en tenant informés les Gouvernements intéressés.

Il peut faire procéder par ses agents aux vérifications nécessaires.

§ 2. A la requête du Commissariat, la Cour peut, dans les conditions fixées par le Statut juridictionnel prévu à l'article 67, prononcer à l'encontre de celles de ces entreprises qui se soustrairaient aux obligations résultant pour elles des décisions prises en application des dispositions du présent article, ou qui fourniraient sciemment des informations fausses, des amendes dont le montant maximum sera de 1 % du chiffre d'affaires annuel et des astreintes dont le montant maximum sera de 5 % du chiffre d'affaires journalier moyen par jour de retard.

Article 109

Un Comité Consultatif est constitué auprès du Commissariat afin de l'aider dans l'accomplissement des tâches visées aux articles 101 et 102 ci-dessus.   Il est composé de vingt membres au moins et de trente-quatre membres au plus.   Il comprend notamment des représentants des producteurs et des représentants des travailleurs; ces représentants sont en nombre égal pour les producteurs d'une part, et pour les travailleurs d'autre part.

Le Comité comprend des nationaux de chacun des États membres.

Les membres du Comité Consultatif sont nommés, à titre personnel et pour deux ans, par le Conseil, à la majorité des deux tiers. Ils ne sont liés par aucun mandat ou instruction.

Le Comité Consultatif désigne parmi ses membres son Président et son bureau pour une durée d'un an. Il arrête son règlement intérieur.

Les indemnités allouées aux membres du Comité Consultatif sont fixées par le Conseil, sur proposition du Commissariat.

Article 110

Le Comité Consultatif est consulté par le Commissariat sur les problèmes de nature économique et sociale posés par la préparation ou l'exécution des programmes communs d'armement, d'équipement, d'approvisionnement et d'infrastructure. Le Commissariat communique au Comité consultatif les informations utiles à ses délibérations.

Le Comité Consultatif est convoqué par son Président à la demande du Commissariat.

Le procès-verbal des délibérations du Comité Consultatif est transmis au Commissariat et au Conseil en même temps que les avis du Comité.

Article 111

Le Commissariat, en consultation avec les Gouvernements des États membres, prépare des plans relatifs à la mobilisation des ressources économiques des États membres.

TITRE VI

DISPOSITIONS GÉNÉRALES

Article 112

Les États membres s'engagent à prendre toutes mesures générales ou particulières propres à assurer l'exécution des obligations résultant des décisions et recommandations des institutions de la Communauté et à faciliter à celle-ci l'accomplissement de sa mission.

Les États membres s'engagent à s'abstenir de toute mesure incompatible avec les dispositions du présent Traité.

Article 113

Toutes les institutions et tous les services de la Communauté et des États membres collaborent étroitement en ce qui concerne les questions d'intérêt commun.

Ils se prêtent une aide mutuelle en matière administrative et judiciaire, dans des conditions qui seront définies par des accords ultérieurs.

Article 114

§ 1. Les États membres s'engagent à mettre à la disposition du Commissariat toutes les informations nécessaires à l'accomplissement de sa mission. Le Commissariat peut demander aux Gouvernements de faire procéder aux vérifications nécessaires. Sur la demande motivée du Commissariat, ses agents peuvent participer aux opérations de vérifications.

Le Conseil, statuant à la majorité des deux tiers, peut formuler des directives générales relatives à l'application de l'alinéa précédent.

Si un État membre estime que les informations qui lui sont demandées par le Commissariat ne sont pas nécessaires à l'accomplissement de la mission de celui-ci, il peut, dans un délai de dix jours, saisir la Cour, qui statue d'urgence. Le recours est suspensif.

§ 2. Les institutions de la Communauté, leurs membres et agents sont tenus de ne pas divulguer les informations qui, par leur nature, sont couvertes soit par le secret professionnel, soit par le secret militaire.

Toute violation desdits secrets ayant causé un dommage peut faire l'objet d'une action en indemnité devant la Cour.

Article 115

Dans la limite des compétences du Commissariat, les agents chargés par lui de missions de contrôle disposent, à l'égard des particuliers, des entreprises privées ou publiques sur le territoire des États membres et dans toute la mesure nécessaire à l'accomplissement de leur mission, des droits et pouvoirs dévolus par les législations de ces États aux agents des administrations dont la compétence est comparable. La mission de contrôle et la qualité des agents chargés de cette mission sont dûment notifiées à l'État intéressé.

Les agents de l'État intéressé peuvent, à la demande de celui-ci ou du Commissariat, participer aux opérations de vérification.

Article 116

La Communauté jouit, sur les territoires des États membres, des immunités et privilèges nécessaires pour remplir sa mission, dans les conditions à définir par une convention entre les États membres.

Article 117

Si le Commissariat estime qu'un État membre a manqué à une obligation qui lui incombe en vertu du présent Traité, il en fait part à cet État et l'invite à formuler ses observations; celles-ci doivent être présentées dans un délai d'un mois.

Si, à l'expiration d'un délai additionnel d'un mois, il subsiste une divergence de vues, le Commissariat ou l'État en cause peut saisir la Cour. Celle-ci doit statuer d'urgence.

La décision de la Cour est notifiée au Conseil.

Article 118

Le siège des Institutions de la Communauté est fixé du commun accord des Gouvernements des États membres.

Article 119

Le régime linguistique des Institutions de la Communauté sera fixé, sans préjudice des dispositions du Titre V du Protocole militaire, par décision du Conseil statuant à l'unanimité.

Article 120

§ 1. Le présent Traité est applicable aux territoires européens des États membres.

§ 2. Par décision du Commissariat, sur avis conforme du Conseil statuant à l'unanimité:

a. Des formations des Forces européennes de défense peuvent être stationnées, avec l'accord du Commandant Suprême compétent relevant de l'Organisation du Traité de l'Atlantique Nord, sur des territoires situés dans la région définie à l'article 6 du Traité de l'Atlantique Nord et non compris dans les territoires visés au paragraphe 1 du présent article:

b. Des écoles, établissements et centres d'entraînement de la Communauté peuvent être installés sur des territoires autres que ceux visés au paragraphe 1, et situés dans la région définie à l'alinéa a du présent paragraphe, ou en Afrique au nord du tropique du Cancer.

§ 3. En vertu d'une décision à cet effet, prise par le Conseil, statuant à l'unanimité, après approbation parlementaire, en tant que de besoin, suivant les règles constitutionnelles de chaque État membre:

— des formations européennes de défense peuvent être stationnées sur des territoires autres que ceux visés au paragraphe 1 et au paragraphe 2, alinéa a;

— des écoles, établissements et centres d'entraînement de la Communauté peuvent être stationnés sur des territoires autres que ceux visés au paragraphe 1 et au paragraphe 2 alinéa b.

Cette décision est prise après consultation avec le Conseil de l'Atlantique Nord et avec l'accord du Commandant Suprême compétent relevant de l'Organisation du Traité de l'Atlantique Nord.

§ 4. Un État membre est autorisé à recruter, pour les besoins du contingent qu'il fournit aux Forces européennes de défense, dans les territoires non visés au paragraphe 1 du présent article, mais relevant de son autorité ou pour lesquels il assume la responsabilité internationale.

Article 121

Les États membres assument l'obligation de ne souscrire aucun engagement international en contradiction avec le présent Traité.

Article 122

Les États membres s'engagent à ne pas se prévaloir des traités, conventions ou déclarations existant entre eux en vue de soumettre un différend relatif à l'interprétation ou à l'application du présent Traité un mode de règlement autre que ceux prévus par celui-ci.

Article 123

§ 1. En cas de nécessité grave et urgente, le Conseil, à titre provisoire, assume ou confère à des institutions de la Communauté ou à tout autre organisme approprié les pouvoirs nécessaires pour faire face à la situation, dans les limites de la mission générale de la Communauté et en vue d'assurer la réalisation des objets de celle-ci; cette décision est prise à l'unanimité.

Le cas de nécessité grave et urgente résulte, soit de la situation prévue à l'article 2, § 3 ci-dessus, au Traité entre les États membres et le Royaume-Uni en date de ce jour[1] ou au Protocole additionnel relatif aux garanties d'assistance entre les États membres de la Communauté européenne de Défense et les États parties à l'Organisation du Traité de l'Atlantique Nord,[2] soit d'une déclaration à cet effet du Conseil statuant à l'unanimité.

§ 2. Les mesures provisionnelles arrêtées en vertu du paragraphe précédent cessent d'être applicables à la date de la fin de l'état de nécessité, déclarée par le Conseil statuant à la majorité des deux tiers.

Les institutions normalement compétentes statuent dans les conditions fixées par le présent Traité sur le maintien des effets de ces mesures.

§ 3. Le présent article n'affecte pas la mise en action des Forces européennes de défense pour répondre à une agression.

Article 124

Dans tous les cas non prévus au présent Traité, dans lesquels une décision ou une recommandation du Commissariat apparaît nécessaire pour assurer le bon fonctionnement de la Communauté et la réalisation de ses objets dans les limites de sa mission générale, cette décision ou cette recommandation peut être prise sur avis conforme du Conseil statuant à l'unanimité.

A défaut d'initiative du Commissariat, le Conseil peut être saisi par l'un des États membres et peut, à l'unanimité, prescrire au Commissariat de prendre cette décision ou de formuler cette recommandation. Faute par le Commissariat de donner suite aux délibérations du Conseil dans le délai fixé par celui-ci, le Conseil est habilité à prendre lui-même ces mesures à la majorité simple.

[1] See below, p. 167.
[2] See below, p. 164.

Article 125

Si des difficultés imprévues, révélées par l'expérience, dans les modalités d'application du présent Traité, exigent une adaptation des règles relatives à l'exercice, par le Commissariat, des pouvoirs qui lui sont conférés, des modifications appropriées peuvent y être apportées par décision unanime du Conseil, sans qu'elles puissent porter atteinte aux dispositions de l'article 2 ci-dessus, ou au rapport des pouvoirs respectivement attribués au Commissariat et aux autres institutions de la Communauté.

Article 126

Le Gouvernement de chaque État et le Commissariat pourront proposer des amendements au présent Traité. Cette proposition sera soumise au Conseil. Si celui-ci émet, à la majorité des deux tiers, un avis favorable à la réunion d'une Conférence des représentants des Gouvernements des États membres, celle-ci est immédiatement convoquée par le Président du Conseil, en vue d'arrêter d'un commun accord les modifications à apporter aux dispositions du présent Traité.

Ces amendements entreront en vigueur après avoir été ratifiés par tous les États membres, en conformité de leurs règles constitutionnelles respectives.

Article 127

Dans les dispositions du présent Traité, les mots « le présent Traité » doivent être entendus comme visant les clauses du Traité et celles:

1° du Protocole militaire;

2° du Protocole juridictionnel;

3° du Protocole relatif au droit pénal militaire;[1]

4° du Protocole financier;

5° du Protocole sur les conditions de rémunération des personnels militaires et civils de la Communauté et sur leurs droits à pension;

6° du Protocole relatif au Grand Duché de Luxembourg;[2]

7° du Protocole relatif aux relations entre la Communauté européenne de Défense et l'Organisation du Traité de l'Atlantique Nord;[3]

8° du Protocole relatif aux engagements d'assistance des États membres de la Communauté envers les États parties au Traité de l'Atlantique Nord.

Article 128

Le présent Traité est conclu pour une durée de cinquante années à dater de son entrée en vigueur.

Si, avant la réalisation d'une Fédération ou Confédération européenne,

---

[1] See *Traité instituant la Communauté européenne de défense et Documents annexes*, p. 43.

[2] Ibid. p. 51.

[3] See below, p. 165.

le Traité de l'Atlantique Nord cessait d'être en vigueur ou la composition de l'Organisation du Traité de l'Atlantique Nord subissait une modification essentielle, les Hautes Parties Contractantes examineraient en commun la situation nouvelle ainsi créée.

Article 129

Tout État européen peut demander à adhérer au présent Traité. Le Conseil, après avoir pris l'avis du Commissariat, statue à l'unanimité et fixe, également à l'unanimité, les conditions de l'adhésion. Celle-ci prend effet du jour où l'instrument d'adhésion est reçu par le Gouvernement dépositaire du présent Traité.

Article 130

Le présent Traité, rédigé en un seul exemplaire original, sera déposé dans les archives du Gouvernement de la République Française, qui en remettra une copie certifiée conforme à chacun des Gouvernements des autres États signataires.

Dès son entrée en fonctions, le Conseil établira les textes authentiques du présent Traité dans les langues autres que celle de l'exemplaire original. En cas de divergence, le texte de l'exemplaire original fait foi.

Article 131

Le présent Traité sera ratifié et ses dispositions exécutées suivant les règles constitutionnelles de chaque État membre. Les instruments de ratification seront déposés dans les archives du Gouvernement de la République Française, qui notifiera leur dépôt aux Gouvernements des autres États membres.

Article 132

Le présent Traité entrera en vigueur le jour du dépôt de l'instrument de ratification de l'État signataire qui procèdera le dernier à cette formalité.

Au cas où tous les instruments de ratification n'auraient pas été déposés dans un délai de six mois à dater de la signature du présent Traité, les Gouvernements des États ayant effectué le dépôt se concerteraient sur les mesures à prendre.

En foi de quoi les Plénipotentiaires soussignés ont apposé leur signature au bas du présent Traité et l'ont revêtu de leur sceau.

Fait à Paris, le vingt-sept mai mille neuf cent cinquante-deux.

Konrad ADENAUER.
Paul VAN ZEELAND.
Robert SCHUMAN.
Alcide DE GASPERI.
Joseph BECH.
Dirk STIKKER.

(b) Protocol on the relations between the European Defence Community and the North Atlantic Treaty Organization[1]

Les États membres de la Communauté européenne de défense,

Désireux de voir les relations entre l'Organisation du Traité de l'Atlantique Nord et la Communauté européenne de défense conserver la plus grande souplesse et tendre à éviter, dans toute la mesure du possible, le chevauchement des responsabilités et des fonctions,

Conviennent de ce qui suit:

§ 1. Pour les questions concernant les objectifs communs des deux Organisations, des consultations mutuelles auront lieu entre le Conseil de l'Atlantique Nord et le Conseil de la Communauté européenne de défense et, chaque fois que l'un ou l'autre Conseil l'estimera souhaitable, les deux Conseils tiendront des réunions communes.

Chaque fois que l'une des Parties au Traité de l'Atlantique Nord ou l'une des Parties au Traité instituant la Communauté européenne de défense considérera qu'il existe une menace contre l'intégrité territoriale, l'indépendance politique ou la sécurité de l'une quelconque d'entre elles ou contre l'existence ou l'unité de l'Organisation du Traité de l'Atlantique Nord ou de la Communauté européenne de défense, une réunion commune sera organisée, à la requête de ladite Partie, afin que soient étudiées les mesures à prendre pour faire face à la situation.

§ 2. En vue d'une coordination étroite sur le plan technique, chaque Organisation communiquera à l'autre les informations appropriées et un contact permanent sera établi entre le personnel des Services du Commissariat de la Communauté européenne de défense et le personnel des Services des Organismes civils de l'Organisation du Traité de l'Atlantique Nord.

§ 3. Dès que les forces de la Communauté européenne de défense auront été placées sous le commandement d'un Commandant relevant de l'Organisation du Traité de l'Atlantique Nord, des membres des Forces européennes de défense deviendront membres de son propre quartier général et des quartiers généraux subordonnés appropriés. Les Commandants relevant de l'Organisation du Traité de l'Atlantique Nord assureront toutes liaisons nécessaires entre ces forces et les autres organismes militaires du Traité de l'Atlantique Nord.

§ 4. Le Conseil de la Communauté européenne de défense et le Conseil de l'Atlantique Nord peuvent, d'un commun accord, apporter aux dispositions qui précèdent des aménagements relatifs aux modalités des rapports ci-dessus définis.

§ 5. Le présent Protocole entrera en vigueur en même temps que le

---

[1] *Traité instituant la Communauté européenne de défense et Documents annexes*, p. 52.

Traité instituant la Communauté européenne de défense, dont il fera partie intégrante.

Fait à Paris, le vingt-sept mai mille neuf cent cinquante-deux.

Konrad ADENAUER.

Paul VAN ZEELAND.

Robert SCHUMAN.

Alcide DE GASPERI.

Joseph BECH.

Dirk STIKKER.

(c) Protocol on guarantees of assistance by members of the European Defence Community to members of the North Atlantic Treaty Organization[1]

Les États membres de la Communauté Européenne de Défense,

Convaincus que la création de la Communauté Européenne de Défense instituée en vertu du Traité signé à Paris, le vingt-sept mai mille neuf cent cinquante-deux, renforcera la Communauté Nord Atlantique et la défense en commun de la zone de l'Atlantique Nord, et encouragera une association plus étroite des pays de l'Europe occidentale,

Conviennent de ce qui suit:

Article premier

Sera considérée comme une attaque armée contre les États membres de la Communauté Européenne de Défense et contre les Forces européennes de défense, toute attaque armée:

1° contre le territoire de l'une ou plusieurs des Parties au Traité de l'Atlantique Nord dans la région définie à l'article 6 (*i*) dudit Traité;

2° contre les forces terrestres, navires ou aéronefs de l'une quelconque des Parties au Traité de l'Atlantique Nord, lorsqu'ils se trouvent dans la région définie à l'article 6 (*ii*) dudit Traité.

En cas d'une telle attaque armée, les États membres de la Communauté Européenne de Défense contractent, tant en ce qui les concerne qu'en ce qui concerne les Forces européennes de défense, des obligations identiques à celles contractées par les États Parties au Traité de l'Atlantique Nord envers les États membres de la Communauté Européenne de Défense et les Forces européennes de défense en vertu du Protocole signé entre les États Parties au Traité de l'Atlantique Nord, et visé à l'article 2 ci-dessous.

L'expression «États Parties au Traité de l'Atlantique Nord» s'entend des États Parties audit Traité à la date d'entrée en vigueur du présent Protocole.

---

[1] *Traité instituant la Communauté européenne de défense et Documents annexes,* p. 53.

Article 2

Le présent Protocole entrera en vigueur en même temps que le Protocole signé par les États Parties au Traité de l'Atlantique Nord qui accorde des garanties réciproques aux États membres de la Communauté Européenne de Défense et aux Forces européennes de défense.

Article 3

Le présent Protocole restera en vigueur pour autant que le Traité instituant la Communauté Européenne de Défense et le Traité de l'Atlantique Nord resteront eux-mêmes en vigueur, et que les États Parties à ce dernier Traité continueront à accorder, en ce qui les concerne et en ce qui concerne leurs forces, des garanties aux États membres de la Communauté Européenne de Défense et aux Forces européennes de défense qui équivalent aux garanties figurant au présent Protocole.

Article 4

Le présent Protocole sera déposé dans les archives du Gouvernement de la République Française, qui en transmettra des copies certifiées conformes aux Gouvernements de tous les États Parties au Traité instituant la Communauté Européenne de Défense et de tous les États Parties au Traité de l'Atlantique Nord.

Fait à Paris, le vingt-sept mai mille neuf cent cinquante-deux.

Konrad ADENAUER.
Paul VAN ZEELAND.
Robert SCHUMAN.
Alcide DE GASPERI.
Joseph BECH.
Dirk STIKKER.

(d) Protocol to the North Atlantic Treaty extending guarantees of assistance to the European Defence Community[1]

The Parties to the North Atlantic Treaty, signed at Washington on April 4, 1949,

Being satisfied that the creation of the European Defense Community set up under the Treaty signed at Paris on May 27, 1952, will strengthen the North Atlantic Community and the integrated defense of the North Atlantic area, and promote the closer association of the countries of Western Europe, and

Considering that the parties to the treaty setting up the European

---

[1] *Department of State Bulletin*, 9 June 1952, pp. 896–7. For Article 5 of the North Atlantic Treaty see *Documents* (R.I.I.A.) for 1949–50, p. 258; for Article 6, as revised in 1951, see *Documents* (R.I.I.A.) for 1951, p. 66.

Defense Community have signed a protocol, which will enter into force at the same time as the present protocol, giving to the parties to the North Atlantic Treaty guarantees equivalent to the guarantees contained in Article 5 of the North Atlantic Treaty,

Agree as follows:

ARTICLE I

An armed attack

(i) on the territory of any member of the European Defense Community in Europe or in the area described in Article 6 (i) of the North Atlantic Treaty, or

(ii) on the forces, vessels or aircraft of the European Defense Community when in the area described in Article 6 (ii) of the said Treaty, shall be considered an attack against all the Parties to the North Atlantic Treaty, within the meaning of Article 5 of the said Treaty, and Article 5 shall apply accordingly.

The expression 'member of the European Defense Community' in paragraph (i) of this Article means any of the following states which is a member of the European Defense Community, namely Belgium, France, German Federal Republic, Italy, Luxembourg and the Netherlands.

ARTICLE II

The present Protocol shall enter into force as soon as each of the Parties has notified the Government of the United States of America of its acceptance, and the Council of European Defense Community has notified the North Atlantic Council of the entry into force of the Treaty setting up the European Defense Community. The Government of the United States of America shall inform all the Parties to the North Atlantic Treaty of the date of the receipt of each such notification and of the date of the entry into force of the present Protocol.

ARTICLE III

The Protocol shall remain in force for so long as the North Atlantic Treaty and the Treaty signed at Paris on May 27, 1952, setting up the European Defense Community remain in force, and the Parties to the latter treaty continue to give in respect of themselves and the European Defense Forces guarantees to the Parties to the North Atlantic Treaty equivalent to the guarantees contained in the present Protocol.

The present Protocol, of which the English and French texts are equally authentic, shall be deposited in the Archives of the Government of the United States of America. Duly certified copies thereof shall be transmitted by that Government to the Governments of all the Parties to the

North Atlantic Treaty and of all the Parties to the Treaty establishing the European Defense Community.

In witness whereof, the undersigned plenipotentiaries have signed the present Protocol.   (Representatives of the 14 NAT countries.)

Done at Paris the 27th day of May 1952.

(*e*) *Treaty between the United Kingdom and the member states of the European Defence Community*[1]

The President of the Federal Republic of Germany, His Majesty the King of the Belgians, the President of the French Republic, the President of the Italian Republic, Her Royal Highness the Grand Duchess of Luxembourg, Her Majesty the Queen of the Netherlands and Her Majesty the Queen of Great Britain, Ireland and the British Dominions beyond the Seas,

Desiring, in the interests of the defence of Western Europe, to extend, as between the United Kingdom and the states members of the European Defence Community established by the Treaty signed at Paris on the 27th day of May 1952, the guarantees of assistance against aggression given in Article IV of the Treaty signed at Brussels on the 17th March 1948,[2]

Have appointed as their plenipotentiaries for this purpose,

The President of the Federal Republic of Germany,

Dr. Konrad Adenauer, Chancellor, minister for Foreign Affairs;

His Majesty the King of the Belgians,

M. Paul van Zeeland, minister for Foreign Affairs;

The President of the French Republic,

M. Robert Schuman, minister for Foreign Affairs;

The President of the Italian Republic,

M. de Gasperi, minister for Foreign Affairs;

Her Royal Highness the Grand Duchess of Luxembourg,

M. Bech, minister for Foreign Affairs;

Her Majesty the Queen of the Netherlands,

M. Stikker, minister for Foreign Affairs;

Her Majesty the Queen of Great Britain, Ireland and the British Dominions beyond the Seas,

M. Anthony Eden, Foreign Secretary.

Who, having exhibited their full powers, found in good and due form, have agreed as follows:

ARTICLE I

If at any time, while the United Kingdom is party to the North Atlantic

---

[1] *Traité instituant la Communanté européenne de défense et Documents annexes*, pp. 68–69.

[2] See *Documents* (R.I.I.A.) for 1947–8, p. 227.

Treaty, any other party to the present Treaty which is at that time a member of the European Defence Community, or the European Defence Forces, should be the object of an armed attack in Europe, the United Kingdom will, in accordance with Article 51 of the United Nations Charter, afford the Party or the Forces so attacked all the military and other aid and assistance in its power.

ARTICLE II

If at any time while Article I remains in force the United Kingdom or its armed forces should be the object of an armed attack in Europe, the other Parties to the present Treaty which are at that time members of the European Defence Community, and the European Defence Forces, will afford the United Kingdom and its forces all the military and other aid and assistance in their power.

ARTICLE III

The present Treaty shall be ratified and its provisions carried out by the signatories in accordance with their respective constitutional processes. The instruments of ratification shall be deposited with the Government of the United Kingdom, which shall notify the Governments of the other signatories of each deposit. The Treaty shall enter into force when all the signatories have deposited their instruments of ratification and the Council of the European Defence Community has notified the Government of the United Kingdom that the Treaty establishing the European Defence Community has entered into force.

ARTICLE IV

The present Treaty, of which the English and French texts are equally authentic, shall be deposited in the archives of the Government of the United Kingdom which shall transmit a certified copy thereof to the Government of each of the other signatories.

In witness whereof the undersigned plenipotentiaries have signed the present Treaty and have affixed thereto their seals.

Done at Paris, on the 27th day of May 1952.

Konrad ADENAUER.
Paul VAN ZEELAND.
Robert SCHUMAN.
Alcide DE GASPERI.
Joseph BECH.
Dirk STIKKER.
Anthony EDEN.

(f) *Declaration by the Governments of the U.S.A., the United Kingdom and France on their interest in the strength and integrity of the European Defence Community*[1]

The Governments of the United States of America, the United Kingdom of Great Britain and Northern Ireland, and France have signed conventions with the German Federal Republic which will establish a new relationship with that country. These conventions, as well as the treaties for a European Defense Community and a European coal and steel community, of which France is a signatory, provide a new basis for uniting Europe and for the realization of Germany's partnership in the European community. They are designed to prevent the resurgence of former tensions and conflicts among the free nations of Europe and any future revival of aggressive militarism. They make possible the removal of the special restraints hitherto imposed on the Federal Republic of Germany and permit its participation as an equal partner in Western defense.

These conventions and treaties respond to the desire to provide by united efforts for the prosperity and security of Western Europe. The Governments of the United States and the United Kingdom consider that the establishment and development of these institutions of the European community correspond to their own basic interests and will therefore lend them every possible co-operation and support.

Moreover, Western defense is a common enterprise in which the Governments of the United States and the United Kingdom are already partners through membership of the North Atlantic Treaty Organization.

These bonds are now strengthened by the system of reciprocal guarantees agreed to between the member states of the European Defence Community, between these member states and the United Kingdom and also between these member states and the member states of the North Atlantic Treaty Organization.

For these various reasons, including the fact that these new guarantees will apply to the states concerned only as members of one or the other of these organizations, the Governments of the United States and the United Kingdom have an abiding interest, as has the Government of France, in the effectiveness of the treaty creating the European Defense Community and in the strength and integrity of that community. Accordingly, if any action from whatever quarter threatens the integrity or unity of the community, the two Governments will regard this as a threat to their own security. They will act in accordance with Article 4 of the North Atlantic Treaty.[2] Moreover, they have each expressed their resolve to station such forces on the continent of Europe, including the Federal

---

[1] *Department of State Bulletin*, 9 June 1952, p. 897.

[2] 'The Parties will consult together whenever, in the opinion of any of them, the territorial integrity, political independence or security of any of the Parties is threatened.'

Republic of Germany, as they deem necessary and appropriate to contribute to the joint defense of the North Atlantic Treaty area, having regard to their obligations under the North Atlantic Treaty, their interest in the integrity of the European Defense Community, and their special responsibilities in Germany.

The security and welfare of Berlin and the maintenance of the position of the Three Powers there are regarded by the Three Powers as essential elements of the peace of the free world in the present international situation. Accordingly they will maintain armed forces within the territory of Berlin as long as their responsibilities require it. They therefore reaffirm that they will treat any attack against Berlin from any quarter as an attack upon their forces and themselves.

These new security guarantees supersede the assurances contained in the declaration of the Foreign Ministers of the United Kingdom, the United States, and France at New York on September 19, 1950.[1]

3. After signature

(i) Communiqué issued after talks between M. Schuman and Mr. Acheson, Paris, 29 May 1952[2]

Conformément à l'usage désormais consacré, qui fait suivre les réunions internationales de conversations entre ministres responsables, un échange de vues franco-américain sur la situation internationale considérée dans son ensemble a eu lieu à la faveur de la présence à Paris du secrétaire d'État des États-Unis.

Le président du Conseil français, assisté de membres de son gouvernement, a examiné avec M. Acheson un certain nombre de problèmes d'intérêt commun, parmi lesquels la situation en Extrême-Orient et en Afrique du Nord, ainsi que la question des commandes américaines en France.

Les ministres français et américains se sont déclarés extrêmement satisfaits des échanges de vues aussi francs que complets qui se sont poursuivis dans une atmosphère de grande cordialité à l'occasion de ces conversations.

(ii) Letter from President Truman to the United States Senate transmitting the Contractual Agreements and the Protocol to the North Atlantic Treaty for ratification, 2 June 1952[3]

I transmit herewith for the consideration of the Senate a copy of the Convention on Relations between the Three Powers and the Federal Republic of Germany, signed by the United Kingdom, the French Republic, the United States, and the Federal Republic of Germany at Bonn

---

[1] *Documents* (R.I.I.A.) for 1949–50, p. 333.   [2] *Le Populaire*, 30 May 1952.
[3] *Department of State Bulletin*, 16 June 1952, pp. 947–9.

on May 26, 1952, to which is annexed the Charter of the Arbitration Tribunal. I also transmit a copy of a protocol to the North Atlantic Treaty covering security guarantees to the members of the European Defense Community by the Parties to the North Atlantic Treaty, signed at Paris on May 27, 1952. I request the advice and consent of the Senate to the ratification of these two documents.

In addition, I transmit for the information of the Senate a number of related documents, including a report made to me by the Secretary of State;[1] three additional Conventions with the Federal Republic of Germany related to the main Convention; the Treaty Constituting the European Defense Community; a declaration made by the United States, the United Kingdom and the French Governments at the time of the signing of this Treaty; and the Treaty Constituting the European Coal and Steel Community.

Together these documents constitute a great forward stride toward strengthening peace and freedom in the world. They are all concerned directly with Europe, but they have world-wide significance.

Three main purposes will be accomplished by these documents:

First, they will restore the Federal Republic of Germany to a status which will enable it to play a full and honorable part in the family of nations.

Second, they will create a common defense organization for six European countries, including the Federal Republic of Germany, and associate that common defense organization with the North Atlantic Treaty. This will greatly strengthen the defense of Europe and the free world against any aggression.

Third, they will constitute additional major steps toward unity among the countries of Western Europe—which is so important for peace and progress in that area.

These purposes are all interrelated, and they all serve the common objective of the free nations to create conditions of peace, based on freedom and justice, in accordance with the principles of the United Nations Charter.

It has been a major objective of the United States to help bring about an independent, democratic, and united Germany, and to conclude a treaty of peace with such a Germany. That is still our policy, and will continue to be. Unfortunately, as all the world knows, the Soviet Union, while professing a desire for German unification, has by its action and policies prevented unification and the creation of a free all-German Government with which a treaty of peace could be negotiated.

Under these circumstances, the United States, France and Great Britain, four years ago, gave the people in Western Germany the chance

[1] Ibid. pp. 949–51.

to create their own democratic Government. They worked out their own constitution, and since September 1949, the Federal Republic of Germany has taken an increasing responsibility for governing the three-fourths of the German people who are free from Soviet control. During this time, the German Government has demonstrated that it is democratic and responsive to the will of the free people of Germany, and that it is able and ready to take its place in the community of free nations and to do its share toward building peaceful and cooperative relationships with other free countries.

Over the last three years, there has been a continuing process of relaxing occupation controls on the one hand and increasing the scope of the German Federal Government's responsibilities on the other. Last October, the United States and many other countries concerned ended the technical state of war which had existed with Germany.[1] In these ways, we have gradually been moving away from the original relationship of conqueror and conquered, and moving toward the relationship of equality which we expect to find among free men everywhere.

Now we are taking another major step in this direction. By the Convention on Relations between the Federal Republic and the United States, France, and Great Britain, we are restoring to the free German people control over their domestic and external affairs, subject only to certain limited exceptions made necessary by the present international situation. These exceptions relate to the stationing and security of Allied forces in Germany, to Berlin, and to questions of unification, a peace settlement, and other matters concerning Germany as a whole. When the new Convention goes into effect, the Occupation Statute will be repealed, the Allied High Commission will be abolished, and relations between the Federal Republic and other countries will be placed on the customary diplomatic basis.

But the Convention on Relations was not, and could not be, prepared as an isolated document, because it does not meet the full problem confronting the free people of Germany and those of other free countries. In order to provide for the security of the Federal Republic, and to ensure against any revival of militarism, arrangements were worked out under which the Federal Republic is joining in establishing the European Defense Community—the common defense organization of six continental European countries. As a member of this Community, the Federal Republic will be able to make a vital contribution to the common defense of Western Europe without the creation of a national German military establishment. The European Defense Community, with a common budget and common procurement of military equipment, common uniforms and common training, is a very remarkable advance, representing

[1] *Documents* (R.I.I.A.) for 1951, pp. 129–33.

as it does a voluntary merging of national power into a common structure of defense.

As an additional vital safeguard for peace and freedom in Europe, the German Federal Republic, as a member of the European Defense Community, is joining in reciprocal commitments between the members of that Community and the members of the North Atlantic Treaty organization. The protocol to the North Atlantic Treaty extends the application of the guarantee of mutual assistance expressed in Article 5 of the Treaty by providing that an attack on the territory of any member of the European Defense Community, including the German Federal Republic, or on the Community's forces, shall be considered an attack against all the parties to the Treaty. A reciprocal guarantee is extended to the North Atlantic Treaty partners by the members of the Community in a protocol to the Treaty Constituting the European Defense Community.

Thus, these various documents constitute an integrated whole. The United States is a party only to the Convention on Relations (and the related Conventions) and to the protocol to the North Atlantic Treaty, but the Treaty Constituting the European Defense Community is an essential factor in the new relationship which the Conventions establish. It is expressly provided that the Conventions with the Federal Republic, the Treaty Constituting the European Defense Community, and the protocol to the North Atlantic Treaty will come into force simultaneously, thus assuring the complete interrelationship of all of them. The participation of the Federal Republic in the European Coal and Steel Community (the Schuman Plan) and the European Defense Community, and the resultant transfer to European agencies of authority over the basic industries of the participating countries and over military activities are the strongest safeguards for the future security of Western Europe. The successful creation of these European institutions makes possible the removal of special restraints which have heretofore been imposed on the Federal Republic and thereby enables the latter to participate in Western defense on a basis of equality.

Thus, while not a party, the United States has a direct and abiding interest in the success and effectiveness of the Treaty Constituting the European Defense Community and in the continuing existence of this Community as constituted. By virtue of the North Atlantic Treaty and the Convention on Relations between the Three Powers and the Federal Republic of Germany, the United States has demonstrated its lasting interest and binding ties with the Atlantic and European communities of nations. By its adherence to the Treaty Constituting the European Defense Community and the Convention on Relations, the Federal Republic has linked its future with that of the Community and of the participating countries. It is therefore evident that the United States has acquired a very great stake in the maintenance of the institutions and relationships thus established and would consider any act which would affect their integrity or existence as a matter of fundamental concern to its own interests and security. I stress this point in order to make clear the relationship between the Conventions, the Treaty Constituting the European Defense Community, and the North Atlantic Treaty, and between the parties to these various agreements.

The documents I am transmitting to the Senate today are real and significant steps forward toward peace and security in Europe and the whole free world. These actions threaten no one; their only targets are fear and poverty. They will allow almost 50 million free German people to take a further great stride toward independence and self-government, and to join with their neighbours in self-defense. These moves are clearly in the direction of a just and lasting peace; only those with aggressive intent could have any objection to them.

The actions represented by these documents will not, of course, wipe out the basic conflicts of policies which underlie the current tense international situation. But they will, when ratified by the various countries concerned, bring about a fundamental change in the relationships between the free people of Germany and their friends in the free countries of the world. Under this new relationship we will all be able to work together more fully and more effectively to combine our strength not only to deter aggression, but also to bring about the economic and social progress, and the more harmonious and friendly international relations, to which all free men aspire.

I recommend that the Senate give early and favorable consideration to the Convention on Relations and to the protocol to the North Atlantic Treaty transmitted herewith, and give its advice and consent to their ratification in order that this great contribution to the strength and unity of the free world can become a reality.

(iii) STATEMENT BY THE FRENCH CABINET ASKING FOR FOUR-POWER DISCUSSIONS ON GERMANY, 11 JUNE 1952[1]

Le gouvernement a donné ses instructions à ses délégués qui auront à discuter le projet de réponse à la note soviétique.

Le gouvernement français est favorable à une discussion à quatre, limitée à des questions précises d'intérêt immédiat, concernant l'unification des deux Allemagnes, occidentale et orientale. La décision appartiendra à l'ensemble des quatre puissances interéssées. Au stade actuel des pourparlers, aucune précision ne peut être donnée à ce sujet.

[1] *Le Populaire*, 12 June 1952.

(iv) UNITED STATES REPLY TO THE RUSSIAN NOTE OF 24 MAY, PROPOSING
A FOUR-POWER MEETING TO DISCUSS THE COMPOSITION OF A COMMISSION
TO INVESTIGATE THE POSSIBILITY OF FREE, ALL-GERMAN ELECTIONS,
10 JULY 1952[1]

In its note of May 13 the United States Government made various
proposals in the hope of facilitating four-power conversations which could
lead to the unification of Germany and to the negotiation with an all-
German Government of a German peace treaty. It observes with regret
that the Soviet Government in its note of May 24 does not answer these
proposals. The United States Government fully maintains the views and
proposals in its note of May 13. On this basis it wishes in its present
note primarily to concentrate attention upon the immediate practical
problem of the procedure for setting up, through free elections, an all-
German Government with which a peace treaty can be negotiated.

In its note the Soviet Government once more proposes simultaneous
discussions on a peace treaty, the unification of Germany, and the formation of an all-German Government. For its part, the United States
Government maintains its position on this question, namely, that an all-
German Government must participate in the negotiation of a peace treaty,
and that, therefore, before undertaking such negotiations Germany must
be unified and an all-German Government established. Unification of
Germany can be achieved only through free elections. The essential first
step is obviously the determination that conditions necessary for such free
elections exist. The second step would be the holding of those elections.

In regard to the first step, the United States Government proposed in
its note of May 13 that an impartial Commission should determine
whether there exist throughout Germany the conditions necessary for the
holding of free elections. While pointing out the great advantages of
using the United Nations Commission, the United States Government
nevertheless offered to consider any other practical and precise proposals
for an impartial Commission which the Soviet Government might advance.
The Soviet Government advances no such proposals and limits itself to
maintaining its position on the appointment of a Commission to carry out
this verification by agreement among the four Powers. It is not clear to
the United States Government whether the Soviet Government considers
that the Commission should be composed of representatives of the four
Powers or merely that the four Powers should agree on its composition,
and the United States Government would be pleased to receive clarification on this point. The United States Government remains convinced
that a Commission composed solely of nationals of the four Powers would

---

[1] *Department of State Bulletin*, 21 July 1952, pp. 92–93. Identical notes were sent by France and
the United Kingdom.

be unable to reach useful decisions since it could only reflect present differences of opinion among the four Powers as to conditions existing in the Federal Republic, in the Soviet Zone and in Berlin. The United States Government considers that if the Commission is to carry out its work effectively, it should be composed of impartial members, should not be subject to veto or control by the four Powers and should be empowered to go freely into all parts of Germany and investigate conditions bearing on the possibility of holding free elections.

In regard to the second step, the United States Government similarly proposed that as soon as the Commission's report was ready there should be a meeting of representatives of the United States, French, Soviet and United Kingdom Governments to discuss the early holding of free elections throughout Germany, including the creation where necessary of appropriate conditions. The United States Government maintains this proposal to which the Soviet Government has not yet replied. The United States Government repeats what it has stated in paragraph 8 of its note of May 13: 'Such free elections can, however, only be held if the necessary conditions exist in all parts of Germany and will be maintained not only on the day of voting, and prior to it, but also thereafter.'

The United States Government further proposed to examine at this same meeting the assurances to be given by the four Powers that the all-German Government formed as a result of these free elections will have the necessary freedom of action during the period before the peace treaty comes into effect. It is the understanding of the United States Government that the only concrete proposal envisaged by the Soviet Government is that the all-German Government must be guided by the Potsdam decisions. This would mean the reestablishment of the quadripartite system of control which was originally designed to cover only 'the initial control period'. An arrangement of this kind would revive a system of control which proved to be impracticable and would, moreover, ignore the whole evolution of events in Germany in recent years. A German Government subjected to such control would in practice enjoy no freedom in its relations with the four Powers and would not be in a position to participate freely with the four above-mentioned Governments in the negotiation of a peace treaty.

The United States Government also observes with concern that while the Soviet Government in its notes repeatedly reaffirms its desire for the unification of Germany, it has recently adopted without any justification a series of measures in the Soviet Zone and in Berlin which tend to prevent all contact between the Germans living in the territory under Soviet occupation and the 50 million Germans in the Federal Republic and in the Western sectors of Berlin. These measures aggravate the arbitrary division of Germany. The United States Government wishes to emphasize that the agreements recently signed with the Federal Republic open up to Germany a wide and free association with the other nations of Europe. The United States Government cannot, as it has already emphasized in its note of May 13, admit that Germany should be denied the basic right of a free and equal nation to associate itself with other nations for peaceful purposes. Furthermore, these agreements reaffirm the determination of the three Powers and the Federal Republic to promote the unification of Germany, and expressly reserve the rights of the three Powers relating to a peace settlement—a peace settlement for the whole of Germany to be freely negotiated by the four Powers and the all-German Government.

In order to avoid further delay, the United States Government, in concert with the French Government and the United Kingdom Government, and after consultation with the German Federal Government and with the German authorities in Berlin, proposes that there should be an early meeting of representatives of the four Governments, provided it is understood that the four Governments are in favor of free elections throughout Germany as described in paragraph 4 of the present note, and of the participation of a free German Government in the negotiation of a German peace treaty. The purpose of this meeting would be to reach agreement on the first question which must be settled if further progress is to be made, namely, the composition and functions of the Commission of investigation to determine whether the conditions necessary for free elections exist. The United States Government proposes that the representatives discuss:

A. The selection of members of the Commission in such a way as to insure its impartiality.

B. The functions of the Commission with a view to insuring its complete independence to make recommendations to the four Powers.

C. The authority of the commission to carry out its investigation in full freedom and without interference.

In order that free elections can be held it will also be necessary to reach agreement on the program for the formation of an all-German Government, as proposed in paragraph 11 (iv) of the United States Government's note of May 13. The United States Government therefore repeats that proposal for the discussion of these further important issues by representatives of the four Powers. When such agreement is reached it will then be possible to proceed to the unification of Germany.

Since the Soviet Government has repeatedly expressed its desire for an early meeting in preference to continued exchanges of notes, the United States Government trusts that the present proposal will commend itself to the Soviet Government.

(v) Resolution asking for four-Power negotiations on German unification, adopted by the Bundestag on 10 July 1952[1]

The Bundestag resolves:

The Federal Government is requested formally to communicate to the
four occupying Powers that the Bundestag and the Federal Government
expect that the Governments of the four occupying Powers shall enter as
soon as possible into negotiations on the reunification of Germany through
free elections.

(vi) Extracts from a speech in the House of Commons by Mr. Eden
during the debate on the Contractual Agreements and the European Defence Treaty, 31 July 1952[2]

I beg to move.

That this House approves the contractual arrangements between Her
Majesty's Government, the Governments of France and the United States of
America and the Government of the German Federal Republic concluded at
Bonn on 26th May, 1952, and the Treaty between Her Majesty's Government
and the European Defence Community together with the Protocol to the North
Atlantic Treaty which were signed at Paris on 27th May, 1952; and affirms that
these instruments give effect to the policy set out in the Declaration signed by
the Foreign Ministers of France, the United Kingdom and the United States
of America at Washington on 14th September, 1951,[3] and pursued by successive
Governments of the United Kingdom for the inclusion of a democratic Germany, on a basis of equality, in a Continental European community, which
itself will form a part of a constantly developing Atlantic community.

The policies for which we ask approval today are embodied in the
documents which were laid before the House in the week preceding the
Whitsun Recess. These documents, as the House knows, are the result
of two sets of negotiations. In Bonn, a new relationship was drawn up
between the Western Powers and the German Federal Republic, and in
Paris the European Defence Community was established. . . .

The guiding principles, as I see them, of these contractual agreements
with Germany are set out in the documents called the Convention on
Relations between the Three Powers and the Federal Republic of Ger-
many. In that Convention, we, in effect, revoke the Occupation Statute.
In this Convention we retain only those rights in the German Federal
Republic which relate to the stationing and protection of our Armed
Forces in Germany, and to our obligations concerning Berlin and the
future Peace Treaty with a united Germany.

[1] Translated from *Deutscher Bundestag, 222. Sitzung*, 10 July 1952, p. 9876.
[2] H.C. Deb. 5th ser. vol. 504, coll. 1699–1725.
[3] *Documents* (R.I.I.A.) for 1951, pp. 133–5.

The central purpose of these Conventions is to create a peaceful and prosperous European community of nations in which a democratic German Federal Republic can play a full and equal part. That is the purpose, and the same purpose underlines the Treaty which sets up the European Defence Community.

There are two other documents to which I must briefly refer. First, the Treaty of Mutual Security between this country and the members of the European Defence Community, and secondly, the Protocol to the North Atlantic Treaty, which establishes reciprocal undertakings between its members and the members of the European Defence Community. The ideas which lie behind these two agreements were set out in the joint declaration made by the three Governments—Her Majesty's Government, the United States Government and the French Government—on the occasion of the signature of these agreements in May. In this declaration, we also reaffirmed our determination to maintain our present position in Berlin, and to treat any attack against Berlin from any quarter as an attack upon our own forces and ourselves.

All these documents, and they are numerous and complicated, give a complex picture, but their meaning is simple and clear. First, it has been agreed that there shall be a European Community of Defence within the North Atlantic Treaty Organisation, and in that European community Western Germany is to play its full part. That is the heart of the matter. The Federal Republic accepts political, economic and certain military obligations towards Europe, and towards the Western world, and in return there is in these agreements a new conception of its rights and sovereignty.

In negotiating all this, it was not our purpose to try to keep as many of our special rights in Germany as possible. That was not what we tried to do. On the contrary, we sought to relinquish as many of them as we could. Those we do retain are not any reflection on the sovereignty or democratic nature of the German Federal Republic. They are there because they are the essential minimum, having regard to the presence of our forces in Germany and the nature of our obligations to Berlin and in other respects.

The policies which these documents finally bring to fruition are not new. They are not the invention of any one Power or any one party. They have been slowly, and I think I might add reluctantly, accepted as inevitable since four-Power co-operation became impossible. So far as this country is concerned, the policy was begun by the late Mr. Ernest Bevin and the then Labour Government. They saw it as the only possible answer to the Soviet policy of obstruction which divided Germany into two. . . .

Now I come to a slightly more controversial note. So far it has been historical. I hope it has been historical; my attempt was to make it such. What are the alternatives to this policy which has been followed by the late Government and by us? Broadly speaking, I think there are two. We could try to hold the present position in Germany under the Occupation Statute. That is one alternative.

That would mean to maintain the allied forces and the allied occupation of Germany in full force. Inevitably this would call for increasingly strict controls and more stringent measures. An occupation cannot be expected to endure indefinitely unless there is a will to enforce it indefinitely. Surely we have learned that from the lessons between the two wars. Does the House really believe that there is such a will now, either in this country or in the United States or in France, to continue indefinitely the occupation forces as they are now? If there is not such a will, would not the attempt to enforce such an occupation merely mean the repetition of the mistakes that were made after the First World War?

The truth is that, ever since we joined in establishing a German Federal Government, as long ago as 1949, we have been committed to a gradual transfer of authority into German hands, quite inevitably. We cannot go back now on that broad decision. If we do not want our relations with Germany to relapse into dangerous antagonism, we have to go forward. Admittedly our forces and the forces of our allies will have to remain in Germany for some considerable time yet, so long as the international situation demands. But surely it is better that they should be there as allies, by agreement with the German Government, than as an occupation force solely dependent upon the right of victory.

If we attempted to prolong the occupation we should encourage all those forces in Germany which it has been our aim since the war to eradicate. We would have to keep the Germans indefinitely in isolation and subjection and we would immediately encourage the more extremist elements. All chance of securing Germany as a partner in European unity and reconstruction would be lost. What is more, we might well be forfeiting the only opportunity of a peaceful reunion of Germany herself in the future.

I believe that, despite Communist propaganda, most thoughtful Germans would now agree that the future of their country does not lie solely in their own hands. They know that their problems can only be solved in close association with the other countries of Western Europe. I am sure that hon. Members opposite who had long and close association with and responsibility for German affairs between 1945 and last year will agree with that summing up.

If that be so, if we cannot have that alternative—continuing occupation as it is now—what other alternative is there? There is certainly one other. We could call a halt to this process in which we have been engaged of building up the unity and strength of the Western countries. We could seek instead to enter into discussions with the Soviet Government with a view to reaching a different settlement. That is possible. But I should like to see where that would lead us. I think that it would lead us to one of two situations.

Either we should have to accept a German settlement on Soviet terms—and I will point out in a moment what those terms would be—or we should be embarking upon a general discussion with the Soviet Union without any clear idea where we hoped to get, and ending up with long and sterile discussions of the type with which we are already only too familiar. If any hon. Members opposite have had no experience of that, they have only to recall what happened at the Palais Rose.[1]

The important consideration which I have to put before the House is that either action would inevitably result in this—that the impetus which we have acquired in Europe to get these agreements through would be lost. The one country which would salute the decision with unbridled enthusiasm would be Soviet Russia; and everyone who feared her in every land would be dismayed. . . .

What would we probably have to face if we got into these four-Power talks? I do not think that it is very difficult to assess what we should be asked to do. One has only to read through the recent Soviet Notes, and one has only to look—and I hope the House will look in the next few days or tomorrow before they vote—at what is going on at present in Eastern Germany.

The first point on which the Soviets place emphasis in their Notes is that we should return to the Potsdam system for Germany, pending a peace settlement. That occurs time and time again in their Notes. This would mean that the system of four-Power controls originally devised for the opening stage of the occupation would have to be re-imposed and maintained by force until a peace treaty was reached. As I have already explained, that would be utterly impracticable at the present time, and certainly it would not be accepted by any political party in Germany.

Secondly, the Soviet Notes suggest that the Soviet Government intend that the peace treaty itself should be worked out by the four Powers and then presented to the German Government. They want a dictated peace treaty and not a negotiated peace treaty. They have persistently and consistently evaded any attempt we have made to ensure that before a treaty can be negotiated a freely elected all-German Government must have been set up. . . .

We have said that we cannot have an all-German Government without free elections. They have always been afraid to contemplate the free election of an all-German Government. It may be that they would be

[1] *Documents* (R.I.I.A.) for 1951, pp. 248–65.

willing to have an all-German Government as contemplated by them. But they have never accepted that we should have a freely elected all-German Government or that we should meet to discuss ways and means by which such a Government should be elected. We put that in our last Note and we have never had an answer. I think I know why. It is because they know perfectly well that an all-German Government, freely elected, could not possibly be a Communist Government, and that is the last thing in the world that they want.

How can we reach a settlement if that continues to be Soviet policy? We think that we can see from their Notes only too clearly what kind of Germany they think the four Powers should create. It would be precluded in advance from entering into regional associations with other Powers. It would be a Germany left in dangerous and irresponsible isolation at the heart of Europe. And it would be a Germany allowed to raise national armed forces, and apparently expected to give free rein to former Nazis and Nationalists in doing so. It almost seems as though the Soviets, conscious of the declining power of Communism in Germany, were seeking to obtain new allies in other circles in that country. If so, it would not be the first time in history that that has happened.

I believe that, fortunately, the Germans are as anxious as we are to avoid these dangers. That is why, as the House will have noted, our position in these diplomatic exchanges has had wide and general acceptance in Germany. All parties of the Federal Government Coalition warmly endorsed our reply to the latest Soviet Note, and the Social Democratic Party—I was coming to that, I am always glad to find that they are in support, too—welcomed the recognition that free elections are the crucial issue. They endorsed the clear order of procedure we set out in the Note.

May I repeat that order so that there may be no doubt where we stand? Free elections first; then the setting up of a free all-German Government; and finally, the negotiation of a peace treaty. That is the order as we see it, and we are prepared to discuss the first of these topics at any time, at any table, if the Soviets are prepared to come. . . .

I am asking hon. Gentlemen opposite whether this is the moment for us to set an example of hesitation and delay. At one point the Opposition were arguing—I do not know whether they are still arguing; but it was in a resolution of the Labour Party Executive—that before the agreements were ratified there should be new elections in Germany. I do not know whether this demand has now been dropped. The idea that we should demand fresh elections in Germany because some people in this country do not like the political complexion of the present Government of Germany is an unacceptable one. It has certainly caused a good deal of embarrassment to right hon. Gentlemen opposite and also to their friends in Germany.

Perhaps we can be told later whether it is still the view of right hon. Gentlemen on the Front Bench opposite that there must first be a general election in Germany. Alternatively, it has been suggested that we must await the decision of the German Constitutional Court on various questions before them. But the Court has decided that Parliament must decide before the Court pronounces, so whatever value there was in that argument seems to have gone by the board. . . .

I have no doubt how one country and one capital would view our delay in ratification. The Soviet would warmly welcome such a delay. They would regard it as a triumph for their policy and redouble their efforts to get the same results in all the capitals of Europe. So far as I am concerned, I signed these documents last May believing that I was expressing the will of the House and of this country and believing that I was fulfilling the policy which the late Government had been pursuing. I do not think that it is unreasonable to ask the House to endorse these signatures more than two months afterwards.

I do not see why there should be any argument about the so-called Attlee conditions which are referred to in the Amendment.[1] We have discussed them before. There is no conflict between them and the steps that we are asking the House to approve. First, the rearmament of the Atlantic Treaty countries must precede that of Germany. Of course it must—and so must the building up of the forces of the democratic States precede that of Germany. Both those conditions are entirely in agreement with the spirit of the N.A.T.O. decisions taken in Brussels in 1950 when the Leader of the Opposition was there.

But 18 months have elapsed and several months more must pass before the E.D.C. Treaty or the Bonn Convention can come into effect. No German units can be formed until that moment. The House will have noted what Herr Blank said on the 13th June. He gave a provisional time-table. He thought that the first call up might take place in the beginning of 1954 and after that a further six months to a year would be needed before units could reach full fighting strength. Could anybody seriously say that that is rushing matters, two years after the decision was taken.

During all this time N.A.T.O. armaments have been turned out. The expenditure on defence of the N.A.T.O. powers is £4,000 million a year at the present time and American equipment is pouring in. Over 1 million tons alone had been supplied to France by spring of this year, and I think that something like 3 million tons collectively have gone to the N.A.T.O. Powers.

There is this further consideration. These German units will not be created and maintained—when they do exist—on a national basis. Under

[1] See below, p. 186.

the E.D.C. system their maintenance and supply, like that of all the other participating forces, have to be organised internationally, as the right hon. Gentleman [Mr. Bellenger] knows. That is clearly set down in the Treaty. Common programmes for armament and supply will be laid down by the International Board of Commissioners. The actual orders for military equipment will be placed by the Board and the forces will be dependent for effective operation on jointly administered common services and support. These services, known as Infrastructure, include communications, aerodromes, and port facilities, and they will be jointly operated by the E.D.C. Without them no Army can act independently. These are all considerations which the House should have in mind.

Throughout the process of creating these German units decisions will have to be taken at every stage by the E.D.C. Powers; by France, Italy and the Benelux countries as well as by Germany herself, and all this in the wider framework of the N.A.T.O. organisation in which we and the Americans are fully engaged.

Surely these are important safeguards for us all. I think it is clear that the first two conditions have been fulfilled. As to the third, the right hon. Gentleman himself admitted that this had been fulfilled. He said:

'The E.D.C. is, in my view, a way of integrating the German contribution of force without raising the danger of a German army.'—[OFFICIAL REPORT, 14th May, 1952; Vol. 92, c. 1482.]

The fourth and remaining condition was that we must have the agreement of the Germans themselves. Every stage in these discussions and endless negotiations has been carried forward in consultation with the German Government.

I say that every one of those conditions has been fulfilled. If it is said that they have not been fulfilled, we shall be glad to know what is the basis of that argument, and if they have been, what is the point of this Amendment and why are we being asked for this further delay? . . .

The decisions which the House takes today can encourage or obstruct the new opportunities which are opening before Europe. The Western nations are engaged in an effort to build up a free and unified Europe in which Germany can play a part. We are not doing that to threaten or challenge the East but to consolidate peace on this Continent. Every measure we approve today is a part of that design. The European Defence Community, the Schuman Plan—they take their place in this broad movement for unity which finds expression in the Council of Europe. That is why we have given approval to those projects. That is why we want to be associated with them as closely as we can.

It is in this spirit that we have recently informed the six Powers participating in these plans that we support their proposals to press forward the work of integration—to advance, as they can and will, to closer political union on the Continent. There is only one condition we have set. It is that that process should be kept within the framework of the Council of Europe, in which this country plays a part. I am hopeful that nothing they do will be incompatible with that plan which we have put forward to link the Council of Europe with these more limited Continental organisations.[1]

The plans of the West are based on the principle of free alliance and close co-operation between peoples. The administration of Eastern Germany today is being more and more centralised and brought more under Communist control. The dark night of Communism is settling on that land. That is not what we want to see in our Western lands, and these agreements, we believe, provide an alternative way of life, an answer to the Communist challenge—an answer which, we believe, is clear, courageous, and encouraging to all free men. They offer a new future for Germany. They offer a new chance for Europe to turn aside from the divisions and disputes which have torn Europe asunder for centuries, and they offer this country the chance of placing our relations with Germany and other Western nations on a basis of friendship and unity.

Those two neighbours, France and Germany, whose destinies have been so often and so tragically in conflict in the past, are now beginning to find means of setting rivalries aside and of working together for a new Europe. We are able to be friends with both. We and the United States support their association with our full strength, and it is for them the chief guarantee of their security, and of the peaceful development of their enterprise. The possibilities of these agreements are in truth revolutionary.

It is not surprising that there should be doubts and hesitations in many countries—in France and Germany. We know that there are Parliamentary obstacles to overcome. Of course, some of the opposition is Communist-inspired—naturally enough, because these agreements place another defensive dyke between the Communists and the West; but some of it, no doubt, is genuine doubt of or lack of faith in this new Europe which is being built.

What is the duty of this country? Surely, it is to lead, to encourage the waverers, to show faith and confidence in the work in which we have been engaged now—all parties—for many years. I do not believe that to delay now is in this country's interests or in Europe's interests. I believe it would damage the cause of peace. I am sure it would encourage our enemies and depress our friends, and, therefore, I invite the House to support this Motion and to empower us to carry forward the constructive work to which we and our Allies have set our hands.

[1] See below, p. 206.

(vii) Motion on the Contractual Agreements and the European Defence Treaty moved by the Labour Opposition in the House of Commons and defeated on 1 August 1952[1]

That this House while accepting the aim of the inclusion of a democratic Germany on a basis of equality, in a Continental European community, which itself will form a part of a constantly developing Atlantic community; and while accepting the principle, subject to proper safeguards and conditions, of a German armed contribution to an international system of collective security, rejects Her Majesty's Government's present proposal as inopportune, particularly at a time when attempts are still being made by the Western Powers to discuss the German problem with the Union of Soviet Socialist Republics, and reaffirms the conditions first laid down in the House by the present Leader of the Opposition on 12th February, 1951.[2]

(viii) Note from the U.S.S.R. to the three western Powers rejecting their proposals of 10 July and presenting the Russian agenda for a four-Power meeting, 23 August 1952[3]

In connection with the note of the Government of the U.S.A. of July 10 of this year, the Soviet Government considers it necessary to state the following:

1. In its note of May 24 as well as in its previous notes, the Soviet Government proposed to the Government of the U.S.A. as well as to the Governments of Great Britain and France to proceed without delay to immediate negotiations concerning a peace treaty with Germany and the formation of an all-German Government. The Soviet Government in order to facilitate the decision of these questions had already on March 10 proposed for joint examination by the four Governments—the U.S.S.R., U.S.A., Great Britain and France—its own draft of the basis for a peace treaty with Germany, expressing at the time its readiness to discuss other possible proposals as well on this question. However, as is known, the Government of the U.S.A. and also the Governments of Great Britain and France evaded immediate negotiations with the Soviet Government on the question mentioned above.

The note of the Government of the U.S.A. of July 10 shows that the three Governments are continuing, just as they formerly did, to delay discussion of such important questions as the question about restoration of unity of Germany and the conclusion of a German peace treaty.

2. The Governments of the U.S.A., Great Britain, and France, while

---

[1] 31 July 1952, H.C. Deb. 5th ser. vol. 504, col. 1725.
[2] See *Documents* (R.I.I.A.) for 1951, pp. 105–6.
[3] *Department of State Bulletin*, 6 October 1952, pp. 518–21.

delaying the exchange of notes with the Soviet Government on the German question, entered into a deal with the Adenauer government. In flagrant violation of the Potsdam Agreement, the Governments of the Three Powers on May 26 concluded with the Bonn Government a separate so-called 'agreement', calling it a convention concerning relations between the three Western Powers and the German Federal Republic, and following that on May 27 there was signed in Paris an 'agreement' concerning a so-called 'European Defense Community'. Having signed these 'agreements', the Governments again demonstrated that they were not at all interested either in unification of Germany or in the conclusion of a peace treaty with Germany, but were aiming at strengthening and deepening of the division of Germany and at tying in West Germany and the West German Army organized by the Governments of the three Western Powers with the North Atlantic bloc and utilizing West Germany more completely for aggressive purposes of that bloc. The separate Bonn 'agreement' of the United States, Great Britain, and France with the Adenauer government represents an open military alliance plainly pursuing aggressive purposes. This 'agreement' legalizes the rebirth of German militarism, the creation of a West German mercenary army, headed by Fascist Hitlerite generals. We place the word 'agreement' in quotation marks, since the separate Bonn 'agreement' was not freely accepted by the Germans of West Germany; it was imposed upon West Germany against the will of the German people.

The Governments of the Three Powers are trying in every way to conceal from the German people the character of the separate Bonn 'agreement', which is one hostile to their national interests and dangerous to the cause of peace. They are trying in this connection to create an impression that the 'agreement' opens up to Germany the possibility for a wide and free association with other nations of Europe, and they wish to make the people believe that the Governments of the United States, Great Britain, and France in some way are striving for the creation of an all-German Government, which, according to their statement, 'must have the necessary freedom of action and powers inherent in a government'. However, the content of the separate Bonn 'agreement' is in direct conflict with these assurances. As is evident from the text of the separate Bonn 'agreement', the Governments of the three Western Powers have fully reserved to themselves the so-called 'special rights', giving as their motives for this the peculiarities of the international position of Germany. These 'special rights' give the Governments of the U.S.A., Great Britain, and France unlimited possibility for stationing their forces on the territory of West Germany, as well as at any time within their own discretion the bringing about in West Germany the establishment of a state of emergency and taking into their own hands full power. The Government of the U.S.A., and also the

Governments of Great Britain and France, have by this 'agreement' assured themselves of the right of intervention on a wide scale in the internal affairs of West Germany up to and including the use of armed forces of the Occupying Powers for the purposes of imposing their *Diktat* on West Germany.

All this is evidence that the Bonn separate 'agreement' does not only not open up for Germany any possibility of future free development, as the Government of the U.S.A. proclaims in its note of July 10, but excludes such a possibility, leaving West Germany in a state of complete subordination and dependence on the Occupying Powers, as this has been under the Occupation Statute.

3. Evading immediate negotiations concerning the formation of an all-German Government and the conclusion of a treaty of peace, the Government of the U.S.A., for the purpose of disguising its position, raises in its note of July 10 the question of guaranties which should be given by the Four Powers to the effect that an all-German Government established as a result of free elections, would have the necessary freedom of action in the course of the period prior to the entry into effect of the peace treaty.

However, there can be no question of any 'freedom of action' of an all-German Government as long as there exists the separate Bonn 'agreement', from article 7 of which it is evident that the very possibility of the creation of a united Germany is made provisional upon the obligatory retention by the Governments of the three Western Powers of all privileges which were envisaged in the Bonn 'agreement' and which deprived Germany of her governmental independence and integrity.

It is entirely clear that the Government of the U.S.A., as well as the Governments of Great Britain and France, in signing the separate Bonn 'agreement', are actually not striving for the unification of Germany, the establishment of an all-German Government, and the extension to that Government in reality freedom of action. The question raised in the note of the Government of the U.S.A. of July 10, concerning the guaranties of 'freedom of action' for the future all-German Government, is a false phrase, designed to conceal the aspirations of the Governments of the three Western Powers to subordinate Germany entirely to themselves, and their aggressive purposes. Insofar as the Government of the U.S.A. raises in its note of July 10 the question concerning the guaranties of freedom of action of an all-German Government, which is immediately connected with the question of the authority of an all-German Government, the Soviet Government finds it necessary to recall that the position of the Soviet Government on this question was exhaustively set forth in its note of May 24. In this note it was stated 'as far as an all-German Government and its powers are concerned this Government must, of course, also be guided by the Potsdam provisions, but after the conclusion of a peace treaty by the provisions of the peace treaty, which must serve the establishment of a firm peace in Europe'. This flows directly from the Potsdam Agreement, which established the principles on which the German state— peace-loving, democratic, independent, united, German state—must be established. The entire activity of the Government of the United States in Western Germany is in plain contradiction to these principles.

In connection with this, the Soviet Government finds it necessary to note that the Government of the United States is interpreting in distorted fashion the reference of the Soviet Government in its note of May 24 to the Potsdam Agreement, making it look as though in this note there was envisaged the 're-creation of a Four Power system of control' although in reality the note of the Soviet Government of May 24 spoke not of the establishment of a Four Power system of control but of the necessity for the observance of the principles of the Potsdam Agreement concerning the reestablishment of Germany as a unified, independent, peace-loving and democratic state.

4. The Government of the United States in its note of July 10 again raises the question regarding the right of the German people to 'join other nations in peaceful aims' and to conclude appropriate agreements. In this regard, the Soviet Government in its note of April 9 pointed out the provision contained in the Soviet draft of a 'basis of a peace treaty' regarding the obligation of Germany 'not to enter into any kind of coalition or military alliance directed against any other power which has participated with its armed forces in a war against Germany'. As is quite evident this provision in no way limits the right of Germany to join other nations for peaceful purposes. But this provision deprives Germany of the possibility of joining such groups as, for instance, the North Atlantic bloc which pursues aggressive aims and the activity of which represents the threat of development of a new world war. The Soviet Government continues to consider that in such provision there is no limitation on sovereign rights of the German state and that such provision is in accordance with the agreements of the Four Powers on the German question and fully responds also to the interests of all states neighboring Germany and is equally to the national interests of Germany itself.

5. The Government of the United States in its note of July 10 refers to the measures carried out at the present time in the German Democratic Republic (GDR) for the strengthening of its security, stating that these measures in some way are 'deepening the division of Germany' and in some way are directed to the prohibition of contact between the Germans living in the GDR and Western Germany.

Such a statement has no foundation. As is known the Government of the GDR has widely published that mentioned measures are taking place at the request of the population which suffers injury on the part of spies, diversionists, terrorists, and contrabandists sent from the Western zone of Germany with provocatory purposes which are directly connected with the policy of remilitarization of Germany and the inclusion of Western Germany in preparation of a new war.

6. In reply to the Soviet Government's proposal in its note of May 24 to enter joint discussion on the questions regarding a peace treaty with Germany without delay and the creation of an all-German Government, the Government of the United States states it considers it impossible for a German peace treaty to be worked out before an all-German Government is created and in view of this, it is necessary to limit itself only to the creation of a commission of investigation in Germany. However, such an assertion does not correspond to the Potsdam Agreement which placed on the Council of Foreign Ministers the obligation to prepare a 'peace settlement for Germany to be accepted by the Government of Germany when a government adequate for the purpose is established'.

The Soviet Government considers as without any kind of foundation the refusal of the Governments of the United States, Great Britain, and France to work out a peace treaty with Germany before an all-German Government is created. It would be incorrect and in no way justified to put off for an indefinite time the discussion of such important questions as the question of a peace treaty with Germany and the reestablishment of the unity of Germany as proposed by the Governments of the United States, Great Britain and France.

As is evident, the proposals of the Government of the United States are designed to continue to prolong for an indefinite time the discussion of the question of a peace treaty with Germany and the reestablishment of the unity of Germany and consequently retain Occupation forces in Germany for an indefinite period.

7. Regarding the question of the creation of a commission to determine the existence of German conditions for the conduct of general free elections, the position of the Soviet Government was set forth already in its notes of April 9 and May 24. The Government of the United States mentions some sort of advantages to the inspection in Germany by such a commission. But the proposal for the creation of an international commission for inspection in Germany and thus to convert Germany into a subject of investigation cannot be considered other than an insult to the German nation. Such a proposal can be brought forward only by those who forget that Germany, in the course of more than 100 years, has lived under conditions of a parliamentary regime with general elections and organized political parties and that therefore it is impossible to put before Germany such requirements which ordinarily are put before backward countries.

As regards the composition of a commission for the investigation of the existence in Germany of conditions for the conduct of general free elections, the most objective such commission would be that created, with the agreement of the Four Powers, by the Germans themselves and composed of Germans representing, let us say, the People's Chamber of the GDR and the Bundestag of Western Germany. Such a commission which would not insult the Germans at the same time would represent the first step of the road toward the unification of Germany.

As regards the inspection of Germany with the aim of determining the existence of conditions for the conduct of free all-German elections, it is self-evident that the first question is to determine in what measure there are being fulfilled the decisions of the Potsdam Conference, the realization of which represent the condition for actual free all-German elections and the formation of an all-German Government representing the will of the German people. Such a decision of the Potsdam Conference is the decision regarding the demilitarization of Germany in order, as mentioned in the Potsdam Agreement 'permanently to prevent the revival or reorganization of German militarism and Nazism', that Germany never again can threaten its neighbors or the maintenance of peace throughout the world. Such a decision is the realization of the political principles enunciated by the Potsdam Agreement regarding Germany which obligate: 'to destroy the National Socialist Party and its affiliated and supervised organizations, to dissolve all Nazi institutions, to ensure that they are not revived in any form, and to prevent all Nazi and militarist activity or propaganda'. To such principles also is related the provision of the Potsdam Conferences 'to prepare for the eventual reconstruction of German political life on a democratic basis and for eventual peaceful cooperation in international life by Germany'.

8. The Governments of the United States, Great Britain, and France propose to convene a meeting of representatives of the four Governments for discussion only of the question of the creation, function, and powers of a commission for the investigation of the existence in Germany of conditions necessary for the conduct of free elections. It may be noted that correspondence on this question has in some measure reconciled the points of view of the Soviet Government on the one hand and the Governments of Great Britain and France on the other hand, but the Soviet Government does not see any foundation for the limitation of the questions set forth for discussion at a meeting of representatives of the Four Powers only to the question of the above-mentioned commission. In limiting the scope of questions put forth for discussion of the representatives of the mentioned Four Powers and to avoid review of the most important questions relating to Germany, the Government of the United States, and also the Governments of Great Britain and France, act as though they were striving that

the meeting of the representatives of the Four Powers should produce the least possible results or should have absolutely no result. Nonetheless, the Soviet Government is prepared to discuss at the meeting of the Four Powers proposed by the Governments of the Three Powers the question of a commission for investigation of conditions for the conduct of free elections in all of Germany. But the Soviet Government, meanwhile, considers that a meeting cannot and should not limit itself to discussion of only this question. The Soviet Government considers it necessary that this meeting as a matter of first importance discuss such important questions as the peace treaty with Germany and the formation of an all-German Government.

Proceeding from the foregoing the Soviet Government proposes to convene at the earliest time and in any case in October of this year a meeting of the representatives of the Four Powers with the following agenda:

A. Preparation of a peace treaty with Germany.
B. Formation of an all-German Government.
C. Conduct of free all-German elections and a commission for the verification of the existence in Germany of conditions for the conduct of such elections, its composition, functions, and powers.

Meanwhile, the Soviet Government proposes to discuss at this meeting of the Four Powers the question of the date of withdrawal from Germany of Occupation troops.

The Soviet Government proposes also that representatives of the German Democratic Republic and the German Federal Republic take part in a meeting to examine appropriate questions.

The Soviet Government has sent similar notes also to the Governments of Great Britain and France.

(ix) RESOLUTION OF THE VOLKSKAMMER REGARDING THE RUSSIAN NOTE OF 23 AUGUST AND APPOINTING A DELEGATION TO NEGOTIATE WITH THE FEDERAL GOVERNMENT ON THE QUESTION OF ALL-GERMAN ELECTIONS, 5 SEPTEMBER 1952[1]

After hearing the declaration of the Government of the German Democratic Republic,[2] the People's Chamber of the German Democratic Republic passed the following motion, which was introduced with the support of all fractions.

The People's Chamber of the German Democratic Republic has repeatedly made proposals to the Bonn Federal Parliament for an understanding on

---

[1] German Democratic Republic: Information Office: *White Book on the Bonn War Treaty* (Berlin, 1952), pp. 223–5.
[2] Ibid. pp. 217–20.

the method of re-establishing Germany's unity as a democratic, peaceable and independent state; on German co-operation in the conclusion of a peace treaty; and on the holding of free all-German elections.

The German people want peace. They desire the unity of their homeland and demand with the greatest emphasis and complete justice, the conclusion of a peace treaty with Germany. The peaceful solution of these questions, vital for our people, entails understanding being reached by the Four Great Powers and amongst the Germans themselves.

The note of the Soviet Government of August 23rd 1952 made new and positive proposals to the governments of the United States, Britain and France for the solution of all questions affecting Germany. In particular it was proposed that a Four Power Conference should be summoned by October this year at the latest. This prospect has given the peaceable German people new courage and new hope in their fight for peace, unity and democracy.

The People's Chamber of the German Democratic Republic therefore regards it as its patriotic duty to hold out the hand of understanding to the Bonn Federal Parliament once again, despite the rejection of its previous proposal.

The German people welcome the proposals of the Soviet Government that a Four Power Conference should discuss the questions of the preparation of a peace treaty with Germany, the creation of an all-German Government, the holding of free, all-German elections and the date for the withdrawal of the occupation troops from Germany. Every German understands that the Soviet Government's proposal that representatives of the German Democratic Republic and the West German Federal Republic should take part in the discussions on the relevant questions is in accordance with the national right of self-determination of the German people and raises prospects of the conclusion of a just peace treaty.

There can be no doubt that an understanding between the Four Great Powers would be made considerably easier by an understanding between the Germans themselves upon the despatch of representatives of the German Democratic Republic and the West German Federal Republic to this Four Power Conference, and also an understanding upon the question of investigating the conditions for holding free all-German elections.

The German people in the East and the West of our homeland are jointly interested in the question to be discussed at the Four Power Conference. Is it not obvious that they should represent these interests together?

Negotiations between representatives of the People's Chamber of the

German Democratic Republic and the West German Federal Parliament could clarify the points of view and could lead to the finding of a joint point of view in the questions vitally affecting our people. This understanding between Germans is most urgent in view of the extraordinary seriousness of the situation created by the signature of the Bonn War Treaty.

According to the plans of Ridgway and Adenauer, the Bonn Federal Parliament should soon ratify the so-called Bonn Treaty and the Military Agreement linked with it. In this way the Bonn War Treaty would be imposed upon West Germany by the governments of the U.S.A., Great Britain and France, even though the Constitution of the Federal Republic is thereby broken.

The initiators of the Bonn War Treaty plan that it should prevent the conclusion of a democratic peace treaty with Germany and the re-establishment of German unity, that it should perpetuate and deepen the partitioning of Germany, and that it should prolong for an unlimited period and aggravate the occupation of West Germany by foreign troops and the national oppression. This Separate Treaty is an undisguised aggressive alliance for war. It would lead to the unleashing of a new massacre of the nations which would be at the same time a murderous blood-letting among the Germans. The Bonn War Treaty thus represents a most serious danger to the existence and future of the German people and to the peace and security of all peace-loving peoples in Europe. For this reason the German people demand the rejection of the Bonn War Treaty and the holding of Four Power negotiations.

For these reasons the People's Chamber of the German Democratic Republic decides:

1. To elect a delegation, charged with delivering to the Presidium of the West German Federal Parliament and to Dr. Ehlers personally, a letter with relevant proposals addressed to all members of the Federal Parliament.

2. To grant the delegation plenipotentiary rights to enter into the necessary discussions regarding the despatch of representatives of the German Democratic Republic and the West German Federal Republic for participation in the Four Power Conference and to discuss the steps to be taken for the establishment of an investigating commission for free all-German elections and the date for it to begin its activity, if the members of the Federal Parliament show the readiness for understanding, which is demanded by the entire people. The establishment of such an investigating commission should be speeded up so that no time is lost in re-uniting Germany.

The following members of the People's Chamber were elected as members of the delegation:

Hermann Matern,	Heinrich Homann,
Otto Nuschke,	Ernst Goldenbaum.
Dr. Karl Hamann,	

The Presidium of the People's Chamber of the German Democratic Republic, the Standing Committee of the People's Chamber and the members of this delegation are charged with drawing up the letter addressed to the West German Parliament.

(x) UNITED STATES REPLY TO THE RUSSIAN NOTE OF 23 AUGUST, 23 SEPTEMBER 1952[1]

The United States Government has carefully considered the Soviet Government's note of August 23 about Germany. It had hoped that the note would have marked some progress towards agreement on the essential question of free all-German elections. This is the first question which must be settled among the four powers so that Germany can be unified, an all-German Government formed and a peace treaty concluded.

Possibly in order to divert attention from this issue, the greater part of the Soviet note of August 23 is, however, devoted to wholly unfounded attacks upon the Atlantic Pact, the European Defense Community and the conventions signed at Bonn on May 26. As the United States Government has often emphasized, these agreements are purely defensive and threaten no one. The Bonn conventions and the EDC treaty, far from being imposed on the German people, are a matter for free decision by freely elected Parliaments, including of course that of the German Federal Republic. Insofar as the Bonn conventions reserve certain strictly limited rights to the three Western powers, a fundamental consideration has been specifically to safeguard the principle of German unity and to keep the door open for agreement with the Soviet Union on the unification of Germany.

The United States Government must insist on the necessity of starting four-power discussions at the only point where they can in fact start, which is the organization of free elections. In its note of July 10, the United States Government drew attention to the obvious fact that this is the first point which must be settled if any progress is to be made towards uniting the Soviet zone with the Federal Republic, which constitutes the greater part of Germany. In its first note, as in its last, the Soviet Government has evaded this clear issue. Instead of putting first things first, it now relegates to the background the problem of elections and

[1] *Department of State Bulletin*, 6 October 1952, pp. 517–18.

proposes that the four-power conference 'should discuss in the first place such important issues as a peace treaty with Germany and the formation of an all-German Government'. But until elections are held, no all-German Government can be formed, nor can Germany be unified.   Until an all-German Government is formed which will be in a position to negotiate freely, it is impossible to discuss the terms of a German peace treaty.

In complete accord with the views of the United States, French and United Kingdom Governments, the Soviet Government originally said that 'the preparation of the peace treaty should be effected with the participation of Germany in the form of an all-German Government'. The Soviet Government has now shifted its ground.   It now substitutes for this, the participation of representatives of the Soviet zone and the Federal Republic in the four-power meetings 'during the discussion of relevant questions'.   The United States Government cannot accept this proposal.   A peace treaty for the whole of Germany cannot be negotiated with, and accepted by, any German representatives other than the all-German Government which would have to carry it out.   Such a government can only proceed ,rom free elections.   It is moreover well known that the East German administration is not representative of the German population of the Soviet zone.   This fact is not controverted by the assertion in the Soviet note of August 23 that this administration acted 'at the request' of that population in enforcing recent measures further dividing East and West Germans in defiance of their clear desire for unity in freedom.

The United States Government is compelled to remind the Soviet Government that conditions have altered radically since the Potsdam Agreement of 1945, which laid down certain political and economic principles to govern the initial control period.   The Soviet conception of a peace treaty drafted by the four powers and imposed upon Germany is entirely unsuitable in 1952.   The United States Government could never agree to a peace treaty being drafted or negotiated without the participation of an all-German Government.   Any other procedure would mean a dictated treaty.   That indeed would be 'an insult to the German nation'.

The United States Government again insists that genuinely free elections with a view to the formation of an all-German Government must come first.   It has however learned by hard experience in recent years that terms such as 'free elections' have one meaning in common parlance and another in the official Soviet vocabulary.   The contrast between the concept of free elections which obtains in West Germany and that which prevails in the Soviet Zone is clear.   It is for the German people to choose between these alternative ways of life.   But they must be able to make their choice in genuine freedom and full responsibility.   Only genuinely free elections can reflect the will of the German people and permit the formation of an all-German Government with the necessary freedom of action to discuss and accept a peace settlement.

In order to create the conditions necessary for free elections, there has been four-power agreement that there should be a commission of investigation. The Soviet Government has now proposed that this commission should be composed of representatives of the People's Assembly of the 'German Democratic Republic' and of the Bundestag of the German Federal Republic. A commission of investigation must, however, be genuinely impartial. A German commission would be no more able than a four-power commission to meet this requirement. The underlying principle of the present Soviet proposal was contained in one which emanated from the Soviet zone on September 15, 1951. This was rejected by the Bundestag, which then suggested investigation by a United Nations Commission. It was thus the freely elected representatives of fifty millions of the German people who themselves proposed the creation of a neutral investigation commission under United Nations supervision. Nevertheless, the United States Government repeats its readiness to discuss any practical and precise proposals, as stated in its note of the tenth of July.

The United States Government continues to seek a way to end the division of Germany. This will not be accomplished by premature discussions about a peace treaty with a Germany not yet united and lacking an all-German Government. The United States Government therefore renews the proposal made in its note of July 10 for an early four-power meeting—which could take place in October—to discuss the composition, functions and authority of an impartial commission of investigation with a view to creating the conditions necessary for free elections. The next step would be to discuss the arrangements for the holding of these elections and for the formation of an all-German Government, as proposed in paragraph 11 (IV) of the United States Government's note of May 13. When free elections have been held and an all-German Government formed, the peace settlement can be negotiated. The United States Government, in concert with the French Government and the United Kingdom Government and after consultation with the German Federal Government and the German authorities in Berlin, most earnestly urges the Soviet Government to reconsider its refusal to join the other powers in a single-minded effort thus to come to grips with the problem of free elections in Germany.

(xi) EXTRACT FROM A SPEECH TO THE ITALIAN CHAMBER BY THE PRIME MINISTER, SIGNOR ALCIDE DE GASPERI, 22 OCTOBER 1952[1]

In conclusion, the proposal put forward on Nenni's initiative cannot be valued as a gesture in itself, but as a step on the way towards an

[1] Translated from *Relazioni Internazionali*, 25 October 1952, pp. 1120–2.

alternative which, deserting western solidarity, would lead Italy into being abandoned and isolated; it would lead her into an impossible neutrality, into a situation of unarmed inertia, incapable of any action for peace, open to all winds and tempests in the midst of a restless and turbulent world.

In contrast to that, our policy is one of international co-operation. In speaking of the Atlantic alliance, great prominence has been given here to the economic and financial difficulties arising out of the financing of the means of defence; much emphasis has been placed upon Europe's revolt against the domination of the dollar and people have been pleased to see its culmination in a diplomatic incident of minor importance which happened recently, on the occasion of a United States' reply which France considered unsatisfactory.

It is undeniable that between the insistence of the United States, who are urging that the armed forces reconstruction programme in the various countries should be realized according to the Lisbon guarantees, and the objections, of an economic nature, which in Europe generally are being raised in order to obtain a delay, it is not easy to reach a compromise at once. But the frequently lively discussions have never cast any doubt on the bond between the alliance and the actual substance of the guarantees. The declarations of President Pinay are a proof of it. In preparation for the meeting of the Council of NATO called for 15 December discussion will soon begin on the replies which the separate states have in the meantime given to a questionnaire which aims at the revision of the objectives laid down at Lisbon, and the reconciliation of such objectives with the financial possibilities.

Discussing, correcting, if need be reconstituting: this is the mark of a democratic régime, all the more understandable when you think that it is a matter of fourteen nations undertaking decisive obligations. That such an organization should function slowly, and that the rhythm of its activities should not bear comparison with that of a dictatorship, is widely appreciated; as it is equally clear that no one could expect a quick and immediate realization of the Atlantic community; that is to say that extension of the military pact into a more living and efficacious co-operation, into an integral community on economic, cultural and social grounds, such as it was envisaged at Ottawa. But we have certainly made some progress, and it may be noted with satisfaction that with the passing of the months, in spite of the naturally greater difficulties due to the fact that the problems which are being gradually tackled, as they come nearer become more concrete, a clearer and more distinct Atlantic conscience is being formed, an Atlantic conscience which we trust will be able to absorb economic and social concepts, so that it may create a real Atlantic community based on common ideals and co-ordinated interests.

Italy will contribute all she can towards a more intensive development of these constructive factors which favour the alliance.

People have been ironical—though it is true that Signor Nenni has refrained—about my presumed catholic 'Europeanism'. Certainly the whole of our social activity contains an aspiration to brotherhood which may derive either from Christianity understood socially, or from a Mazzinian and Socialist humanitarianism; but such aspiration does not in any way coincide with the confession of one particular faith. Let it suffice to recall that the Republic of Bonn is 51% Protestant and 49% Catholic, and certainly no one thinks of establishing the *cuius regio eius religio* of the treaty of Westphalia; and ecclesiastical frontiers and frontiers of thought and culture raise no barriers, as may be seen at these international meetings where we find ourselves side by side with socialists, free thinkers, and —oddly enough—trade union representatives. Why?

Because the necessity of obtaining an expanded market and the free circulation of labour, of overcoming economic frontiers, impells us all irresistibly. This impulse—there is no need to pretend to prophecy to say this—is contained in the nature of things, in the social structure, in the exigencies of labour above all. This impulse, sooner or later, will make itself felt, will find expression, and may find expression in Europe either through a centralization of totalitarian, political power such as Hitler dreamt of, or through a communist régime made up of the various satellite states around the Soviet Republic, commanded by a dictator-like super-marshal; or else, slowly and more gradually, but certainly with less bloodshed, through a federation of free democracies.

This, my friends, this, honourable colleagues, is the goal of European Union, within which we must harmonize social reform, that is the advent of a predominance of labour, without compromising political freedom and free economic enterprise. Moreover, a socialism intent on reform, which would give more thought to political freedom than to the fate of the Soviet Republic, could be introduced into this political structure.

This is how the Europe of tomorrow should be born, and whoever wishes it well or promotes it, is a forerunner of social progress and whoever opposes it may be classed among the bands of wreckers and saboteurs, and be said to lag behind progress. Those who act in this way are not daring; they are reactionaries.

Here too the work will be laborious and slow, a matter of placing stone upon stone. I am not astonished at the difficulties which I foresee, I do not delude myself as to the resentment with which we will meet. I would be surprised if hostilities did not appear, as the building grows and the structure takes shape. The probability of not seeing the walls rise myself, does not distress me. Statesmen, lawyers, economists, representatives of every social class, especially of the economic categories, must all help.

I know well . . . how much this work of placing stone upon stone, of
building a house of concord, in the midst of the ruins of a devastating war,
and the fear of a fresh catastrophe, is as beset with dangers as it is pregnant
with hope. And yet the attempt is being made! The process is under way.
Not only has the Coal and Steel Community begun its activities, giving
life to supranational institutions such as the High Authority, the Assembly
and the High Court (and the Defence Community will soon start upon its
work), but there has been the unanimous decision of the six governments
in question, made at the recent meeting of Foreign Ministers at Luxembourg, to entrust to the said Assembly of the Coal and Steel Community,
appropriately constituted, the task of drafting the plan for a European
political Assembly.[1] The common Assembly immediately understood the
importance of the undertaking, and, in accepting it, brought into being a
definite *ad hoc* assembly, which will be specifically concerned with the plan
in question, which has to be submitted to the governments by 10 March
next year. This Assembly has already begun its studies and we are even
now taking part in the first meetings of study groups which have been
formed for this purpose.

Italy intends to contribute fully and constructively to this activity,
offering the benefit of her judiciary culture, and her knowledge of and
experience in economic, political and social fields.

One cannot, naturally, speak of these matters without also touching
upon the themes discussed at the sittings of what is the oldest European
political forum, the Council of Europe; and several speakers who are here
now have referred to this.

With regard to specific contacts and specific themes, the Council of
Europe, in the past months, has had its ups and downs. Everyone knows
in particular, of those proposals which go under the name of Mr. Eden,
the British Minister who put them forward. They are intended to direct
these communities of six, which are striving towards a more complete and
intimate bond of a political order, in such a way that they may develop
without assuming isolated positions, and be therefore less in contrast with
those of other sectors of Europe.[2]

This is certainly a legitimate concern which we fully share, and it is for
this reason that, from the very beginning, we accepted the spirit of the
Eden proposal, in which, moreover, we appreciated Great Britain's noble
effort not to alienate herself from the old Europe. In any case, in the
interest of western civilization, it seems to us that today the process of the
consolidation of Europe needs a more efficacious propelling power behind
it, and the English are the first to recognize that an undoubtedly favourable
element in the situation is constituted by the fact that six countries of this
Europe, bordering upon each other, and sharing a close affinity, should

[1] See below, p. 214.　　　　　　　[2] See below, p. 206.

anticipate the natural rhythm of the process: not cut off from, or in contrast with, others, but in a sincere spirit of collaboration, leaving the door open to every ulterior development of the process of European consolidation. The six countries can build up, in the meantime, a common voice within the wider sector of the whole of Europe.

Thus the Council of Strasbourg, which was and is a great European tribunal, has given the signal for the constitution of an organization which, far from being in a state of absorption, can absorb all its useful functions in the harmonizing of ideas and initiatives for European union.

I know, when one speaks of European unification and above all, in the concrete, of the defence community, that the question of Germany arises. So, let it be said that democratic Italy is in a position of complete impartiality: she keeps an open mind to the anxieties which have arisen in France over the question of German rearmament, but she has also an ear for the voice of historical reality. We understand some of the anxieties of French public opinion, and if any word of ours should be of use, we would like to express our feelings of sincere brotherly loyalty. Suspicions have arisen over my talks at Bonn, but the French government knows that I have not betrayed the spirit of Santa Margherita[1] and that it may count upon our lively sympathy at any moment.

As for the nations who conquered Germany, these too have come a long way. Let us look, in Churchill's memoirs, at the notes on what happened in Teheran in January 1944. Then all the great powers, particularly Roosevelt and Stalin, were agreed that Germany should be broken up into a series of states, five to be precise, and that the Ruhr should be internationalized. At Yalta, in February 1945, Stalin proposed three states, and at Potsdam they only spoke vaguely of a federation of Bavaria and Austria–Hungary, separately from the other regions.

Then followed another period, the Truman–Attlee–Bevin period: the culminating point of this is 29 August 1950, two months after the outbreak of the war in Korea. (One may note the effects and reactions produced by events.) Adenauer presents the High Commissioner with a memorandum in which he pronounces a sentence truly worthy of a statesman, which recalls certain classical examples which we often quote to prove that to follow your own interest, you must follow that of others.

'We are in danger', says Adenauer, 'and therefore we are prepared to contribute.' Thus we arrive at the Pleven plan for a common army, and Carlo Schmid, who is the technician of the socialist opposition in Germany, says: 'What do you expect to do with the twelve divisions, outlined in the plan? They would no more frighten the Russians than would a pistol shot.' So very small did the military organization seem, so negligible as a threat, the German contribution.

[1] See *Documents* (R.I.I.A.) for 1951, p. 75.

In fact the draft of the Bill which you will shortly discuss, aims, first
and foremost, at linking the disposition of the forces to a collective will
outside Germany and Italy; it aims at reciprocal agreement. Secondly it
aims at organizing these forces in such a way that no withdrawal may be
possible without in itself weakening those very states who were instrumental
in their creation. Here we are faced by convictions. I can understand the
French anxieties, and I also understand the opposition of the extreme left:
I ask you to recognize that this my profound conviction, which is certainly
not mine alone, is held in entire good faith.

Furthermore, it is Europe's participation that reassures the Americans
and encourages moderate policies, because the conviction that Europe is
resistant prevents one from thinking of any form of preventive war. We
must therefore think of the common army as a lesser danger of conquest,
however it may be, as a controlled and regulated development of German
armaments. But above all there are the internal European reasons which
counsel acceptance.

Distinguished colleagues, the common army is the instrument by which
peace may be secured between Germany and France. I know that it is
difficult, I know that there are strong reactions against it both on the
right and the left. But turning back to history, I find no other solution,
history tells me that any other way tragedy repeats itself. And so I say,
that, whatever the difficulties may be, whatever the opposition, they must
be overcome in the name of peace, which is not only the peace of France
and Italy, but is the peace of Europe, and the peace of the world.

On the plane of the realization of the Schuman and Pleven plans, we
have so far met with one characteristic fact, the preliminary agreement of
two governments, the French and the German. So, we, unpreoccupied
by other questions, however important, excepting those concerning these
two states, have seen in this instrument above all the basis, the point of
departure, for a development of the European political authority.

(xii) Resolution protesting against the denial of democratic rights
in the Saar, adopted by the Bundestag on 18 November 1952[1]

The German Bundestag enters a solemn and decided protest against
the suppression of basic democratic rights in the Saar. The German
Bundestag protests against the banning of democratic parties and against
the refusal to allow certain candidates to stand for election, whereby
reputable Germans in the Saar are being prevented from taking part in
legislation and administration. Members of parties which accept a
democratic order have been debarred from issuing electoral manifestoes
merely because they oppose the present régime. The members of their

[1] Translated from *Deutscher Bundestag, 237. Sitzung*, 18 November 1952, p. 10931.

founding committees have been prevented from standing as candidates. Thus it has been made impossible for the Saar's German population to send to the Landtag men and women whom they trust.

The German Bundestag will refuse to recognize the Landtag emerging from sham elections of this kind. A Landtag created by the contrivings of a separatist political machine cannot legitimately represent the population of the Saar.

The German Bundestag welcomes the appeal made by the German parties in the Saar to abstain from voting or spoil their ballot papers.

The German Bundestag assures the oppressed Germans in the Saar of the sincere sympathy of the whole German people. The population's legitimate struggle to give free, unhindered and effective expression to its political wishes has the full support of the German Bundestag.

(xiii) LETTER FROM M. SCHUMAN TO THE SAAR PRIME MINISTER, HERR JOHANNES HOFFMANN, PROPOSING NEGOTIATIONS FOR THE MODIFICATION OF THE FRANCO-SAAR CONVENTIONS OF 1950, 26 NOVEMBER 1952[1]

Monsieur le président,

Comme suite aux délibérations du conseil des ministres en date de ce jour, j'ai l'honneur de vous faire savoir que le gouvernement français est prêt à engager avec le gouvernement sarrois des pourparlers en vue d'apporter aux conventions franco-sarroises, dans le cadre de l'union monétaire et douanière, un certain nombre de modifications dont les principales pourraient être les suivantes:

1. Creation d'une instance arbitrale

Les dispositions des conventions franco-sarroises qui atribuent une voix prépondérante au président des commissions mixtes seront abrogées. Il sera procédé à la création d'une instance arbitrale qui sera saisie en cas de partage des voix au sein d'une commission mixte.

Le président de cette instance arbitrale sera désigné d'un commun accord par les deux gouvernements.

2. Suppression du droit d'opposition du représentant de la France en Sarre

Le droit d'opposition actuellement reconnu par la convention générale au représentant de la France en Sarre sera supprimé.

Corrélativement, il conviendra de déterminer les modalités suivant lesquelles seront évoqués et réglés les différends d'ordre économique.

[1] *Le Monde*, 28 November 1952. For the text of the Conventions see *Documents* (R.I.I.A.) for 1951, pp. 231–40.

3. *Gestion commune franco-sarroise du gisement houiller sarrois*

La France et la Sarre s'associeront pour assurer en commun l'exploitation du gisement houiller sarrois.

A cet effet une entreprise franco-sarroise sera substituée à la régie des mines de la Sarre.

La loi sarroise sur les conventions collectives sera appliquée, dans le cadre du nouveau régime conventionnel, au personnel des mines.

Par ailleurs, et en dehors de ces importantes modifications, le gouvernement français prend les engagements suivants:

1. *Commerce extérieur franco-sarrois*

Les conditions particulières propres aux intérêts économiques sarrois seront prises en large considération, compte tenu des *desiderata* exprimés par les pouvoirs publics sarrois, dans le cadre du commerce extérieur de l'union économique franco-sarroise. Il en sera notamment ainsi en ce qui concerne la répartition des contingents et les conditions d'attribution des licences.

2. *Contribution sarroise aux dépenses d'administration et de défense*

Le gouvernement français est prêt à envisager la modification de la contribution sarroise aux dépenses civiles et militaires effectuées par la France en Sarre.

3. *Réorganisation des entreprises sidérurgiques placées sous séquestre*

Le gouvernement français consultera le gouvernement sarrois au sujet de la réorganisation des entreprises sidérurgiques sarroises placées sous séquestre en vue de mettre fin, dans les délais les plus brefs, à l'administration séquestre de ces entreprises.

4. *Gisement du Warndt*

En ce qui concerne le gisement du Warndt les deux commissions déjà instituées d'un commun accord par nos deux gouvernements poursuivront leurs travaux.

Le gouvernement français s'engage à apporter dans les plus brefs délais aux problèmes posés par l'amodiation du Warndt une solution qui tienne compte du résultat de ces travaux.

Je ne doute pas que les indications contenues dans cette lettre ne répondent aux préoccupations dont votre gouvernement et les partis politiques sarrois m'ont fait part depuis plusieurs mois.

Veuillez agréer, monsieur le président, les assurances de ma très haute considération.

R. Schuman

(xiv) Resolution on the Contractual Agreements and the Defence Treaty, adopted by the Bundestag on 5 December 1952[1]

The Federal Government is requested, on the exchange of the instruments of ratification of the General Agreement and the European Defence Treaty, to communicate in a note to the other contracting parties five stipulations expressing the wish of the German people:

(1) The German people has the inalienable right to unity as a nation and state. It maintains that, in accordance with the Basic Law of the Federal Republic, the present order is to be considered as only temporary until the peaceful attainment of a completely free and united Germany. Hence the German people does not recognize the present frontier lines in the East and West.

(2) It will be the policy of every German Government to proceed as soon as possible to a revision of those clauses of the transitional Treaty which are incompatible with the spirit of true partnership.

(3) The German people, in the consciousness of its responsibilities, will fulfil its obligations under the agreements, but in conformity with the obligations it has assumed, it expects that no burdens or duties will be imposed on it which would tend to lower the standard of living.
The German people expects the psychological conditions to be created to allow the German contribution to rearmament to be satisfactorily carried out.

(4) As regards the links between the member states of the E.D.C. and NATO it is the duty of the German Government to work for the creation of a treaty relationship between NATO and the German Federal Republic which would give the German people rights corresponding to its obligations.

(5) Every German Government will consider it has an inalienable right, as have the other contracting parties, to pursue an independent foreign policy within the framework of the obligations it has assumed.

(xv) Resolution on the European Defence Community adopted by the North Atlantic Council, 17 December 1952[2]

The North Atlantic Council

Recalling the decisions taken by the Council at Brussels and at Lisbon regarding German participation in Western defence, and the resolution of the 26th May, 1952, by which the Council noted that the Treaty establishing the European Defence Community fulfilled the conditions embodied in the Brussels and Lisbon decisions;

[1] Translated from *Neue Zeitung*, 5 December 1952.   [2] Cmd. 8732, p. 8.

TAKING NOTE that this Treaty was signed on the 27th May, 1952;

TAKING NOTE of the progress made towards European integration, in particular in the economic field by the creation of the Coal and Steel Community which is already functioning;

HAVING NOW HEARD the report on the activities of the Interim Committee of the Conference for the Organisation of the European Defence Community submitted by the Chairman of this committee;

REITERATES that the defence of Europe, including Western Germany, calls for the early establishment of the European Defence Community;

RE-AFFIRMS the importance of the reciprocal guarantees exchanged between the parties to the North Atlantic Treaty and the members of the European Defence Community;

STRESSES the paramount importance which the Atlantic Community attaches to the rapid entry into force of the Treaty establishing the European Defence Community and, consequently, to its ratification by all the signatories, as well as to the ratification of the Additional Protocol to the North Atlantic Treaty to members of the European Defence Community.

4. Western European Union

(i) AIDE-MÉMOIRE FROM THE BRITISH GOVERNMENT TO THE GOVERNMENTS OF THE MEMBERS OF THE COUNCIL OF EUROPE ON THE FUTURE ROLE OF THE COUNCIL OF EUROPE, MARCH 1952[1]

1. The Agenda of the meeting of the Committee of Ministers of the Council of Europe which opens in Paris on the 19th March includes a number of items that raise the question of the future rôle of Strasbourg in the development of the European Community, which is gradually taking shape in the form of the European Defence Community and the Schuman Plan.

2. The movement for unity in Europe, which led to the creation of the Council of Europe, is now flowing along two main streams: the Atlantic Community, a wide association of States which, without formal surrender of sovereignty, is achieving increasing unity of purpose and action through the machinery of the North Atlantic Organisation, and the European Community, a smaller group of States which is moving towards political federation by the progressive establishment of organisations exercising supranational powers in limited fields. The Council of Europe seems to be in danger of becoming stranded between these two streams.

3. In an attempt to acquire 'limited authority but real powers' the Assembly has produced a draft new Statute of the Council of Europe,[2] which will

---

[1] Council of Europe: *Consultative Assembly, Fourth Ordinary Session (First Part), 26th–30th May 1952, Documents*, vol. I, Document 11, pp. 288–90.   [2] *Documents* (R.I.I.A.) for 1951, p. 154.

be on the agenda at the next session of the Committee of Ministers. This transforms what is now a purely consultative body into a quasi-federal institution with legislative and executive powers and the right to be consulted by member Governments on certain matters within its competence. If the new Statute were adopted this would undoubtedly make things very difficult for the United Kingdom.

4. In Mr. Eden's view, a more promising future for the Council of Europe would lie in a remodelling of the organisation so that its organs could serve as the institutions of the European Coal and Steel Community, the European Defence Community and any future organisations of the same structure and membership. The advantage would be:

(a) The Council of Europe would be given valuable work to do;

(b) The duplication of European bodies would be avoided;

(c) The European Coal and Steel Community and the European Defence Community would be provided with ready-made machinery.

5. Mr. Eden hopes that the Committee of Ministers will agree that this possibility is worthy of study. The Council of Europe has already served a useful purpose as the mainspring of plans for European unity, and any adjustment which is now made to bring it into focus with the European Community would be a logical development of the rôle that it has so far played. It will, of course, be necessary to consider the position in the reconstituted Council of Europe of those countries which are not members of the Schuman Plan and the E.D.C. But Mr. Eden is confident that a satisfactory 'two-tier' system could be evolved which would enable the Council of Europe to continue its work as an organisation for intergovernmental co-operation in Western Europe. On occasions the Committee of Ministers and the Assembly could meet on a 6-Power basis to transact business connected with the Coal and Steel Community, the Defence Community and any future organisations of the same type and membership. At the same time both the Committee of Ministers and the Assembly would continue to meet on a 15-Power basis as at present for the purposes defined in Article 1 of the Statute. In particular, the present practice of receiving and discussing reports from the O.E.E.C. should be maintained. The full council would also discuss questions relating to the European Community which were of general interest to Western Europe.

6. Mr. Eden is anxious that M . . . should be aware of his views before the meeting of the Committee of Ministers when he hopes that they will serve as a basis for a full and frank discussion on the future of the Council of Europe.

(ii) Resolution adopted by the Committee of Ministers of the Council of Europe on the best means of giving effect to the British proposals, 23 May 1952[1]

The Committee of Ministers,

Having regard to the United Kingdom proposals that arrangements should be made in the Council of Europe to enable the Committee of Ministers and the Consultative Assembly to serve as the Ministerial and Parliamentary institutions of restricted Communities;

Having regard to the questionnaire drawn up by the Ministers' Deputies to enable the various Governments to define their views on these proposals;

Having heard the observations formulated by its Members on this subject;

Approves the principle underlying the United Kingdom proposals that organic liaison should be established between restricted Communities and the Council of Europe;

Declares that this principle applies to the relations between the Council of Europe and the restricted Communities, in particular as regards their Ministerial and Parliamentary institutions; and taking note that at the present stage, and until such restricted Communities have come into being, the mechanism of the relationship to be established between them and the Council of Europe cannot be exactly defined;

Resolves:

1. To transmit to the Consultative Assembly the appropriate documents with a view to obtaining its opinion on the best means of giving effect to the United Kingdom proposals;

2. To instruct the Secretary-General to obtain the views of the Governments taking part in the restricted Communities.

3. To instruct the Secretary-General to obtain the views of the restricted Communities as soon as they have come into existence;

4. To instruct the Deputies of the Ministers to proceed with a detailed examination of the problem on the basis of the opinions obtained;

5. To resume the examination of this question at its next Session.

[1] Council of Europe: *Consultative Assembly, Fourth Ordinary Session (First Part), 26th–30th May 1952, Documents,* vol. I, Document 11, pp. 287–8.

(iii) RESOLUTION CONCERNING THE REQUEST FROM THE COMMITTEE OF MINISTERS FOR AN OPINION ON THE BEST MEANS OF GIVING EFFECT TO THE BRITISH PROPOSALS, ADOPTED BY THE CONSULTATIVE ASSEMBLY OF THE COUNCIL OF EUROPE ON 30 MAY 1952[1]

The Assembly,

Having been requested by the Committee of Ministers to give an opinion on the best means of implementing the proposals of the United Kingdom concerning the role of the Council of Europe;

Expressing its satisfaction that the Committee of Ministers is now proceeding to examine this important question in collaboration with the Assembly, thereby enabling the latter to fulfil the consultative role conferred upon it by the Statute;

Recalling its previous Recommendations concerning the links to be established between the Specialised Authorities and the Council of Europe;

Noting the decisions of a statutory nature on the Specialised Authorities adopted by the Committee of Ministers at its Eighth Session;

Adopts the following Resolution:

1. The Assembly approves the general principle underlying the proposals of the United Kingdom to the effect that organic links be established between the Communities and the Council of Europe.

The Assembly considers that the implementation of the United Kingdom proposals will lessen the risks of a schism in Europe. It emphasises the great symbolic value and practical significance of such a decision.

2. The Assembly suggests that the United Kingdom proposals be implemented on the basis of the following principles:

(i) The action taken should not hamper in any way the normal functioning or development of the Communities, nor the subsequent establishment of other Communities, specifically a Political Community.

(ii) Member states should undertake to link the Communities in which they participate with the Council of Europe, on the understanding that the ways and means of liaison to be established shall in each case be the subject of a special agreement.

(iii) The organic links which may be established between a Community and the Council of Europe should be of such a nature as to enable Member States not participating in the Community to be associated with certain measures which might be contemplated by the latter.

(iv) Such liaison with the Council of Europe would not preclude

[1] Council of Europe: *Consultative Assembly, Fourth Ordinary Session (First Part), 26th–30th May 1952, Texts adopted by the Assembly*, vol. I, Resolution 11, pp. 11–12.

certain Members more directly concerned with the activities of a particular Community from concluding special agreements with the latter in order to achieve a closer degree of liaison.

(v) The forms of association within the Council of Europe should be adjusted so as to enable Member States unwilling to enter into liaison with certain Communities—such as the European Defence Community —to continue to co-operate within the Council for the achievement of the aims laid down in Article 1 of the Statute, without being in any way bound by the agreements concluded between the Council and such Communities.

(vi) It would appear advisable to take suitable steps to standardise the regulations affecting the staff of these Communities and of other European Organisations, in order to prevent the danger of the administration of the said Communities and Organisations being carried on in separate compartments. Steps should be taken to draw up the constitution and rules of a real 'European Civil Service'.

3. If the Council of Europe is to be in a position to fulfil the new tasks which would devolve on it as a result of the implementation of the United Kingdom proposals, it would be highly desirable to achieve a suitable measure of integration between the Council of Europe and the Organisation for European Economic Co-operation. The Assembly urges that negotiations to this end be undertaken at the same time as the study of the United Kingdom proposals.

4. The concentration of the institutions of the European Communities and of the Council of Europe at a single Seat would appear to be a step to which consideration must be given in the interest both of the Communities and of Europe as a whole.

The Assembly urges the States participating in the Coal and Steel and in the European Defence Communities to bear in mind the overriding interests of Europe as a whole when deciding upon the headquarters of the Organs of these Communities.

5. The Assembly requests the Committee on General Affairs, bearing in mind the principles of this Resolution and in collaboration with any other competent European body, to give detailed study to the 'Questionnaire' drawn up by the Ministers' Deputies in order, with the approval of the President of the Assembly, to inform the Deputies of its conclusions, and to establish such form of future co-operation with them as may be considered suitable.

(iv) Extracts from the inaugural address of the Chairman, M. Jean Monnet, at the first meeting of the High Authority of the European Coal and Steel Community, Luxembourg, 10 August 1952[1]

Pour la première fois les relations traditionnelles entre les États sont transformées. Selon les méthodes du passé, même lorsque les États européens sont convaincus de la nécessité d'une action commune, même lorsqu'ils mettent sur pied une organisation internationale, ils réservent leur pleine souveraineté.

Aussi l'organisation internationale ne peut-elle ni décider ni exécuter, mais seulement adresser des recommandations aux États. Ces méthodes sont incapables d'examiner nos antagonismes nationaux, qui s'accusent inévitablement, tant que les souverainetés nationales elles-mêmes ne sont pas surmontées.

Aujourd'hui, au contraire, six Parlements ont décidé, après mûre délibération et à des majorités massives, de créer la première communauté européenne qui fusionne une partie des souverainetés nationales et les soumet à l'intérêt commun.

Dans les limites de la compétence qui lui est conférée par le traité,[2] la Haute Autorité a reçu des six États le mandat de prendre en tout indépendance des décisions qui deviennent immédiatement exécutoires dans l'ensemble de leur territoire. Elle est en relations directes avec toutes les entreprises. Elle obtient ses ressources financières non de contributions des États mais de prélèvements directement établis sur les productions dont elle a la charge.

Elle est responsable non devant les États mais devant une assemblée européenne. L'Assemblée a été élue par les Parlements nationaux; il est déjà prévu qu'elle pourra l'être directement par les peuples. Les membres de l'Assemblée ne sont liés par aucun mandat national; ils votent librement et par tête, et non par nation. Chacun d'eux ne représente pas son pays mais la communauté entière. L'Assemblée contrôle notre action, elle a le pouvoir de nous retirer sa confiance. Elle est la première assemblée européenne dotée de pouvoirs souverains.

Les actes de la Haute Autorité sont susceptibles de recours en justice. Ce n'est pas devant des tribunaux nationaux que de tels recours seront portés, mais devant un tribunal européen: la Cour de Justice.

Toutes ces institutions pourront être modifiées et améliorées à l'expérience. Ce qui ne sera pas remis en question, c'est qu'elles sont des institutions supranationales et, disons le mot, fédérales. Ce sont des institutions qui, dans la limite de leur compétence, sont souveraines, c'est-à-dire dotées du droit de décider et d'exécuter.

Le charbon et l'acier ne sont toutefois qu'une partie de la vie écono-

[1] *Le Monde*, 12 August 1952.   [2] See *Documents* (R.I.I.A.) for 1951, pp. 173–215.

mique. C'est pourquoi une liaison constante doit être assurée entre la Haute Autorité et les gouvernements, qui demeurent responsables de la politique économique d'ensemble de leurs États. Le conseil des ministres a été créé, non pour exercer un contrôle ou une tutelle mais pour établir cette liaison et assurer l'harmonie entre la politique de la Haute Autorité et celle des États membres.

La tâche qui nous est confiée par le traité est lourde. Nous devons établir et maintenir un marché unique du charbon et de l'acier sur tout le territoire de la communauté. Dans quelques mois toutes les entraves douanières, toutes les restrictions quantitatives, toutes les discriminations, seront éliminées. Le charbon et l'acier ne connaîtront plus de frontières à l'intérieur de la communauté, ils seront à la disposition de tout acheteur dans les mêmes conditions.

Le traité, qui est la première loi antitrusts de l'Europe, nous donne mandat de dissoudre les cartels, d'interdire les pratiques restrictives, d'empêcher toute concentration excessive de pouvoirs économiques. Ainsi dans un régime de saine concurrence la production du charbon et de l'acier sera véritablement au service des consommateurs.

Le traité nous prescrit d'intervenir, s'il est nécessaire, pour atténuer les effets des fluctuations économiques, pour faciliter le développement et la modernisation des ces industries. Dans le grand effort de développement économique qui va être poursuivi nous aurons particulièrement à l'esprit la préoccupation de promouvoir l'amélioration des conditions de vie et de travail de la main-d'œuvre, permettant leur égalisation dans le progrès.

Que signifiera dans la vie quotidienne des citoyens de nos six pays ce marché unique du charbon et de l'acier pour 150 millions de consommateurs?

On dira sans doute que peu d'entre eux achètent du charbon et de l'acier en quantités importantes. Mais le charbon et l'acier interviennent dans la fabrication de tout ce dont l'homme moderne a besoin: le gaz, l'électricité, les outils, les machines, les automobiles. Par la charrue et le tracteur, par l'équipement textile ou la machine à coudre, par l'armature du béton, par l'échafaudage ou la charpente métallique, ils ont leur part essentielle jusque dans nos maisons, nos vêtements et notre nourriture.

Le charbon et l'acier plus abondants, de meilleure qualité, à un prix plus bas, c'est la possibilité pour chacun d'acheter davantage et pour chaque famille d'obtenir un niveau de vie plus élevé. C'est l'ampleur et la liberté du marché unique qui permettront de développer une production de masse, seul moyen d'obtenir la diminution des prix de revient, le développement des débouchés et l'expansion de la production.

Mais ce marché unique qui englobe les territoires de nos six pays a encore une autre signification.

Comment ne pas être frappé en considérant les activités soumises à la communauté par cette extraordinaire concentration de fer et de charbon, par la densité de ces ressources minières et de ces installations industrielles qui dans un espace aussi limité constituent sans doute un ensemble unique au monde?

Voyez comme le bassin du nord de la France se prolonge vers la Belgique, comment les charbonnages belges se raccordent aux charbonnages d'Aix et de la Ruhr. Regardez la campine partagée entre la Belgique et les Pays-Bas, et ce même charbon réparti entre la Sarre et la Lorraine, ce même minerai de fer entre la Lorraine et le Luxembourg. Ces ressources dont la nature a fait l'actif industriel essentiel de l'Europe ont été l'enjeu des luttes entre États et des entreprises de domination. En effaçant les divisions que les hommes ont arbitrairement introduites il s'agit aujourd'hui de recréer ce bassin naturel dont ils ont morcelé l'unité et limité le développement.

Pour atteindre ces objectifs le traité et la convention ont prévu des étapes. Pleinement conscients des adaptations nécessaires, nous remplirons le mandat qui nous est confié avec détermination et prudence.

Il ne nous appartient pas de diriger la production du charbon et de l'acier: c'est là le rôle des entreprises. Notre tâche est d'établir et de maintenir les conditions dans lesquelles la production se développera au mieux de l'avantage commun.

Nous allons immédiatement établir des liaisons avec les gouvernements, avec les producteurs, avec les travailleurs, avec les utilisateurs et les négociants, avec les associations qu'ils ont constituées. Nous placerons ainsi, dès le début, le fonctionnement de la communauté sur une base de consultation constante. Nous établirons entre tous une vue commune et une connaissance mutuelle.

Ainsi se dégagera une connaissance d'ensemble de la situation de la communauté et des problèmes qu'elle comporte, ainsi pourra être préparée la forme concrète des mesures qui devront être prises pour y faire face.

Nous soumettrons le bilan ainsi dressé à l'assemblée commune au cours de la deuxième réunion qu'elle doit tenir dans cinq mois. Dans les toutes prochaines semaines nous réunirons le comité consultatif, composé de chefs d'entreprise, de travailleurs, d'utilisateurs et de négociants.

Dans tous les cas prévus par le traité nous soumettrons nos décisions à l'épreuve de la discussion et en rendrons public les motifs.

La prospérité de notre communauté européenne est indissolublement liée au développement des échanges internationaux. Notre communauté contribuera à régler les problèmes d'échanges qui se posent dans le monde.

Nous sommes déterminés à rechercher sans délai, dans des conversations directes, les moyens de mettre en œuvre l'intention déclarée du gouvernement britannique d'établir l'association la plus étroite avec la communauté.

Nous sommes convaincus que dans l'exécution du mandat qui nous a été confié par les Parlements de nos six pays nous pouvons envisager une collaboration étroite et fructueuse avec les États-Unis, qui, depuis la proposition faite par M. Schuman le 9 mai 1950,[1] nous ont donné des preuves répétées de leur sympathie active.

Nous assurerons toutes liaisons utiles avec les Nations unies et l'Organisation européenne de coopération économique. Nous développerons avec le Conseil de l'Europe toutes les formes de collaboration et d'assistance mutuelle prévues par le traité.

Nous ne sommes qu'au début de l'effort que l'Europe doit accomplir pour connaître enfin l'unité, la prospérité et la paix.

Les obligations qui nous sont assignées nous imposent de nous mettre au travail sans délai. Nous avons à la fois des responsabilités immédiates et celle de préparer des transformations si importantes qu'aucun temps ne doit être perdu pour les mettre en œuvre. La construction de l'Europe ne tolère plus de retard.

(v) Resolution adopted by the Foreign Ministers of the six Schuman Plan Powers inviting the members of the Coal and Steel Assembly to draft a Treaty constituting a European Political Authority, 10 September 1952[2]

Considering that the final aim of the six governments has been and remains the establishment of as widespread a European Political Community as possible;

Bearing in mind that at the request of the Italian Government there has been included in the Treaty constituting a European Defence Community, signed on 27th March 1952,[3] an Article 38, the purpose of which was to entrust the Assembly of that Community with the task of studying the constitution of a new Assembly elected on a democratic basis in such a way as to be able to form part of a subsequent federal or confederal system based on the principle of separate powers and, in particular, on a dual chamber system of representation;

Recalling that in its Resolution No. 14, adopted on 30th May, 1952, the Consultative Assembly of the Council of Europe requested the Governments of the States participating in the European Defence Community to choose, by the adoption of whichever of the procedure was the more rapid, the Assembly to be responsible for drafting the Statute of a supranational Political Community open to all Member States of the

---

[1] *Documents* (R.I.I.A.) for 1949–50, pp. 315–17.
[2] *Ad Hoc* Assembly instructed to work out a draft treaty setting up a European Political Community: *Debates, Official Report of the Sitting of 15th September 1952*, pp. 6–8.
[3] See above, p. 128.

Council of Europe and offering opportunities of association to such of these States as were not full members of the Political Community;

Realising that the constitution of a European Political Community of a federal or confederal nature is bound up with the establishment of common bases of economic development and a merging of the essential interests of Member States;

The Six Ministers for Foreign Affairs of the countries participating in the Coal and Steel Community, met together at Luxembourg 10th September, 1952, have taken the following decision, which takes into account previous considerations as well as their desire to expedite the study of the proposed draft, by ensuring that it possesses the maximum authority:

A.—The Members of the Coal and Steel Assembly are invited, on the basis of the principles contained in Article 38 of the Treaty establishing the European Defence Community and without prejudice to the provisions of that Treaty, to draft a Treaty constituting a European Political Authority. With this in view, the Members of the Assembly, grouped together in national delegations, shall co-opt, from among the Representatives to the Consultative Assembly who are not already members of the Coal and Steel Assembly as many additional members as shall be necessary to make up the total number laid down for each country to the Assembly of the European Defence Community;

B.—The Assembly thereby fully and finally constituted shall meet together in plenary sessions at the Seat of the Council of Europe. It may also meet in committee.

It shall determine the conditions under which representatives of other countries, especially those which are Members of the Council of Europe, may be associated with the work as observers;

It shall periodically report to the Consultative Assembly on the progress of such work.

C.—The Ministers for Foreign Affairs met together within the Council of the European Coal and Steel Community shall be associated with the work of the Assembly along lines which shall be laid down by mutual agreement.

In order to facilitate such work, they shall draw up a list of questions for submission to the Assembly, bearing on such matters as:

—the spheres in which the institutions of the European Political Community shall be competent to operate;

—measures necessary to ensure a merging of the interests of Member States in those spheres;

—the powers to be vested in institutions of the Community.

The Ministers shall periodically report to the Committee of Ministers of the Council of Europe.

D.—Within six months of the convening of the Coal and Steel Assembly, that is by 10th March, 1953, the results of the surveys referred to above should be transmitted to the Assembly of the European Defence Community, responsible for carrying out the tasks laid down in Article 38 of the Treaty establishing the European Defence Community, as well as to the Ministers for Foreign Affairs of the six countries concerned.

E.—The Governments hereby reaffirm that they have based themselves upon the proposals of the United Kingdom Government for the establishment of the closest possible relations between the future Political Community and the Council of Europe.

It is with this in view that the drafting of the Statute of that Community should be undertaken and pursued in constant co-operation with the institutions of the Council of Europe.

F.—The Consultative Assembly of the Council of Europe shall be informed of the above decision.

G.—The procedure laid down above shall in no way prejudice the Treaty establishing the European Defence Community.

(vi) Opinion adopted by the Consultative Assembly of the Council of Europe on the best means of giving effect to the British proposals, with special reference to relations between the Council of Europe and the European Coal and Steel Community, 30 September 1952[1]

The Assembly,

Having received from the Committee of Ministers a request for an Opinion on the best means of giving effect to the United Kingdom proposals,

Reserving the possibility of continuing its examination of this question during future Sessions,

Submits to the Committee of Ministers the following Opinion:

The Assembly,

Considering that the intention underlying the United Kingdom proposals is that the pattern of the restricted Communities, including a Political Authority, should be worked out, and that they should develop, within the orbit of the Council of Europe,

Considering that appropriate measures should be taken so that the United Kingdom proposals may be made applicable as fully and as quickly as possible.

Section A

Welcomes the decision of the *Ad Hoc* Assembly to invite observers from non-participating countries to join in the work of preparing plans for a European Political Community.

---

[1] Council of Europe: *Consultative Assembly, Fourth Ordinary Session (Second Part), 15th–30th September 1952, Texts adopted by the Assembly*, pp. 35–38.

Section B

Considering that it is of the highest importance that the United Kingdom proposals should be made applicable to the European Coal and Steel Community, the first Community to be established,

Emphasising the political significance of the establishment of organic links between the Council of Europe and the European Coal and Steel Community, which would prepare the way for those Members of the Council of Europe that do not participate in the restricted Communities to enter into close association with such Communities as may be created later, in particular with the Political Community.

1. Suggests that the following measures should be taken immediately in the matter of the relations between the Council of Europe and the European Coal and Steel Community;

(a) All Member States of the Council of Europe which do not accede to the European Coal and Steel Community should be invited to establish permanent delegations to the High Authority. These delegations might, in the case of States so desiring, be the delegations already accredited to the Council of Europe.

(b) The six Governments should permanently maintain the seat of the Assembly of the European Coal and Steel Community at the Seat of the Council of Europe, so that the latter's buildings and Secretariat may be utilised by the new Assembly,

(c) As far as possible the same Representatives should in future be appointed to the Assemblies of the European Coal and Steel Community and of the Council of Europe,

(d) By agreement between the Assemblies of the European Coal and Steel Community and the Council of Europe, and on conditions to be jointly decided, the following measures should be taken:

  (i) Representatives to the Assembly of the Council of Europe of countries not participating in the European Coal and Steel Community shall be able, as observers, to take part in the proceedings of the Assembly of the European Coal and Steel Community and have the right to speak but not to vote.
  (ii) Close co-ordination shall be secured in respect of the proceedings of the Assemblies with regard to matters of common interest.

(e) That the Committee of Ministers should open discussions with the High Authority and the Council of Ministers of the European Coal and Steel Community for the purpose of:

  (i) deciding upon the conditions under which Member States of the Council of Europe not participating in the European Coal and

Steel Community could be represented by observers on the Council of Ministers of the European Coal and Steel Community, and also the mutual obligations thereby entailed,

(ii) defining the conditions under which the High Authority might be authorised to take part in certain meetings of the Committee of Ministers and the Assembly of the Council of Europe, especially when consideration is being given to its reports submitted to the Council of Europe.

2. Reserving to itself the right to pursue a more detailed examination of the relationship to be established between the European Coal and Steel Community and the Council of Europe, requests the Committee of Ministers to keep it informed of the progress of negotiations with the European Coal and Steel Community.

Section C

1. Recalls that it is the wish of the Assembly that all Governments of Member States be invited to attend the negotiations for the establishment of the restricted Communities and, in particular, the Political Community.

2. Considers that the appropriate changes should be made in the Statute of the Council of Europe, so that negotiations on the Political Community may more easily be initiated within the orbit of the Council of Europe.

3. Submits to the Committee of Ministers the following Draft Protocol:

Draft Protocol

The Member States of the Council of Europe,

Considering that the Statutory Resolutions on the Specialised Authorities and partial agreements adopted at the Eighth and Ninth Sessions of the Committee of Ministers allow of negotiations being held within the orbit of the Council of Europe, with a view to setting up European Communities whose aims lie within the limits of Article 1 of the Statute, or the linking of such Communities with the Council of Europe,

Considering that it is essential to extend these possibilities so as to include European Communities whose objects go further than the present Statute, while maintaining the co-operation of all Member States within the Council,

Have agreed as follows:

(a) the Committee of Ministers and the Consultative Assembly may be empowered to act as the Ministerial and Parliamentary organs of any European Community whose aims are within the scope of Article 1(a) of the Statute,[1] and in which Members of the Council of Europe alone participate,

[1] *Documents* (R.I.I.A.) for 1951, p. 155.

(*b*) when the Committee of Ministers and the Consultative Assembly act as organs of a European Community:

(i) their competence shall extend to all matters within the competence of that Community and their powers, functions, composition and procedure shall be determined by the provisions of the instrument establishing that Community and of any relevant statute, rules or regulations which may be in force within it;

(ii) they shall meet in restricted session. Only the Members of the Community shall be entitled to representation; it shall rest with them to determine the conditions on which other Member States of the Council of Europe may be invited to send observers to such restricted meetings or to participate in them as associate Members;

(iii) the measures taken by the Council of Europe, sitting with restricted membership, involve the responsibility only of those States participating in the decision, other Member States and the Council of Europe as a whole being in no way committed;

(*c*) any additional expense incurred by the Council of Europe in connection with the measures taken in giving effect to the present Protocol shall be borne exclusively by the Member States which shall have participated therein or by the communities concerned.

4. Requests the Committee of Ministers to consider the possibility of increasing the number of Representatives of all Member States in the Assembly, taking as a basis the number of seats proposed for the Common Assembly of the E.D.C.

Section D

Secretariat

Considering:

(*a*) that its policy is to establish organic liaison between the European Communities and the Council;

(*b*) that it is necessary, in the interests of the unity of Europe and of the effectiveness and good repute of international administration, and also with the object of economy, to avoid a multiplication of machinery such as would impair its efficiency and be disheartening to public opinion;

Suggests that:

1. The Assemblies of the Council of Europe and of the Communities should each have a Clerk appointed by itself and responsible only to it. He would deal with procedural matters, the conduct of business appropriate to the Assembly, and day to day administration.

2. The Clerk to the Assembly of the Council of Europe should assume the functions of Director of European Parliamentary Services.

3. The primary duties of the Director should be:

(*a*) to act as a medium of liaison between the Assemblies on administrative matters of common concern.

(*b*) to provide, from amongst the personnel and material facilities at his disposal, the necessary services for each Assembly.

4. In the interests of economy and efficiency, and pending the creation of a unified Civil Service for Europe, the Director should draw to the greatest possible extent on the staff and material resources of the Council of Europe. Where it proves necessary to engage additional staff, the latter would be recruited by the Council of Europe under conditions of service and remuneration similar to its own.

5. The Council of Europe and the European Coal and Steel Community should share in the expense involved in these services according to proportions to be determined. Any Community subsequently utilising these services should also make an appropriate contribution.

6. These proposals should be the subject of negotiation between the Bureau of the Assembly of the Council of Europe and the Bureau of the Common Assembly of the Coal and Steel Community. Any agreement thus reached should be subject to confirmation, so far as the Council of Europe is concerned, by its Committee of Ministers.

Section E

Requests the Committee of Ministers to consider what amendments to the Statute would be required in order to put into effect the foregoing measures.

(vii) Extract from a speech to the Consultative Assembly of the Council of Europe by the British Foreign Secretary, Mr. Eden, 15 October 1952[1]

It is, of course, well known that my country has not felt able to pursue the course of federation. At the same time, we have been anxious that this should not divide us from those of our European friends who feel that they can do so. We have repeatedly expressed our wish to be closely associated with them in their work. We have taken positive steps to make this possible. Inevitably the existence of supranational or federal arrangements amongst a group of members of the Council of Europe creates a problem of their relationship with the others. I know that you have all given a great deal of thought, as we have, to this very real

[1] Council of Europe: *Consultative Assembly, Fourth Ordinary Session (Second Part), 15th–30th September 1952, Official Report of Debates*, vol. 3, pp. 281–2.

difficulty. Failure to solve it would not only be frustrating to the hopes and enthusiasms which have been built here in Strasbourg. It would be dangerous for Europe. If we cannot maintain harmony between the various approaches to the common objective, the result may be separation.

It was in an effort to find a solution of this problem that I put forward to the Committee of Ministers in Paris last March certain proposals on behalf of Her Majesty's Government in the United Kingdom. You are already familiar with them. Indeed you have been generous enough to approve them in principle. They have since been studied in detail by your Committee on General Affairs, whose Report will be a basis for your discussion during the present Session. For my part, I should like at once to declare my entire agreement with the general conclusions of that Report and to express the hope that this Assembly will find it possible to endorse them.

Our suggestions were designed, as I have explained, to meet a situation of fact. They were not intended to be a rigid or sensational plan. Their purpose was simply to help reconcile the aim of the six Powers to create a supranational community with the need to keep Europe united. The essential idea is very simple. Briefly, it is this: that all European restricted Communities, such as the Coal and Steel Community, which require Ministerial or Parliamentary institutions, should draw upon the facilities existing here in the Council of Europe. In other words, that they should make use, as far as is compatible with their own smaller membership, of the Ministerial and Parliamentary machinery which you have evolved here. That is the idea in its simplest terms. Of course, it is not suggested that our Assembly or our Committee of Ministers, sitting with full membership, should take over control of the restricted Communities. Not at all. When they are functioning as the organs of a restricted Community, obviously their membership would be limited to representatives of the countries concerned. But the fact that they were established here, and formed part of the facilities of the Council of Europe, would enable the new Communities to develop in harmony with the wider European work.

Nor are these proposals, as I have seen it suggested, simply a device to find new activities for the Council of Europe. They would, if adopted, certainly give impetus and direction to its work. But this is not their central purpose. It is, above all, as a practical means of preserving the essential unity of Europe that I commend these proposals to you.

Notable progress has been made in Europe during the last year. We have seen the signature of a treaty setting up the European Defence Community. Another treaty, signed at the same time, has established new contractual relations between the German Federal Republic and the three Occupying Powers.[1] By these instruments, when they enter into force,

[1] See above, pp. 105–13.

the Federal Republic will become an equal partner in our joint enterprise.

And now the treaty setting up the Coal and Steel Community has come into operation. It will be for ever associated with the name and fame of my colleague and friend, M. Robert Schuman, the wise and far-seeing Foreign Minister of France. The High Authority has been established. The Community's Council of Ministers and its Assembly have met. Moreover, a Special Assembly, appointed to prepare plans for a European Political Authority, has met here in Strasbourg this morning. It has taken practical decisions which will ensure that all Members of the Council of Europe will be in continuous touch with the development of this project. This is in full accord with the spirit of our proposals. Meanwhile other projects, such as that relating to the creation of a European Agricultural Pool, are also under close study.

But there are other and wider achievements embracing Western Europe as a whole which must not be forgotten. The Brussels Treaty, the O.E.E.C., the North Atlantic Treaty—in all these we have learned the benefits of close co-operation and the need to reconcile our own interests with those of our neighbours. These great organisations secure the fabric of Western Europe. They express the realities of our European life. Our safety and economic well-being are bound up with them.

Thus, each one of the member countries of the Council of Europe is working towards the essential unity of our Continent.

All of us here want to see Europe develop, and believe that our Continent has a special message for the world to-day. It would be sad, if as a consequence of these valuable new ideas, new divisions were created.

It was with these thoughts in mind that I put forward our proposals. They do not lay down detailed machinery, nor do they dictate constitutional doctrine. Their purpose is to link the communities with the rest of Western Europe without impairing their independence. There is no intention of subordinating them to the Council of Europe, still less to make the Council of Europe a court of appeal against them. They would retain their full independence to develop freely, and to exercise the powers and functions which have been conferred on them by the six nations. They would be free to decide to what extent and in what way other countries should be associated with their work. None of us who are not members of the Six could expect to have the right to attend their meetings unless invited to do so. But I would hope that the link with the Council of Europe which I have proposed would make it easy and natural for the Communities to share a great deal of their thought with the rest of us.

These proposals are flexible. They do not attempt to lay down rigid lines on which the relationship between the Council of Europe and the Communities should develop. Our object was to suggest the means, and promote the action, by which the two main trends towards European unity, the supranational and the intergovernmental, could be linked together. We did not expect immediate or spectacular results. The restricted Communities are only just coming into being. Their institutions are experimental. It will be some time before we can see exactly how they will develop. The links with the Council of Europe must therefore be established gradually. The most we can do at present is to provide facilities here which the Communities can use as they see fit. But, once these links are created, the institutions of Western Europe will be closely interlocked, with, I am convinced, real advantage to us all.

PART III

THE U.S.S.R.

A. STATE AND PARTY

(i) Answers by Marshal Stalin to questions put by a group of American newspaper editors, published on 1 April 1952[1]

Question: Is a third world war nearer at the present time than two or three years ago?
Answer: No, it is not.

Q. Would a meeting between the heads of the great Powers be beneficial?
A. Possibly it would be beneficial.

Q. Do you consider the present moment suitable for the unification of Germany?
A. Yes, I do.

Q. On what basis is the co-existence of capitalism and communism possible?
A. The peaceful co-existence of capitalism and communism is fully possible given the mutual desire to co-operate, readiness to perform obligations which have been assumed, observance of the principle of equality and non-interference in the internal affairs of other States.

(ii) The Nineteenth Congress of the Communist Party

(a) Extract concerning the crisis in world capitalism and the inevitability of war between the capitalist states, taken from an article by Marshal Stalin published in Bolshevik *on 15 September 1952*[2]

Disintegration of the Single World
Market and Deepening of the Crisis
of the World Capitalist System

The disintegration of the single, all-embracing world market must be regarded as the most important economic sequel of the Second World War and of its economic consequences. It has had the effect of further deepening the general crisis of the world capitalist system.

---

[1] *Soviet News*, 2 April 1952.
[2] J. V. Stalin: *Economic Problems of Socialism in the U.S.S.R.* (Moscow, Foreign Languages Publishing House, 1952), pp. 34–41.

The Second World War was itself a product of this crisis. Each of the two capitalist coalitions which locked horns in the war calculated on defeating its adversary and gaining world supremacy. It was in this that they sought a way out of the crisis. The United States of America hoped to put its most dangerous competitors, Germany and Japan, out of action, seize foreign markets and the world's raw material resources, and establish its world supremacy.

But the war did not justify these hopes. It is true that Germany and Japan were put out of action as competitors of the three major capitalist countries: the U.S.A., Great Britain and France. But at the same time China and other, European, people's democracies broke away from the capitalist system and, together with the Soviet Union, formed a united and powerful socialist camp confronting the camp of capitalism. The economic consequence of the existence of two opposite camps was that the single all-embracing world market disintegrated, so that now we have two parallel world markets, also confronting one another.

It should be observed that the U.S.A., and Great Britain and France, themselves contributed—without themselves desiring it, of course—to the formation and consolidation of the new, parallel world market. They imposed an economic blockade on the U.S.S.R., China and the European people's democracies, which did not join the 'Marshall plan' system, thinking thereby to strangle them. The effect, however, was not to strangle, but to strengthen the new world market.

But the fundamental thing, of course, is not the economic blockade, but the fact that since the war these countries have joined together economically and established economic co-operation and mutual assistance. The experience of this co-operation shows that not a single capitalist country could have rendered such effective and technically competent assistance to the People's Democracies as the Soviet Union is rendering them. The point is not only that this assistance is the cheapest possible and technically superb. The chief point is that at the bottom of this co-operation lies a sincere desire to help one another and to promote the economic progress of all. The result is a fast pace of industrial development in these countries. It may be confidently said that, with this pace of industrial development, it will soon come to pass that these countries will not only be in no need of imports from capitalist countries, but will themselves feel the necessity of finding an outside market for their surplus products.

But it follows from this that the sphere of exploitation of this world's resources by the major capitalist countries (U.S.A., Britain, France) will not expand, but contract; that their opportunities for sale in the world market will deteriorate, and that their industries will be operating more and more below capacity. That, in fact, is what is meant by the deepening of the general crisis of the world capitalist system in connection with the disintegration of the world market.

This is felt by the capitalists themselves, for it would be difficult for them not to feel the loss of such markets as the U.S.S.R. and China. They are trying to offset these difficulties with the 'Marshall plan', the war in Korea, frantic rearmament, and industrial militarization. But that is very much like a drowning man clutching at a straw.

This state of affairs has confronted the economists with two questions:

(*a*) Can it be affirmed that the thesis expounded by Stalin before the Second World War regarding the relative stability of markets in the period of the general crisis of capitalism is still valid?

(*b*) Can it be affirmed that the thesis expounded by Lenin in the spring of 1916—namely, that, in spite of the decay of capitalism, 'on the whole, capitalism is growing far more rapidly than before'—is still valid?

I think that it cannot. In view of the new conditions to which the Second World War has given rise, both these theses must be regarded as having lost their validity.

Inevitability of Wars
Between Capitalist Countries

Some comrades hold that, owing to the development of new international conditions since the Second World War, wars between capitalist countries have ceased to be inevitable. They consider that the contradictions between the socialist camp and the capitalist camp are more acute than the contradictions among the capitalist countries; that the U.S.A. has brought the other capitalist countries sufficiently under its sway to be able to prevent them going to war among themselves and weakening one another; that the foremost capitalist minds have been sufficiently taught by the two world wars and the severe damage they caused to the whole capitalist world not to venture to involve the capitalist countries in war with one another again—and that, because of all this, wars between capitalist countries are no longer inevitable.

These comrades are mistaken. They see the outward phenomena that come and go on the surface, but they do not see those profound forces which, although they are so far operating imperceptibly, will nevertheless determine the course of developments.

Outwardly, everything would seem to be 'going well': the U.S.A. has put Western Europe, Japan and other capitalist countries on rations; Germany (Western), Britain, France, Italy and Japan have fallen into the clutches of the U.S.A. and are meekly obeying its commands. But it would be mistaken to think that things can continue to 'go well' for 'all eternity', that these countries will tolerate the domination and oppression of the United States endlessly, that they will not endeavour to tear loose from American bondage and take the path of independent development.

Take, first of all, Britain and France. Undoubtedly, they are imperialist countries. Undoubtedly, cheap raw materials and secure markets are of paramount importance to them. Can it be assumed that they will endlessly tolerate the present situation, in which, under the guise of 'Marshall plan aid', Americans are penetrating into the economies of Britain and France and trying to convert them into adjuncts of the United States economy, and American capital is seizing raw materials and markets in the British and French colonies and thereby plotting disaster for the high profits of the British and French capitalists? Would it not be truer to say that capitalist Britain, and, after her, capitalist France, will be compelled in the end to break from the embrace of the U.S.A. and enter into conflict with it in order to secure an independent position and, of course, high profits?

Let us pass to the major vanquished countries, Germany (Western) and Japan. These countries are now languishing in misery under the jackboot of American imperialism. Their industry and agriculture, their trade, their foreign and home policies, and their whole life are fettered by the American occupation 'regime'. Yet only yesterday these countries were great imperialist powers and were shaking the foundations of the domination of Britain, the U.S.A. and France in Europe and Asia. To think that these countries will not try to get on their feet again, will not try to smash the U.S. 'regime', and force their way to independent development, is to believe in miracles.

It is said that the contradictions between capitalism and socialism are stronger than the contradictions among the capitalist countries. Theoretically, of course, that is true. It is not only true now, today; it was true before the Second World War. And it was more or less realized by the leaders of the capitalist countries. Yet the Second World War began not as a war with the U.S.S.R. but as a war between capitalist countries. Why? Firstly, because war with the U.S.S.R., as a socialist land, is more dangerous to capitalism than war between capitalist countries; for whereas war between capitalist countries puts in question only the supremacy of certain capitalist countries over others, war with the U.S.S.R. must certainly put in question the existence of capitalism itself. Secondly, because the capitalists, although they clamour for 'propaganda' purposes about the aggressiveness of the Soviet Union, do not themselves believe that it is aggressive, because they are aware of the Soviet Union's peaceful policy and know that it will not itself attack capitalist countries.

After the First World War it was similarly believed that Germany had been definitely put out of action, just as certain comrades now believe that Japan and Germany have been definitely put out of action. Then, too, it was said and clamoured in the press that the United States had put Europe on rations; that Germany would never rise to her feet again, and that there would be no more wars between capitalist countries. In spite of this, Germany rose to her feet again as a great power within the space of some fifteen or twenty years after her defeat, having broken out of bondage and taken the path of independent development. And it is significant that it was none other than Britain and the United States that helped Germany to recover economically and to enhance her economic war potential. Of course, when the United States and Britain assisted Germany's economic recovery, they did so with a view to setting a recovered Germany against the Soviet Union, to utilizing her against the land of socialism. But Germany directed her forces in the first place against the Anglo-French-American bloc. And when Hitler Germany declared war on the Soviet Union, the Anglo-French-American bloc, far from joining with Hitler Germany, was compelled to enter into a coalition with the U.S.S.R. against Hitler Germany.

Consequently, the struggle of the capitalist countries for markets and their desire to crush their competitors proved in practice to be stronger than the contradictions between the capitalist camp and the socialist camp.

What guarantee is there, then, that Germany and Japan will not rise to their feet again, will not attempt to break out of American bondage and live their own independent lives? I think there is no such guarantee.

But it follows from this that the inevitability of wars between capitalist countries remains in force.

It is said that Lenin's thesis that imperialism inevitably generates war must now be regarded as obsolete, since powerful popular forces have come forward today in defence of peace and against another world war. That is not true.

The object of the present-day peace movement is to rouse the masses of the people to fight for the preservation of peace and for the prevention of another world war.[1] Consequently, the aim of this movement is not to overthrow capitalism and establish socialism—it confines itself to the democratic aim of preserving peace. In this respect, the present-day peace movement differs from the movement of the time of the First World War for the conversion of the imperialist war into civil war, since the latter movement went farther and pursued socialist aims.

It is possible that in a definite conjuncture of circumstances the fight for peace will develop here or there into a fight for socialism. But then it will no longer be the present-day peace movement; it will be a movement for the overthrow of capitalism.

What is most likely is that the present-day peace movement, as a move-

---

[1] See further below, p. 252.

ment for the preservation of peace, will if it succeeds, result in preventing a *particular* war, in its temporary postponement, in the temporary preservation of a *particular* peace, in the resignation of a bellicose government and its suppression by another that is prepared temporarily to keep the peace. That, of course, will be good. Even very good. But, all the same, it will not be enough to eliminate the inevitability of wars between capitalist countries generally. It will not be enough, because, for all the successes of the peace movement, imperialism will remain, continue in force—and, consequently, the inevitability of wars will also continue in force.

To eliminate the inevitability of war, it is necessary to abolish imperialism.

(*b*) *Extracts from Mr. G. M. Malenkov's report to the Nineteenth Congress of the Communist Party of the Soviet Union, 5 October 1952*[1]

The basic line of the Party in the sphere of foreign policy was and remains a policy of peace among nations and of guaranteeing the security of our socialist motherland.

Since the first days of the existence of the Soviet State the Communist Party has proclaimed, and has pursued in practice, a policy of peace and friendly relations among nations. Throughout the period between the two world wars the Soviet Union persistently upheld the cause of peace and fought in the international arena against the danger of another war; it worked for a policy of collective security and collective rebuff to aggressors. It was no fault of the Soviet Union that the reactionary circles in the United States and the countries of Western Europe frustrated the policy of collective security, encouraged Hitlerite aggression and led to the unleashing of the Second World War.

While unswervingly upholding a policy of peace, our Party, keeping in mind the hostile encirclement, tirelessly strengthened the country's defence in order to meet the enemy fully prepared. . . .

After the Second World War, the Party continued to pursue a foreign policy of ensuring a lasting and stable peace and of promoting international co-operation. The Soviet Government advanced its widely-known programme of measures to avert war.

The peacefulness of the Soviet Union is illustrated not only by its proposals but also by its deeds. After the war the Soviet Union considerably reduced its armed forces, which are now numerically not superior to the forces it had before the war. In the briefest period of time after the war the Soviet Government withdrew its troops from the territory of China, Korea, Norway, Czechoslovakia, Yugoslavia and Bulgaria, whither those troops had been moved in the course of military operations against the

[1] *Soviet News*, 18, 21 and 23 October 1952.

fascist aggressors. The Supreme Soviet of the U.S.S.R., holding that the fight against the man-hating propaganda for another war plays a big role in easing international tension, adopted, on March 12, 1951, the Law in Defence of Peace and proclaimed war propaganda the gravest of crimes against humanity. It thereby set an example for other countries.

During the most serious complications which have arisen in the international arena in recent years, it was the Soviet Union that advanced proposals providing a basis for a peaceful settlement of outstanding questions. It suffices to recall that it was the Soviet side which advanced the proposals that served as the basis for the truce talks in Korea.[1]

The Government of the U.S.S.R. attaches much importance to the United Nations Organisation, holding that it could be an important instrument for maintaining peace. But at present the United States is turning the United Nations from the organ of international co-operation which it should be according to the Charter, into an organ of its dictatorial policy in the struggle against peace, and is using it as a screen for its aggressive actions. However, notwithstanding the tremendous obstacles put in its way by the voting machine which the United States has set up in the United Nations, the Soviet Union upholds peace there and works for the adoption of realistic proposals arising from the present-day international situation; proposals aimed at curbing the aggressive forces, at preventing another war, and at stopping hostilities where they are already in progress.

It would be incorrect to consider that war would be directed only against the Soviet State. The First World War, as we know, was unleashed by the imperialists long before the U.S.S.R. came into being. The Second World War began as a war among capitalist States, and the capitalist countries themselves suffered heavily from it. The contradictions which today rend the imperialist camp may lead to war between one capitalist State and another. Taking all these circumstances into consideration, the Soviet Union is working to prevent any war among States and is acting for a peaceful settlement of international conflicts and disagreements.

However, in pursuing its policy of ensuring lasting peace, the Soviet Union finds itself up against the aggressive policy pursued by the ruling circles of the United States of America.

Moreover, bellicose American circles are endeavouring to put the blame where it does not belong. They are inflating in every possible way their propaganda of lies about a supposed threat on the part of the Soviet Union. As for these lies and inventions about the Soviet Union, it would be ridiculous to go into them, for they completely lack foundation. Indisputable facts show who really is the aggressor.

[1] *Documents* (R.I.I.A.) for 1951, p. 633.

Everybody knows that the United States of America is intensifying its armaments drive, refuses to ban the atomic and germ weapons and to reduce conventional armaments, while the Soviet Union proposes a ban on the atomic and germ weapons and a reduction of other armaments and armed forces.[1]

Everybody knows that the United States refuses to conclude a Peace Pact, while the Soviet Union proposes the conclusion of such a Pact.

Everybody knows that the United States is forming aggressive blocs against the peace-loving peoples, while the exclusive object of the treaties concluded between the Soviet Union and foreign States is to combat revival of Japanese or German aggression.

Everybody knows that the United States attacked Korea and is trying to enslave it, while the Soviet Union has not conducted any hostilities anywhere since the end of the Second World War.

The United States is carrying out aggression also against China. It had seized ancient Chinese territory—the island of Taiwan [Formosa]. Its air force is bombing Chinese territory in violation of all accepted standards of international law. Everybody knows that the air force of the U.S.S.R. is not bombing anybody and that the U.S.S.R. has not seized any foreign territory.

Such are the indisputable facts.

Passing over to our relations with Britain and France, it must be said that these relations ought to be in keeping with the spirit of the treaties we concluded with those countries during the Second World War, and which stipulate co-operation with them in the post-war period. However, the British and French Governments are grossly violating these treaties. Contrary to the solemn pledges of post-war co-operation which they gave to the Soviet Union at the time it was waging a bloody war to liberate the peoples of Europe from German fascist enslavement, the rulers of Britain and France have joined completely in carrying out the American imperialists' aggressive plans against the peace-loving States. It is clear that in view of such a stand taken by the Governments of Britain and France, our relations with these countries leave much to be desired.

The position of the U.S.S.R. as regards the United States, Britain, France and the other bourgeois States is clear, and our side has stated that position on many occasions. Now, as well, the U.S.S.R. is ready for co-operation with these States, having in mind the observance of peaceful international standards and the guaranteeing of a stable and lasting peace. . . .

The Soviet Government considers that Japan should also become an independent, democratic peace-loving State, as envisaged by joint decisions of the Allies. The Soviet Government refused to sign the one-sided

[1] For disarmament proposals see further below, p. 279.

treaty which the American dictators forced upon the San Francisco Conference since that treaty tramples upon the principles of the Cairo and Potsdam declarations and the Yalta Agreement, and is aimed at turning Japan into an American Far Eastern military base. The peoples of the Soviet Union have deep respect for the Japanese people who have to endure the yoke of foreign bondage, and they believe that the Japanese people will achieve national independence for their homeland and take the path of peace.

The Soviet policy of peace and security of the peoples proceeds from the fact that the peaceful co-existence of capitalism and communism and their co-operation are quite possible provided there is mutual desire to co-operate, readiness to adhere to commitments entered into, and observance of the principle of equality and non-interference in the internal affairs of other States.

The Soviet Union has always stood, and stands today, for the development of trade and co-operation with other countries notwithstanding differences in social systems. The Party will pursue this policy, in the future as well, on the basis of mutual advantage.[1]

While bellicose American and British circles keep reiterating that only the armaments drive keeps industry in the capitalist countries going at full capacity, there is in actual fact another prospect: the prospect of developing and extending trade relations between all countries—irrespective of differences in their social systems—which could keep the factories and mills in the industrially developed countries working to capacity for years, that could ensure markets in other countries for the goods in which some countries are rich, promote economic advance in the under-developed countries and thereby establish lasting economic co-operation. . . .

In the period since the XVIII Party Congress, our Soviet State has continued to grow, develop and gain strength.

The economic foundation of our State—socialist ownership of the means of production—has grown and gained in strength. In this period the friendly co-operation of the workers, peasants and intelligentsia, comprising the Soviet socialist society, has become still stronger.

In the face of the greatest difficulties, our social and State system proved, as the experience of the war showed, to be the firmest, the most resilient and stable in the world. The indestructible might of the Soviet socialist system is due to the fact that it is a genuine people's system, created by the people themselves, that it enjoys their powerful support and ensures the progress of all the material and spiritual forces of the people.

The enemies and vulgarisers of Marxism advocated the theory, most

[1] See further below, p. 242.

harmful to our cause, of the weakening and withering away of the Soviet State in conditions of capitalist encirclement. Smashing and rejecting this rotten theory, the Party advanced and substantiated the thesis that in conditions when the socialist revolution has been victorious in one country while capitalism dominates in the majority of others, the country where the revolution has triumphed must not weaken, but must strengthen its State to the utmost, that the State is preserved even under communism should the capitalist encirclement remain. We could not have achieved the successes in our peaceful construction of which we are proud today had we allowed our State to be weakened. We would have found ourselves disarmed in the face of the enemy and in danger of military defeat if we had not strengthened our State, our Army, our punitive and security organs. The Party has made the Soviet land an indestructible fortress of socialism because it strengthened in every way and continues to strengthen the socialist State. . . .

The tasks of the Party in the sphere of internal policy are:

(1) To continue steadfastly to strengthen the economic might of our State, organising and directing the peaceful labour of the Soviet people towards fulfilment and over-fulfilment of the great tasks set forth in the Fifth Five-Year Plan for the development of the U.S.S.R. which constitutes an important stage in the transition from socialism to communism;

(2) To promote the further advance of industry and transport. To introduce more widely into industry, building and transport the latest achievements of science and technique, to increase in every way the productivity of labour, to strengthen discipline in fulfilling State plans, to ensure high quality production. To reduce costs of production steadily, this being the basis for systematic reduction of wholesale and retail prices for all goods;

(3) To bring about a further advance in agriculture in order to create in our country within a short period of time an abundance of foodstuffs for the population and of raw materials for light industry; to ensure the absolute fulfilment of the principal task in agriculture—the utmost increase in yields of all crops and growth in the head of livestock while simultaneously raising its productivity, an increase in gross and marketable production of crop growing and animal husbandry. To improve the work of the machine and tractor stations and State farms. To raise the labour productivity of the collective farmers, further to strengthen the commonly-owned economy of the collective farms, multiply their wealth and on this basis ensure further improvement of the material well-being of the collective farm peasantry;

(4) To effect the strictest regime of economy in all spheres of the national economy and in all branches of administration;

(5) To develop further the advanced Soviet science with the object of

advancing it to first place in world science. To direct the scientists' efforts towards a more rapid solution of scientific problems pertaining to utilisation of the tremendous natural resources of our country, to strengthen the creative co-operation of scientists and industrial workers, remembering that this co-operation enriches science with practical experience, and helps practical workers to solve more rapidly the tasks facing them;

(6) To develop to the utmost the creative initiative of the working people of our country, broaden the socialist emulation movement, work tirelessly for the purpose of multiplying the positive model examples of organisation of labour in a new way in all fields of socialist construction, disseminate these examples of model work persistently among all working people so that the example of the best workers of our society is followed by more and more men and women on the labour front;

(7) To improve further the material well-being of our people; to increase steadily the real wages of factory and office workers, improve housing conditions for the working people; to help in every way to increase the incomes of the peasants. To develop Soviet culture; to improve public education and the health services; to give constant attention to the further development of Soviet literature and the arts;

(8) To strengthen to the utmost our social and State system. To develop further the political activity and patriotism of Soviet people, to strengthen the moral and political unity and friendship of the peoples of our country;

(9) To keep vigilant watch for intrigues of the warmongers. To strengthen in every way the Soviet Army, Navy and security organs. . . .

The strength of our Party lies in its organic ties with the broad masses, in the fact that it is a genuine people's party, whose policy corresponds to the vital interests of the people. Such mass organisations as the Soviet trade unions and the Komsomol are now playing a much bigger role in rallying the working people around the Party and training them in the spirit of communism. The struggle for the liberty and independence of our motherland, for the building of communist society, has brought our Party into even closer kinship with the people and has strengthened its ties with the broad masses of the working people. The Soviet people unanimously support the policy of the Party and place complete confidence in it.

Striking evidence of the closer ties between the Party and the masses, of its growing prestige among the Soviet people, is provided by the growth of Party membership. At the XVIII Congress, the Party had 1,588,852 members and 888,814 probationer members, making a total of 2,477,666. On October 1, 1952, the figure was 6,882,145 of whom 6,013,259 are members and 868,886 probationer members.

During the Great Patriotic War, despite the heavy losses the Party suffered at the battlefronts, its membership, far from declining, actually increased by more than 1,600,000. The Party was joined by the staunchest fighters in the Soviet Army and Navy who displayed bravery in battle, by advanced members of the working class, of the collective farm peasantry and of the Soviet intelligentsia whose self-sacrificing labour in the rear paved the way for victory over the enemy.

After the war, the Central Committee of the Party decided to slow down somewhat the admission of new members, but admission still proceeded at an accelerated pace. The Party could not but notice that this rapid growth in its ranks had certain negative features, which tended to lower somewhat the level of political understanding, with a decline in the general quality of the membership. A certain disparity appeared between the Party's quantitative growth and the level of political training of its members and probationer members. To eliminate this disparity and to improve the qualitative composition of the Party further, the Central Committee decided not to boost the growth of membership, but to concentrate the attention of Party Organisations on raising the political level of members and probationer members. On the instructions of Central Committee, Party organisations began to select new members more carefully, raising the requirements for applicants and undertaking extensive work to promote political training. The result has been an undoubted advance in the political level of Party members in the Marxist-Leninist consciousness of our cadres. However, it cannot be said that the task set by the Party of eliminating the lag in political training, compared with the growth of the Party's ranks, has already been accomplished. That being the case, we must continue the policy of restricting admission and improving the work of political education and the tempering of Party members, for the Party's strength lies not only in the size of its membership, but above all in its quality.

The strengthening of Party bodies, improving their activities and intensifying the work of Party organisations, has acquired special importance in the post-war period.

The new tasks confronting the country in connection with the ending of the war and the transition to peaceful construction, called for a serious improvement in inner-Party work and a higher standard of leadership of State and economic activity by Party organisations. The fact of the matter is that wartime conditions had made necessary certain specific methods of Party leadership and had given rise to serious shortcomings in the work of Party bodies and Party organisations. This found expression, above all, in the fact that Party bodies paid less attention to organisational and ideological work, with the result that in many Party organisations this work was neglected. There was some danger that Party bodies would lose contact with the masses, and that, from being militant organs of political leadership, displaying their own initiative, they would turn into something in the nature of administrative management offices, incapable of countering all kinds of local, narrow departmental and other tendencies against the interests of the State, and failing to observe outright distortions of the party's economic policy and violations of the national interest.

In order to avert this danger and to cope successfully with the work of strengthening local Party bodies and advancing the activities of Party organisations, it was necessary to overcome the neglected state of organisational and ideological work, and to put an end to such practices as introducing administrative methods of leadership into Party organisations, for this led to bureaucracy in Party work and lessened the activity and initiative of the Party membership.

The Central Committee focused the attention of Party organisations on the task of the consistent carrying out of inner-Party democracy and the encouragement of criticism and self-criticism and on this basis of enhancing control by the Party membership over the work of Party bodies. This was the key to heightening the entire work of the Party, to raising the activity and initiative of Party organisations and members. The measures carried out by the Party to develop inner-Party democracy and self-criticism helped its organisations to overcome, to a considerable degree, the defects in Party political work and played an important part in raising this work to a higher level. This led to greater activity and initiative by Party members, strengthened the lower Party organisations in industry, in the collective farms and in offices, invigorated their activities, increased the membership's control over the work of Party bodies and enhanced the part played by plenary meetings of Party committees and by meetings of the Party *active*.

We would, however, be making a mistake if we failed to see that the level of Party political work still lags behind the requirements of the situation and the tasks set by the Party. It must be admitted that there are shortcomings and errors in the work of the Party organisations, that there are still no small number of negative and, not infrequently, of unhealthy practices in the life of our Party organisations, and these must be seen, known and exposed so that they can be eliminated and overcome, and the road cleared for further progress. . . .

Our tasks in the matter of further strengthening the Party are the following:

1. To continue to improve the qualitative composition of the Party, not to permit any drive for numbers but to concentrate on raising the political level and Marxist training of members and probationer members of the Party; to enhance the political activity of the members, make them all staunch fighters for the fulfilment of Party policy and decisions, to be

uncompromising toward shortcomings in work and capable of persistent work for the elimination of these shortcomings; to improve and perfect the work of the trade unions and of the Komsomol, to strengthen ties with the masses day in and day out, remembering that the strength and invincibility of our Party lies in its unbreakable bonds of kinship with the people.

2. To put an end to the self-satisfaction and smugness which are so harmful and dangerous for our cause; to eliminate manifestations of ostentation and complacency in the ranks of the Party; boldly and resolutely to disclose and eliminate shortcomings and weaknesses in our work; consistently to carry out inner-Party democracy, to broaden self-criticism and criticism from below, to ensure to all honest Soviet people the opportunity of criticising shortcomings in the work of our organisations and institutions boldly and fearlessly; to wage relentless struggle against all attempts at suppressing criticism, against persecution and reprisals for criticism; to strengthen in every way Party and State discipline; to eradicate the formal approach to decisions of the Party and the Government; to wage resolute struggle against lack of discipline, against violation of the interests of the State;

3. To raise to a higher plane the work of Party organs as regards correct selection, allocation and training of cadres; strictly to observe the principles laid down by the Party for the correct selection of cadres, to wage irreconcilable struggle against those who violate these principles; to fight relentlessly any bureaucratic approach to the choice of cadres; to improve the qualitative composition of leading cadres; to promote more boldly to leading posts people devoted to the interests of the Party and the State, who know their work well and are able to advance it further; to remove incapable, unsuitable, backward and unconscientious workers; to strengthen in every way control and checking up on the fulfilment of decisions throughout the entire chain of leadership, from top to bottom; to increase the personal responsibility of the heads of all organisations and institutions for checking up on the fulfilment of the decisions of the Party and the Government; to combine such verification from above with verification from below on the part of the Party and non-Party masses; to ensure that the correct selection of people and verification of fulfilment of decisions really become the main elements in the leadership exercised by the central and local Party, Soviet and economic organisations;

4. To put an end to underestimation of ideological work, to wage resolute struggle against liberalism and heedlessness with regard to ideological mistakes and distortions; systematically to improve and perfect the ideological and political training of our cadres; to direct all means of ideological influence, our propaganda, agitation and the Press, towards the communist education of the Soviet people; to raise Soviet science to a still

higher level, promoting criticism and the battle of opinions in scientific work, and remembering that only in this way can Soviet science fulfil its mission of occupying first place in world science;

5. To continue to guard as the apple of its eye the Leninist unity of the Party's ranks, which is the foundation of the strength and invincibility of our Party.

(c) *Speech by Marshal Stalin in reply to the greetings of foreign delegates to the Nineteenth Congress, 15 October 1952*[1]

Comrades! Permit me to express the thanks of our Congress to all the fraternal parties and groups, representatives of which have honoured our Congress by their presence or which have sent greetings to the Congress— thanks for their friendly greetings, for their wishes of success, for their trust.

To us this trust is especially valuable. It denotes the readiness to support our party in its struggle for the bright future of the peoples, in its struggle against war, in its struggle to safeguard peace. It would be erroneous to think that our party, which has become a mighty force, does not need support any more. This is not true. Our party and the country always needed and will need the trust, sympathy, and support of fraternal peoples abroad. The peculiarity of this support lies in the fact that every kind of support for the peaceful strivings of our party on the part of any fraternal party signifies, at the same time, the support of its own people in the struggle for the preservation of peace.

When British workers, in 1918–19, during the armed attack by the British bourgeoisie on the Soviet Union, organized a struggle against the war under the slogan 'Hands off Russia', this was a support, primarily of their own people for peace and, furthermore, also a support of the Soviet Union. When Comrade Thorez[2] and Comrade Togliatti[3] declare that their people will not fight against the Soviet Union, we recognize in such statements, in the first place, the support of the workers and peasants of France and Italy for peace and the support of the peace-loving efforts of the Soviet Union. Such mutual assistance is explained by the fact that the interests of our party, far from being opposed to the interests of peace-loving peoples, merge with them.

As regards the Soviet Union, its interests are generally indivisible from the cause of peace the world over. Our party cannot remain indebted to fraternal parties and it must, in its turn, render support both to them and to their peoples in their struggle for liberation, for the preservation of peace. After our party had come to power in 1917, and after the party had undertaken real measures for the liquidation of the capitalist and landowners'

---

[1] *Manchester Guardian*, 16 October 1952.
[2] Secretary-General of the French Communist Party.
[3] Secretary-General of the Italian Communist Party.

oppression, the representatives of fraternal parties, admiring the courage and successes of our party, had given it the name of 'shock brigade of the world revolutionary and workers' movement'. This name was a symbol of hope to other fraternal parties which expected that the successes of our party would make their tasks easier.

We did what was expected by our friends. This was noticeable especially during the Second World War when the Soviet Union crushed the German and Japanese Fascist tyrannies and liberated several peoples of Europe and Asia from Fascist slavery. Our task was difficult because the shock brigade was alone. Now all that belongs to the past. From China and Korea to Czechoslovakia and Hungary there spreads a chain of new shock brigades.

Careful attention must be paid to the situation of those workers' and peasants' parties which are still suffering under the heel of the cruel bourgeois law. Their task is difficult but not as difficult as was ours in the period of Tsardom, when every move on the people's side had been considered a crime. Russian Communists were not afraid of difficulties and they have become victorious at the end. The same lot awaits other Communist parties.

The bourgeoisie is now different from what it was. It has considerably changed; it has become more reactionary and has lost its ties with the people, thereby weakening itself. It is clear that such circumstances must necessarily facilitate the work of revolutionary and democratic parties. Once upon a time the bourgeoisie could afford to be liberal and to defend the bourgeois democratic freedoms, and thus it could build for itself popularity among the people.

Now there are no more traces of liberalism. There is no longer any so-called freedom of the individual. Personal rights are now recognized only for those who possess capital, while all other citizens are regarded as human raw material fit only for exploitation. The principle of equality of men and nations has also been discarded. It has been replaced by the principle of the exploitation of the majority who have no rights by the minority who have them all.

The banner of bourgeois democratic freedoms has been thrown overboard. I believe that it devolves on you—the representatives of Communist and democratic parties—to raise that banner and carry it forward if you wish to rally around you the majority of the people. There is no one else to raise it.

In the past the bourgeoisie was regarded as the head of the nations. It was defending the rights and independence of nations, placing these above everything else. Now no trace is left of the national principle. Today the bourgeoisie sells out its rights and independence, and national sovereignty has been thrown overboard. There is no doubt that this banner must be raised by you—the representatives of Communist and democratic parties —and carried forward if you wish to be true patriots of your countries, if you wish to become the leading force of nations. There is no one else to raise that banner.

Such is the situation at present. It is understandable that all these circumstances are bound to facilitate the work of Communist and democratic parties which have not yet been in power. Consequently there is every reason to count on the successes and victory of fraternal parties in countries under the domination of capital.

Long live our fraternal parties. . . . Long life and success to the leaders of the fraternal parties. . . . Long live peace among nations. . . . Down with the warmongers.

(iii) ANSWERS BY MARSHAL STALIN TO QUESTIONS PUT BY AN AMERICAN JOURNALIST, PUBLISHED ON 25 DECEMBER 1952[1]

Question. At the arrival of the New Year and at the beginning of the new administration in the United States, is it still your conviction that the Union of Soviet Socialist Republics and the United States can live peacefully in the coming years?

Answer. I still believe that war between the United States of America and the Soviet Union cannot be considered inevitable, and that our countries can continue to live in peace.

Question. Wherein lie the sources of the present international tension in your judgment?

Answer. Everywhere and in everything wherever the aggressive actions of the policy of the 'cold war' against the Soviet Union find their expression.

Question. Would you welcome diplomatic conversations with representatives of the new Eisenhower administration, looking towards the possibility of a meeting between yourself and General Eisenhower on easing world tensions?

Answer. I regard such a suggestion favourably.

Question. Would you co-operate in any new diplomatic approach designed to bring about an end to the Korean war?

Answer. I agree to co-operate, because the U.S.S.R. is interested in ending the war in Korea.

[1] *Soviet News,* 30 December 1952.

(iv) ANNOUNCEMENT BY *TASS* OF THE ARREST OF NINE RUSSIAN DOCTORS ON CHARGES OF THE MURDER AND ATTEMPTED MURDER OF RUSSIAN LEADERS, 13 JANUARY 1953[1]

Some time ago the State security organs uncovered a terrorist group of doctors, who had set themselves the task of shortening the life of Soviet leaders by means of harmful treatment.

Among the members of this terrorist group were: Professor M. S. Vovsi, therapeutist; Professor V. N. Vinogradov, therapeutist; Professor M. B. Kogan, therapeutist; Professor B. B. Kogan, therapeutist; Professor P. I. Yegorov, therapeutist; Professor A. I. Feldman, otolaryngologist; Professor Y. G. Etinger, therapeutist; Professor A. M. Grinshtein, neuropathologist; G. I. Mayorov, therapeutist.

The documents, investigations, the opinion of medical experts and the confessions of those arrested prove that the criminals, secret enemies of the people, subjected their patients to harmful treatment and undermined their health.

As a result of investigation it was established that the members of the terrorist group, utilising their positions as doctors and abusing the trust of their patients, deliberately and villainously undermined their health; purposely ignored the results of objective examinations of the patients; made incorrect diagnoses which did not correspond to the actual nature of the illnesses; and then killed them by means of incorrect treatment.

The criminals confessed that, having availed themselves of Comrade A. A. Zhdanov's illness, they made an incorrect diagnosis of his disease and, concealing the myocardial infarction from which he suffered, prescribed a regimen which was contra-indicated for this serious illness, and thereby killed Comrade A. A. Zhdanov. It has been established through investigation that the criminals also shortened the life of Comrade A. S. Shcherbakov, by incorrectly applying powerful drugs for his treatment introducing a detrimental regimen and thus causing his death.

The criminal doctors tried first of all to undermine the health of leading Soviet military cadres, to disable them and to weaken the defence of the country. They tried to disable Marshal A. M. Vasilevsky, Marshal L. A. Govorov, Marshal I. S. Koniev, Army General S. M. Shtemenko, Admiral G. I. Levchenko and others but arrest thwarted their villainous plans and the criminals failed to achieve their end.

It has been established that all these doctors—murderers who became fiends in human form, trampled underfoot the sacred banner of science and desecrated the honour of scientists—were paid agents of a foreign intelligence service.

Most of the participants in the terrorist group (M. S. Vovsi, B. B. Kogan,

[1] Ibid., 22 January 1953.

A. I. Feldman, A. M. Grinshtein, Y. G. Etinger and others) were connected with 'Joint',[1] an international Jewish bourgeois nationalist organisation, set up by the U.S. intelligence service, allegedly to render material aid to Jews in other countries. Actually, however, this organisation, under the guidance of the U.S. intelligence service, conducts large-scale espionage, terrorist and other subversive activities in a number of countries, including the Soviet Union. The arrested Vovsi stated during the interrogation that he had received a directive from the United States 'to exterminate the leading cadres of the U.S.S.R.' from the 'Joint' organisation through a Moscow doctor Shimelyovich and the well-known Jewish bourgeois nationalist, Mikhoels.[2]

Other members of the terrorist group (V. N. Vinogradov, M. B. Kogan, P. I. Yegorov) proved to be agents of the British intelligence service of long standing.

Investigation will be completed in the very near future.

B. THE MOSCOW ECONOMIC CONFERENCE

(i) Statement issued by the Preparatory Commission of the International Economic Conference in Moscow, published on 15 February 1952[3]

The Preparatory Commission of the International Sponsoring Committee for the convocation of the International Economic Conference in Moscow from April 3 to 10, 1952, met in Copenhagen from February 10 to 12.

The Commission noted with satisfaction that the initiative taken in convening the conference has been received with great interest in many countries among commercial and industrial circles, trade unions, scientific and civic leaders and organisations.

The International Sponsoring Committee, set up in Copenhagen on October 27 and 28, 1951, is the sole body responsible for preparing the International Economic Conference.

The Conference is not convened by Government bodies. Industrialists, businessmen, farmers, economists, engineers and trade union and co-operative leaders will take part in it.

The Preparatory Commission recalls the statement made by the Sponsoring Committee which met in Copenhagen on October 27 and 28, 1951, to the effect that the conference is of an economic character and aims to promote co-operation among countries irrespective of the difference in

---

[1] The Jewish Joint Distribution Committee, an American charitable organization.
[2] Solomon Mikhoels, Director of the Jewish Theatre in Moscow until his death in 1948.
[3] *Soviet News*, 20 February 1952.

their economic systems by bringing to light possibilities for expanding trade and economic relations among countries and on this basis to improve people's living conditions.

The agenda of the Conference is as follows:

'To find ways to improve people's living conditions through peaceful co-operation among different countries and various systems, through the development of economic relations among all countries.'

The Conference will discuss the present-day situation in international trade and will assist in removing existing difficulties in this sphere, in finding ways and means for the expansion of international trade relations and the alleviation of the economic difficulties experienced by many countries of late.

The Conference will consider how the development of normal trade relations among countries and an increase in foreign trade can facilitate the expansion of national production, increase employment of the population and reduce the high cost of living.

The Conference will examine in particular the possibilities for expanding trade between East and West and between economically developed and under-developed countries, as well as any other proposals which may be submitted by the conference participants in conformity with the agenda.

The Commission has taken note of the suggestions received from representatives of national Preparatory Committees of certain countries concerning the inexpediency of presenting special reports at the Conference from groups of countries, as was contemplated earlier. It seems more expedient to discuss the question on the conference agenda on the basis of the speeches of all the participants in the Conference who wish to speak, and not on the basis of one or several reports from groups of countries.

In order to enable a greater number of participants to state their points of view and to discuss more concretely the problems of interest to them, it is planned to organise, in addition to plenary meetings, panels on separate problems, for example: development of international trade, assistance in the development of trade with economically under-developed countries, international economic co-operation with the object of solving social problems, etc.

Assistance is envisaged in the establishment of business ties among representatives of commercial and industrial circles of the various countries.

The Conference will provide an opportunity for the broad and free exchange of opinions and will not take any decisions binding upon its participants, but will limit itself to the adoption of recommendations.

The Preparatory Commission invites all circles concerned to take part in the Conference. The representatives of industrialists, businessmen and farmers, chambers of commerce, industrial associations, financiers and co-operative associations are invited to the Conference.

Invitations are also being sent to economic agencies of the United Nations.

The Conference will be attended by representatives of trade unions irrespective of their trends, and by scientists, economists, and scientific and civic leaders. Thus a place at the Conference is ensured for all persons desiring, irrespective of their political views and convictions, to promote trade and other economic relations among countries.

The Commission recalls the statement made by the Soviet Preparatory Committee that during their stay on the territory of the U.S.S.R., those taking part in the Conference will be accorded the necessary assistance and hospitality and, should they so desire, will have the opportunity to establish contact with representatives of Soviet trade, industrial and co-operative organisations.

(ii) EXTRACTS FROM A SPEECH TO THE INTERNATIONAL ECONOMIC CONFERENCE BY THE RUSSIAN DELEGATE, MR. MIKHAIL NESTEROV, 5 APRIL 1952[1]

As President of the U.S.S.R. Chamber of Commerce, the chief task of which is that of facilitating the development of foreign trade, I am happy today to tell this esteemed gathering that the move to convene the International Economic Conference met with favour among Soviet trade and industrial representatives. Since a desire to extend trade with the Soviet Union has been revealed by certain trading circles in a number of countries, it can be stated definitely that there are suitable opportunities for this.

The fact, known to all present here, that the lead for the convening of the present Conference was so actively supported in many countries is an indication that the extension of economic co-operation and trade ties among the countries is a pressing, vital need; and an indication that the weakening of these ties in recent years and the creation of artificial difficulties in this field are causing no little disquiet.

While, in the period immediately following the end of the Second World War, international trade was successfully restored and developed, over the past three or four years the conditions for its development have deteriorated sharply, and trade is falling into a state of increasing dislocation.

The deterioration in international economic relations is resulting in the restriction of civilian production, and has a harmful effect on the conditions of life of the peoples of many countries. A reduction has occurred in the sales of many commodities important for the development of the civilian economy and for the satisfaction of the needs of the population, particularly since the switch to a war economy began in a number of countries. Gathered here are people who are well aware of facts of this kind. We cannot shut our eyes to these facts.

[1] *Soviet News*, 16 April 1952.

The dislocation of world economic relations also has a harmful effect on the position of the economically under-developed countries. The necessary delivery of equipment to these countries are lacking, and this delays the development of their national economy. The stringent foreign control which operates in practice over the raw material resources of the economically under-developed countries is an obstacle to their mutually advantageous trade with other countries.

The restoration and extension of normal trade and other economic relations among the countries could help to improve the state of affairs in many countries, could help to raise the living standards of the people.

Our country, for her part, could make her contribution to the extension of normal economic relations and thereby help to strengthen international co-operation. Soviet trading organisations will not refuse to extend relations with the trade and industrial circles of other countries if these relations are based on mutual advantage and scrupulous fulfilment by all parties of the obligations they assume. As for the Soviet Union, it is common knowledge that Soviet trading organisations always scrupulously observe any obligations they assume.

In speaking of the favourable attitude of Soviet trading organisations to the development of international trade, I consider it necessary to emphasise that our trading organisations have no intention of squeezing anyone out of world markets, or of obtaining any privileges for themselves. They proceed from the fact that, in normal conditions, foreign trade is advantageous for all the countries taking part in it, making possible the more productive use of those economic opportunities which are created by an international division of labour. World trade, in this way, can serve as an additional factor in the economic development of the countries which take part in it. In this, clearly, differences in economic systems cannot constitute obstacles to the development of co-operation among the countries.

The development of the Soviet Union's national economy is based on a constantly expanding home market and the steady increase in the purchasing capacity of its population. Because of the variety and richness of her natural resources, and the development of industry and agriculture achieved during the years of Soviet power, the U.S.S.R. possesses everything necessary for her economic development and for extending trade with other countries.

There is no need to prove that our country is in favour of developing international economic ties and that in the post-war years she has greatly extended her trade with the outside world—although for reasons beyond our control trade with certain Western countries has fallen off, and in some instances even has completely stopped.

The Soviet Union's foreign trade turnover, according to the Customs authorities' figures, at the present time exceeds 18,000 million roubles a year; moreover, the present volume of trade in comparable prices is approximately three times the pre-war level. . . .

The U.S.S.R. Chamber of Commerce has carried out a survey to ascertain the possibilities of increasing trade between Soviet economic organisations and the countries of Western Europe, the Americas, South-East Asia, the Middle East, Africa and Australia.

Provided the business circles of other States have serious intentions of expanding trade with the Soviet foreign trade organisations, then the Soviet foreign trade organisations express their readiness to increase substantially the volume of export–import operations with those countries.

The Chamber of Commerce has collected the necessary information to show definitely what could be accomplished in this respect.

Soviet foreign trade organisations would be able to buy from the countries of Western Europe, the Americas, South-East Asia, the Middle East, Africa and Australia their usual exports; and would be able to sell to those countries the Soviet-produced goods in which they were interested, in quantities by which the total trade of the U.S.S.R. with those countries over the next two or three years would amount to 30,000–40,000 million roubles, or from 10,000 to 15,000 million roubles a year, compared with the maximum post-war turnover, reached in 1948, of approximately 5,000 million roubles.

This indicated increase in trade between the U.S.S.R. and the countries of Western Europe, the Americas, South-East Asia, the Middle East, Africa and Australia is not the limit, if it be borne in mind that in 1931, for instance, the Soviet Union's trade turnover with these countries, in present-day prices, amounted to approximately 11,000 million roubles, and that at the present time the Soviet Union's possibilities, both as exporter and importer, are incomparably greater.

The aforementioned programme for developing trade signifies that, as a whole, the annual foreign trade turnover of the Soviet Union could increase by half within the next two or three years alone, or could even be doubled compared with the present trade turnover—which, as has already been stated, amounts to 18,000 million roubles a year. Of course, Soviet trade organisations would also examine with interest any proposal which covered a longer period of time.

Increased employment would be one important result of the extension in trade. The aforementioned expansion of trade between the Soviet Union and other countries would result in increased employment for about $1\frac{1}{2}$ to two million persons in countries which expanded their trade with the U.S.S.R. Both large-scale Soviet purchases in the Western European countries, and, at the same time, these countries' greatly increased imports of raw materials and semi-manufactures from the Soviet Union would be of considerable importance for increasing employment in their industries.

In this period, Soviet foreign trading organisations could buy consumer goods, mainly from West European firms. Along with this also would be purchases of raw materials, metals and other materials, including raw materials for the production of consumer goods, first and foremost in the countries of South-East Asia, the Near and Middle East. These purchases could reach a total sum of 8,000–12,000 million roubles. In contrast to previous years, Soviet foreign trade organisations would be able, provided the conditions were suitable, to make, in particular, large purchases of textile, leather, food and other consumer goods; and, moreover, in increasing amounts.

It also appears from information received from the foreign trade organisations that orders for machinery and equipment, merchant ships and fishing vessels could in the next two or three years amount to 7,000–10,000 million roubles. The engineering and metal industries and a whole number of other industries of Britain, Belgium, France, Italy, Western Germany, the United States and other countries would acquire a stable market and far wider possibilities than at present for the sale of their products.

Provided appropriate conditions existed to make world trade normal, Soviet foreign trade organisations, for their part, would be able at the same time to increase sales of grain, timber, pulp and paper, metal ores, fertilisers, coal oil products, flax, various kinds of industrial equipment, agricultural machinery, means of transport, and also products of light industry, to the countries which need these goods. In particular, Soviet foreign trade organisations could, in the next two or three years, supply machinery and equipment to the value of up to 3,000 million roubles to the countries of South-East Asia, the Near and Middle East. . . .

Representatives of both West and East who are at present in Moscow should by now have learned the addresses of the Soviet firms in which they are interested. At all events, circumstances favour the making of new acquaintanceships in Moscow between persons interested in trade and the conclusion of new trade transactions.

The terms of settlement used in the practice of Soviet trade organisations, if one refers to the facts which are commonly known, are not merely no worse than those in other countries but are more flexible. As has been proved in practice, Soviet foreign trade organisations can, in many instances, without great difficulty, reach agreement on terms of settlement with foreign firms on a mutually acceptable and advantageous basis.

Soviet trade organisations express their readiness to conclude barter transactions. They could also carry out sales of goods in the national currencies, using the proceeds in the same countries. Taking into account the currency difficulties in many countries, barter transactions and sales of goods for local currency could greatly promote the expansion of trade.

Our trade organisations could effect settlements for transactions through the national banks, without having recourse to the agency of foreign banks, which would increase the turnovers of the local banks and their interest in foreign trade operations.

For most West European countries the problem of balancing their accounts with countries in the dollar zone is particularly acute. This problem would not be so acute if the countries of Western Europe, besides trading with America, were to restore and develop trade with the countries of Eastern Europe on the basis of mutual supplies of goods. Yet trade between these countries and the countries of Eastern Europe is now practically down to a mere third of the pre-war volume.

In conclusion, permit me to observe once more that in order to restore and expand international economic relations it is necessary first of all to renounce all forms of discrimination in international trade. I do not have to enlarge about such intolerable things as the United States' declaration of a trade blockade against China, which is a senseless manifestation of an aggressive policy.[1]

The serious dislocation of world trade caused by the armaments drive and the policy of discrimination applied by the ruling circles of certain countries, leads inevitably to the deterioration of the economic position and the lowering of the living standards of the population in many countries, it has a harmful effect on the economy of under-developed countries and threatens a further worsening of economic difficulties.

That is why we must raise here the question which millions of ordinary people are now asking every day: What is being done to lessen existing difficulties in economic relations between the countries?

The possibility of lessening these difficulties is to be found through restoring and expanding trade and economic ties between the countries, with a corresponding restoration and expansion of the civilian branches of industry which have recently been cut.

The development of world trade would be furthered by the conclusion of trade agreements among the countries, including multilateral and long-term agreements, for the purpose of increasing the trade in food, timber, coal, fertilisers, metals, machinery, textile and other products.

The expansion of world trade would also be furthered by the conclusion of agreements with under-developed countries to supply them with industrial equipment and the materials they require in exchange for raw materials and other goods they produce. Such agreements, based on principles of mutual advantage, observance of respect for national sovereignty and non-interference in the internal affairs of economically backward countries, would have a good effect on the development of national economies and on the raising of the living standards of the populations of those countries.

[1] *Documents* (R.I.I.A.) for 1951, pp. 560–72.

This Conference must help to extend world trade. Many millions of people are interested in this. The trade policy of our country meets these aspirations. This is only natural. Our trade policy corresponds to the essence of the Soviet State. In this connection, I should like to recall the following words pronounced by J. V. Stalin, the head of the Soviet Government: 'Those who want peace and seek business relations with us will always have our support.'

The carrying out of a programme of expanding trade relations between the Soviet Union and other countries, together with a general increase in world trade turnover will be an important contribution to the cause of international co-operation and will help to ease economic difficulties, to create the conditions for improving the living standards of people, to improve relations among the States, and thereby lead to greater stability in international relations.

(iii) COMMUNIQUÉ ISSUED AT THE END OF THE INTERNATIONAL ECONOMIC CONFERENCE, MOSCOW, 12 APRIL 1952[1]

An International Economic Conference was held in Moscow from April 3 to 12, consisting of industrialists, businessmen, economists, trade union and co-operative leaders, which discussed 'the possibilities of improving the living conditions of the peoples, through the peaceful co-operation of the various countries and different systems, through the development of economic ties'.

The Conference was attended by 471 persons from 49 countries, namely: Australia, Austria, Albania, Argentina, Belgium, Burma, Bulgaria, Brazil, Great Britain, Hungary, Venezuela, Viet Nam, the German Democratic Republic, the Netherlands, Greece, Denmark, Egypt, Western Germany, Israel, India, Indonesia, Iran, Iceland, Italy, Canada, the Chinese People's Republic, Cyprus, the Korean People's Democratic Republic, Cuba, Lebanon, Luxembourg, Mexico, the Mongolian People's Republic, Norway, Pakistan, Paraguay, Poland, Rumania, the United States of America, the Union of Soviet Socialist Republics, Uruguay, Finland, France, Ceylon, Czechoslovakia, Chile, Switzerland, Sweden, Japan.

The Conference thoroughly examined the present state of world trade, and established that the deterioration in international relations, which has been particularly intensified in recent years, has increased the artificial obstacles standing in the way of trade among the countries. Traditional trading ties among countries have been interrupted, geographical spheres of trade have been restricted and there has been a sharp break in trade between the West and the East.

---

[1] *Soviet News*, 18 April 1952.

The dislocation of world trade is doing serious damage to the development of the economies of a number of countries, interrupts the equilibrium of trade and payment balances and has a detrimental effect on the living standards of people, giving rise to a worsened food situation, increased prices, mounting unemployment, and hampers the carrying out of social measures, particularly housing construction.

As a result of a wide and free exchange of opinion, the Conference has unanimously established that the volume of world trade can be increased considerably, and that the expansion of trading ties among the countries would be advantageous to industrialists, traders, and farmers. It would lead to a better use of the economic resources of all the countries and would mean increased employment and improved living standards for the broad masses of the population.

Statements by participants in the Conference who have come from various countries make it possible to record that the differences of economic and social systems do not constitute an obstacle to extending world economic ties, based on equality and mutual advantage.

At the Conference, great and concrete opportunities were revealed for expanding trade between the countries of Western Europe, the United States, Canada, the countries of Latin America, Asia, Africa, the Soviet Union, the Chinese People's Republic and the countries of Eastern and Central Europe.

The work of the Conference has demonstrated that economic progress in the under-developed countries and the supply of machines and industrial equipment to them, as well as mutually advantageous correlation of the prices of raw materials they export and the goods they import, are of vital importance for the development of international trade and peaceful economic co-operation.

The Conference considers that the rapid industrialisation of the under-developed countries, and international co-operation for this purpose, are very necessary, and this should be given every assistance.

The participants in the Conference made proposals for increasing the volume of foreign trade and named the lines they could buy and sell on mutually advantageous terms. A number of concrete proposals were made with the aim of facilitating the conditions of world trade and, in particular, concluding trade transactions in the national currencies.

During the period of work of the Conference, the representatives of business circles of various countries were given the opportunity of establishing personal contact, discussing on a broad basis questions of interest to them and of conducting commercial talks. As a result of the talks a large number of transactions have been concluded between firms of various countries represented at the Conference. The commercial talks started at the Conference are continuing, showing that there is a great desire among the business leaders to take advantage of every opportunity to expand foreign trade.

In these circumstances, the Governments, and also the United Nations Organisation, should take appropriate action. In this connection the participants in the Conference have decided to propose to the United Nations General Assembly that it call in the near future an inter-governmental conference on questions of world trade, with the participation of representatives of business circles, trade unions and other public organisations.

The Conference revealed the unanimous desire of all taking part to continue and develop the work they had begun for the expansion of world trade. In particular, it was considered desirable to hold another International Economic Conference based on the self-same principle of economic co-operation among the countries, irrespective of their economic and social systems, which guided the International Economic Conference in Moscow. It was also resolved to continue the exchange of information with regard to export and import possibilities in the various countries.

To carry out these proposals the Conference elected a committee to promote the development of world trade. The Committee consists of the following persons: Antoine Allard (Belgium), Paul Bastid (France), Oliver Vickery (U.S.A.), Victor Manuel Gutierrez (Guatemala), Josef Dobretsberger (Austria), Imre Degen (Hungary), Hosein Daryush (Iran), Henri Jourdan (W.F.T.U.), Main M. Iftikharuddin (Pakistan), Greta Kuckhoff (German Democratic Republic), Hirachand Lalchand (India), Oscar Lange (Poland), Pierre Lebrun (France), Lu Ning-i (W.F.T.U.), D. P. Mukerjee (India), Nan Han-chen (Chinese People's Republic), M. V. Nesterov (U.S.S.R.), Antonio Pesenti (Italy), Jack Perry (Britain), Otakar Phol (Czechoslovakia), Joan Robinson (Britain), Otto Rocha e Silva (Brazil), Sergio Steve (Italy), Suchjar Tedjasukmana (Indonesia), Felipe Freire Florencio (Argentina), Karl Wilhelm de Vries (Netherlands), I. S. Khokhlov (U.S.S.R.), Edmund von Henke (U.S.A.), Tsi Chao-tin (Chinese People's Republic), Robert Chambeiron (France).

The Conference participants appeal to business people of all countries and to scientific and technical workers, to the trade unions and co-operatives, irrespective of their views, to support the move to develop trade relations among the countries and to remove the obstacles standing in the way of such relations.

The Conference expresses the conviction that the development of world trade under mutually advantageous conditions, on the basis of equality and with due consideration for the requirements of industrialisation of the under-developed countries, will serve the cause of strengthening economic co-operation among the nations, and improving the living conditions of people.

Adopted at the plenary meeting of the International Economic Conference in Moscow, April 12, 1952.

C. THE WORLD PEACE MOVEMENT

(i) Resolution on Germany adopted by the World Peace Council at its meeting in Berlin, 1–6 July 1952[1]

Appeal to the Governments of the four great Powers and to all Peoples

Seven years after the crushing of the Hitlerite regime the Peace Treaty with Germany has still not been concluded.

The World Peace Council, interpreting the aspirations of millions of men and women throughout the world, addresses itself to the Governments of the four great Powers, the U.S.A., France, Great Britain, the U.S.S.R., which, by the Potsdam agreements, assumed a special responsibility for the peaceful solution of the German problem.

It says to them that the time has come to assume their responsibility fully and collectively.

In fundamental contradiction to such a duty, the separate agreements concluded in Bonn and Paris on May 26 and 27[2] aim at a one-sided settlement. The agreements carry within themselves the rebirth of militarism and of fascism, deepen the division of Germany and of Europe, and are an obstacle to all practical efforts to promote general disarmament.

The peoples know well that apart from a negotiated solution with the firm determination to succeed, there is the danger of no other outcome but war.

The World Council considers the best solution to be the immediate convening of a four-Power conference, the object of which will be to take all decisions with a view to the peaceful solution of the German problem.

It considers, as the best solution, that the German people themselves, through free elections, achieve their unity and give themselves the Government which will conclude a peace treaty with all the States against which Hitlerite Germany made war.

This treaty will have to recognise the right to sovereignty of a unified, democratic, independent and peaceful Germany.

This treaty, in which Germany will agree not to enter into any military coalition, will fix the methods and times of evacuation of the foreign armies of occupation. It will thus help restore to the nations of Europe the choice of their destiny in security, co-operation and respect for their independence.

The World Peace Council, at the same time as it calls upon the Governments of the four great Powers, also calls on the peoples of all countries.

It salutes the great movement of public opinion and the different actions which are developing, unhindered by frontiers and beyond divergencies

---

[1] *Soviet News*, 19 July 1952.   [2] See above, pp. 105–70.

of ideas or beliefs, against the danger which the ratification and carrying out of the Bonn and Paris agreements will involve.

It salutes through its support those vigilant and courageous men and women who in all countries, and especially in Germany, are demonstrating their determination to join forces against this peril and demand an explanation of the members of their Governments, leaders or members of Parliament who bear the responsibility of supporting the realisation of these agreements.

The World Peace Council solemnly declares that the co-operation of all men of good will is indispensable to the development of effective action without delay.

It calls upon the trade unions, political parties, organisations and churches, particularly upon those of Germany, Great Britain, France, Italy, the Scandinavian countries and all the nations neighbouring on Germany. It appeals to the rising generation whose future would be ruined for ever by war. It appeals to all those who are conscious of the threat which is hanging over the homes of the world, to all those who believe that disaster is not inevitable, and that the gravity of the hour demands the greatest confidence in the capacity of the peoples to listen to one another and to find a common path of action.

With all their assembled strength the peoples can, in the months facing us, prevent the ratification of the separate agreements, impose the holding of a meeting of the four Powers and make it reach a peaceful solution that corresponds to their own security as well as to the national interests of the German people.

(ii) Resolution on Japan adopted by the World Peace Council at its meeting in Berlin, 1–6 July 1952[1]

The San Francisco Treaty, which was signed under pressure of the United States, and the Japanese-American Security Treaty have provoked, only two months after their being declared effective (April 28, 1952), the strong opposition of the Japanese people who consider that these acts have been forced on them in violation of their vital interests and their desire for peaceful development.

Millions of people throughout the world support the Japanese people in their opposition to these Treaties and the Administrative Agreement following them, because they constitute a danger to the peace, not only of the Japanese people and the people of Asia and of the Pacific, but also those in the rest of the world.

Events have confirmed the view expressed in the resolution of the World Peace Council passed at its Vienna meeting, November 1 to 6, 1951. The

[1] *Soviet News*, July 19, 1952.

rapid expansion of Japanese rearmament, the maintenance of U.S. occupation troops and of numerous war bases on Japanese territory, the signing of a so-called peace treaty with the puppet regime of Chiang Kai-shek accompanied by the American support of aggressive groups in other parts of Asia, can only point to Japan as a base for aggression.

Faced with this threat of the extension of the war in Asia, the World Peace Council is of the opinion that:

the San Francisco Treaty and the dependent agreements are not valid because of their disregard of international agreements, and must be replaced by a genuine treaty, signed by all interested States.

That treaty should provide:

(a) for the withdrawal of all occupation troops and prohibit the establishment of foreign military bases in Japan;

(b) for the full sovereignty of the Japanese people and the necessity for their democratic and peaceful development.

The World Peace Council salutes the heroic struggle of the Japanese people for peace, independence and democracy against the forces of militarism and war, and appeals to all other peoples of Asia and the Pacific to give them the maximum support in this struggle, thereby helping to ensure their own peaceful and democratic development. It further appeals to peace-loving peoples in all countries whose Governments signed the San Francisco Treaty to struggle for its replacement by a genuine peace treaty.

Towards this end, the World Peace Council calls on the peoples of Asia and the Pacific to make the greatest effort to mobilise the forces of peace and democracy at the Asian and Pacific Peace Conference to be held in Peking in the autumn of 1952, which will help to find a satisfactory solution to the Japanese problem and other problems concerning Peace in the regions of Asia and the Pacific.

(iii) Appeal for peace adopted by the Congress of Peoples for Peace, Vienna, 12–19 December 1952[1]

By proposing the convocation of the Congress of the Peoples for Peace, the World Council of Peace showed its desire to unite the noble efforts of the various movements, organisations and viewpoints which, though they differ on many matters, long for agreement between the peoples and desire to struggle jointly against war and to build peace.

Free discussion has demonstrated a unanimous desire to put an end to the policy of force that has brought so much misery to mankind and risks leading mankind to catastrophe.

We hold that there are no differences between States that cannot be settled by negotiation.

[1] *Soviet News*, 1 January 1953.

Enough of destroying towns and countries, enough of piling up weapons of slaughter, enough of preaching hate and calling for war! It is high time to discuss, high time to agree!

We call on the Governments of the five great Powers, the U.S.A., the U.S.S.R., Great Britain, the People's Republic of China, and France, on whom so largely depends the peace of the world; we call on them at once to start negotiating to conclude a Pact of Peace.

A tremendous responsibility rests on the Governments of the five great Powers. The peoples await their answer. The peoples will do their utmost to make the spirit of negotiation prevail.

We call for all hostilities in Korea to cease immediately. While towns are shattered and blood flows, agreement becomes impossible. When hostilities have ceased, the parties will more easily reach agreement on the questions at issue between them.

We are convinced that this impartial, just and humane call will evoke support from every person of good will.

We call also for the immediate ending of hostilities in Viet Nam, Laos, Cambodia and Malaya, with unqualified respect for the right to independence of the peoples concerned.

We call for an end to the violence employed to stifle the lawful national aspirations of peoples to independence, as in Tunisia and Morocco.

The Congress of the Peoples for Peace proclaims the right of all peoples to self-determination and to choose their own way of life without any interference in their internal affairs, whatever motive be invoked in justification. The national independence of every State constitutes the essential condition of peace.

We protest against all racial discrimination which, an insult to the human conscience, aggravates the danger of war.

We are convinced that military pacts whereby the stronger involves the weaker, the presence on one nation's territory of the bases and troops of another, constitute a serious danger to the security of that nation, which might find itself involved in a war against its will. We hold that a State which takes no part in a coalition and accepts no foreign troops on its territory must be guaranteed against the threat of aggression, declared or hidden.

The ashes of the last war risk bursting into flame in both Europe and Asia. However, negotiation can and must achieve a peaceful solution of the German problem and the Japanese problem. We consider that a Peace Treaty, excluding its participation in any military alliance directed against any country whatsoever, must be concluded at the earliest possible moment with a united, democratic Germany, a Germany where there shall be no room for the Nazism and militarism that have brought such woe to Europe. We propose the conclusion of a Peace Treaty with Japan, that

shall end its occupation and allow the Japanese people to return into the
fellowship of peaceful nations. We hold that negotiation must be resumed on a state treaty for Austria which shall free the country from
foreign occupation.

We have heard the reports on the use of bacteriological warfare, made
by famous experts from different countries, who went to Korea and China.
Deeply concerned by these reports, we categorically demand the immediate prohibition of biological warfare and the adherence of all States to
the Geneva Protocol of 1925. The great achievements of science must not
become a means to destroy millions of defenceless human beings. At the
same time we demand an absolute ban on atomic, chemical and all other
means of exterminating civil populations.

We criticise the short-sighted who claim that the arms drive is capable
of strengthening a country's security. We are convinced that the arms
drive strengthens, on the contrary, the threat to all countries, great and
small.

Interpreting the will of the peoples, we urge the immediate opening of
negotiations for a disarmament that shall be fair and not unilateral. We
are sure that effective international control would make possible the carrying out of general, simultaneous, progressive and proportional disarmament.

We support the desire of the representatives of the peoples, who urge
that exchange of material and cultural values between States be renewed
as soon as possible. The obstacles to international trade, to the exchange
of achievements of science, literature and the arts, place in jeopardy the
well-being and progress of mankind.

We hold that the Charter of the United Nations offers a guarantee of
security for all the countries of the world but this Charter is being infringed
in spirit and letter. We urge that the People's Republic of China be enabled to take its rightful seat at the United Nations. We urge likewise
the admission of the fourteen nations who have as yet been unable to raise
their voices there.

We urge, finally, that the United Nations become once more a place for
finding agreement between the Governments and not disappoint for much
longer the hopes reposed in it by all the peoples of the world. The peoples
long to live in peace, whatever their regimes or loftiest ideals. War is
hated by every people, war throws its shadow over every cradle. It is in
the power of the peoples to change the course of events, to give back to
mankind its confidence in a peaceful tomorrow.

We call on the peoples of the world to struggle for the spirit of negotiation
and agreement, for the right of man to peace.

D. THE U.S.S.R. AND ITS SATELLITES

1. Industry and Agriculture

(i) Extract from a report by the Hungarian President of the Economic Council, Mr. Erno Gerö, on the fulfilment of the Hungarian plan for 1951 and on the necessity for a more constant rhythm of production in industry, 12 January 1952[1]

Nous avons donc réalisé le plan dans son ensemble. Nous l'avons même dépassé. Mais nous ne devons pas oublier que dans certains domaines, malgré les progrès réalisés, nous n'avons pas réussi à exécuter les tâches fixées par le plan augmenté. Et ce sont là faits d'autant plus graves, qu'il s'agit du domaine de la production de matières premières de base, sur lequel le IIe Congrès de notre Parti avait tout particulièrement attiré l'attention. C'est ainsi que la production du charbon a augmenté de presque 15 %, c'est-à-dire 2 millions de tonnes, en 1951, par rapport à 1950, ce qui constitue en soi un progrès sérieux, pour un petit pays comme la Hongrie.

Mais les mines n'ont pas exécuté le plan augmenté et il faut reconnaître que, au début de 1952, la production dans les mines ne démarre qu'avec une relative lenteur. Pourtant nous avons besoin de toujours plus de charbon et il faut que nous assurions à tout prix, en 1952, une augmentation de 3 millions de tonnes par rapport à la production effective de 1951.

Il y a eu également des retards dans la production du pétrole brut, en dépit de la tendance positive marquée au cours des derniers mois. Mais il faut noter que la production pétrolière au cours du quatrième trimestre a dépassé la tâche fixée pour elle par le plan.

Quant à l'industrie métallurgique du fer, nous avons enregistré une certaine amélioration à partir du troisième trimestre. Cette industrie, dans l'ensemble, a réalisé son plan. Nous devons consacrer une grande attention à la métallurgie, afin que celle-ci ne se contente pas d'une exécution *globale* du plan mais qu'elle le réalise dans ses détails également. Ceci d'ailleurs ne concerne pas seulement la métallurgie, mais les autres branches industrielles également, notamment l'industrie légère qui ne devrait pas fabriquer ce qu'il lui plaît de produire, ce qui est facile, mais qui doit produire ce dont le pays a besoin et ce qui lui a été prescrit par le plan.

Nous devons accélérer en 1952 le développement de notre industrie de l'aluminium, ainsi que l'extraction et la métallurgie des métaux non ferreux.

Les décisions fondamentales de notre IIe Congrès sur la nécessité

---

[1] *Szabad Nep*, 13 January 1952, reproduced in France: Ministère des Affaires Étrangères: Documentation Française: *Problèmes Économiques*, no. 220, 18 March 1952.

S

absolue d'accroître notre production de matières premières, et de courant électrique, demeureront en vigueur en 1952. C'est pourquoi je dois souligner que la réalisation de notre plan économique augmenté, 'tendu', pour 1952, la réalisation de ce plan dans son ensemble, dépend d'une manière décisive de la réalisation des prévisions pour la production du charbon, de la métallurgie du fer, de la production du pétrole, de matériaux de construction, d'aluminium et du courant électrique. C'est de cette réalisation que dépendent l'exécution du plan de notre industrie mécanique qui est la force motrice de toute notre industrialisation, l'exécution du plan de notre industrie légère, de notre industrie de produits de consommation de masse. Elle est la condition préalable du succès de nos investissements, du développement progressif de la mécanisation et de la modernisation de notre agriculture, ainsi que du développement, de l'adaptation au nouveaux besoins, de notre réseau de communications.

Certes, nous avons dépassé dans son ensemble le plan de production de 1951. Mais nous avons eu beaucoup de difficultés en cours de route en raison du *rythme inégal* de la production. Nous avons eu au début de 1951 un certain retard. Puis vint le Congrès du Parti qui inspirait un puissant élan à la production. Ensuite, en été, nous connûmes une nouvelle baisse; ensuite, à partir du mois d'août, le rythme de la production s'est accéléré, nous avons exécuté toujours mieux et mieux, pour enfin dépasser le plan. Eh bien, en 1952, nous devons mettre tout en œuvre pour transformer cette courbe ondoyante tantôt ascendante, tantôt descendante de la production, en une ligne montant d'une manière continue.

La production de l'industrie devra s'accroître en 1952 de 25 % par rapport à la production effective en 1951, ce qui veut dire que l'augmentation sera un peu inférieure en pourcentage à celle de 1951 par rapport à 1950. Mais il serait erroné de penser qu'il sera plus facile d'obtenir cette augmentation moindre en 1952 que de réaliser l'augmentation plus importante en 1951. N'oublions pas que si nous disposons toujours de réserves importantes, si certaines de nos réserves se reproduisent, — nous avons cependant utilisé en 1951 et au cours des années précédentes une partie considérable des réserves facilement mobilisables. D'où la nécessité d'un effort plus méthodique, d'un élan plus soutenu encore, et ceci dès le début de 1952. Nous devons renforcer les mesures prises pour économiser les matières premières, nous devons continuer la lutte pour une exécution conséquente du décret ministériel concernant ces économies; nous devons consacrer une attention renouvelée au mouvement Gazda qui au cours des dernières semaines semble un peu battre de l'aile. Nous devons organiser une coopération plus étroite, dans les différents ateliers de la même usine, comme entre les usines individuelles, les branches industrielles, et les différents ministères.

Nous le devons d'autant plus que la valeur absolue de la production devra augmenter considérablement par rapport à 1951, même si cette augmentation se chiffre par un pourcentage relativement inférieur. . . .

Nous devons assurer une augmentation continue, à rythme égal, de la production. C'est pourquoi nous devons mettre fin, une fois pour toutes, à la course effrénée pour rattraper le retard qui a lieu vers la fin de tous les mois. Nous devons établir des 'plans de dix jours'; dans certaines branches nous devons même aller plus loin, en établissant des plan détaillés pour chaque jour, ou même pour chaque heure de la journée de travail.

Actuellement, la plupart de nos usines travaillent à un rythme tout à fait inégal. C'est ainsi que nos mines de charbon ont produit au cours de la première décade de novembre, 29·8 %, au cours de la deuxième décade 32·4 % et au cours de la troisième décade 37·8 % de la production mensuelle, ce qui est assurément une chose anormale. La fabrique d'automobiles *Csepel* a livré dans la première décade de novembre 1951, 55 camions, dans la seconde décade 113, et 256 camions au cours de la troisième décade. C'est à peu près le même tableau qu'offre la production des tracteurs, dans la fabrique de tracteurs *Étoile rouge*. Cette situation caractérise non seulement notre industrie lourde et mécanique, mais en partie également l'industrie légère, notamment celle du textile. Et le rythme n'est pas seulement inégal selon les décades. On peut constater les mêmes fluctuations entre les époques différentes de l'année ou même au cours de la semaine, au cours de la journée de travail. Le matin, le travail démarre lentement, en traînant, puis il augmente d'intensité; ensuite, après l'interruption de midi, il retombe, puis il monte à nouveau, pour retomber à la fin de la journée. Cette précipitation du travail qui est l'une de nos plus grandes déficiences, fait qu'au début de chaque mois, l'équipement et la main-d'œuvre ne sont pas pleinement utilisés, qu'une partie des ouvriers n'a pas de travail. En revanche, à la fin de chaque mois, il y a pénurie de main-d'œuvre; on fait constamment des heures supplémentaires, en dépassant ainsi le fonds de salaires autorisé. On peut donc dire que nous possédons des réserves immenses dans la production organisé suivant des plans de décades qui prévoient une augmentation continue.

Nous devons donc en 1952 liquider toute précipitation, toute course de la fin du mois et assurer une production conforme aux courbes représentées par les graphiques. C'est ainsi que nous devons nous assurer, dès le mois de janvier, que dans toutes les branches de notre industrie, à l'exception des branches ayant un caractère expressément saisonnier, la production augmente d'une manière continue, de décade en décade, de mois en mois, de trimestre en trimestre.

(ii) Appeal to peasants, issued by the Polish United Workers' Party and United Peasants' Party, in connexion with the law on the compulsory delivery of livestock, 15 February 1952[1]

The National Assembly has promulgated a law on the sale and compulsory delivery of animals for slaughter: this is an important law, which concerns both peasants and workers, dwellers in the country as well as in the town. What is its aim and what advantages are to be derived from it?

The above-mentioned law imposes on everyone alike in the country the obligation to provide sufficient supplies of meat for the working people. Hitherto the majority of working peasants have honestly fulfilled their duty to provide the state with the produce of their own growing, conscious of their social and patriotic duty towards the country and the nation. But some of the farmers have favoured the speculators and, with consequent harm to society, have supported them in their efforts to raise the prices of agricultural produce. In this way they have impaired the provision of food for the towns, taking no account of the enormous losses such speculation causes the national economy, the whole country and the peasants themselves.

Every farmer should now keep in mind that it is not possible to fulfil the great task of industrializing our country—parallel with the development of science, education and culture—nor to raise the technical and economic level of the nation, according to the objectives of the six-year plan, nor to manufacture tractors, agricultural machinery, fertilizers and everything else needed for the people in country and town unless at the same time there is a sharp struggle against speculators, kulaks and the other harmful elements which work to stop the economic development of the people's Poland. These speculators wish our country to remain undefended, backward and poor as it was before the war. . . .

The law assures favourable conditions for breeders, renders stockbreeding extremely profitable and encourages farmers to develop breeding in accordance with the country's needs. Apart from the compulsory deliveries, which for the majority of small and middle farms will not exceed one fattened pig a year, every breeder can contract to sell such animals, obtaining a premium of 30 per cent. on the price, great facilities for obtaining coal and fodder, and also a reduction in the compulsory harvesting and delivery of grain. . . .

The people's state helps the small farms in particular. The owners of less than two hectares have the right to carry out the whole delivery with another kind of animal, or with fowls, but they should do their best to deliver and sell pigs because this is in their own interests; in fact the fattening of pigs is no obstacle to the breeding of cattle or of farmyard animals,

[1] Translated from *Relazioni Internazionali*, 8 March 1952, pp. 277–8.

indeed the breeding of cows on the farm is a help towards the breeding of pigs. It is to the interest of the small and middle-holding peasants to sell pigs for food for the towns since they have the highest interest in the development of industry, which works for them and provides occupation for their friends. The new system brings advantages and help to those who manage their own farms for the benefit of the state and of their own families.

(iii) Extracts from a report by President Boleslaw Bierut to the Central Committee of the Polish United Workers' Party on the development of agriculture and the necessity for increased collectivization, 14 June 1952[1]

A thorough analysis of the social and economic changes which have been taking place in the Polish countryside since the liberation should be the basis for outlining the party's policy in the countryside. These are profound and fundamental changes, proceeding in a direction completely opposite to that of pre-war days. In the past, an increasingly rapid degradation and ruin of the majority of the peasants could be registered; today, the material prosperity of the countryside and its standard of living are undoubtedly rising and so is the social and political activity of the peasants and the level of their cultural development.

These gains of the working people are being consolidated and expanded through the industrialisation of Poland and the realisation of the Six-Year Plan, the socialisation of the means of production in key branches of our national economy, by exerting a momentous influence on the life and work of the peasants.

Is not this, for instance, borne out by the fact that thanks to rising labour productivity in agriculture and the absorption by industry of formerly 'redundant' people, the number of people engaged in farming (individual, co-operative and State), which is today 46 per cent. lower than before the war, produces more or less the same amount of agricultural crops as the entire pre-war landowner economy and peasant economy put together? If we compare the present total of agricultural production per capita, we find that it is one-third higher than before the war.

This has been brought about by the influence of planned economy and State assistance in raising the production of peasant farms. Thus, this is an economic effect of the political worker–peasant alliance which, at the present stage, is expressed in the joint efforts of the working people of the entire country to realise the economic and cultural plans and, in the political sphere, is reflected in the slogan of the national front of the fight for peace and the Six-Year Plan.

[1] *Polish Facts and Figures*, 28 June 1952.

But we must clearly realise the different character of the present economic structure of the countryside as compared with the structure of industry and the remaining branches of our national economy. This is a problem which assumes particular importance at the present period. As we advance in the realisation of our plan of socialist building, the backward and different nature of the economic structure of the countryside, based on smallholder methods of production, does not allow for an adequate rise in agricultural production and is, to an increasing extent, influencing the growth of disproportion between the requirements of the national economy for agricultural production, on the one hand, and the development of this production, on the other. In other words, the rate of increase in agricultural production is still excessively lagging behind in relation to the needs of the national economy. . . .

What are the measures which the State can take to ensure indispensable stocks adequate to safeguarding normal supplies of agricultural products for the working population so as to avoid dislocations resulting from the spontaneity of small commodity production?

One such indispensable measure was the introduction of quota deliveries of part of the commodities produced by farms. These quota deliveries include cereal grains, livestock or meat, potatoes and milk—that is the most basic agricultural products indispensable for the regular supply of foodstuffs for the working people.

It is characteristic that the vast majority of working peasants showed full understanding of the advisability and justness of the decision of the people's authorities introducing quota deliveries of a part of their agricultural products. In the economic year, 1951–1952, grain deliveries were carried out successfully, in accordance with the planned quantity of grain, despite kulaks' attempts at resistance. Deliveries of livestock and animal produce, introduced only a few months ago (milk as late as May), are on the whole also being carried out successfully.

Does the introduction and expansion of quota deliveries to include part of agricultural production indicate a change in the policy of the People's State in relation to the working peasants? Does this policy aim at abolishing a free commodity circulation in agricultural articles? These are questions to which the working peasants would like to have a clear answer.

Now the task of the State is not to abolish free commodity circulation in agricultural products. Quota deliveries include and will include also in the future only a part of the commodities produced on peasant farms but in no case will they include all products. Peasants may exchange their surplus produce at will on the open market and nobody will restrain them from doing so. . . .

One of the sources of our difficulties which we are at present experiencing and which we can and shall effectively overcome is, as is known, an excessive disproportion between the rate of development of our socialist industry and the rate of development of our agriculture.

An excessive disproportion in the sphere of agriculture is a symptom all the more dangerous and threatens our national economy with serious dislocations since it is precisely this disproportion which directly affects the threads existing between various economic sectors—between the socialist sector and the small commodity sector—directly affecting the economic union between the working class and peasantry.

By allowing an excessive disproportion to occur between the growth of agricultural production, and the growth in demand for agricultural products, we are not only creating dangerous gaps in economic planning, but we are also weakening the regulating role of the State in the sphere of commodity exchange between town and country. But what does a weakening of the regulating role of the State in the sphere of commodity exchange between town and country lead to? It strengthens elements of spontaneity, free market anarchy and speculation—that is it strengthens capitalist elements.

The problem lies, above all, in the fact that economic unity between the working class and peasants, which is the basic political union of these classes—the foundation of the worker–peasant alliance—can grow stronger and develop only under conditions of restricting capitalist elements. It is, however, exposed to danger under conditions where these elements are reviving and growing stronger.

An excessive disproportion in the sphere of agriculture, accentuated last autumn as the result of the catastrophic drought and by reducing the supply of agricultural products, sharpened the difficulties in supplying the working class with food. As a consequence of a marked rise in free market prices for agricultural commodities, heightened by wild speculation and hostile rumours, a considerable rise in the profits of wealthier peasants took place, causing a drop in working class incomes.

Thus, instead of the peasants also contributing in an equitable and justified degree to socialist accumulation, since they are particularly interested in the industrialisation of the country, exactly the reverse process could be noted. Part of the working class income was diverted to the countryside where it found its way into the pockets of the kulaks and wealthier medium-holders who had at their disposal greater surpluses of produce, and a part of the working class income found its way into the coffers of urban capitalists who again became active and grew fat.

At the same time, the kulaks preyed on the waverings of the medium-holders and, by creating speculation fever, attempted to infect the medium-holders with it. In the last analysis it was precisely these manœuvres of the kulaks which caused a certain disproportion—incompatible with the entire meaning of our policy of worker–peasant alliance—in the distribution of the national income at the cost of the working class and to the detriment of the People's State.

This moved the Party to take a number of steps such as the partial rationing and introduction of free market controlled prices. Steps were also taken to expand quota deliveries. At the same time, contracts for delivery were appreciably expanded and the trade network improved.

The purpose of all this is to even out irregularities existing in commodity circulation between town and country. . . .

Are there any concrete possibilities for speeding up the development of agricultural production, for a marked increase in this production? There is no doubt that such possibilities exist and that too little use has so far been made of them.

The share of the socialist sector in the total value of production of all agriculture amounted in 1949 to barely 6 per cent., in 1950 to 8 per cent., in 1951 to 12 per cent. and, according to the plan for the current year, it should amount to 16 per cent. These figures point to considerable possibilities for developing socialist forms of farming. In barely three years the share of the socialist sector in the total production of agriculture is to rise from 6 to 16 per cent. But a number of other observations indicate that this rise could be considerably greater. For instance, since the middle of last year, the number of co-operative farms remained more or less on the level of 3,000, and it was only in spring of this year that it increased by about 300.

During that period a further marked strengthening of existing co-operatives took place, but in the quantitative development of peasant co-operative farming one could see in the second half of last year a certain stagnation. How can this be explained?

This can be explained by the fact that Party organisers turned their attention to other campaigns and neglected, so far as work in the countryside is concerned, their propaganda and organisational efforts in increasing co-operative farming.

The secret of the weakening rate of development of socialising life in the countryside lies, as it seems, in the conviction of some comrades that the development of the co-operative movement among the peasants can take place either spontaneously or under pressure of administrative means, pressure from above.

But the Central Committee agrees neither to administrative measures of pressure nor does it wish to wait patiently for spontaneous processes; it does not wish to tolerate spontaneity in any sphere of party work.

It is not a single campaign that is at stake but the most important and at the same time the most difficult task, a task of fundamental character— the socialist transformation of the countryside as a basic pre-requisite for the development of the country towards socialism.

(iv) Extract from a speech by Mr. Gheorghe Gheorghiu-Dej, Rumanian Prime Minister, on the currency reform in Rumania, 29 June 1952[1]

In January this year the Central Committee of the Rumanian Workers' Party and the Council of Ministers decided to carry out a currency reform designed to strengthen the purchasing power of the lei and ensure better supplies for the working class and urban working people.

What are the results of the currency reform today, five months after it was effected?

In the first place, the purchasing power of the lei remains on the level established when the currency reform was introduced. Prices for manufactured goods remain stable and firm. There has been no rise in prices for manufactured goods. Prices of agricultural products on the open market fell sharply as a result of the reform and in most cases remain at this level which signifies greater purchasing power of earnings of factory and office workers. Only on certain products (meat, fats, milk) are the prices above the level of state commercial prices and this is only because we lack these products in sufficient quantity to cause a price reduction on the open market. This is due to the fact that the purchasing plan for these products was not fully fulfilled.

Secondly, food supplies have improved. February, March, and April were always the worst months from the standpoint of food supplies. The market experienced a shortage of many products. This year, as a result of the currency reform, contrary to previous years, foodstuffs were fairly abundant on the market during February, March and April. At present all the conditions exist for further improving food supplies in view of the prospect of a good harvest.

Thirdly, currency circulation is effected according to plan as established and approved by the Government. The level of currency circulation is quite satisfactory. After the currency reform and removal of the former leadership of the Ministry of Finances—the unhealthy tendencies in currency circulation were eliminated.

Fourthly, the rate fixed for the lei proved to be correct, the lei has become a stable currency on the international market.

The currency reform effected by the Party and Government can be regarded as a complete success, signifying a big victory of our Party and State, a victory gained in struggle against the class enemy and the capitulatory elements—the Right deviators. . . .

[1] *For a Lasting Peace, For a People's Democracy!*, 11 July 1952.

(v) Extract from a speech by the Czechoslovak Minister of National Security, Mr. Karol Bacilek, on the problem of the elimination of sabotage in Czechoslovak agriculture and industry, 8 August 1952[1]

What is the present situation in Czechoslovakia? That of transition from capitalism to socialism. Planned economy is making possible the development of our industry, the increase of culture and the raising of the standard of living of the workers, and also the building of socialism in both towns and villages. Our bourgeoisie, defeated in 1948, lost the possibility and the hope of being able to endanger our régime in any way by their own power. They therefore turned their eyes to the west and entrusted themselves to American imperialism, being ready for any low action and to execute any order which might come from their allies. . . .

Given this situation we must not in the slightest degree weaken our armed forces, our national and state security, to which every honourable citizen of the Republic has the duty to give full and direct help in the present stage of our fight against the enemy. Neither should we for a moment deny that among us there still lives a considerable remnant of the capitalist classes: there are still landed proprietors, industrialists, bankers, whose power we have smashed by nationalizing the banks and factories, but who still have—as recently discovered crimes have shown—wealth hidden away which they use for their subversive activities.

A great help to the Republic, in the fight against the enemies of our State in the villages, is provided by the new organization of national security, the so-called district representatives, who are to make themselves well-informed on local conditions, get to know the people in the district assigned to them, know how to distinguish a friend from a foe, and support our people's administration, the working people of the village, in impeding the activities of the enemies of the Republic.

The auxiliary guards constitute a notable aid to public security: with their creation the collaboration of the security organs with the citizens assumes a concrete form. In every village in which there is state property (machine and tractor stations, unified agricultural co-operatives) auxiliary guards are to be created in groups of from 3 to 10 persons who are members of co-operatives or employed at the stations, and whose task is to defend the common property, disclose wastage, collaborate with the state security organization in the execution of its duty, interrogate suspected persons, etc. Thus it will be even more evident that the security organs are organs of the people, serve the people and work with the people.

[1] Translated from *Relazioni Internazionali*, 13 September 1952, p. 972.

2. Politics

(i) Extracts from a speech by Mr. Gheorghiu-Dej regarding deviations by Mrs. Ana Pauker, Mr. Vasile Luca and Mr. Teohari Georgescu, 29 June 1952[1]

V. Luca denied the decisive role of industry in socialist construction. It is known that without socialist industry and its development socialist exchange between town and countryside is impossible, exchange which would serve the purpose not of the growth of capitalist, profiteering elements, but of restricting and ousting them, of raising the living standard of the working class and of the toiling peasantry.

Proceeding from his harmful views which ran counter to the Party line and working people's interests, V. Luca, with the aid of the hostile elements whom he entrusted with leading posts in the spheres of state activity for which he was responsible, pursued a policy of retarding development of heavy industry, a policy which aimed at slowing down the tempo of socialist industrialisation of the country.

The anti-Party line of retarding development of heavy industry conducted by Vasile Luca also affected the coal industry.

V. Luca tried to hold up the policy of our Party in the sphere of capital investments. This also found expression in efforts to reduce the planned capital investments in the coal industry. Intervention by the leadership of the Party and Government was required in order to prevent this. However, the anti-Party and anti-State line of V. Luca in relation to capital investments, the undermining activity of the hostile elements in the leadership of the finance-banking apparatus, and the sabotage of certain hostile elements in the administrative and technical organs of the mining industry resulted in underfulfilment of the 1951 plan for capital investments in the coal industry. . . .

At the same time V. Luca, as Finance Minister, pursued a policy of encouraging kulak and other capitalist elements. He carried out numerous measures in favour of the kulaks: they were granted credits which, for the most part, were never recovered; tens of thousands of kulaks were masked as middle peasants; non-collection of taxes and even exemption from taxation for kulak households, etc.

In this way the Right deviators sought to pump material means from the State and the people into the private-capitalist sector for the purpose of enriching the capitalist elements in town and countryside.

V. Luca, who was responsible for internal trade and co-operation,

[1] *For a Lasting Peace, For a People's Democracy!*, 11 July 1952. Mrs. Pauker was the Rumanian Foreign Minister, Mr. Luca the Minister of Finance and Mr. Georgescu the Minister of the Interior.

by means of fixing speculative prices on the open market in purchasing
and contracting for agricultural products, encouraged capitalist trade and
profiteering on the open market. Giving encouragement to the kulaks and
conniving with them, demanding for them the right to sell their products
'anywhere, to anyone and at whatever price they please', Luca acted
against the regulating role of the state in the exchange of goods between
town and countryside, pursued a policy of fostering profiteering, of enriching the kulaks, hoarders and other speculator elements whose purpose was
to starve the industrial workers and plunder the toiling peasants. . . .

While striking at the interests of the working class V. Luca's anti-Party
and anti-State activity also delivered a serious blow at the working
peasantry who are interested in developing the exchange of goods between
town and countryside, in developing socialist industry—the basis for the
building of Socialism, the basis for improving the wellbeing of the workers,
the toiling peasantry and all the people.

The currency reform, from the very beginning, encountered the frantic
resistance of the enemies of the people who had wormed their way to
responsible posts in the finance-banking system, the resistance of the
opportunist deviators and capitulatory elements. The currency reform
encountered the most bitter resistance on the part of V. Luca who sought
to frustrate it. . . .

Conciliation, as Comrade Stalin points out, is the concealed form of
opportunism. When opportunism has been exposed and discredited it
masks itself in the toga of conciliation, liberalism and connivance in
relation to the deviators, in the toga of sentimentalism, it begins to bemoan
and pity those who are guilty before the Party, before the State of the
working people, before the proletariat. Consequently, conciliation in relation to opportunism is a danger which must be combated with the same
determination with which we do away with naked opportunism.

Such a conciliatory attitude which, in fact, turned out to be nothing
more than concealed opportunism, was displayed by Ana Pauker and
Teohari Georgescu. Their conciliatory attitude in relation to the anti-
Party and anti-State line of V. Luca prevented the Party from exposing
in good time and eliminating the Right deviation and its harmful consequences. Theirs is a serious guilt, because at bedrock of the conciliation
of A. Pauker and T. Georgescu towards V. Luca's deviation is the fact
that they pursued the same policy of opposition to the Party line. In the
case of Ana Pauker this policy manifested itself in that she actually im-
mobilised the state organs called upon to carry out the plan for purchasing
agricultural products, held up the organisation of more agricultural co-
operatives, neglected the question of organising new collective farms,
tolerated kulak penetration into the collective farms and agricultural
co-operatives, neglected the state-socialist sector of agriculture (machine

and tractor stations and state farms) with the result that numerous hostile and subversive elements wormed their way into these bodies.

As for Teohari Georgescu, he, having been placed by the Party at a post where he should have safeguarded the interests of the state of people's democracy and of the working people, showed that he had lost revolutionary vigilance, lost militancy and class sense, which enabled hostile elements to unfold activity inimical to the interests of the state.

Meeting on the platform of the Right deviation from the Party line Ana Pauker, Teohari Georgescu and Vasile Luca introduced factionalism into the Party thereby violating one of the basic principles of the Marxist-Leninist Party—the principle that the strength of the Party is determined by its unity of will, incompatible with the existence of factions. Violation of the iron unity of the Party, of its internal unity, is serious guilt before the Party, before the working class.

The deviators have been exposed. They tried to continue the anti-Party policy and to extend it. The leadership of our Party exposed the deviators. Everybody knows of the measures taken by the Party and the Government in relation to the opportunists and conciliators. These measures reflect the great strength and lofty principledness of the Party of the working class—the Party which demands from each member, irrespective of his post, loyalty to the Party and to its unity, revolutionary irreconcilability in relation to the class enemy, loyalty to the Marxist-Leninist teaching.

(ii) Extract from the sentence pronounced on Mr. Rudolf Slansky, former Secretary-General of the Czechoslovak Communist Party, 27 November 1952[1]

As a trotzkyist, during the second World War he [Slansky] carried on harmful activities against the people and the Czechoslovak Republic. In agreement and collaboration with other imperialist agents he tried to weaken and harm the liberation movement during the Slovak rising against the Nazi occupiers. He knowingly caused the death of the head of this rising, Comrade Sverma, in order to rid himself of a witness to his criminal activity, to make himself popular, by taking the other's place as hero of the revolution, and to be able better to hide his activities as an agent.

After the liberation of the Czechoslovak Republic by the Soviet army, Slansky joined the spies and agents, purchased on instructions from Dulles[2] from among the émigrés to the west, and other active elements of a reactionary and nationalistic mentality who carried on activity hostile to the working classes, all being people who called themselves communists.

[1] Translated from *Relazioni Internazionali*, 6 December 1952, pp. 1261–2.
[2] This reference is not to Mr. John Foster Dulles, but to his brother, Mr. Allen Dulles.

These agents returned to Czechoslovakia from London in the company of Benes, with the task of separating the Czechoslovak Republic from the friendship of the Soviet Union and making it part of the imperialist Anglo-American block opposed to the U.S.S.R.

As Secretary-General of the Communist Party Slansky was in a position to use trotzkyist methods for causing the infiltration of hostile elements into the machinery of the party and of the state. The people he had gathered round him were suitable for this purpose: they were war criminals, agents of the Gestapo, capitalists, spies, trotzkyists, zionists, nationalists of all types, sworn enemies of the working classes and of the Soviet Union.

The aim of these criminals was to execute a *coup d'état* at a suitable moment, after the manner of Tito. To this end, with the help of the renegades who served him, Slansky had created his own organization within the party and the state which, under the appearance of various committees and sections, weakened the control of the party and the government. These committees were responsible only to Slansky himself. With this violation of the principles of party organization Slansky estranged the party cadres from the masses, and systematically undermined the party's guiding power, in order to prepare his own plan, or rather the annihilation of the People's Democracy.

As the traitors knew well that socialism could be realized only through the continued planned increase of socialist production they sabotaged development and the economic plans. The methods of this economic sabotage were revealed in detail during the trial.

At the same time their intention was to weaken the armed forces of the Republic. The infiltration of thousands of enemy émigrés into the sphere of the foreign trade of the Republic of Czechoslovakia, the continuous thefts of and damage to the people's property, by which immense sums accrued to these enemies, all this constituted only one of the methods which were used to overthrow the People's Republic.

E. THE U.S.S.R. AND ITS ADVERSARIES

(i) NOTE FROM THE RUSSIAN GOVERNMENT TO THE UNITED STATES GOVERNMENT PROTESTING AGAINST THE PROVISIONS OF THE MUTUAL SECURITY ACT, 1951, 9 JANUARY 1952[1]

In connection with the Note of the United States Government dated December 19, 1951, the Soviet Government considers it necessary to state that it cannot recognise as satisfactory the reply of the United States

[1] *Soviet News*, 16 January 1952. For the provisions of the Act and for previous Russian protests, together with the United States reply, see *Documents* (R.I.I.A.) for 1951, pp. 317–21.

Government to the Note of the Soviet Government dated November 21 with regard to the so-called Mutual Security Act adopted in the United States on October 10, 1951.

As is known, the law provides for the appropriation of one hundred million dollars to finance 'any selected persons who are residing in or escapees from the Soviet Union, Poland, Czechoslovakia, Bulgaria, Hungary, Rumania, Albania . . . either to form such persons into elements of military forces supporting the North Atlantic Treaty Organisation or for other purposes.'

Thus the law adopted in the United States on October 10, 1951, and the funds appropriated under this law provide for the formation both on the territory of the U.S.S.R. and beyond its borders of 'elements of military forces' of 'any selected persons' who are residing on Soviet territory or escapees from the U.S.S.R. and for utilising these persons and armed groups against the U.S.S.R. This means that the above-mentioned United States law sets itself the object of creating on U.S.S.R. territory underground gangs for subversive sabotage and terrorist activity, as well as utilising all kinds of mercenary people who have escaped from the U.S.S.R. for criminal actions against the Soviet Union.

That these activities provided for by the above-mentioned United States law are precisely of such a nature, is confirmed also by the statement of one of the authors of this law—a member of the American Congress—Kersten, who, speaking in the House of Representatives on October 20, 1951, stated outright that this law envisaged methods by which the United States would be able to help underground movements in communist countries. This provision, according to Kersten, is contained in an amendment which he moved in the House of Representatives and which was adopted.

In connection with the Note of the United States Government dated December 19, 1951, the Soviet Government considers it necessary again to call the attention of the Government of the United States to the commitments which the United States assumed under the Soviet-American Agreement of November 16, 1933.[1]

Under this Agreement the United States and the Soviet Union have mutually commited themselves to refrain from any interference in each other's internal affairs and from any act having the purpose of arousing or encouraging armed intervention or changing by force the political or social system of the contracting parties, and have also committed themselves to restrain from similar activity governmental organisations and organisations receiving financial assistance from the Government. Under this Agreement the United States and the Soviet Union have also undertaken not to permit the formation or residence on their territories of, and

[1] See *Survey* for 1933, pp. 530 seqq.

not to subsidise, any organisations or groups pursuing the above-mentioned aims, including military organisations or groups having the object of armed struggle against the other side. Besides, the Government of the United States and the Government of the U.S.S.R. under the said Agreement committed themselves to prevent any recruiting intended for such organisations and groups.

The adoption of the Act of October 10, 1951, indicates that the Government of the United States, in violation of the Soviet-American Agreement of 1933, sets itself the aim of organising and financing underground gangs and criminal elements for subversive espionage and sabotage activity against the Soviet Union. Such actions on the part of the United States representing gross interference in the internal affairs of the Soviet Union testify that the Government of the United States is brazenly trampling underfoot the commitments it assumed under the Soviet-American Agreement of November 16, 1933.

The adoption by the United States Government of the law of October 10 also constitutes an unprecedented act in relations between States, a most flagrant violation of the standards of international law and is in no way compatible with normal relations between countries. The adoption of this law by the United States cannot be regarded as other than an aggressive act having the object of further complicating relations between the United States and the Soviet Union and rendering the international situation more acute. Gross interference in the internal affairs of other States by means of setting up underground bands of hired agents and utilising criminal elements for sabotage and terrorist purposes on the territories of other States cannot have anything in common with 'defensive' purposes or with the interests of 'European freedom' to which the United States Government refers in its Note of December 19.

In its reply the Government of the United States has not fortuitously passed by in silence the fact that the law adopted by the United States provides for the financing and arming of criminal elements and underground groups on the territory of the Soviet Union and other States to carry through subversive and sabotage activity inside these States. The circumstance that the United States Government has remained silent on this is quite understandable, as the above-mentioned activity provided for by the law of October 10, 1951, being direct interference of the United States Government in the internal affairs of the Soviet Union, exposes the United States Government as an enemy of peace and as a violator of commitments assumed, trampling underfoot the universally recognised standards of international law in relations between States.

Unable to deny the indisputable statements contained in the Soviet Government's Note of November 21, 1951, the United States Government in its reply Note resorted to fabrications and slanders against the Soviet

Union with regard to some 'support' by the Soviet Union of subversive activity directed against the United States and other States. The Soviet Government sweeps aside such fabrications intended, as is obvious, to divert the attention of public opinion from the incontrovertible facts which expose the organisers of underground bands for carrying through sabotage and terrorist activity against the Soviet Union and the people's democratic States.

Considering that the adoption by the United States of the law of October 10, 1951, represents an unheard of violation of the standards of international law and a gross violation of the Soviet-American Agreement of November 16, 1933, the Soviet Government deems it necessary again to declare that responsibility for such actions rests wholly with the Government of the United States and insists on the repeal of the above-mentioned law.

(ii) RESOLUTION CALLING FOR AN INVESTIGATION BY THE INTERNATIONAL COMMITTEE OF THE RED CROSS OF THE CHARGES AGAINST UNITED NATIONS FORCES OF USING BACTERIOLOGICAL WARFARE IN KOREA, DEFEATED IN THE SECURITY COUNCIL ON 3 JULY 1952[1]

THE SECURITY COUNCIL,

NOTING the concerted dissemination by certain governments and authorities of grave accusations charging the use of bacteriological warfare by United Nations forces in Korea;

NOTING that the Government of the U.S.S.R. has repeated these charges in organs of the United Nations;

RECALLING that when the charges were first made the Unified Command for Korea immediately denied the charges and requested that an impartial investigation be made of them;

REQUESTS the International Committee of the Red Cross, with the aid of such scientists of international reputation and such other experts as it may select, to investigate the charges and to report the results to the Security Council as soon as possible;

CALLS UPON all governments and authorities concerned to accord to the International Committee of the Red Cross full cooperation, including the right of entry to, and free movement in, such areas as the Committee may deem necessary in the performance of its task.

REQUESTS the Secretary General to furnish the Committee with such assistance and facilities as it may require.

[1] S/2671, 20 June 1952. The resolution was vetoed by the U.S.S.R.

(iii) Resolution condemning the dissemination of false charges of using bacteriological warfare, defeated in the Security Council on 9 July 1952[1]

The Security Council,

Noting the concerted dissemination by certain Governments and authorities of grave accusations charging the use of bacteriological warfare by United Nations Forces,

Recalling that when the charges were first made the Unified Command for Korea immediately denied the charges and requested that an impartial investigation be made of them,

Noting that the Chinese Communist and North Korean authorities failed to accept an offer by the International Committee of the Red Cross to carry out such an investigation but continued to give circulation to the charges,

Noting that the World Health Organization offered to assist in combating any epidemics in North Korea and China, and that the Unified Command for Korea agreed to co-operate,

Noting with regret that the Chinese Communist and North Korean authorities rejected the offer and refused to permit the entry of the World Health Organization teams into territories controlled by these authorities,

Noting that the Government of the Union of Soviet Socialist Republics has, in the United Nations, repeated the charges that United Nations Forces were engaging in bacteriological warfare,

Noting that the draft resolution submitted by the Government of the United States proposing an impartial investigation of these charges by the International Committee of the Red Cross was rejected by the Union of Soviet Socialist Republics, and that by reason of the negative vote of the Union of Soviet Socialist Republics the Security Council was prevented from arranging for such an impartial investigation,

Concludes, from the refusal of those Governments and authorities making the charges to permit impartial investigation, that these charges must be presumed to be without substance and false.

Condemns the practice of fabricating and disseminating such false charges, which increases tension among nations and which is designed to undermine the efforts of the United Nations to combat aggression in Korea and the support of the people of the world for these efforts.

[1] S/2688, 3 July 1952. The resolution was vetoed by the U.S.S.R.

(iv) Note from the United States Government to the Russian Government asking for the return of an aircraft detained in Hungary in 1951 and for damages on account of the detention of the aircraft, 10 December 1952[1]

The Government of the United States of America draws the attention of the Government of the Union of Soviet Socialist Republics to the case of the four United States Air Force personnel, Captain Dave H. Henderson, Captain John J. Swift, Sergeant Jess A. Duff, and Sergeant James A. Elam, who were brought down on Hungarian territory by a Soviet airplane on November 19, 1951, were detained by Soviet and Hungarian authorities within Hungary, and were thereafter tried and convicted of crime by Hungarian authorities, and to effect whose release the United States Government paid to the Government of the Hungarian People's Republic on December 28, 1951, under protest, the sum of $123,605.15.

It will be recalled that the Soviet Government did not disclose to the United States authorities prior to December 3, 1951, that the Soviet Government had seized and detained the airmen and their airplane, C-47 type USAF 6026, bearing the identification symbol 43-16026, and both the Soviet and Hungarian authorities prevented access to the airmen by United States authorities at all times until the release of the airmen on December 28, 1951. The United States was therefore unable to determine whether any evidence whatever existed, of however doubtful validity or credibility, to justify or sustain any of the allegations of fact, charges, and findings announced by the Soviet and Hungarian authorities at various times in the matter or what acts had been engaged in by the Soviet and Hungarian Governments with respect to the incident. Since the return of the airmen, the United States has engaged in an exhaustive inquiry to ascertain all the essential facts with respect to the entire incident. As the United States is separately informing the Hungarian Government, this inquiry has disclosed so serious a variance between the actual facts as now ascertained and the representations with respect to these facts theretofore made by the Hungarian and Soviet Governments that the United States is compelled to consider whether it should not now take further action in this matter.

The United States finds, as a result of the inquiry, that as to certain important issues of fact the best legal documentary evidence was seized by the Soviet Government from the aircraft and its crew or has otherwise come into the possession of the Soviet Government. The United States desires to defer the taking of further action in this matter until it has been able to review that evidence, if the Soviet Government will make all such

---

[1] *Department of State Bulletin*, 22 December 1952, pp. 981–2. A note was also sent to the Hungarian Government, asking for details of the trial in Hungary of the four American airmen: ibid. pp. 982–4.

evidence in its possession available to the United States Government for that purpose.

1. The United States Government has confirmed in the course of this investigation that it was the Soviet authorities stationed in Hungary who on November 19, 1951, seized C-47 type USAF airplane 6026 and its contents from the custody of the United States Air Force personnel above named, who had unwittingly become lost over Hungarian territory, and whom a Soviet plane had shown to a landing field in Hungary. The property seized was and is property of the United States Government. It consisted of:

(1) United States Air Force airplane 6026, C-47 type and its equipment, value $96,436.40.

(2) Cargo thereof, itemized in the manifests on board the airplane when seized by the Soviet authorities, value $2,342.89.

Total value $98,779.29.

The United States Government requests the Soviet Government to make prompt return of the airplane, its equipment and its cargo, or to make prompt provision for the payment of the value thereof as shown above, with interest at 6 per cent from November 19, 1951, in the event that the return should not for any valid reason be possible.

2. In particular, and apart from the foregoing, the United States requests the Soviet Government to return to it specifically certain articles, property of the United States, which were on board the airplane when it was seized by the Soviet authorities and which are known by the United States Government to have been and are therefore believed still to be in the possession of the Soviet authorities. These articles are:

(1) Aeronautical charts entitled 'World Aeronautical Charts' published by the United States Government, Forms Nos. WAF 230, 231, 252, 253, 320, 321, 343, 423, 424, 425; and two aeronautical planning charts, Nos. 11 and 12.

(2) A *Radio Facilities Chart of Europe*, published by the United States.

(3) The flight plan, bearing the signatures of the pilot, Captain Dave Henderson, and other United States Air Force personnel.

(4) The navigation log, as filled out by United States Air Force personnel, showing the details of the anticipated flight from Erding, Germany, to Belgrade, Yugoslavia.

(5) AF Form No. 1, being the log of aircraft 6026, showing number of passengers carried, place and time of take-off, landings et cetera, kept by the engineer and the pilot.

(6) AF Form 35, being the log kept by the radio operator, Sergeant James A. Elam, and all notes of the same radio operator, whether or not in the log.

(7) AF Form 75, being the retained copy of the pilot, Captain Henderson,

of the clearance form issued by American authorities at Erding, Germany, on the aircraft's leaving that place November 19, 1951, showing the persons carried, the weather briefing, the route to be flown, the estimated time of flight, the amount of fuel carried by the plane and other flight information.

(8) Navigation computer, described as Form E6B.

(9) *Pilot's Handbook* published by the United States.

(10) AF Form 15 and pad, showing the condition of the plane on departure.

(11) Leather brief case, called a navigator's kit, and all other contents thereof in addition to these described above.

(12) One portable United States Air Force emergency radio transmitter.

(13) Twenty-one blankets.

The Soviet Government, in replying to the foregoing request, is asked to specify whether the maps (in item 1 above), the radio transmitter (in item 12 above) and the blankets (in item 13 above) are those to which Mr Andrei Y. Vyshinsky, Minister of Foreign Affairs of the Soviet Government, referred to in his several speeches on this subject in the course of the meetings of the General Assembly of the United Nations at Paris in December 1951 and January 1952.

3. The United States is informed further, as a result of the investigation, that the Soviet authorities in Hungary interrogated the four United States Air Force personnel mentioned above from November 19 to December 3, 1951. The United States Government requests the Soviet Government to provide the United States Government with:

(1) Duly authenticated copies of each statement made by each of the four airmen, however taken from them, whether in writing or by other forms of transcription.

(2) Duly authenticated copies of all reports with respect to the facts of the case made by the interrogators and other investigators to the Soviet Government.

Should the Soviet Government prefer, the United States is prepared to make copies of the contents of the dossiers of the case and of the documents to which reference is made, upon the representation of the Soviet Government that the dossiers and the documents under reference are complete and intact, and if reasonable access thereto for the purpose is provided by the Soviet authorities.

4. With further respect to the facts in the case the United States makes reference to various statements on this subject by Soviet authorities and particularly Mr Andrei Y. Vyshinsky, Minister of Foreign Affairs of the Soviet Government, during the course of the United Nations General Assembly held in Paris in December 1951 and January 1952. In this respect the United States Government requests the Soviet Government to provide the United States Government with the specific provisions of

all treaties, agreements and other arrangements between the Soviet Government and the Hungarian Government by which, in the Soviet Government's view, Soviet authorities were legally entitled to bring down and detain the aircraft 6026, its personnel, cargo and other contents, to interrogate the personnel, to refrain from informing the United States of such facts and from returning the airmen, the plane, or the cargo and other contents, to the United States authorities, and to turn the airmen, and to the extent it has done so any of the property described, over to the Hungarian authorities.

5. The Soviet Government is further informed that should it fail promptly to effect the return of the property requested, or promptly to make available for the examination of the United States the documentary evidence as requested, or promptly to provide the information requested, the United States Government will consider itself entitled to take such substantive action on account of such failure as it may then find appropriate, and also to rely on and produce secondary evidence, to the extent available to the United States, in any proceedings hereafter in which the property, the documents, or the information, as original or best legal evidence, may be relevant. The United States Government reserves the right to proceed upon the premise that return of the articles, examination of the documents and provision of the information, so requested and not made, would be unfavorable to the Soviet Government and the United States Government will consider and contend whenever and wherever appropriate that the Soviet Government should be estopped from producing as evidence in its behalf the original or best legal evidence thus concealed from the United States or from contesting the admissibility or value of the secondary evidence.

6. The United States wishes to make clear that the return of the airplane, its equipment and its cargo, or their value, and the documents and other property taken by the Soviet Government in connection therewith will not be considered by the United States to relieve the Soviet Government or the Hungarian Government in any way of liability for damages caused by either government to the United States or its nationals in this matter and remaining unsatisfied.

The United States Government requests the favor of a reply from the Soviet Government at the Soviet Government's earliest convenience.

(v) STATEMENT BY THE RUSSIAN MINISTRY OF FOREIGN AFFAIRS REGARDING THE UNITED STATES NOTE OF 10 DECEMBER, PUBLISHED ON 16 DECEMBER 1952[1]

On December 10, 1952, Mr O'Shaughnessy, United States Chargé d'Affaires in the U.S.S.R., addressed a Note to Y. A. Malik, Deputy

---

[1] *Soviet News*, 16 December 1952.

Minister of Foreign Affairs of the U.S.S.R., conveying the demand of the United States Government for the return of an American C47 military transport plane, with all the objects it contained.

It will be recalled that, on November 19, 1951, the plane mentioned in this Note violated the Hungarian border, penetrated to the zone of the Soviet air unit maintained in Hungary in accordance with Article 22 of the Peace Treaty, and was forced to land on Hungarian territory by a Soviet fighter patrol.

Y. A. Malik returned this Note to Mr O'Shaughnessy with the following letter:

'Your Note No. 473 of December 10, 1952, is returned herewith as one that was wrongly addressed, since it deals with the American C47 military transport plane which in November, 1951, violated the border of the Hungarian People's Republic, and was confiscated by the Hungarian authorities together with the objects it contained, in accordance with the ruling of the Budapest Military Tribunal.'

F. DISARMAMENT

(i) Draft Russian resolution on disarmament submitted to the Political Committee of the United Nations on 12 January 1952[1]

1. The General Assembly declares participation in the aggressive Atlantic bloc and the creation by certain States, and primarily by the United States of America, of military, naval and air bases in foreign territories incompatible with membership of the United Nations.

2. The General Assembly recognizes it to be essential that:

(a) The countries taking part in the Korean war should immediately end military operations, conclude an armistice and withdraw their forces from the 38th parallel within a period of ten days;

(b) All foreign troops and also foreign volunteer units should be withdrawn from Korea within a period of three months.

3. The General Assembly, considering the use of atomic weapons, as weapons of aggression and of the mass destruction of people, to be at variance with the conscience and honour of peoples and incompatible with membership of the United Nations, proclaims the unconditional prohibition of atomic weapons and the establishment of strict international control over the enforcement of this prohibition, it being understood that the prohibition of atomic weapons and the institution of international control shall be put into effect simultaneously.

[1] A/C. 1/698.

The General Assembly instructs the Disarmament Commission to prepare and submit to the Security Council, not later than 1 June 1952, for its consideration, a draft convention providing measures to ensure the implementation of the General Assembly decision on the prohibition of atomic weapons, the cessation of their production, the use of already-manufactured atomic bombs exclusively for civilian purposes, and the establishment of strict international control over the observance of the above-mentioned convention.

4. The General Assembly recommends the permanent members of the Security Council—the United States of America, the United Kingdom, France, China and the Union of Soviet Socialist Republics—to reduce the armaments and armed forces in their possession at the time of the adoption of this recommendation by one-third during a period of one year from the date of its adoption.

5. The General Assembly recommends that forthwith, and in any case not later than one month after the adoption by the General Assembly of the decisions on the prohibition of atomic weapons and the reduction by one-third of the armaments and armed forces of the five Powers, all States should submit complete official data on the situation of their armaments and armed forces, including data on atomic weapons and military bases in foreign territories. These data shall be submitted with reference to the situation obtaining at the time when the above-mentioned decisions are adopted by the General Assembly.

6. The General Assembly recommends the establishment within the framework of the Security Council of an international control organ, the functions of which shall be to supervise the implementation of the decisions on the prohibition of atomic weapons and the reduction of armaments and armed forces, and to verify the data submitted by States regarding the situation of their armaments and armed forces.

With a view to the establishment of an appropriate system of guarantees for the observance of the General Assembly's decisions on the prohibition of atomic weapons and the reduction of armaments, the international control organ shall have the right to conduct inspection on a continuing basis; but it shall not be entitled to interfere in the domestic affairs of States.

7. The General Assembly calls upon the Governments of all States, both Members of the United Nations and those not at present in the Organization, to consider at a world conference the question of the substantial reduction of armed forces and armaments and also the question of practical measures for prohibiting the atomic weapon and establishing international control over the observance of such prohibition.

The General Assembly recommends that the above-mentioned world conference should be convened at the earliest possible date and, in any case, not later than 15 July 1952.

8. The General Assembly calls upon the United States of America, the United Kingdom, France, China and the Soviet Union to conclude a peace pact, and to combine their efforts for the achievement of this high and noble aim.

The General Assembly also calls upon all other peace-loving States to join in the peace pact.

(ii) UNITED STATES PROPOSALS FOR THE DISCLOSURE AND VERIFICATION OF ARMED FORCES AND CONVENTIONAL AND ATOMIC ARMAMENTS, SUBMITTED TO THE DISARMAMENT COMMISSION ON 5 APRIL 1952[1]

ANNEX I

Proposed stages of disclosure and verification of Armed forces and non-atomic armaments

STAGE I

Disclose

(a) Over-all manpower strength of regular and reserve military forces and para-military organizations, including training establishments and security and police forces, broken down into each category.

(b) Location of all operational military installations.

Verify

(a) By examination and cross-checks of central records to include personnel, disbursement, medical and procurement supplemented by access to and spot checks of records at selected installations.

(b) By direct examination, location, manpower used, power input and physical dimensions of installations.

(a) and (b): Inspectors will have access to entire national territory to extent necessary to determine that all facilities and installations have been declared. Aerial surveys will be permitted for same purpose and to same extent.

STAGE II

Disclose

(a) Organization, composition and disposition of units making up over-all strengths disclosed in stage I.

(b) Over-all annual capacity of heavy industry relating to armaments to include coal, steel, aluminium and electricity.

[1] DC/C. 2/1, Annexes I and II: *Disarmament Commission, Supplement for April, May and June 1952*, pp. 15–18.

Verify

(a) By quantitative analysis of records pertaining to personnel, movement of units and administrative support supplemented by access to and spot checks of selected units and installations

(b) By cross-checks of pertinent statistics and employment records, access to plants, and analysis of operation with respect to materials used.

(a) and (b): By aerial survey as stated in stage I.

Stage III

Disclose

(a) Equipment (including reserve equipment of units making up over-all strengths disclosed in stages I and II except units equipped with novel weapons).

(b) Production facilities for manufacture of weapons and heavy equipment for units making up over-all strengths disclosed in stages I and II (excluding novel weapons), giving location, type and capacity.

Verify

(a) By quantitative analysis of records pertaining to table of organization and equipment, and repair and overhaul of equipment supplemented by access to and spot checks of selected units and installations.

(b) By inspection of physical dimensions of plants and examination of records pertaining to consumption of power and raw materials, available labour force, and finances, and by access to and spot checks of selected units and installations.

(a) and (b): By aerial survey as stated in stage I.

Stage IV

Disclose

(a) Information as to equipment of units equipped with novel weapons to include biological warfare, chemical warfare, radiological warfare and atomic weapons.

(b) Installations and facilities devoted to manufacture of novel weapons.

Verify

(a) By cross-checks with stages I and II and quantitative inspection of units disclosed.

(b) By inspection of physical dimensions of plants and examination of records pertaining to consumption of power and raw materials, available labour force, and finances, and by access to and spot checks of selected units and installations.

(a) and (b): By aerial survey as set forth in stage I.

STAGE V

Disclose

(*a*) Quantities of novel weapons on hand by types.

Verify

(*a*) By physical count of stockpiles of finished novel weapons cross-checked with information disclosed in stages I, II, III and IV.

ANNEX II

Proposed stages of disclosure and verification of Atomic armaments

STAGE I

Disclose

(*a*) Location of all installations directly concerned with production of atomic energy, or the product of which is primarily useful in the production of atomic energy. Also manpower employed, physical dimensions and power input of each installation. (Excluding weapon storage sites.)

(*b*) Uses or functions of these installations. This should be confined to a statement giving the input material, the produce material and the process used in each instance.

Verify

(*a*) By direct examination, location, manpower used, power input and physical dimensions of installation. (Inspectors will have access to entire national territory to the extent necessary to determine through such means as aerial survey, inspection of water and railways and power lines, that all atomic energy installations have been declared.)

(*b*) Uses and functions in so far as revealed by external examination of all structures and unhoused equipment. Detailed interior inspection shall take place in subsequent stages, the particular stage in which it will take place depending upon the function of the plant. (Verification of (*a*) above will be of value as partial verification of plant use or function.)

(*a*) and (*b*): By aerial survey in all stages for same purposes and to same extent as permitted with armed forces and non-atomic armaments. (See annex I.)

STAGE II

Disclose

(*a*) Details of design and operation, including present and past output, of all those installations or parts of installations concerned with preparation of atomic energy, raw or feed materials (and such auxiliary materials as graphite, heavy water and beryllium), from mines up to but not including reactors, isotope separation plants, and similar nuclear conversion devices used to produce fissionable or fusionable material.

Verify

(*a*) By direct and detailed inspection of all aspects the installations and appropriate records. Cross-checks with stage I.

STAGE III

Disclose

(*a*) Details of design and operation, including present and past output of all those atomic energy installations, or parts of installations, concerned with the conversion of feed materials to fissionable or fusionable materials or with the preparation of radioactive materials in large quantities.

(*b*) Amounts and types of fissionable or fusionable material on hand or in process; amounts and types of radioisotopes on hand or in process.

(*c*) General design and operational characteristics of research laboratories involving reactors operating at a power level of 1 MW or more, including amounts of radioactive, or fissionable or fusionable materials produced.

Verify

(*a*) By direct and detailed inspection of all aspects the installations and appropriate records. Cross-checks with stages I and II.

(*b*) By direct and detailed inspection of fissionable or fusionable material, or radioactive materials, installations for production thereof, and appropriate records.

(*c*) By survey of facilities associated with reported reactors, by detailed inspection of reactors themselves.

STAGE IV

Disclose

(*a*) Details of design and operation, including past and present output of all those atomic energy establishments and installations concerned with the fabrication of atomic or radioactive weapons from fissionable or other materials.

Verify

(*a*) By direct and detailed inspection of installations and appropriate records. Cross-checks with stages I, II and III.

STAGE V

Disclose

(*a*) Location, numbers and types of atomic and radioactive weapons on hand. Weapon storage sites.

Verify

(*a*) By direct inspection. Cross-checks with stages I, II and III and (*a*) above.

(iii) UNITED STATES PROPOSAL OF SIX ESSENTIAL PRINCIPLES FOR A DISARMAMENT PROGRAMME, SUBMITTED TO THE DISARMAMENT COMMISSION ON 24 APRIL 1952[1]

The Disarmament Commission accepts as a guide for its future work the following principles as the essentials of a disarmament programme:

1. The goal of disarmament is not to regulate but to prevent war by relaxing the tensions and fears created by armaments and by making war inherently, as it is constitutionally under the Charter, impossible as a means of settling disputes between nations.

2. To achieve this goal, all States must co-operate to establish an open and substantially disarmed world:

(*a*) In which armed forces and armaments will be reduced to such a point and in such a thorough fashion that no State will be in a condition of armed preparedness to start a war, and

(*b*) In which no State will be in a position to undertake preparations for war without other States having knowledge of such preparations long before an offending State could start a war.

3. To reach and keep this goal, international agreements must be entered into by which all States would reduce their armed forces to levels, and restrict their armaments to types and quantities, necessary for:

(*a*) The maintenance of internal security,

(*b*) Fulfilment of obligations of States to maintain peace and security in accordance with the United Nations Charter.

4. Such international agreements must ensure by a comprehensive and co-ordinated programme both:

(*a*) The progressive reduction of armed forces and permitted armaments to fixed maximum levels, radically less than present levels and balanced throughout the process of reduction, thereby eliminating mass armies and preventing any disequilibrium of power dangerous to peace, and

(*b*) The elimination of all instruments adaptable to mass destruction.

[1] DC/C. 1/1: *Disarmament Commission, Supplement for April, May and June 1952*, pp. 8–9.

5. Such international agreements must provide effective safeguards to ensure that all phases of the disarmament programme are carried out. In particular, the elimination of atomic weapons must be accomplished by an effective system of international control of atomic energy to ensure that atomic energy is used for peaceful purposes only.

6. Such international agreements must provide an effective system of progressive and continuing disclosure and verification of all armed forces and armaments, including atomic, to achieve the open world in which alone there can be effective disarmament.

(iv) Proposals on the numerical limitation of armed forces submitted to the Disarmament Commission by the U.S.A., the United Kingdom and France on 28 May 1952[1]

A. *Introduction*

1. Paragraph 3 of General Assembly resolution 502 (VI) of 11 January 1952:

'*Directs* the Disarmament Commission to prepare proposals to be embodied in a draft treaty (or treaties) for the regulation, limitation and balanced reduction of all armed forces and all armaments, for the elimination of all major weapons adaptable to mass destruction, and for the effective international control of atomic energy to ensure the prohibition of atomic weapons and the use of atomic energy for peaceful purposes only.'

2. Paragraph 6 of the resolution:

'*Directs* the Commission, in working out plans for the regulation, limitation and balanced reduction of all armed forces and all armaments:

'(*a*) To determine how over-all limits and restrictions on all armed forces and all armaments can be calculated and fixed;
'(*b*) To consider methods according to which States can agree by negotiation among themselves, under the auspices of the Commission, concerning the determination of the over-all limits and restrictions referred to in sub-paragraph (*a*) above and the allocation within their respective national military establishments of the permitted national armed forces and armaments.'

3. The present working paper presents a plan for the determination of over-all numerical limitations on the size of the armed forces of States. Obviously some over-all limitations on the size of the armed forces of States are an essential part of any comprehensive plan for the regulation,

---

[1] DC/10: *Disarmament Commission, Supplement for April, May and June 1952*, pp. 2–5.

limitation and balanced reduction of armed forces and armaments. The working paper is not intended to exclude, but to facilitate the development of other essential components which must be included in what the preamble of the General Assembly resolution refers to as 'comprehensive and co-ordinated plans, under international control, for the regulation, limitation and balanced reduction of all armed forces and armaments, for the elimination of all major weapons adaptable to mass destruction, and for the effective control of atomic energy to ensure the prohibition of atomic weapons and the use of atomic energy for peaceful purposes' including 'safeguards that will ensure the compliance of all . . . nations [whose military resources are such that their failure to accept would endanger the system]'. Proposals have already been submitted on certain other essential components, i.e. the control of atomic energy and disclosure and verification of all armed forces and armaments. By submitting this working paper and focusing attention on another component we hope to facilitate progress toward an agreed comprehensive program.

B. *Standards for determining numerical limitations of all armed forces*

4. In fixing numerical limitations on the armed forces of States a number of factors, demographic, geographic, political and economic, have to be considered. The Charter responsibilities of States and the need of balanced power-relationships among States must also be taken into account. There is no one automatic formula which can inflexibly be applied in all cases. The objective must be to reduce the possibility and the fear of successful aggression and to avoid a disequilibrium of power dangerous to international peace and security.

5. The following working formula is suggested as a basis of discussion:

(*a*) There should be fixed numerical ceilings for China, France, the Union of Soviet Socialist Republics, the United Kingdom, and the United States of America which should be worked out with a view of avoiding a disequilibrium of power dangerous to international peace and security among themselves or with other States and thus reducing the danger of war. It is tentatively suggested that the maximum ceilings for the Union of Soviet Socialist Republics, the United States of America and China should be the same and fixed at, say, between 1 million and 1.5 million, and the maximum ceilings for the United Kingdom and France should be the same and fixed at, say, between 700,000 and 800,000.

(*b*) For all other States having substantial armed forces there should be agreed maximum ceilings fixed in relation to the ceilings agreed upon for the five Powers. Such ceilings should be fixed with a view to avoiding a disequilibrium of power dangerous to international peace and security in any area of the world and thus reducing the danger of war. The ceilings would normally be less than one per cent of the population. Moreover, they should be less than current levels except in very special circumstances.

C. *Significance of over-all numerical limitations*

6. While a nation's armed forces are not the only measure of its armed strength, and other elements of armed strength will have to be considered in any comprehensive programme for the balanced reduction of armed forces and armaments, nevertheless a numerical limitation on armed forces is a major element in any such programme for the following reasons:

(*a*) All armaments programmes depend upon man-power and therefore must to a greater or less degree be affected by limitations on permitted armed forces.

(*b*) A substantial reduction of armed forces as here suggested in itself would tend to reduce the likelihood of successful aggression.

(*c*) Agreement on a substantial and balanced reduction of armed forces, minimizing the likelihood and fear of successful aggression, should greatly facilitate agreement reducing and restricting the armaments supporting these armed forces.

D. *Implementation of proposals for numerical limitations of all armed forces*

7. In determining the numbers in the armed forces, all kinds of armed forces, including para-military and security forces, must be included.

8. Adequate provision must be made to ensure that the maximum limitation on armed forces is not circumvented through building up large forces of trained reserves or militarily trained police.

9. This system must be accepted by all States, whether or not Members of the United Nations, whose military resources are such that their failure to accept would endanger the system.

10. There should be adequate safeguards throughout the process of reduction to ensure that limitations are put into effect and observed as agreed and that violations can be promptly detected.

11. The implementation of the reductions should be closely related to progress in connexion with other phases of the programme for regulation, limitation and balanced reduction of armed forces and armaments, such as the control of atomic energy and the system of progressive and continuing disclosure and verification.

12. The reduction should be carried through in a manner and in accordance with a time schedule prescribed by the international control organ

and should be completed within the shortest feasible time after its commencement.

13. In the future, further numerical limitation of permitted armed forces would be contemplated as substantial progress is achieved toward the easing of international tensions, and the agreed ceilings would be subject to review at stated intervals.

14. The proposed limitations—including their relationship to other components of the programme for regulation, limitation and balanced reduction of armed forces and armaments and the elimination of weapons adaptable to mass destruction—should be comprehended within the treaty or treaties required under paragraph 3 of General Assembly resolution 502 (VI) of 11 January 1952.[1]

[1] *Documents* (R.I.I.A.) for 1951, pp. 356–8.

PART IV

THE MIDDLE EAST AND THE ARAB WEST

A. EGYPT

(i) DRAFT OF THE SELF-GOVERNMENT STATUTE FOR THE SUDAN, LAID BEFORE THE SUDAN LEGISLATIVE ASSEMBLY ON 2 APRIL 1952[1]

An Order to provide for full Self-Government in the Sudan

WHEREAS by the Executive Council and Legislative Assembly Ordinance 1948 measures were taken to promote the realisation of the desire of the peoples of the Sudan to attain full self-government by the creation of an Executive Council and Legislative Assembly and delegation thereto of executive and legislative power.

AND WHEREAS the Governor-General is of opinion that measures may now be taken to complete the realisation of the said desire for full self-government by the creation in place of the said Council and Assembly of fully self-governing institutions, with all powers necessary to that end, as a prelude to the exercise by the Sudanese of self-determination in due course.

Now THEREFORE in exercise of the powers conferred upon him by Section 66 of the said Ordinance and of all other powers enabling him in that behalf the Governor-General of the Sudan having taken into consideration the views thereon of the said Assembly and Council

HEREBY MAKES THE FOLLOWING ORDER:—

CHAPTER I

PRELIMINARY

(Title and Commencement)

1. This Order may be cited as 'the Self-Government Statute', and shall come into force on the   day of   1952.

(Interpretation)

2. In this Order, unless the context otherwise requires, the following

---

[1] Great Britain: Foreign Office: *Documents concerning Constitutional Development in the Sudan and the Agreement between the Government of the United Kingdom of Great Britain and Northern Ireland and the Egyptian Government concerning Self-Government and Self-Determination for the Sudan, 17th February 1953* (Cmd. 8767). (London, H.M.S.O., 1953), pp. 18–45.

expressions shall have the meanings hereby respectively assigned to them:—

'The appointed day' means the day upon which the Governor-General by writing under his hand certifies that the self-governing institutions intended to be hereby created, namely the Council of Ministers, the House of Representatives, and the Senate, have been duly constituted in accordance with the provisions of this Order.

'House' includes, where the context so requires, the Senate.

'Chief Justice' includes a person appointed to act as Chief Justice.

'The Council' means the Council of Ministers constituted by this Order.

'Governor-General' includes the person from time to time appointed by the Governor-General to perform the functions of his office.

'Grand Kadi' includes a person appointed to act as Grand Kadi.

'Member of the Judiciary' means any of the following persons, namely:—

Chief Justice, Grand Kadi, Mufti, Members of the High Courts, District Judges, Kadis, Resident Magistrates, Police Magistrates, Legal Assistants, and the Chief Registrar.

'Members of Subsidiary Courts' means members of the Judiciary inferior to members of the High Courts.

'Money bill' means any bill making any provision for expenditure to be charged to or an allocation to be made from revenue, or Government reserves, any bill imposing altering or repealing any tax, and any bill authorising the raising of loans or the issue of bonds.

'The Ordinance' means the Executive Council and Legislative Assembly Ordinance 1948.

'Parliament' means the Senate and the House of Representatives.

'Pensions' includes gratuities and other post-service benefits.

'Southern Constituency' means, in the case of the Senate, one of the Southern Provinces, and in the case of the House of Representatives, a constituency in any of such Provinces.

'Southern Provinces' means the Provinces of Equatoria Bahr El Ghazal and Upper Nile.

'Tax' means any tax, whether general local or special, and includes royalties, import, export, consumption and excise duties.

(Effect of Appointed Day)

3.—(1) Upon the appointed day the provisions of the Ordinance and all orders prior to this present Order made thereunder shall be replaced by the provisions of this Order, which incorporates the said first-mentioned provisions as hereby extended modified and varied.

(2) From and after the appointed day, references in any existing legisla-

tion to the Legislative Assembly shall be read and construed as meaning Parliament or either House of Parliament as the context may require; and references to the Governor-General's Council, or to the Governor-General in Council, or to the Executive Council, or to the Governor-General acting on the advice of the Executive Council, or any expressions of the like nature, shall be read and construed as meaning the Council of Ministers. Provided that whenever such legislation confers a power to make regulations rules or orders with or subject to the consent or approval of the Governor-General in Council or of the Executive Council, the consent or approval of the Council of Ministers thereto shall not be required; but all such regulations rules or orders shall be laid upon the table of each House, and the House of Representatives may within one month by resolution cancel the same, but so that such cancellation shall not have retrospective effect.

(Effect of Order on Existing Legislation)

4. In the case of any repugnancy or inconsistency between the provisions of this Order and any existing legislative enactment, the provisions of this Order shall prevail, and such legislative enactment shall be read and construed as repealed, cancelled, or amended so far only as may be necessary for the purpose of removing such repugnancy or inconsistency; but without prejudice to the right of Parliament, or the Council, or other body or person having legislative authority with regard thereto, in due course specifically to repeal cancel or amend any such legislative enactment for the purpose aforesaid.

CHAPTER II

FUNDAMENTAL RIGHTS

(Right to Freedom and Equality)

5.—(1) All persons in the Sudan are free and are equal before the law.

(2) No disability shall attach to any Sudanese by reason of birth religion race or sex in regard to public or private employment or in the admission to or in the exercise of any occupation, trade, business or profession.

(Freedom from Arrests and Confiscations)

6. No person may be arrested detained imprisoned or deprived of the use or ownership of his property except by due process of law.

(Freedom of Religion, Opinion and Association)

7.—(1) All persons shall enjoy freedom of conscience, and the right freely to profess their religion, subject only to such conditions relating to morality, public order, or health as may be imposed by law.

(2) All persons shall have the right of free expression of opinion, and the right of free association and combination, subject to the law.

(The Rule of Law)

8. All persons and associations of persons, official or otherwise, are subject to the law as administered by the Courts of Justice, saving only the established privileges of Parliament.

(Independence of Judiciary)

9. The Judiciary shall be independent and free from interference or control by any organ of the Government, executive or legislative.

(Right to Constitutional Remedy)

10. Any person may apply to the High Court for protection or enforcement of any of the rights conferred by this Chapter, and the High Court shall have power to make all such orders as may be necessary and appropriate to secure to the applicant the enjoyment of any of the said rights.

CHAPTER III

THE GOVERNOR-GENERAL

(Position of Governor-General as Military Commander-in-Chief)

11. The Supreme military command in the Sudan shall remain vested in the Governor-General, who shall be Commander-in-Chief of the Sudan Defence Force.

(Position of Governor-General as Constitutional Authority)

12. The Governor-General shall be the Supreme Constitutional Authority within the Sudan, but, save as expressly in this Order provided to the contrary, shall act upon the advice of the Prime Minister or the Council of Ministers as the case may be.

CHAPTER IV

THE EXECUTIVE

(The Prime Minister)

13. The Governor-General shall appoint as Prime Minister such person as may from time to time be elected for the purpose by the House of Representatives from amongst the existing members of Parliament.

(Ministers)

14.—(1) The Prime Minister shall be appointed Minister to one or more of the several Departments of Government, or Minister without Portfolio.

(2) The Governor-General on the advice of the Prime Minister shall appoint not less than ten nor more than fifteen Ministers to other Departments, or Ministers without Portfolio, of whom not less than two Ministers in each Council shall be members of Parliament representing Southern constituencies. Provided that the Governor-General may at his discretion dispense with such last-mentioned requirement if he is at any time satisfied that the right of special representation on the Council hereby granted in respect of the Southern Provinces is being abused.

(Qualifications)

15.—(1) No person shall be appointed Minister unless he is qualified for membership of Parliament.

(2) A person who is party to an existing contract with the Government shall not be eligible for appointment unless he shall have disclosed to the Prime Minister the existence and nature of such contract and of his interest therein, and either the Prime Minister shall have raised no objection thereto, or he shall at the request of the Prime Minister have terminated his interest therein.

(Ministerial Oath)

16. Every Minister shall on appointment take an oath or make a declaration before the Governor-General in the form set out in Part I of the Third Schedule.

(Remuneration)

17. The salaries to be paid to the Prime Minister and other Ministers shall be such as may from time to time be laid down by Parliament by ordinance, and in the meantime shall be those respectively payable to the Leader of the Assembly and the other Ministers immediately before the appointed day.

(Vacation of Office)

18.—(1) The Prime Minister shall cease to hold office in the following events, namely:—

(a) if he shall cease to be qualified for membership of Parliament; or
(b) on acceptance by the Governor-General of his resignation, duly tendered in writing to the Governor-General; or
(c) upon the first sitting of the first session of a new House of Representatives; or
(d) upon the proclamation of a Constitutional Emergency under Section 102.

(2) A Minister shall cease to hold office in the following events, namely:—

(a) if, not being a member of Parliament at the date of his appointment, he shall have failed to be elected a member within six months of such date. Provided that not more than three Ministers in any one Council may, at the discretion of the Prime Minister, be exempted from the obligation to vacate office under this paragraph; or

(b) if he shall cease to be qualified for membership of Parliament; or

(c) if he shall place his resignation in the hands of the Prime Minister for submission to the Governor-General, and the Governor-General on the advice of the Prime Minister shall accept the same; or

(d) if his appointment shall be terminated by the Governor-General on the advice of the Prime Minister; or

(e) if the Prime Minister shall cease to hold office.

(The Council of Ministers)

19. The Prime Minister and other Ministers shall together constitute a Council of Ministers, which shall be responsible to Parliament for the executive and administrative functions of government.

(Responsibility of Ministers)

20. Ministers shall be individually responsible to the Prime Minister for the conduct of their Ministries.

(Collective Responsibility of Council)

21. The Ministers shall be collectively responsible for the policy decisions and acts of the Council. Provided that where in the opinion of the Prime Minister any such matter does not involve an issue of confidence in the Council as a whole, it shall lie within the discretion of the Prime Minister whether an adverse vote thereon in the House of Representatives shall entail the resignation of the Council, the resignation or termination of appointment of the Minister responsible, or the withdrawal or revocation of the matter in question.

(Parliamentary Under-Secretaries)

22.—(1) The Prime Minister may appoint a Parliamentary Under-Secretary to such of the Ministries as he may think fit.

(2) A Parliamentary Under-Secretary shall be responsible to his Minister.

(3) No person shall be appointed Parliamentary Under-Secretary unless he is eligible for membership of Parliament.

(4) A Parliamentary Under-Secretary who at the date of his appointment is not a member of Parliament shall cease to hold office if he fails

to be elected a member within six months of such date. Provided that not more than three Parliamentary Under-Secretaries at any one time may, at the discretion of the Prime Minister, be exempted from the obligation to vacate office under this sub-section.

(5) The salaries to be paid to Parliamentary Under-Secretaries shall be such as may from time to time be laid down by Parliament by ordinance, and in the meantime shall be those payable to Under-Secretaries immediately before the appointed day.

(6) The Prime Minister may from time to time at his discretion terminate such appointments and make fresh appointments to the same or other Ministries.

(7) All appointments hereunder shall forthwith lapse upon the Prime Minister ceasing to hold office.

(Filling of vacancies)

23. If a Minister other than the Prime Minister ceases to hold office, the vacancy may be filled by fresh appointment made in accordance with the provisions of section 14 (2); but so that, subject only to the power of dispensation conferred upon the Governor-General by that sub-section, no appointment shall be made, or vacancy left unfilled for more than three months, the effect of which would be to leave the Council without at least two Ministers who are members of Parliament representing Southern constituencies.

(Presidency of Council)

24.—(1) The Prime Minister shall be President of the Council, and if present shall preside over its meetings.

(2) The Prime Minister may appoint a member of the Council to preside in his absence, and in default of such appointment, the Council shall elect a person to preside at each such meeting.

(Quorum)

25. Unless more than half the total number of Ministers are present at a meeting, there shall not be a quorum, and no business save that of adjournment shall be transacted thereat.

(Rules of conduct for Ministers and Parliamentary Under-Secretaries)

26.—(1) The proceedings and deliberations of the Council shall be secret, and every Minister shall be under an obligation not to disclose the same outside the Council Chamber. Provided always that a Minister may be expressly authorised by the Council in the exercise of his official duties to make public any decision of the Council.

(2) A Parliamentary Under-Secretary shall likewise be under an obliga-

tion not to disclose secret or confidential information coming to his knowledge by virtue of his office or in the course of his official duties.

(3) Ministers and Parliamentary Under-Secretaries shall so conduct themselves in office that no conflict of duty or interest shall arise, or appear to arise, between their official and their private duties and interests; and in particular they shall not make use of their official positions for private advantage, or to further private interests.

(4) A Minister or Parliamentary Under-Secretary who commits a breach of his obligations hereunder shall be liable to have his appointment terminated by the Governor-General on the advice of the Prime Minister; and may, if the breach is capable of remedy, be called upon by the Prime Minister to remedy the same as a condition of retaining his appointment. Provided that any such action by the Governor-General or the Prime Minister shall be without prejudice to any other proceedings which may lie in respect of such breach against the Minister or Parliamentary Under-Secretary concerned.

(Standing Orders of Council)

27. The Council may make standing orders for the regulation and orderly conduct of its proceedings and the despatch of its business, including the determination of the places and times at which the Council shall meet, the conditions under which persons not members of the Council may be invited to attend and address meetings thereof, and the appointment and duties of officials and servants of the Council.

(Duty of Prime Minister to Report to Governor-General)

28. It shall be the duty of the Prime Minister to communicate to the Governor-General all decisions of the Council (other than decisions on purely formal or routine matters) relating to the administration of the Sudan, or to proposed legislation, and to give to the Governor-General all such information relating thereto as the Governor-General may from time to time require.

CHAPTER V

THE LEGISLATURE

(Creation of Parliament)

29. There shall be constituted a Parliament for the Sudan, which shall consist of two Houses, namely a Senate, and a House of Representatives.

(Constitution of Legislature)

30. The Governor-General the Senate and the House of Representatives shall together constitute the Legislature for the Sudan.

(Composition of Senate)

31. The Senate shall be composed of 50 members, of whom 20 shall be nominated by the Governor-General at his discretion, and 30 shall be elected to represent constituencies in accordance with the provisions of Part I of the First Schedule.

(Composition of House of Representatives)

32. The House of Representatives shall be composed of elected members only, who shall be elected to represent the constituencies specified in Part II of the First Schedule, in accordance with the provisions of Part III of that Schedule.

(Qualifications of Voters)

33. The qualifications of voters in elections to the House of Representatives shall be those specified in Part IV of the First Schedule.

(Qualifications for Membership of Parliament)

34.—(1) Sudanese who are not less than 40 years of age shall be eligible for membership of the Senate. Provided that Sudanese standing for Southern constituencies shall be eligible if not less than 30 years of age.

(2) Sudanese who are not less than 30 years of age shall be eligible for membership of the House of Representatives.

(Members' Oath)

35. Every Member of each House shall, before taking his seat, take an oath or make a declaration in the form set out in Part II of the Third Schedule, before the Speaker, or, in the case of the Speaker, before the assembled Members of that House.

(Disqualifications)

36.—(1) The following persons shall be disqualified from membership of either House:—

(a) Members of the Judiciary.
(b) The Auditor General.
(c) Government servants.
(d) Undischarged bankrupts or persons whose property is subject to a composition or arrangement with creditors.
(e) Persons who have within the past seven years been sentenced to a term of imprisonment for a period of not less than two years.
(f) Persons who have within the past seven years been convicted of a corrupt practice or any abetment thereof at any Parliamentary or Local Government election.

(*g*) Persons of unsound mind.

(*h*) Illiterates.

(2) No person shall be a member of more than one House at the same time.

(Vacation of Seats)

37. The seat of a member of either House shall become vacant in any of the following events:—

(*a*) Upon his death.

(*b*) If without leave of the House he shall be absent from 25 consecutive Sittings of the House.

(*c*) If he shall become subject to any of the disqualifications specified in the preceding Section.

(*d*) If any other person is convicted of any corrupt practice carried out on his behalf or with his knowledge or connivance in respect of the election at which he was elected.

(*e*) If he shall become a member of the other House.

(*f*) If he shall give to the Speaker of the House written notification of his resignation from membership.

(Filling of Vacancies)

38.—(1) Whenever the seat of an elected member becomes vacant, a fresh election shall be held to fill the vacancy in accordance with the procedure appropriate to such seat.

(2) Whenever the seat of a nominated member of the Senate becomes vacant, the vacancy shall be filled by nomination by the Governor-General.

(Decision of Questions as to Membership of Parliament)

39. Any question which may arise as to the right of any person to be or remain a Member of either House shall be referred to the Speaker who may if he thinks fit submit the same to the Civil High Court for determination.

(Sessions of Parliament)

40.—(1) The Governor-General shall on the advice of the Prime Minister appoint the date and place for the commencement of each session of Parliament. Provided that Parliament shall be summoned by the Governor-General to meet twice at least in every year, and so that the commencement of a new session shall be appointed to take place within six months of the last sitting of the preceding session.

(2) A session of Parliament shall continue until determined by the Governor-General, on the advice of the Prime Minister, by prorogation of

both Houses or by dissolution of the House of Representatives. Provided that the Governor-General may in the exercise of his discretion decline to prorogue Parliament or dissolve the House of Representatives on the advice of the Prime Minister if by reason of either—

(*a*) the defeat in that House of a bill or motion (or an essential part thereof) initiated by the Council and declared by the Prime Minister to involve an issue of confidence in the Council, or

(*b*) a vote of censure passed in that House against the Council, or the Prime Minister, or against an individual Minister in a matter involving an issue of confidence in the Council as a whole,

the Governor-General is satisfied that the Prime Minister or the Council no longer enjoys the support of the House of Representatives.

(3) If the Governor-General declines for the reasons aforesaid to prorogue Parliament or dissolve the House of Representatives, the Prime Minister and other Ministers shall forthwith resign, and the Governor-General shall thereupon call upon the House of Representatives to elect a new Prime Minister.

(Duration of Senate)

41.—(1) Every Senate shall continue for a period of three years from the beginning of its first session, and save as hereinafter mentioned shall not be subject to dissolution.

(2) On the expiration of a Senate, the Governor-General shall direct fresh elections to be held for the purpose of filling the seats of elected members, and thereafter shall make fresh nominations for the purpose of filling the seats of nominated members.

(Duration of House of Representatives)

42.—(1) Unless sooner dissolved, every House of Representatives shall continue for a period of three years from the beginning of its first session.

(2) On the expiration or dissolution (other than a dissolution under the following section) of a House of Representatives, the Governor-General shall direct fresh elections to be held for the purpose of constituting a new House.

(3) Notwithstanding the expiration or dissolution of the House, the Prime Minister and other Ministers shall continue in office until the first sitting of the first session of the new House.

(4) The Governor-General shall call upon the new House of Representatives at the first sitting of its first session to elect a new Prime Minister.

(Special Dissolution of Parliament prior to Self-Determination)

43.—(1) The Governor-General may at his discretion dissolve the Senate together with the House of Representatives should it appear necessary or expedient so to do for the special purpose of facilitating the exercise by the Sudanese of self-determination.

(2) In such case the Governor-General may at his discretion dispense with or postpone the holding of fresh elections to either or both Houses pending the exercise of self-determination.

(Remuneration of Members)

44. Members of the Senate and of the House of Representatives who are not also either Ministers or Parliamentary Under-Secretaries shall be entitled to receive such salaries and allowances for their services as may from time to time be laid down by Parliament by ordinance; and in the meantime shall receive remuneration at the rate payable to members of the Legislative Assembly immediately before the appointed day.

(Presidency of Houses)

45.—(1) Each House shall be presided over by a Speaker.

(2) In the case of a joint sitting of both Houses, the Speaker of the House of Representatives, or in his absence the Speaker of the Senate shall preside.

(3) The Speaker of each House shall be elected by its members from amongst members or persons qualified to be members of that House.

(4) The name of the Speaker-elect shall be submitted to the Governor-General, who may at his discretion give or withhold his approval, and so that no person shall act as Speaker until the approval of the Governor-General has been signified.

(5) If the Speaker is not an existing member of the House, he shall become a member thereof *ex officio*.

(6) The Speaker may resign office by notice in writing addressed to the Clerk of the House and may be removed from office by the Governor-General on the recommendation of the House.

(7) There shall be a Deputy Speaker of each House, elected by the House from amongst its members. He shall preside at meetings of the House in the absence of the Speaker.

(8) The Deputy Speaker may resign office by notice in writing addressed to the Speaker, and may be removed from office by resolution of the House.

(9) The salaries to be paid to the Speakers and Deputy Speakers shall be such as may from time to time be laid down by Parliament by ordinance; and in the meantime the salary to be paid to the Speaker of the House of Representatives shall be that payable to the Speaker of the Legislative Assembly immediately before the appointed day. Provided that the Speaker's salary shall not be varied to his disadvantage after his appointment.

(Clerk of Parliament)

46.—(1) There shall be a Clerk of the Parliament, who shall be responsible for the administration of the Parliament, the general control of the offices of the Senate, and of the House of Representatives, and, in consultation with Speakers of both Houses, the staffing of the Parliament. The Clerk of the Parliament shall be entitled to sit and act as clerk in either House.

(2) The first Clerk of the Parliament shall be appointed by the Governor-General at his discretion; thereafter Clerks of the Parliament shall be so appointed by the Governor-General after consultation with the Speakers of both Houses.

(3) The Clerk of the Parliament shall hold office until he attains the age of 55 years, or such later age in any particular case as the Governor-General may approve, but may resign from office at any time by notice in writing addressed to the Governor-General; and may be removed from office by the Governor-General, for conduct unfitting his office, in pursuance of a recommendation to that effect passed by a three-quarters majority at a joint sitting of both Houses.

(4) On ceasing to hold office, a Clerk of the Parliament shall not be eligible for employment by the Sudan Government unless the Governor-General gives his consent in writing thereto.

(5) The salary and pension rights of the Clerk of the Parliament shall be such as may be laid down by Parliament by Ordinance; and in the meantime shall be those payable and applicable to the Clerk of the Assembly immediately before the appointed day. Provided that neither salary nor pension rights of the Clerk of Parliament shall be varied to his disadvantage after his appointment.

(Voting)

47.—(1) All questions proposed for decision in either House shall be determined by a majority of the votes of the members of that House present and voting.

(2) In the case of a joint sitting of both Houses, the question shall be determined by such majority as is hereinafter specified of the votes of the total number of members of both Houses present at such joint sitting, whether voting or not.

(3) The Speaker shall have neither an original nor a casting vote.

(4) If upon any question before either House the votes are equally divided, the motion shall be deemed to be lost.

(Quorum)

48.—(1) Two fifths of the members of each House shall constitute a quorum in that House.

(2) In the case of a joint sitting of both Houses, two thirds of the members of each House shall together constitute a quorum.

(Language of Parliament)

49. Subject to the provisions of their respective Standing Orders, proceedings in each House shall be conducted in the Arabic language, but without prejudice to such use of the English language as may be convenient.

(Freedom of Speech in Parliament)

50. Subject to the provisions of this Order and of any Standing Orders made hereunder, there shall be freedom of speech in each House, and no member thereof shall be liable to any proceedings in any Court in respect of anything said or of any vote given by him in either Chamber or any Committee thereof.

(Right of Debate)

51.—(1) Subject only as provided in Chapter XI, each House shall be entitled to hold debates and pass resolutions on any subject.

(2) Resolutions may, if the House in question thinks fit, be submitted to the Council for consideration.

(Right of Question)

52. A member of either House may, subject to its Standing Orders, address questions on any subject to the Council or the Minister concerned.

(Right of Ministers and Parliamentary under-Secretaries to take part in Proceedings of Parliament)

53. Every Minister and Parliamentary Under-Secretary shall have the right to speak in and otherwise take part in the proceedings of either House, any joint sitting of both Houses, and any Parliamentary committee of which he may be appointed a member. Provided that he shall not vote in a House of which he is not a member.

(Right of Governor-General to Address Parliament)

54.—(1) The Governor-General may at his discretion at any time address either the Senate or the House of Representatives, or both Houses in a joint sitting, and may for that purpose require the attendance of members.

(2) The Governor-General shall address the Senate and the House of Representatives, either separately or in a joint sitting at his discretion, at the beginning of every session.

(3) The Governor-General may at his discretion send messages to either House concerning pending legislation or business or on any other matter,

whether then pending before the House or otherwise, and such message shall thereupon be considered by the House in question with all convenient despatch.

(Standing Orders)

55.—(1) The Governor-General shall by order prescribe Standing Orders for the regulation and orderly conduct of the proceedings of Parliament and the despatch of its business, including provision for the setting up of such standing, select, or other committees of Parliament as may from time to time appear necessary or expedient; Parliament may thereafter from time to time add to, amend, or revoke such Standing Orders.

(2) The Governor-General in consultation with the Speaker of each House shall make Standing Orders for the regulation of joint sittings of the two Houses.

CHAPTER VI

LEGISLATION

(Legislative Procedure)

56.—(1) Subject only as provided in Chapter XI, legislation (other than subsidiary legislation) shall be initiated by bill or provisional order.

(2) A bill other than a money bill may originate in either House. A money bill may originate only in the House of Representatives.

(3) Subject as in this Section mentioned, a bill shall not become law unless it has been passed by both Houses, either without amendment, or with amendments agreed to by both Houses, and has received the Governor-General's assent. On receipt of the Governor-General's assent, the bill shall become law as an ordinance.

(4) A bill passed by the House in which it originated shall be sent to the other House, which may either pass the bill without amendment, reject the bill, or amend the bill and return it as amended to the originating House.

(5) If the Senate rejects a Bill passed by the House of Representatives, or returns such bill to the House of Representatives with amendments unacceptable to that House, or fails to pass such bill in due course, the following provisions shall apply:—

(a) in the case of a money bill, after the expiration of three months from the date of its introduction into the Senate, the bill may be presented to the Governor-General for his assent, and on receipt of his assent shall become law notwithstanding such rejection, amendment or failure to pass the same by the Senate.

(b) in the case of any other bill, if the bill is passed by the House of Representatives in two successive sessions, and the Senate rejects such bill, or returns such bill to the House of Representatives with amendments unacceptable to that House, or fails to pass such bill, in each of those sessions, then if one year shall have elapsed between the date of the introduction of the bill into the House of Representatives in the first session, and the date on which it was passed by the House of Representatives in the second session, the bill may be presented to the Governor-General for his assent, and on receipt of his assent shall become law notwithstanding such rejection, amendment, or failure to pass the same by the Senate.

(6) If a Government bill is passed by Parliament with amendments which are not acceptable to the Council, the Council may withdraw the bill.

(Joint Sittings)

57.—(1) The Governor-General may at his discretion summon both Houses to meet in a joint sitting to consider legislation in either of the following events:—

(a) when a bill, other than a money bill, passed by one House is either rejected by the other House, or passed by the other House with amendments unacceptable to the first House, or not passed by the other House within six months of its introduction into that House (excluding any period during which that House was prorogued),

(b) when a bill passed by the House of Representatives is, before its introduction into the Senate, declared by the Governor-General to be a measure of major importance.

(2) If the bill is passed by a three-quarters majority at such joint sitting, it shall be presented to the Governor-General for his assent.

(Urgent Legislation by Provisional Order)

58.—(1) If at any time when Parliament is not sitting the Council shall resolve that the passing of any Government legislation is a matter of urgency, the Council may make a provisional order enacting the same, and submit such order to the Governor-General for his assent.

(2) On receipt of the Governor-General's assent, the provisional order shall have the force of law.

(3) Every such order shall be submitted by the Council to Parliament as soon as practicable for confirmation.

(4) If the order be confirmed by resolution of each House, it shall thereupon become an ordinance.

(5) If either House refuses to confirm the provisional order, the order shall forthwith lapse and cease to have effect, but without prejudice to the right of the Council to introduce a bill to the same or a similar effect.

(6) Any enactment repealed or amended by a provisional order shall as from the date of the lapse of such order be revived and have effect as if such order had not been made.

(7) The lapse of any such order shall not have retrospective effect.

(8) The Governor-General may at his discretion withhold his assent under Subsection (1) if he is satisfied in any case that procedure by provisional order is an abuse of the legislative rights of Parliament.

(Confirmation of Provisional Orders made before the Appointed Day)

59. Provisional orders which have received the Governor-General's assent but have not been confirmed by the Legislative Assembly prior to the appointed day shall be deemed to have been made under this Order, and shall be dealt with in accordance with the provisions of Subsections (2) to (5) of the preceding Section.

CHAPTER VII

FINANCE

(Definition of Year)

60. In this Chapter the expression 'year' means the financial year, which shall be the 12 months ending on the 30th day of June in each calendar year.

(The Budget)

61. The annual budget, which shall consist of estimates of revenue and of expenditure (other than expenditure from reserves), shall be prepared by the Minister of Finance and shall, when passed by the Council, be laid before Parliament.

(Appropriation Bills)

62.—(1) The proposals of the Council for all such expenditure (other than expenditure hereinafter declared to be excepted expenditure) shall be submitted to the vote of Parliament by means of an Appropriation Bill which shall contain estimates under appropriate heads for the several services required.

(2) The following expenditure shall be excepted expenditure and shall not be submitted to the vote of Parliament but shall be paid out of revenue under the authority of this Order, namely:—

(a) Debt service charges for which the Sudan Government is liable by virtue of obligations incurred by it before the appointed day.

(b) The salaries payable to members of the Judiciary.

(c) The salaries payable to the members of the Public Service Commission.

(*d*) The salary payable to the Auditor-General.

(*e*) The expenditure of the Governor-General's office.

(3) The decision of the Governor-General whether any proposed expenditure falls under any of the above heads shall be conclusive.

(4) Parliament may assent or refuse its assent to any estimate included in the Appropriation Bill or may vote a lesser amount than that included therein but it may not vote an increased amount or an alteration in its destination.

(Advance Appropriation Bills)

63.—(1) The Council may present to Parliament by means of an Advance Appropriation Bill estimates of the amounts required to provide for the maintenance of government services from the first day of the financial year until the Appropriation Bill receives the Governor-General's assent.

(2) Advance Appropriation Bills shall be dealt with in the same way as Appropriation Bills.

(Supplementary Appropriation Bills)

64.—(1) The Council may present to Parliament supplementary estimates of expenditure whenever:—

(*a*) the amount voted by Parliament proves insufficient for the purpose of the current year; or

(*b*) a need arises during the current year for expenditure, for which the vote of Parliament is necessary, upon some new service not provided for in the budget for that year.

(2) Supplementary estimates shall be dealt with in the same way as estimates, save only that if Parliament is not then sitting the additional expenditure may in cases of urgency be authorised by provisional order.

(Allocations to Government Reserves)

65. Whenever the Council proposes to make allocations from revenue to Government reserves, or to make a transfer from one reserve to another, it shall present to Parliament a bill to cover such allocation or transfer; and such bill shall be dealt with in all respects as an Appropriation Bill, save only that if Parliament is not then sitting such allocation or transfer may in cases of urgency be authorised by provisional order. Provided that it shall not be necessary for the Council to present a separate bill to Parliament under this Section for any allocation which has been included as expenditure in an Appropriation Bill or a Supplementary Appropriation Bill.

(Expenditure to be Charged to Government Reserves)

66. Whenever the Council proposes to expend moneys to be charged to Government reserves, it shall present to Parliament a bill to cover such expenditure, and such bill shall be dealt with in all respects as an Appropriation Bill, save only that if Parliament is not then sitting, such expenditure may in cases of urgency be authorised by provisional order.

(Imposition, Alteration and Repeal of Taxes)

67. Proposals for the imposition of new or the alteration or repeal of existing taxes shall be submitted to the vote of Parliament by means of a bill. Provided that the Council may, where in its opinion the public interest so requires, provide by Order in Council that any proposed new tax or alteration in or repeal of an existing tax shall come into operation on the day on which the bill is presented to the House of Representatives; but every such order shall be without prejudice to the right of Parliament to vote in due course on any such proposal. An order made under this subsection may be revoked by the Council and, unless sooner revoked, shall expire upon the coming into operation of the bill as an ordinance, or upon the rejection by the House of Representatives of the bill; but its revocation or expiration shall not have retrospective effect, and no revenue collected under such order shall in any event be repayable. Provided further that if Parliament is not then sitting, any new tax or alteration to or repeal of an existing tax may in cases of urgency be authorised by provisional order.

(Consent by Minister of Finance to Financial Legislation)

68.—(1) No member of Parliament shall introduce any bill, or move any amendment to a bill, having the object or effect of imposing or increasing any tax, or imposing any charge upon the revenue, or upon Government reserves, save with the prior consent of the Minister of Finance. Provided that a bill or amendment shall not be deemed to have such object or effect by reason only that it includes provision for the imposition of fines or penalties, or for the payment of fees for licences, or fees for services rendered.

(2) A certificate by the Minister of Finance that a proposed bill has such object or effect shall be conclusive.

(Final Accounts)

69.—(1) The final accounts of Government revenue and expenditure, including expenditure charged to reserves, for each year shall be laid before Parliament by the Council.

(2) The Auditor-General shall submit his report on the accounts to Parliament at the same time as the accounts are laid before it, or as soon as practicable thereafter.

(3) If the accounts show that expenditure was incurred in excess of the appropriation made by Parliament in respect of any head, the Council shall present to Parliament a bill to cover the excess, and such bill shall be dealt with in all respects as an Appropriation Bill.

CHAPTER VIII

The Auditor-General

(Constitution of Post of Auditor-General)

70. There shall be an Auditor-General for the Sudan, who shall be the servant of and directly responsible to Parliament.

(Appointment)

71.—(1) The Auditor-General shall be appointed by the Governor-General at his discretion, after consultation with the retiring Auditor-General if any.

(2) An Auditor-General holding office immediately before the appointed day shall continue in office and shall be deemed to have been appointed under this Order.

(Tenure of Office)

72.—(1) The Auditor-General shall hold office until he attains the age of 55 years, or such later age in any particular case as the Governor-General may approve, but may resign from office at any time by notice in writing addressed to the Governor-General; and may be removed from office by the Governor-General for conduct unfitting his office in pursuance of a recommendation to that effect passed by a three-quarters majority at a joint sitting of both Houses.

(2) On ceasing to hold office, an Auditor-General shall not be eligible for employment in the Sudan Government service.

(Salary)

73. The salary and pension rights of the Auditor-General shall be such as may be laid down by Parliament by ordinance, and in the meantime shall be those in force immediately before the appointed day. Provided that neither salary nor pension rights of the Auditor-General shall be varied to his disadvantage after his appointment.

(Functions)

74.—(1) The Auditor-General shall perform such duties and exercise such powers in relation to the accounts of the Sudan Government and every department or board thereof as may be laid down by Parliament by ordinance; and in the meantime shall perform such duties and exercise such powers as were conferred on or exerciseable by the Auditor-General by or under the Audit Ordinance 1933 immediately before the appointed day.

(2) Any such ordinance may confer on the Auditor-General similar duties and powers in relation to such other accounts as may be therein specified.

(3) The Auditor-General shall not be concerned with matters of financial policy.

(Audit Reports)

75. The reports of the Auditor-General relating to the accounts specified in the preceding Section shall be submitted to Parliament.

CHAPTER IX

The Judiciary

(Powers of the Governor-General to be Discretionary)

76. In exercising his powers under this Chapter, the Governor-General shall act at his discretion.

(Preliminary)

77.—(1) The administration of justice in the Sudan shall be performed by a separate and independent department of state, which shall be called 'the Judiciary'.

(2) The Judiciary shall also assume responsibility for the Land Registries, the office of the Administrator-General, and such other quasi-judicial branches or departments of the Government service as the Governor-General after consultation with the Council of Ministers may from time to time direct.

(3) The Judiciary shall be directly and solely responsible to the Governor-General for the performance of its functions.

(4) The general administrative supervision and control of the Judiciary shall be vested in the Chief Justice.

(5) There shall be vested in the Chief Justice all the powers conferred upon the Governor-General or the Legal Secretary by the Civil Justice Ordinance, the Penal Code, the Code of Criminal Procedure, the Chiefs' Courts Ordinance 1931 and the Native Courts Ordinance 1932 save only such of the same as are specified in the First Part of the Second Schedule (which powers shall lapse and cease to be exercisable) and in the Second Part thereof (which powers shall remain vested in and exerciseable by the Governor-General at his discretion).

(6) There shall further be vested in the Chief Justice all the powers conferred upon Governors by the Chiefs' Courts Ordinance 1931 and the Native Courts Ordinance 1932. Provided that:—

(*a*) the Chief Justice may delegate all or any of the said powers to the Governor concerned:

(*b*) the Chief Justice may delegate any power, other than the powers of establishing and convening Courts and of appointing Presidents and members of Courts, to the Judge of the Civil High Court of a Province:

(*c*) neither the Chief Justice nor a Judge of the Civil High Court shall exercise any of the said powers except after consultation with the Governor concerned.

(Divisions of Judiciary)

78. The Judiciary shall consist of two divisions, the Civil division, and the Sharia division, of which the Chief Justice and the Grand Kadi shall be the respective Presidents and judicial heads.

(Jurisdiction of Civil Division)

79. The Civil division shall comprise the Courts and shall exercise the jurisdiction specified in the Civil Justice Ordinance, the Penal Code, the Code of Criminal Procedure, the Chiefs' Courts Ordinance 1931 and the Native Courts Ordinance 1932, or any amendment of the same, and such other Courts and jurisdiction as may from time to time be conferred upon it by ordinance.

(Jurisdiction of Sharia Division)

80. The Sharia division shall comprise the Courts, and shall exercise the jurisdiction, specified in the Sudan Mohammedan Law Courts Ordinance 1902.

(Conflict of Jurisdiction)

81. In the event of any conflict of jurisdiction arising between the Civil and the Sharia divisions, the same shall be referred for decision to a Court of Jurisdiction, which shall consist of the Chief Justice as President, the Grand Kadi, two judges of the Civil High Court and one judge of the Sharia High Court.

(Delegation of Powers by Chief Justice)

82. The Chief Justice may delegate to the Grand Kadi or to a member or members of the Civil High Court or the Chief Registrar or the Commissioner of Local Courts such of the powers vested in him as administrative head of the Judiciary as he may think fit: and may delegate to a member

or members of the Civil High Court or the Chief Registrar or the Commissioner of Local Courts such of the powers vested in him as judicial head of the Judiciary as he may think fit. Provided that he shall not delegate his powers under Subsection (5) of Section 77, or under Section 81.

(Custody of the Constitution)

83.—(1) The Judiciary shall be the custodian of the Constitution, and shall have jurisdiction to hear and determine any matter involving the interpretation of the Constitution hereby established, or the enforcement of the rights and freedoms conferred by Chapter II.

(2) The jurisdiction with regard to the interpretation of the Constitution shall be exercised by the Civil High Court.

(Judicial Appointments)

84.—(1) The Chief Justice, the Grand Kadi, and members of the High Courts shall be appointed by the Governor-General, after consultation with the appropriate President or retiring President.

(2) Members of subsidiary courts shall be appointed by the appropriate President.

(3) Members of the Judiciary holding office immediately before the appointed day shall continue in office, and shall be deemed to have been appointed under this Order.

(4) No appointment may be made which would effect an increase in the number of judges as established on the appointed day unless such increase is authorised by ordinance.

(The Judicial Oath)

85.—(1) The Chief Justice and members of the Civil High Court shall on appointment take an oath or make a declaration before the Governor-General in the form set out in Part III of the Third Schedule. Members of subsidiary civil courts shall take the said oath or make the said declaration before the Chief Justice.

(2) Any such person holding office immediately before the appointed day and continuing in office by virtue of Subsection (3) of the preceding section shall take the said oath or make the said declaration before the Governor-General or the Chief Justice, as the case may be, within 12 months of the appointed day.

(Tenure of Office)

86.—(1) The Chief Justice, the Grand Kadi, and members of the High Courts shall hold office until they attain the age of 55 years, or such later age in any particular case as the Governor-General may approve. Provided that they may at any time resign office by notice in writing addressed to the Governor-General; and may be removed from office by the Governor-General for conduct unfitting the office of a Judge in pursuance of a recommendation to that effect, either made by the appropriate President and all other members of that High Court (except the member, if any, whose conduct is in question), or carried by a three-quarters majority at a joint sitting of both Houses.

(2) Members of subsidiary Courts shall hold office until they attain such age as may be prescribed by regulations made by the Chief Justice, with the consent of the Governor-General and, in the case of members of subsidiary Sharia Courts, of the Grand Kadi, and in the meantime shall hold office in accordance with the terms of service applicable to them immediately before the appointed day. Provided that they may at any time resign office by notice in writing addressed to the appropriate President, and may be removed from office by the appropriate President with the consent of the Governor-General.

(3) No person who has held office as Chief Justice, Grand Kadi, or a member of a High Court may plead or act before any Court in the Sudan unless the Governor-General gives his consent in writing thereto.

(Salaries and Conditions of Service of Judiciary and Staff)

87.—(1) The salaries and pension rights of members of the Judiciary shall be such as may be laid down by Parliament by ordinance, and in the meantime shall be those in force immediately before the appointed day. Provided that neither salary nor pension rights of a member of the Judiciary shall be varied to his disadvantage after his appointment.

(2) The salaries and pension rights of the secretarial and non-judicial staff of the Judiciary, and of the members and staff of any quasi-judicial branch or department for which the Judiciary shall assume responsibility in pursuance of Subsection (2) of Section 77, shall continue to be those in force immediately before the appointed day until varied by or under the authority of an ordinance.

(3) Save in so far as the same are hereby in this Chapter expressly laid down or otherwise provided for, the conditions of service of members of the Judiciary, and of the members and staff mentioned in the preceding Subsection, including provisions as to recruitment, appointment, promotion, transfer, retirement, discipline and pension shall be such as may be laid down by regulations made by the Chief Justice, in consultation with the Grand Kadi so far as concerns the Sharia division, and with the consent of the Governor-General; and in the meantime shall be those in force immediately before the appointed day and applicable to all Government servants, as amended from time to time.

(4) The said regulations may provide for the creation of a Judicial Service Board, of which the Chief Justice shall be President, and the Grand

Kadi a member ex-officio, and for the delegation thereto of such powers and functions in respect of any of the matters mentioned in the preceding Subsection as may be thought appropriate.

CHAPTER X

THE PUBLIC SERVICE COMMISSION

(Powers of Governor-General to be Discretionary)

88. In exercising his powers under this Chapter, the Governor-General shall act at his discretion.

(Creation of Public Service Commission)

89.—(1) There shall be a Public Service Commission (in this Chapter referred to as 'the Commission'), the chairman and other members whereof shall be appointed by the Governor-General after consultation with the Council.

(2) The Governor-General may make regulations determining the number of members of the Commission, their tenure of office, and their remuneration, and making provision for the Commission's staff.

(General Functions of Commission)

90. The Commission shall be consulted by the Council of Ministers, or the Minister concerned, and shall make recommendations to the Council or Minister in respect of the principles to be observed in the following matters:—

(a) the recruitment, appointment, promotion, transfer and retirement of Government servants,
(b) the holding of examinations for entry to or promotion in the public service,
(c) the Sudanisation of the public service,
(d) the enforcement of discipline in the public service.

Provided that the Governor-General may by order specify the matters (not being matters of major importance) on which either generally, or in any particular class of case, or in any particular circumstances, it shall not be necessary for the Commission to be consulted.

(Special Functions of Commission)

91. The Council or the Minister concerned shall submit the following matters to the Commission, which may make recommendations to the Council or Minister thereon:—

(a) Proposals for regulations affecting the salaries or conditions of service of Government servants.

(*b*) Proposals for the creation of new posts to which super-scale salaries are to be allotted.

(*c*) Proposals for the promotion of Government servants to posts to which super-scale salaries are allotted.

Provided that the Governor-General may by order specify the matters (not being matters of major importance) which either generally, or in any particular class of case, or in any particular circumstances, it shall not be necessary for the Council or Minister to submit to the Commission.

(Transfer of Powers and Duties to Commission)

92. The Governor-General after consultation with the Council may by order direct that all or any of the following powers and duties shall be transferred to and vested in the Commission:—

(*a*) the powers and duties vested in the Central Board of Discipline under the Officials Discipline Ordinance 1927,

(*b*) the powers and duties vested in all or any of the Councils constituted under the several Sudan Government Pensions and Provident Fund Ordinances.

(Power of Governor-General to confer Additional
Functions on the Commission)

93. The Governor-General with the consent of the Council may by order confer upon the Commission such additional functions, of a like nature to those hereby specified, in respect of the public service as he may from time to time think fit.

(Conferment of Subsidiary Powers on Commission by Regulations)

94. In order to enable the Commission to perform its functions and exercise its powers hereunder, the Governor-General may make regulations:—

(*a*) authorising the Commission to require the production before it of any Government documents or records, and to require any person to appear before the Commission to give evidence on any matter which is under consideration or investigation by the Commission.

(*b*) providing for all other necessary subsidiary matters, including the prescribing of offences and the imposition of penalities in respect of any of the matters mentioned in the preceding paragraph.

(Non-Acceptance of Commission's Recommendation
to be Reported to the Governor-General)

95. In any case where the Council or a Minister does not accept a recommendation of the Commission, the Council or Minister shall forthwith report the fact to the Governor-General, giving the reasons for such non-acceptance.

(References to Commission by Governor-General)

96. The Governor-General may refer to the Commisssion for its advice:—

(*a*) petitions submitted to him by Government servants, and

(*b*) any other matter which in his opinion affects the public service.

(Annual Report)

97. The Commission shall submit to the Governor-General an annual report on its work, and the Governor-General shall cause a copy of the report to be laid before Parliament.

CHAPTER XI

TRANSITIONAL PROVISIONS

(Powers of Governor-General During Transitional Period)

98.—(1) Pending the exercise by the Sudanese of self-determination, the Governor-General shall retain the powers specified in this Chapter.

(2) Within the scope of his authority the Governor-General shall act at his discretion in exercising his powers under this Chapter.

(Responsibility of Governor-General for External Affairs)

99.—(1) The Governor-General shall remain responsible for external affairs. If and so far as legislation with regard thereto shall in his opinion be necessary or expedient, the same shall be enacted by the Governor-General by order.

(2) Every such order shall be in writing under the Governor-General's hand, and, unless otherwise expressly provided in the order, shall come into force on publication in the Sudan Government Gazette.

(3) An order hereunder may revoke modify or extend any existing enactment dealing with external affairs.

(4) Notwithstanding that the Council has no executive powers and Parliament has no legislative powers with regard to external affairs, nevertheless:—

(*a*) the Governor-General shall keep the Council informed thereon;

(*b*) the Council may make representations to the Governor-General with regard thereto, and it shall be the duty of the Governor-General to take the same into consideration:

(*c*) either House may, if the prior consent of the Governor-General has been obtained, hold debates or pass resolutions on any such matter. Any such resolution may, if the House thinks fit, be submitted to the Governor-General for his consideration, and it shall be the duty of the Governor-General to take the same into consideration accordingly.

(5) A declaration in writing by the Governor-General that a matter falls within his responsibility under this Section shall be conclusive and shall bind the Council and Parliament.

(Special Responsibilities of Governor-General)

100.—(1) The Governor-General shall have a special responsibility for the public service and for the Southern Provinces. It shall be his duty to ensure fair and equitable treatment both for members of the public service, whose contractual rights and interests shall be safeguarded, and for the Southern Provinces, whose special interests shall be protected.

(2) The Governor-General may refuse his assent to any bill which would in his opinion adversely affect the performance by him of his duties under the preceding Sub-section; and may from time to time make such orders as may appear to him to be necessary in the performance of the said duties.

(3) Every such order shall be in writing under the Governor-General's hand, and shall recite the purpose of the order.

(4) An order hereunder shall have the force of law, and to the extent of any repugnancy or inconsistency between any such order and any existing or future legislative enactment, or administrative or executive act of the Government, the order shall prevail, and the Courts shall give effect thereto accordingly.

(Responsibility of Governor-General for Constitutional Amendments)

101.—(1) The Governor-General may, if so requested by a joint resolution carried by a three-quarters majority at a joint sitting of both Houses, by order revoke modify or extend all or any of the provisions of this Order, and, if all its provisions shall have been revoked, may repeal the Ordinance.

(2) In order to remove unforeseen difficulties or rectify errors anomalies or omissions, the Governor-General may at the instance of the Council or of the Senate or of the House of Representatives by order make such amendments to the provisions of this Order as may from time to time appear to him to be essential for any of those purposes.

(3) The provisions of this Order may not be amended or revoked, and the Ordinance shall not be repealed, save in accordance with the procedure laid down by this Section.

(Responsibility of Governor-General in event of Constitutional Breakdown)

102.—(1) If at any time the Governor-General is satisfied:—

(a) that by reason of political deadlock, non-co-operation, boycott, or otherwise the government of the Sudan cannot be carried on under the Constitution hereby established, or (*b*) that imminent financial collapse or breakdown of law and order necessitates his immediate intervention in the interests of the good government of the Sudan,

he may proclaim a Constitutional Emergency.

(2) Parliament shall thereupon stand suspended, and the Prime Minister and other Ministers shall vacate office; and the Governor-General shall, if practicable, appoint a Council of State, with such membership as he shall think fit. The Council of State shall be charged with the duty of seeking means of restoring effective Parliamentary government under the Constitution at the earliest opportunity, and in the meantime, of assisting the Governor-General in maintaining the good government of the Sudan.

(3) So long as a proclamation hereunder remains in force, the government of the Sudan shall be carried out by means of orders made by the Governor-General after consultation with the Council of State, if any.

(4) Every such order shall have the force of law, and may revoke or amend any existing enactment other than the Ordinance or this Order.

(5) A proclamation hereunder may be revoked by a subsequent proclamation, and unless sooner revoked shall cease to operate at the expiration of six months from the date thereof, but without prejudice to the power of the Governor-General to make a fresh proclamation.

(Appointment of Officials to assist Governor-General)

103.—(1) To assist him in the performance of his responsibilities under this Chapter, the Governor-General may appoint such officials as he may consider necessary, and may determine their salaries and conditions of service.

(2) The said salaries shall form part of the expenditure of the Governor-General's office.

THE FIRST SCHEDULE

PART I

(Section 31)

ELECTIONS TO THE SENATE

1. Each Province shall form a constituency.
2. The thirty seats for elected members shall be divided amongst the constituencies as follows:—

Name of Constituency.	Seats allotted.
Bahr el Ghazal Province	3
Blue Nile Province	5
Darfur Province	4

Equatoria Province	2
Kassala Province	3
Khartoum Province	2
Kordofan Province	5
Northern Province	3
Upper Nile Province	3

3. The members for each Province Constituency shall be elected by all the Sudanese members of recognised Local Government Councils in the province, and by all the Sudanese members of the Province Council (if there be one), voting as a single electoral college.

4. There shall be no residential qualification for candidates for the Senate.

5. The Governor-General may at his discretion make rules for the regulation and conduct of elections to the Senate. . . .[1]

PART III

(Section 32)

ELECTIONS TO THE HOUSE OF REPRESENTATIVES

In this Part, 'qualified elector' means a person qualified to vote by virtue of the provisions contained in the following Part.

A. DIRECT ELECTIONS

1.—(1) In those constituencies listed in Part II A of this Schedule, elections shall be direct, that is to say that qualified electors shall vote for the election of one of the nominated candidates for membership of the House of Representatives in a single stage by secret ballot.

(2) A President of a Court constituted under the Native Courts Ordinance 1932 shall be eligible to stand for and to represent such constituency notwithstanding that the constituency or any part thereof lies within the area for which the Court has jurisdiction; but after nomination he shall cease to exercise his functions as President or as a member of such Court, and shall not resume the same until he has either failed to secure election, of, if elected, has ceased to be a member of the House of Representatives.

B. INDIRECT ELECTIONS

2.—(1) In those constituencies listed in Part II B of this Schedule, elections shall be indirect, that is to say in two stages, namely a primary election and a secondary election.

[1] Part II of the First Schedule (not printed here) contains a list of the constituencies for the House of Representatives.

(2) For each such constituency there shall be an electoral college which shall be composed of the following members:—

    (a) One to ten delegates from each Omodia or similar local administrative unit in accordance with its population, to be elected by vote or by acclamation by qualified electors of such Omodia or unit.

    (b) One or more delegates from any town within the constituency which has been authorised by the Governor to hold secret ballots in Local Government Elections, in accordance with the proportion which its population bears to that of the rest of the constituency, to be elected by secret ballot by the qualified electors residing in that town.

(3) The first stage shall consist of the election of delegates to the electoral college as provided by the preceding paragraph.

(4) The second stage shall consist of the election by the electoral college of the member who is to represent the constituency in the House of Representatives by secret ballot, which shall take place on the day or days appointed for the election in that constituency.

(5) A person shall not be eligible to represent such constituency unless he has during the last ten years been resident for not less than two years in the province within which that constituency lies.

(6) The mandate of the electoral colleges shall continue till the expiration or dissolution of the House of Representatives, that is to say that a by-election shall necessitate a fresh election at the second stage only, by the same electoral college as at the previous election. If a by-election is to be held, any casual vacancy in the electoral college shall be filled by election in accordance with the appropriate sub-paragraph of paragraph (2) above.

(7) The Governor-General may at his discretion, in such constituencies as he thinks fit, by order declare that the first stage of the election shall not take place and that the electoral college shall consist of the Local Government body, or in the absence of a single Local Government body covering the constituency, of such Local Government representatives as the Governor may at his discretion appoint for the purpose.

C. ELECTIONS FOR THE GRADUATES' CONSTITUENCY

3. The members for the Graduates' Constituency shall be elected by qualified electors, voting through the post and using the method of the single transferable vote.

D. GENERAL

The Governor-General may at his discretion make rules for the regulation and conduct of elections to the House of Representatives, and may by such rules make provision for:—

    (a) the appointment of Returning Officers
    (b) the appointment of Electoral Committees

(c) the preparation and maintenance of electoral rolls
(d) the nomination of candidates
(e) the conduct of direct elections, indirect elections, both primary and secondary, and postal elections
(f) the conduct of by-elections
(g) any other electoral matter requiring to be regulated by rules.

PART IV

(Section 33)

QUALIFICATIONS OF VOTERS
IN CONSTITUENCIES FOR HOUSE OF REPRESENTATIVES

1.—(1) A person shall be qualified to vote in the Constituencies specified in Part II A and B if he:—

(a) is a Sudanese, and
(b) is a male, and
(c) is not less than 21 years of age, and
(d) is of sound mind, and
(e) has been ordinarily resident in the constituency for a period of not less than six months before the closing of the electoral roll.

(2) No person shall be qualified to vote in more than one of the said constituencies or in more than one electoral division of any such constituency.

2.—(1) A person shall be qualified to vote in the Graduates' Constituency if he:—

(a) is a Sudanese, and
(b) is not less than 21 years of age, and
(c) is of sound mind, and
(d) is not a student at any recognised school, university or university college whether in the Sudan or elsewhere, save in the capacity of post-graduate student, and
(e) holds one of the following educational qualifications, namely:—

(i) has completed the full course at a recognised secondary school, or
(ii) holds a degree or diploma from a recognised university or university college, or
(iii) has passed the Cambridge School Certificate examination, or an equivalent or higher examination, or
(iv) holds an Alimiya Certificate from the Maahad el Ilmi, or
(v) has completed the course in the Teachers' and Kadis' Section of the old Gordon Memorial College.

(2) A person may vote in the Graduates' Constituency in addition to voting in a constituency specified in the preceding paragraph. . . .[1]

(ii) THE MILITARY *Coup*

(*a*) *Proclamation by General Muhammad Nagīb to the Egyptian people after the military* coup, *23 July 1952*[2]

Egypt has undergone a critical time in its recent history. It has been a period of gross corruption and government instability, and these factors had a great influence on the Army. People who received bribes contributed towards our defeat during the Palestine war. Traitors plotted against the Army after the Palestine war, but now we have purged ourselves, and our affairs within the Army have been placed in the hands of men in whose ability, character and patriotism we have faith.

The whole of Egypt will welcome this news. No harm will be done to former military personnel who have been arrested. The entire Army is working for the interests of Egypt within the constitution and without any designs of its own.

I appeal to all Egyptians not to resort to any acts of sabotage or violence. These would not be in the interests of Egypt. Any such action will be met with unparalleled firmness, and the offender will be punished immediately for treason. The Army will undertake responsibility for law and order in co-operation with the police, and I want to assure our brother foreigners of the safety of their lives and property for which the Army considers itself responsible.

(*b*) *Ultimatum from General Nagīb demanding the abdication of King Fārūq, 26 July 1952*[3]

Du férik d'état-major Mohamed Naguib, au nom des officiers de l'armée et de ses hommes, à S.M. le Roi Farouk I[er.]

Étant donné que, ces derniers temps, l'anarchie générale règne dans tous les domaines de la vie du pays, et cela en conséquence de votre mauvaise gestion et du peu de cas que vous faites de la Constitution et de la volonté du peuple, de sorte que nul ne pouvait être sans inquiétude pour sa vie, ses biens et sa dignité:

Étant donné que la réputation de l'Égypte déclinait par suite de votre persistance dans cette conduite au point que les traîtres et les prévaricateurs trouvaient auprès de vous protection, sécurité et richesse excessive et se permettaient des gaspillages scandaleux — et cela aux dépens du peuple pauvre, affamé:

---

[1] The Second and Third Schedules (not printed here) deal respectively with the powers of the Legal Secretary and Governor-General and with the form of oath to be taken by Ministers, Members of Parliament, and members of the judiciary.

[2] *The Times*, 24 July 1952.   [3] *Bourse Égyptienne*, 1 August 1952.

Étant donné que tout ce qui précède s'est manifesté durant la guerre de Palestine, et les scandales des armes défectueuses qui en découlèrent, suivis de jugements au cours desquels vous êtes intervenu ouvertement, déformant de la sorte la vérité et ébranlant la confiance en la justice, et encourageant les traîtres à suivre votre exemple et à s'enrichir sans réserve ni décence et mener une vie de libertinage:

Étant donné tout cela, j'ai été délégué, par l'armée qui représente la force du peuple, pour demander à Votre Majesté d'abdiquer en faveur de votre fils, le Prince Héritier Ahmed Fouad, et cela aujourd'hui (samedi 26 juillet 1952) le 4 zoul Kaada 1371; et de quitter le territoire, cet après-midi avant 6 heures.

L'Armée rejette sur Votre Majesté la responsabilité des conséquences de votre refus éventuel de vous soumettre aux désirs du peuple.

Férik d'état-major
MOHAMED NAGUIB

(c) Statement by King Fārūq announcing his abdication in favour of his son, 26 July 1952[1]

We, Farouk I, King of Egypt and the Sudan, since we have always sought the welfare, happiness and progress of our country, since we honestly wish to save the country from the difficulties she faces in these critical circumstances, and submitting to the will of the people, we have decided to abdicate the throne in favor of our Crown Prince, Ahmed Fuad.

We have issued an order to this effect to Premier Aly Maher Pasha for action accordingly.

FAROUK.

(d) Statement by the Secretary of State, Mr. Acheson, on the attitude of the U.S.A. towards the military coup *and on the relations between the U.S.A. and Egypt, 3 September 1952*[2]

There have been some encouraging developments in Egypt since we last met together, including the reform program announced by the Egyptian Government. We are following events with much interest and we wish Prime Minister Ali Maher and his civilian and military colleagues every success in their efforts to solve the internal problems of their country.

Relations between the United States and Egypt remain most friendly and cooperative. I am hopeful that in the interest of our two countries these relations, as well as those between Egypt and all the nations of the

---

[1] *New York Times*, 27 July 1952.
[2] *Department of State Bulletin*, 15 September 1952, p. 406.

free world, will be increased and strengthened. We look forward to an era in which new areas of cooperation and mutual benefit can be brought into being.

(iii) Letter from General Nagīb to the Regency Council accepting the Council's request to him to form a Cabinet, 7 September 1952[1]

La mission d'assumer les responsabilités du pouvoir dans cette étape bénie de notre révolution réformatrice entreprise par l'armée du pays exprimant les aspirations des habitants de la Vallée du Nil et réalisant leurs vœux pour une vie pleine de dignité, de prestige et de fraternité, afin de leur donner la liberté, sans distinction de classe ou de fortune, tout en renforçant le sentiment du patriotisme dans les âmes, avec tout ce que cela comporte d'honnêteté d'intentions, d'intégrité et de disposition au sacrifice, sans attendre une récompense et aussi d'asseoir les bases de la Constitution, rempart des libertés et garant des droits :

Cette noble mission dont je remercie le Conseil de Régence est une preuve nouvelle que cette révolution réformatrice n'est pas le mouvement de l'armée seule, mais aussi celui de la nation, qui a hérité des traditions les plus nobles. La constitution d'un ministère présidé par un militaire de l'armée de la patrie, aidé par des frères non militaires est la preuve la plus convaincante que ce mouvement peut donner, que le peuple et l'armée ne forment qu'un seul bloc.

Dès le début, nous avions convenu, mes collègues et moi, de laisser le pouvoir aux hommes politiques. En cela, nous proclamions ce que nous pensions. Mais la nécessité de hâter les travaux auxquels tend le mouvement a exigé de coordonner les relations entre l'armée et la politique. J'ai accepté de présider le ministère et d'assumer les charges du ministère de la Guerre et de la Marine, tout en conservant le commandement général des forces armées, afin de ne pas perdre de temps dans des consultations inévitables entre le Haut Commandement et le Ministère. Il est possible maintenant, par économie du temps, que ces consultations se fassent à l'intérieur du ministère que je préside. Cette exigence même a amené l'ancien Président Ali Maher à présenter sa démission après avoir aidé le mouvement, depuis son début, avec un esprit en harmonie avec son passé honorable au service de son pays.

En ayant l'honneur de déclarer que je suis prêt à assumer les charges du gouvernement, continuant la révolution réformatrice et licite que nous avons commencée, je remercie le Tout-Puissant pour m'avoir accordé l'honneur de la confiance de votre honorable Conseil. Je le prie de m'aider, ainsi que mes collègues qui ont accepté de s'associer avec moi

[1] France: Ministère des Affaires Étrangères: La Documentation Française: *Notes et Études Documentaires*, No. 1682, 24 November 1952, p. 15.

dans le gouvernement, à aller fermement de l'avant avec la chère patrie et faire sentir à chacun que sa vie, ses ressources, son avenir et celui de ses enfants ainsi que la garantie de leur instruction et la protection de leurs libertés, de leurs opinions et de leurs convictions sont un dépôt entre les mains d'un gouvernement vigilant dont la devise est de s'acquitter de son devoir entre les enfants de la patrie et les hôtes étrangers, quelles que soient les difficultés qu'il devra supporter.

[There follows a list of the members of General Nagīb's Cabinet.]

(iv) Official communiqué from the Egyptian Army headquarters on the dismissal of Colonel Rashād Muhannā, one of the three Regents, 14 October 1952[1]

Lorsqu'elle entreprit son mouvement révolutionnaire, l'armée avait pour premier objectif la suppression de la tyrannie. Elle a écarté un roi tyran, qui ne tenait aucun compte des pouvoirs et intervenait constamment dans les affaires du gouvernement.

L'armée ayant proposé un de ses officiers au conseil de régence provisoire, officier auquel il fut demandé de se maintenir strictement dans le cadre de ses fonctions, et de ne pas intervenir dans les affaires du gouvernement, nous avons le regret d'annoncer que le régent kaimakam Mohamed Rachad Mehanna a perdu de vue les limites de ses attributions. Souvent, il adressait au ministère des demandes constituées en général de recommandations pour ses amis. Souvent aussi, il se mettait en contact avec les membres de l'administration dans le même but.

Un jour, il ordonna directement la confiscation d'un journal et même le retrait du permis du journal.

Nous lui avons adressé plusieurs avertissements à ce sujet. Mais il n'en tint aucun compte.

De plus, il a été jusqu'à s'opposer à la promulgation de la loi sur la limitation de la propriété, bien que n'ignorant pas que cette loi est la pierre angulaire de la réforme totale que désirent le peuple, l'armée et son commandement lequel a dirigé le mouvement.

Bien plus, il faisait des déclarations et accordait des interviews aux journaux égyptiens et étrangers. Ces déclarations constituaient des interventions directes dans la politique nationale, ce qui n'est nullement permis à un régent.

Il exprima son opinion sur le Soudan et d'autres questions intérieures. Il se mit en contact avec les journaux pour se placer au premier plan. Il essaya aussi de pousser l'armée à la division, au point que certains eurent

[1] *Bourse Égyptienne*, 14 October 1952. As a result of Colonel Muhannā's dismissal Dr. Bahi ud-Din Barakāt resigned from the regency council, leaving Prince 'Abd ul-Mun'im as sole Regent.

l'impression qu'il existait plusieurs tendances au sein de l'armée et non un seul but, bien précis.

Le quartier-général a supporté ces agissements, semaine après semaine, jusqu'à ce que, il y a quelques jours, le kaimakam Mehanna ait demandé officiellement de pouvoir intervenir dans toutes les affaires du gouvernement. Tout cela nous a montré qu'il n'était pas capable de concilier son attitude avec les buts du mouvement et ses principes.

En conséquence, nous avons décidé de le dispenser du poste de régent.

Que chacun sache que ce mouvement est basé sur des principes et qu'il ne saurait être entravé par des considérations de personnes ou des ambitions individuelles. Dieu est garant du succès.

> Léwa d'état-major
> MOHAMED NAGUIB
> commandant en chef
> des forces armées

Mardi, 24 Moharram 1372
14 octobre 1952.

(v) STATEMENT IN THE HOUSE OF COMMONS BY THE FOREIGN SECRETARY, MR. EDEN, ON BRINGING INTO FORCE THE SELF-GOVERNMENT STATUTE FOR THE SUDAN, 22 OCTOBER 1952[1]

Last May the Governor-General of the Sudan submitted to Her Majesty's Government and to the Egyptian Government a draft Statute designed to bring about internal self-government. The Statute had been drawn up in the light of discussions in the Constitutional Amendment Commission, composed of Sudanese with a British chairman, and was later discussed and approved in the Sudanese Legislative Assembly.

Her Majesty's Government have today informed the Acting Governor-General that they give their consent to his making the Proclamation necessary to bring the Self-Government Statute into force. Her Majesty's Government's approval is given on the understanding that:

(i) the provisions of the draft concern only the relations between the Governor-General and the other organs of government set up under the Statute—that is to say, the Council of Ministers and the Parliament. This state of affairs will continue until, as a result of self-determination, or at some earlier date by agreement between the two Governments, alternative provisions are made for the exercise of these powers;

(ii) except in regard to technical and administrative matters, responsibility for the external affairs of the Sudan belongs as before to the two Governments.

[1] H.C. Deb. 5th Ser. vol. 505, coll. 1014–15.

There is an Article in the Statute laying down that no disability shall be attached to Sudanese by reason of sex, and that all persons shall enjoy freedom of conscience and the right freely to confess their religion. With respect to the second of these principles, Her Majesty's Government have expressed the hope that as liberal an interpretation as possible may be given to the freedom of all persons to profess their religion.

The Acting Governor-General's attention has also been drawn to the views recently expressed to me by representatives of various parties in the Sudan on the desirability of increasing the number of direct elections to be held under the new constitution.

The views of the Egyptian Government on the draft Statute have not yet been received. I hope that they may be in time for consideration by Her Majesty's Government and the Sudan Government before the Statute is brought into effect.

I should like to take this opportunity to express Her Majesty's Government's pleasure in congratulating the people of the Sudan upon what we hope will be a momentous step forward in the history of their country. The House will, I am sure, want to join me in this. The Sudanese are now proceeding to self-government, that is to say, government by an all-Sudanese Parliament to the Sudanese people. This is a prelude and a preparation for the exercise by them of self-determination. Her Majesty's Government look forward to the Sudanese exercising self-determination at an early date. In my view, however, this is a matter for the Sudanese Parliament, elected under the provisions of this Statute, to discuss and to decide.

(vi) Note from the Egyptian Government to the British Government concerning Self-Government and Self-Determination for the Sudan, 2 November 1952.[1]

1. The Egyptian Government firmly believes in the right of the Sudanese to self-determination and the effective exercise thereof in the proper time and with the necessary safeguards.

2. To attain the above-mentioned object, there should begin forthwith a transitional period envisaging two objectives:

(a) To secure full self-government for the Sudanese.
(b) To provide the requisite free and neutral atmosphere for the Sudanese to exercise self-determination.

3. The transitional period, being a preparation for the effective termination of the Dual Administration, shall be considered as a liquidation of that administration. The Egyptian Government declares that the sovereignty

[1] Cmd. 8767, pp. 47–49.

of The Sudan shall be kept reserved for the Sudanese, during this transitional period, until self-determination is achieved.

4. The Governor-General shall be during the transitional period the supreme constitutional Authority within The Sudan and shall exercise his powers according to Paragraph (5) below with the aid of a five-member Commission, consisting of two Sudanese, proposed by agreement between the Egyptian and British Governments and subject to the subsequent approval of the elected Sudanese Parliament which shall be entitled to nominate them in case of disapproval, one Egyptian, one British, and one Indian or Pakistani, each proposed respectively by his own Government. The five-member Commission, to be appointed by the Egyptian Government by decree. In the absence of the Governor-General, the elder of the two Sudanese Commissioners shall act in his place.

5. The Governor-General shall exercise his powers in the manner set out in the Statute, save as regards the discretional powers delineated in the appended amendments, which he shall exercise subject to the approval of his Commission.

6. The Governor-General shall remain responsible to the two liquidating Governments as regards:

(a) Any affairs which are not strictly internal.
(b) Any change requested by the Sudanese Parliament as regards any part of the Statute for Self-Government.
(c) Any resolution passed by the Commission which he might regard as inconsistent with his responsibilities. In this case the two Governments must give an answer within one month of the date of formal notice. The Commission's resolution shall stand unless the two Governments agree to the contrary.

7. There shall be constituted a mixed Commission of seven members: three Sudanese appointed by the Governor-General after the approval of his Commission, one Egyptian, one British, one American, and one Indian or Pakistani nominated by their respective Governments. The Indian or Pakistani shall be Chairman of the Commission. The functions of this Commission shall be to appoint sub-commissions for each electoral constituency, to decide on its own rules of procedure and methods of work in order to observe effectively the preparations for and the conduct of the elections and to ensure their impartiality.

8. Direct-Election Constituencies shall be increased to comprise all constituencies throughout The Sudan except the following provinces:—

(a) Bahr-el-Ghazal.
(b) Equatoria.
(c) Upper Nile.

However, the election in the Yei constituency, together with the constituencies comprising the towns of Waw, Juba and Malakal shall be direct.

9. Subject to the preparations to be made by the mixed Commission, the Egyptian Government hopes that the elections shall begin before the end of 1952, in the following order:

(a) The 24 direct-election constituencies, listed in the draft submitted to the Legislative Assembly.

(b) The indirect-election constituencies.

(c) The remaining constituencies which are changed from indirect to direct; together with the eleven direct-election constituencies, listed in the draft submitted to the Egyptian Government and which have not as yet been officially published.

10. 'To provide the free and neutral atmosphere requisite for self-determination' being a prime objective, there shall be established a Sudanisation Committee, consisting of:

(a) An Egyptian and a British member to be proposed by their respective Governments and subsequently appointed by the Governor-General, together with three Sudanese members to be selected from a list of five members submitted by the Sudanese Prime Minister. The selection and appointment of these three Sudanese members shall have the prior approval of the Governor-General's Commission.

(b) One or more members from the Civil Service Commission, to act in a purely advisory capacity without the right to vote.

The functions of this Committee shall be:

(a) To speed up the Sudanisation of the Administration, the Police, the Sudan Defence Force, and any other Government posts, that may affect the freedom of the Sudanese at Self-Determination.

(b) The Committee may co-opt one or more members as they deem fit, to act in an advisory capacity, without the right to vote.

(c) The Committee shall take its decisions by majority vote, which shall be submitted to the Governor-General for his assent.

The Sudanisation Committee shall complete its duties within three years.

11. The Egyptian Government strongly recommends the creation of a post for a Sudanese Under-Secretary to act as liaison between the Governor-General and the Council of Ministers, the functions of whom shall be to prepare for the representation of The Sudan only in International Technical Conferences.

12. The transitional period shall begin with the appointment of the five-member Commission, and shall not exceed three years, subject to the completion of the Sudanisation explained in Article (10) above. It shall end following a move by the Sudanese Parliament expressing that desire with the agreement of and the ratification by the two liquidating Governments.

13. On the ratification by the two liquidating Governments of the date on which the transition period is to be terminated, the Sudanese Government, then existing, shall draw up a draft law for the election of a constituent assembly which it shall submit to Parliament for approval. The Governor-General shall ratify the law with the agreement of the Commission referred to in paragraph (4).

Safeguards assuring the freedom and impartiality of the elections shall then be agreed upon.

14. British and Egyptian Military Forces shall be withdrawn from The Sudan at least one year before the elections of the Constituent Assembly.

15. The Constituent Assembly shall have two duties to discharge: the first is to decide on the future of The Sudan as one integral whole. The second is to draw up a constitution for The Sudan compatible with the decision to be taken in regard to that future as well as electoral law for a permanent Sudanese Parliament. Deciding the future of The Sudan shall be made:

(a) either by the Constituent Assembly choosing to link up The Sudan with Egypt in any form:

(b) or by the Assembly choosing a Sudan completely independent of the United Kingdom, Egypt or any other country.

16. The Egyptian Government trusts that the British Government will agree to join in undertaking to respect the decision taken by the Constituent Assembly in connection with the future of The Sudan, and that each Government shall, on its part, take all necessary measures to give effect to this decision.

Cairo, November 2nd, 1952.[1]

B. ISRAEL

(i) Speech to the Knesset by the Israeli Prime Minister, Mr. David Ben-Gurion, on the relations between Israel and the Arab states, 18 August 1952[2]

Perhaps the rulers of the new Egypt are now dedicating themselves in particular to the consolidation of their authority within the country. This period of transition in Egypt is full of possibilities, both favourable and unfavourable, and we must watch the situation closely. I welcome some of the developments which are now taking place in Egypt. I accept General Nagīb's statement according to which he and other friends were opposed to the invasion of Israel by Egypt, an invasion which

---

[1] There follow two appendixes, not printed here, giving the proposed alterations to the draft Statute for Self-Government.

[2] Translated from *Relazioni Internazionali*, 30 August 1952, p. 921.

undoubtedly represents one of the gravest errors committed by the Egyptian rulers four years ago. Then, as now, there were no reasons for discord between Egypt and Israel. A great desert divides the two countries, and there is therefore no territorial problem. There are no reasons, political, economic, or territorial, for conflict. We nourish no hostile feelings towards Egypt for the injury that was done to our ancestors in the time of the Pharaohs, nor even for that which was done to us four years ago. We have shown our goodwill towards Egypt because we have never exploited her differences with a great power, to attack her and take our revenge on her. In contrast to Nagīb, Colonel Shishakly did not oppose the invasion of Israel but rather guided the attack, and saved himself with difficulty. Perhaps the Syrian dictator's recent threats were destined for internal use, but Israel cannot permit herself to be so complacent. Many of the United Nations, both eastern and western, wish to see peace established between us and the Arabs, because peace in the Middle East would further world peace, and the social, cultural, and economic development of the peoples in this sector. Co-operation between Israel and the Arab peoples would be a great blessing for the two semitic nations that history has constrained to live together, and would strengthen the real independence of the Arab states. And yet there is no peace. The only stable forces in the Middle East are Israel and Turkey. The tense and confused atmosphere is so explosive that the least spark could set it off. The lessons to be drawn from the situation are that together with military preparation it is necessary to maintain a sincere desire for peace. As for military preparation I think that what was sufficient in 1948 may not be so to-day. Many considered Israel's victory four years ago as a miracle. If by a miracle we mean something unusual, I am ready to accept it; if something unnatural, then it constitutes a danger. The enemy powers have learnt their lesson from their defeat and have strengthened their army in quality and in quantity, in equipment, training, and contingents of troops. As for the proposed amendments to the security services Law, there are two essential reasons for extending the period of military service by six months:

1) The eighteen-year-old national servicemen do not constitute a sufficient contingent of troops for the army and, 2) the immigrants from Islamic countries have had no opportunity of obtaining adequate education.

I do not mean thereby to establish a supremacy of the Western Jews over the Eastern. A Persian Jew with a higher education could easily keep abreast of a German or a Russian Jew, but the difference lies in the fact that in the West there have been greater possibilities for educating oneself. There is not the slightest doubt that the sons of eastern immigrants will not be inferior to the sons of western ones.

(ii) Comment by the Secretary-General of the Arab League, 'Abd ur-Rahman 'Azzām Pasha, on Mr. Ben-Gurion's speech of 18 August, 19 August 1952[1]

The Prime Minister, Ben Gurion, stated yesterday in the Israeli Parliament, that Israel wishes to make peace with Egypt; we, all the same, have received no official invitation. It is unthinkable that Egypt could resume friendly relations with Israel when more than a million Arabs have been driven out of their native country and are living in miserable conditions. Moreover Israel is increasing her potential military strength, and continually threatening Syria and Colonel Shishakly. I cherish the hope that the Defence Council of the Arab League, including the Foreign Ministers, War Ministers, and Heads of State of the member countries, will meet in the second half of September. We shall be able to profit from the occasion to call in session at the same time the Political Committee and the Council of the League.

(iii) Resolution urging the Arab States and Israel to enter into negotiations for a settlement of their differences, adopted by the United Nations Ad Hoc Political Committee on 11 December 1952[2]

The General Assembly,

Recalling that it is the primary duty of all Members of the United Nations, when involved in an international dispute, to seek the settlement of such a dispute by peaceful means, in accordance with Article 33 of the Charter,

Recalling the existing resolutions of the General Assembly and the Security Council on Palestine,

Recalling especially those resolutions which call upon the parties to achieve at any early date agreement on a final settlement of their outstanding differences,

Taking note of the twelfth progress report (A/2216) of the United Nations Conciliation Commission for Palestine in which it is suggested that 'general or partial agreement could be sought through direct negotiations, with United Nations assistance or mediation',

1. Expresses its appreciation of the efforts made to date by the United Nations Conciliation Commission for Palestine in the discharge of its mandate;

2. Calls upon the parties to honour fully their undertaking to refrain from any acts of hostility against each other;

3. Reaffirms the principle that the Governments concerned have the

[1] Translated from *Relazioni Internazionali*, 30 August 1952, p. 921.

[2] A/2310, 15 December 1952, pp. 6–7. This resolution was not adopted by the General Assembly as it failed to secure a two-thirds majority.

primary responsibility for reaching a settlement of their outstanding differences, and with this in view;

4. *Urges* the Governments concerned to enter at any early date, without prejudice to their respective rights and claims, into direct negotiations for the establishment of such a settlement, bearing in mind the resolutions as well as the principal objectives of the United Nations on the Palestine question, including the religious interests of third parties;

5. *Requests* the Conciliation Commission for Palestine to continue its efforts to fulfil the tasks entrusted to it under General Assembly resolutions and to be available for assistance in the negotiations if so desired;

6. *Requests* the Conciliation Commission for Palestine to render progress reports periodically to the Secretary-General for transmission to the Members of the United Nations;

7. *Requests* the Secretary-General to continue to provide the necessary staff and facilities for carrying out the terms of the present resolution.

C. PERSIA

1, American Aid

(i) Letter from the Persian Prime Minister, Dr. Muhammad Musaddiq, to the United States Ambassador in Tehrān, Mr. Loy Henderson, giving the assurances on Persia's adherence to the United Nations Charter required by the Mutual Security Act of 1951[1] for the renewal of United States economic aid, 6 January 1952[2]

Pursuant to our discussions relative to the economic situation of Iran and the readiness of the United States Government to extend its financial aid to various development projects, particularly public health, agriculture and education, I have the honor to state that my Government is prepared to accept most gratefully any aid, whether in cash or in goods, and to insure effective utilization thereof. Further, with reference to the same discussions, I wish to point out that the Iranian Government, without assuming new obligations, as a signatory of the United Nations Charter gives its allegiance to the principles contained in the said Charter.

(ii) Letter from Dr. Musaddiq to Mr. Henderson giving the assurances required by the Mutual Security Act of 1951[3] for the resumption of United States military aid to Persia, 24 April 1952[4]

Pursuant to our oral conversations, I find it necessary to inform Your Excellency that my Government, in view of its financial and economic

---

[1] Under Section 511 (*b*): see *Documents* (R.I.I.A.) for 1951, p. 52.
[2] *New York Times*, 7 January 1952.
[3] Under Section 511 (*a*): see *Documents* (R.I.I.A.) for 1951, p. 51.
[4] *New York Times*, 26 April 1952.

situation, welcomes the assistance which Your Excellency's Government is prepared to extend to this country.

Iran supports and defends the principles of the United Nations to the extent that its resources and general conditions permit.

It is also doing what it can to strengthen its defensive possibilities.

And if it should be attacked from any direction, it shall defend its freedom and independence with all its might.

(iii) NOTE FROM THE U.S.S.R. TO PERSIA PROTESTING AGAINST THE PERSIAN MILITARY AID AGREEMENT WITH THE U.S.A. AS A BREACH OF THE RUSSO-PERSIAN TREATY OF 1921, 21 MAY 1952[1]

In connection with the exchange of letters that took place at the end of April, 1952, between the Iranian Prime Minister, Mr. Mossadek, and the United States Ambassador to Iran, Mr. Henderson, on the question of the United States of America rendering so-called aid to Iran, the Minister of Foreign Affairs of the Union of Soviet Socialist Republics has the honour to inform the Government of Iran of the following:

From the above-mentioned exchange of letters it is seen that an agreement has been reached between the Governments of Iran and the United States on the rendering of military and financial aid to Iran by the United States of America and that the Government of Iran, for its part, undertook definite commitments of a military and political nature.

As follows from reports in the Iranian Press, as well as from statements of representatives of the Iranian Government and the Government of the United States, the Iranian Government committed itself under this agreement to renew the contracts with American military advisers in Iran. This was confirmed in the official statements by Mr. Bushechri, Minister of Communications of Iran, on April 27 this year, on the one hand, and by Mr. McDermott, United States Assistant Secretary of State, on April 25, on the other. It is also known that the American military mission which ended its activities in January this year, as a result of the exchange of letters between Mr. Mossadek and Mr. Henderson, has resumed its work; and, at the same time, the agreement between the United States and Iran of May 23, 1950, concerning military aid and the American military mission in Iran, has again gone into force.

Thus, as a result of the above-mentioned exchange of letters and the re-entry into force of the Iranian-American military agreement, the Iranian Government places the Iranian army under the control of the United States Government. Thereby the Iranian army loses its character as the national army of an independent, sovereign State.

---

[1] *Soviet News*, 28 May 1952. For the Treaty of 1921 see *British and Foreign State Papers*, vol. cxiv, pp. 901–7.

The Soviet Government deems it necessary to call the attention of the Iranian Government to the fact that, in agreeing to accept American so-called aid and, in this connection, assuming definite commitments of a military nature towards the United States of America, the Iranian Government is in fact setting out on the path of helping the United States Government to carry out its aggressive plans directed against the Soviet Union.

Such actions of the Iranian Government cannot be regarded otherwise than as actions incompatible with the principles of good neighbourly relations, the maintenance and consolidation of which is the duty of the parties who signed the Soviet-Iranian Agreement of February 26, 1921.

2. Persian oil

(i) NOTE FROM THE BRITISH GOVERNMENT TO THE PERSIAN GOVERNMENT REGARDING THE BRITISH ATTITUDE TO THE NATIONALIZATION OF THE OIL INDUSTRY IN PERSIA AND REPEATING ITS READINESS TO SETTLE THE DISPUTE BY NEGOTIATION, 19 MARCH 1952[1]

H.M. Government observe that in their Note of the 12th January, 1952, the Imperial Government repeat earlier arguments to the effect that the nationalisation of the oil industry in Iran is an internal matter solely connected with the sovereignty of Iran, that it is of no concern to H.M. Government in the United Kingdom and that, despite the reference of the matter to the International Court of Justice by H.M. Government in the United Kingdom, the Court has no competence to adjudicate upon it. H.M. Government in the United Kingdom have however on many occasions made clear to the Imperial Government that, in taking up the case of the Anglo-Iranian Oil Company when the Company was divested of its concession in a manner contrary to the principles of international law and contrary to the treaty obligations undertaken by Iran towards the United Kingdom, H.M. Government were not interfering in a matter solely connected with the sovereignty of Iran but were proceeding in virtue of the right, which all States claim, to accord diplomatic protection to their nationals when their nationals are treated in a manner contrary to the principles of international law. On the 26th May, 1951, H.M. Government instituted proceedings by means of an Application before the International Court of Justice and on 10th October, 1951, filed a Memorial with the Court setting out the reasons why they maintained that the enforcement of the Iranian Oil Nationalisation Act of the 1st May, 1951,[2] is not a matter within the exclusive domestic jurisdiction of Iran but is an international matter on which the Court is competent to adjudicate. The Imperial Government may contend that the Court is not competent to

---

[1] *Foreign Office Press Release*, 5 April 1952, no. 8.
[2] *Documents* (R.I.I.A.) for 1951, p. 481.

adjudicate upon the merits of this question. The Imperial Government cannot deny, however, that the Court is competent to decide the question of its own competence in the matter, as this is expressly provided for in Article 36 (6) of the Statute of the Court, which is an annex of the Charter of the United Nations. H.M. Government wish therefore to place firmly on record that they cannot accept the contention of the Imperial Government, made in their Note of the 12th January, 1952, that this question is not one to be regarded as under judicial consideration. In the view of H.M. Government, it follows from Article 36 of the Court's Statute that, until the Court has given its decision, the whole matter must necessarily be regarded as *sub judice*.

The Imperial Government in their recent Note also state that they view with great surprise that in their Note of the 22nd December, 1951, H.M. Government expressed their inability to agree to the purchase of Persian oil by British nationals and also their refusal to recognise that the Imperial Government had any legal right to sell the said oil, having regard to the fact that, in a Note dated 3rd August, 1951, H.M. Government officially recognised on their own behalf and on behalf of the Anglo-Iranian Oil Company the nationalisation of the oil industry throughout Iran. The Imperial Government will recall however that this recognition by H.M. Government of the principle of the nationalisation of the oil industry in Iran was for the purpose of negotiation only. This is made quite clear in the first two paragraphs of the Note of the 3rd August, 1951, which read as follows:

'I have the honour to inform your Excellency, on instructions from my Government, that they have received through Mr. Harriman, *the Imperial Government's formula for negotiations* between the Imperial Government and H.M. Government on behalf of the Anglo-Iranian Oil Company and for discussion on matters of mutual interest to the Governments.

'H.M. Government are desirous of availing themselves of this formula and *are prepared to negotiate in accordance with it*. But it will be appreciated by the Imperial Government that *negotiations* which H.M. Government for their part will enter into with the utmost good will cannot be conducted in a satisfactory manner unless the present atmosphere is relieved. On the assurance that the Imperial Government recognise this fact and will enter into discussions in the same spirit a mission headed by a Cabinet Minister will immediately set out.'[1]

Neither in their Note of the 3rd August, 1951, nor on any other occasion have H.M. Government ever recognised that the oil industry in Iran has been lawfully nationalised or that the enforcement of the Iranian Oil Nationalisation Act of the 1st May 1951, represented a lawful exercise of

[1] *Documents* (R.I.I.A.) for 1951, p. 502.

Iranian sovereignty. As the Imperial Government well know, H.M. Government have always challenged, and continue to challenge in proceedings before the International Court of Justice—proceedings in which the Imperial Government are now taking part—the validity in international law of the unilateral abrogation by Iran of the 1933 agreement negotiated between the two countries under the auspices of the League of Nations. In their Note of the 3rd August, 1951, H.M. Government did no more than place on record their readiness to negotiate with the Imperial Government on the basis that the oil industry, operated in Iran by the Anglo-Iranian Oil Company, should be nationalised in a manner acceptable to them and to the Company. As the Imperial Government are aware, the acceptance of a certain formula as a basis for negotiations in no way constitutes a binding acceptance of the provisions of that formula regardless of the outcome of the negotiations. In interpreting the Note of the 3rd August, 1951, as an acceptance by H.M. Government of the *fait accompli* brought about in Iran by the unlawful enforcement of the Iranian Oil Nationalisation Act of the 1st May, 1951, the Imperial Government have therefore completely misrepresented the position.

H.M. Government remain ready to settle the dispute by negotiation and for the purpose of further negotiations to accept the same formula as a basis of discussion, but must emphasise that they accept it as a basis for negotiation only which does not prejudice the rights of either side if the negotiations are not successful.

(ii) STATEMENT BY THE UNITED STATES DEPARTMENT OF STATE ON PERSIAN REQUESTS FOR FINANCIAL AID AND EXPRESSING HOPES FOR THE SETTLEMENT OF THE ANGLO-PERSIAN OIL DISPUTE, 20 MARCH 1952[1]

The United States has received several requests, both written and oral, from the Iranian Government for loans for direct financial assistance to ease the acute situation in which the Iranian Government finds itself as a result of the loss of its oil revenues. The U.S. position in reponse to these requests has been that while the United States desires to be in a position to render Iran any proper and necessary assistance, it could not justify aid of the type requested at a time when Iran has the opportunity of receiving adequate revenues from its oil industry without prejudice to its national aspirations. It has been pointed out that the United States is bearing a heavy financial burden in its efforts to help bring about a stable and lasting peace and that it is most difficult to undertake additional commitments to a country which has the immediate means of helping itself.

The United States has not, as indicated in press reports originating in

---

[1] *Department of State Bulletin*, 31 March 1952, p. 494.

Iran, established as a condition for granting financial aid to Iran that the Iranian Government should accept any particular proposals. The United States has consistently maintained that a settlement is possible in which the legitimate interests of both Iran and the United Kingdom will be protected and which will make the resumption of the oil-industry operation feasible and practicable from the economic viewpoint. We believe that the offer of the International Bank to assist in this matter has provided a good opportunity to reach this objective, even though on an interim basis. We continue to hope that a formula will be found which will be acceptable to both parties.

(iii) The Anglo-American proposals

(a) *Statement by the Foreign Office reviewing recent negotiations with the Persian Government and announcing the joint Anglo-American proposals sent to Dr. Musaddiq by President Truman and Mr. Churchill, 30 August 1952*[1]

In its Note of August 7, 1952, addressed to her Majesty's Chargé d'Affaires at Teheran, the Persian Government announced that, with a view to finding a solution for investigating the just claims of the Anglo-Iranian Oil Company and the reciprocal claims of the Persian Government within the framework of the Persian Nationalization law of May 1, 1951, it was prepared to enter into negotiations with the representatives of the company. It proposed that, if no agreement was reached by direct negotiations, the company should pursue its claims in the Persian courts.

On August 14 her Majesty's Chargé d'Affaires at Teheran called on Dr. Moussadek to seek clarification of this Note. During the interview the Persian Prime Minister said that if her Majesty's Government wished to submit the question of compensation to arbitration, he was prepared for his part to agree that the International Court of Justice should be asked by both parties to settle the question of compensation, though the Court could not be asked to adjudicate on 'the question of the 1933 agreement or on the validity of the nationalization laws'.

He also asked that her Majesty's Government should examine, as a matter of urgency, whether some sum could be made immediately available to the Persian Government, and he proposed that the Anglo-Iranian Oil Company or its nominee should get in touch with the Persian oil sales commission to discuss the purchase of oil.

Her Majesty's Government, while not prepared to accept the Persian view that the 1933 concession agreement was invalid or that the Persian nationalization law was in conformity with Persia's international obliga-

[1] *The Times*, 1 September 1952. See also Great Britain: Foreign Office: *Correspondence between Her Majesty's Government in the United Kingdom and the Iranian Government, and Related Documents, concerning the Joint Anglo-American proposals for the Settlement of the Oil Dispute, August 1952 to October 1952* (Cmd. 8677) (London, H.M.S.O., 1952), p. 3.

tions, have always been anxious that discussions should be started with the Persian Government on a basis which might lead to an acceptable solution of this dispute, including the acceptance by her Majesty's Government of the fact of the Persian nationalization.

They were determined therefore not to neglect the opportunity which Dr. Moussadek's proposals appeared to present. The United States Government also wished to see a settlement of the dispute, and accordingly the representatives of the two Governments in Teheran were instructed to deliver to Dr. Moussadek a joint message from the President of the United States and the Prime Minister:—

'We have reviewed the messages from our two embassies in Persia regarding recent talks with you, as well as your communication of August 7, 1952, to her Majesty's Government. It seems clear to us that to bring about a satisfactory solution to the oil problem will require prompt action by all three of our Governments.

'We are attaching proposals for action which our two Governments are prepared to take and which we sincerely hope will meet with your approval and result in a satisfactory solution. We are motivated by sincere and traditional feelings of friendship for the Persian nation and people and it is our earnest desire to make possible an early and equitable solution of the present dispute.

HARRY S. TRUMAN.
WINSTON S. CHURCHILL.'

The proposals referred to were in an annexe to the message, and are as follows:—

(1) There shall be submitted to the International Court of Justice the question of compensation to be paid in respect of the nationalization of the enterprise of the Anglo-Iranian Oil Company in Persia, having regard to the legal position of the parties existing immediately prior to nationalization, and to all claims and counter-claims of both parties.

(2) Suitable representatives shall be appointed to represent the Persian Government and the Anglo-Iranian Oil Company in negotiations for making arrangements for the flow of oil from Persia to world markets.

(3) If the Persian Government agrees to the proposals in the foregoing two paragraphs, it is understood that: (a) representatives of the A.I.O.C. will seek arrangements for the movement of oil already stored in Persia, and as agreements are reached upon price, and as physical conditions of loading permit, appropriate payment will be made for such quantities of oil as can be moved; (b) her Majesty's Government will relax restrictions on exports to Persia and on Persia's use of sterling; and (c) the United States Government will make an immediate grant of $10 m. to the Persian Government to assist in the budgetary problems.

These proposals were communicated to Dr. Moussadek by her Majesty's Chargé d'Affaires and the United States Ambassador at 3.30 p.m. (local time) today. They have been presented in a sincere effort to offer to Dr. Moussadek a means of meeting his present difficulties and are thought to constitute the most positive and helpful reply possible to his Note of August 7.

(b) Statement by Mr. Acheson regarding the joint proposals, 3 September 1952[1]

The joint message and proposals from President Truman and Prime Minister Churchill to Prime Minister Mossadegh on the oil situation were, we believe, fair and reasonable and had no strings attached. It may be useful to clarify certain points which have been raised in the press.

There has been question raised regarding British recognition of the nationalization of the oil industry in Iran. The joint United States–United Kingdom proposals to Mr. Mossadegh accept the nationalization of the oil industry in Iran as a fact and propose a forum for the determination of compensation.

Another question concerns the part which the Anglo-Iranian Oil Company (AIOC) is to play in making arrangements for the flow of Iranian oil to world markets. In this connection I refer to the Nine-Point law implementing the nationalization of the Iranian oil industry. Article 7 of this law provides that purchasers of Iranian oil products during the 2 years immediately preceding the nationalization of the oil industry shall receive certain priority rights of purchase. The AIOC, as the principal former customer, would seem, therefore, to be the logical entity to open such negotiations with the Iranians. The joint message does not propose that the AIOC should be the sole purchaser of Iranian oil.

It is recognized that there must be a fair settlement of the claims and counterclaims arising from the nationalization of the oil industry in Iran. The Iranian Nine-Point Nationalization law accepts this principle in article 2 which takes cognizance of the fact that funds should be set aside 'to secure' such claims.

What we are proposing is that the International Court of Justice, as an impartial body, be asked to consider all claims of both parties. We believe that this proposal should be acceptable to the Iranians, especially in view of the recent decision of the International Court of Justice which was favorable to Iran.

There has been some question regarding the U.S. offer of a grant of 10 million dollars. I would like to point out that the purpose of this grant would be to provide Iran with funds for a short term to assist that nation financially until flow of Iranian oil to world markets could be resumed. The availability of oil revenue should not be long delayed in view of the

[1] *Department of State Bulletin*, 15 September 1952, pp. 405–6.

proposal for the early sale of the oil already stored in Iran. The figure of 10 million dollars was based on such information as we had of current Iranian budgetary deficits.

I sincerely believe that the proposals meet the outstanding issues in the oil dispute and deserve careful consideration as a basis for negotiations to end the unhappy dispute between two good friends of the United States.

(c) *Letter from Dr. Musaddiq to Mr. Churchill replying to the message of 30 August and presenting the Persian counter-proposals, 24 September 1952*[1]

Your Excellency's message, which was received in the form of a proposal for the solution of the oil problem and the settlement of the dispute between the former company and the Iranian Government, has been carefully considered and examined. Although one would have thought that after having spent a year and a half, the British Government should have appreciated the real meaning of the national movement of Iran, and should have ceased giving improper protection to the former company, unfortunately, contrary to expectations, the effort, which ever since the approval of the law nationalizing the oil industry of Iran, has been made by the former company to revive the invalid 1933 agreement, is plainly noticeable and obvious in the latest message in changed terms of phraseology.

Since it was certain that such a proposal would never be accepted nor approved by the Iranian nation, I pointed out immediately to your Government's Chargé d'Affaires that if a solution of the oil problem was desired, it would be better if this proposal were withdrawn and drafted in such a way that it could be presented to Iranian public opinion, and could be used as a basis for further negotiations. This request had no result and after a few days, that is on Sharivar 8, 1331 (August 30, 1952) the message was delivered to me without any change whatsoever.

Before proceeding with the transmission of a counter proposal, I find it necessary to explain briefly the position of the Iranian Government in regard to the message. The said message, like previous proposals, is inconsistent with the laws of nationalization of the oil industry. Of course, whatever has been mentioned in the beginning of the message concerning the creation of friendly relations for the early solution of the dispute between the two countries is in conformity with the wishes and aspirations of the Iranian nation, which has always endeavoured and is still endeavouring to strengthen friendly relations with the British people, notwithstanding the heavy damages and innumerable injuries that it has suffered during recent centuries from the imperialistic policy of the British Government. My Government, as shown by documents and other proofs, has from the very beginning not neglected this matter in any way

[1] *The Times*, 26 September 1952; Cmd. 8677, pp. 4–8.

whatsoever, and has always been prepared to negotiate within the limits of legal principles for the settlement and solution of the oil problem.

The failure to achieve any result up to this time has been due to the fact that the British Government have desired to retain the influence of the former company under other titles in the same shape and form as before, in violation of the laws and of the rights and desires of the Iranian nation. This has been and still is intolerable to the Iranian nation.

Another point worthy of attention in this message is the word 'equitable' which has been included therein and the solution which has been proposed following this word, which solution is not only inequitable but far more inequitable than previous solutions and proposals. In its latest message, the British Government have wanted to convert the oil question, which is an internal affair and which has been confirmed as such by the decision of The Hague Court, into a dispute between two Governments through the signing of an agreement.

Article 1 of the annex to the message speaks of compensation which should be paid to the former company for the nationalization of the oil industry. This article has been drawn up in such a manner that it is feared that it is desired thereby to legalize the invalid 1933 agreement which has never been acceptable to the Iranian people, because reference has been made to the legal position of both parties immediately prior to the nationalization of the oil industry. If it were intended that compensation for the property of the former oil company in Iran should be paid, my Government has always been prepared to enter into negotiations with due regard to the claims of both parties and to find a just and equitable solution.

If it were meant that in the event of disagreement the question should be referred to the International Court of Justice, such procedure should be agreed to between the Iranian Government and the former oil company and there would be no need of an agreement between the two Governments. If by Article 2 of the annex the purchase of oil is intended, the Iranian Government has always been prepared to sell and has repeatedly declared this to the world. If, however, it is intended that a purchase monopoly be given to a specific company and interference in the management of the oil industry be renewed, this will never be approved by the Iranian nation, for, as a result of such monopoly and interference, economic crises and difficulties might be created which would lead to the same situation which existed before the nationalization of the oil industry.

It is in fact admitted in Article 3 that the British Government's motive in its previous measures was to bring economic pressure on the Iranian nation in order that the latter should submit to the unfair terms of that Government. In paragraph A of this article it is stated that if the other terms are accepted they would be prepared to move the oil stored at

Abadan, but nothing is said about the price, the fixing of which is post-poned until subsequent agreement is reached. If the object of this were to aid and assist they should have specified their views about the price as well, in order that the Iranian Government would be able to make a definite decision.

In paragraph B of this article mention is made of existing restrictions on exports of commodities and the use of sterling funds by Iran which have repeatedly been the subject of protests by the Iranian Government. It has been expressly admitted that such restrictions which have been imposed until now do exist, and it has been promised that in the event of the other terms being accepted these restrictions will be removed. Contrary to what has been claimed in the message, it is neither friendly nor equitable to make the removal of illegal restrictions contingent upon the acceptance of certain terms; furthermore, the restrictions by the British Government directed against the Iranian Government and nation are not confined to these two instances.

After having stated briefly the objections of the Iranian Government, I wish to inform your Excellency that the Iranian people, after suffering innumerable hardships, have unanimously nationalized the oil industry in the country, which is a sovereign right of every nation. It had two motives in taking this action, namely:—

1.—To eradicate foreign influence and agents in the country and thus take charge of its own destiny and ensure the political independence of the country while cooperating shoulder to shoulder with the other freedom-loving nations in maintaining world peace. During the half-century of the former company's domination, it has never been possible for the Iranian Government to make a free decision in its internal affairs and its foreign policy. Your Excellency having been at the head of the British Government over a long period of years is, of course, aware, as was once expressly admitted by his Excellency Mr. Eden, Foreign Secretary in your Cabinet, after the cruel occupation of Iran during the last world war, that the attitude of the British Government towards Iran was not just and should be changed, and that England must take useful and effective steps to win over the public opinion of the Iranian nation and to make up for the past. Unfortunately, however, this promise was never kept and no sign of a change in the British attitude became apparent and, as soon as signs of the awakening of the Iranian nation were noticed, British capitalists persuaded the British Government to employ all kinds of pressure so that the Iranian nation should never be able to check their covetous aims.

Consequently, after the Iranian nation decided to nationalize the oil industry the British Government, instead of appreciating the true desires of the Iranian people, against principles intervened in the dispute and gave protection to the former company, doing everything they could to put obstacles and difficulties in the way of the carrying out of the desires of the Iranian people. They wrongfully dragged the case before the Security Council and from there to the International Court of Justice in The Hague, and, now that it has been proved in both places that the Iranian nation is justified, they are not prepared to abandon their old attitude in order that an agreement may be reached between the former company and the Iranian Government for the settlement of the dispute.

2.—The Iranian nation's other motive in taking this action was to improve economic conditions, because during the period when the former company was engaged in exploiting the resources of Iran it was never prepared to consider and observe the rights of the nation, even in conformity with the D'Arcy concession and the invalid 1933 agreement. During this time the taxes which the company paid a British Government and which were wrongfully assessed on the royalties accruing to the Iranian Government, were several times the income paid to the original owners of the oil, i.e., the Iranian nation. It is surprising that, in spite of its participation in the profits, the Iranian nation was never able to ascertain the quantity of oil which the British Admiralty had obtained from the company, nor the amount of money which had been paid.

By nationalizing the oil industry the Iranian people wanted to take for themselves the maximum profits made from their resources by a foreign company over a long period of years, and by making up for the past injustices by recouping its losses to make every effort to provide for the welfare of the people, 90 per cent. of whom are deprived of all the advantages of life in human society.

In the present circumstances, the Iranian nation may follow one of two roads; either it must endeavour to improve the social conditions and ameliorate the situation of the deprived classes, something that would be impossible without the income from oil; or, if this road should remain blocked, it should surrender itself to probable future events which would be to the detriment of world peace. I have repeatedly stated, and I explicitly declare once more, that the Iranian Government is exceedingly eager that the existing differences be removed as soon as possible in order that the two nations may, as a mark of good understanding, enjoy the results of cooperation and mutual assistance, and fulfil their duty for the preservation of world peace in the best manner.

With reference to the above, I bring the following to your Excellency's attention. The Iranian courts are the only competent channel for investigating the former company's claims and are prepared to adjudicate them, but should the company not wish to refer its claims to the above-mentioned competent authorities, and should the International Court of Justice at The Hague be able to deal with the dispute between the Iranian Government and the former company on the basis of an agreement between the two parties, and should there be no illusion that such action recognizes the existence of a dispute between two Governments, my Government, in order to show its complete good will, after agreement on the four articles below, is prepared to agree to the judgment of the International Court, and in this case the International Court will be requested to issue its final verdict as soon and as far as possible within six months.

Article 1.—COMPENSATION

Determination of the amount of compensation to be paid for property belonging to the former oil company at the time of the nationalization of the oil industry in Iran, and arrangements for paying this by instalments based on any law carried out by any country for nationalizing its industries in similar instances which may be agreed to by the former oil company. This is the only compensation which the Iranian Government will pay to the former company and the company will have no right to make any further claims whatsoever.

Article 2.—BASIS OF EXAMINATION OF CLAIMS

Examination of claims of both parties on the basis of one of the following three provisions to be recognized by the International Court of Justice as fair and just for settling the parties' claims and used by it as the basis for judgment.

(a) Examination of claims of the two parties up to the date of nationalization of the oil industry on the basis of the d'Arcy agreement, with due regard to the calculation of income-tax which the Iranian Government should have received in accordance with the country's enacted laws. The above-mentioned agreement is referred to only for the purpose of settling the financial differences up to the date of the nationalization of the oil industry (9th of Ordibehesht 1330, which is equivalent to April 30, 1951). As from that date this agreement ceases to apply and can in no way be used or invoked by either of the parties, and from that date the company has been acting as a trustee.

(b) Examination of claims of both parties from 1933 to the end of 1947 on the basis of the invalid 1933 agreement and from the beginning of 1948 to April 30, 1951, on the basis of the above-mentioned invalid agreement and the Gass–Golshayan supplementary draft agreement which was agreed to and signed by the former company but which both Houses of the Iranian Parliament did not consider adequate for obtaining the Iranian nation's rights. Reference to the 1933 agreement is solely and exclusively for the purpose of solving financial differences between the parties up to the end of 1947 and the above-mentioned invalid agreement, with the addition of the Gass–Golshayan supplementary draft agreement, is solely and exclusively for solving financial differences from the beginning of 1948 to

April 30, 1951. All effects of the agreements cease from the date of nationalization of the oil industry and cannot be used or invoked in any way by either of the parties, and from that date the company has been acting as a trustee.

(c) Examination of the claims of both parties on the basis of the fairest concession agreements of other oil-producing countries in the world, where the cost of producing oil, according to that concession, is not cheaper than the cost of producing Iranian oil during a corresponding period. Obviously, from the date of nationalization of the oil industry, the company is acting as a trustee. There is no need to mention that the use of any of the three above-mentioned provisions as a basis is merely in order to calculate the financial claims of the parties up to the date of the nationalization of the oil industry and has no connexion with the articles of the above-mentioned agreements which refer to the investigation of differences. The claims of both parties as specified above should be judged directly by the International Court of Justice.

Article 3.—Determination of Damages

Examination and determination of the amount of damages caused to the Iranian Government resulting from the difficulties and obstacles put in the way of the sale of Iranian oil by direct and indirect activities of the former oil company, as well as losses resulting from the delay in payment of funds, which are definitely debts owed by the company.

Article 4.—Payment in Advance and on Account

Payment in advance and on account of £49 m. shown on the former oil company's balance-sheet for 1950 as increases in royalty, taxes and dividends due to Iran from the reserves. From this amount any part due from royalty and tax as it was guaranteed on a gold basis, must be paid in sterling convertible into dollars. Although the said amount is definitely owing to the Iranian Government by the company, in order to show its utmost good will the Iranian Government agrees that if the International Court of Justice does not consider Iran entitled to all the amount or any part of it, sums received in this connexion will be regarded as the Iranian Government's debt to the former oil company and will be settled without delay by delivery of oil. Reference to the judgment of the International Court of Justice on the basis of the four articles mentioned above, which is a sign of extraordinary concessions on the part of the Iranian Government, is binding on the latter only when they are accepted in their entirety.

None of these articles can be invoked separately. Of course the Iranian Government will take up through the International Court of Justice, as a case between two Governments, the question of losses caused by various difficulties and obstacles created by the British Government in their attempt to support the former company, as well as losses resulting from restrictions imposed on exports to Iran and on the use of sterling which the British Government have acknowledged in sub-paragraph B of Article III of the annex to the joint message. This proposal is valid for 10 days from the date of delivery. In conclusion, I bring to your Excellency's attention the fact that the National Iranian Oil Company is always prepared to sell its oil products.

(d) Reply from Mr. Eden to Dr. Musaddiq, 5 October 1952[1]

Mr. Churchill and I and our colleagues in Her Majesty's Government are disappointed to see from your message that our latest proposals for a settlement of the oil dispute should have been misunderstood in so many ways. The fears which you express are without foundation. The proposals in no way fail to recognise the fact of Persia's nationalisation of her oil industry or seek to revive the 1933 Concession. There was no suggestion that there should be foreign management of the oil industry, still less was this put forward as a condition. We did not contemplate a monopoly of the purchase of oil.

The proposals suggested an equitable method, not necessarily the only method, of settling all claims and counter-claims of both sides by impartial adjudication. We said nothing about price of oil because that falls to be discussed between seller and purchaser and not between governments.

I am sending you this message in order that whether or not you accept the proposals you and your countrymen may know exactly what we had in mind.

(e) Letter from Dr. Musaddiq to Mr. Eden, reaffirming his counter-proposals, 7 October 1952[2]

Your Note dated October 5, 1952, which recognized in its entirety the action of the Iranian Government in nationalizing its oil industry, and stated that it did not intend to revive the invalid 1933 Concession Agreement, nor to interfere in the administration of the Iranian oil industry, and recognized the Iranian Government's freedom to sell its oil products, was handed to me by the British Chargé d'Affaires in Teheran.

While taking into consideration the fact that the text of the Note in question in the parts mentioned above is in accordance with the indisputable rights of the Iranian nation, and the same above-mentioned facts are taken as documentary evidence, at the same time it is a matter of regret that in this Note, which was in answer to my Note of Mehr 2, 1331 (September 24, 1952), you did not make any reference to the counter-proposals dated Mehr 2, 1331 (September 24, 1952). I find it necessary

[1] *Foreign Office Press Release*, 5 October 1952, no. 4; Cmd. 8677, p. 9.
[2] *The Times*, 9 October 1952; Cmd. 8677, pp. 10–11.

to inform you again that the object of my counter-proposals was to avoid wasting time and to find an equitable way of investigating the claims of the former oil company and the counter-claims of the Iranian Government.

Now I once again, with the same object in view, declare my readiness for discussion and settlement of this problem. In order that it should be finally quite clear how this dispute stands, representatives of the former A.I.O.C. invested with full powers are invited to leave for Teheran within a week as from today's date, for the purpose of necessary discussions concerning the Iranian Government's counter-proposals. Taking into consideration the several years' delay by the former company in paying its debts to the Iranian Government and also the Iranian Government's need for immediate aid, before the departure of its representatives for Iran the former oil company should put at the disposal of the Iranian Ministry of Finance the sum of £20 m. convertible into dollars, out of the £49 m. mentioned in Article 4 of my counter-proposals dated Mehr 2, 1331 (September 24, 1952). The remainder of the above-mentioned sum should be placed to the credit of the Iranian Government at the end of negotiations, for which a maximum period of three weeks is envisaged.

In conclusion, it is expected that the complete good will of the Iranian Government towards a just solution of differences, which has been reaffirmed in this Note, will be well received and made use of. Your Excellency's attention is particularly drawn to the point that the Iranian Government has always indicated the serious consequences of delay in reaching a rapid and final solution of the differences. You are now once again reminded of the impossibility of the continuation of this state of affairs and any eventuality arising from pursuit of this policy is not the responsibility of the Iranian Government.

(f) Note from the British Government to the Persian Government rejecting the Persian claims of 24 September and 7 October, 14 October 1952[1]

Her Majesty's Government note with regret that in spite of the recent messages from Mr. Acheson on behalf of the President of the United States and from Mr. Eden on behalf of Her Majesty's Government in the United Kingdom correcting certain misunderstandings which appear to exist in the mind of the Persian Government as to the meaning of the joint proposals put forward on 26th August, 1952, the Persian Government should still be unwilling to regard these proposals as an equitable basis for the solution of the oil dispute and should revert to the counter-proposal contained in the Persian Government's note of 24th September, 1952. The Persian counter-proposal was not referred to in Mr. Eden's message of

---

[1] *Foreign Office Press Release*, 14 October 1952, no. 5; Cmd. 8677, pp. 12–14.

4th October, 1952, since that message was sent with the sole purpose of enabling the Persian Government to understand the joint proposals correctly, and in the hope that these proposals would be re-examined by the Persian Government in the spirit in which they were intended. But since the Persian Government now insist on putting forward their counter-proposal as the only basis for a settlement of the dispute, Her Majesty's Government feel obliged to state in some detail why this counter-proposal is unreasonable and unacceptable. Moreover, the terms in which the Persian Government now purport to describe the joint proposals show that the joint proposals are still not understood and make it necessary for Her Majesty's Government once more to place their views and intentions on record.

The Persian Government state in their counter-proposal that the question of claims by the Anglo-Iranian Oil Company and counter-claims by the Persian Government may be referred to the International Court of Justice provided that agreement is previously reached on four conditions. They now invite the Company to send representatives to Tehran within seven days to discuss these conditions while at the same time they demand the partial fulfilment of one of the conditions even before the Company's representatives set out.

By the first and second of their conditions the Persian Government seek to limit the question of claims by the A.I.O.C. to the value of the Company's property in Persia and expressly rule out all possibility of any claim on behalf of the A.I.O.C. relating to the period subsequent to the date of nationalisation. In the Joint Proposals H.M.G. accept the nationalisation of the Persian oil industry as a fact but in return claim just compensation on behalf of the A.I.O.C., the question of such compensation being referred in its entirety to the impartial judgment of the highest judicial tribunal in the world. The International Court should be asked to consider all claims and counter-claims of both parties without limitation and to have regard to the legal position existing immediately prior to nationalisation. Her Majesty's Government would, when presenting claims on behalf of the Company, ask the Court to consider what compensation was due, not for the mere loss of the Company's installations in Persia, but for the unilateral termination of the 1933 Concession Agreement contrary to the explicit undertaking in the Agreement that it would not be so terminated. As was made clear in Mr. Eden's message of 4th October, Her Majesty's Government did not seek to revive the Concession Agreement in other respects. Naturally it would be for the Court to decide whether and to what extent a claim to compensation on the basis indicated above was justified and Her Majesty's Government would, of course, be bound by its decision. Her Majesty's Government could in no circumstances agree to debar themselves from raising such a claim before proceedings had even begun and as a condition for reference to the Court as the Persian Government demand.

With regard to the third stipulation, Her Majesty's Government cannot admit that Persia has any claim against the A.I.O.C. in respect of Persia's failure to sell oil abroad. The A.I.O.C. have merely exercised their legal rights in regard to oil they regard as theirs, an attitude in which they have the full support of Her Majesty's Government, and they have declared their intention of defending those rights throughout the world.

The fourth stipulation refers to the payment in advance and on account of £49 million erroneously stated to be shown in the A.I.O.C.'s balance sheet for 1950 as 'due to Iran'. The Persian Government now insist that of this sum £20 million should be paid within seven days. The Supplemental Oil Agreement, as is well known, was intended to modify the 1933 Concession Agreement in such a way as to entitle the Persian Government to considerable additional payments from the Company. There would have been increases in the tonnage royalty and in the annual payments in respect of Persian taxation. In addition, by very considerably bringing forward the date of payment and by altering the method of assessing the amount of the payments in respect of sums allocated to the General Reserve, the Supplemental Agreement would have ensured to the Persian Government a greater and more certain and more immediate benefit in respect of sums so allocated. The additional financial benefits to the Persian Government would have amounted to some £49 million up to the end of 1951 solely by reason of the terms of the Supplemental Agreement and not by those of the 1933 Agreement. It was a condition of the Supplemental Agreement that the 1933 Agreement, revised in this manner, should remain in full force and effect. Persia rejected the Supplemental Agreement and wrongfully terminated the 1933 Agreement. It is therefore clear that the sums are in no sense due to the Persian Government. Her Majesty's Government are thus being asked to agree, before a given date in the immediate future, that the A.I.O.C. should pay a fictitious debt of £49 million, nearly half of which is to be largely convertible into dollars (a demand not previously made by the Persian Government), in return for the Company's abandoning its right to claim just compensation. Her Majesty's Government are not prepared to entertain this request.

As stated above, the Persian Government have, in the first sentence of their note, described the joint proposals in terms which suggest that misunderstandings still exist. Her Majesty's Government therefore wish to make it abundantly clear that

(i) Her Majesty's Government and the A.I.O.C. accept the nationalisation of the Persian oil industry as a fact, but in return Her Majesty's Government claim just compensation on behalf of the Company.

(ii) Her Majesty's Government consider that the question of compensation should be referred to the impartial adjudication of the International Court.

(iii) Her Majesty's Government claim compensation on behalf of the A.I.O.C. for the unilateral termination of the 1933 Concession Agreement contrary to the explicit undertaking in the Agreement that it will not be so terminated.

(iv) Neither Her Majesty's Government nor the A.I.O.C. seek to revive the 1933 Concession Agreement in any other respect.

(v) As soon as agreement is reached as to the terms on which the question of compensation is to be adjudicated, the A.I.O.C. will be ready to open negotiations as indicated in the Joint Proposals. As already stated, neither Her Majesty's Government nor the A.I.O.C. insist on the Company securing a monopoly of the purchase of Persian oil.

(vi) Pending agreement as to the terms on which the question of compensation is to be adjudicated, Her Majesty's Government on their own behalf and on behalf of the A.I.O.C. reserve their full legal rights.

(iv) NOTE FROM PERSIA TO THE UNITED KINGDOM ANNOUNCING THE BREAKING OF DIPLOMATIC RELATIONS BETWEEN THE TWO COUNTRIES, 22 OCTOBER 1952[1]

I have the honour to inform you of the Persian Government's decision to sever diplomatic relations with the British Government. The Persian Government greatly regrets that it has been obliged to adopt such a decision.

In the course of the dispute with the former oil company my Government always made every effort to ensure that this dispute should not damage the friendly relations between the two Governments.

My Government is convinced that if the British Government had paid proper attention, consistent with justice and friendship, to the aims of the Persian nation and Government, who have only been seeking and are still seeking to secure their rights, which had been infringed, the relations between the two countries would never have reached such a stage.

It is regretted, however, that your Government not only refrained from helping to solve the dispute in this matter, which is vital for our nation, but also prevented an agreement by unlawfully supporting the former company.

Moreover, some of the official representatives of the British Government, through intrigues and improper interference, created difficulties aimed at disturbing this country's order and security.

[1] *The Times*, 23 October 1952.

The Persian Government hopes that the British Government will realize the nature and the truth underlying the movement and the aspirations of the Persian nation and that they will revise their policy.

Should such a favourable atmosphere and good understanding be created, the Persian Government, which has always been interested in the existence of good relations between the two Governments, will be very glad to take action to renew diplomatic relations.

In conclusion I wish to inform you that instructions have been given to the members of the Persian Embassy staff in London to leave for Teheran within one week from October 22, 1952.

(v) Statement by the United States Department of State regarding its attitude towards the purchase of Persian oil by American firms, 6 December 1952[1]

Questions have been raised regarding the present attitude of the U.S. Government toward the purchase of oil from Iran by American nationals or American firms. It would seem advisable at this time to clarify the Department's position on this matter.

Prior to the passing of the oil nationalization law in Iran, some 32 million tons or approximately 240 million barrels of oil and refined products were produced in that country and marketed per year. The gross income on royalties, taxes, and wages received by Iran exceeded 100 million dollars. As will be recognized at once, this constituted a vast commercial operation engaging the world's largest fleet of tankers and required the services of an enormous distributing and marketing organization.

Ever since the oil ceased to flow and the refinery at Abadan was shut down, the United States has made every effort to assist in resolving the differences between the parties to this dispute. The United States wished to see as rapidly as possible the resumption of Iran's revenue. Also in the interests of the entire free world, the United States wished to minimize the dislocation of a great industry and avoid the attendant waste in manpower and monetary resources.

Since the passing of the oil nationalization law in Iran the Anglo-Iranian Oil Company (AIOC) has turned to other sources for its supplies, and in the absence of an over-all settlement, facilities of the AIOC have not been available to move and market oil from Iran. The question of moving relatively small quantities of oil or oil products has seemed to us as of minor importance in comparison with the necessity to find some solution which could drive to the heart of the matter and result in resumption of large-scale movement of Iranian oil. Thus we believe that the

---

[1] *Department of State Bulletin,* 15 December 1952, p. 946.

relatively small amount of oil which could be moved without the assistance of large tanker fleets and distribution and marketing organization will not solve the problem nor enable Iran to benefit from significant revenues from its great resources. Indeed on occasions it has seemed to us more likely than not that such shipments with the attendant legal complexities involved could be harmful to a general settlement of the major problem.

Under present circumstances, this Government believes that the decision whether or not such purchases of oil from Iran should be made must be left to such individuals or firms as may be considering them, and to be determined upon their own judgment. The legal risks involved are matters to be resolved by the individuals or firms concerned.

The Department of State will continue to address itself to the main problem which is the resolution of the dispute so that the essential international principle of adequate and effective compensation may be given effect and Iran may again benefit from the large scale resumption of its oil production.

D. THE MAGHRIB

1. Tunisia

(i) SEVEN-POINT PROGRAMME FOR TUNISIA DEFINED BY DR. HABIB BORGUIBA, LEADER OF THE NEW DASTŪR PARTY, 14 APRIL 1950[1]

1. Revival of the Tunisian Executive, trustee of Tunisian sovereignty. At the present time such sovereignty is non-existent, the Prime Minister of a Tunisian Cabinet being no other than the representative of France.

2. Setting up of a Tunisian Government responsible for law and order, headed by a Tunisian Minister appointed by the Bey, who in his quality as Chief of State, presides over the Cabinet.

3. Discontinuance of the Secretariat-General, which controls all the administration and holds, in practice, all the power.

4. Suppression of Civil Controllers, who practise direct administration, which is incompatible with Tunisian sovereignty.

5. Suppression of the French constabulary (gendarmerie) which, being answerable to the French Ministry of National Defence, stands out as a symbol of the military occupation of the country.

6. Institution of elected municipal councils, allowing for the representation of French interests wherever there are French minorities.

7. On the legislative level, creation of a National Assembly elected by universal suffrage, whose task shall be the preparation of a democratic

---

[1] *Recent Developments in Tunisia (April 1950–May 1951)* (Paris, Neo-Destour of Tunisia, 1951), p. 18.

Constitution, and the re-adjustment of the relationship between France and Tunisia on a new basis of mutual respect for the legitimate interests of France and for the sovereignty of Tunisia.

(ii) Decrees giving effect to the proposals of the French Government regarding administrative reforms in Tunisia, approved by the Bey of Tunis, 8 February 1951[1]

(a) Decree setting up a personal Cabinet for the Bey

Article Premier: Il est créé, au sein du Palais, un Cabinet attaché à Notre Personne et relevant directement de Nous.

Art. 2: Ce Cabinet est chargé de l'examen de toutes les affaires intéressant Notre Maison.

Il coordonne, à cet effet, l'action de tous les Services du Palais et maintient une étroite liaison avec Notre Premier Ministre pour tout ce qui concerne le Protocole et le Cérémonial de Notre Cour.

Art. 3: Les membres de ce Cabinet sont nommés par décret.

Ils comprennent:

1. Directeur du Cabinet;
2. Adjoints.

Le Cabinet dispose également d'un personnel d'exécution (1 interprète, 1 commis, 1 dactylographe).

Art. 4: Notre Premier Ministre et le Secrétaire Général du Gouvernement Tunisien sont chargés de l'exécution du présent décret.

(b) Decree regarding the constitution of the Council of Ministers

Article premier: Le Conseil des Ministres, avec Notre approbation, définit l'orientation et dirige l'action générale du Gouvernement de Notre Royaume.

Le Conseil des Ministres est, en outre, l'organe de travail en commun des Ministres, Directeurs et Commissaire pour le règlement des affaires administratives. Chacun d'eux peut soumettre au Conseil des Ministres les affaires les plus importantes concernant son département.

Les décisions du Conseil des Ministres font, le cas échéant, l'objet de décrets soumis à Notre Sceau.

Art. 2: Le Conseil des Ministres comprend, sous la présidence de Notre Premier Ministre:

le Secrétaire Général du Gouvernment Tunisien;
le Secrétaire Général Adjoint du Gouvernment Tunisien;
le Ministre de la Justice;
le Ministre d'État;
le Ministre des Affaires Sociales;

[1] *Middle East Journal*, Summer 1951, pp. 354–9.

le Ministre du Commerce et de l'Industrie;

le Ministre de la Santé Publique;

le Ministre de l'Agriculture;

le Directeur des Finances;

le Directeur des Travaux Publiques;

le Directeur de l'Instruction Publique;

le Directeur de l'Office Tunisien des Postes, Télégraphes et Téléphones;

le Commissaire à la Reconstruction et au Logement.

Art. 3: Le Président arrête l'ordre du jour et fixe la date des séances du Conseil des Ministres.

Communication de l'ordre du jour est donnée par le secrétariat au Résident Général et à tous les membres du Conseil des Ministres 48 heures avant la réunion.

Art. 4: Le secrétariat du Conseil des Ministres est assuré par le Secrétaire Général du Gouvernement Tunisien.

Art. 5: Le décret du 7 août 1947 portant réorganisation du Conseil des Ministres et instituant un Conseil de Cabinet est abrogé.

Art. 6: Notre Premier Ministre et le Secrétaire Général du Gouvernement Tunisien sont chargés de l'exécution du présent décret.

(c) Decree making provision for action in a state of emergency

Article Premier: En cas d'événements graves susceptibles de mettre en œuvre les hautes obligations derivant des Traités et de compromettre l'administration générale de Notre Royaume, le Résident Général et Notre Gouvernement se concertent au sein d'un Haut Comité en vue de définir les mesures justifiées par ces circonstances exceptionnelles.

Art. 2: Le Haut Comité se réunit sur l'initiative du Résident Général qui en assure la présidence.

Ses décisions font, le cas échéant, l'objet de décrets soumis à Notre Sceau.

Art. 3: Notre Premier Ministre et le Secrétaire Général du Gouvernement Tunisien sont chargés de l'exécution du présent décret.

(d) Decree regarding budgetary procedure

Article Premier: Le troisième alinéa de l'article 3 du décret susvisé du 12 mai 1906 est abrogé et remplacé par les dispositions suivantes:

Art. 3: Troisième alinéa (nouveau): Les divergences entre les Chefs d'Administration et le Directeur des Finances sont soumises, en vue de leur règlement, au Premier Ministre, assisté du Secrétaire Général du Gouvernement Tunisien, puis, le cas échéant, et successivement, au Conseil des Ministres et au Résident Général. Dans le cadre des solutions intervenues, le projet de budget est arrêté par le Conseil des

Ministres, examiné par le Grand Conseil de la Tunisie, présenté au contrôle du Ministre des Affaires Étrangères de la République Française, approuvé ensuite par Nous et promulgué au 'Journal Officiel Tunisien'.

Art. 2: La procédure prévue au 3ème alinéa de l'article 3 du décret du 12 mai 1906 est applicable à tout projet relatif à un emprunt publique contracté ou garanti par l'État.

Art. 3: Les articles 76 et 77 du décret susvisé du 15 septembre 1945 sont abrogés et remplacés par les dispositions suivantes:

Art. 76 (nouveau): Les questions pour le règlement desquelles aucune majorité prévue à l'article précédent n'a pu être réunie, font alors l'objet d'un tableau portant indication:

— d'une part, des propositions du Gouvernement;

— d'autre part, des propositions de chacune des Sections; et sont soumises aux délibérations d'un Comité Supérieur Budgétaire composé:

— du Résident Général, Président;

— du Premier Ministre;

— du Président de chacune des deux Sections du Grand Conseil;

— du Président et du Rapporteur Général de la Commission des Finances de chacune des deux Sections du Grand Conseil.

Les membres du Conseil des Ministres ont accès auprès du Comité Supérieur Budgétaire pour lui apporter toutes informations touchant les questions qui les concernent.

Art. 77 (nouveau): Le Comité Supérieur Budgétaire règle les questions qui lui sont soumises à la majorité des voix. En cas de partage égal, la voix du Président est prépondérante.

Art: 4: Notre Premier Ministre, le Secrétaire Général du Gouvernement Tunisien et le Directeur des Finances sont chargés, chacun en ce qui le concerne, de l'exécution du présent décret.

(*e*) *Decree regarding the general administration of Tunisia*

Article Premier: L'Administration générale de Notre Royaume est assurée, sous l'autorité de Notre Premier Ministre, par:

(1) Une Administration centrale comprenant:

— le Ministère de la Justice;

— le Ministère d'État;

— le Ministère des Affaires Sociales;

— le Ministère du Commerce et de l'Industrie;

— le Ministère de la Santé Publique;

— le Ministère de l'Agriculture;

— la Direction des Finances;

— la Direction des Travaux Publiques;

— la Direction de l'Instruction Publique;

— la Direction de l'Office Tunisien des Postes, Télégraphes et Téléphones;

— le Commissariat à la Reconstruction et au Logement.

(2) Un corps de caïds qui Nous représent dans les circonscriptions administratives de Notre Royaume où, en cette qualité, ils sont délégataires des pouvoirs de Notre Premier Ministre.

Notre Premier Ministre est assisté, pour l'administration générale de Notre Royaume, du Secrétaire Général du Gouvernement Tunisien.

TITRE I

Du Premier Ministre

Art. 2: Le Premier Ministre Nous propose les décrets et actes soumis à Notre Sceau. Il en surveille et en assure l'exécution.

Il préside le Conseil des Ministres.

Il coordonne l'action des Ministères, Directions et Commissariat.

Art. 3: Le Premier Ministre est également compétent pour tout ce qui concerne:

— le protocole et le cérémonial de Notre Cour; les intérêts du patrimoine de Notre Famille;

— le protocole de la Présentation des décrets et maroudhs et la chancellerie de Notre Sceau;

— le règlement des affaires concernant la direction, le contrôle et la discipline des agents de Notre Autorité et de leurs auxiliaires (Caïds, Kahias, Khalifats et Cheiks);

— la garde et la conservation des archives de l'État.

Art. 4: Lorsque le Premier Ministre se trouve absent ou empêché, le Ministre chargé de son intérim est désigné par décret.

TITRE II

Du Secrétariat Général du Gouvernement Tunisien

Art. 5: Le Secrétaire Général du Gouvernement Tunisien est nommé par Nous sur la présentation du Résident Général.

Il assure auprès du Premier Ministre, dans les conditions prévues à l'article 1er (dernier alinéa) et à l'article 7 du présent décret:

(1) la centralisation des affaires civiles et administratives et notamment des décrets et actes proposés à Notre Sceau, ainsi que des arrêtés;

(2) l'inspection générale des services administratifs;

(3) l'exercice du contrôle du personnel et du contrôle des dépenses publiques des administrations civiles; le Premier Ministre est tenu régulièrement informé de l'activité de ces contrôles administratifs;

(4) la gestion du service tunisien des statistiques;

(5) l'élaboration du plan économique dont il surveille l'exécution après son approbation par le Conseil des Ministres.

Il est chargé de la publication des décrets et arrêtés, pour les actes qui ne sont pas publiés au *Journal Officiel Tunisien* de leur enregistrement, avant notification, sur un registre coté et paraphé à cet effet.

Art. 6: Le Secrétaire Général Adjoint du Gouvernement Tunisien est nommé par Nous, sur la présentation du Résident Général.

Il assiste le Secrétaire Général qui peut lui déléguer certaines de ses attributions.   Il le remplace en cas d'absence ou d'empêchement.

TITRE III
Des Ministères, Directions et Commissariat

Art. 7: Les Ministres, Directeurs et Commissaire placés à la tête des Administrations énumérées à l'article 1er sont nommés par décret.

Chacun d'eux a seul qualité pour instruire et conclure les affaires relevant de son département.

Il nomme, par arrêté, le personnel recruté par son Administration. Toutefois, la délégation dans les fonctions de chef de service et de Sous-Directeur ou la nomination à un poste équivalent sont prises par décret.

Il engage, liquide et ordonnance les dépenses de ses services dans les conditions fixées par les règlements relatifs à la compatibilité publique.

Art. 8: Lorsqu'un des Ministres, Directeurs ou Commissaire, visés au présent décret se trouve absent ou empêché, le Chef d'Administration chargé de l'intérim est désigné par décret.

Art. 9: L'organisation, les cadres et les effectifs des Ministères, Directions et Commissariat énumérés à l'article 1er sont fixés par décret.

TITRE IV
Dispositions Générales

Art. 10: Les membres du Conseil des Ministres exercent, dans le cadre de leurs attributions, sauf dispositions législatives spéciales, le pouvoir réglementaire.

Tous les projets d'arrêtés réglementaires ou individuels, centralisés dans les conditions prévues à l'article 5, sont communiqués par les soins du Secrétaire Général du Gouvernement Tunisien au Résident Général qui les renvoie avec son assentiment ou, le cas échéant, et préalablement à celui-ci, ses recommandations.

Art. 11: Tous les actes réglementaires ou individuels sont exécutoires du seul fait de leur publication ou, pour ceux qui ne sont pas publiés, de leur notification, compte tenu des dispositions du dernier alinéa de l'article 5 ci-dessus.

Art. 12: Le décret du 9 août 1947, portant réorganisation de l'Administration de la Tunisie, est abrogé.

Art. 13: Notre Premier Ministre et le Secrétaire Général du Gouvernement Tunisien sont chargés de l'exécution du présent décret.

(f) Decree regulating employment in the civil service

Article Premier: L'accès pour l'avenir aux Administrations publiques de Régence, définies à l'article 1er, (1°), de Notre décret susvisé du 8 février 1951, est régi par les dispositions ci-après.

Art. 2: Les candidats français et les candidats tunisiens, répartis en deux séries, subissent les mêmes épreuves et sont notés par les mêmes jurys. L'arrêté déterminant les conditions du concours fixe la note moyenne minimum exigée pour l'admission.

Art. 3: Les places mises au concours sont réparties en deux contingents affectés à chacune des séries de candidats. Si le nombre des candidats ayant obtenu dans chaque série, ou dans l'une d'entre elles, la note moyenne exigée pour l'admission, est inférieur au nombre de places affectées à la série, il n'est pas pourvu aux places en excédent qui, s'ajoutant, le cas échéant, aux nouvelles places vacantes, seront remises au concours selon les proportions prévues à l'article 4 ci-après.

Art. 4: Les contingents définis à l'article 3 ci-dessus comprennent respectivement:

Pour les candidats de nationalité française, la moitié des places dans les concours donnant accès aux emplois de la catégorie A et de la catégorie B, le tiers des places dans les concours donnant accès aux emplois de la catégorie C, le quart des places dans les concours donnant accès aux emplois de la catégorie D.

Pour les candidats de nationalité tunisienne, la moitié des places dans les concours donnant accès aux emplois de la catégorie A et de la catégorie B, les deux tiers des places dans les concours donnant accès aux emplois de la catégorie C, les trois quarts des places dans les concours donnant accès aux emplois de la catégorie D.

Art. 5: Les concours donnant accès aux emplois de la catégorie D comprennent une épreuve facultative de langue arabe. Les candidats qui n'ont pas subi cette épreuve ou qui, l'ayant subie, n'ont pas obtenu une note au moins égale à la moyenne, ne peuvent être titularisés qu'après avoir justifié de connaissances élémentaires de langue arabe leur permettant de tenir une conversation simple, sur des sujets de vie courante ayant trait notamment à la fonction exercée.

Art. 6: En vue de l'application du présent décret, il est tenu compte, pour le classement des emplois dans les catégories A, B, C et D, telles qu'elles sont définies à l'article 104 du décret susvisé du 23 mai 1949, de l'indice affecté au grade de début dans le cadre qui est rapproché à cette fin de l'indice de début desdites catégories.

Art. 7: Les pourcentages prévus à l'article 4 sont applicables aux emplois accessibles sans concours aux candidats qui n'appartiennent pas à l'Administration.

Art. 8: Il n'est pas dérogé par le présent décret:

— aux dispositions de l'article 2 du décret susvisé du 3 juin 1937;

— aux dispositions instituant des règles particulières concernant les personnels de l'Office Tunisien des Postes, Télégraphes et Téléphones.

Art. 9: Sont abrogées toutes dispositions contraires à celles du présent décret et notamment l'article 1er du décret susvisé du 3 juin 1937.

Art. 10: Notre Premier Ministre et le Secrétaire Général du Gouvernement Tunisien sont chargés de l'exécution du présent décret.

(iii) Memorandum from the Tunisian Government to the French Government regarding the realization of self-government for Tunisia, 31 October 1951[1]

L'expérience entreprise le 17 août 1950[2] visait un double but: créer d'abord la détente politique dans le pays, hâter ensuite la mise en œuvre d'un ensemble de réformes de structure devant conduire, par étapes, la Tunisie vers l'autonomie interne. D'où l'accession au gouvernement d'une équipe chargée de négocier avec la République française les modalités d'application de la nouvelle politique.

Il avait été bien question, préalablement à la constitution du ministère, de contacts mensuels à Paris avec le Gouvernement français en vue de préciser le contenu et la durée des étapes à franchir.

Malheureusement, il s'est avéré que le vague dans lequel se sont tenus les accords intervenus permit leur interprétation dans un sens restrictif qui en réduisit à pratiquement peu de chose la portée et la valeur. On avait négligé de définir le contenu des étapes et de préciser leur durée.

En même temps, on n'était pas parvenu, du côté français, à se libérer suffisamment des anciennes pratiques. On pensait que les mesures à introduire pouvaient s'inscrire dans le cadre de la législation et des institutions existantes. Les réformes de février 1951 s'en sont, de ce fait, fortement ressenties; elles devaient, du reste, se révéler inopérantes, voire génératrices de conflit, qui, très vite, altérèrent les rapports franco-tunisiens.

La timidité du partenaire français, l'obstruction systématique de certains hauts fonctionnaires, amenèrent, du côté tunisien, une crise de confiance qui est allée sans cesse croissant.

[1] *L'Année politique, 1951* (Paris, Éditions du Grand Siècle, Presses Universitaires de France, 1952), pp. 588–9.

[2] The formation of a new Tunisian Government under Mr. Muhammad Chenik.

On ne pouvait vraiment faire du neuf en maintenant intact un statut politique qui, depuis longtemps, jurait avec le degré d'évolution du peuple tunisien et dont l'anachronisme avait été explicitement reconnu par le Gouvernement français, en la personne de M. le Ministre des Affaires étrangères.

Il suffit, pour en juger, d'en faire une étude succincte, mais objective.

Le Traité de 1881,[1] qui a épousé la forme d'une convention entre deux États, a réservé au Bey sa souveraineté interne. Par la suite, la Convention du 8 juin 1883,[2] où pour la première fois il fut question de 'protectorat', avait stipulé que, 'afin de faciliter au Gouvernement français l'accomplissement de son protectorat, S. A. le Bey s'engage à procéder aux réformes administratives, judiciaires et financières que le Gouvernement français jugera utiles'.

Ce n'était donc pas une délégation de pouvoirs consentie par le Souverain tunisien au profit du Gouvernement français, mais simplement un engagement de ce même Souverain d'effectuer telle réforme que le Gouvernement français estimerait utile.

C'est encore moins une abdication de l'autonomie beylicale, Son Altesse gardant toujours l'initiative des lois tant qu'elles n'étaient pas contraires aux engagements pris dans l'acte du 12 mai 1881. Cette interprétation découle des travaux préparatoires et notamment du refus de ratification par le Parlement français de la Convention élaborée par M. Paul Cambon, le 30 octobre 1882.

Dans son esprit, la Convention de la Marsa, nonobstant ses vices originaux, suppose une collaboration entre deux gouvernements et non pas une administration directe de la Tunisie par la France, encore moins l'adjonction à la souveraineté tunisienne, seule légale et légitime, d'une autre souveraineté. Ceci est si évident que le pouvoir législatif du Bey est resté intact.

Cependant, le Souverain auquel il a été reconnu le droit d'effectuer toutes les réformes, ne peut les effectuer que si leur opportunité a été préalablement appréciée par le représentant de la France.

De sorte qu'en même temps que le Gouvernement acquérait un droit de contrôle sur le pouvoir législatif, le Souverain se voyait restreindre l'exercice de sa souveraineté interne.

Par la suite, une interprétation extensive de la Convention de la Marsa permit par un acte unilatéral — décret présidentiel du 10 novembre 1884 — de déléguer le Résident général à 'l'effet d'approuver au nom du Gouvernement français la promulgation et la mise à exécution dans la Régence de Tunis de tous les décrets rendus par Son Altesse le Bey', faisant pratiquement de ce haut fonctionnaire français le véritable chef

---

[1] The Bardo Treaty: *British and Foreign State Papers*, vol. lxxii, pp. 247–9.
[2] The Convention of La Marsa: ibid. vol. lxxiv, pp. 743–4.

de l'État. Il est seul, désormais, à pouvoir donner aux lois une forme exécutoire.

Ce premier pas vers le partage de l'exercice de la souveraineté interne une fois franchi, nous avons assisté à la naissance de l'inconsistante théorie du 'protectorat, création continue' aboutissant, par une confusion de souveraineté, à la gestion directe.

Les modifications de détail introduites de temps à autre dans l'appareil gouvernemental ou administratif, les innovations apportées au fonctionnement de nos institutions, légalisaient ces empiètements et faussaient toujours davantage les rapports de la Tunisie avec la France.

La promesse d'autonomie interne devait, dans l'esprit des Tunisiens, redresser totalement la situation. Mais, faute d'avoir clairement défini cette autonomie interne, d'en avoir fixé les modalités d'application, on retombe de nouveau dans les errements du passé. Il s'en suivit un flottement tel que ce fut de nouveau l'immobilisme.

Cependant, nous sommes persuadés que le Gouvernement français, fort de tous ces enseignements, a fini par être convaincu de la nécessité de rompre résolument et définitivement avec les demi-mesures. La nouvelle orientation à prendre ne saurait se manifester autrement que par le dégagement complet de la souveraineté tunisienne.

L'autonomie interne que la France entend réaliser jure avec la persistance de l'état de choses actuel tant dans le domaine législatif et gouvernemental qu'administratif.

L'autonomie interne veut dire une Tunisie intérieurement souveraine, jouissant du 'Self-Government' et faisant évoluer ses institutions selon sa propre vocation.

Cette autonomie interne, gage de l'amitié franco-tunisienne, doit être réalisée dans un temps minimum. Elle doit, d'ores et déjà, recevoir une consécration sur le triple plan gouvernemental, législatif et administratif.

Sur le plan gouvernemental, l'homogénéité du Gouvernement tunisien s'est révélée une nécessité. Les ministres, chefs des départements, s'entoureront, s'il en était besoin, de techniciens français, pour mener à bien leur tâche et former à l'école de la technique administrative française des administrateurs avisés et compétents. L'on évitera ainsi une dualité de fait au sein du Gouvernement tunisien, préjudiciable à l'évolution, à la bonne marche des affaires et aussi de l'amitié franco-tunisienne.

Sur le plan législatif, l'institution d'une Assemblée représentative tunisienne, élaborant les lois et contrôlant la gestion et la politique générale du Gouvernement, sera un pas appréciable dans la voie de la démocratie. Pour une période transitoire, l'initiative des lois peut être réservée exclusivement à l'exécutif; les membres de cette Assemblée auront toutefois le droit d'un amendement.

Enfin, sur le plan administratif, tout en sauvegardant aux fonctionnaires français, au service de l'État tunisien, leurs situations acquises, il est indispensable de doter la fonction publique tunisienne d'un statut compatible avec le nouveau régime. Le Gouvernement tunisien s'engage, par ailleurs, à ne recruter qu'en France et par l'intermédiaire du Gouvernement français les techniciens dont la Tunisie aura besoin.

Cette souveraineté interne restaurée n'interdit pas à la Tunisie de passer avec la France des accords de nature à maintenir sur les plans culturel, économique et stratégique les relations les plus étroites et de garantir aux ressortissants français résidant en Tunisie la jouissance de leurs droits civils, et la pleine sécurité de leurs biens et de leurs personnes.

Telles sont les propositions que le Gouvernement tunisien, au nom de Son Altesse le Bey, a l'honneur de soumettre à l'accord du Gouvernement français; elles constituent une étape vers la réalisation de l'autonomie interne.

La restitution des responsabilités se fera, à propos de chaque domaine, suivant des accords particuliers.

Si les présentes propositions sont agréées, dans leur principe, une commission composée de représentants des Gouvernements français et tunisien en mettra au point, aussitôt que possible, les textes à soumettre à l'assentiment du Gouvernement français et à la sanction de S. A. le Bey.

(iv) Reply by M. Schuman, the French Foreign Minister, to the Tunisian Prime Minister, 15 December 1951[1]

J'ai l'honneur de faire savoir à Votre Excellence que le Conseil des ministres réuni le 15 décembre a étudié, sur ma proposition et comme suite à nos récentes conversations, le mémoire que vous m'avez remis le 31 octobre dernier pour préciser les vues de S. A. le Bey sur le problème des rapports franco-tunisiens.

Tout en recherchant les possibilités de faire évoluer le protectorat dans le sens souhaité par Son Altesse, le gouvernement s'est tout d'abord étonné qu'on pût faire abstraction de l'œuvre passée et présente accomplie en Tunisie par la France: celle-ci croit pouvoir tirer une légitime fierté des progrès réalisés depuis soixante-dix ans avec le concours éclairé des chefs de la dynastie husseinite par un pays dont elle a créé l'administration, organisé la justice ainsi que l'enseignement et assuré le développement économique et social. Cette évolution a seule permis de faire face à la poussée démographique que connaît la Tunisie, dont la population a triplé depuis l'instauration du protectorat.

Cette œuvre s'est poursuivie ces dernières années à un rythme accéléré. Comme ne l'ignore pas le gouvernement, c'est une aide directe de la France qui finance la quasi-totalité du budget extraordinaire tunisien, soit le tiers des dépenses budgétaires.

[1] *L'Année politique 1951*, pp. 591-2.

Elle assure ainsi la réalisation d'un vaste programme d'équipement, sans lequel la Régence ne pourrait s'adapter aux conditions d'une économie mondiale en pleine évolution. Les réalisations déjà accomplies, telles que les grands barrages de la Medjerdah, appelés à donner une impulsion nouvelle à l'œuvre hydraulique agricole, ainsi que l'importance des crédits affectés à la modernisation du paysannat, au développement de l'enseignement et de l'hygiène sociale, sont là pour attester l'ampleur de l'effort fourni par la puissance protectrice.

Le gouvernement français, conscient de remplir une mission conforme à l'acception la plus haute du traité du protectorat, n'entend pas se départir à l'avenir d'une action qui s'exerce au bénéfice de l'ensemble des populations de la Régence.

Dans cette œuvre civilisatrice les Français de Tunisie ont joué un rôle essentiel que nul ne saurait songer à contester. La part qu'ils prennent par leur travail à la vie économique du pays, l'importance de leur contribution au budget de l'État tunisien, ne permettent pas d'écarter leur participation au fonctionnement des institutions politiques.

Le gouvernement français est fermement attaché à ce principe, qui lui paraît seul être susceptible d'assurer, par une association féconde franco-tunisienne, le développement harmonieux de ces institutions.

Il importe de garder ces considérations présentes à l'esprit en étudiant les rapports futurs de nos deux pays, qui ne peuvent être fondés que sur la reconnaissance du caractère définitif du lien qui les unit.

Le gouvernement de la République reste d'autre part animé du désir de répondre aux aspirations des populations de Tunisie. Il a marqué à plusieurs reprises qu'il était disposé à introduire dans la Régence des réformes compatibles avec l'accomplissement de sa mission.

C'est dans cet état d'esprit qu'a été rédigé d'un commun accord le programme d'une première série de réformes qui a fait l'objet du communiqué du 17 août 1950. Les décrets du 8 février ont permis une réorganisation de l'exécutif et une réforme de la fonction publique conformes au vœu de la population tunisienne, et qu'il ne saurait être question de remettre aujourd'hui en cause.

Le gouvernement français, conscient d'avoir pour sa part rempli les termes de l'accord du 17 août 1950, se trouve en droit de demander à S.A. le Bey de donner suite aux engagements librement souscrits au sujet de la réforme municipale, qui constitue aux yeux du gouvernement français une première mesure indispensable au développement de la démocratie tunisienne.

Peut-être n'est-il pas superflu de marquer une fois encore que la réalisation de cette réforme, dont le caractère démocratique ne vous aura pas échappé, constitue la condition préalable à la mise en application de toute autre réforme qui pourrait être envisagée.

C'est avec le même souci d'amener le peuple tunisien à assumer la gestion des affaires publiques en association avec les Français que le gouvernement de la République avait obtenu de S. A. le Bey la création du Grand Conseil de la Tunisie. Le mandat de l'Assemblée actuelle est arrivé à expiration le 9 de ce mois, et vous m'avez saisi à cette occasion du vœu de S.A. le Bey de voir réformer ce système législatif. Le gouvernement français ne refuse pas d'envisager l'étude d'une modification de l'institution actuelle, tout en maintenant qu'il est indispensable de préserver la continuité de la représentation des Français et des Tunisiens auprès du gouvernement de S. A. le Bey.

A cet effet je crois devoir insister sur la nécessité d'assurer le vote du budget de 1952 par une mesure qui pourrait prendre la forme d'une prorogation du Grand Conseil pour une durée qui suffise à garantir la permanence de la fonction représentative.

Sous ces réserves ainsi indiquées, et compte tenu des considérations générales développées plus haut, j'ai l'honneur de vous faire savoir que le gouvernement français donne pour instructions à son représentant à Tunis de constituer dès le mois de janvier prochain une commission mixte franco-tunisienne destinée à étudier les modalités d'un système représentatif qui pourrait être appelé à remplacer le Grand Conseil de la Tunisie, et dont les conclusions devraient être remises dans un délai déterminé.

Le gouvernement français reste convaincu que S. A. le Bey, dans sa grande sagesse, prêtera un concours éclairé au résident dans la recherche des améliorations qu'il est possible d'apporter au fonctionnement du protectorat. L'intérêt qui s'attache en effet pour la France comme pour la Tunisie à ce que cette évolution s'accomplisse dans la concorde et dans la paix ne saurait vous échapper.

Le gouvernement de la République, pour sa part, considère que l'amitié sincère qui s'est développée entre nos deux pays grâce à l'œuvre commune poursuivie pendant près de trois quarts de siècle est un bien trop précieux pour que notre premier devoir ne soit pas de maintenir plus étroite que jamais la solidarité franco-tunisienne, dont les résultats furent si féconds dans le passé, dont la confiance mutuelle demeure la condition première et dont la situation présente du monde souligne clairement la nécessité.

(v) LETTER FROM THE TUNISIAN PRIME MINISTER, MR. MUHAMMAD CHENIK, TO THE PRESIDENT OF THE SECURITY COUNCIL BRINGING TO THE NOTICE OF THE COUNCIL A DISPUTE BETWEEN FRANCE AND TUNISIA, 12 JANUARY 1952[1]

Sir,

I have the honour to request you to bring to the notice of the Security

[1] S/2571, 31 March 1952, pp. 3-5.

Council the application of the Tunisian Government regarding a dispute between the Tunisian Government and the Government of the French Republic.

On 12 May 1881, the French State and the Tunisian State signed 'a treaty of friendship and of bon voisinage' under which the Tunisian State authorizes the French Government provisionally to occupy certain points in the Territory of Tunisia.

The above Treaty maintained intact for His Highness the Bey the enjoyment and exercise of domestic sovereignty.

The French authorities in Tunisia have in practice replaced the Tunisian Sovereign in the exercise of this sovereignty and established a system of direct administration.

The result has been constant unrest and an ever deepening crisis in Franco-Tunisian relations.

To remedy this state of affairs and to bring about normal relations between the two countries, the French Government has solemnly undertaken to abandon direct administration in Tunisia and to permit the development of Tunisian political institutions to the point of achieving internal autonomy.

On the basis of these undertakings, His Highness the Bey entrusted me in August 1950 with the task of forming 'a Ministry for negotiations to lead Tunisia to internal autonomy'.

On 15 May 1951, His Highness the Bey solemnly proclaimed his purpose 'to endow his people with representative, democratic assemblies' and expressly instructed his Ministers 'to prepare the texts relating thereto'.

Difficulties due to the non-fulfilment of the undertakings given having prevented the Tunisian Ministry from carrying out the task assigned to it, the latter proceeded to Paris for conversations with the French Government regarding the necessity for the fulfilment of its undertakings.[1]

The French Government, after long and difficult negotiations both in Paris and at Tunis, replied in a note of 15 December 1951 by rejecting the memorandum presented to it on 31 October 1951.[2]

In its reply, the French Government affirmed the necessity for 'the participation of the French citizens in Tunisia—a foreign colony—in the working of the political institutions of Tunisia'. The anti-legal position is in obvious contradiction with the provisions of the Treaty of 12 May 1881 cited above.

---

[1] An Italian text of this document includes here a paragraph which does not appear in S/2571: 'Il governo tunisino, in un memoriale del 31 ottobre 1951, ha esposto le modalità per realizzare l'autonomia interna prommessa dalla Francia; queste modalità si riassumono nell'istituzione di un governo tunisino omogeneo e di un organo rappresentativo tunisino sorto da libere elezioni e incaricato di elaborare le leggi: ciò in conformità del desiderio espresso da Sua Altezza il bey nella sua proclamazione': *Relazioni Internazionali*, 26 January 1952, p. 90.

[2] See above, pp. 360–3.

Moreover, by opposing the establishment of a specifically Tunisian political assembly, the French Government impairs the principle of the unity of sovereignty in Tunisia.

Further, since the bond between France and Tunisia is regarded as 'definitive' by the French Government, the latter violates the provisions of the Treaty of 12 May 1881, the provisional character of which is solemnly affirmed (Article 2, 2).

In view of these considerations and France's desire to impede the establishment of true democracy in the Kingdom of Tunisia, the Tunisian Government considers that this situation creates a dispute between the French State and the Tunisian State, the settlement of which by direct contact and negotiation has proved impossible.

The attitude of the French Government calls into question the very foundations of Franco-Tunisian relations. Its persistence in maintaining a policy of direct administration in a State which has never abdicated its sovereignty and in opposing democratic institutional reforms is likely to prejudice the development of 'friendly relations among nations based on respect for the principle of equal rights and self-determination of peoples'. (Charter of the United Nations, Article 1, paragraph 2.)

The Tunisian Government availing itself of Article 35, paragraph 2, of the Charter of the United Nations and accepting the obligations deriving therefrom is justified in bringing before the Security Council the dispute between the French State and the Tunisian State with a view to its solution in conformity with equity and its adjustment by means likely to safeguard good relations between nations.

The Tunisian Government, in accordance with Article 32 of the Charter requests you to permit it 'to participate in the discussion relating to the dispute'.

I have the honour, etc.

s/M'HAMMED CHENIK
Prime Minister of the Kingdom of
Tunisia
Head of the Tunisian Government

(vi) SPEECH IN THE FRENCH NATIONAL ASSEMBLY BY THE PRIME MINISTER, M. EDGAR FAURE, ON THE GOVERNMENT'S POLICY IN TUNISIA, 22 JANUARY 1952[1]

J'aborde maintenant le fond du problème: notre politique franco-tunisienne.

Cette politique n'a pas changé; elle est telle qu'elle a été pleinement explicitée par M. le ministre des affaires étrangères M. Robert Schuman,

[1] *Journal Officiel, Débats*, 23 January 1952, pp. 294–6.

au cours d'un débat qui s'est déroulé devant l'autre Assemblée, et dont le compte rendu a paru au *Journal officiel.*

Cette politique, vous le savez, avait pris, depuis près de deux ans, l'aspect plus particulier de ce qu'on a appelé la politique de réformes et dont voici les étapes. Le 17 août 1950, formation d'un gouvernement, que vous connaissez. Le 8 février 1951, deuxième étape, annonce des réformes que l'on a parfois appelées les 'réformettes' et qui, cependant, avaient leur importance et leur sincérité; désignation d'un premier ministre tunisien, désignation de six ministres tunisiens, établissement de l'égalité, suppression des visas.[1]

Nous nous souvenons tous, surtout ceux d'entre nous qui connaissent la Tunisie, de l'époque où l'on était loin de ce régime et où uniquement des directeurs français faisaient fonction de ministres en Tunisie.

Voilà donc les premières réformes. Suffisantes? Définitives? Ce n'est pas ainsi qu'elles étaient conçues. Ce n'était qu'une première étape, d'accord, mais une étape tout de même, une étape sérieuse et réelle, gage précis, effectif de notre volonté.

Les autres étapes, vous les connaissez. Il y a, d'abord, celle de la fonction publique, car il faut que l'accès des Tunisiens à la fonction publique soit plus largement favorisé.

Il a donc été décidé par le Gouvernement, à juste titre, qu'une règle arithmétique empêcherait de donner une proportion trop forte aux effectifs français dans le cadre de la fonction publique. Et puisque nous sommes ici pour dire la vérité, j'estime qu'il y a actuellement une surabondance de fonctionnaires français et qu'il faut développer l'accession des Tunisiens aux cadres de la fonction publique.

Une autre étape a été l'organisation municipale. C'est celle sur laquelle nous sommes, c'est l'obstacle devant lequel nous nous trouvons.

Cela paraît aride et abstrait, une organisation municipale. Pourtant, c'est là que se noue le conflit, comme je l'indiquerai.

Troisième étape: L'Assemblée représentative.

Le grand conseil, quelques services qu'il ait pu rendre, n'est plus, en effet, exactement adapté aux nécessités actuelles.

C'est au cours de la discussion de ces points que des difficultés se produisent, que des impatiences s'opposent à des prudences et que l'on arrive à ce que je peux appeler la tension des mémorandums, tension qui se produit entre les dates du 31 octobre — mémorandum des ministres tunisiens — et du 16 décembre — réponse française[2] — qui n'est elle-même suivie d'une réponse, notez-le, mesdames, messieurs, que le 9 janvier.

Une première question se pose: Y a-t-il ou non un malentendu?

Je crois qu'il y a un malentendu parce que je veux le croire, parce que

---

[1] See above, p. 354.
[2] See above, p. 360.

je l'espère. Et, s'il y a malentendu, il ne faut pas hésiter à le dissiper et, même, à le dissiper plusieurs fois.

Je m'appuie, là encore, sur des textes, je parle en présence de mon ministre des affaires étrangères qui a, depuis si longtemps, la charge de cette lourde gestion et qui s'est exprimé ainsi:

'On nous a reproché d'avoir indiqué pour la première fois, dans un texte officiel, la notion de la co-souveraineté. Nous n'avons pas employé le terme. Nous n'avons même pas exprimé cette idée.'

Je voudrais maintenant résumer notre position dans la politique tunisienne par les quelques idées suivantes, sur lesquelles je me permets de demander l'attention de l'Assemblée.

Le premier principe, je l'énoncerai ainsi: pas de départ, pas d'abandon de la présence française. . . .

Donc, pas d'abandon de la présence française pour toutes les raisons que vous connaissez, et dont certaines ont trait à la stratégie. Au moment où nous demandons au pays un très lourd effort pour la défense nationale, nous serions, entre autres inconvénients, dans l'illogisme si nous négligions les positions qui font partie du domaine de la stratégie.

Puisque nous sommes ici pour dire la vérité, je dois reconnaître, en manifestant quelque satisfaction, que dans le mémorandum tunisien du 31 octobre, la nécessité du maintien de cette position est expressément reconnue. Mais si la présence française répond à la nécessité de la stratégie, elle répond également à la nécessité de la vie, à la formation de l'histoire, à cette longue imbrication de la vie de la Tunisie avec tous les progrès que nous lui avons connus depuis longtemps.

Je ne peux, sur ce point, que faire miennes à nouveau, en m'excusant de ces lectures qui sont destinées à peser les termes de la pensée, les réponses de M. le président Schuman dans le même débat:

'Vous avez dit que nous accepterions l'idée de notre départ de Tunisie, disait-il à un orateur. Comment pouvez-vous supposer cela de la part du Gouvernement français ou de la part d'un membre du Gouvernement?

'Ce serait renier ainsi une politique française faite de sacrifices, de courage, de grands espoirs, non seulement pour les intérêts français mais aussi pour les populations que nous avons prises en charge.'

Tel est donc notre premier principe: pas de départ et pas d'abandon.

Voici le second: pas de renversement de la politique des réformes; au contraire, son maintien et sa continuation.

Permettez-moi de le dire tout de suite, abandonner la politique des réformes, ce serait donner raison à l'agitation et non pas lui donner tort . . .

Ce principe est d'ailleurs conforme à la leçon de notre Constitution: 'Fidèle à sa mission traditionnelle, la France entend conduire les peuples dont elle a pris la charge à la liberté de s'administrer eux-mêmes et de gérer démocratiquement leurs propres affaires.'

Voici maintenant la question qui est le butoir, l'épreuve des bonnes volontés et des sincérités respectives. Elle se présente à propos de l'organisation municipale. Elle est à l'origine du malentendu, si malentendu il y a, du conflit, si conflit il y a. Elle est grave et délicate. Elle ne doit pas être dissimulée.

Cette question, c'est celle de la participation des Français aux institutions publiques dont la mise en train s'avère nécessaire dans l'étape actuelle de l'organisation vers l'autonomie interne.

C'est là que se produit la discussion possible sur cette participation des Français de Tunisie à des institutions publiques dont l'organisation municipale sera le premier développement.

Car nous n'entendons pas accepter — cela a déjà été dit et doit être répété encore — ce que l'on a appelé l'inversion du protectorat, c'est-à-dire qu'il n'y ait plus d'autre notion à l'égard de la population française de Tunisie que celle d'une protection, leur fût-elle juridiquement bien assurée.

Cette association de la population française dans l'organisation démocratique, dans les institutions publiques, est-elle ou non contraire à la notion de souveraineté?

Il faut poser comme principe qu'elle ne doit pas l'être, que ce n'est pas parce que nous parlons de cela que nous nions la souveraineté beylicale et que, bien que plusieurs souverains de la dynastie husseinite aient prononcé le terme de souveraineté indivisible, nous, nous ne le revendiquons pas, nous ne contestons pas la souveraineté beylicale et nous ne réclamons pas, nous ne réclamerons jamais la co-souveraineté . . .

Et maintenant, quel est notre projet, quel demeure notre projet immédiat? C'est de reprendre nos conversations dans le cadre opportun et convenable de la commission mixte dont les membres français allaient être désignés au moment de la crise ministérielle.

Voilà, ramenés à l'essentiel, quels nous paraissent les grands traits de notre politique tunisienne.

Y en a-t-il une autre? Deux autres sont concevables: l'une est la politique de l'abandon, l'autre est celle qu'on appelle la politique du poing sur la table.

Nous n'admettons ni l'une, ni l'autre, et nous croyons d'abord qu'elles sont peut-être plus proches qu'on ne le pense parfois.

Des noms, des souvenirs sont encore présents à nos mémoires.

Abordons franchement maintenant l'aspect politique qui se pose le jour même où, pour la première fois, paraît devant vous le Gouvernement . . .

Je crois qu'il est impossible de poursuivre une politique franco-tunisienne loyale et bonne si nous retranchons l'assentiment d'une partie importante de l'opinion publique française.

Si je sépare la question de l'assentiment du groupe communiste — qui vient de me le refuser sans me créer beaucoup de surprise — j'estime qu'il est impossible que, parmi les partis républicains et les partis dévoués à la nation, nous acceptions l'idée qu'une politique tunisienne soit établie en retranchant l'un de ces partis.

Si, tout à l'heure, bien que portant sur la date, un vote minoritaire était émis, alors, je vous le demande, comment espérez-vous convaincre la majorité des Tunisiens si vous ne pouvez pas réunir la majorité des Français?

Faisons un effort. Il y a évidemment des traditions différentes, les unes plus prudentes ou plus rigoureuses, les autres plus généreuses. Il faut unir toutes nos voix pour leur donner plus de résonance, pour porter au delà des fronts figés, des rancunes et des concurrences, dans ces populations françaises et tunisiennes qui ont tout de même longuement appris à se connaître, à s'interpénétrer, pour essayer d'éveiller en elle des idées vivantes, des idées dynamiques, pour porter, dis-je, auprès d'elles le souffle des grandes compréhensions.

Tout à l'heure, M. Caillavet — je ne veux pas le lui reprocher mais je m'excuse de le citer — a dit: trop de faiblesse.

Faiblesse ou fermeté? La fermeté, il la faut dans le maintien de l'ordre public et il la faut dans les desseins.

Il faut de la fermeté dans les desseins de conciliation qui sont les nôtres. Il faut souvent plus de fermeté pour concilier que pour refuser et pour ne rien faire.

Si, cependant, certains esprits se laissaient attirer par une sorte de nostalgie du passé, des temps où l'on pensait que toutes ces questions étaient moins importantes qu'elles ne le paraissent aujourd'hui, où il y avait peut-être un complexe de supériorité d'un côté, un complexe d'infériorité de l'autre et où toutes les questions paraissaient se ramener à la force et au prestige, je dirais que si l'on en éprouve le regret — et je ne discute pas le fond — ce regret est inutile, car ce temps est révolu. Si nous étions incapables de chercher les formules nouvelles qu'exige l'évolution nécessaire des temps, si nous nous révélions incapables de concevoir cette évolution, là serait la véritable faiblesse que l'histoire n'excuserait pas.

(vii) Exchange of telegrams between the Bey of Tunis and the French President, M. Auriol, regarding a complaint by the Bey of interference by the French Resident-General, M. Jean de Hautecloque[1]

(a) *Telegram from the Bey, 25 March 1952*

M. Vincent Auriol, président de
la République française, Paris.

Depuis que notre dynastie est en rapport avec la République française,

[1] *Le Monde*, 5 April 1952.

et plus particulièrement depuis notre accession au trône tunisien, nous nous sommes toujours plu à reconnaître la courtoisie dont le gouvernement français a eu le souci d'entourer ses interventions auprès de nous dans les circonstances les plus diverses.

Le ton comminatoire employé au cours de l'audience de ce jour par M. l'ambassadeur de Hautecloque tranche avec les traditions de la France et nous autorise à douter qu'un tel comportement puisse être celui de la France vis-à-vis du monarque qui lui a donné en toutes circonstances les preuves d'une sincère amitié.

25 mars 1952,
LAMINE IER.

(b) M. Auriol's reply, 27 March 1952

Cher ami,

Le ton et la forme du télégramme que Votre Altesse m'a adressé m'ont vivement surpris.

Pour m'en déclarer blessé je n'invoquerai pas seulement nos relations personnelles, nouées à une époque où les agitateurs qui troublent en ce moment la Tunisie menaçaient votre trône, et où vous exprimiez chaleureusement votre confiance en notre amitié. Je veux simplement rappeler que rien ne peut rompre les liens d'affection qui unissent traditionnellement la Tunisie et la France, que rien ne peut interrompre, sans nuire à nos deux peuples, l'œuvre magnifique de civilisation humaine qu'avec votre dynastie la France a édifiée dans votre royaume, et dont ceux-là mêmes qui inconsidérément se dressent aujourd'hui contre notre coopération ont, dans tous les domaines, le plus largement bénéficié.

L'interruption de cet effort nuirait à la cause même qu'ils prétendent défendre, et les troubles sanglants qui meurtrissent nos cœurs montrent en quelle anarchie votre royaume, si on le livrait à l'agitation, ne tarderait pas à sombrer.

La France ne nie certes pas l'évolution. Elle en a donné le signal. Et le gouvernement de la République a, ces jours-ci encore, affirmé sa volonté, non seulement de s'y adapter, mais de la favoriser. Il a établi un programme de réformes, dont certains peut-être regretteront la hardiesse, mais qui, conduit par étapes, trouvera, dans le succès et la rapidité de sa réalisation, sa justification et son rythme.

Mais cette œuvre ne peut être accomplie que dans le même esprit de sagesse, de confiance, de constante collaboration que celui qui, jusqu'à ces derniers temps, a permis d'amener la Tunisie au degré de prospérité et de civilisation où elle se trouve.

Or au moment même où le gouvernement de la République affirmait cette volonté, en accord avec nos Assemblées parlementaires, quelques-uns des hommes que Votre Altesse, détentrice de la souveraineté tunisienne que personne ne conteste, avait choisis pour l'assister dans son action gouvernemental ont, sans prévenir ni Votre Altesse ni le gouvernement de la République, déposé contre la France une plainte devant l'Organisation des Nations unies, qui siégeait dans notre propre capitale.[1] Cet acte de défiance et d'hostilité rendait dès lors impossible tout travail fructueux avec eux. Et j'ai été surpris que, n'ayant pas signé ce recours, Votre Altesse n'ait pas aussitôt désavoué ces ministres—et d'abord le premier aux responsabilités — qui ont abusé de votre confiance puisqu'ils ont agi sans votre signature et au mépris de vos droits souverains.

Depuis ce jour, le sang coule dans votre royaume. Des attentats contre les personnes et les biens assombrissent le présent et compromettent l'avenir. Chargée de la sécurité et de l'ordre, la France fait son devoir. Mais, possesseur de royaume de Tunis, Votre Altesse a la responsabilité morale la plus lourde dans le rétablissement du calme et de l'union.

J'ai longtemps espéré qu'Elle ferait entendre sa voix devant son peuple. Je l'espère encore et je fais appel à son auguste sagesse pour qu'Elle ordonne à tous le calme et la raison.

Puisqu'Elle s'adresse à moi, je lui demande de former, en accord avec le représentant de la France, un gouvernement d'union et d'apaisement afin que soit constituée la commission franco-tunisienne chargée de mettre au point, au plus tôt, les réformes envisagées par le gouvernement de la République.

Ainsi, la Tunisie sera-t-elle conduite, dans le respect de sa souveraineté, de votre dynastie et des intérêts légitimes de la France et des Français de Tunisie, vers cette autonomie intérieure dont l'heureuse réalisation dépendra surtout de la sagesse de ses dirigeants.

J'espère que Votre Altesse ne démentira pas la confiance que je place encore en sa haute clairvoyance et en l'amitié dont Elle veut bien rappeler qu'elle fut toujours fidèle et confiante et dont je lui renouvelle, en terminant, l'expression.

Signé: Vincent Auriol.

(viii) Extract from a speech in the National Assembly by M. Schuman outlining the French Government's programme of reforms for Tunisia, 19 June 1952[2]

I. — *Réforme de l'exécutif.*

1) Le Gouvernement.

L'homogénéité du Gouvernement ne peut être envisagée dans une première étape. Elle constituerait, à l'heure actuelle, une solution inadaptée et nous serions obligés de l'assortir de tellement de réserves que

[1] See above, p. 365.   [2] *Journal Officiel, Débats*, 20 June 1952, pp. 3054–6.

la mesure perdrait sa raison d'être.   Il faut tenir compte, au surplus, de l'évolution très rapide, déjà intervenue dans la composition du gouvernement tunisien au cours de ces dernières années.   Il n'est pas inutile de redire que la parité entre membres français et tunisiens au conseil des ministres est réalisée depuis moins de deux ans.

Par contre, il y a lieu de préciser que dans la seconde phase la composition du conseil des ministres sera modifiée dans le sens d'un nouvel élargissement des departments ministériels attribués aux Tunisiens:

Dans le présent:

Seront gérés par les ministres tunisiens:

Le premier ministère, dont le titulaire est désormais le chef du gouvernement.

Le ministère d'État, chargé du contrôle des administrations locales.

Le ministère de la justice.

Le ministère de la santé publique.

Le ministère de l'agriculture.

Le ministère du commerce.

Le ministère du travail.

Demeurent provisoirement gérés par les directeurs français, les départements ministériels suivants:

Finances.

Travaux publics.

Instruction publique.

ainsi que l'office tunisien des postes, télégraphes et téléphones, et le commissariat à la reconstruction et au logement.

Toutefois, dans les départements ministériels qui resteront sous l'autorité de directeurs français, il est institué des directeurs adjoints tunisiens investis de réelles attributions.

Afin de prouver que l'homogénéité du gouvernement tunisien est l'objectif de l'évolution en cours, les ministres tunisiens vont assumer de plus larges responsabilités que par le passé.   A cet effet, un projet de décret accorde aux chefs d'administration tunisienne une complète autonomie dans la gestion de leurs services, c'est-à-dire que:

a) L' 'assentiment', par le résident général, des arrêtés ministériels est supprimé; les arrêtés sont donc rendus publics et éxecutoires sans aucun contrôle préalable de l'autorité française;

b) Le contrôle du personnel qui appartenait jusqu'ici au secrétaire général est laissé désormais à chaque chef d'administration.

En même temps, le premier ministre reçoit la présidence des commissions interministérielles et le directeur des finances le contrôle des dépenses engagées.   Un nouveau pas est ainsi franchi dans la voie qui conduit, depuis plusieurs années, à faire du secrétaire général le 'premier collaborateur du premier ministre'.   Il conserve, à titre de chef d'administration, les attributions propres suivantes: service de la fonction publique, élaboration et contrôle du plan économique.

2) Création d'un tribunal administratif.

Cette création constitue une réforme essentielle: l'institution d'un tribunal compétent pour connaître toutes actions dirigées contre l'État et pour apprécier la légalité des décisions administratives, est dans tout pays moderne une des premières garanties à accorder aux particuliers.

La compétence du tribunal s'étend à tous les actes émanant des autorités administratives de la régence, ce qui couvre notamment les autorités de police.

Par contre, cette juridiction est incompétente pour tous les décrets beylicaux à caractère judiciaire et religieux ou ayant valeur législative. En ce qui concerne les autres décrets, il est entendu, pour réserver les pouvoirs du souverain, qu'elle émettra seulement des avis. Au contraire, les arrêtés des ministres et des directeurs pourront faire l'objet d'une annulation.

Dans le cadre de son pouvoir de contrôle, le résident général dispose du droit de saisir le tribunal administratif de tous les arrêtés qu'il estime illégaux. Ce recours, qui doit être exercé dans un délai d'un mois, est suspensif.

Le tribunal administratif, présidé par un Français, choisi parmi les membres du Conseil d'État, compte huit juges, dont quatre de nationalité française et quatre de nationalité tunisienne.

Appel peut être interjeté des décisions du tribunal administratif de Tunisie devant une commission d'appel, qui est une juridiction tunisienne. Celle-ci est présidée par le président de la section du contentieux du Conseil d'État et comprend trois membres français choisis parmi les conseillers d'État, et trois membres tunisiens nommés par décret beylical. Elle tient ses séances à Paris.

Cette composition du tribunal et de la commission d'appel nous est imposée sur le plan international par les engagements pris par la France à l'égard des pays qui ont renoncé au régime capitulaire.

3) Réforme de la fonction publique.

Dans ce domaine, le texte envisagé donne dès maintenant les satisfactions les plus larges aux revendications tunisiennes.

Aux 'pourcentages' établis par les décrets de février 1951,[1] on a substitué une formule plus favorable aux Tunisiens: l'accès à la fonction publique est dorénavant ouvert, en principe, aux seuls Tunisiens, sous réserve du respect des situations acquises et de la détermination par

---

[1] See above, p. 359.

décret beylical d'un certain nombre d'emplois qui seront obligatoirement attribué à des fonctionnaires de nationalité française, en considération, notamment, des engagements pris par la France sur le plan financier et sur celui de la défense nationale.   En vue de garantir la qualité du recrutement, des dispositions sont prévues, qui tendent à maintenir le niveau des concours, d'une part, en fixant les programmes par analogie avec ceux des concours correspondants de France, et, d'autre part, en maintenant l'exigence de jurys mixtes pour examiner les candidats. Les épreuves de ces concours ont lieu en français pour les emplois supérieurs et principaux, au choix des candidats, en français ou en arabe, pour les autres emplois.   L'usage exclusif de la langue arabe est maintenu pour les concours d'accès aux emplois traditionnels.

Le texte prévoit enfin des dispositions transitoires en faveur des agents contractuels et des agents temporaires en service depuis un certain délai dans l'administration tunisienne.

Pendant toute la période où les Tunisiens risquent de ne pas être en mesure de pourvoir toutes les places vacantes, des fonctionnaires français pourront être placés en service détaché et mis à la disposition du gouvernement tunisien selon des modalités fixées par les autorités françaises.

II. — *Procédure législative.*

Actuellement, le pouvoir législatif appartient exclusivement au Bey. Dans l'état actuel des institutions tunisiennes, il n'est pas envisagé de donner à une assemblée législative un pouvoir de décision et d'instituer une sorte de régime parlementaire avant d'avoir mis en place des assemblées locales élues qui en sont l'infrastructure nécessaire et dont la création est d'ailleurs envisagée par le présent programme de réformes.

Pour l'instant, il n'est donc pas permis d'aller au delà d'assemblées simplement consultatives.   Afin de tenir compte à la fois de certaines aspirations tunisiennes et de la sauvegarde nécessaire des intérêts des Français de la régence, nous envisageons deux assemblées ayant une compétence distincte.

1) Le Conseil législatif.

Ce conseil, composé exclusivement de Tunisiens, a une compétence législative générale, exception faite des décrets d'ordre financier ou budgétaire.   Il ne peut être saisi que par le Bey et il doit donner son avis sur les textes qui lui sont soumis.   Il propose les amendements qui lui paraissent souhaitables.

Les membres, au nombre de trente en principe, seront à l'origine nommés par décret beylical.   Après la mise en place des conseils de caïdat et des conseils municipaux, des membres élus par ces organismes locaux pourront être progressivement substitués.

2) Le Conseil financier.

Le Conseil financier est de composition mixte, les membres français et tunisiens y siègent en commun. Le Conseil financier est paritaire. Cette parité est justifiée par l'importance de la part contributive des Français aux charges budgétaires et par la participation financière de la métropole aux charges locales, sous forme de prêts ou de subventions.

Il connaît seul du budget et de toute mesure de caractère financier ou budgétaire, mais il est incompétent en toute autre matière législative.

Ses membres sont désignés pour partie dans le cadre de la représentation des intérêts économiques.

Le Conseil financier dispose du droit d'amendement, mais le Gouvernement, s'il est en désaccord sur les modifications proposées, pourra demander une seconde lecture.

Précisons enfin qu'aucune disposition du texte ne fait intervenir, dans les majorités requises, la notion de deux collèges ou de deux sections.

III. — Les collectivités locales.

La réforme qui est envisagée ici est d'une réelle importance puisqu'elle substitue l'élection à la désignation par décret des membres des conseils municipaux et qu'elle institue, dans chaque caïdat, une assemblée délibérante.

La Tunisie est aujourd'hui un État très centralisé.

Hormis les conseils municipaux qui fonctionnent dans 70 agglomérations, il n'existe dans la régence aucune collectivité chargée de la gestion de l'ensemble des intérêts locaux et le budget de l'État est ainsi encombré de chapitres qui traitent d'affaires qui seraient bien plus normalement examinées sur place.

Par la réforme municipale et par la création dans le cadre du caïdat d'assemblées chargées d'établir un budget, de gérer un domaine et d'instituer certains services publics locaux, il s'agit tout à la fois de familiariser les Tunisiens avec l'exercice du droit de vote et d'initier les élus aux responsabilités qui découlent d'un mandat représentatif.

Cette expérience se fera dans les grandes villes en collaboration entre Français et Tunisiens élus par deux collèges distincts; dans les villes ou les localités où la population européenne est de peu d'importance, comme dans la majorité des conseils de caïdat, les élus seront tous ou presque tous Tunisiens. Du résultat de ces diverses expériences, il sera possible de tirer des conclusions particulièrement valables quant aux possibilités de hâter l'acheminement du pays vers son autonomie interne.

Ce plan de réformes s'inscrit, sans équivoque possible, dans le cadre de la politique que s'est assignée la France en Tunisie. Il institue, dès maintenant, un véritable régime d'autonomie interne non seulement dans les collectivités locales mais dans des secteurs importants de l'administration centrale tunisienne. Sur la base des réformes ainsi réalisées, et en tenant compte de l'expérience acquise, il sera possible, par étapes successives, d'étendre ce régime des institutions tunisiennes.

Il n'est pas exclu que ces projets, auxquels certains reprocheront leur hardiesse, d'autres leur timidité, suscitent des réserves ou des oppositions. Toutefois, le Gouvernement fera tout ce qui dépendra de lui, dans les limites et dans les délais qu'il s'est fixé, pour que ces réformes et les principes qu'elles consacrent soient inscrits dans les institutions du royaume.

(ix) Explanatory memorandum sent to the United Nations by thirteen Arab and Asian states together with a request for the inclusion of the Tunisian question on the agenda of the General Assembly, 30 July 1952[1]

French penetration of Tunisia, which commenced in the middle of the 19th century as a sequence to the conquest of contiguous Algeria, culminated in 1881 in an armed invasion of the country. Ostensibly this invasion was undertaken by France to protect the frontiers of Algeria from the depredations of lawless tribes, but in reality it was a premeditated attempt to bring Tunisia under French domination. By virtue of the Treaty of Bardo, which the Bey was forced to sign in 1881, France assumed responsibility to act for Tunisia in its external relations; the principle of Tunisian sovereignty, however, remained intact, and its separate statehood was explicitly recognized in the Treaty. The La Marsa Convention of 1883—again signed by the Bey under duress—for the first time mentioned the term 'Protectorate', without, however, calling into question the statehood of Tunisia. Thereafter, French control was extended, unilaterally, by the Presidential Decree of 1 November 1884, and the Announcement of 23 June 1885, which in effect invested the Resident-General (the representative of the French Government in Tunisia) with all the powers of a Head of Government.

Henceforth, France contrived to assure, to herself and her nationals, domination in every field of Tunisian life. A policy of peopling the country with French settlers was adopted. This was done partly to counterbalance the already existing large Italian colony; the main considerations, however, were political and economic. Hence the policy of generous grants of crown lands, accompanied by subsidies and many privileges, to those French citizens who wished to settle in Tunisia; hence also the introduction of steadily growing numbers of French officials into the Tunisian administration. The result was the growth of an artificially

[1] A/2152, 6 August 1952. The thirteen countries were Afghanistan, Burma, Egypt, India, Indonesia, 'Irāq, Lebanon, Pakistan, Persia, the Philippines, Sa'ūdī Arabia, Syria and Yemen.

inflated French colony that was sustained by grants of land, concessions of various kinds, and lucrative jobs, the whole cost being borne by the State of Tunisia and the Tunisian people.

This policy was translated into legislation. Under it, all the best land in Tunisia passed into the hands of French colonists. A typical example of the method employed was illustrated in the matter of the so-called 'juridical forests'. Thousands of acres of cultivable land were arbitrarily classed as forests and thus passed into the hands of the State. Once this operation was completed, a second law reclassified the 'forests' as agricultural land, and it was put back into circulation for the benefit of the French colonists.

As regards public finance, it is only necessary to glance through the budgets for the last twenty years to see how State expenditure has continuously grown to maintain the army of officials required to uphold French administration of Tunisia. Its cost amounts to two-thirds of the total budget. Of the 30,000 public officials in Tunisia (that is to say, one for a little over 100 inhabitants) about three-quarters are of French nationality. All the key positions are reserved for Frenchmen; Tunisian officials hold almost without exception only subordinate posts.

The financial and economic policy carried out by the French in the country has channelled the wealth of Tunisia into the hands of the French settlers. The nature of the tax system is the best illustration of this. Two-fifths of the Tunisian budget is made up of indirect taxes, i.e. those that hit the mass of the people and do not really affect the well-to-do. For the rest, the land tax and capitulation tax hold a high place in the revenues of the State. To this must be added the exploitation of the natural resources of the country by the great French companies, the mines, ports, public utilities, transports, banks, cement works, agricultural estates, and so on. Between them they have drained and are draining the greater part of the country's wealth into the coffers of metropolitan big business, thus converting Tunisia into a vast commercial enterprise.

National awakening came early in the 20th century. Although the Tunisian people are well known for their mild temperament and genial ways, French colonial policies gradually roused them to organized national struggle. This struggle was suspended during World War I and the succeeding years (until 1921), for the Tunisians hoped that their whole-hearted support of the Allied cause would bring them the reward of independence. But the French did not change their policy. The national movement assumed thereupon a more definite shape under the leadership of the Destour Party which was founded in 1920. After a period of intermittent agitation, the Neo-Destour Party came into being in 1934 and began an organized, country-wide campaign to bring home to the people the fact of their political dependence. Bourguiba was deported by the

French authorities in 1936, but was released a year later under the orders of the Popular Front Government then in power in France, only to be rearrested in 1939. A state of siege was imposed on the country in 1938.

The outbreak of World War II did not stop either the popular agitation or the military repression. This continued until the Vichy Government permitted in 1942 the landing of Axis troops on Tunisian territory. The Tunisian leaders were released by the Axis authorities. Acute pressure was being brought to bear upon them and upon the then ruler of Tunisia, Monsef Bey, to throw in their lot with the Axis Powers for a promise of independence after the war. Monsef Bey, however, decided to remain neutral and this was the more remarkable as at that time the Axis Powers were at the peak of their military successes. The later French regime, however, chose to ignore this loyalty. Action against the Neo-Destour Party was intensified; but this only strengthened the national movement. On 23 August 1946, a congress of all the national organizations in Tunisia passed a unanimous resolution condemning the French Protectorate and demanding complete independence. The meeting was broken up by the police and all the leaders were arrested.

In April 1950, the Bey, in a letter addressed to the President of the French Republic, launched a fervent appeal to France to grant Tunisia her rights and thus to lay a durable foundation of friendship between the two countries. In the same month Bourguiba, the Neo-Destour leader, proposed in Paris the following seven-point programme as the basis of a French-Tunisian settlement:[1]

(1) Revival of Tunisian sovereignty.
(2) Setting up of a homogenous Tunisian Government headed by a Tunisian Prime Minister nominated by the Bey.
(3) Abolition of the post of Secretary-General, who had always been a Frenchman and had by now assumed full administrative authority.
(4) Elimination of the French Civil Controllers, who had been placed over the Tunisian Kaids (district officers).
(5) Elimination of the French gendarmerie which is responsible to the Minister of National Defence in France and is one of the main props of the military occupation.
(6) Establishment of municipal councils, allowing for representation of French interests.
(7) Creation of a National Assembly elected by universal suffrage whose task should be the preparation of a Constitution defining Tunisia's future relations with the French on the basis of 'mutual respect for each others' legitimate interests'.

The strength and persistence of the national movement gradually forced

[1] See above, p. 353.

the French to take cognizance of the Tunisian demands. On 11 June 1950, Mr. Schuman, the French Foreign Minister, declared that independence was the final goal for all territories of the French Union. This was confirmed by the French Resident-General, Mr. Périllier, in his speech in Tunis two days later. The political tension was considerably lessened and negotiations began immediately between the French and Tunisian Governments in an atmosphere of hopefulness. These preliminary negotiations culminated, on 17 August 1950, in what the French termed an 'experiment'. A new Tunisian cabinet, presided over by a Tunisian Prime Minister and comprising six Tunisian Ministers and six French Directors, was appointed by the Bey. The Tunisian Ministers were the recognized leaders of the people, while the French Directors were nominees of France. This new government was formed with the express purpose of 'negotiating such institutional modifications as are required to lead the Tunisians by successive steps towards internal autonomy'.

Two months later, however, the trend of the discussions between the French and Tunisian Governments changed completely and disagreements became more and more acute, the reason being the strong pressure which was brought to bear on the French Government by the French colonists in Tunisia, who were afraid of losing their predominant position in the Protectorate. In addition to this, the insubordination of French officials in Tunisia defeated the genuine endeavours of the Tunisian Ministers to co-operate with the French element in the administration.

A second attempt at internal reforms was made early in 1951, but the relevant Decree (dated 8 February 1951)[1] made only superficial concessions to the Tunisian demands and did not constitute any marked advance towards the country's autonomy. The arbitrary powers of the Secretary-General were reduced—but most of them were transferred to the Resident-General, thus leaving, in effect, all administrative control in the hands of the French authorities in Tunisia.

In an endeavour to come to a friendly settlement with France, the Bey instructed his Prime Minister to present on his behalf an *Aide Mémoire* to the French Government. This document, dated 31 October 1951, outlined the legitimate demands of the Tunisian people. In his reply of 15 December 1951,[2] the French Foreign Minister made it clear that while the French Government admitted the necessity of reforms, these should be formulated in such a manner as not to deprive the French minority in Tunisia of the political and administrative prerogatives which they had enjoyed in the past. As this was the very crux of the Tunisian objections to French domination, Mr. Schuman's letter constituted a rejection of the Tunisian demand for real self-government.

Realizing that no useful purpose could be served by further negotiations

---

[1] See above, p. 356.   [2] See above, pp. 363–5.

so long as the French were not prepared to concede the fundamental principle of Tunisian self-government, the Tunisian Prime Minister appealed on 14 January 1952[1] to the President of the Security Council to intervene in the dispute. The French authorities tried to get the Tunisian Government to withdraw their complaint from the Security Council, but in vain. Thereupon, all Tunisian political leaders were arrested on 18 January 1952. The number of French troops was increased to between 40,000 and 50,000. Stern repressive measures were taken whenever there was any expression of popular feeling. It may be mentioned here that the state of siege now in operation in Tunisia continues, unrevoked, since 1938. Many Tunisians were killed, thousands arrested (it is estimated that about 8,000 to 10,000 political detenues are kept in the various concentration camps scattered all over the country), acts of violence became frequent, and whole villages—especially in the Cap Bon area—were razed to the ground.

This unhappy state of affairs reached its climax in March 1952, when the Prime Minister and other Tunisian Ministers were arrested and the Bey was forced to dissociate himself from the leaders he had himself chosen to guide his people towards independence.

In April 1952, the Tunisian question was brought to the notice of the Security Council by eleven Member States of the United Nations, as the situation in Tunisia, in their view, constituted a threat to international peace and security. Never before in the history of the United Nations had so many Member nations approached the Security Council in such unison on a single issue.

The Security Council, contrary to all precedent, rejected the adoption of the agenda. It rejected the Chilean proposal to place the item on the agenda and to postpone discussion. It also rejected the request that the complainants should be given an opportunity to reply to the doubts cast on their *bona fides* by the representative of France on the Security Council.

Members of the Security Council who did not favour the adoption of the agenda reiterated one after another that their stand was actuated by their anxiety not to jeopardize the negotiations that, according to them, were taking place or were about to take place between the French and the Tunisians. In reality, the French authorities hoped to 'negotiate' reforms with a nominal government set up for that purpose without, however, any popular backing.

Since then the situation in Tunisia has deteriorated further. The expected negotiations have not materialized because the acknowledged representatives of the Tunisian people, with whom alone any negotiations can prove fruitful, are in prison or exile, and the Bey is virtually a prisoner

[1] See above, p. 365.

of the French authorities with no means of consulting his national advisers or the leaders amongst his people or of acting in an independent manner.

There is no visible relaxation of repression in Tunisia, and on account of the heavy censorship that prevails, no free flow of information. It appears, however, that the French authorities, having failed to 'negotiate' even with a Tunisian 'government' of their own contrivance, are proposing to impose dubious reforms of their choice on the Tunisian people and to back their implementation with military force. This would be far from the so-called negotiations for the hopeful outcome of which some Members of the United Nations opposed discussion in the Security Council.

Since April 1952, therefore, French authorities have not taken any successful step towards either the restoration of civil liberties or the beginning of negotiations. On the other hand, the tension in Tunisia has increased and there is a deep sense of frustration among people in many countries of the world, and especially in Asian and African countries.

Following the unprecedented action of the Security Council in refusing even to place the Tunisian question on its agenda, thirteen delegations representing African-Asian countries in the United Nations made a request to the Secretary-General for convening a special session of the General Assembly to consider the question. This request received the support of no less than twenty-three countries, representing more than half the population of the world, and comprising almost all the Member States of Asia and several from South America and Europe. Although the request for the special session thus received such wide support in terms of world public opinion, the special session failed to be called because the technical majority required under the rules of procedure of the General Assembly was not forthcoming.

As the situation in Tunisia continues to be serious, the question is being referred to the General Assembly in order that a just and peaceful settlement may be achieved. Article 11, paragraph 2, of the Charter confers on the General Assembly the power to discuss any question relating to the maintenance of international peace and security and to make appropriate recommendations.

(x) EXTRACTS FROM A LETTER FROM THE BEY OF TUNIS TO M. AURIOL, REFUSING TO SIGN THE REFORM DECREES SUBMITTED TO HIM BY THE FRENCH GOVERNMENT, 9 SEPTEMBER 1952[1]

. . . Une fois en possession des projets de décrets nous avons remarqué tout d'abord que, par les nombreuses dispositions qui en restreignaient la portée, ils étaient loin de traduire toutes les assertions contenues dans les

[1] *Le Monde*, 13 November 1952.

exposés des motifs qui nous avaient été communiqués quelques jours auparavant, et au vu desquels on nous demandait une adhésion anticipée à des textes non encore connus de nous. Nous avons noté également que la lettre résidentielle qui accompagnait les décrets soumis à notre sceau, reprenant une idée exprimée par le président du conseil à la tribune de l'Assemblée et dans sa lettre du 4 juillet 1952, disait explicitement que les dispositions proposées constituaient 'l'extrême limite' de ce que la France pouvait consentir pour satisfaire aux revendications tunisiennes.

Cette précision excluait pour nous la possibilité de prendre d'autres initiatives et nous plaçait devant l'alternative d'entériner les textes en l'état ou de les rejeter. . . .

Les personnalités musulmanes et israélites que nous avons réunies à cet effet ont, à notre demande, procédé chacune dans son milieu à une étude des projets de réformes. En conclusion de leurs travaux elles nous ont présenté un rapport pertinent.[1]

Ce document fait ressortir que les réformes proposées constituent une atteinte à la souveraineté tunisienne; consacrent le maintien de l'administration directe; aggravent la confusion et l'irresponsabilité des pouvoirs; n'apportent aucun progrès dans le sens de la démocratisation des institutions tunisiennes.

Ainsi ces réformes se révèlent impropres à satisfaire les aspirations de la population tunisienne, elles ne répondent d'ailleurs pas aux objectifs minima que nous avons nous-même définis, notamment le 15 mai 1951 et le 31 octobre de la même année. Au surplus elles ne constituent nullement un acheminement vers l'autonomie interne, solennellement promise par le gouvernement français.

Il nous paraît donc difficile dans ces conditions de les revêtir de notre sceau . . .

(xi) M. Auriol's reply, 15 September 1952[2]

A S. A. Mohammed Lamine pacha bey, possesseur du royaume de Tunis.

Monseigneur,

J'ai l'honneur de vous accuser réception de votre lettre du 9 septembre 1952 et du document joint, et de vous informer que, selon les règles constitutionnelles, je les ai transmis à M. le président du conseil des ministres.

Je laisse au governement le soin d'y donner telle suite qui lui paraîtra utile et conforme aux intérêts des deux peuples, ainsi que de rectifier les erreurs et de réparer les omissions qui altèrent votre exposé des faits et lui donnent un caractère regrettable de polémique.

---

[1] Not printed; see *Le Monde*, 13 September 1952.
[2] Ibid, 13 November 1952.

Je dois déplorer, pour ma part, que mes appels répétés à votre sagesse, dans un esprit de sincère amitié, n'aient eu d'autre réponse que l'intransigeance d'un refus et l'interruption des conversations, car l'expérience et de glorieux précédents montrent que seuls une coopération confiante et l'accord des volontés peuvent maintenir en Tunisie la prospérité que la France y a par de lourds et constants sacrifices assurée, et conduire le peuple tunisien vers les hautes destinées humaines qui doivent lui être réservées.

Je vous prie d'agréer, monseigneur, avec les regrets d'une amitié assombrie, les assurances de ma très haute considération.

V. Auriol.

(xii) Extracts from a speech in the General Assembly by M. Schuman, explaining the French Government's reasons for opposing discussion by the General Assembly of the Tunisian and Moroccan questions, 10 November 1952[1]

In spite of the objections we have expressed, the Assembly has decided to include in its agenda two complaints concerning the situation in Tunisia and Morocco.[2] I shall speak of these in all candour, without failing at any time in the respect we owe to a great idea and the confidence we have in the institution which embodies it.

The representative of France is compelled to warn this Assembly not only against the injustice which some persons would have it commit, against the insult which this accusation represents to his country, against the repercussions which any intervention, whatever form it took, would inevitably have outside the United Nations, but also and above all against the harm which would thereby be done to the Organization itself.

It is the Assembly's duty, in its wisdom, to remain within the confines of its duties and not to assume before history the responsibility, fraught with incalculable consequences, of exceeding its powers and thereby jeopardizing a task which France has undertaken, is continuing to perform and will pursue in North Africa with faith and pride.

I must emphasize, in the first place, that our Organization is incompetent to discuss these questions; doubly so, it might be said, because of the nature of the treaties which bind France to Tunisia and Morocco, and of the very text which defines the competence of the United Nations— that is to say, the Charter.

France is bound to Tunisia and Morocco by treaties concluded as between sovereign States. In accordance with those treaties, the foreign relations of Morocco and Tunisia can be conducted only within the

[1] *General Assembly, Seventh Session, 392nd Plenary Meeting*, pp. 193–9. For Morocco see also below, pp. 417 seqq.
[2] A/2152 and A/2175.

framework provided for in the treaties, that is to say, through France. The treaties also provide that the reforms to be carried out in the two countries are to be effected in close and exclusive co-operation with France and on the latter's initiative.   Thus we are faced with bilateral treaties which establish a special legal system and constitute the charter of the contracting States, defining the relations between them and their relations with the international community.   It is a frequent occurrence for two States to set up special arrangements under contractual agreements, and no one would think of conceding a general right of intervention or interference in such arrangements either by a third State or by an international organization.

As the Assembly is aware, the United Nations has not been given competence to proceed in any manner, even indirectly, with the revision of treaties.   This is apparent not only from the preparatory work of the San Francisco Conference, but also from the discussions which have already taken place on specific issues.   No intervention or interference is possible, therefore, in the situation created by the two treaties between France and Tunisia and Morocco respectively.   What State, among those here represented, would accept the principle of such intervention, of supervision of the application of any bilateral treaties it had concluded or might conclude?

This is clearly one of the situations referred to in Article 2, paragraph 7, of the Charter, which was designed to prevent the Organization from exceeding its competence.   What, indeed, is the competence of the United Nations?   It is defined by the Charter itself and only by the Charter.   It does not exist by presumption.   It is a competence that is actually granted and that can derive only from an explicit text.   Its authors undoubtedly wanted it to be very broad, but it was never conceived as being unlimited.

The sovereign States which signed the Charter thereby assumed commitments which represented considerable limitations on their sovereignty and provided for intervention by the United Nations in matters formerly within the exclusive domestic jurisdiction of those States.   These limitations of sovereignty are expressly and exhaustively stated.   To avoid any ambiguous interpretation, the list of fundamental principles in Article 2 includes that of non-intervention by the United Nations 'in matters which are essentially within the domestic jurisdiction of any State'.   The text of Article 2, paragraph 7, originated in the joint amendment to the original Dumbarton Oaks draft submitted by the four Powers which sponsored the San Francisco Conference.   The text of this amendment, which became paragraph 7 of Article 2 of the Charter, is as follows:

'Nothing contained in the present Charter shall authorize the United Nations to intervene in matters which are essentially within the domestic jurisdiction of any State or shall require the Members to submit such matters to settlement under the present Charter; but this principle shall not prejudice the application of enforcement measures under Chapter VII.'

In contrast to the former Article 15 of the Covenant of the League of Nations, this new text does not constitute a mere procedural exception whose sole effect would be to prohibit the recommendation of a solution. It goes much further. It forestalls any action, precluding not only any resolution or recommendation, but even any consideration of such a question. It applies automatically to all matters which are essentially within the domestic jurisdiction of any State.

This rule applies even where a question has or assumes international implications. These international implications are not sufficient to destroy the basic character of the question, since the national aspect remains the essential factor. The only eventuality in which the United Nations could be led to intervene is that provided for in Chapter VII, that is, in the case of 'threats to the peace, breaches of the peace, and acts of aggression'. No one, however, either here in this Assembly or elsewhere, whatever his prejudices, can claim with any semblance of justification that the present situation in North Africa in any way constitutes a threat to international peace, that is, a threat to the security of other States, or that it is likely to provoke a breach of the peace. In the absence of any such situation, which is expressly provided for, though by way of exception, the United Nations is not competent to examine the situations brought about by the two treaties or to intervene to any extent whatever in the relations existing between the two North African States and France. . . .

In 1881, France concluded the Treaty of Bardo and later, in 1883, the Treaty of La Marsa with the Bey of Tunis. In 1912, France's concern, then developing rapidly, for the security of North Africa, induced it to intervene in unhappy and strife-torn Morocco and to conclude the Treaty of Fez with the Sultan.[1]

What is the general relationship between France on the one hand and Tunisia and Morocco on the other, first, as embodied in those treaties and secondly, in practice? Essentially, there is an exchange of reciprocal rights and duties between the signatory States. In return for the special powers conferred by the treaties on France as possessing sovereignty over Tunisia and Morocco, those two territories receive various kinds of advantages.

In the first place, in dealings with other States, they are represented by France, and their citizens, when abroad, are protected in the same way and to the same extent as French citizens.

As to security, Tunisia and Morocco are included in France's national defence perimeter and plans. This is an economic advantage to the two

[1] *British and Foreign State Papers*, vol. cvi, pp. 1023–4.

territories and relieves them of the crushing burden that States must bear in these times.

As to the national economy, the economic systems of those countries were originally quite rudimentary, but through the efforts of France have now become prosperous, complex and stable. They are now developing with the aid of France, and find markets and economic assistance within the more extensive economic system of our country, which equips them, balances their budget, and stabilizes their balance of trade and of payments. . . .

All aspects of this joint undertaking, which is constantly developing, are closely linked to each other, and it is hard to imagine on what theory some persons base their claim to isolate political problems and ignore their close connexion with economic, social and cultural development. Political institutions must be an expression of that development and of the increasing maturity of a people. France has undertaken to educate and initiate those peoples in democracy, as provided in the treaties, and it is responsible for completing its task. Considerable strides have already been made. Many, of even greater importance, are being prepared, and France is ready to discuss them with properly authorized representatives.

Everything is done completely in the open. These are not secret negotiations carried out under cover to force the weaker party to agree. The Sultan of Morocco and the Bey of Tunis are perfectly free to make their attitude known, and can state it formally in public. Who, then, can allege that freedom is being stifled? The fact that lengthy and laborious discussions are sometimes inevitable in matters of this complexity is no cause for surprise; still less should it arouse indignation, in which passion plays a greater part than reason. Simple solutions can doubtless be applied in countries still in the initial stages of their economic and social evolution, but no longer in Tunisia and Morocco, because of the great complexity of their problems, which cannot be dealt with by improvisation or by a breach in continuity.

Is it really intended to challenge France's right to discuss the various stages and the pace of this evolution, seeing that France first started and directed the process? Who, then, is to take these decisions in France's stead? Without going back to the legal aspect which I dealt with a moment ago, without asking under what power, what text, the United Nations would seize itself of these problems, I should like to know how our Organization could possibly define what reforms should be undertaken, by what stages, and through what institutions. For that is the proposal. You are to be made the judges, not only of the existing situation, but also of what should be done in the future; that is to say, of the way to protect the interests of 3 million Tunisians, 8 million Moroccans,

500,000 and 150,000 other Europeans who are at present working hard together to lead the two territories towards a maximum of prosperity and welfare.

The Moroccan and the Tunisian problems alike consist basically of how to ensure for the future, as in the past, that all these elements in the population, each essential to the life of the country, shall be able to live and work together in peace and friendship. The indigenous populations themselves are not homogeneous; they differ in their origins, traditions, beliefs and aspirations. The successes achieved under the authority, the responsibility and the protection of France in the past must be maintained and guaranteed by a new régime. That is the political problem before us. . . .

With regard to Tunisia, the French Government has submitted to the Bey a detailed programme of new reforms which would constitute a step forward towards internal self-government.[1] They would bring about extensive participation by the Tunisians in public affairs. Our purpose is that the Tunisians should be able to assume ever-increasing responsibilities. We particularly want the support of young Tunisians, who are given priority in all the administrative careers in their country. In this way we are trying to spread democratic organization at all levels, starting at the bottom, in the municipalities and other local communities. Then, as these reforms are gradually put into effect and tested in practice, France will be prepared gradually to give up the powers which it holds under the treaties and exercises at present on behalf of sovereign Tunisia by virtue of a contractual delegation.

In Morocco, the development started thirty years later than in Tunisia and has proceeded along very different lines. The final objective, however, is the same: to establish Morocco with its dynasty as a sovereign State, to develop its political and social institutions on democratic foundations within a progressively expanding area of self-government, to protect all interests, and to make the best use of all resources and help, so that, working harmoniously together, we may ensure the welfare of Morocco and all its inhabitants. We have recently given an assurance of these aims to His Majesty the Sultan, and we are always prepared to reach an understanding on these principles and the methods of applying them, just as we have been and still are prepared to do in Tunisia.

In Tunisia, unfortunately, some have preferred violence and intimidation to free and friendly understanding. Terrorism is always a most hateful method; it will never serve as an argument against us. It is criminal and cowardly to murder innocent victims, women and children, the great majority of them Tunisians, by the haphazard explosion of bombs thrown or placed by ill-doers who have been turned into fanatics

[1] See above, p. 373.

or hired by those who prefer to remain under cover. Those who organize terrorism do irreparable damage to the cause they claim to serve.

You could not be deceived by such methods, become the pawns of coldly premeditated terrorism, or give way to such criminal blackmail. France alone is responsible for the maintenance of order and security; it protects both French and Tunisians impartially and will continue to do so firmly and with composure in spite of provocations.

An assembly such as this must weigh its responsibilities very carefully, for they are commensurate with its high authority. The mere possibility that the Assembly might intervene in Tunisian affairs has encouraged the agitators. It has caused great bewilderment and has troubled the negotiations, which were previously conducted quite calmly. A minority of extremists would like to delude the masses by the mirage of a fruitless debate in this Assembly. Foreign propaganda is also being used to mislead people, and the result is the useless sacrifice of several dozen human lives, loss of time, and a slowing down of activities at a time when the people as a whole want merely to work and live in peace and security. Some persons are fostering the dangerous illusion of being granted an audience by the Assembly; they are speculating about your possible intervention against us. This is the only remaining expedient, the last resort of those who have undertaken the serious responsibility of breaking off the negotiations in which the French Government has never ceased to associate with them.

You owe it to yourselves to put an end to these speculations, to this uncertainty. As long as you go on discussing, as long as there remains the slightest chance of your intervening, the fanatics will do everything to prevent the possibility of a friendly solution.

This is the case with Tunisia, this could become the case with Morocco, but it would also end by being the case with other States as well.

Is there a single country without any difficulties arising out of antagonisms based on race, language or religion? Let me ask whether such countries believe that they could remain free from all outside interference or from any attempt at interference if the United Nations admitted the principle, or even the possibility, of such interference in the case of Tunisia or Morocco? Sooner or later the United Nations would be asked to set itself up as the judge of these extremely delicate problems of minorities. Does anyone really believe that that would serve the cause of peace among nations, in accordance with Article 1 of the Charter?

To take action on the suggestions made to you would, moreover, jeopardize the internal cohesion of States by giving rise within them to misgivings and dissensions which would thenceforth be encouraged from outside. The more I think of it, the more I am convinced that what is involved in this matter is not only North Africa, not only the interests of France—vital interests which France is entitled to protect and will protect with all its strength—but also a sound conception of the United Nations itself. The Organization is threatened by a distortion which would be pernicious to itself, to the Member States and to the cause of peace. . . .

France considers that it would be making a serious and unpardonable mistake if territories still imperfectly developed, for which it is now responsible in varying degrees, set themselves up as independent States before they were able to meet the heavy responsibilities which that would imply. The dangerous mirage of a premature independence, fictitious rather than real, would imperil not only the legitimate interests of France and of others, which France has undertaken to safeguard, but also the further development of those same territories, which we cannot expose to chance and anarchy.

For all these reasons, which we have frankly explained to you, my Government declares itself compelled in all conscience to warn the Assembly against the consequences of an interference to which in no case and under no conditions could it consent. Consequently my Government can agree to discuss neither the principle nor the manner of such inter-ference.

(xiii) RESOLUTION ASKING FOR THE DISPATCH OF A COMMISSION TO TUNISIA, SUBMITTED TO THE POLITICAL COMMITTEE BY THE ARAB AND ASIAN STATES AND DEFEATED ON 12 DECEMBER 1952[1]

The General Assembly

1. *Recalling* (*a*) the communications addressed to the President of the Security Council on 2 April 1952 by the Governments of Afghanistan, Burma, Egypt, India, Indonesia, Iran, Iraq, Pakistan, the Philippines, Saudi Arabia and Yemen on 'The Tunisian Question', and (*b*) the com-munication addressed to the Secretary-General on 20 June 1952 by the Governments of Afghanistan, Burma, Egypt, India, Indonesia, Iran, Iraq, Lebanon, Pakistan, the Philippines, Saudi Arabia, Syria and Yemen pro-posing a special session of the General Assembly to consider 'The Tunisian Question',

2. *Taking note* of the communication addressed to the Secretary-General on 30 July 1952 by the Governments of Afghanistan, Burma, Egypt, India, Indonesia, Iran, Iraq, Lebanon, Pakistan, the Philippines, Saudi Arabia, Syria and Yemen regarding the present serious situation in Tunisia,

3. *Recalls* that the Charter of the United Nations affirms the equal rights of nations large and small and that among the purposes of the United

[1] A/C. 1/736, 2 December 1952.

Nations is the development of friendly relations among nations based on respect for the principle of equal rights and self-determination of peoples;

4. *Considers* that the continuance of the present situation in Tunisia is detrimental to those rights and purposes and also endangers international peace and security;

5. *Recalling* further that all Members shall refrain in their international relations from the threat or use of force,

6. *Urges* upon the Government of France to establish normal conditions and normal civil liberties in Tunisia;

7. *Recommends* that negotiations be resumed between the Government of France and the true representatives of the Tunisian people for the purpose of implementing the right of self-determination and the fulfilment of the national aspirations of the Tunisian people;

8. *Decides* to appoint a commission of good offices consisting of A, B and C to arrange and assist in the proposed negotiations;

9. *Requests* the commission to take all necessary steps for the aforesaid purposes and to report to the General Assembly on the progress made;

10. *Invites* all concerned to give the commission their full co-operation;

11. *Requests* the Secretary-General to provide the commission with the necessary staff and facilities; and

12. *Decides* to include this item on the provisional agenda of the eighth regular session of the General Assembly.

(xiv) Resolution expressing confidence in the French Government's policies for Tunisia and calling for continued negotiations for the settlement of disputes, adopted by the General Assembly on 17 December 1952[1]

The General Assembly

Having debated the question proposed by thirteen Member States in document A/2152,

Mindful of the necessity of developing friendly relations among nations based on respect for the principle of equal rights and self-determination of peoples,

Considering that the United Nations, as a centre for harmonizing the actions of nations in the attainment of their common ends under the Charter, should strive towards removing any causes and factors of misunderstanding among Member States, thus reasserting the general principles of co-operation in the maintenance of international peace and security,

---

[1] *General Assembly, Seventh Session, Supplement No. 20, Resolutions*, 611 (VII).

Expresses the confidence that, in pursuance of its proclaimed policies, the Government of France will endeavour to further the effective development of the free institutions of the Tunisian people, in conformity to the purposes and principles of the Charter,

Expresses the hope that the parties will continue negotiations on an urgent basis with a view to bringing about self-government for Tunisians in the light of the relevant provisions of the Charter of the United Nations,

Appeals to the Parties concerned to conduct their relations and settle their disputes in accordance with the spirit of the Charter and refrain from any acts or measures likely to aggravate the present tension.

(xv) Decree regarding municipal organization and administration in Tunisia, 20 December 1952[1]

Louanges à Dieu!

Nous, Mohamed Lamine Pacha Bey, Possesseur du Royaume de Tunis,

Vu le décret du 14 janvier 1914 (17 safar 1332) sur l'organisation des Communes, modifié ou complété par les décrets du 29 décembre 1934 (23 ramadan 1353), du 10 août 1938 (19 rabia II 1352), du 17 avril 1941 (20 rabià I 1360) et du 8 novembre 1945 (3 doul hidja 1364);

Vu le décret du 29 décembre 1934 (22 ramadan 1353), modifié ou complété par le décret du 11 janvier 1945 (27 moharem 1364), sur l'organisation des communes rurales;

Vu le décret du 15 septembre 1945 (10 chaoual 1364) sur l'élection du conseil municipal de Tunis;

Considérant l'importance des intérêts de la population française et la participation de celle-ci aux budgets municipaux;

Après Nous être assuré de l'assentiment du Gouvernement Français;

Sur avis du Conseil des Ministres;

Sur la proposition de Notre Premier Ministre;

Avons pris le décret suivant:

TITRE I

Principes généraux

ARTICLE PREMIER. — Les communes sont des collectivités de droit public dotées de la personnalité civile et de l'autonomie financière. Elles sont chargées de la gestion des intérêts municipaux.

ART. 2. — Chaque commune est gérée par un conseil municipal et par un président assisté d'un vice-président et d'un ou de plusieurs adjoints.

Le nombre des adjoints est fixé par délibération du conseil. Il ne peut

---

[1] *Notes et études documentaires*, no. 1696, 18 January 1953, pp. 6–15. For the decree on the reorganization of the *caïdats*, signed at the same time, see ibid. pp. 2–5.

être supérieur à deux que dans les localités expressément désignées par arrêté du Ministre d'État.

ART. 3. — Les communes sont constituées, délimitées, modifiées ou supprimées par décret. Leur territoire peut s'étendre sur tout ou partie d'un ou plusieurs cheikhats.

Le décret constitutif attribue un nom à la commune; le changement de nom est décidé en la même forme, le conseil intéressé préalablement consulté. Il fixe le lieu où doit siéger le conseil.

ART. 4. — Le nombre des conseillers dans chaque conseil et éventuellement leur répartition entre conseillers français et conseillers tunisiens, sont fixés conformément aux indications du tableau annexé au présent décret.

ART. 5. — Les conseillers sont élus au suffrage direct par deux collèges désignant respectivement les conseillers tunisiens et les conseillers français.

TITRE II
Du conseil

CHAPITRE PREMIER
De la composition du conseil

ART. 6. — Peut être conseiller municipal, toute personne ayant la capacité électorale, âgée de vingt-cinq ans au moins, à l'exception de:

1° celles qui sont pourvues d'un conseil judiciaire;

2° celles qui sont dispensées de subvenir aux charges communales et celles qui sont secourues par les bureaux de bienfaisance;

3° les domestiques attachés exclusivement à la personne.

ART. 7. — Ne sont pas éligibles aux conseils municipaux dans toute l'étendue de la Tunisie:

1° les fonctionnaires du corps du contrôle civil et les agents du cadre supérieur des caïdats;

2° les magistrats de la justice française et les magistrats de la justice tunisienne, religieuse et séculière;

3° les commissaires et les agents de la force publique;

4° les employés de contrôle civil, des caïdats et du service des communes.

ART. 8. — Ne sont pas éligibles aux conseils municipaux dans le ressort où ils exercent leurs fonctions:

1° les ingénieurs et les conducteurs de travaux publics chargé du service de la voirie municipale;

2° les comptables des deniers communaux et les concessionnaires de services municipaux ainsi que les administrateurs des sociétés concessionnaires de ces services;

3° les agents salariés de la collectivité, parmi lesquels ne sont pas compris ceux qui, étant fonctionnaires publics ou exerçant une profession indépendante, ne reçoivent une indemnité de la collectivité qu'en raison des services qu'ils lui rendent dans l'exercice de cette profession.

ART. 9. — Les ascendants et les descendants, les frères et les alliés au même degré ne peuvent être simultanément membre du même conseil; le mandat demeure à celui d'entre eux qui a priorité pour l'inscription au tableau du conseil.

ART. 10. — Nul de peut être membre de plusieurs conseils.

Si plusieurs déclarations de candidatures sont déposées par le même candidat en violation de l'alinéa précédent, elles sont toutes nulles.

ART. 11. — Les conseillers sont inscrits à l'ordre du tableau selon l'ancienneté de leurs fonctions. A égalité d'ancienneté, la préférence est donnée à celui qui a bénéficié proportionnellement au nombre d'électeurs inscrits dans chaque collège du plus grand nombre de voix; en cas d'égalité dans le nombre de voix, il est tenu compte de l'âge.

Les conseillers siègent dans l'ordre du tableau.

ART. 12. — Sauf cas prévus aux articles 14 à 16, chaque conseil est renouvelé par moitié tous les trois ans.

Les membres du premier conseil dont le mandat viendra à expiration au bout de trois ans, seront désignés par le sort, proportionnellement à leur nombre, parmi les conseillers français ou tunisiens.

ART. 13. — Lorsque le conseil a perdu, par l'effet des vacances survenues, le tiers soit des membres français, soit des membres tunisiens, il est procédé dans le délai de deux mois, à dater de la dernière vacance, à des élections complémentaires.

Toutefois, dans l'année qui précède le renouvellement partiel, les élections complémentaires ne sont obligatoires dans chaque collège qu'au cas où le conseil a perdu plus de la moitié des membres de chaque collège.

ART. 14. — Le conseil ne peut être dissous que par décret délibéré en Conseil des Ministres et publié au *Journal officiel tunisien.*

S'il y a urgence, il peut être provisoirement suspendu par arrêté motivé de Notre Ministre d'État délibéré en Conseil des Ministres.

La durée de la suspension ne peut excéder trois mois.

ART. 15. — En cas de dissolution d'un conseil ou de démission de tous ses membres en exercice et lorsqu'un conseil ne peut être constitué, une délégation spéciale en remplit les fonctions.

Dans le mois qui suit la dissolution ou l'acceptation de la démission, cette délégation spéciale est nommée par décret.

Le nombre des membres de la délégation spéciale ne peut être inférieur à trois ni supérieur à sept.

Le décret instituant la délégation spéciale désigne son président.

Les pouvoirs de cette délégation spéciale sont limités aux actes de pure administration conservatoire et urgente.

En aucun cas, il ne lui est permis d'engager les finances de la collectivité au delà des ressources disponibles de l'exercice courant. Elle ne peut ni préparer le budget, ni recevoir les comptes du président ou du receveur de la commune, ni modifier le statut du personnel.

Art. 16. — Toutes les fois que le conseil a été dissous ou que, par application de l'article précédent, une délégation spéciale à été nommée, il est procédé — sauf s'il en est autrement ordonné par décret délibéré en Conseil des Ministres — à la réélection du conseil dans les deux mois à dater de la dissolution, ou de la date d'acceptation de la démission, à moins que l'on se trouve dans les trois mois qui précèdent le renouvellement général des conseils municipaux.

Les fonctions de la délégation spéciale expirent de plein droit dès que le conseil est reconstitué.

Art. 17. — Tout membre du conseil qui, sans motif reconnu légitime par le conseil, a manqué à trois convocations successives, peut être, après avoir été admis à fournir ses explications, déclaré démissionnaire par Notre Ministre d'État, sauf recours dans les dix jours de la notification devant le Premier Ministre.

Art. 18. — Tout membre du conseil qui, pour une cause survenue postérieurement à son élection, se trouve dans un des cas d'incapacité prévus par les articles 6 à 8, est immédiatement déclaré démissionnaire par Notre Ministre d'État.

La réclamation introduite auprès de Notre Ministre d'État dans les dix jours de la notification vaut recours devant le Premier Ministre, qui statue.

Art. 19. — Les démissions volontaires sont adressées au Président, qui les transmet à Notre Ministre d'État par l'intermédiaire du caïd.

Elles sont définitives à partir de l'accusé de réception de Notre Ministre d'État et, à défaut d'accusé de réception, un mois après un nouvel envoi, constaté par lettre recommandée, de la démission à Notre Ministre d'État.

CHAPITRE II

FONCTIONNEMENT DES CONSEILS

Art. 20. — Les conseils tiennent obligatoirement quatre sessions ordinaires en février, mai, juillet et novembre. Les séances se tiennent à la municipalité.

La durée de chaque session ordinaire est de dix jours au plus. Elle peut être, toutefois, prolongée avec l'autorisation du caïd.

Pendant les sessions ordinaires, le conseil peut s'occuper de toutes les matières qui entrent dans ses attributions.

Art. 21. — Les sessions extraordinaires peuvent être tenues en vertu d'un arrêté motivé du caïd, soit sur la demande du président, soit sur la demande du tiers des membres en exercice du conseil.

L'arrêté du caïd autorisant la session extraordinaire en fixe la date d'ouverture, la durée et l'ordre du jour. Avis en est donné au Ministre d'État.

ART. 22. — Il n'est pas fait de distinction entre les sessions ordinaires et les sessions extraordinaires pour le délai qui doit s'écouler entre la convocation et la réunion du conseil.

Ce délai est de trois jours francs dans tous les cas.

Le caïd informé, obligatoirement, de toute convocation du conseil, conserve le droit d'abréger ce délai en cas d'urgence.

Le délai de trois jours étant un délai franc, ni le jour de la convocation, ni celui de la réunion n'y sont compris.

Toute convocation est faite par le président.

Elle est mentionnée au registre des délibérations, affichée à la porte de la municipalité et adressée par écrit et à domicile à tous les membres du conseil.

ART. 23. — Le conseil ne peut valablement délibérer que lorsque la majorité des membres en exercice assiste à la séance. Quand, après deux convocations successives, à trois jours d'intervalle, et dûment constatées, le conseil n'est pas réuni en nombre suffisant, la délibération est valable quel que soit le nombre des membres présents.

ART. 24. — Le président dirige les débats. Dans les séances où les comptes d'administration du président sont débattus, le conseil élit un président provisoire.

ART. 25. — Au début de chaque session et pour sa durée, le conseil nomme un ou plusieurs de ses membres pour remplir les fonctions de secrétaire.

Il peut s'adjoindre des auxiliaires pris hors de ses membres, qui assistent aux séances, mais sans participer aux délibérations.

ART. 26. — Les délibérations sont prises à la majorité absolue des votants.

En cas de partage, sauf le cas de scrutin secret, la voix du président est prépondérante.

Le vote a lieu au scrutin public sur la demande du quart des membres présents; les noms des votants avec la désignation de leurs votes, sont insérés au procès-verbal.

Il est voté au scrutin secret toutes les fois que le tiers des membres présents le réclame, ou qu'il s'agit de procéder à une nomination ou à une présentation.

Dans ces derniers cas, si aucun des candidats n'a obtenu la majorité absolue, il est procédé à un deuxième tour de scrutin et l'élection a lieu à la majorité relative; à égalité de voix, l'élection est acquise au plus âgé.

La demande de scrutin secret a toujours la priorité sur la demande de scrutin public.

Art. 27. — Les délibérations sont inscrites par ordre de date sur un registre, coté et paraphé au service des communes. Les délibérations sont signées par tous les membres présents à la séance, ou mention est faite de la cause qui les empêche de signer.

Le compte rendu analytique en français et en arabe de la séance sera affiché à la porte de la municipalité.

Art. 28. — Les habitants ou contribuables de chaque collectivité peuvent demander communication et prendre copie des délibérations du conseil.

Cette faculté est étendue aux budgets, aux comptes et aux arrêtés.

La communication est faite sans déplacement des documents consultés.

Art. 29. — Le conseil peut former, au cours de chaque session, des commissions d'études chargées de l'examen préalable des affaires soumises au conseil, soit par l'administration soit en vertu du droit d'initiative qui appartient à chaque membre du conseil.

Ces commissions tiennent leurs séances pendant les sessions du conseil; elles peuvent, toutefois, sur la demande du conseil municipal et avec l'accord du caïd, se réunir dans l'intervalle des sessions du conseil.

Les commissions formées au sein du conseil ne peuvent être que des commissions d'études; elles n'ont pas de pouvoir propre et ne peuvent exercer, même en vertu de délégation, aucune des attributions réservées par la législation au conseil.

Elles devront se borner à préparer et à instruire les affaires qui leur auront été renvoyées.

Art. 30. — Les séances des conseils sont publiques.

Néanmoins, sur la demande du tiers de ses membres ou du président, le conseil décide s'il se formera en séance secrète.

Le président a seul la police de l'assemblée.

Il peut faire expulser de l'auditoire ou arrêter tout individu qui trouble l'ordre.

En cas de crime ou délit, il en dresse procès-verbal et le parquet compétent en est immédiatement saisi.

CHAPITRE III

ATTRIBUTIONS DES CONSEILS

Art. 31. — Le conseil règle par ses délibérations dans le cadre des lois et règlements en vigueur les affaires de la commune énumérées ci-après:

1° le budget de la collectivité et, en général, les dépenses et les recettes ordinaires ou extraordinaires;

2° le mode d'administration du patrimoine de la collectivité;

3° le tarif des droits et produits locaux dont la perception est autorisée par les dispositions législatives ou réglementaires;

4° les acquisitions, aliénations et échange des propriétés de la commune, leur affectation à des services publics, et les mesures tendant à leur entretien, à leur amélioration ou à leur accroissement;

5° les conditions de baux des biens donnés ou pris à ferme ou à loyer par la commune;

6° l'acceptation des dons et legs faits à la commune;

7° la désignation des chemins ou portions de chemins à ouvrir ou à entretenir ou réparer par la commune;

8° les projets de constructions, grosses réparations, entretien, démolition et tous travaux à entreprendre dans l'intérêt de la commune et, plus généralement, les plans d'aménagement;

9° les travaux d'utilité commune, comme la création et l'entretien des points d'eau, citernes, abreuvoirs, travaux de captage, de retenue ou d'irrigation dont la commune prend l'initiative ou la charge; les conditions de mise en valeur des terres incultes, brousses ou marais, ou nappes alfatières, appartenant à la commune;

10° la réglementation du parcours, de la vaine pâture, de la jouissance et de la répartition des pâturages et des fruits; les conditions à imposer aux parties prenantes;

11° les mesures de protection des populations civiles intéressant la commune qui sont effectuées dans le cadre d'un programme établi pour l'ensemble du territoire;

12° l'établissement, la suppression ou les changements des foires et marchés;

13° les actions en justice et les transactions;

14° les emprunts.

ART. 32. — Les conseils émettent des avis sur les objets que prévoient les décrets ou règlements ou que leur propose l'administration supérieure.

ART. 33. — Il est interdit au conseil soit de publier des proclamations ou adresses, soit d'émettre des vœux politiques, soit, hors des cas prévus par le présent décret, de se mettre en communication avec un ou plusieurs autres conseils.

ART. 34. — Les délibérations du conseil sont, dans les quinze jours qui suivent la clôture de la session où elles ont été prises, adressées en expéditions authentiques, par le président au caïd, qui en transmet, après consultation des services techniques intérieurs, un exemplaire au Ministre d'État et, pour les questions relevant de sa compétence, au Directeur des Finances. Il en communique un exemplaire au contrôleur civil.

ART. 35. — Sont nulles de plein droit:

1° les délibérations d'un conseil portant sur un objet étranger à ses attributions définies ci-dessus ou prises hors de sa réunion légale;

2° les délibérations prises en violation des textes législatifs ou réglementaires;

La nullité de droit est déclarée, par arrêté motivé du Ministre d'État; elle peut être prononcée, proposée ou opposée à toute époque.

Art. 36. — Sont annulables les délibérations auxquelles auront pris part les membres du conseil intéressés soit en leur nom personnel, soit comme mandataires à l'affaire qui en fait l'objet.

L'annulation d'une délibération doit être prononcée par un arrêté motivé du Ministre d'État dans les deux mois qui suivront la transmission que lui en fait le caïd; elle est prononcée soit d'office, soit sur la proposition du caïd.

Art. 37. — Les délibérations qui ont pour objet l'établissement du budget, celui des taxes, de droits divers ou de contributions, la fixation des statuts du personnel titulaire investi d'emplois permanents, l'élaboration des règlements généraux d'hygiène, le classement ou le déclassement des ouvrages du domaine public, l'exercice d'actions judiciaires ou des transactions d'un taux supérieur à 50.000 francs ne sont exécutoires que si elles sont approuvées par Notre Ministre d'État.

Les délibérations relatives à la composition, aux effectifs et à la rémunération du personnel des communes ne sont exécutoires qu'après avoir été approuvées conjointement par Notre Ministre d'État et le Directeur des Finances.

Art. 38. — Les délibérations des conseils qui ont pour objet des acquisitions ou des échanges d'immeubles ou des transactions dont les prix ou les valeurs ne dépassent pas cinquante mille francs, ou des baux dont la durée n'excède pas neuf ans et le loyer vingt mille francs, sont exécutoires de plein droit. Toutefois, leur exécution est suspendue, si le caïd fait connaître au président, dans les quinze jours qui suivent leur transmission, qu'il poursuit leur annulation en vertu de l'article 36 ci-dessus.

Art. 39. — Toutes les autres délibérations légalement prises par le conseil sont rendues exécutoires par l'approbation que leur donne le caïd dans le délai d'un mois qui suit la communication que lui en a faite le président. Le silence du caïd vaut approbation. Si le caïd n'approuve pas la délibération il notifie et motive son refus au président et en rend compte au Ministre d'État. Si, dans un nouveau délai d'un mois, il n'est pas statué par le Ministre d'État sur le refus opposé par le caïd, la délibération devient exécutoire de plein droit.

Le Ministre d'État peut faire inscrire à l'ordre du jour des séances du conseil toutes questions intéressant la commune.

Art. 40. — Si le Ministre d'État refuse son approbation à une délibération d'un conseil, il peut présenter à celui-ci des propositions et l'inviter à reprendre l'examen de la question.

TITRE III
DE L'ADMINISTRATION DES COMMUNES

CHAPITRE PREMIER
DU PRÉSIDENT DU CONSEIL MUNICIPAL

Art. 41. — Le conseil municipal est présidé par un président assisté d'un vice-président et d'un ou de plusieurs adjoints chargés de l'exécution des décisions du conseil. Le président est en outre le représentant local du pouvoir central.

Art. 42. — Le président est seul chargé de l'administration, mais il peut, sous sa surveillance et sa responsabilité, déléguer, soit à titre temporaire, soit à titre permanent, ses fonctions au vice-président.

La délégation est faite par arrêté transcrit au registre des arrêtés municipaux; elle subsiste lorsqu'elle est permanente, tant qu'elle n'a pas été rapportée; elle est rapportée dans la même forme qu'elle a été donnée.

Le vice-président doit toujours mentionner dans les actes qu'il accomplit en qualité de délégué la délégation en vertu de laquelle il agit.

Art. 43. — Le président est nommé par décret beylical parmi les membres du corps caïdal, autres que le caïd, qui a la tutelle des communes, le vice-président et les adjoints sont élus par le conseil municipal parmi ses membres. La délibération doit être prise à la majorité absolue, au début de la première session qui suit chaque renouvellement partiel.

Si deux tours de scrutin n'ont pas permis de désigner le vice-président et les adjoints, au troisième tour la délibération est prise à la majorité relative.

Dans les communes ayant au moins trois conseillers municipaux français, le premier adjoint sera de droit de nationalité différente du vice-président.

De même, lorsqu'un conseil municipal comprenant au moins trois conseillers français désigne une délégation, celle-ci sera composée selon des proportions analogues à celles du conseil et comprendra, en tout état de cause, un membre français.

Art. 44. — La délibération portant désignation du vice-président et des adjoints est affichée à la porte de la municipalité.

Art. 45. — La délibération portant désignation du vice-président ou des adjoints, peut être arguée de nullité par les membres du conseil municipal dans un délai de cinq jours.

Le Conseil des ministres statue sur les recours formés contre ces propositions qui sont adressées au caïd.

Lorsque la délibération est annulée par le Conseil des Ministres ou que, pour toute autre cause, le vice-président ou les adjoints ont cessé leurs fonctions, le conseil est convoqué par le caïd pour procéder dans le délai d'un mois à de nouvelles élections.

Art. 46. — Les fonctions de président, de vice-président ou d'adjoints sont gratuites. Cependant le conseil peut, sur les ressources ordinaires de la commune, attribuer à ceux-ci, dans les conditions définies ci-après, des indemnités dont les taux maxima sont fixés, pour l'ensemble de la Régence, par arrêté de Notre Ministre d'État et du Directeur des Finances. Elles ne sont accordées que lorsque la situation des bénéficiaires le rend nécessaire. Elles peuvent être réduites de moitié lorsque les intéressés sont investis d'un autre mandat électoral rémunéré.

Art. 47. — Les présidents, vice-présidents et adjoints peuvent être suspendus de leurs fonctions pour la durée d'un mois par le caïd après approbation par le Ministre d'État; cette suspension peut être portée à trois mois par arrêté du Ministre d'État.

La décision de suspension désignera les membres du conseil municipal chargés d'assurer les intérims.

Art. 48. — Les présidents, vice-présidents et adjoints peuvent être révoqués par décret sur le rapport du Ministre d'État.

La révocation comporte de plein droit l'incapacité d'exercer les fonctions de président, de vice-président ou d'adjoint, pendant une année à compter du décret de révocation, même s'il était procédé auparavant au renouvellement du conseil.

Art. 49. — Ne peuvent être vice-présidents ou adjoints ni en exercer temporairement les fonctions:

1° les agents et employés de l'Administration des Finances;

2° les agents des Forêts;

3° les agents des Postes et Télégraphes;

4° les gardes des établissements publics;

5° les agents salariés de la commune sans distinction.

CHAPITRE II

DES ATTRIBUTIONS DES PRÉSIDENTS

Art. 50. — Le vice-président peut, sous sa surveillance et sa responsabilité, et après accord du président, déléguer à un ou plusieurs des adjoints, par arrêté approuvé par Notre Ministre d'État, une partie des attributions dont il est lui-même délégataire.

Cette délégation existe tant qu'elle n'est pas rapportée.

Les actes accomplis en vertu d'une délégation doivent, à peine de nullité, mentionner l'arrêté de délégation, sa date et son objet.

Art. 51. — Dans les cas où les intérêts du président ou du vice-président se trouvent en opposition avec ceux de la commune, le conseil désigne un autre de ses membres de même nationalité pour représenter la commune soit en justice, soit dans les contrats.

Les adjoints sont dans les mêmes conditions remplacés par un conseiller de leur nationalité.

ART. 52. — Dans le cas où le président ou son délégué refuserait ou négligerait de faire un des actes qui lui sont prescrits par la loi, Notre Ministre d'État peut, après l'en avoir requis par l'intermédiaire du caïd, y procéder d'office par lui-même ou par un délégué spécial.

ART. 53. — Le président est chargé, sous le contrôle du conseil:

1° de conserver et d'administrer le domaine de la commune et de faire en conséquence tous actes conservatoires;

2° de gérer les revenus, de surveiller les établissements et la comptabilité de la commune;

3° de préparer, proposer et exécuter le budget;

4° de lancer les adjudications et de passer les marchés;

5° de passer, dans les formes établies par la législation, les actes de vente, location, échange, partage, acceptation de dons et legs, acquisitions, transactions, lorsque ces actes ont été autorisés;

6° de diriger les travaux avec le concours des agents techniques mis à sa disposition;

7° d'assurer, en ce qui concerne l'exécution du plan d'aménagement de la commune, le contrôle des lotissements et des constructions entreprises sur son territoire;

8° de représenter la commune, soit en demandant, soit en défendant;

9° et d'une manière générale, d'exécuter les décisions du conseil.

Les actes du président pris en exécution des délibérations du conseil sont exécutoires dans les mêmes formes que les délibérations correspondantes.

ART. 54. — Le président est chargé, sous l'autorité de l'administration supérieure:

1° de la publication et de l'exécution des lois, décrets et règlements;

2° de la police municipale;

3° des fonctions particulières qui lui sont attribuées par des dispositions législatives et réglementaires spéciales.

ART. 55. — La police municipale a un triple but: elle consiste à assurer le bon ordre, la sûreté et la salubrité publiques.

Elle comprend notamment:

1° tout ce qui intéresse la sûreté et la commodité du passage dans les rues, quais, places et voies publiques, ce qui comprend le nettoiement, l'éclairage, l'enlèvement des encombrements, la démolition ou la réparation des édifices menaçant ruine, l'interdiction de rien exposer aux fenêtres ou aux autres parties des édifices qui puisse nuire par sa chute, ou celle de rien jeter qui puisse endommager les passants ou provoquer des exhalations nuisibles; le contrôle du respect de la réglementation concernant l'alignement et le nivellement ainsi que des dispositions du décret d'aménagement;

2° le soin de réprimer les atteintes à la tranquillité, telles que les rixes et disputes dans les rues, le tumulte excité dans les lieux d'assemblée publique, les attroupements, les bruits et rassemblements nocturnes qui troublent le repos des habitants et tous actes de nature à compromettre la tranquillité publique;

3° le maintien du bon ordre dans les endroits où il se fait de grands rassemblements de personnes, tels que foires, marchés, réjouissances et cérémonies publiques, spectacles, jeux, cafés et autres lieux publics;

4° le mode de transport des personnes décédées, des inhumations, des exhumations; le maintien du bon ordre et de la décence dans tous les cimetières, privés ou publics, dans le cadre du décret du 30 juillet 1884;

5° l'inspection sur la fidélité du débit des denrées qui se vendent au poids ou à la mesure et la salubrité des comestibles exposés en vente;

6° le soin de prévenir, par des précautions convenables, et celui de faire cesser par la distribution des secours nécessaires, les accidents et les fléaux calamiteux, tels que les incendies, les inondations, les maladies épidémiques ou contagieuses, les épizooties, en provoquant, s'il y a lieu, l'intervention de l'autorité supérieure;

7° le soin de prendre provisoirement les mesures nécessaires contre les aliénés dont l'état pourrait compromettre la morale publique, la sécurité des personnes et la conservation des propriétés;

8° le soin d'obvier ou de remédier aux événements fâcheux qui pourraient être occasionnés par la divagation des animaux malfaisants ou féroces.

ART. 56. — Le service de la police est assuré dans chaque commune par des commissaires, inspecteurs et agents de police relevant de l'État.

Ce service est chargé de l'exécution des décisions prises par le président en application de l'article précédent ainsi que par des agents assermentés des collectivités.

ART. 57. — Les commissaires et agents de police, ainsi que les agents assermentés constatent, par des procès-verbaux, les contraventions aux règlements.

Les délinquants sont déférés à l'autorité judiciaire française ou tunisienne, selon leur nationalité.

ART. 58. — Le président prend des arrêtés à l'effet:

1° de donner une publicité locale aux lois et règlements de police et de rappeler les habitants à leur observation;

2° d'assurer la police et, d'une façon générale, d'ordonner toute mesure dans le cadre de ses attributions.

ART. 59. — Les arrêtés doivent être portés à la connaissance du public par voie de publication et d'affiches toutes les fois qu'ils contiennent des dispositions générales et, dans les autres cas, par voie de notifications individuelles.

La publication est constatée par une déclaration certifiée par le président.

La notification est établie par le récépissé de la partie intéressée ou, à défaut, par l'original de la notification conservé dans les archives de la commune.

Les arrêtés, actes de publication et de notification sont inscrits à leur date, sur le registre des arrêtés de la commune.

Art. 60. — Le président désigne par arrêté les lieux qui, conformément aux dispositions de l'article 16 du décret du 6 août 1936 (12 djoumada I 1355) sur la presse, sont exclusivement destinés à recevoir les affiches de lois et autres actes de l'autorité publique. Il est interdit d'y placarder des affiches particulières.

Les affiches des actes émanés de l'autorité publique sont seules imprimées sur papier blanc.

Art. 61. — Les arrêtés intéressant la circulation, l'occupation du domaine public ou l'hygiène ne sont exécutoires qu'après approbation de Notre Ministre d'État.

Les arrêtés intéressant la sécurité locale sont soumis au visa de l'autorité de contrôle.

Art. 62. — Le président pourvoit d'urgence à ce que toute personne décédée soit ensevelie et inhumée.

Dans le cas où, au sujet de l'ensevelissement et de l'inhumation d'une personne décédée, des difficultés s'élèvent, le président prend les mesures qu'exige soit le bon ordre, soit la décence publique.

Les dispositions du décret du 30 juillet 1884 (6 chaoual 1301), modifié par le décret du 15 mars 1932 (7 doul kaada 1350) sur la police des cimetières de la ville de Tunis, sont étendues à toutes les communes de la Régence.

Le président ne doit délivrer de permis d'inhumer que sur la production d'un certificat de décès. Le certificat sera dressé par un médecin.

Art. 63. — Le président a la police des routes dépendant du domaine public de l'État dans l'intérieur du périmètre de la commune mais seulement en ce qui touche la circulation, l'hygiène et la sécurité publiques sur lesdites voies. Il a, en outre, la police de la voirie de la commune.

Art. 64. — Les pouvoirs de police attribués aux présidents, tels qu'ils résultent des dispositions du présent décret, ne font pas obstacle au droit, pour le Directeur des Services de Sécurité, de prendre, conformément au décret du 30 octobre 1941 (9 chaoual 1360), dans tous les cas où il n'y aurait pas été pourvu par les autorités locales, toutes mesures relatives au maintien de la salubrité, de la sûreté et de la tranquillité publiques, à l'intérieur des périmètres de la commune.

CHAPITRE III

Du personnel de la commune

Art. 65. — Le président est secondé pour l'administration par un personnel local qui a à sa tête un secrétaire.

Dans les villes désignées par arrêté conjoint de Notre Ministre d'État et du Directeur des Finances, ce fonctionnaire prend le titre de secrétaire général.

Art. 66. — Le président nomme à tous les emplois pour lesquels les dispositions législatives ou réglementaires en vigueur ne fixent pas un droit spécial de nomination.

Le conseil n'est jamais appelé à donner son avis sur les nominations aux emplois de la commune.

Art. 67. — Sont nommés par arrêté de Notre Ministre d'État :

— les secrétaires généraux, secrétaires généraux adjoints, secrétaires et receveurs ;

— les médecins et vétérinaires au service de la collectivité ;

— les chefs de service.

Art. 68. — Dans toute commune où il existe des emplois confiés à titre permanent à un personnel exclusivement local, ainsi que dans toute commune où il en est créé, le conseil détermine, dans le cadre d'un statut général fixé par arrêté de Notre Ministre d'État et sous réserve de l'application des art. 69, 70 et 71, par délibération soumise à l'approbation de Notre Ministre d'État, les règles concernant le recrutement, l'avancement et la discipline des titulaires de ces emplois.

Faute, par le conseil, d'avoir délibéré, il pourra être statué d'office par arrêté de Notre Ministre d'État, qui rendra applicable dans la commune un statut-type.

Art. 69. — Les peines comportant retard dans l'avancement, réduction de traitement, suppression totale ou partielle du congé annuel, suspension ou révocation, ne peuvent être prononcées qu'après avis d'un conseil de discipline.

Sauf en ce qui concerne la révocation, qui est toujours prononcée par Notre Ministre d'État, les peines disciplinaires sont prononcées par l'autorité investie du pouvoir de nomination.

Art. 70. — Sont toutefois maintenues en vigueur :

1° en ce qui concerne les secrétaires et receveurs, les dispositions du décret du 12 juillet 1929 (4 safar 1348) portant statut de ces catégories de personnel ;

2° en ce qui concerne le personnel ouvrier permanent et employé des communes, les règles fixées par le décret du 19 mai 1938 (10 rabia I 1357) ou prises pour son application.

Art. 71. — Il est interdit aux communes d'accorder à leurs personnels des traitements, salaires, indemnités ou allocations ayant pour objet de leur créer une situation plus avantageuse que celle des fonctionnaires, agents, ouvriers de l'État exerçant une fonction équivalente.

Art. 72. — Les arrêtés du président fixant, en exécution de l'article 68, le statut des agents titulaires de la commune, investis d'emplois permanents, sont visés par Notre Ministre d'État, ceux relatifs à la composition, aux effectifs et à la rémunération du personnel de la commune sont visés conjointement par Notre Ministre d'État et le Directeur des Finances.

Les arrêtés individuels du président relatifs à la nomination, l'avancement et la discipline du personnel sont visés par le caïd et approuvés par Notre Ministre d'État.

TITRE IV

DE LA GESTION DES COMMUNES

CHAPITRE PREMIER

DU DOMAINE

Section I. — *De la consistance du domaine*

Art. 73. — Le domaine de la commune comprend un domaine public et un domaine privé.

Art. 74. — Font partie du domaine public communal :

1° les parcelles lui appartenant qui ont reçu de droit ou de fait une affectation comme rues, places, jardins publics ou routes, à l'exception des routes de grand parcours et des routes de moyenne communication dont la création et l'entretien incombent à l'État;

2° les parcelles lui appartenant qui supportent des ouvrages de distribution d'eau, de gaz, d'électricité ou d'assainissement, des plates-formes de voies de tramways ou tous autres ouvrages d'intérêt public chaque fois que la charge en aura été expressément remise à la commune;

3° les autres biens compris dans le domaine public par application du décret du 24 septembre 1885 (3 djoumada I 1282) lorsqu'ils auront été remis à la commune dans les conditions prévues à l'article 80 ci-après;

4° les parcelles appartenant à la commune et constituant l'assiette d'un ouvrage prévu au plan d'aménagement régulièrement approuvé ou ayant fait l'objet d'une déclaration d'utilité publique spéciale, le décret d'aménagement ou la déclaration d'utilité publique pris dans les formes qui sont définies dans chaque cas particulier valant affectation.

Art. 75. — Le domaine public est inaliénable et imprescriptible. Il peut être déclassé par arrêté du président conformément à une délibération du conseil et sous réserve d'approbation par le Ministère d'État.

Art. 76. — Les rues et routes incorporées dans le domaine communal sont classées en voiries urbaines et en voiries vicinales. La voirie urbaine assure la desserte à l'intérieur des agglomérations et la voirie vicinale assure la liaison entre les diverses agglomérations d'une même commune ou les divers points de son territoire.

Le classement d'une voie dans la voirie urbaine ou la voirie vicinale résulte soit du décret d'aménagement de la commune, soit, à défaut, d'un arrêté du président pris en exécution de délibérations du conseil sous réserve de l'approbation du Ministre d'État.

Art. 77. — Le tracé et l'emplacement des voies urbaines et des voies vicinales sont constatés ou modifiés par le décret d'aménagement ou, à défaut, par l'arrêté de classement.

L'alignement et le nivellement de ces voies résultent d'arrêtés pris conformément à une délibération du conseil sur l'avis du représentant local de la Direction des Travaux Publics, sous réserve de l'approbation conjointe du Ministre d'État et du Commissaire à la Reconstruction et au Logement.

Art. 78. — Il est procédé par les administrations responsables à la remise aux services de chaque commune des parties du domaine public de l'État dont la gestion et la conservation leur sont confiées par application de l'article 74 ci-dessus.

Les pouvoirs d'administration définis ci-après prendront leur origine du jour de cette remise.

Art. 79. — Le domaine privé des communes comprend:

1° les biens affectés à un service public (maison communale, cimetières, halles, marchés, etc.);

2° les biens patrimoniaux.

Section II. — *De la gestion du domaine*

Art. 80. — Les règles édictées par la législation en vigueur ou à intervenir, pour la conservation et la police du domaine public de l'État sont applicables au domaine public des communes, sous réserve des dispositions du présent décret.

Sous réserve des dispositions législatives ou réglementaires existantes, des autorisations d'occupation provisoire du domaine public peuvent être données par arrêté du Président. Ces occupations sont précaires et révocables; elles donnent lieu à perception d'une redevance.

Dans les voies dépendant du domaine public de la commune et moyennant le paiement de droits fixés par un tarif régulièrement approuvé, les alignements individuels et les permissions de voirie sont délivrés par le président conformément aux arrêtés d'alignement et de nivellement.

Les autorisations de bâtir ou modifier ou réparer une construction sur le territoire de la commune sont délivrées par le président conformément à la législation en vigueur.

Art. 81. — Le service de voirie comprend:

1° l'entretien, la réparation et la construction des chaussées, trottoirs, promenades, plantations, jardins, squares et de leurs accessoires et dépendances;

2° l'entretien, la réparation, le curage ou la construction des égouts;

3° le nettoiement et l'arrosage des voies et espaces libres publics;

4° l'éclairage des voies publiques et des établissements de la commune;

5° le service des eaux, quand remise en a été faite à la commune;

6° la construction, l'entretien ou la réparation des bâtiments de la collectivité, abattoirs, halles, marchés, fourrières, postes de police, cimetières, théâtres, kiosques, horloges publiques, bibliothèques, maisons communales, etc.;

7° les travaux d'assainissement de toute nature;

8° l'inscription des noms des rues et des numéros des maisons;

et en général tout ce qui se rattache aux travaux dont les dépenses sont imputables sur les fonds de la commune.

Sont également rattachés à ce service:

a) tout ce qui concerne l'exécution du plan d'aménagement, les alignements, les constructions particulières, les bâtiments menaçant ruine, etc.;

b) l'application des règlements sur les établissements dangereux, incommodes ou insalubres.

Toutefois, dans les grandes villes, il pourra être créé pour ces deux derniers objets un ou des services distincts.

Art. 82. — Le service des travaux municipaux est confié:

A Tunis, au chef du service des travaux municipaux qui est un ingénieur spécialement désigné;

Dans les communes, sièges d'un arrondissement des Travaux Publics, à l'ingénieur des Travaux Publics de l'arrondissement;

Dans les communes, sièges d'une subdivision des Travaux Publics, à l'ingénieur ou à l'agent des Travaux Publics chargé de la subdivision;

Enfin, dans les autres localités, à l'ingénieur ou à l'agent des Travaux Publics de la subdivision dont dépendent ces localités.

Toutefois, une commune peut être autorisée, par arrêté conjoint de Notre Ministre d'État et du Directeur des Finances pris sur avis du Directeur des Travaux Publics, à organiser un service autonome de travaux communaux, à condition de prévoir l'inscription des dépenses correspondantes à son budget.

Les communes peuvent, après autorisation du Ministre d'État, faire exécuter, sous le contrôle de l'agent des Travaux Publics chargé de la direction des travaux, soit par leurs propres moyens, soit par l'entreprise privée, les travaux que les agents de la Direction des Travaux Publics se trouveraient dans l'impossibilité d'exécuter dans les conditions et délais jugés nécessaires par les administrations municipales. Les travaux de bâtiment, grosses réparations, transformations et constructions doivent être confiés à un architecte agréé.

Art. 83. — Les projets, plans et devis de travaux à exécuter en régie, les projets de concession des services publics ou portant sur des parcelles du domaine public ou privé, les projets de marchés de travaux, fournitures ou transports à exécuter par l'entreprise, sont établis sur la demande du président et soumis à l'examen du conseil en même temps que les voies et moyens affectés à leur financement.

Ces projets sont soumis aux dispositions du décret du 29 janvier 1934 (13 chaoual 1352) instituant la commission des marchés, tel qu'il a été modifié ou complété et à celles du décret du 16 décembre 1948 (14 safar 1368) instituant un conseil supérieur des bâtiments civils.

Lorsqu'ils requièrent soit l'accord préalable de l'administration supérieure, soit l'approbation de Notre Ministre d'État, soit l'intervention d'un décret, ils doivent être accompagnés de la délibération correspondante, rappelant l'inscription au budget des crédits correspondants et être appuyés, s'il y a lieu, des observations de l'ingénieur ou agent chargé du service de la voirie et des travaux.

Ils deviennent exécutoires dans les mêmes formes et délais que les délibérations correspondantes.

Les projets de traités portant concession des grands services municipaux et notamment l'alimentation en eau, les transports publics, l'éclairage, sont soumis à l'avis du Conseil des Ministres et approuvés par décret.

Art. 84. — Les marchés de travaux, fournitures ou transports à exécuter par l'entreprise sont passés dans les formes prévues pour les marchés de l'État, sous réserve des adaptations qui pourraient être édictées par arrêtés conjoints de Notre Ministre d'État, du Directeur des Finances et du Directeur des Travaux Publics.

Les receveurs sont responsables des paiements qu'ils effectueraient pour des travaux non autorisés.

Art. 85. — Les cautionnements des soumissionnaires ne portent pas intérêt lorsqu'ils sont versés en numéraire.

Si le cautionnement est fait en obligations tunisiennes, les coupons seront détachés et remis aux adjudicataires à leur échéance.

Les dépôts préalables des soumissionnaires sont pris en recette par le receveur, qui en délivre quittance. Les remboursements des dépôts provisoires sont constatés par un reçu des parties souscrit au verso des quittances à souche qui leur ont été délivrées et qu'elles doivent restituer au receveur municipal. Les recettes et les dépenses sont portées au compte de gestion du receveur.

Les remboursements de cautionnement sont effectués sur le vu d'un certificat délivré par le chef de service des travaux constatant que l'adjudicataire a satisfait à tous ses engagements et contresigné par le président.

ART. 86. — La création ou l'amélioration des voies urbaines entraîne une participation des riverains aux dépenses en résultant dans des conditions qui seront définies par décret.

L'établissement des égouts, des réseaux de distribution d'eau, de gaz, d'électricité, l'établissement d'ouvrages de défense contre les inondations, le remblaiement des terres inondables et, d'une façon générale, tous les travaux dont peuvent bénéficier plus spécialement certains propriétaires, donnent lieu à une participation de ces derniers aux dépenses correspondantes dans des conditions qui seront définies par décret.

ART. 87. — Le président a pouvoir pour constater les infractions aux arrêtés d'alignement et de nivellement ainsi que toutes les contraventions aux dispositions législatives et réglementaires intéressant la voirie.

Il peut également commissionner un agent assermenté aux fins de constater ces infractions.

ART. 88. — Les délibérations du conseil portant acceptation de dons ou legs faits à la commune lorsqu'il y a des charges ou conditions ou qu'ils donnent lieu à des réclamations des familles, sont approuvées par décret.

Lorsque la délibération porte refus de dons ou legs, Notre Ministre d'État peut, après avoir requis une nouvelle délibération du conseil municipal, être autorisé par décret à accepter dans l'intérêt de la commune, si l'assemblée maintient sa première décision.

Section III. — *De l'aménagement de la commune.*

ART. 89. — Toute commune et, éventuellement, les fractions du territoire non érigées en communes, fait l'objet d'un décret particulier d'aménagement du territoire de la collectivité.

La réalisation du plan d'aménagement nécessite:

1° l'exécution des ouvrages publics prévus; la réalisation de ces ouvrages appartient aux diverses collectivités publiques intéressées;

2° le contrôle des lotissements constitués sur le territoire de la collectivité, conformément à la législation en vigueur;

3° le contrôle des constructions soumises à autorisation de bâtir délivrée par le président conformément à la réglementation applicable en la matière.

CHAPITRE II
DU BUDGET

ART. 90. — Le budget de chaque commune est préparé et proposé par le président, voté par le conseil et arrêté conjointement par Notre Ministre d'État et le Directeur des Finances.

ART. 91. — Sont obligatoires pour les communes et peuvent être inscrites d'office à leur budget, les dépenses suivantes;

— la rémunération du personnel de la commune;

— les frais de bureau;

— l'acquittement des dettes exigibles et des annuités d'emprunt;

— les frais d'impression et de conservation des actes et documents qu'il leur incombe d'établir ou de conserver;

— les dépenses d'installation, d'entretien et de grosses réparations des édifices, bâtisses et établissements immobiliers ou fonciers qui composent leur patrimoine;

— les frais d'établissement et conservation des plans d'aménagement urbains et ruraux;

— les frais d'entretien, d'alignement, de nivellement, des voies, chemins ou rues, des aqueducs, canaux, points d'eau, fontaines, canaux d'évacuation des eaux usées ou de pluies, classés dans le domaine de la commune;

— la quote-part des frais d'hospitalisation des indigents et semi-indigents;

— plus généralement, les dépenses qu'un décret met à la charge des communes.

ART. 92. — Les recettes des communes sont constituées par:

a) des taxes locales;

b) une quote-part de l'actif des divers fonds communs institués par la réglementation en vigueur;

c) les revenus du patrimoine de la collectivité et des services publics payants qu'elle assume;

d) éventuellement, des subventions pour emprunts imputables aux fonds communs susvisés et des subventions en capital de l'État.

ART. 93. — Le Président est seul ordonnateur des crédits ouverts au budget.

Si, après mise en demeure restée sans effet dans un délai d'un mois, il néglige d'ordonnancer une dépense régulièrement exigible et prévue au budget, un arrêté de Notre Ministre d'État prescrivant le paiement tient lieu de mandat dans les écritures du comptable, qui effectue le paiement dans les formes habituelles.

ART. 94. — Les recettes et les dépenses de la commune sont exécutées par un comptable, chargé seul et sous sa responsabilité de poursuivre la rentrée de tous les revenus de la commune et de toutes les sommes qui seraient dues à celle-ci ainsi que d'acquitter toutes les dépenses mandatées par le président jusqu'à concurrence des crédits ouverts au budget.

Le comptable a seul la faculté, et sous sa responsabilité, d'accorder des sursis ou d'échelonner les paiements des droits et produits dont il assure le recouvrement.

ART. 95. — Lorsque le budget ne peut être arrêté pour une cause indépendante du conseil avant le commencement de l'exercice, le budget de l'exercice précédent est provisoirement reconduit jusqu'à l'approbation du nouveau budget.

Il en est de même lorsque, du fait du refus ou de la négligence du conseil, le budget n'a pas été établi ou n'a pas été voté en équilibre.

Dans les deux cas visés à l'alinéa précédent, le conseil est convoqué en session extraordinaire. Si celle-ci n'est pas suivie d'effet, le nouveau budget est arrêté d'office par Notre Ministre d'État après avis du Directeur des Finances. Notre Ministre d'État reçoit à cet effet tous les pouvoirs dévolus au conseil en matière fiscale et budgétaire. Il ne peut toutefois augmenter le taux des taxes ou en instituer de nouvelles que dans la mesure où, après suppression de tout ou partie des dépenses facultatives, le produit des taxes existantes serait insuffisant pour couvrir les dépenses obligatoires. Les relèvements fiscaux sont rendus applicables par arrêté de Notre Ministre d'État pris sur la proposition du Directeur des Finances et affiché au siège de la commune.

Les dispositions du premier alinéa du présent article sont applicables en cas de dissolution du conseil jusqu'à la formation d'une nouvelle assemblée.

CHAPITRE III

Des actions judiciaires

Art. 96. — Le conseil délibère sur les actions à intenter ou à soutenir au nom de la commune.

Le président, en vertu de la délibération du conseil, représente la commune en justice.

Nulle commune ne peut ester en justice sans y être autorisée par Notre Ministre d'État. Elle doit justifier des chances de succès et d'un intérêt suffisant.

Après tout jugement intervenu, la commune ne peut se pourvoir devant un autre degré de juridiction qu'en vertu d'une nouvelle autorisation de Notre Ministre d'État.

Dans les cas prévus par les deux paragraphes précédents, la décision de Notre Ministre d'État doit être rendue dans les deux mois à compter du jour de la demande en autorisation. A défaut de décision rendue dans ledit délai, la commune est autorisée à plaider.

Le président peut toujours, sans autorisation préalable du conseil et de Notre Ministre d'État, intenter toute action possessoire ou y défendre et faire tous actes conservatoires ou interruptifs de déchéance. Il peut, sans autre autorisation, interjeter appel de tout jugement et se pourvoir en cassation; mais il ne peut ni suivre sur son appel, ni suivre sur le pourvoi en cassation qu'en vertu d'une nouvelle autorisation.

Art. 97. — Aucune action judiciaire, autre que les actions possessoires et les oppositions au recouvrement de droits, produits et revenus de la commune, lesquelles sont régis par des règles spéciales, ne peut, à peine de nullité, être intentée contre une commune qu'autant que le demandeur a préalablement adressé à Notre Ministre d'État un mémoire exposant l'objet et les faits de sa réclamation.

Il lui en est donné récépissé.

L'action ne peut être portée devant les tribunaux que deux mois après la date du récépissé, sans préjudice des actes conservatoires.

La présentation du mémoire du demandeur interrompt toute prescription ou déchéance si elle est suivie d'une demande en justice dans le délai de trois mois.

TITRE V

Du régime électoral

ART. 98. — Nul ne peut, à peine de nullité de chacune des inscriptions, être porté sur plus d'une liste d'électeurs. Aucun électeur aux conseils municipaux ne peut, à peine de la même sanction, figurer sur une liste établie en vue des élections aux conseils de caïdat.

ART. 99. — Les élections aux conseil municipal ont lieu au scrutin de liste majoritaire à deux tours. Les listes de candidature peuvent comprendre un nombre de candidats égal ou inférieur au nombre de sièges à pourvoir. Nul n'est élu au premier tour s'il n'a réuni:

1° plus de la moitié des suffrages;

2° le nombre de suffrages égal au $1/4$ de celui des électeurs inscrits.

Au second tour de scrutin, qui a lieu à une semaine d'intervalle, l'élection a lieu à la majorité relative, quel que soit le nombre des votants. Si plusieurs candidats obtiennent le même nombre de suffrages, l'élection est acquise au bénéfice de l'âge.

Pour l'élection des membres du conseil municipal, la commune peut être divisée en sections électorales, dont chacune élit un nombre déterminé de conseillers. La division en sections électorales est fixée par arrêté résidentiel pour l'élection des conseillers français, et par arrêté de Notre Premier Ministre pour l'élection des conseillers tunisiens.

ART. 100. — Sont électeurs dans leur collège respectif, les Français des deux sexes et les Tunisiens de sexe masculin, âgés de 21 ans accomplis, jouissant de leurs droits civiques et politiques et remplissant l'une des deux conditions suivantes:

— avoir leur domicile réel dans la commune depuis deux ans au moins, ce délai n'étant pas exigé toutefois de toute personne dont la résidence est imposée du fait de ses fonctions;

— avoir acquitté pour la cinquième année consécutive à l'année de l'élection un impôt pour des biens situés ou pour une activité exercée sur le territoire de la commune.

Ne peuvent être inscrites sur les listes électorales les personnes qui ont été condamnées à une peine d'emprisonnement.

ART. 101. — Dans le cadre des dispositions du présent décret, les conditions d'application de l'article précédent sont fixées, pour les conseillers français par arrêté du Résident Général et pour les conseillers tunisiens par arrêté de Notre Premier Ministre.

Les dispositions relatives au contentieux de l'inscription sur les listes électorales et à celui des élections seront fixées, par décret, dans le cadre du présent texte.

TITRE VI
DES ORGANISMES COMMUNS À PLUSIEURS COMMUNES

ART. 102. — Deux ou plusieurs conseils peuvent provoquer entre eux, par l'entremise de leurs présidents et après en avoir averti Notre Ministre d'État, une entente sur les objets compris dans leurs attributions et qui intéressent à la fois leurs communes respectives.

Ils peuvent passer des conventions à l'effet d'entreprendre ou de conserver à frais communs des ouvrages ou des institutions d'utilité commune.

Les questions d'intérêt commun seront débattues dans des conférences où chaque conseil sera représenté par trois de ses membres.

Les décisions qui y seront prises ne seront exécutoires qu'après avoir été ratifiées par tous les conseils intéressés.

La mise en discussion de toutes questions autres que celles prévues au paragraphe 1er du présent article entraîne la dissolution de la conférence; la dissolution est prononcée par arrêté de Notre Ministre d'État.

ART. 103. — Lorsque les conseils de deux ou plusieurs communes ont fait connaître, par délibérations concordantes, leur volonté d'associer les communes qu'ils représentent en vue d'une œuvre d'une utilité commune et qu'ils ont décidé de consacrer à cette œuvre des ressources suffisantes, un décret autorise, s'il y a lieu, la création d'un syndicat.

Le décret désigne le président et les membres du syndicat, il en détermine le but et le mode de fonctionnement.

TITRE VII
DISPOSITIONS DIVERSES

ART. 104. — Sous réserve des dispositions transitoires ci-après, le présent décret remplace, pour l'avenir:

1° le décret du 14 janvier 1914 (16 safar 1332) sur l'organisation des communes, tel qu'il a été modifié ou complété par les textes subséquents;

2° le décret du 29 décembre 1934 (22 ramadan 1353) instituant les communes rurales, tel qu'il a été modifié ou complété par les textes subséquents.

ART. 105. — Dans les communes instituées en vertu du décret susvisé du 14 janvier 1914 (16 safar 1332), les dispositions du présent décret s'appliquent immédiatement, à l'exception de celles relatives à l'élection des corps municipaux.

La substitution, pour la formation des corps municipaux, du régime de l'élection à celui de la nomination, se fera par étapes progressives et devra être édictée pour chaque commune, par un décret particulier.

Jusqu'à l'intervention de ce décret particulier, les règles de formation des corps municipaux prescrites par le décret susvisé du 14 janvier 1914 (16 safar 1332) sont maintenues en vigueur.

Art. 106. — Dans les communes instituées en vertu du décret du 29 décembre 1934 (22 ramadan 1353), l'application totale ou partielle des dispositions du présent décret sera, pour chaque commune, édictée par un décret particulier.

Art. 107. — En ce qui concerne Notre capitale de Tunis, il n'est rien modifié aux dispositions des décrets du 22 février 1913 (16 rabia I 19313, fixant les attributions du Cheikh El-Médina et du 15 septembre 1945 (10 chaouat 1364) sur l'élection du conseil municipal de Tunis.

Les pouvoirs dévolus aux caïds par le présent décret seront pour Tunis exercés par Notre Ministre d'État.

Art. 108. — Sont également maintenues les dispositions législatives et réglementaires en vigueur concernant les attributions des communes en matière d'état civil et, notamment, le décret du 30 septembre 1929 (14 rabia II 1347).

Art. 109. — Les Présidents ont la franchise postale avec Nous, Notre Premier Ministre et les membres de Notre Gouvernement, le Secrétaire Général du Gouvernement Tunisien et le Trésorier Général de la Tunisie.

Les receveurs ont droit aux mêmes privilèges.

Art. 110. — Notre Premier Ministre, le Secrétaire Général du Gouvernement Tunisien, Notre Ministre d'État et le Directeur des Finances sont chargés de l'exécution du présent décret.

Notre Ministre d'État et le Directeur des Finances sont autorisés à pourvoir à cette exécution par voie d'arrêtés réglementaires.

Vu pour promulgation et mise à exécution:

Tunis, le 20 décembre 1952.

L'Ambassadeur de France
Résident Général
de la République Française à Tunis:
J. de Hauteclocque.

2. Morocco

(i) Proclamation by the Sultan of Morocco appealing for calm and warning the people of Morocco against communism, Rabat, 25 February 1951[1]

Louange à Dieu! Les derniers événements et leurs échos, tant à l'intérieur qu'à l'extérieur du pays, ont ému notre peuple fidèle et troublé sa sérénité. Pour dissiper toute inquiétude morale ainsi causée, apaiser l'opinion publique et chercher à éviter que la situation ne continue à se développer dans un sens préjudiciable à l'intérêt du pays, il a été jugé opportun de faire une déclaration qui rendra au peuple sa sérénité et lui confirmera ce qu'il a toujours constaté en nous: l'effort persévérant et l'action continue en sa faveur et pour le bien du pays, par les moyens que nous avons adoptés pour nous-mêmes, et qui s'appuient sur les prescriptions de notre religion et sur ce que réclame la responsabilité du souverain.

Le sentiment du père et la tendresse du bon pasteur poussent Notre Majesté, symbole de l'unité du pays, à assurer le relèvement de la nation et à la conduire à la place qui lui convient sur les plans scientifique, littéraire, social et économique. C'est en raison de ce sentiment paternel, de cette tendresse et des impératifs religieux que nous n'avons jamais cessé de nous placer au-dessus des partis et des organisations politiques, à l'écart de toutes les querelles partisanes.

Les conjonctures actuelles exigent de recommander à notre peuple de s'attacher à la morale de l'islam, à ses idéaux, à ses hautes traditions; de se parer constamment des qualités de pondération, de circonspection et de sagesse, et de suivre le droit chemin. Ainsi il pourra suivre l'exemple des nations mûres dans la voie du progrès, en harmonie avec l'esprit du siècle et l'évolution moderne.

L'islam est et ne cesse d'être hostile à l'animosité et à la violence. Il prêche les bonnes relations et recommande l'esprit de conciliation: c'est une religion de haute morale, de civilité et de tolérance. En florissant, ces prescriptions donnent naissance à l'amour, à la concorde et à la paix. Les mêmes conjonctures commandent également de mettre notre peuple en garde contre l'idéologie subversive du communisme, incompatible avec les principes de l'islam et les traditions de notre empire.

Le Maroc a franchi des étapes, dans le domaine notamment de l'évolution économique et sociale, grâce à l'action généreuse de la République française démocratique, dont la devise est: 'Liberté, Égalité, Fraternité'. Il est normal que de cette évolution naissent des problèmes dont la solution donne lieu à des divergences de vues. La meilleure voie

[1] *Le Monde*, 28 February 1951.

à adopter en ce cas est celle de la saine compréhension avec sagesse, bonne volonté et bonne foi, tout en suivant une politique de douceur.

Des relations franco-marocaines le Maroc attend l'avènement d'une ère nouvelle, et il est convaincu que l'amitié franco-marocaine assurera la réalisation de ses aspirations et de ses vœux. Lorsque les intentions sont pures et les volontés bonnes, que les buts ne sont entachés ni de passion ni d'égoïsme, et que les relations sont fondées sur le respect réciproque, il est plus facile de vaincre les difficultés et d'atteindre les nobles objectifs. Il revient à notre grand vizir de faire une déclaration en considération des circonstances actuelles. Salut!

(ii) Declaration by the Grand Vizier of Morocco condemning the methods of the Istiqlal Party, Rabat, 25 February 1951[1]

Louange à Dieu! Sa Majesté le sultan a honoré le peuple par une proclamation rappelant à chacun de ses sujets ses devoirs moraux: être modéré, éviter le recours à la violence. En conséquence nous nous engageons, suivant notre habitude, à agir loyalement selon les principes du souverain du pays, nous efforçant d'atteindre tout noble objectif en vue de l'essor de ce cher pays, dans le cadre des lois et des règlements, fruits d'une longue expérience et conformément aux saintes traditions impériales.

Nous affirmons que nous ne subissons dans l'exercice de nos fonctions aucune influence étrangère, et que nous ne sommes à la remorque d'aucun parti, quelle que soit son étiquette, et considérons une telle dépendance comme une atteinte à nos aptitudes et aux responsabilités qui nous sont confiées.

Nous vous convions à entretenir des relations de nature à consolider les rapports d'amitié entre l'Empire chérifien et la République française, et condamnons tout ce qui pourrait troubler le climat de cette amitié ou porter atteinte à la dignité des deux nations; de même que nous condamnons les méthodes d'un certain parti, méthodes qui, se fondant sur l'intimidation et la contrainte, aboutissent à l'obstruction politique et à la paralysie d'institutions vivantes et saines, et qui tendent à aggraver la division entre les habitants de ce pays.

(iii) Statement in the National Assembly by M. Schuman on the French Government's policy in Morocco, 22 November 1951[2]

En ce qui concerne le Maroc, je répondrai à M. Raymond-Laurent qu'il est exact que nous avons eu à nous défendre devant les Nations Unies contre une tentative d'ingérence dans les relations qui existent entre la France et le Maroc.

Aujourd'hui, je ne veux pas parler du débat qui s'est instauré devant cette

---

[1] *Le Monde*, 28 February 1951.   [2] *Journal Officiel, Débats*, 23 November 1951, pp. 8323–4.

organisation internationale, mais je crois utile de définir ici, devant vous, devant le Parlement français, ce qu'est la politique de la France à l'égard du Maroc et je ne pourrai mieux le faire qu'en citant un passage de la réponse qui a été faite par le Gouvernement français, le 31 octobre 1950, au mémoire de S.M. le sultan.

Voici cette réponse:

'Fidèle au traité et aux principes inscrits dans la Constitution de 1946, le Gouvernement constate que le Maroc est entré dans une nouvelle phase d'une évolution qui, suivant les propres expressions de S.M. le sultan, amènera le peuple marocain à s'administrer lui-même et à gérer démocratiquement ses propres affaires.

'Le Gouvernement tient à affirmer que tel est le principe qui régit sa politique. Il convient donc d'aménager les institutions en vue de cette étape de la coopération franco-marocaine dont le caractère essentiel consistera à accroître progressivement les responsabilités marocaines dans la gestion du pays.'

Cette politique se fonde donc et continuera de se fonder sur une entente réciproque, librement débattue et conclue, sans ingérence extérieure d'aucune sorte.

S.M. le sultan a, il y a quelques jours, exprimé publiquement sa confiance que la France tiendra ses promesses. Elle les tiendra conformément à son habitude et à une tradition plus que séculaire. Elle désire qu'aboutissent rapidement des réformes dont l'étude pourrait, d'après la proposition faite par le Gouvernement français, être confiée à une commission mixte franco-marocaine.

On oublie parfois, dans certains discours que nous avons entendus ces jours-ci, l'œuvre immense accomplie par la France au Maroc durant un demi-siècle de présence.

Cette œuvre et la conscience que nous avons de la mission accomplie justifient la confiance que la France place en une coopération franco-marocaine garantie par des institutions adaptées à la fois aux exigences démocratiques et aux légitimes aspirations de la nation marocaine.

Cette déclaration, je la fais au nom du Gouvernement parce qu'il est nécessaire que notre politique soit définie devant le Parlement français.

(iv) Explanatory memorandum adjoined to the request by thirteen Arab and Asian states for the inclusion of the question of Morocco in the agenda of the General Assembly,[1] 15 September 1952[2]

The methods adopted by France in bringing Morocco under her political subjugation were the same as were so successfully adopted earlier in

---

[1] A/2175, 8 September 1952. The thirteen states were Afghanistan, Burma, Egypt, India, Indonesia, 'Irāq, Lebanon, Pakistan, Persia, the Philippines, Saudi Arabia, Syria and Yemen.

[2] A/2175/Add. 1, 16 September 1952.

Algeria and Tunisia. The country was invaded to vindicate a trifling incident as a pretext to force on the unwilling and besieged Sultan of Morocco the Treaty of Fez on 20 March 1912 which gave France a foothold in Morocco. Earlier in 1906 the Act of Algeciras, to which thirteen nations were party, had reaffirmed Morocco's sovereign integrity and internal independence. The Treaty of Fez, therefore, coming so soon after the solemn assurances of a contrary nature, was the more flagrant. Although Moroccan sovereignty was ostensibly unassailed, means were used by the French administration to undermine the Sultan's internal administration, with the result that today a negligible minority of Frenchmen enjoy the benefits of the country in a grossly disproportionate manner.

The Moroccan Government, or the Makhzen, has been stripped of its powers and prerogatives and the authority of the Sultan reduced to a farce. The real power is exercised by the French Resident General, who controls the entire administration, the finances and the policing of the country. In 1950, France needed nearly 14,000 of her own policemen, apart from her army contingents, to maintain peace and order and the extraordinary number of policemen can only be rivalled by thrice that number of civil servants, also predominantly French, who fill the 'administrative honeycomb' of a comparatively small and poor country.

Before the advent of French rule, a recognized system of Islamic law obtained in meting out justice to all alike. Today, although the French colons enjoy the privilege of being tried under a separate code of laws based on the French system and more lenient and emancipated than the one applied even to their compatriots in their mother country, for the rest of the population there is no recognized, adequate or impartial system by which justice may be obtained. *Habeas corpus* is not known, a diversity of jurisdictions makes the exercise of justice a travesty. The executive and judicial powers of the officials are not separated, and the French *Contrôleur*, who is the public prosecutor, also controls the judges! It is therefore not unfair to claim that justice is dispensed arbitrarily and may be used as a political weapon. The budget for maintaining the French judiciary was 609 million francs, whereas the total expenditure on the maintenance of the entire Makhzen, including all the departments (Justice, Education, etc.) was only 350 million francs.

After forty years of progressive French administration 92 per cent. of the native population is illiterate. Child mortality is 283 per thousand, which is understandable when it is considered that in 1951 there were only 235 doctors for a population of nearly nine million people.

Perhaps the most injurious effects of the protectorate are seen in the economic backwardness of the native Moroccans, because the resources of the country are exploited almost exclusively by foreigners and mainly in the interests of France. Moroccan economy is subordinated to the economy of France, and Morocco is restrained from competing in world markets as 70 per cent. of Moroccan exports are diverted to the franc areas. The Moroccan franc has been artificially linked to the French franc and, as a consequence, all the evils of inflation have been attracted to Morocco in the wake of the economic instability of France. Agriculture is important in Morocco, where four-fifths of the population depend upon it for their livelihood. But of the 15 million hectares of arable land only a third is cultivated, and of this a fifth is held by the French colonists, who number a little over 4,000. This result has been achieved by systematic expropriation of land from native holders and its transfer on attractive terms to French colonists, who are induced to settle in Morocco by lavish technical and financial aid paid for from the Moroccan exchequer. Hence, the lot of the native farmer has deteriorated steadily and a dissatisfied rural proletariat numbering 1,500,000 has been created, with a low standard of living which is a potential danger to the well-being of the State. So far as the use to which the exiguous revenues of the State are put, it is significant to note that 80·2 per cent. of the revenues go towards defraying the cost of maintaining an army of French civil servants.

The occupation of Morocco by the French was not accepted uncontested, for during the twenty-two years from 1912–34 national insurrections against invaders constantly occurred but were put down with a firm and ruthless hand. The so-called reforms aim merely at decentralizing the government and placing the authority in local councils or 'djemas'. These Councils will be virtually composed of French nominees; the exercise of the vote by the native citizen will be denied him, while the French settler who possesses French nationality is to be allowed to vote and allotted 50 per cent. of the representation against his numerical strength of only 0·5 per cent. of the population.

As grave questions of principle are involved in these unfair 'democratic reforms', the Sultan of Morocco has not agreed to them. The aspirations of the people for freedom from foreign interference are wholeheartedly supported by the Sultan, as is evidenced by the two memoranda presented by him to the French Government in October 1950 and March 1952. He has received no answer to these, and despite his best endeavours to negotiate with the French Government on an equitable basis, the latter's intransigence has not resulted in any progress so far. The Sultan, in the second memorandum, has claimed the following prerogatives for his people:

1. The right to fundamental liberties (assembly, expression and travel, and the lifting of martial law in force since 1914);

2. The right to form a completely Moroccan Government having the

confidence of the people expressed through recognized democratic methods;

3. The right to negotiate the terms on which the relationship between France and Morocco shall be based, without an enforced discrimination against the interest of Morocco.

It will be recalled that, when the question of Morocco was raised in the last session of the General Assembly, it was not inscribed on the agenda after the French Foreign Minister had declared that negotiations between France and Morocco had never been interrupted. This statement was immediately contradicted by the Sultan in a speech dealing with his request that negotiations be commenced, when he said: 'We have been hoping for the opening of negotiations concerning this matter. We are still awaiting these negotiations while remaining firmly attached to our high ideals and fundamental principles.'

The so-called contemplated reforms, if foisted on Morocco, would establish the right of the French residents to a voice in the government of the country out of all proportion to their population; they would create labour unions with a fictitious representation, as 75 per cent. of Moroccan labour are farm workers and would be excluded by statute; they would legalize the private Council of the French Resident General, called the 'Council of Government', which has been instituted by a unilateral decree of the Resident General and is not recognized by the Sultan; they would revive local councils called 'djemas' which would be so composed as to be subservient to French dictates.

Meanwhile, the denial of human rights in Morocco continues in direct opposition to the principles and obligations embodied in the United Nations Charter. In the face of the rising tide of nationalism in Africa, continued denial of human rights and continued disrespect for the principle of self-determination cannot but constitute a mounting threat to the peace. It is to eliminate this threat and to ensure the basic political and social rights of the Moroccan people that the Moroccan question is brought before the Assembly.

(v) COMMUNIQUÉ ISSUED BY THE SULTAN OF MOROCCO REVIEWING THE COURSE OF FRANCO-MOROCCAN NEGOTIATIONS FROM OCTOBER 1950, 8 OCTOBER 1952[1]

Being responsible for the destiny of this country, as its Sovereign, and being bound by Our obligations to the Nation to watch over its rights and interests and to work for the accomplishment of its legitimate aspirations, We believe it Our duty to give an account at this juncture of the

[1] A/2175/Add. 2, 16 October 1952.

steps which We have taken to these ends, in obedience to the following considerations:

The degree of progress achieved by the Moroccan people in various spheres.

The world-wide changes brought about by the last war, which was waged to secure the triumph of the principles of justice and democratic freedom and the firm establishment of individual and collective rights, and which has resulted in an awakening of national consciousness of constantly broadening scope.

The ardent desire of Our people to enjoy its rights and freedoms, a desire all the more legitimate in that the Moroccan people took an active part in the war at the side of France and its Allies and voluntarily placed its men and resources at their disposal.

The essential purpose of Our journey to Paris in 1950 was to present to the Government of the French Republic a memorandum (30 Hidja 1369—3 October 1950) in which We stated that the Moroccan problem was no longer a question of piecemeal reform within the framework of the present system, but rather the problem of a people desirous of a new system corresponding to its aspirations and adapted to the changed international situation.

In reply to that memorandum (31 October 1950), the Government of the French Republic expressed the view that any modification of the established regime would be premature, and went no further than to propose piecemeal reforms within the framework of the Protectorate Treaty.

In view of the divergence between Our views and those of the French Government, the gravity of the political crisis, which seemed likely to endanger Franco-Moroccan relations, and the absence of the negotiations the initiation of which We so earnestly desired, We submitted to the Government of the French Republic another memorandum (14 March 1952) in which We reiterated, in the light of experience, that the wisest solution of the Moroccan problem lay in a re-definition of Franco-Moroccan relations guaranteeing to Morocco its sovereignty and to the French their legitimate interests, within a framework of fruitful economic, cultural and international co-operation between Morocco and France, due provision being made for protection of the interests of the other foreign minorites. With a view to the achievement of this objective, We proposed:

The improvement of the political atmosphere;

The granting of private and public freedoms, and particularly of trade union rights;

The constitution of a provisional Moroccan government with instructions in Our name and under Our authority to negotiate with the Government of the French Republic the terms of a new Franco-Moroccan treaty.

Our proposals aim at the attainment of the ideal objective of enabling the Moroccan people to administer the affairs of the country through a representative parliament and a constitutional government, in accordance with modern democratic processes, it being recognized that the institution of such a regime is not incompatible with the continuance of co-operation, between France and Morocco.

On 17 September 1952, the French Government transmitted to Us through the intermediary of General Guillaume, Resident Commissioner-General of France in Morocco, its reply to Our last memorandum.

After enumerating, in the first part of its reply, all the achievements of the Protectorate in Morocco in various spheres, including public education, health, economic development and industrial production, the French Government set forth, in the second part, a plan of reforms the main lines of which are as follows:

Institution of elective administrative Djemas[1] in rural districts;

Establishment of mixed municipal commissions in the towns and of Franco-Moroccan commissions in the rural centres, a measure which would give French residents in Morocco the right to secure representation in these assemblies by election and to exercise deliberative functions in them on the same terms as Moroccan nationals.

In regard to the executive authority, the French note mentions the existence of the Council of Viziers and Directors established in 1947 and suggests that the Secretary-General of the Protectorate should be placed under the Grand Vizier to assist him in discharging his functions as Head of the Administration.

The reply also asserted that the administration in Morocco is mixed, i.e. Franco-Moroccan under the supervision of the French authorities.

With regard to the organization of the judiciary, the French Government promises to submit to Us in the near future draft legislation on that subject.

It should be noted that the reform plan that the French Government has submitted to Us contains no new elements.

The Dahir concerning administrative Djemas was promulgated in June 1951 and steps have already been taken to carry it into effect.

The plan for municipal reform was first studied by a makhzen [government] commission on 8 May 1948. On 26 June 1951 it was submitted to the Council of Viziers which rejected it on the grounds that it was calculated to infringe Moroccan sovereignty, the integrity of which has been guaranteed by international treaties.

Plans for the reorganization of the judiciary were submitted by the Resident-General in 1947. They were studied by a makhzen technical commission which made a number of recommendations, most of which were not adopted by the administration.

[1] Local councils.

The French reply did not mention the proposals that We had made in Our memorandum of 14 March 1952 concerning the constitution of a Moroccan government, the improvement of the political atmosphere and the granting of certain essential liberties which Our subjects do not enjoy, such as freedom of trade union organization.

In short, the French Government reiterated its determination to maintain the Protectorate Treaty in force, and presented to us a plan of reforms which were stated to be inseparable and based on an over-all view, so that they formed a whole and could not be dealt with in isolation.

Lastly, the French Government stated that it was willing, once the principle and general tendency of the reforms were accepted, to proclaim in a solemn instrument the principles of a friendly association and interdependence of interests and responsibilities which would serve as the basis for the future relations between Morocco and France, without prejudice to the purposes and the specific powers defined in the Treaty of Fez.

In a reply sent to the French Government on 3 October 1952 We expressed Our deep regret that it had not seen fit to accept Our proposals.

We also drew attention to the fact that by their spirit and their content alike, the practical effect of the reform proposals submitted to Us would be a partition of Moroccan sovereignty.

(vi) RESOLUTION EXPRESSING CONFIDENCE IN THE FRENCH GOVERNMENT'S POLICIES IN MOROCCO AND CALLING FOR RENEWED NEGOTIATIONS FOR THE SETTLEMENT OF DISPUTES, ADOPTED BY THE GENERAL ASSEMBLY ON 19 DECEMBER 1952[1]

THE GENERAL ASSEMBLY

Having debated the 'Question of Morocco', as proposed by thirteen Member States in document A/2175,

Mindful of the necessity of developing friendly relations among the nations based on respect for the principle of equal rights and self-determination of peoples,

Considering that the United Nations, as a centre for harmonizing the actions of nations in the attainment of their common ends under the Charter, should strive towards removing any causes or factors of misunderstanding among Member States, thus reasserting the general principles of co-operation in the maintenance of international peace and security,

1. *Expresses the confidence* that, in pursuance of its proclaimed policies, the Government of France will endeavour to further the fundamental liberties of the people of Morocco, in conformity with the Purposes and Principles of the Charter;

2. *Expresses the hope* that the parties will continue negotiations on an

[1] *General Assembly, Seventh Session, Supplement No. 20, Resolutions*, 612 (VII), p. 5.

urgent basis towards developing the free political institutions of the people of Morocco, with due regard to legitimate rights and interests under the established norms and practices of the law of nations;

3. *Appeals* to the parties to conduct their relations in an atmosphere of goodwill, mutual confidence and respect and to settle their disputes in accordance with the spirit of the Charter, thus refraining from any acts or measures likely to aggravate the present tension.

407th plenary meeting
19 December 1952.

PART V

THE FAR EAST

A. KOREAN NEGOTIATIONS

1. At Panmunjom

(i) Proposals for the repatriation of prisoners of war submitted by the United Nations Command on 2 January 1952[1]

1. POWs who elect repatriation shall be exchanged on a one-for-one basis until one side has exchanged all such POWs held by it.

2. The side which thereafter holds POWs shall repatriate all those POWs who elect to be repatriated in a one-for-one exchange for foreign civilians interned by the other side, and for civilians and other persons of the one side who are at the time of the signing of the armistice in the territory under control of the other side, and who elect to be repatriated. POWs thus exchanged shall be paroled to the opposing force, such parole to carry with it the condition that the individual shall not again bear arms against the side releasing him.

3. All POWs not electing repatriation shall be released from POW status and shall be paroled, such parole to carry with it the condition that the individual will not again bear arms in the Korean conflict.

4. All remaining civilians of either side who are, at the time of the signing of the armistice, in territory under control of the other side, shall be repatriated if they so elect.

5. In order to insure that the choice regarding repatriation is made without duress, delegates of the ICRC[2] shall be permitted to interview all POWs at the points of exchange, and all civilians of either side who are at the time of the signing of the armistice in territory under the control of the other side.

6. For the purposes of paragraphs 2, 4 and 5, civilians and other persons of either side are defined as those who on 25 June 1950 were bona-fide residents of either ROK or the DPRK.[3]

(ii) Communist proposals regarding the convening of a political conference, 16 February 1952[4]

In order to reach speedily a fair and reasonable settlement on agenda item five, recommendations to the governments of the countries concerned

---

[1] *Department of State Bulletin*, 21 January 1952, p. 106.
[2] International Committee of the Red Cross.
[3] Republic of Korea and Democratic People's Republic of Korea.
[4] S/2619, 29 April 1952.

on both sides, our side, the delegation of the Korean Peoples Army and the Chinese Peoples Volunteers, now submits a revised draft of the principle.

The revised draft of the principle proposed by the delegation of the Korean Peoples Army and the Chinese Peoples Volunteers on agenda item five, recommendations to the governments of the countries concerned on both sides, is as follows:

In order to ensure the peaceful settlement of the Korean question, the military commanders of both sides hereby recommend to the governments of the countries concerned on both sides that, within three months after the armistice agreement is signed and becomes effective, a political conference of a higher level of both sides be held by representatives appointed respectively to settle through negotiation the questions of the withdrawal of all foreign forces from Korea, the peaceful settlement of the Korean question, et cetera.

(iii) UNITED NATIONS COMMAND ACCEPTANCE OF THE COMMUNIST PRO-POSALS OF 16 FEBRUARY, 17 FEBRUARY 1952[1]

We have carefully considered your revision of the principle proposed by you as the solution of item five of the agenda. In order to give you concrete evidence of the sincerity of the United Nations Command delegation and to eliminate entirely any pretexts for further delay on your part in reaching agreement on unresolved issues in items three and four, the United Nations Command delegation accepts your proposal of 16 February as the solution of this item of the agenda, subject to the following remarks:

So that there may be no question regarding the understanding of the United Nations Command delegation as to the meaning of your proposal, we deem it advisable to make certain explanations at this time. First, we desire to point out that this recommendation will be made by the Commander in Chief, United Nations Command, to the United Nations as well as to the Republic of Korea. Second, in accepting the term Foreign Forces, we are doing so in the basis for your statement that this term means non-Korean Forces. And third, we wish it clearly understood that we do not construe the word et cetera to relate to matters outside of Korea.

(iv) STATEMENT BY THE SENIOR UNITED NATIONS COMMAND DELEGATE, VICE-ADMIRAL CHARLES TURNER JOY, PRESENTING THE UNITED NATIONS PROPOSALS FOR A SOLUTION OF THE OUTSTANDING QUESTIONS IN THE ARMIS-TICE NEGOTIATIONS, 28 APRIL 1952[2]

For more than nine months our two delegations have been negotiating for an armistice which will bring a cessation to hostilities in Korea. We

[1] S/2619.   [2] S/2715, 21 July 1952.

have progressed to the point where only three issues remain between us and final agreement on an armistice. These three issues concern, first, whether there will or will not be restrictions on the rehabilitation and construction of military airfields; second, the basis of exchange of Prisoners of War; and third, the nations to compose the Neutral Nations Supervisory Commission.

As for the first issue, for many weeks the United Nations Command Delegation has stated that in order to maintain the stability of the armistice and prevent the creation of tension that might lead to a resumption of hostilities it is highly desirable that restrictions be placed on the rehabilitation and construction of military airfields. Your side has opposed this limitation on what would be a manifest increase of offensive potentiality upon the ground that it would constitute interference by one side in the internal affairs of the other. Yet, if your side is moving in good faith toward an armistice, you should have no hesitation in agreeing not to build up your military air potential.

As for the second issue I have referred to, for many weeks the United Nations Command Delegation has stated that all Prisoners of War must be released but that only those should be repatriated or turned over to the other side who can be delivered without the application of force. Your side has opposed this principle and has, instead, insisted that certain Prisoners of War must be repatriated even if physical force is necessary, asserting that to accord respect to the feelings of the individual prisoner is unprecedented and deprives a Prisoner of War of his rights. Your current attitude on this question is inconsistent with the historical facts that during the Korean War your side has followed the practice of inducting captured personnel into your armed forces, and that you have in this and other ways disposed of approximately four-fifths of the military personnel of our side who fell into your custody.

The United Nations Command holds as Prisoners of War 116,000 North Koreans and Chinese People's Volunteers; 59,000, or more than fifty percent of this number held by our side, will return to your side without being forced. In addition, some 11,000 citizens of the Republic of Korea, now in our custody, have elected to go to your side under the principle of free choice. This is in marked contrast to the 12,000 captured personnel of our side whom you have stated you will repatriate, a figure which is less than twenty percent of those you have admitted having taken into your custody.

The foregoing figures are now a basic factor in the Prisoner of War question. It was with the full concurrence of your side that the Prisoners of War in our custody were screened to determine their attitude as regards repatriation. Once screened, Prisoners of War had to be segregated in accordance with their individual determination. No action can now be taken by either side to alter materially this situation. It is an accomplished fact. For you to pretend otherwise would be completely unrealistic.

Moreover, our side has indicated our willingness to send to your side any Prisoners of War who may change their views on repatriation between the time of the initial determination and the completion of the exchange of Prisoners of War. We have also informed you that, if you wish, you may verify the results of our screening processes after the armistice is signed. Your side can at that time interview those persons held by the United Nations Command who have indicated that they would violently oppose being returned to your side. If any indicate that they are not still so opposed, the United Nations Command will return them promptly to your side.

Lastly, in regard to the third issue, although both sides agreed to nominate mutually acceptable nations to compose the Neutral Nations Supervisory Commission you have continued to insist on membership for a nation which the United Nations Command will not accept.

The issues are clearly drawn. The discussions of the past several months have clearly defined the differences on the issues, but such discussions have failed to develop any common meeting ground for resolving these differences. Within the limit of these discussions each side has indicated that its position is firm and unshakeable. We believe that because of the strong views already set forth by both sides in the respective meetings, we will only prolong the stalemate on each of the three differences if we attempt to discuss them further or to settle them separately. Therefore, we believe it absolutely essential that the three remaining issues be settled together. It is evident that if both sides remain adamant in their present position on the three issues, these negotiations will be deadlocked indefinitely. If an armistice agreement is to result from our efforts here, if we are to bring about the long-awaited cessation of hostilities in Korea, if we are to build the bridge which is to lead to a solution of the Korean problem, the three issues must be resolved at the earliest practicable date. There are two ways to accomplish this objective: either one side could concede on all issues, or each side could concede to the position taken by the other side on some of the remaining issues. The only alternative to the foregoing is for these delegations to admit that they have failed to accomplish their mission.

I state categorically that the United Nations Command will not accede to your demands on all matters at issue. I assume that you would make a similar statement on behalf of your delegation. It is clear, then, that unless you are willing to accept the entire responsibility for the failure of these negotiations, you must join us in seeking a compromise solution which both sides may accept in the interest of reaching an early agreement on an armistice.

The United Nations Command has carefully reviewed the positions taken by both sides on the three issues. It remains our conviction that the stability of an armistice would be increased by restricting rehabilitation and construction of military airfields. We are fully aware that you consider that any such restriction constitutes interference in your internal affairs. We utterly disagree with your contention in this regard, since this is a military armistice, designed to freeze the military situation in *status quo* pending a final peaceful settlement. However, in the interest of reaching an early armistice agreement, we are willing to accede to your stand that no restriction be placed on the rehabilitation and construction of airfields.

I must make it absolutely clear, however, that our acceptance of your position regarding airfields is contingent upon your acceptance of our positions regarding Prisoners of War and the composition of the Neutral Nations Supervisory Commission. As you know, our position regarding Prisoners of War is the exchange of 12,100 Prisoners of War of our side for approximately 70,000 of your side. You also know that our position regarding the Neutral Nations Supervisory Commission is that this Commission shall be composed of representatives from the four neutral nations which are acceptable to both sides.

The United Nations Command Delegation submits a draft wording for the entire armistice agreement. This draft wording incorporates all the agreements hitherto reached on agenda items 2, 3, 4, and 5. It omits any restriction on the rehabilitation and construction of military airfields. It provides a specific agreement on the nations composing the Neutral Nations Supervisory Commission. Lastly, it provides a practical and realistic basis for the exchange of Prisoners of War.

We formally propose that this draft armistice wording be approved *in toto* by our delegations and that the liaison officers be directed to prepare the formal armistice agreement documents for signature by our respective commands. Our liaison officers will be prepared to discuss details concerning minor changes in wording and necessary administrative matters.

The United Nations Command has now made its final offer in an effort to reach an armistice. The United Nations Command Delegation desires to make it unmistakably clear to you that we will not agree to any substantive change in this proposal, and that we are absolutely firm that this proposal must be considered as a whole. The fate of this armistice conference, and future peace in Korea, now rest fully and exclusively with you.

(v) FURTHER PROPOSALS FOR THE REPATRIATION OF PRISONERS OF WAR PRESENTED BY THE SENIOR UNITED NATIONS DELEGATE, GENERAL WILLIAM HARRISON, 28 SEPTEMBER 1952[1]

A. Proposal Number One:

As soon as the armistice agreement goes into effect all prisoners of war

[1] *Department of State Bulletin*, 6 October 1952, pp. 549–50.

in the custody of each side shall be entitled to release and repatriation. Such release and repatriation of prisoners of war shall begin in accordance with the provisions of article three of the armistice agreement. Both sides agree that the obligation to exchange and repatriate prisoners of war shall be fulfilled by having them brought to an agreed exchange point in the demilitarized zone. The prisoner of war shall be identified and his name checked against the agreed list of prisoners of war in the presence, if desired, of one or a combination of the International Committee of the Red Cross, joint Red Cross teams, or joint military teams. The prisoner of war shall thereupon be considered as fully repatriated for the purposes of the agreement. Both sides agree, however, that any prisoner of war who at time of identification states that he wishes to return to the side by which he had been detained shall immediately be allowed to do so.

Such former prisoner of war shall thereupon go into the custody of the side to which he wishes to go, which side shall provide him with transportation from the demilitarized zone to territory under its control in Korea. Such individual, of course, shall not be detained as a prisoner of war but shall assume civilian status, and, in accordance with paragraph 52 of the armistice agreement, shall not again be employed in acts of war in the Korean conflict.

B. Proposal Number Two:

As soon as the armistice agreement goes into effect all prisoners of war who desire repatriation will be exchanged expeditiously. All prisoners objecting to repatriation will be delivered to the demilitarized zone in small groups where, at a mutually agreeable location, they will be freed from military control of both sides and interviewed by representatives of a mutually agreed country or countries whose forces are not participating in the Korean hostilities, such persons being free to go to the side of their choice as indicated by such interview. The foregoing procedure will be accomplished, if desired, with or without military representation from each side and under the observation of one or a combination of the following:

1. International Committee of the Red Cross
2. Joint Red Cross teams
3. Joint military teams

C. Proposal Number Three:

As soon as the armistice is signed and becomes effective, all prisoners· of war who desire repatriation will be exchanged expeditiously. Concurrently, if logistical capability permits, or as soon as possible thereafter, those prisoners of war who have previously expressed their objections to repatriation will be delivered in groups of appropriate size to a mutually agreed upon location in the demilitarized zone and there freed from the military control of both sides. Without questioning, interview, or screening, each individual so released will be free to go to the side of his choice. We will agree, if desired, to have this movement and disposition of non-repatriates accomplished under the observation of one or a combination of the International Committee of the Red Cross, joint teams of military observers, or Red Cross representatives from both sides.

(vi) LETTER TO THE COMMANDER-IN-CHIEF, UNITED NATIONS COMMAND, GENERAL MARK CLARK, FROM THE COMMUNIST COMMANDERS, GENERALS KIM IL SUNG AND PENG TEH-HUAI, REGARDING THE REPATRIATION OF PRISONERS OF WAR, 16 OCTOBER 1952[1]

When the people throughout the world including the people of the United States of America were eagerly awaiting the realization of peace in Korea, when a complete agreement was nearly reached in the Korean armistice negotiation, your delegation, in disregard of the proposal put forth by our delegation, suddenly declared unilaterally an indefinite recess on 8 October 1952, refused to negotiate and broke up the negotiations. This unreasonable action is in itself sufficient to prove that your side has no sincerity at all for an armistice in Korea, and that your side should bear the total responsibility for the disruption of the armistice negotiations.

The Korean armistice negotiations have gone on for fifteen months. During these fifteen months, your side has made various unreasonable demands, including that of drawing the military demarcation line between both sides deep in the area of our side, dispatching military personnel to conduct ground and air inspection in our rear following the armistice, interfering in the construction of air fields by our side, and other unreasonable demands. In the meantime, your side incessantly violated the agreement of neutrality in the conference site area and resorted to the so-called military pressure outside of the conference, even resorting to the bombing of peaceful inhabitants and peaceful towns and villages with germ bombs, napalm and poison gas bombs, in an attempt thereby to force our side into submission. But what your side has not been able to gain on the battlefield is likewise never to be gained by your side in the conference. These unreasonable actions and attempts of your side have failed and will continue to fail. On the other hand, our side had, during these fifteen months, maintained the principle of fairness and reasonableness with great effort and patience so that the draft armistice agreement of sixty-three paragraphs including the nine agreed paragraphs pertaining to the arrangements relating to prisoners of war was finally completed in the armistice negotiations. Had there not been the

[1] *Department of State Bulletin*, 10 November 1952, pp. 752–4.

deliberate obstruction by your side to the settlement of the question of prisoners of war, the Korean armistice should certainly have been realized long ago, peace should certainly have been restored long ago in South Korea and North Korea, and the prisoners of war of both sides should certainly have returned home long ago to lead a peaceful life.

The proposition held by your side on the question of prisoners of war is that of the so-called 'no forced repatriation'. But this proposition is devoid of any basis either in law or in facts; it is a pretext fabricated by your side purely for the purpose of delaying and disrupting the negotiations. As everybody knows, prisoners captured in war are totally different from political refugees. Therefore, it is especially stipulated in article 118 of the 1949 Geneva Convention relating to the treatment of prisoners of war that 'prisoners of war shall be released and repatriated without delay after the cessation of active hostilities'; it is further laid down in article 7 that 'prisoners of war may in no circumstances renounce in part or in entirety the rights secured to them by the present Convention'. These stipulations are obviously designed to prevent either belligerent from taking the inhuman action following the armistice of retaining prisoners of war by force and refusing to repatriate them home under the pretext of the so-called principle of voluntary wishes. Actually, in past international wars, prisoners of war of both belligerents were always repatriated in toto after the cessation of hostilities. That is why your delegation could not but agree to the following provisions in the draft armistice agreements: 'All prisoners of war held in the custody of each side at the time this armistice agreement becomes effective shall be released and repatriated as soon as possible' (paragraph 51), 'within this time limit (referring to the time limit of two months after the armistice agreement becomes effective) each side undertakes to complete the repatriation of all of the prisoners of war in its custody at the earliest practicable time' (paragraph 54).

In fact of international practice, the stipulations of the Geneva Convention, and the paragraphs already agreed upon by both sides in the draft Korean armistice agreement, your side has already no reason whatsoever to oppose the principle that prisoners of war of both sides shall be repatriated in toto. Yet your side dogmatically asserts that there are captured personnel of our side who indicate that they are unwilling to rejoin their beloved ones to lead a peaceful life and, on the contrary, wish to remain as refugees and cannon fodder under the dark tyranny of their enemy, notorious to the whole world, to which they have also been opposed. This is utterly against commonsense of human beings and is therefore wholly incredible. In order to expose the falsity of your assertion, it is sufficient to cite the facts that to date, in the prisoner of war camps of your side, day after day, our captured personnel are still being slaughtered, persecuted, tattooed and forced to make finger-printing and they are protesting against these atrocities. The message addressed by your Brigadier General Colson to our captured personnel is a definite proof of these facts.

When the classification of the war prisoners was being discussed, in view of the fact that your side had raised the matter of there being Korean prisoners of war of both sides whose homes were in the area of the detaining side, our side proposed to recheck the name lists in accordance with the principles of classification according to nationality and area, that is, armed personnel of foreign nationality captured by either side, i.e., captured personnel of the United Nations Forces or of the Chinese People's Volunteers, shall all be repatriated home; of the Korean armed personnel captured by either side, i.e. of the captured personnel of the South Korean Army of the Korean People's Army, those whose homes are in the area of the side to which they belong shall all be repatriated home, while the others whose homes are in the area of the detaining side may be permitted to return home directly without having to be repatriated. It is also stipulated in the draft Korean armistice agreement that 'the release and repatriation of such prisoners of war shall be effected in conformity with lists which have been exchanged and have been checked by the respective sides prior to the signing of this armistice agreement' (paragraph 51) and that 'each side insures that it will not employ in acts of war in the Korean conflict any prisoner of war released and repatriated incident to the coming into effect of this armistice agreement' (paragraph 52).

However, when the name lists were actually checked, your side on both occasions did not follow the principle of classification proposed by our side, but applied to the prisoners of war the so-called principle of screening, which is in actuality forcible retention, in total violation of the provisions of the Geneva Convention and the draft armistice agreement concerning the total repatriation of war prisoners and the assurance that they will return home to lead a peaceful life. Therefore, no ground whatsoever can be found either for your so-called principle of voluntary wishes or for your so-called principle of screening in international practice or the Geneva Convention, or even in the draft armistice agreement agreed upon by both sides; in contradistinction, the proposition firmly maintained by our side that prisoners of war of both sides shall all be repatriated home is a principle recognized by the whole world. It is solely due to the obstinate insistence of your side upon its unreasonable proposition that the only remaining question in the Korean armistice negotiations, that is, the question of repatriation of war prisoners, had dragged on for five months since May this year and has been prevented from attaining any settlement.

Recently, because the people throughout the world, and firstly the people of Asia and the Pacific area, have become increasingly impatient with the delay of the Korean armistice negotiations, because even the American people have come to consider the war of intervention against Korea a 'damned war', and because the meeting of the General Assembly of the United Nations and the United States presidential Election have approached, your delegation on 28 September spuriously put forth three proposals for the repatriation of war prisoners in an attempt to hoodwink the people of the world with the words of the so-called 'total repatriation', but in substance, these proposals are still run through by your unreasonable demand of the so-called 'no forced repatriation' which is in fact forcible retention of war prisoners. In the meantime, your side audaciously and unilaterally disposed of our captured personnel without waiting for the conclusion of an agreement on the question of repatriation of war prisoners. It can be seen from this that you are not even prepared to carry out your own proposals.

Yet on our part, in order to hold firmly to our stand for a peaceful settlement of the Korean question and to meet the eager desire of the world people for an armistice in Korea, we still adopted certain reasonable factors from your proposals in spite of the fact that the principle underlying your three proposals was wholly unacceptable, and on 8 October we put forth our new proposal.

On the basis of the just demand that war prisoners of both sides shall all be repatriated home to lead a peaceful life, our side proposed that when the armistice agreement becomes effective, all war prisoners may be brought to the agreed exchange point in the demilitarized zone as soon as your side has proposed, to be delivered to and received by the other side. After they are delivered and received, the Joint Red Cross Teams will visit the war prisoners of both sides in accordance with paragraph 57 of the draft Korean Armistice Agreement as your side has proposed, to explain to them that they are insured to return home to lead a peaceful life and not to participate again in hostilities in Korea. Thereafter considered classification of the war prisoners will be carried out in accordance with the above-mentioned principle of classification according to nationality and area as proposed by our side. Repatriation will be carried out immediately after the classification; these tasks of exchange, visit, classification and repatriation may be accomplished under the observation of Neutral Nations Inspection Teams.

The above-mentioned proposal of ours is in full accord with the provisions of the Geneva Convention and the draft Korean Armistice Agreement. At the plenary conference of the delegations on 8 October, your delegation not only ignored this reasonable proposal of ours and refused to conduct discussion, but immediately read a statement prepared beforehand and unilaterally declared an indefinite recess; furthermore, your delegation left the conference in the middle without waiting for our reply and categorically broke off the Korean armistice negotiations in which the people of the whole world are concerned. This unreasonable action of disrupting the negotiations taken by your side is obviously premeditated. Your side possibly attempts thereby to press the General Assembly of the United Nations to endorse your plot to violate international conventions, to disrupt the armistice negotiations and to extend the war. But it can be definitely said that the peace-loving people all over the world absolutely will not permit your plot to win through.

The situation is already very clear, but we are still willing to make our greatest effort to promote an armistice in Korea. We hereby put forth to you the following requests:

1. That the unreasonable action of breaking off the armistice negotiations taken by your delegation be stopped immediately.

2. That total repatriations of war prisoners must be carried out in accordance with international practice, of the 1949 Geneva Convention and with the already agreed draft Korean Armistice Agreement. The method and the procedure of its concrete implementation can be settled through consultation in the negotiations.

3. That an armistice in Korea be realized speedily on the basis of the draft Korean Armistice Agreement.

If your side still has the slightest sincerity for an armistice in Korea and a peaceful settlement of the Korean question, you should give an affirmative reply to the above-mentioned reasonable request by our side. The peace-loving people and nations all over the world are focusing their attention on this action of your side.

(vii) REPLY FROM GENERAL CLARK TO GENERALS KIM AND PENG, 20 OCTOBER 1952[1]

Your letter of 16 October 1952 has been received. I regret that you have seen fit to use this means to repeat completely false and unfounded charges and to indulge generally in a pointless harangue. I have no intention of replying in kind.

For fifteen months the United Nations Command, acting in good faith, has made an honest effort to negotiate an armistice that is fair and reasonable to both sides. A great deal of progress has been achieved and the people of the world have looked with hope for an armistice which would end the bloodshed in Korea. This hope could have become a reality many months ago had your side exhibited similar good faith and been willing to accept the humane principle of not forcing prisoners who feared for their lives to be returned to you against their will.

[1] *Department of State Bulletin*, 10 November 1952, p. 754.

The United Nations Command Senior Delegate presented to your delegation three additional proposals on 28 September 1952, any one of which could have led to a fair and just armistice. Your side summarily rejected these reasonable proposals without offering any constructive counterproposal which would recognize the individual's right of self-determination. One of the proposals offered by the United Nations Command provided for the release of those prisoners of war who had previously expressed their objections to repatriation by their delivery in groups of appropriate size to a mutually agreed-upon location in the demilitarized zone to be there freed from the military control of both sides. This proposal further provided that without questioning, interview or screening, each individual so released would be free to go to the side of his choice, and that, if desired, this movement and disposition of non-repatriates would be accomplished under the observation of one or a combination of the International Committee of the Red Cross, joint teams of military observers, or Red Cross representatives from both sides. This procedure parallels in principle the action which your side claims it took in releasing some 50,000 unaccounted for United Nations Command personnel admittedly captured by your side and allegedly 'released at the front'. The fact that your side claims to have previously followed such a practice makes your present position in refusing to accept the United Nations Command proposal completely inconsistent and clearly exposes the fraudulent nature of your charge that the United Nations Command desires to forcibly retain any prisoners. Each of our proposals submitted on 28 September refutes this false charge. Each abounds with absolute safeguards which would preclude any possibility of coercion by either side.

Your delegation, by refusing to accept any obviously fair and just proposals offered by the United Nations Command, has created grave doubt in the minds of people everywhere concerning the sincerity of your expressed desire for an end to the bloodshed in Korea.

The United Nations Command Senior Delegate made it completely clear in his statement at the 8 October session and in his letter of 16 October that the United Nations Command delegation was not terminating the negotiations but stood ready to meet with your delegation at any time it is ready to accept any one of the United Nations Command proposals or to submit in writing a constructive proposal which would meet the reasonable requirements of the United Nations Command. The United Nations Command did not break off negotiations as you falsely charge and the United Nations Command delegation is ready and willing to meet with your delegation as soon as you indicate willingness to negotiate in good faith on the basis indicated by the United Nations Command delegation in the plenary session of 8 October 1952.

I consider that your letter of 16 October 1952 contains nothing new nor constructive. Although for your own devious reasons you have sought to embellish your so-called new proposal with tinsel trimmings, claiming that you have adopted 'certain reasonable factors' from our proposals, in fact, your so-called proposal bears not the slightest resemblance to the United Nations Command proposals of 28 September. The underlying nature of your proposal is clearly revealed in your demand that 'all war prisoners . . . be delivered to and received by' your side. This is nothing more than a demand that the United Nations Command turn over to your custody by force thousands of prisoners of war who have stated positively that they would violently resist repatriation to your side. You further glibly propose that after the United Nations Command has forced unwilling prisoners into your hands you would then carry out a classification according to nationality and area of residence and repatriate prisoners in accordance with this classification. As far back as July you proposed such a classification, knowing full well that irrespective of nationality many prisoners were determined not to go back to your side. The United Nations Command exposed the falseness of this device of yours months ago. Thus, when all is said and done your so-called new proposal is nothing more than the same old package containing your time-worn demand that the United Nations Command drive unwilling prisoners back to your custody. It should be clear to you by now that the United Nations Command will never agree to nor negotiate further on the basis of any proposal that would require the United Nations Command to use force to repatriate prisoners to your side. Accordingly, the United Nations Command considers that your letter of 16 October 1952 does not constitute a valid basis for resumption of delegation meetings.

2. In the United Nations

(i) Draft resolution on a Korean armistice submitted by 21 nations to the Political Committee of the General Assembly on 24 October 1952[1]

The General Assembly,

1. *Having received* the special report of the Unified Command of 18 October 1952 on the status of military action and the armistice negotiations in Korea,

---

[1] A/C. 1/725: *General Assembly, Seventh Session, Annexes, Agenda item 16*, p. 29. The sponsoring nations were Australia, Belgium, Canada, Colombia, Denmark, Ethiopia, France, Greece, Honduras, Iceland, Luxembourg, the Netherlands, New Zealand, Nicaragua, Norway, the Philippines, Siam, Turkey, the United Kingdom, the U.S.A. and Uruguay. It was agreed on 2 December that further consideration of this resolution should be deferred until the President of the General Assembly had made his report in accordance with the Indian resolution adopted by the Committee: see below, p. 446.

2. *Noting* with approval the efforts of the United Nations negotiators to achieve a just and honourable armistice to bring an end to the fighting in Korea in accordance with United Nations principles,

3. *Noting further* that disagreement on one remaining issue has prevented the achievement of such an armistice,

4. *Reaffirms* the earnest intention of the United Nations to reach a just and honourable settlement of the Korean conflict;

5. *Notes with approval* the tentative agreements which the United Nations Command has reached on behalf of the United Nations;

6. *Notes with approval* the principle followed by the United Nations Command with regard to the question of repatriation of prisoners of war, and the numerous proposals which the United Nations Command has made to solve the questions in accordance with this humanitarian principle;

7. *Notes further* that other suggestions consistent with the basic humanitarian position of the United Nations Command have been made by various Members of the United Nations;

8. *Calls upon* the Central People's Government of the People's Republic of China and upon the North Korean authorities to avert further bloodshed by having their negotiators agree to an armistice which recognizes the rights of all prisoners of war to an unrestricted opportunity to be repatriated and avoids the use of force in their repatriation;

9. *Requests* the President of the General Assembly to transmit this resolution to the Central People's Government of the People's Republic of China and to the North Korean authorities, and to make a report to the General Assembly as soon as he deems appropriate during the present session on the result of his action.

(ii) MEXICAN DRAFT RESOLUTION ON THE REPATRIATION OF PRISONERS OF WAR SUBMITTED TO THE POLITICAL COMMITTEE ON 3 NOVEMBER 1952[1]

THE GENERAL ASSEMBLY,

Whereas it is the purpose of the United Nations to restore peace and, therefore, to achieve the cessation of hostilities in Korea through the conclusion of a just and honourable armistice;

Whereas from official reports at the disposal of the General Assembly it follows that the only obstacle to the conclusion of the armistice lies in the fact that it has not been possible to reach an agreement in regard to the exchange of prisoners of war;

Whereas the United Nations must safeguard the application of the

---

[1] A/C. 1/730, 1 November 1952: *General Assembly, Seventh Session, Annexes, Agenda item 16*, pp. 30–31. It was agreed on 2 December that further consideration of this resolution should be deferred until the President of the General Assembly had made his report in accordance with the Indian resolution adopted by the Committee: see below, p. 446.

humanitarian principles that underlie the international instruments in force relating to prisoners of war;

A

Requests the President of the General Assembly to invite, through the channels that he may deem appropriate, the Military Commanders of the North Korean and Chinese forces in Korea to consider the following general bases for the exchange of prisoners of war, with a view to facilitating the early conclusion of the armistice:

1. Prisoners of war held by either of the parties, who have voluntarily expressed their desire to return to the country of their origin, shall be repatriated without delay upon the conclusion of the armistice.

2. Other prisoners of war held by either of the parties, and desirous of establishing temporary residence in other States, would not return to the country of their origin until the coming into force of the decisions that, in order to achieve a peaceful settlement of the Korean question, might be adopted in the political conference that would take place after the armistice, in conformity with the agreement reached by the military Commanders on point 5 of the Armistice agenda.

3. Pending the entry into force of the above-mentioned decisions, the situation of the prisoners of war referred to in paragraph 2 shall be governed by the following rules:

(*a*) The General Assembly, acting in the manner and through the channel it may deem appropriate, shall negotiate with each State agreeing to participate in the plan envisaged in this resolution on the number of prisoners which such a State may be prepared to receive in its territory, as well as on the conditions essential to their admission.

(*b*) Once they are in the country of temporary residence, the authorities of that country shall grant them a migratory status which will enable them to work in order to provide for their needs.

4. When the situation foreseen for their repatriation arises as described in paragraph 2 above, the authorities of the countries of origin shall grant facilities for the return of the ex-prisoners of war and shall furnish guarantees for the subsequent protection of their freedom and their lives.

5. In the case of those ex-prisoners of war who, by virtue of the present Resolution, would be provisionally residing in another country and might express their will to return to their country of origin before the situation foreseen for their repatriation in the terms of paragraph 2 had arisen, the United Nations would provide the means to carry their wishes into effect.

B

Requests the President of the General Assembly to report to the Assembly in due course concerning the result of the steps which he is asked to take by this resolution.

(iii) Indian draft resolution on the repatriation of prisoners of war submitted to the Political Committee on 17 November 1952[1]

The General Assembly,

Having received the special report of the United Nations Command of 18 October 1952 on 'the present status of military action and armistice negotiations in Korea' and other relevant reports relating to Korea;

Noting with approval the considerable progress made by negotiation and the tentative agreements to end the fighting in Korea and to reach a settlement of the Korean question;

Noting further that disagreement between the parties on one remaining issue, alone, prevents the conclusion of an armistice and that a considerable measure of agreement already exists on the principles on which this remaining issue can be resolved;

Mindful of the continuing and vast loss of life, devastation and suffering resulting from and accompanying the continuance of the fighting;

Deeply conscious of the need to bring hostilities to a speedy end and of the need for a peaceful settlement of the Korean question;

Anxious to expedite and facilitate the convening of the political conference as provided in article 60 of the draft Armistice Agreement;

Affirms that the release and repatriation of prisoners of war shall be effected in accordance with the Geneva Convention relative to the Treatment of Prisoners of War, dated 12 August 1949, the well-established principles and practice of international law and the relevant provisions of the draft Armistice Agreement;

Affirms that force shall not be used against prisoners of war to prevent or effect their return to their homelands, and that they shall at all times be treated humanely in accordance with the specific provisions of the Geneva Convention and with the general spirit of the Convention;

Accordingly requests the President of the General Assembly to transmit the following proposals to the Central People's Government of the People's Republic of China and to the North Korean authorities as forming a just and reasonable basis for an agreement and to invite their acceptance of these proposals and to make a report to the General Assembly during its present session and as soon as appropriate:

Proposals

1. In order to facilitate the return to their homelands of all prisoners of war, there shall be established a Repatriation Commission consisting of representatives of Czechoslovakia, Poland, Sweden and Switzerland, that is, the four States constituting the Neutral Nations Supervisory Com-

[1] A/C. 1/734: *General Assembly, Seventh Session, Annexes, Agenda item 16,* pp. 32–34. For the revised version of this resolution adopted by the General Assembly, see below, p. 446.

mission referred to in paragraph 37 of the draft Armistice Agreement, or constituted alternatively, of representatives of four States not participating in hostilities, two nominated by each side, but excluding representatives of States that are permanent members of the Security Council.

2. The release and repatriation of prisoners of war shall be effected in accordance with the 'Geneva Convention relative to the treatment of prisoners of war', dated 12 August 1949, the well-established principles and practice of International Law and the relevant provisions of the draft Armistice Agreement.

3. Force shall not be used against the prisoners of war to prevent or effect their return to their homelands and no violence to their persons or affront to their dignity or self-respect shall be permitted in any manner or for any purpose whatsoever. This duty is enjoined on and entrusted to the Repatriation Commission and each of its members. Prisoners of war shall at all times be treated humanely in accordance with the specific provisions of the Geneva Convention and with the general spirit of that Convention.

4. All prisoners of war shall be released to the Repatriation Commission from military control and from the custody of the detaining side in agreed numbers and at agreed exchange points in agreed demilitarized zones.

5. Classification of prisoners of war according to nationality and domicile as proposed in the letter of 16 October from General Kim Il Sung, Supreme Commander of the Korean People's Army, and General Peng Teh-huai, Commander of the Chinese People's Volunteers, to General Mark W. Clark, Commander-in-Chief, United Nations Command, shall then be carried out immediately.

6. After classification, prisoners of war shall be free to return to their homelands, forthwith, and their speedy return shall be facilitated by all parties concerned.

7. In accordance with arrangements prescribed for the purpose by the Repatriation Commission, each party to the conflict shall have freedom and facilities to explain to the prisoners of war depending upon them their rights and to inform the prisoners of war on any matter relating to their return to their homelands and particularly their full freedom to return.

8. Red Cross teams of both sides shall assist the Repatriation Commission in its work and shall have access, in accordance with the terms of the draft Armistice Agreement, to prisoners of war while they are under the temporary jurisdiction of the Repatriation Commission.

9. Prisoners of war shall have freedom and facilities to make representations and communications to the Repatriation Commission and to bodies and agencies working under the Repatriation Commission, and to inform any or all such bodies of their desires on any matter concerning them-

selves, in accordance with arrangements made for the purpose by the Commission.

10. Notwithstanding the provisions of paragraph 3 above, nothing in this Repatriation Agreement shall be construed as derogating from the authority of the Repatriation Commission (or its authorised representatives) to exercise its legitimate functions and responsibilities for the control of the prisoners under its temporary jurisdiction.

11. The terms of this Repatriation Agreement and the arrangements arising therefrom shall be made known to all prisoners of war.

12. The Repatriation Commission is entitled to call upon parties to the conflict, its own member governments, or the Member States of the United Nations for such legitimate assistance as it may require in the carrying out of its duties and tasks and in accordance with the decisions of the Commission in this respect.

13. When the two sides have made an agreement for repatriation based on these proposals, the interpretation of that agreement shall rest with the Repatriation Commission. In the event of disagreement in the Commission, majority decision shall prevail. When no majority decision is possible, an umpire agreed upon in accordance with the succeeding paragraph and with article 132 of the Geneva Convention of 1949 shall have the deciding vote.

14. The Repatriation Commission shall at its first meeting and prior to an armistice proceed to agree upon and appoint an umpire. If agreement on the appointment of an umpire cannot be reached by the Commission within a period of three weeks after the date of the first meeting, this matter shall be referred to the General Assembly.

15. The Repatriation Commission shall also arrange after the armistice for officials to function as umpires with inspecting teams or other bodies to which functions are delegated or assigned by the Commission or under the provisions of the draft Armistice Agreement, so that the completion of the return of prisoners of war to their homelands shall be expedited.

16. When the Repatriation Agreement is acceded to by the parties concerned and when an umpire has been appointed under paragraph 14 above, the draft Armistice Agreement, unless otherwise altered by agreement between the parties, shall be deemed to have been accepted by them. The provisions of the draft Armistice Agreement shall apply except in so far as they are modified by the Repatriation Agreement. Arrangements for repatriation under this agreement will begin when the armistice is thus concluded.

17. At the end of ninety days, the disposition of any prisoners of war whose return to their homelands has not been effected in accordance with the procedure set out above shall be referred by the Repatriation Commission to the political conference to be called under article 60 of the draft Armistice Agreement.

(iv) Russian draft resolution on Korean unification submitted to the Political Committee on 17 November 1952[1]

The General Assembly,

Having considered the report of the Commission for the Unification and Rehabilitation of Korea,

Considers it necessary:

To establish a Commission for the peaceful settlement of the Korean question with provision for the participation of the parties directly concerned and of other States, including States which have not taken part in the Korean war. The Commission shall consist of the following members: the United States of America, the United Kingdom, France, the Union of Soviet Socialist Republics, the People's Republic of China, India, Burma, Switzerland, Czechoslovakia, the People's Democratic Republic of Korea and South Korea;

To instruct the said Commission to take immediate steps for the settlement of the Korean question on the basis of the unification of Korea— to be effected by the Koreans themselves under the supervision of the above-mentioned Commission, such steps to include extending all possible assistance in the repatriation of all prisoners of war by both sides.

(v) Addendum to the Russian resolution of 17 November, 23 November 1952[2]

Insert as first paragraph of the operative part of the revised draft resolution submitted by the Union of Soviet Socialist Republics (A/C. 1/729/Rev. 1/Corr. 1) the following:

'To recommend to the belligerents in Korea an immediate and complete cease-fire, i.e., the cessation of military operations by both sides on land, by sea and in the air, on the basis of the draft armistice agreement already approved by the belligerents, the question of the complete repatriation of prisoners of war to be referred for solution to the Commission for the peaceful settlement of the Korean question provided for in the USSR draft resolution, in which Commission questions shall be decided by two-thirds majority vote of its members.'

[1] A/C. 1/729/Rev. 1/Corr. 1, 17 November 1952: *General Assembly, Seventh Session, Annexes, Agenda item 16*, p. 30. This resolution, together with the following addendum, was defeated in the Political Committee on 2 December 1952.
[2] A/C. 1/729/Rev. 1/Add. 1: *General Assembly, Seventh Session, Annexes, Agenda item 16*, p. 30.

(vi) Resolution on the release and repatriation of prisoners of war in Korea, proposed by India and adopted by the General Assembly on 3 December 1952[1]

The General Assembly,

Having received the Special Report of the United Nations Command of the 18th October 1952 on 'the present status of military action and armistice negotiations in Korea'[2] and other relevant reports relating to Korea;

Noting with approval the considerable progress towards an armistice made by negotiation at Panmunjom and the tentative agreements to end the fighting in Korea and to reach a settlement of the Korean question;

Noting further that disagreement between the parties on one remaining issue, alone, prevents the conclusion of an armistice and that a considerable measure of agreement already exists on the principles on which this remaining issue can be resolved;

Mindful of the continuing and vast loss of life, devastation and suffering resulting from and accompanying the continuance of the fighting;

Deeply conscious of the need to bring hostilities to a speedy end and of the need for a peaceful settlement of the Korean question;

Anxious to expedite and facilitate the convening of the political conference as provided in Article 60 of the Draft Armistice Agreement;

Affirms that the release and repatriation of Prisoners of War shall be effected in accordance with the 'Geneva Convention relative to the treatment of Prisoners of War', dated Twelfth August 1949, the well-established principles and practice of International Law and the relevant provisions of the Draft Armistice Agreement;

Affirms that force shall not be used against Prisoners of War to prevent or effect their return to their homelands, and that they shall at all times be treated humanely in accordance with the specific provisions of the Geneva Convention and with the general spirit of the Convention;

Accordingly requests the President of the General Assembly to communicate the following proposals to the Central People's Government of the People's Republic of China and to the North Korean Authorities as forming a just and reasonable basis for an agreement so that an immediate cease-fire would result and be effected; to invite their acceptance of these proposals and to make a report to the General Assembly during its present session and as soon as appropriate:

PROPOSALS

1. In order to facilitate the return to their homelands of all Prisoners of War, there shall be established a Repatriation Commission consisting of

[1] *General Assembly, Seventh Session, Supplement No. 20, Resolutions,* 610 (VII), pp. 3–4.
[2] A/2228.

representatives of Czechoslovakia, Poland, Sweden and Switzerland, that is, the four States agreed to for the constitution of the Neutral Nations Supervisory Commission and referred to in paragraph 37 of the Draft Armistice Agreement, or constituted, alternatively, of representatives of four States not participating in hostilities, two nominated by each side, but excluding representatives of States that are permanent members of the Security Council.

2. The release and repatriation of Prisoners of War shall be effected in accordance with the 'Geneva Convention relative to the treatment of Prisoners of War', dated Twelfth August 1949, the well-established principles and practice of International Law and the relevant provisions of the Draft Armistice Agreement.

3. Force shall not be used against the Prisoners of War to prevent or effect their return to their homelands and no violence to their persons or affront to their dignity or self-respect shall be permitted in any manner or for any purpose whatsoever. This duty is enjoined on and entrusted to the Repatriation Commission and each of its members. Prisoners of War shall at all times be treated humanely in accordance with the specific provisions of the Geneva Convention and with the general spirit of that Convention.

4. All Prisoners of War shall be released to the Repatriation Commission from military control and from the custody of the detaining side in agreed numbers and at agreed exchange points in agreed demilitarized zones.

5. Classification of Prisoners of War according to nationality and domicile as proposed in the letter of October 16th from General Kim Il Sung, Supreme Commander of the Korean People's Army, and General Peng Teh-Huai, Commander of the Chinese People's Volunteers, to General Mark W. Clark, Commander-in-Chief, United Nations Command, shall then be carried out immediately.

6. After classification, Prisoners of War shall be free to return to their homelands, forthwith, and their speedy return shall be facilitated by all parties concerned.

7. In accordance with arrangements prescribed for the purpose by the Repatriation Commission, each party to the conflict shall have freedom and facilities to explain to the Prisoners of War 'depending upon them' their rights and to inform the Prisoners of War on any matter relating to their return to their homelands and particularly their full freedom to return.

8. Red Cross teams of both sides shall assist the Repatriation Commission in its work and shall have access, in accordance with the terms of the Draft Armistice Agreement, to Prisoners of War while they are under the temporary jurisdiction of the Repatriation Commission.

9. Prisoners of War shall have freedom and facilities to make representations and communications to the Repatriation Commission and to bodies and agencies working under the Repatriation Commission, and to inform any or all such bodies of their desires on any matter concerning themselves, in accordance with arrangements made for the purpose by the Commission.

10. Notwithstanding the provisions of paragraph 3 above, nothing in this Repatriation Agreement shall be construed as derogating from the authority of the Repatriation Commission (or its authorised representatives) to exercise its legitimate functions and responsibilities for the control of the prisoners under its temporary jurisdiction.

11. The terms of this Repatriation Agreement and the arrangements arising therefrom shall be made known to all Prisoners of War.

12. The Repatriation Commission is entitled to call upon parties to the conflict, its own member governments, or the Member States of the United Nations for such legitimate assistance as it may require in the carrying out of its duties and tasks and in accordance with the decisions of the Commission in this respect.

13. When the two sides have made an agreement for repatriation based on these proposals, the interpretation of that agreement shall rest with the Repatriation Commission. In the event of disagreement in the Commission, majority decision shall prevail. When no majority decision is possible, an umpire agreed upon in accordance with the succeeding paragraph and with Article 132 of the Geneva Convention of 1949 shall have the deciding vote.

14. The Repatriation Commission shall at its first meeting and prior to an armistice proceed to agree upon and appoint an umpire who shall at all times be available to the Commission and shall act as its chairman unless otherwise agreed. If agreement on the appointment of an umpire cannot be reached by the Commission within the period of three weeks after the date of the first meeting, this matter should be referred to the General Assembly.

15. The Repatriation Commission shall also arrange after the armistice for officials to function as umpires with inspecting teams or other bodies to which functions are delegated or assigned by the Commission or under the provisions of the Draft Armistice Agreement, so that the completion of the return of Prisoners of War to their homelands shall be expedited.

16. When the Repatriation Agreement is acceded to by the parties concerned and when an umpire has been appointed under paragraph 14 above, the Draft Armistice Agreement, unless otherwise altered by agreement between the parties, shall be deemed to have been accepted by them.

The provisions of the Draft Armistice Agreement shall apply except in so far as they are modified by the Repatriation Agreement. Arrangements for repatriation under this agreement will begin when the armistice agreement is thus concluded.

17. At the end of ninety days, after the Armistice Agreement has been signed, the disposition of any Prisoners of War whose return to their homelands may not have been effected in accordance with the procedure set out in these proposals or as otherwise agreed, shall be referred with recommendations for their disposition, including a target date for the termination of their detention to the political conference to be called as provided under Article 60 of the Draft Armistice Agreement. If at the end of a further thirty days there are any Prisoners of War whose return to their homelands has not been effected under the above procedures or whose future has not been provided for by the political conference, the responsibility for their care and maintenance and for their subsequent disposition shall be transferred to the United Nations, which in all matters relating to them shall act strictly in accordance with international law.

(vii) Extracts from a cable sent by General Chou En-lai, Minister for Foreign Affairs of the Chinese People's Republic, to Mr. Lester Pearson, President of the General Assembly, commenting on the Assembly's resolution of 3 December, 14 December 1952[1]

(1) The General Assembly of the United Nations, after illegally adopting in February 1951 the shameful and calumnious resolution slandering China as an aggressor,[2] has now, in the absence of the representatives of the People's Republic of China and the Korean Democratic People's Republic, discussed the Korean question and adopted a resolution supporting the United States Government's position of forcibly retaining in captivity prisoners of war in contravention of international conventions, and facilitating its continuation and expansion of the war now raging in Korea. Such an action is clearly illegal and void and is firmly opposed by the Chinese people.

(2) This illegal resolution, adopted by the General Assembly and based on the Indian draft resolution, having as its basic content the question of the repatriation of prisoners of war, does not correspond to the description in your cable that it deals with the question of the repatriation of prisoners of war 'under the terms of the Geneva Convention relative to the Treatment of Prisoners of War of 12 August 1949, under the well-established principles and practice of international law and under the relevant provisions of the draft armistice agreement'.

[1] A/2354, 20 December 1952: *General Assembly, Seventh Session, Annexes, Agenda item 16*, pp. 47–50.
[2] *Documents* (R.I.I.A.) for 1951, p. 547.

Quite to the contrary, it is entirely based on the so-called principles of 'voluntary repatriation' or 'no forcible repatriation', all of which are in essence the 'principle' of forcibly retaining in captivity prisoners of war, a principle which the United States side has unjustifiably maintained ever since 11 December 1951, when the Korean armistice negotiations entered into discussion on the prisoner-of-war item on the agenda, and which is universally recognized as violating the Geneva Convention and international law.

No matter how it claims to be in conformity with the Geneva Convention and international law, this illegal resolution, stripped of its disguise, is actually nothing but a revamped version of the 'twenty-one nation proposal' submitted by Mr. Acheson of the United States to the First Committee of the General Assembly on 24 October 1952.[1]

On this score, official spokesmen of the United States, Britain and other countries have not only repeatedly and openly admitted but also expressed approval of the fact that this illegal resolution 'staunchly and firmly establishes the principle of voluntary repatriation'.

All countries, in and outside the United Nations, whether they are for or against the Indian draft resolution, consider that this draft resolution supports the 'principle of no forcible repatriation' maintained by the United States Government. Even Mr. Krishna Menon, the Indian delegate to the United Nations, who tabled the illegal resolution, himself makes no attempt to hide this. And even you, Mr. Pearson, did you not in your report of 8 December to the Canadian House of Commons on the progress of the General Assembly also frankly admit 'the principle of no forcible repatriation' maintained by the United States still served as the sole basis of negotiations for the United Nations in the Korean armistice negotiations?

Such an illegal resolution, based on the so-called principle of 'voluntary repatriation' or 'no forcible repatriation', cannot possibly settle what you describe in your cable as 'the sole remaining issue which has not been settled in the course of these armistice negotiations', namely, 'the principles and procedures by which the repatriation of prisoners of war can be effected'. The fact is that with regard to this remaining issue, both parties to the Korean armistice negotiations have, in accordance with the principle of the total repatriation of prisoners of war as accepted in international practice and the Geneva Convention, established concrete and scrupulously detailed measures and procedures in article III of the agreed draft armistice agreement. Article III consists not only of what you refer to in your cable as terms acceptable to both sides for bringing the Korean war to an end, but also of the terms already accepted by both sides for bringing the Korean war to an end.

[1] See above, p. 439.

If the United States had adhered to the draft armistice agreement instead of deliberately inventing the so-called principle of 'voluntary repatriation' or 'no forcible repatriation' as an excuse to obstruct an armistice in Korea, then this 'sole remaining issue which has not been settled' would long ago have been satisfactorily settled, and the Korean war, which is a matter of common concern to the people of the world, would long ago have been brought to an end.

The people of the world know that it is the United States Government which has, by maintaining the so-called principle of 'voluntary repatriation' or 'no forcible repatriation'—in essence the 'principle' of forcibly retaining in captivity prisoners of war—violated the terms of the Geneva Convention and the provisions of the draft armistice agreement and broken off the Korean armistice negotiations, hence made it impossible over a long period of time to settle the question of prisoner-of-war repatriation. These criminal violations of the United States are even supported by the General Assembly.

This is a situation which the Chinese people absolutely cannot tolerate. The Central People's Government of the People's Republic of China has always firmly adhered to and upheld the basic principle of the total repatriation of prisoners of war after an armistice is effected, as established in the Geneva Convention, and will continue to do so.

(3) The resolution which you forwarded bases itself not only on the so-called principle of 'voluntary repatriation' or 'no forcible repatriation', but also on the hypothesis that there are actually some among the Korean and Chinese captured personnel who 'refuse to return home' to rejoin their families and lead a peaceful life. This does not accord in the slightest with human nature; still less does it square with facts.

The facts are that the United States has long since flagrantly cast aside the provisions of article 17 and other articles of the Geneva Convention regarding the humane treatment of prisoners of [war] and has in the prisoner-of-war camps under its control placed large numbers of United States, Syngman Rhee and Chiang Kai-shek special agents in responsible posts, and has even planted Syngman Rhee and Chiang Kai-shek special agents posing as Korean and Chinese prisoners of war to coerce prisoners of war to make declarations 'refusing repatriation' and of 'unwillingness to return home', by frequent recourse to so-called 'persuasion', 'screening', 'rescreening', and 'interrogation' of the Korean and Chinese prisoners of war—measures effected by such utterly savage and inhuman methods as torture, massacre and mass starvation.

Prisoners of war who refused to submit were viciously beaten up by these special agents and, while these prisoners of war lay unconscious as a result of their serious injuries, these special agents took advantage of this either to tattoo these prisoners of war with humiliating marks of treason against their mother-land contrary to their will, or to dip the fingers of the prisoners of war in blood from their wounds, to forcibly affix their fingerprints to 'screening' petitions allegedly expressing 'unwilling-ness to return home'.

These special agents even stained their own fingers with blood from the wounds of prisoners of war who had been cruelly beaten unconscious, to forge fingerprints. All of this has, over the past year and more, been conclusively and in every detail corroborated by United States and British news agency dispatches; the Press of India, Canada, Britain and other participants in the war on the United States side; the admissions of former commandants of the United States prisoner-of-war camps, Brigadier Generals Colson and Dodd; the accounts of Korean and Chinese prisoners of war who were fortunate enough to have escaped from the death camps; the report of the International Committee of the Red Cross; and even by the recent statement to the Press made by United States Secretary of Defense Robert Lovett on 2 December.

The United States, sinking to the lowest depths of moral depravity, turns these tattooings and petitions in blood of its own making into a pre-text for its noisy claim that 'some Koreans and Chinese prisoners of war are unwilling to be repatriated'.

And now this illegal resolution which you forwarded even sustains this claim, ranting that 'the Geneva Convention cannot be construed as authorizing a detaining Power to employ force to effect the return of individual prisoners of war to their homelands'.

In reality, prisoners of war are those combatants of one side who are under the armed control and at the forcible disposal of their enemy and have no freedom. Release and repatriation is a right to which all prisoners of war of both sides are entitled as soon as an armistice comes into effect, that is, they should be freed from the armed control of the enemy and be returned to their own side so that they may regain their freedom and return to their homeland to lead a peaceful life.

Since prisoners of war are entitled to such rights, how can [there] be such a question as 'forcible repatriation' or 'return to their homelands effected by force'? The unfounded argument that 'a detaining Power may not employ force to effect the return of individual prisoners of war to their homelands' cannot hold water. It can find no basis whatever in the Geneva Convention. On the contrary, article after article of the Geneva Convention lays down that the detaining Power is charged with the responsibility of speedily releasing and repatriating all prisoners of war after the armistice comes into effect and has absolutely no right to use force and special agents to insult and retain in captivity prisoners of war.

It is evident that the adoption of the illegal resolution by the General

Assembly aims to divert the indignation and attention of the people of the world from the criminal terrorism, as evidenced in the 'screening' of prisoners of war by the United States, to the so-called question of 'forcing prisoners of war to return to their homes' or 'force shall not be used to effect the return of prisoners of war to their homelands'. All of you who have taken this action are indeed 'challenging the fundamental humanitarian instincts'. . . .

(4) The illegal resolution which you forwarded prescribes that the Korean and Chinese prisoners of war, numbering more than 100,000, shall be 'released' to a Repatriation Commission, composed of neutral nations, in a demilitarized zone; that those who are 'willing to go home' shall be allowed to return to their homes, and those who are 'unwilling to go home' shall be delivered to the Repatriation Commission and handed over to the United Nations at the end of 120 days for disposal. It is also prescribed that an umpire shall be appointed to the Repatriation Commission and that, if agreement on the appointment of an umpire cannot be reached, this matter should be referred to the General Assembly. The umpire is given a decisive role to play in the Repatriation Commission. The proposal to give the United Nations the final authority of appointing the umpire and the final authority of disposing of those prisoners of war allegedly 'unwilling to go home' is really extremely absurd. Can it be that those delegates who sponsored and adopted the illegal resolution in the United Nations have really forgotten that the United Nations is one of the belligerent parties in the Korean war?

To put it more frankly, having passed through a circuitous course in which resort was made to many deceitful tactics, these provisions actually adopt in full the three proposals put forward at Panmunjom on 28 September 1952 by the United States. None the less, these provisions are couched in terms more sly in order to deceive more easily the people of the world and to facilitate the realization of the United States Government's scheme to forcibly retain in captivity prisoners of war in violation of international conventions. . . .

General Kim Il Sung, Supreme Commander of the Korean People's Army, and General Peng Teh-huai, Commander of the Chinese People's Volunteers, in their letter of 16 October 1952 to General Clark of the United States, proposed that all prisoners of war be brought to a demilitarized zone to be handed over directly to and accepted by the other side, and that repatriation be effected after visits and explanations. Taking into account the complicated situation mentioned above, these proposals, first of all, enable prisoners of war to be released from the armed control of the opposite side, to give them the protection of their own side, so that the total repatriation of prisoners of war in accordance with humanitarian principles, international practice, the Geneva Convention and the [draft armistice] agreement can be assured. If the General Assembly of the United Nations is not a sounding board for the United States Government, it has no reason whatever to decline this sensible and reasonable proposal of the Korean and Chinese side for the repatriation of prisoners of war.

(5) From the above, it can be clearly seen that the illegal resolution which you forwarded is not only unfair but also unreasonable. The illegal resolution is unreasonable because it runs counter to the conscience of man, completely violates humanitarian principles, international practice, as well as the provisions of the Geneva Convention and the draft armistice agreement; it is unreasonable because it recognizes the 'desire' of the prisoners of war to 'refuse repatriation', a 'desire' created by the United States side by the most brutal methods; it is unreasonable because it insists on the retaining in captivity of tens of thousands of Korean and Chinese prisoners of war as hostages in order to force the Korean and Chinese side to yield to the United States. It is unfair because it deliberately attempts to impose on the Korean and Chinese side the utterly groundless 'principle of voluntary repatriation' which the United States has maintained throughout, and because it rejected without any reason the proposal of the Korean and Chinese side for the repatriation of all prisoners of war in adherence to the Geneva Convention and the proposal of the delegation of the Soviet Union for the immediate and complete cessation of hostilities in Korea prior to the settlement of the question of the repatriation of all prisoners of war.

In view of these facts, I cannot but inform you solemnly that the Central People's Government of the People's Republic of China considers that such an illegal resolution cannot possibly provide 'a just and reasonable basis for an agreement'.

On the question of the repatriation of prisoners of war, the Central People's Government considers that the Korean and Chinese side is at once correct and just, fair and reasonable, in insisting on the principle of total repatriation, a principle which is in conformity with humanitarian principles and the Geneva Convention. The settlement of the question of the repatriation of prisoners of war in the Korean armistice negotiations must and can only be achieved on the basis of the Geneva Convention. Any illegal principles cannot and should not be allowed to serve as a basis. Acting on the principles of the Geneva Convention, the Korean and Chinese side has repeatedly declared that, as soon as the armistice in Korea comes into effect, both sides should immediately effect the unconditional, speedy and total repatriation of prisoners of war, and, furthermore, is prepared to receive the joint Red Cross teams for visits to the prisoner-of-war camps in order to expedite the return of the prisoners of war of the other side to their homes.

It is obvious that the Korean and Chinese side is indeed, to use the phraseology of your cable, willing to make every possible effort to ensure that all prisoners of war shall return to their homes and that their speedy return be facilitated. But to accept the illegal resolution forwarded by you, which is neither fair nor reasonable, would make it impossible to ensure the speedy return of all prisoners of war to their homes. To accept it would be to capitulate before the bestial violence of the United States, which tramples on the human rights of the prisoners of war. It would therefore be absolutely impossible that an actual cease-fire would result and be effected. Furthermore, if we permit the realization of the 'principle of voluntary repatriation' held by the United States Government and embodied in the illegal resolution forwarded by you, if we permit the ruthless subversion by the United States Government of the principles of international law which safeguard international order and the human rights of prisoners of war, then the sufferings now visited on the Korean and Chinese prisoners of war will be visited tomorrow on the people of other nations who may become prisoners of war; likewise, the calamities today endured by Korea and China as victims of aggression will tomorrow befall any other nation in the world.

(6) Your cable devoted considerable verbiage to an attempt to show that by adopting this illegal resolution, which has as its basic content the United States 'principle of voluntary repatriation' under an Indian cloak, all of you earnestly desire a speedy conclusion to the Korean war. However, this illegal resolution which you forwarded fully demonstrates that it abjectly submits to the brutal will of the United States Government, which uses violence to carry through the forcible retaining in captivity of prisoners of war so that the Korean armistice negotiations might be broken off and sabotaged and that the Korean war might be prolonged and expanded. All of you are not doing everything possible to bring the fighting to an end in Korea. You are doing everything possible to induce and coerce some of the nations represented in the General Assembly to endorse jointly the policy of the United States of no armistice, no negotiations, and no peaceful settlement, but the prolongation and expansion of the Korean war. At the same time, all of you attempt further to shift the responsibility for the failure to end the war to the Korean and Chinese side. It can be positively stated that this attempt of yours to shift responsibility will be of no avail.

If, as you said in your cable, the General Assembly's 'unanimous desire is to bring peace to Korea', then it should insist upon the principle of the total repatriation of prisoners of war as embodied in the Geneva Convention and international law. It should sternly demand that the United States side immediately resume the negotiations at Panmunjom and, with the proposal for the peaceful settlement of the Korean question submitted by Mr. Vyshinsky, delegate of the Soviet Union, on 10 and 24 November,[1] as a basis, bring about the accomplishment of a complete cease-fire on the part of the belligerent parties in accordance with the draft Korean armistice agreement already agreed upon by both sides as a first step, and then refer for settlement the question of the total repatriation of prisoners of war, together with the peaceful settlement of the Korean question, to the 'commission for the peaceful settlement of the Korean question', composed of the United States, Britain, France, the Soviet Union, the People's Republic of China, India, Burma, Switzerland, Czechoslovakia, the Korean Democratic People's Republic and South Korea. The commission is of the same nature as the political conference provided for in article 60 of the draft Korean armistice agreement, which you mentioned in your cable, and its composition is at once the fairest possible and the most reasonable.

If such a procedure is followed, an armistice in Korea can be immediately achieved, and the distress of the Korean peoples as well as the casualties on both sides can be brought to an end. Thus, the General Assembly can indeed speedily 'bring peace to Korea'.

However, the present session of the General Assembly has already rejected such a fair and reasonable proposal which can really lead to peace. I hereby once again make the following proposal: to realize the fervent desire for peace of the people of the world, to demonstrate the sincerity of the Chinese people for an early restoration of peace in Korea, and to preclude the further use of the prisoner-repatriation issue as an obstacle and pretext in the realization of an armistice in Korea, the Central People's Government of the People's Republic of China requests that the General Assembly rescind the illegal resolution which you forwarded, call upon the United States Government to resume immediately the negotiations at Panmunjom and, with the draft Korean armistice agreement as a basis, to bring about the realization of a complete armistice as a first step and then to refer for settlement the question of total repatriation of prisoners of war to the above-mentioned 'commission for the peaceful settlement of the Korean question'.

If the General Assembly agrees to discuss this request, then representatives of the People's Republic of China and the Korean Democratic People's Republic must take part in the discussions. Should the General Assembly reject even such a just request, and still persist in maintaining the illegal resolution which aims at supporting the United States Government in forcibly retaining in captivity prisoners of war in violation of international conventions, then it would further demonstrate that your purpose, far from being the achievement of peace in Korea and the Far East, is nothing but the continuation and expansion of the Korean war

[1] See above, p. 445.

so that peace in the Far East and throughout the world can be further disrupted at some future date. This would all the more expose the United Nations as increasingly becoming a tool of the ruling clique of the United States in its preparations for war and for the extension of aggression.

(viii) TELEGRAM TO THE PRESIDENT OF THE GENERAL ASSEMBLY FROM MR. PAKH HEN EN, MINISTER FOR FOREIGN AFFAIRS OF THE PEOPLE'S DEMOCRATIC REPUBLIC OF KOREA, REGARDING THE ASSEMBLY'S RESOLUTION OF 3 DECEMBER, 17 DECEMBER 1952[1]

We have the honour to acknowledge receipt of the telegram dispatched by you concerning the adoption at the 399th plenary meeting of the seventh session of the General Assembly of the United Nations of the so-called draft resolution on the Korean question of 3 December 1952 in connexion with item 16 of the agenda. In this connexion I am empowered to state that the Government of the People's Democratic Republic of Korea considers that not only does the above-mentioned draft resolution lack the legal basis which a genuine draft resolution on the solution of the Korean question must have but is also an unjust decision resulting from the hypocritical policy of the U.S.A. which is aiming at intrigues behind the scenes designed to secure a further continuation and expansion of the criminal and aggressive war in Korea. The resolution is therefore absolutely powerless to bring about an immediate end of the criminal and aggressive war which the United States is waging in Korea and a peaceful and just settlement of the Korean question. The Government of the People's Democratic Republic of Korea, acting in accordance with the peaceful desires and insistent demands of the Korean people and of peace loving peoples throughout the world who have raised their voice against war and in defense of peace considers this draft resolution to be unacceptable.

On the instructions of the Government of the People's Democratic Republic of Korea a statement was sent by me on 17 October to the effect that the Government of the People's Democratic Republic of Korea requests that the interested party—the legal representatives of the People's Democratic Republic of Korea—be given an opportunity of participating in the discussion of the Korean question at the General Assembly and at the same time stating that it will regard as illegal any discussion and any decision taken without the participation of its representatives. It is an elementary truth to every educated person of today that the grant to the interested parties and legal representatives of an opportunity to express the views of their people at an international conference at which the fate

[1] A/2354, 20 December 1952.

of interested states and peoples is being discussed is not only a basic pre-
requisite for a just solution of the question but is a principle which is
fundamental to international conferences claiming to defend freedom and
democracy. The so-called majority group in the United Nations, acting
upon instructions of the ruling circles of the United States has nevertheless declined to permit our legal representatives and the representatives
of the Chinese People's Republic an opportunity to participate in the
discussion of the Korean question, despite the just request of our government and has invited only representatives of the puppet regime of Syngman Rhee, who have absolutely no legal right to represent the Korean
people and are an object of hatred to the entire Korean people.

What is the explanation for the fact that the majority group in the
United Nations, obedient to the dictates of the United States, declined
to admit representatives of the People's Democratic Republic of Korea
to the General Assembly despite the fact that the presence of both
interested parties is essential to a just solution of the Korean question?
The explanation is first, that the majority group in the United Nations
is not interested in a just solution of the Korean question; second, this
group fears that representatives of the People's Democratic Republic of
Korea will expose the crimes committed by the Americans in Korea under
the United Nations flag. In those circumstances the draft resolution on
the Korean question manufactured behind the scenes in the United
Nations by means of American dollars not only has no legal force but is
an unprecedented document in that it constitutes a crime against the
moral principles and conscience of mankind; I therefore protest against
this illegal draft resolution fabricated on the instructions of the United
States in order to deceive public opinion and all people of goodwill
throughout the world. The decision you have adopted cannot be
accepted by our government from the standpoint of a solution of the
question of the repatriation of the prisoners of war. Contrary to established international standards and despite the existing principles clearly
laid down in the Geneva Convention of 12 August 1949, the decision
taken by you is based on the principle of so-called voluntary repatriation
dictated by the Americans. This unprecedented demand, as the whole
world now knows, in fact signifies the use of force and the exertion of
pressure on our country's patriots now in captivity. It means compulsory
'screening' and 'interrogation' by the use of severe repressive measures,
even the mass shooting of unarmed men. The purpose of this inhuman
principle is merely to retain a large proportion of the Korean and Chinese
prisoners of war on their side by any method. Such a principle corresponds to the aggressive purposes and intentions of the United States and
its satellites which are aiming at ending the Korean war not by peaceful
means but by a military decision. It is time it was realized that no

deception and no military threat on the part of the United States military speculators can ever intimidate or subjugate the Korean people, which knows full well that it is fighting for its freedom and independence. If the United Nations really intends to do everything possible to achieve the rapid conclusion of the war in Korea, as emphasized in your cablegram, this should not be merely a good intention [? of no practical value][1] but a real effort must be made to achieve a genuinely just solution of the Korean question and, above all, to secure an immediate cease-fire in Korea.

In view of the foregoing I request you, as President of the present session of the General Assembly, to take the following appropriate steps forthwith: 1. To revoke the above-mentioned 'resolution' illegally adopted by the General Assembly to camouflage the aggressive United States policy of prolonging and extending the Korean war; 2. To condemn the fighting in Korea and to take the necessary steps to bring about an immediate cease-fire in Korea and achieve a peaceful settlement of the Korean question on the basis of the U.S.S.R. proposals of 10 and 24 November 1952 which are whole-heartedly supported and approved by all peace-loving nations; 3. To give representatives of the People's Democratic Republic of Korea an opportunity to participate in the discussion on the Korean question in the organs of the United Nations, as the true representatives of the Korean people; 4. To call to account the representatives of the American side who are responsible for the breakdown of the Panmunjom negotiations, having unilaterally broken off indefinitely the truce negotiations in Korea which had succeeded in settling the fundamental issues except for the sole remaining question of prisoners of war; 5. To put an end to the barbarous bombing of the peaceful populations, towns and villages of North Korea by the American aggressors under the flag of the United Nations; 6. To cease immediately the barbarous procedure of forcibly detaining our prisoners of war and the inhuman treatment and mass murder of and brutality towards the inmates of prisoner-of-war camps; 7. In accordance with international law and the conscience of mankind, to punish severely the American war criminals who, hypocritically trampling upon the standards of international law and the principles of human morality, are using bacterial, chemical and other weapons for the mass slaughter of the peaceful inhabitants of North Korea, so that a repetition of such barbarous crimes may be impossible in the future. If these just proposals which accord with the aspirations of the Korean people and of all peace-loving nations are rejected by the (majority) group in the United Nations, may the entire responsibility for the continuation of the war in Korea rest with those members of the United Nations which overtly or covertly are supporting the United States aggression in Korea.

[1] Text not clear.

I have the honour, Mr. President, to request you to make this statement known to all members of the United Nations.

I have the honour to be, etc.

PAKH HEN EN
*Minister of Foreign Affairs of the People's
Democratic Republic of Korea*

B. CHINA

1. Relations with the West

(i) NOTE FROM THE BRITISH CHARGÉ D'AFFAIRES IN PEKING TO THE CHINESE PEOPLE'S GOVERNMENT REGARDING THE DIFFICULTIES OF BRITISH FIRMS IN CHINA, 12 APRIL 1952[1]

Peking, 12th April, 1952.

British firms have been facing increasing difficulties in China which have been handicapping them in carrying out their legitimate trading activities. Among these difficulties are the following:—

(i) The making of each individual manager *personally* responsible for the policy and acts of his company, in some cases for acts before he became manager.

(ii) The increasing restrictions on the entry and exit of foreign staff.

(iii) The cancellation by the Chinese Government's trading organisations of former contracts, even though raw materials have been paid for and processed.

(iv) Taxation and legal judgments which both appear to be discriminatory against foreigners.

(v) Uncertainty caused to British subjects by the fear of arrest and detention *incommunicado* and without charges being preferred.

(vi) Pressure by the labour unions and reluctance by the local authorities to give any protection to firms who are being accused by the unions of malpractice.

If this situation continues it can only result, sooner or later, in the elimination of British business interests in China to the detriment of friendly relations between China and the United Kingdom. I am therefore instructed by Her Majesty's Government, at the request of the British firms principally concerned, to bring this unsatisfactory state of affairs to the notice of the Chinese Government.

I have, &c.
L. H. LAMB.

[1] Great Britain: Foreign Office: *Correspondence between the Government of the United Kingdom of Great Britain and Northern Ireland and the Central People's Government of China on British Trade in China, Peking, 12th April–5th July 1952, with Statement by the Secretary of State for Foreign Affairs in the House of Commons on 20th May 1952* (Cmd. 8639) (London, H.M.S.O., 1952), pp. 2–3.

(ii) Statement to the House of Commons by Mr. Eden on the detention of foreign nationals in China, 21 April 1952[1]

The House will wish to know that Her Majesty's Chargé d'Affaires in Peking has been instructed to address a Note to the Chinese Government today bringing to their notice all cases of Australian, Canadian, United Kingdom and United States citizens reported to be under detention in China, requesting information about those who have been arrested, the nature of the charges, what sentences, if any, have been passed on them, and their present whereabouts and welfare, and requesting facilities to enable Her Majesty's Chargé d'Affaires to communicate with them.

Her Majesty's Government in the United Kingdom is in charge of Australian, Canadian and United States interests in China. This step has, therefore, been taken on behalf of and with the approval of the Governments of Canada, Australia and the United States as well as on our own account.

There are believed to be 55 citizens of the countries in question who are at present in gaol. Five of these are citizens of the United Kingdom and Colonies, five of Canada, three of Australia and 42 of the United States. A further 20 United States citizens are reported to be under house arrest.

Others are known to have died in prison, though no satisfactory details have been obtained from the Chinese authorities, and several have been released in such a poor state of health, due to neglect of their special ailments, that they died shortly after release. The figures given are subject to correction, since in most cases persons under detention have not been permitted to get in touch with their national representative, families or friends.

General representations on behalf of those detained were made by Her Majesty's Chargé d'Affaires in August last year and the attention of the Central People's Government has repeatedly been drawn to the various individual cases by separate communications. I regret to inform the House that these representations do not so far appear to have effected any improvement in the situation. Hence the Note which Her Majesty's Chargé d'Affaires has been instructed to address today to the Chinese Government.

(iii) Note from the British Chargé d'Affaires in Peking to the Chinese People's Government regarding the closing of British firms in China, 19 May 1952[2]

Peking, 19th May, 1952.

As stated in my note of 12th April, 1952, British firms in China have for a long time and for reasons beyond their control been facing increasing

---

[1] H.C. Deb. 5th ser. vol. 499, coll. 51–52. [2] Cmd. 8639, pp. 3–4.

difficulties. The increasing extent to which many of the functions formerly handled in China by private merchants and industrialists are being taken over by organisations operating on a State basis is correspondingly reducing need for maintenance in their existing form of many British owned and established enterprises.

2. Nearly all, if not all, of the British companies in China, have come to the conclusion that this change in conditions necessitates a corresponding change in the nature of their organisations and in the scope of their activities. Many feel they can no longer operate satisfactorily in China and can serve no useful purpose in the future. Consequently they feel that the proper course is for them to arrange for the transfer as going concerns, custody or closure, of their businesses. The needs of individual companies will vary with their particular circumstances, and applications appropriate thereto will be made by them in due course.

3. A number of important British companies, whilst recognising that in existing conditions their present organisations are or may become redundant, believe that they can still perform a useful service in the interests of Sino-British trade. They therefore contemplate setting up a new form of organisation which is better suited to current conditions. This would take the form of an association of representatives of manufacturers and overseas buyers, who would maintain direct contact with the appropriate Chinese authorities. This body could, in fact, act as a permanent Trade Mission.

4. Her Majesty's Government trust that the Central People's Government will issue appropriate instructions to the departments concerned to facilitate the measures for which individual British companies will make application in pursuance of the above decisions. The particular points in respect of which the good offices of the Central People's Government are requested are:—

(*a*) approval of the termination of the services of redundant staff;
(*b*) the issue of exit permits for non-Chinese staff;
(*c*) the setting up of machinery to deal with custody or transfer as going concerns of any businesses to which this treatment is appropriate;
(*d*) taking of the necessary steps to deal with the suggestion in paragraph 3 above.

5. In view of the prolonged period during which many companies have been operating under economically adverse circumstances, Her Majesty's Government request that early and favourable consideration will be given to the representations made herein.

I have, &c.
L. H. LAMB.

(iv) Statement on British business interests in China made by Mr. Eden to the House of Commons, 20 May 1952[1]

With your permission Mr. Speaker and that of the House I should like to make a statement.

The House will be aware that British firms in China have for reasons beyond their control been facing for some time past increasing difficulties so far as trade and industry inside China are concerned. These difficulties are partly due to the increasing extent to which many of the functions formerly handled in China by private merchants and industrialists are being taken over by organisations operating on a State basis. There are, however, other difficulties, for example the increasing restrictions on the entry and exit of foreign staffs, arbitrary taxation demands and compulsion to retain and pay redundant labour. In these circumstances many firms have been operating at a loss for a considerable period. For these reasons most of the British companies have reluctantly come to the conclusion that they can no longer operate satisfactorily inside China, and that the time has come to arrange for the disposal of their businesses. Many have already decided to apply for closure, custody, transfer, or lease of their various interests, as may be appropriate in each case. There are likely to be many problems involved and, at the request of the China Association, acting on behalf of the firms concerned, Her Majesty's Government have presented a note to the Central People's Government of China requesting that all the necessary facilities be made available to ensure that these problems are dealt with expeditiously. Both Her Majesty's Government and the firms themselves remain convinced of the need and desirability for British trade with China to be continued. The suggestion has been conveyed to the Central People's Government that the requirements of this trade under the changed conditions in China might perhaps be met by setting up a new form of organisation. The firms feel that this could take the form of an association of representatives of manufacturers and overseas buyers, who would maintain direct contact with the appropriate Chinese authorities. This body, could, in fact, act as a permanent trade organisation.

I should like to take this opportunity to pay tribute to the skill, tenacity and courage of the British Community in the Far East. During the course of their long and honourable connexion with China they have contributed greatly to the prosperity of both countries, and much of the traditional goodwill and mutual understanding which has existed between our two countries is also due to them. The firms concerned have recently had to face increasingly heavy losses, as I have explained, and have been, in many cases, unable to replace their foreign staffs in China who, as may

[1] Cmd. 8639, p. 7.

be imagined, have been working under conditions of acute strain and anxiety. In these circumstances it is difficult to see how the firms could have made any other decision. Her Majesty's Government for their part fully realise the gravity of this step, but they feel that, having regard to the factors which I have outlined, they can only endorse the decision which the firms have taken.

(v) STATEMENT BY THE CHINESE VICE-MINISTER FOR FOREIGN AFFAIRS, MR. CHANG HAN-FU, ON BRITISH TRADE WITH CHINA, 5 JULY 1952[1]

The Ministry of Foreign Affairs of the Central People's Government of the People's Republic of China has already received from Mr. Lamb, the representative for negotiations of the British Government, Note No. 53 of 18th April, 1952,[2] on Sino-British trade, and Note No. 69 of 19th May, 1952, on the suggestions of the British industrial and commercial firms in China to wind up their business and to set up a new form of organisation, and has further taken notice of the related statement made by Mr. Eden, the Secretary of State for Foreign Affairs of the British Government, on 20th May, in the House of Commons of Britain.

Mr. Chang Han-fu, Vice-Minister for Foreign Affairs of the Central People's Government considers it necessary to issue the following statement:—

(1) The Central People's Government has repeatedly declared: China is willing to restore and develop international trade relations with Governments and peoples of other countries, on a basis of equality and mutual benefit; all foreign residents and firms in China, who abide by the laws of the Chinese Government, will receive protection from the people's governments of all levels. In accordance with this policy of the Central People's Government, all the private and State trade organisations of China have been and still are striving to establish normal trade connections with foreign industrial and commercial firms.

Since October 1949, the trade between China and Britain has had a considerable revival and development. Consequently, the activities of the British firms in China have gradually become brisk. For more than two years, the private and State trade organisations of China have further signed trade contracts of various forms and contracts for processing and orders with foreign industrial and commercial firms in China, among which chiefly are the British.

Recently, at the International Economic Conference, convened in April of this year in Moscow, the Chinese and British delegations reached an agreement for trade exchange to the amount of £10,000,000 on either side in 1952. On the basis of this agreement, the Chinese and British repre-

---

[1] Cmd. 8639, pp. 5–6. [2] Not printed here: see ibid. p. 2.

sentatives for trade negotiations signed on 9th June, in Berlin, a pro-forma contract to the amount of £6,500,000 for the first instalment of goods. All these facts amply prove that the Chinese Government and people are willing to develop between China and Britain, a normal trade relationship on an equal and mutually beneficial basis.

(2) However, the British Government has persistently carried out a discriminatory trade policy against China, thus hindering the establishment of a normal economic relationship between the British people and the People's Republic of China. It can be recalled that since 1950, under the incessant pressure of the United States, the British Government has adopted a series of unfriendly measures of control in respect of trade against the People's Republic of China. On 18th May, 1951, in the United Nations Assembly, under the domination and coercion of the United States Government, the delegate of the British Government voted for the preposterous proposal of the United States for an embargo against the People's Republic of China. Immediately afterwards, on 19th June, 1951, the British Government further declared all the export items to China and Hong Kong to be under the control of special permits. The British Government has thus followed the United States Government in carrying out the policy of trade control and embargo, hostile to the People's Republic of China, and calculated to obstruct the trade exchange between China and Britain. Since then, the trade between China and Britain has abruptly declined in volume.

Under such a trade policy of the British Government, the British industry and commerce have met serious but unnecessary difficulties. This is especially so in the case of the British companies and manufacturing firms in China, many of which have been reduced to the straits of retrenchment or closure of their business by the depressed state of the trade between the two countries, in addition to their bad management. For some time in the past, they have taken a wait-and-see attitude with anxiety. The Government authorities of all levels of the People's Republic of China have taken such measures as the advancing of loans and supplying of raw materials in order to aid them. However, the measures of trade control and embargo taken by the British Government have not shown the least sign of relenting, and the resulting difficulties, before which the British firms in China are powerless, have shown the tendency to become increasingly greater, instead of the slightest sign of abating.

The predicament of the British firms in China is the bitter fruit of the policy of trade control and embargo of the British Government. This alone suffices to prove that by following the United States in carrying out the trade control and embargo, the British Government not only contravenes but also jeopardises the interests of the British people.

(3) Due protection shall be afforded to the British companies and

H h

manufacturing firms in the territories of the People's Republic of China by the authorities of the people's governments of all levels, provided that they abide by the laws of the Chinese Government. In case they wish to wind up their business voluntarily, no matter what form of wind up they may take, they may apply at the people's government at their respective localities, and the competent authorities will deal with each case according to its own merits and the regulations. In the course of winding up, any question that may arise relating to the termination of services of employees and workers, the application for exit permit, and the disposal of the enterprises, may be expeditiously and reasonably settled on the merits of each case and in accordance with the regulations.

(4) The Central People's Government considers that the active promotion of the trade relations between China and Britain on a basis of equality and mutual benefit is conducive to the recovery and development of industrial and agricultural production in both countries, as well as to the improvement of the living conditions of the peoples of both countries. Therefore, any British companies and manufacturing firms, or any such in the territory of China, as well as any organisation jointly formed by the British companies and manufacturing firms, provided that they do not harbour monopoly designs and are willing to trade with China on a basis of equality and mutual benefit, may all approach at any time the private and State trade organisations of China, establish contacts with them, and conduct specific business negotiations with them.

(vi) Appeal from the Asian and Pacific Region Peace Conference to the peoples of the world, Peking, 12 October 1952[1]

We, the 367 delegates from 37 countries, assembled at the Peace Conference of the Asian and Pacific Regions, have met together in an atmosphere of goodwill and mutual trust; belonging to different nations and races, holding various religious beliefs and political views, but expressing the determined will for peace of over 1,600 million people, we are fully agreed that to win and preserve peace is an urgent task which must and can be accomplished by the joint efforts of all.

The ruthless war in Korea has been waged for more than two years. Bacteriological weapons, napalm bombs, indiscriminate bombing and other methods of mass slaughter are being unscrupulously employed. Peaceful cities and villages are being burnt and destroyed; horrible atrocities are being inflicted upon innocent men, women and children. This war has already taken a heavy toll of human life and happiness. The U.S. government's refusal to repatriate the prisoners of war in accordance

---

[1] *New China News Agency*, 21 October 1952. For the other resolutions passed by the conference see ibid. 17 and 21 October 1952.

with the principles of international law prevents the conclusion of a truce in Korea. The repeated disruption of the Korean truce talks by the U.S. Military Command, the use of illegal methods of warfare, the encroachments on China's sovereignty, are acts of provocation which threaten to spread the war.

At the same time, armed intervention in Viet Nam, Malaya and other countries, seeking to crush the people's desire for freedom, continues.

The revival of Japanese militarism, in violation of solemn international agreements, by the U.S. government, in order to convert Japan into a war base for launching a new war against the Asian and Pacific regions, resurrects the spectre of war for the whole area.

In many countries of this area, the struggle to win liberation and to preserve national independence is being subjected to foreign intervention. National sovereignty and territorial integrity are being violated by the acquisition of military bases and the imposition of military alliances. The national wealth of many lands is being plundered, and their economic resources diverted to serve the plans for aggressive foreign wars. In countries that are being compelled to join the arms drive, high prices and inflation have adversely affected the people's living standards. Blockades and embargoes impose further unnecessary hardships, dislocating economies which have not even fully recovered from the effects of World War Two. In many lands, cultural undertakings and programmes of social betterment are having to be curtailed, and, in large parts of this area, the rights of women are being flouted and child welfare is neglected. In order to justify and promote war policies international suspicions are fanned through lying propaganda, racist theories are propounded, and disunity among nations is fostered by every possible means.

In glaring contrast with the frenzied drive towards war, is the earnest desire of the peoples of the whole world that existing conflicts should be brought to an end, that the energy and resources devoted to the destruction of life should be spent in building and beautifying life, and that the human race should be guaranteed a permanent peace.

Peoples that are still subject to foreign rule realise that the struggle for national liberation is inseparably linked with the struggle against war, that war preparations strengthen the chains of their slavery.

Peoples whose governments lead the preparation for war live in fear and insecurity; and the peoples are realising that security and stability can only be achieved through peaceful development. Countries with vast plans for peaceful economic reconstruction eagerly desire peace to continue with the task of improving their people's standards of living.

The peoples of the Asian and Pacific regions firmly adhere to a common aim, namely, to oppose war and defend peace.

We reaffirm our firm conviction that countries with different social systems and ways of life can co-exist in peace and mutually beneficial co-operation.

We realise keenly that peace cannot be awaited, it must be won. In order to win lasting peace, we must unite and wage tireless struggles.

The peace of this area and the world demands:

Immediate peace in Korea on a just and reasonable basis, an end to the wars in Viet Nam, Malaya and other regions, and the withdrawal of all foreign troops from these regions.

A halt to the revival of Japanese militarism; conclusion of a genuine peace treaty between Japan and the countries concerned; and establishment of an independent, democratic, free and peaceful new Japan.

Opposition to intervention in the internal affairs of one country by another and the encroachment on the sovereignty of one country by another. Defence and achievement of national independence.

Opposition to blockade and embargo. Promotion of economic co-operation and cultural exchange between the countries on the basis of equality and mutual benefit.

Prohibition of incitement to war, opposition to racial discrimination, and protection of women's rights and the promotion of child welfare.

Speedy conclusion of a Five-Power Peace Pact. Arms reduction and a ban on the use of atomic, bacteriological, and chemical weapons and other weapons of mass murder.

In the struggle for the defence of peace in Asia and the Pacific regions and throughout the world, the people of the United States bear an especially great responsibility.

The acts of war and preparations for war now being carried out in these regions, as well as in other parts of the world, by the government of the United States, are disastrous to the peoples of the Asian and Pacific regions, and disastrous to the people of the world. Though committed in their name, these acts do not serve the will or the interests of the people of the United States.

Hence it is the urgent need and solemn obligation of the people of the United States to put an end to these acts of their government and to lead the country to follow the path of peace.

The Peace Conference of the Asian and Pacific regions greets the people of the United States, who are struggling for peace amidst great difficulties. We express the hope that they will intensify their struggle and strengthen their unity in defence of peace. In this noble task, we wish them every success, and offer them our hand of friendship.

We realise that the people of Japan have suffered terribly under United States occupation and their own militarist rulers. We know they will struggle, along with the other peoples of Asia and the Pacific, for national independence, and to escape being used as cannon-fodder. The peoples of Asia and the Pacific will whole-heartedly support the heroic fight of the Japanese people in defence of peace and independence. We wish them success and offer them our hand of friendship.

The monstrous cruelties which accompany the wars of today have roused the consciences of every decent man and woman. The mass killing of civilians, the senseless destruction of peaceful towns and villages, the infliction of untold horrors on innocent women and children, make modern war an instrument of total annihilation. This genocide, by the use of the most fiendish weapons ever invented by man, threatens to reach other lands and peoples. If the cultural achievements of long centuries are not to be wiped out, if life is not to become a bestial struggle for existence, if the life of man is to retain any element of humanity, the orgy of bloodshed in Korea, Viet Nam, Malaya and other countries, must be stopped. The grim prospect of a world war imperils the life of every man, woman and child. It is, therefore, a common duty to struggle for peace and halt the world's steady drift towards war. The peoples of the Asian and Pacific areas are determined to wage a relentless struggle against the forces of war, and are convinced that, by the co-operation of all persons of goodwill, they will be able to avert the threatening catastrophe, dispelling the dark clouds of war and clearing man's horizons for the dawn of universal friendship and a lasting peace.

2. Relations with the U.S.S.R.

(i) Exchange of messages between Mr. Mao Tse-tung and Marshal Stalin on the anniversary of the defeat of Japan, 2 September 1952[1]

(a) Mr. Mao's telegram

On the occasion of the seventh anniversary of victory in the anti-Japanese war, permit me on my own behalf and on behalf of the People's Liberation Army of China and of the Chinese people as a whole, to convey to you, to the armed forces of the Soviet Union and to all the Soviet people cordial congratulations and heartfelt gratitude.

The great aid rendered by the Soviet Union to the Chinese people in the anti-Japanese war and the rout by the Soviet Army of the main forces of the Japanese Army—the Kwantung Army—enabled the Chinese people to achieve final victory in the anti-Japanese war. The Soviet Union is rendering fraternal assistance to the Chinese people in restoring and developing China and is thereby contributing to the rapid growth and strengthening of the forces of the Chinese people.

Today, when Japanese militarism is reviving and the aggressive forces

---

[1] *Soviet News*, 6 September 1952.

of Japan are again rearing their heads, the unbreakable friendship and alliance between China and the Soviet Union constitutes the firm guarantee for preventing a recurrence of aggression on the part of Japan or any other State which might unite with Japan in acts of aggression, the firm guarantee for preserving peace in the East and throughout the world.

Long live the great unbreakable friendship between the Chinese People's Republic and the Union of Soviet Socialist Republics!

(Sgd.) Mao Tse-tung

(b) Marshal Stalin's reply

I beg you, Comrade Chairman, to accept my gratitude for the sentiments you have expressed with regard to the Soviet people and the Soviet Army in connection with the seventh anniversary of the victory over the Japanese imperialists.

In this historic victory a great part was played by the Chinese people and their People's Liberation Army whose heroism and selflessness facilitated the cause of liquidating Japanese aggression.

The great friendship between the Soviet Union and the Chinese People's Republic is the reliable guarantee against the threat of another aggression, the powerful bulwark of peace in the Far East and throughout the world.

Accept, Comrade Chairman, the congratulations of the Soviet Union and the Soviet Army on the occasion of the seventh anniversary of the liberation of the Chinese people from the yoke of Japanese imperialism.

Long live the unbreakable friendship of the Chinese People's Republic and the Soviet Union!

Long live the People's Liberation Army of the Chinese People's Republic!

(Sgd.) J. Stalin

(ii) Sino-Russian agreements of 15 September 1952[1]

(a) Communiqué on the negotiations in Moscow between the Chinese and Russian Governments

Recently negotiations were held in Moscow between J. V. Stalin, Chairman of the Council of Ministers of the U.S.S.R.; A. Y. Vyshinsky, Minister of Foreign Affairs of the U.S.S.R., and P. N. Kumykin, Minister of Foreign Trade of the U.S.S.R., on the one hand, and the Government delegation of the Chinese People's Republic headed by Chou En-lai, Premier of the State Administrative Council and Minister of Foreign Affairs, and composed of Chen Yun, Vice-Premier of the State Administrative Council; Li Fu-chun, vice-chairman of the Financial and Economic

[1] *Soviet News*, 20 September 1952.

Committee; Chang Wen-tien, Ambassador Extraordinary and Pleni-potentiary of the Chinese People's Republic to the U.S.S.R., and Su Yu, Deputy Chief of the General Staff, on the other hand.

During these negotiations, important political and economic questions of relations between the Chinese People's Republic and the Soviet Union were discussed. The negotiations, which proceeded in an atmosphere of friendly mutual understanding and cordiality, confirmed the determina-tion of both parties to direct their efforts towards further consolidation and development of friendship and co-operation between them, at the same time helping in every way to preserve and strengthen peace and international security.

Both parties agreed, in the course of the negotiations, to commence carrying out measures to effect, towards the end of 1952, the transfer by the Soviet Government to the Government of the Chinese People's Republic without compensation, of all its rights to joint administration of the Chinese Changchun Railway, together with all property belonging to the railway.

At the same time, Chou En-lai, Premier of the State Administrative Council and Minister of Foreign Affairs of the Chinese People's Republic, and A. Y. Vyshinsky, Minister of Foreign Affairs of the U.S.S.R., ex-changed Notes on the question of extending the term of joint use of the Chinese naval base of Port Arthur.

The following are the aforementioned Notes, as well as the Soviet-Chinese communiqué on the Chinese Changchun Railway.

(b) Communiqué on the transfer of the Chinese Changchun Railway to the Chinese People's Government

In accordance with the established relations of friendship and co-operation between the U.S.S.R. and the Chinese People's Republic, an agreement on the Chinese Changchun Railway was signed in Moscow on February 14, 1950, under which the Soviet Government transfers without compensation to the Government of the Chinese People's Republic all its rights to joint administration of the Chinese Changchun Railway, together with all property belonging to the railway. Under this agree-ment the transfer of the aforementioned Chinese Changchun Railway must be effected not later than by the end of 1952.

At present the Soviet Government and the Government of the Chinese People's Republic have begun carrying out measures for implementing this agreement and with this end in view agreed to form a joint Soviet-Chinese Commission.

The joint Soviet-Chinese Commission must complete the transfer of the Chinese Changchun Railway to the Chinese People's Republic not later than by December 31, 1952.

(c) Note from General Chou to Mr. Vyshinsky

Dear Comrade Minister!

Inasmuch as Japan refused to conclude an overall peace treaty but has concluded a separate treaty with the United States and certain other countries, as a result of which Japan has not and apparently does not want to have any peace treaty with the Chinese People's Republic and the Soviet Union, conditions dangerous to the cause of peace and favourable for the recurrence of Japanese aggression have arisen.

In view of this and for the purpose of ensuring peace, and also on the basis of the Treaty of Friendship, Alliance and Mutual Assistance between the Chinese People's Republic and the Union of Soviet Socialist Republics, the Government of the Chinese People's Republic suggests and asks the Soviet Government to agree to postpone the date of withdrawal of the Soviet troops from the jointly used Chinese naval base of Port Arthur, provided for in Article 2 of the Chinese-Soviet Agreement on Port Arthur, until such time as a peace treaty between the Chinese People's Republic and Japan and a peace treaty between the Soviet Union and Japan are concluded.

If the Soviet Government agrees to the aforementioned proposal of the Government of the Chinese People's Republic, the present Note and your Reply Note will be regarded as a component part of the agreement of February 14, 1950, between the Chinese People's Republic and the U.S.S.R. concerning the naval base of Port Arthur, and will go into force on the day of the exchange of Notes.

I beg you, Comrade Minister, to accept assurances of my profound respect for you.

(Sgd.) CHOU EN-LAI

September 15, 1952.

(d) Mr. Vyshinsky's reply

Dear Comrade Premier and Minister,

I acknowledge the receipt of your Note of September 15 of the current year, which says:

Inasmuch as Japan refused to conclude an overall peace treaty but has concluded a separate treaty with the United States and certain other countries, as a result of which Japan has not and apparently does not want to have any peace treaty with the Chinese People's Republic and the Soviet Union, conditions dangerous to the cause of peace and favourable for the recurrence of Japanese aggression have arisen.

In view of this and for the purpose of ensuring peace, and also on the basis of the Treaty of Friendship, Alliance and Mutual Assistance between the Chinese People's Republic and the Union of Soviet Socialist Republics, the Government of the Chinese People's Republic suggests and asks the

Soviet Government to agree to postpone the date of withdrawal of the Soviet troops from the jointly used Chinese naval base of Port Arthur, provided for in Article 2 of the Chinese-Soviet Agreement on Port Arthur, until such time as a peace treaty between the Chinese People's Republic and Japan and a peace treaty between the Soviet Union and Japan are concluded.

The Soviet Government agrees to the aforestated proposal of the Government of the Chinese People's Republic and also to the proposal that your Note and this reply to it become a component part of the aforementioned agreement of February 14, 1950, concerning the naval base of Port Arthur as from the day of the exchange of these Notes.

I beg you, Comrade Premier and Minister, to accept assurances of my profound respect for you.

(Sgd.) A. VYSHINSKY

September 15, 1952.

C. JAPAN

(i) NEW YEAR'S MESSAGE TO THE JAPANESE PEOPLE SENT BY MARSHAL STALIN TO MR. KIISHI IWAMOTO, EDITOR-IN-CHIEF OF THE KYODO NEWS AGENCY, 31 DECEMBER 1951[1]

Dear Mr. K. Iwamoto,

I have received your request to send a New Year's message to the Japanese people.

It is not a tradition with Soviet leaders that the Premier of a foreign State should address his wishes to the people of another State. However, the profound sympathy of the peoples of the Soviet Union for the Japanese people who are in straits owing to foreign occupation, impels me to make an exception to the rule and to meet your request.

Please convey to the Japanese people that I wish them freedom and happiness, that I wish them full success in their gallant struggle for the independence of their homeland.

In the past the peoples of the Soviet Union themselves experienced the horrors of foreign occupation in which the Japanese imperialists also took part. Therefore they fully understand the sufferings of the Japanese people, deeply sympathise with them and believe that they will achieve the regeneration and independence of their homeland as the peoples of the Soviet Union achieved it in the past.

I wish the Japanese workers deliverance from unemployment and low wages, elimination of high prices of consumer goods and success in the struggle for the preservation of peace.

---

[1] *Soviet News*, 5 January 1952.

I wish the Japanese peasants deliverance from landlessness and land shortage, elimination of high taxes and success in the struggle for the preservation of peace.

I wish the entire Japanese people and their intelligentsia full victory of the democratic forces of Japan, revival and advance of the country's economic life, the flowering of national culture, science and art and success in the struggle for the preservation of peace.

With respect,

(Signed) J. STALIN

December 31, 1951.

(ii) EXCHANGE OF LETTERS BETWEEN THE JAPANESE PRIME MINISTER, MR. SHIGERU YOSHIDA, AND MR. JOHN FOSTER DULLES, REGARDING JAPAN'S POLICY TOWARDS CHINA[1]

(a) *Mr. Yoshida's letter, 24 December 1951*

Dear Ambassador Dulles,

While the Japanese Peace Treaty and the U.S.–Japan Security Treaty were being debated in the House of Representatives and the House of Councillors of the Diet, a number of questions were put and statements made relative to Japan's future policy toward China. Some of the statements, separated from their context and background, gave rise to misapprehensions which I should like to clear up.

The Japanese Government desires ultimately to have a full measure of political peace and commercial intercourse with China which is Japan's close neighbour.

At the present time it is, we hope, possible to develop that kind of relationship with the National Government of the Republic of China, which has the seat, voice and vote of China in the United Nations, which exercises actual government authority over certain territory, and which maintains diplomatic relations with most of the members of the United Nations. To that end my Government on November 17, 1951, established a Japanese Government Overseas Agency in Formosa, with the consent of the National Government of China. This is the highest form of relationship with other countries which is now permitted to Japan, pending the coming into force of the multilateral Treaty of Peace. The Japanese Government Overseas Agency in Formosa is important in its personnel, reflecting the importance which my government attaches to relations with the National Government of the Republic of China. My government is prepared as soon as legally possible to conclude with the National Government of China, if that government so desires, a Treaty which will re-

---

[1] *Department of State Bulletin*, 28 January 1952, p. 120.

establish normal relations between the two Governments in conformity with the principles set out in the multilateral Treaty of Peace. The terms of such bilateral treaty shall, in respect of the Republic of China, be applicable to all territories which are now, or which may hereafter be, under the control of the National Government of the Republic of China. We will promptly explore this subject with the National Government of China.

As regards the Chinese Communist regime, that regime stands actually condemned by the United Nations of being an aggressor and in consequence, the United Nations has recommended certain measures against that regime, in which Japan is now concurring and expects to continue to concur when the multilateral Treaty of Peace comes into force pursuant to the provisions of Article 5(a) (iii), whereby Japan has undertaken 'to give the United Nations every assistance in any action it takes in accordance with the Charter and to refrain from giving assistance to any State against which the United Nations may take preventive or enforcement action'. Furthermore, the Sino-Soviet Treaty of Friendship, Alliance and Mutual Assistance concluded in Moscow in 1950 is virtually a military alliance aimed against Japan. In fact there are many reasons to believe that the Communist regime in China is backing the Japan Communist Party in its program of seeking violently to overthrow the constitutional system and the present Government of Japan. In view of these considerations, I can assure you that the Japanese Government has no intention to conclude a bilateral Treaty with the Communist regime of China.

Yours sincerely,
SHIGERU YOSHIDA

(b) Mr. Dulles's reply, 16 January 1952

My dear Mr. Prime Minister,

I acknowledge the receipt by pouch of your letter of December 24, 1951, in which you express the intentions of your Government with reference to China.

This clear statement should dispel any misapprehensions which, as you suggest, may have arisen from statements, separated from their context and background, made during the course of debate in Japan on the ratification of the Japanese Peace Treaty and the U.S.–Japan Security Treaty.

I am grateful to you for your letter and I respect the courageous and forthright manner in which you face up to this difficult and controversial matter.

Sincerely yours,
JOHN FOSTER DULLES

(iii) Treaty of Peace between Japan and Nationalist China, Taipei, 28 April 1952[1]

Japan and the Republic of China.

Considering their mutual desire for good neighborliness in view of their historical and cultural ties and geographical proximity;

Realizing the importance of their close cooperation to the promotion of their common welfare and to the maintenance of international peace and security;

Recognizing the need of a settlement of problems that have arisen as a result of the existence of a state of war between them;

Have resolved to conclude a Treaty of Peace and have accordingly appointed as their Plenipotentiaries,

The Government of Japan:
Mr. Isao Kawada;

His Excellency the President of the Republic of China:
Mr. Yeh Kung Chao.

Who, having communicated to each other their full powers found to be in good and due form, have agreed upon the following articles:

Article I

The state of war between Japan and the Republic of China is terminated as from the date on which the present Treaty enters into force.

Article II

It is recognized that under Article 2 of the Treaty of Peace with Japan signed at the city of San Francisco in the United States of America on September 8, 1951 (hereinafter referred to as the San Francisco Treaty),[2] Japan has renounced all right, title and claim to Taiwan (Formosa) and Penghu (the Pescadores) as well as the Spratly Islands and the Paracel Islands.

Article III

The disposition of property of Japan and its nationals in Taiwan (Formosa) and Penghu (the Pescadores), and their claims, including debts, against the authorities of the Republic of China in Taiwan (Formosa) and Penghu (the Pescadores) and the residents thereof, and the disposition in Japan of property of such authorities and residents and their claims, including debts, against Japan and its nationals, shall be the subject of special arrangements between the Government of Japan and the Government of the Republic of China. The terms nationals and residents whenever used in the present Treaty include juridical persons.

[1] *Contemporary Japan* (Tokyo, Foreign Affairs Association of Japan), vol. xxi, nos. 1–3, 1952, pp. 160–3.
[2] For the San Francisco Treaty see *Documents* (R.I.I.A.) for 1951, pp. 611–25.

ARTICLE IV

It is recognized that all treaties, conventions and agreements concluded before December 9, 1941, between Japan and China have become null and void as a consequence of the war.

ARTICLE V

It is recognized that under the provisions of Article 10 of the San Francisco Treaty, Japan has renounced all special rights and interests in China, including all benefits and privileges resulting from the provisions of the final Protocol signed at Peking on September 7, 1901, and all annexes, notes and documents supplementary thereto, and has agreed to the abrogation in respect to Japan of the said protocol, annexes, notes and documents.

ARTICLE VI

(a) Japan and the Republic of China will be guided by the principles of Article 2 of the Charter of the United Nations in their mutual relations.

(b) Japan and the Republic of China will cooperate in accordance with the principles of the Charter of the United Nations and, in particular, will promote their common welfare through friendly cooperation in the economic field.

ARTICLE VII

Japan and the Republic of China will endeavour to conclude, as soon as possible, a treaty or agreement to place their trading, maritime and other commercial relations on a stable and friendly basis.

ARTICLE VIII

Japan and the Republic of China will endeavour to conclude, as soon as possible, an agreement relating to civil air transport.

ARTICLE IX

Japan and the Republic of China will endeavour to conclude, as soon as possible, an agreement providing for the regulation or limitation of fishing and the conservation and development of fisheries on the high seas.

ARTICLE X

For the purpose of the present Treaty, nationals of the Republic of China shall be deemed to include all the inhabitants and former inhabitants of Taiwan (Formosa) and Penghu (the Pescadores) and their descendants who are of the Chinese nationality in accordance with the laws and regulations which have been or may hereafter be enforced by the Republic of China in Taiwan (Formosa) and Penghu (the

Pescadores) ; and juridical persons of the Republic of China shall be deemed to include all those registered under the laws and regulations which have been or may hereafter be enforced by the Republic of China in Taiwan (Formosa) and Penghu (the Pescadores).

ARTICLE XI

Unless otherwise provided for in the present Treaty and the documents supplementary thereto, any problem arising between Japan and the Republic of China as a result of the existence of a state of war shall be settled in accordance with the relevant provisions of the San Francisco Treaty.

ARTICLE XII

Any dispute that may arise out of the interpretation on application of the present Treaty shall be settled by negotiation or by other pacific means.

ARTICLE XIII

The present Treaty shall be ratified and the instruments of ratification shall be exchanged at Taipei as soon as possible. The present Treaty shall enter into force as from the date on which such instruments of ratification are exchanged.

ARTICLE XIV

The present Treaty shall be in the Japanese, Chinese and English languages. In case of any divergence of interpretation, the English text shall prevail.

IN WITNESS WHEREOF, the respective Plenipotentiaries have signed the present Treaty and have affixed thereto their seals.

Done in duplicate at Taipei, this 28th day of the fourth month of the Twenty Seventh year of Showa of Japan corresponding to the 28th day of the fourth month of the Forty First year of the Republic of China and to the 28th day of April in the year One Thousand Nine Hundred and Fifty Two.

For Japan: (signed) ISAO KAWADA
For the Republic of China: (signed) YEH KUNG CHAO

PROTOCOL

At the moment of signing this day the Treaty of Peace between Japan and the Republic of China (hereinafter referred to as the present Treaty), the undersigned Plenipotentiaries have agreed upon the following terms which shall constitute an integral part of the present Treaty:

1. The application of Article XI of the present Treaty shall be subject to the following understandings:

(a) Wherever a period is stipulated in the San Francisco Treaty during which Japan assumes an obligation or undertaking, such period shall, in respect of any part of the territories of the Republic of China, commence immediately when the present Treaty becomes applicable to such part of the territories.

(b) As a sign of magnanimity and good will towards the Japanese people, the Republic of China voluntarily waives the benefit of the services to be made available by Japan pursuant to Article 14 (a) of the San Francisco Treaty.

(c) Articles 11 and 18 of the San Francisco Treaty shall be excluded from the operation of Article XI of the present Treaty.

2. The commerce and navigation between Japan and the Republic of China shall be governed by the following Arrangements:

(a) Each Party will mutually accord to nationals, products and vessels of the other Party:

(i) Most-favored-nation treatment with respect to customs duties, charges, restrictions and other regulations on or in connection with the importation and exportation of goods; and

(ii) Most-favored-nation treatment with respect to shipping, navigation and imported goods, and with respect to natural and juridical persons and their interests—such treatment to include all matters pertaining to the levying and collection of taxes, access to the courts, the making and performance of contracts, rights to property (including those relating to intangible property and excluding those with respect to mining), participation in juridical entities, and generally the conduct of all kinds of business and professional activities with the exception of financial (including insurance) activities and those reserved by either Party exclusive to its nationals.

(b) Whenever the grant of most-favored-nation treatment by either Party to the other Party, concerning rights to property, participation in juridical entities and conduct of business and professional activities, as specified in sub-paragraph (a) (ii) of this paragraph, amounts in effect to the grant of national treatment, such Party shall not be obliged to grant more favorable treatment than that granted by the other Party under most-favored-nation treatment.

(c) External purchases and sales of government trading enterprises shall be based solely on commercial considerations.

(d) In the application of the present arrangements, it is understood:

(i) that vessels of the Republic of China shall be deemed to include all those registered under the laws and regulations which have been or may hereafter be enforced by the Republic of China in Taiwan

(Formosa) and Penghu (the Pescadores); and products of the Republic of China shall be deemed to include all those originating in Taiwan (Formosa) and Penghu (the Pescadores); and

(ii) that a discriminatory measure shall not be considered to derogate from the grant of treatments prescribed above, if such measure is based on an exception customarily provided for in the commercial treaties of the Party applying it, or on the need to safeguard that Party's external financial position or balance of payments (except in respect to shipping and navigation), or on the need to maintain its essential security interests, and provided such measure is pro-portionate to the circumstances and not applied in an arbitrary or unreasonable manner.

The Arrangements set forth in this paragraph 2 shall remain in force for a period of one year as from the date on which the present Treaty enters into force.

Done in duplicate at Taipei, this 28th day of the fourth month of the Twenty Seventh year of Showa of Japan corresponding to the 28th day of the fourth month of the Forty First year of the Republic of China and the 28th day of April in the year One Thousand Nine Hundred and Fifty Two.

(iv) MEMORANDUM REGARDING THE DISSOLUTION OF THE FAR EASTERN COMMISSION FROM MR. A. S. PANYUSHKIN, THE RUSSIAN MEMBER, TO MR. MAXWELL HAMILTON, THE UNITED STATES MEMBER AND CHAIRMAN, 28 APRIL 1952[1]

In connection with the letter of the United States representative in the Far Eastern Commission with regard to the dissolution of the Far Eastern Commission, the Soviet delegation in the Far Eastern Commission deems it necessary to declare the following:

The statement of the United States representative concerning the dis-solution of the Far Eastern Commission is another illegal act on the part of the Government of the United States. The illegality of this act is determined by the fact that it is taken in connection with the unlawful separate peace treaty with Japan, concluded in violation of the corre-sponding international agreements on Japan—the Cairo and Potsdam declarations, the Yalta agreement, the decisions of the Far Eastern Com-mission and the Declaration of the United Nations of January 1, 1942.

It is not the first time that the United States Government has had recourse to flagrant violation of the above-mentioned agreements of the Powers in relation to Japan. Long before the signing of the separate

[1] *Soviet News*, 10 May 1952.

peace treaty it had become clear that the United States objectives in Japan had nothing in common with the commitments assumed as regards the prevention of the revival of Japan as an aggressive State. In carrying through the occupation of Japan, the American occupation authorities, instead of fulfilling the decisions on the democratisation of Japan, helped to establish a regime of arbitrary police rule against the democratic organisations and democratic leaders.

As early as 1948, the Soviet delegation, coming out against the issuing by the Commander-in-Chief of the Allied Powers in Japan of a directive to the Japanese Government on the revision of the 'Law on State and Public Service', pointed out that the measures of the occupation authorities violated the rights of the Japanese working people and were contrary to the Potsdam declaration and the political decisions of the Far Eastern Commission on the question of the democratisation of Japan.

In subsequent statements repeatedly made on this question, the Soviet delegation showed by concrete facts that the policy of the American occupation authorities is aimed at encouraging the Japanese Government to intensify the pressure on the democratic rights of the Japanese people, to suppress the lawful activity of trade unions and other organisations of the working people and to establish a regime of arbitrary police rule in Japan.

Today the consequences of this policy of the United States are universally known. Even the American Press is compelled to admit that fundamental human rights are being violated in Japan. Japanese workers, peasants, intellectuals and students are subject to brutal police persecution. It is sufficient to recall the mass police reprisals against democratic organisations in Japan on February 21–22 this year, the use by the police of arms, tear gas and even torture against the Japanese people.

It is known that the international agreements on Japan devoted particular attention to the task of demilitarisation and of the prevention of the resurgence of Japanese militarism—a task inseparably connected with that of democratising the political life of the country.

Facts, however, prove that in violation of these international agreements the American occupation authorities have carried out a policy of encouraging and supporting militarist and revanchist elements in Japan, instead of preventing the resurgence of Japanese militarism. The American authorities long ago began the unlawful practice of releasing Japanese war criminals before their sentences had been served—including chief war criminals sentenced by International Military Tribunal for the Far East.

Encouraging the persecution of democratic organisations in Japan, the occupation authorities have helped in every way to revive the militarist and ultra-nationalist organisations. They have openly supported Japanese political leaders who are propagating revanchist ideas. It is sufficient to recall that, after making openly revanchist statements in 1947, the then Foreign Minister of Japan, Ashida, became in 1948 Prime Minister of Japan with the support of the Commander-in-Chief of the Allied Powers. This is not surprising, since it is commonly known today that the United States Government, in order to carry out its war plans in Japan, is basing itself, not on the democratic forces of Japan, but on the same military circles who have more than once impelled Japan on to the path of aggression.

The Soviet representatives in the Far Eastern Commission and in the Allied Council for Japan have more than once declared that such a policy is contrary to the international commitments assumed by the United States Government and violates the agreements of the Powers on the formation of a peaceful, democratic Japan.

The conclusion of the separate peace treaty with Japan was a continuation of this policy by the United States. The conclusion of this treaty shows how far the United States Government has gone in its policy of converting Japan into a military bridgehead of the United States in the Far East. That is precisely why the separate peace treaty with Japan and the so-called 'security pact' with the help of which Japan is being turned into a State dependent on the United States, a State which must subordinate its national interests to the aggressive purposes of the United States ruling circles, cannot be qualified otherwise than as treaties directed towards the preparation of another war in the Far East.

The statement on the liquidation of the Far Eastern Commission consummates the U.S. Government's policy of gross violation by the United States of its obligations with regard to Japan. This statement has been made despite the fact that the Far Eastern Commission, as is known, was far from having discharged the functions entrusted to it by the decision of the Moscow Conference of Foreign Ministers of the U.S.S.R., the United States and Great Britain in 1945, to which China adhered. As a result of the separate peace treaty imposed upon Japan and the above-mentioned 'security pact', American troops remain in Japan, emphasising the dependent position of that country. Thus the status of Japan has actually not changed. She remains an occupied country, with all the adverse consequences for her national independence and State sovereignty. It goes without saying that responsibility for such a situation rests primarily with the United States Government. The Soviet Government, which insists on the withdrawal of all occupation forces from Japan and on a truly peaceful settlement with Japan, with the participation of all the States concerned, cannot bear any responsibility for the situation created.

(v) Treaty of Peace between Japan and India, Tokyo, 9 June 1952[1]

Whereas the Government of India have by public notification issued on the 28th day of April, 1952, terminated the state of war between Japan and India;

And whereas the Government of Japan and the Government of India are desirous of co-operation in friendly association for the promotion of the common welfare of their peoples and the maintenance of international peace and security, in conformity with the principles of the Charter of the United Nations;

The Government of Japan and the Government of India have therefore determined to conclude this Treaty of Peace, and to this end have appointed as their Plenipotentiaries:

The Government of Japan, Katsuo Okazaki, Minister for Foreign Affairs of Japan, and

The Government of India, K. K. Chettur, Ambassador Extraordinary and Plenipotentiary to Japan,

Who, having indicated to each other their respective Full Powers, and found them good and in due form, have agreed on the following articles:—

Article 1

There shall be firm and perpetual peace and amity between Japan and India and their respective peoples.

Article 2

(a) The Contracting Parties agree to enter into negotiations for the conclusion of treaties or agreements to place their trading, maritime, aviation and other commercial relations on a stable and friendly basis.

(b) Pending the conclusion of the relevant treaty or agreement, during a period of four years from the date of issue of the notification by the Government of India terminating the state of war between Japan and India—

(1) The Contracting Parties shall accord to each other most-favoured-nation treatment with respect to air traffic rights and privileges;

(2) the Contracting Parties shall accord to each other most-favoured-nation treatment also with respect to customs duties and charges of any kind and restrictions and other regulations in connection with the importation and exportation of goods or imposed on the international transfer of payments for imports or exports and with respect to the method of levying such duties and charges and with respect to all rules and formalities in connection with importation and exportation and charges to which customs clearing operations may be subject; and any advantage,

[1] *Nippon Times*, 10 June 1952.

favour, privilege or immunity granted by either of the Parties to any product originating in or destined for any other country shall be accorded immediately and unconditionally to the like products originating in or destined for the territory of the other Party;

(3) Japan will accord to India national treatment, to the extent that India accords Japan the same, with respect to shipping, navigation and imported goods, and with respect to natural, and juridical persons and their interests—such treatment to include all matters pertaining to the levying and collection of taxes, access to the courts, the making and performance of contracts, rights to property (tangible and intangible), participation in juridical entities constituted under Japanese law, and generally the conduct of all kinds of business and professional activities.

Provided that in the application of this Article, a discriminatory measure shall not be considered to derogate from the grant of national or most-favoured-nation treatment, if such measure is based on an exception customarily provided for in the commercial treaties of the Party applying it, or on the necessity of safeguarding that Party's external financial position or balance of payments, or on the need to maintain her essential security interests, and provided such measure is proportionate to the circumstances and is not applied in an arbitrary or unreasonable manner.

Provided further that nothing contained in sub-paragraph (2) above shall apply to the preferences or advantages which have existed since before the 15th August, 1947, or which are accorded by India to contiguous countries.

(c) No provision of this Article shall be deemed to limit the undertakings assumed by Japan under Article 5 of this Treaty.

Article 3

Japan agrees to enter into negotiations with India, when India so desires, for the conclusion of an agreement providing for the regulation or limitation of fishing and the conservation and development of fisheries on the high seas.

Article 4

India will return or restore in their present form all property, tangible and intangible, and rights of interests of Japan or her nationals which were within India at the time of the commencement of the war and are under the control of the Government of India at the time of the coming into force of this Treaty; provided that the expenses which may have been incurred for the preservation and administration of such property shall be paid by Japan or her nationals concerned. If any such property has been liquidated, the proceeds thereof shall be returned, deducting the above-mentioned expenses.

Article 5

Upon application made within nine months of the coming into force of this Treaty, Japan will, within six months of the date of such application, return the property tangible and intangible, and all rights of interests of any kind in Japan of India and her nationals which were within Japan at any time between the 7th December, 1941, and the 2nd September, 1945, unless the owner has freely disposed thereof without duress or fraud.

Such property will be returned free of all encumbrances and charges to which it may have become subject because of the war, and without any charges for its return.

Property the return of which is not applied for by or on behalf of its owner or by the Government of India within the prescribed period may be disposed of by the Japanese Government in its discretion.

If any such property was within Japan on the 7th December, 1941, and cannot be returned or has suffered injury or damage as a result of the war, compensation will be made on terms not less favourable than the terms provided in the Allied Powers Property Compensation Law of Japan (Law No. 264, 1951).

Article 6

(a) India waives all reparation claims against Japan.

(b) Except as otherwise provided in this Treaty, India waives all claims of India and Indian nationals arising out of action taken by Japan and her nationals in the course of the prosecution of the war as also claims of India arising from the fact that she participated in the occupation of Japan.

Article 7

Japan agrees to take the necessary measures to enable nationals of India to apply within one year of the coming into force of this Treaty to the appropriate Japanese authorities for review of any judgment given by a Japanese Court between the 7th December, 1941, and such coming into force, if in the proceedings in which the judgment was given any Indian national has suffered injury by reason of any such judgment, he shall be restored to the position in which he was before the judgment was given or shall be afforded such relief as may be just and equitable in the circumstances of the case.

Article 8

(a) The Contracting Parties recognise that the intervention of the state of war has not affected the obligation to pay pecuniary debts arising out of obligations and contracts (including those in respect of bonds) which existed and rights which were acquired before the existence of the state of war, and which are due by the Government or nationals of Japan to the Government or nationals of India, or are due by the Government or nationals of Japan; nor has the intervention of the state of war affected the obligation to consider on their merits claims for loss or damage to property or for personal injury or death which arose before the existence of a state of war, and which may be presented or represented by the Government of India to the Government of Japan or by the Government of Japan to the Government of India.

(b) Japan affirms her liability for the pre-war external debt of the Japanese State and for debts of corporate bodies subsequently declared to be liabilities of the Japanese State, and expresses her intention to enter into negotiations at an early date with her creditors with respect to the resumption of payments on those debts.

(c) The Contracting Parties will encourage negotiations in respect to other pre-war claims and obligations and facilitate the transfer of sums accordingly.

Article 9

(a) Japan waives all claims of Japan and her nationals against India and her nationals arising out of the war or out of actions taken because of the existence of a state of war, and waives all claims arising from the presence, operations or actions of forces or authorities of India in Japanese territory prior to the coming into force of this Treaty.

(b) The foregoing waiver includes any claims arising out of actions taken by India with respect to Japanese ships between the 1st September, 1939, and the coming into force of this Treaty, as well as any claims and debts arising in respect to Japanese prisoners of war and civilian internees in the hands of India, but does not include Japanese claims specifically recognized in the laws of India enacted since the 2nd September, 1945.

(c) Japan recognizes the validity of all acts and omissions done during the period of occupation under or in consequence of directives of the occupation authorities or authorized by Japanese law at that time, and will take no action subjecting Indian nationals to civil or criminal liability arising out of such acts or omissions.

Article 10

Any dispute arising out of the interpretation or application of this Treaty or one or more of its Articles shall be settled in the first instance by negotiation, and, if no settlement is reached within a period of six months from the commencement of negotiations, by arbitration in such manner as may hereafter be determined by a general or special agreement between the Contracting Parties.

Article 11

This Treaty shall be ratified and shall come into force on the date of exchange of ratifications which shall take place as soon as possible at New Delhi.

IN WITNESS WHEREOF the undersigned Plenipotentiaries have signed this Treaty.

DONE in duplicate at Tokyo, this ninth day of June 1952, Japanese and Minder texts of this treaty will be exchanged by the two Governments within a month of this date.

9th June, 1952.

(vi) STATEMENT BY THE JAPANESE FOREIGN OFFICE ON THE STATUS OF UNITED NATIONS FORCES IN JAPAN, 14 NOVEMBER 1952[1]

1. With regard to the provisions pertaining to criminal jurisdiction in the agreement regarding the status of the United Nations forces in Japan, negotiations carried on between the representatives of Japan and the United Nations forces have not yet come to agreement. The Japanese Government, considering the fact that, although the Agreement between the Parties to the North Atlantic Treaty regarding the Status of their Forces, 1951,[2] (NATO Agreement) has not yet entered into force, its provisions pertaining to criminal jurisdiction are the newest and most reasonable formula on such matter in accord with the principles of international law, and further, that the relevant provisions of the Administrative Agreement between Japan and the United States are to be revised along the line of the NATO Agreement when the latter comes into force, has deemed it appropriate to work out a formula patterned after the NATO Agreement for the United Nations forces and, has, accordingly, presented to the United Nations side such a proposal with minor alterations. Its main point is to the effect that Japan shall have the primary right, in principle, to exercise jurisdiction on all offenses, committed by members of the United Nations forces or of their civilian components, other than (a) those against the security or property of sending States, (b) those against the life, person or property of members of the United Nations forces or of their civilian components, (c) those committed inside of the facilities in use by the United Nations forces, and (d) those committed by members of the United Nations forces or of their civilian components in the performance of their official duties.

In this connection, the Japanese representative expressed the opinion in the course of the negotiations that it was desirable to revise along the line of the Japanese proposal the provisions pertaining to criminal jurisdiction in the Administrative Agreement between Japan and the United

[1] *Nippon Times*, 15 November 1952.

[2] Great Britain: Foreign Office: *Agreement regarding the Status of Forces of Parties to the North Atlantic Treaty* (Cmd. 8279) (London, H.M.S.O., 1951).

States in order to meet the request of the Commonwealth countries for 'equal treatment'.

2. In reply, the representatives of the United Nations forces verbally stated their views at the informal meeting with Foreign Minister Okazaki on November 12 and presented the Memorandum setting forth the main points of their views, the gist of which is as follows:

(1) Since the NAT formula has not come into force, the Unified Command seeks a jurisdictional arrangement, as an interim measure, which would accord the United Nations forces in Japan the same treatment as that now granted to the United States forces under the Administrative Agreement between the United States and Japan, until such time as that Agreement is amended either by the coming into force of the NAT formula for the United States, or otherwise. The United Command position is designed to achieve equality of treatment for the forces in Japan of the United Nations and United States.

(2) Any difference in treatment concerning criminal jurisdiction which is so closely related to the maintenance of military discipline, constitutes discrimination which would adversely affect the morale of the United Nations Command and reduce its military effectiveness.

(3) The present Japanese position is considered to be inconsistent with Japan's obligation to give the United Nations every assistance in the action it has undertaken to repel aggression. Such obligation is clearly set forth in Article 5 of the Treaty of Peace signed at San Francisco on September 8, 1951, and in the exchange of notes of the same date in which Japan specifically undertook to permit and facilitate the support in and about Japan of the forces engaged in the United Nations action in Korea.

(4) Failure to achieve equality of treatment in jurisdictional matters would be cause for justifiable criticism by the Governments and public opinion in those States subscribing to the United Nations' action in Korea.

If provisions substantially similar to the NAT agreement were now adopted, many of the Governments concerned might feel constrained, in view of the fact that the NAT agreement has not yet entered into force, to delay the deposit of their instruments of acceptance of the proposed agreement. The ensuing delays would not be conducive to the best interests of Japan and the Governments participating in the United Nations action in Korea.

(5) The forces of the United Nations Command, by repelling armed aggression in Korea and the forces of the United States in Japan, by deterring armed attack upon it, are making contributions to the preservation of international peace and security in the Far East, as well as to the security of Japan. The direct and material benefits to Japan are apparent. In return, the granting by Japan of equality of treatment would represent

but a small contribution in comparison with the great sacrifices of men
and money that other free nations are making.

(6) It is therefore urged that, in the light of these considerations, Japan
review its position on criminal jurisdiction for the purpose of arriving at
a mutually satisfactory solution on the basis of equality of treatment.

3. There are not a few points in the Memorandum on which we cannot
agree. However, this memorandum being the one presented by them to
express their views in the course of friendly and informal conversations,
we are prepared to continue similar informal conferences and fully set
forth our views and position in order to obtain their better understanding.

Further, the Japanese Government is willing to carry on negotiations
with the United Nations side in a friendly manner, the Ministries of
Foreign Affairs and Justice and other Government agencies concerned,
on our part, cooperating in close contact with each other as heretofore.

PART VI
SOUTH-EAST ASIA

1. General Survey

(i) Communiqué issued after talks on South-East Asia and other subjects between Mr. Acheson, Mr. Eden and M. Schuman, London, 27 June 1952[1]

M. Acheson, secrétaire d'État américain, et M. Schuman, ministre français des affaires étrangères, se sont entretenus aujourd-hui, au Foreign Office, avec M. Anthony Eden. Ils ont été rejoints dans le courant de l'après-midi par M. Jean Letourneau, ministre français des États associés.

Les conversations ont porté sur de nombreux sujets concernant l'Europe, la Corée et le Sud-Est asiatique.

Les ministres ont passé en revue les événements qui se sont déroulés dans ces régions depuis leur dernier entretien à Paris en mai.

Les ministres ont réaffirmé leur accord concernant la nécessité de consultations et d'une coopération étroite en ce qui concerne, à la fois, la Corée et l'Asie du Sud-Est, et ils ont étudié les moyens de la réaliser.

Les trois ministres ont étudié le projet de réponse à la dernière note soviétique préparé par les experts à Washington. Un accord complet est intervenue sur le fond de cette réponse, qui va maintenant être établie sous sa forme définitive.

(ii) Communiqué issued after the first meeting of the Foreign Ministers of Australia, New Zealand and the U.S.A.—the ANZUS Council—at Kaneohe, Hawaii, 4 August 1952[2]

ANZUS treaty recognizes that an armed attack in the Pacific area on any of the parties would be dangerous to the peace and security of all signatories and declares that each would act to meet the common danger in accordance with constitutional processes. The treaty also establishes the Council as the means for a closer consultative relationship among the three governments. We believe that the Council will afford each of us the opportunity to achieve more effective cooperation as members of the free world. We take this occasion to reaffirm the principles of the treaty.

At this first meeting we have established the necessary organization to implement the treaty. In following the provision of the treaty which

[1] *Le Monde*, 29–30 June 1952.
[2] *Department of State Bulletin*, 18 August 1951, pp. 244–5.

states that the Council is to consist of the three foreign ministers or their deputies we have agreed that the Council of Ministers should meet annually one year in the United States and the alternate year in Australia or New Zealand. The Council also agreed that special meetings normally attended by the Deputies will be held in Washington to provide for continuing consultation and to provide a focus where existing channels and agencies may be utilized in the implementation of the treaty.

The deputy members of the Council will be: For Australia, The Honorable Sir Percy C. Spender, Ambassador to the United States; for New Zealand, The Honorable Leslie K. Munro, Ambassador to the United States; and for the United States, the Honorable David K. Bruce, Under Secretary of State.

To ensure that effective measures are taken to implement Article III of the treaty the Council will have the advice of appropriate military officers of the three governments. Admiral Arthur W. Radford USN has been designated as the United States military representative accredited to the Council. The Australian and New Zealand military representatives will soon be designated. An early meeting of these officers will be held at Honolulu to work out details of the military machinery the general nature of which was agreed to.

The Council considered the responsibilities devolving upon it in the light of Article VIII of the treaty which authorizes it to maintain a consultative relationship with other states and regional organizations. The Council discussed the ways and means by which it might contribute to the growth of the system of regional security referred to in this article and reaffirmed on behalf of the three governments the need for collective defense in the Pacific area. The Council examined the possibility of providing arrangements for the association of other governments in its work. Recognizing that the Council is just beginning to evolve its own tripartite organization and program it came to the conclusion that it would be premature at this early stage in its own development to attempt to establish relationships with other states or regional organizations. The Council agreed, however, that in the meantime the members of the Council would continue to keep in close touch through existing channels with other states concerned to preserve peace in the Pacific area.

We reaffirm that our governments are dedicated to the strengthening and furtherance of friendly and peaceful relationships among nations in the Pacific area. In so doing we emphasize that the purpose of the ANZUS treaty is solely the defense of its members against aggression. As is clear from the treaty itself this is fully consistent with the principles of the United Nations Charter and with the obligations of the members under the charter. The ANZUS Council is dedicated to help support and implement the principles and responsibilities of the United Nations.

The principle of collective security is the common objective of both and the security system of the United Nations which we are seeking to build will be made stronger by the steps which we have taken here. Furthermore, in our discussion of how best to contribute by constructive measures to the security of the Pacific area we have taken into account the membership of Australia and New Zealand in the British Commonwealth and United States participation in the North Atlantic Treaty organization and its association by treaty with the other American republics and with Japan and the Philippines.

We have taken the opportunity to review situations of mutual concern. We exchanged views on the operations of the United Nations in Korea and the problem of assisting the free nations of Asia to resist Communist imperialism.

We emphasize, however, that we neither reached any decisions nor undertook any commitments regarding matters of direct concern to our friends in the Pacific area or elsewhere.

(iii) COMMUNIQUÉ ISSUED BY THE PRIME MINISTERS OF THE UNITED KINGDOM, AUSTRALIA AND NEW ZEALAND REGARDING THE SITUATION IN THE PACIFIC AND SOUTH-EAST ASIA. LONDON, 14 DECEMBER 1952[1]

The Prime Ministers of the United Kingdom, Australia and New Zealand took the opportunity provided by the Commonwealth Economic Conference to discuss the situation in the Pacific and the problems of South-East Asia.

They reached complete understanding with regard to certain fundamental propositions which will, in due course, be the subject of friendly discussion with their allies, the United States.

2. Indo-China

(i) EXTRACTS FROM A SPEECH IN THE FRENCH NATIONAL ASSEMBLY BY M. JEAN LETOURNEAU, MINISTER FOR THE ASSOCIATED STATES AND HIGH COMMISSIONER IN INDO-CHINA, ON THE GOVERNMENT'S POLICY IN INDO-CHINA, 10 APRIL 1952[2]

Le b, a, ba de la politique française en Indochine, même et surtout lorsque vous avez l'esprit constamment préoccupé de chercher une solution, c'est que soit clairement affirmée, sans faille, la résolution de la France de rester là-bas tout le temps nécessaire. Sinon, vous n'avez plus l'ombre d'une solution possible.

Dès que vous laissez semer je ne sais quel doute dans les esprits sur la

[1] Financial Times, 15 December 1952.
[2] Journal Officiel, Débats, 11 April 1952, pp. 2102-4.

résolution française, il n'y a plus l'ombre d'une solution possible, et je voudrais vous dire pourquoi.

Je parlerai très franchement à l'Assemblée. Encore une fois, elle sait avec quelle attention je me suis penché sur ces problèmes, combien j'en subis le poids; elle peut donc me faire confiance pour que je lui parle en toute franchise.

On m'a dit parfois que j'étais très optimiste et j'ai répondu aussi que je ne le croyais pas. Les optimistes sont ceux qui, trop souvent, par générosité d'esprit, pensent que leur rêve pourrait demain devenir la réalité.

Je pense, moi — et c'est cruel à dire — que dans l'immédiat la seule chose à faire pour la France, c'est de tenir, car nous n'avons pas les moyens aujourd'hui de faire autre chose.

Prenons, en effet, l'un des aspects de ce problème, sur lequel M. Christian Pineau a si justement insisté.[1] Nous avons dit, nous avons répété — et nous avons bien fait, puisque c'est la vérité — que le corps expéditionnaire français défendait là-bas un des bastions avancés du monde libre. D'avoir affirmé aussi nettement, je puis dire, notre désintéressement dans cette affaire — puisque, si nous défendons le monde libre auquel nous appartenons, nous rendons service à un nombre considérable de nations qui, d'ailleurs, pourraient parfois en prendre un compte plus exact — cela nous a permis tout de même d'obtenir, en particulier des États-Unis, une aide militaire et financière qui devient chaque jour de plus en plus substantielle et dont nous devons les remercier.

Ce qu'ils font là, et qui concourt d'une manière si efficace à la défense du monde libre et à la diminution des pertes de notre corps expéditionnaire, mérite que le Parlement français les en remercie.

Mais est-ce une raison pour penser, même si cela est agréable, que nous pouvons du jour au lendemain abandonner le combat et, alors que nous sommes si engagés partout dans la défense des libertés, pour abandonner à l'esclavage communiste, pour commencer, 25 millions de Cambodgiens, de Laotiens et de Vietnamiens? Est-ce comme cela que nous commencerons la campagne pour le monde libre? A partir de ce jour-là, qui donc, dans le camp du monde libre, nous croirait et qui donc, dans cette coalition des nations libres, prêterait la moindre attention aux promesses et aux engagements que nous pourrions prendre?

Si vraiment, comme nous l'avons dit, nous croyons — et personnellement, après avoir longuement étudié ce problème et regardé les cartes, j'en suis absolument certain — que le verrou tonkinois est indispensable, même à long terme, pour la sécurité de l'Europe, ne pensons pas nous débarrasser allègrement de ce fardeau, par ailleurs pour nous si redoutable.

---

[1] M. Pineau had presented to the National Assembly the report of a parliamentary mission to Indo-China earlier in the year.

Nous devons, au surplus, nous rappeler que nous sommes au milieu de ces peuples d'Indochine, non pas depuis cinq ans, mais depuis près d'un siècle. Or, pendant plus de quatre-vingts ans nous leur avons dit: Nous vous protégerons contre les invasions extérieures; nous nous chargerons de vous garantir d'abord contre les pirateries intérieures, ensuite contre les dangers venus de l'extérieur.

Depuis la Constitution de 1946, comme le rappelait hier M. Massot, et depuis les accords de 1949,[1] nous avons par surcroît affirmé à ces peuples: Nous vous donnons et nous vous garantissons votre indépendance dans le cadre de l'Union française, sans aucune espèce de réticence et sans vouloir la diminuer. Et parce que vous appartenez à l'Union française, nous sommes vos amis, nous sommes à côté de vous et nous vous protégerons contre les risques que court votre jeune indépendance.

Je vous le demande, que resterait-il de l'Union française à partir du jour où vous auriez délibérément déclaré que décidément vous allez quitter l'Indochine?

Et si l'on me dit: 'Vous retrouverez des troupes disponibles qui pourront assurer le maintien de l'ordre dans d'autres secteurs où vous pourrez rencontrer des difficultés', je répondrai que j'attache infiniment plus d'importance aux hommes qui, en Afrique du Nord, comme en Afrique noire, comme ailleurs, ont confiance dans la parole de la France.

Que resterait-il de cette confiance le jour où, parce que le poids de notre fardeau est lourd, nous aurions abandonné nos amis du Viet-Nam, du Cambodge, du Laos, auxquels nous avons donné aussi notre parole?

Je crois qu'à partir de ce jour-là, il ne resterait plus grand-chose de l'Union française.

Je le répète, l'Indochine n'est pas pour nous ce que la Corée peut être pour les États-Unis d'Amérique. L'Indochine, encore une fois, est une terre où nous sommes depuis près d'un siècle, où se sont créés entre la vieille terre de France et ces vieilles terres d'Asie mille et un liens. Une contexture extrêmement étroite y lie non seulement les intérêts, mais les familles, et toute une structure d'œuvres de tous genres et en particulier d'actions culturelles y a été édifiée. Nous ne pouvons pas rayer tout cela d'un trait de plume. Des citoyens français vivent dans ces pays, où vivent aussi des Eurasiens sur lesquels l'Assemblée, avec tant de raison, attire très souvent l'attention du Gouvernement, et des citoyens français d'origine vietnamienne. Qui donc peut imaginer que tout cela ne représente subitement rien pour la France, que cela ne représente pas non seulement un capital économique mais un capital moral énorme et qu'on peut ainsi, tout d'un coup, déclarer qu'on va s'en aller?

Devant un certain nombre de considérations de ce genre, les optimistes sont ceux qui voudraient faire croire à l'Assemblée qu'on peut s'en aller

---

[1] *Documents* (R.I.I.A.) for 1949–50, p. 596.

ainsi de l'Indochine, un beau matin, alors que la vérité est parfaitement opposée. Si désagréable, si dure qu'elle soit, il vaut mieux la regarder en face et prendre les dispositions nécessaires pour y faire front, plutôt que de laisser croire au pays que je ne sais quelle lassitude justifierait brusquement tous les abandons.

Cela dit, que faut-il alors faire?

Il faut, tout en recherchant avec une attention sans défaillance — et là je suis pleinement d'accord avec M. Defferre — toutes les occasions possibles d'une solution convenable, pour suivre notre effort.

Je dois dire, parce que je veux être franc, qu'il est une solution à laquelle je ne puis me rallier, et pourtant elle m'a parfois été suggérée par des esprits dont la générosité et l'honnêteté n'étaient pas douteuses et j'ai parfois été tenté de les suivre.

On m'a dit souvent: Pourquoi ne faites-vous pas appel à Ho Chi Minh? Pourquoi ne lui déclarez-vous pas que nous sommes prêts à traiter? S'il ne vous répond pas — et, m'ont dit beaucoup de ces amis, nous croyons qu'il ne vous répondra pas — du moins notre conscience sera-t-elle soulagée d'un grand poids; nous serons assurés que ce combat, ce n'est pas nous qui l'avons recherché et l'avons voulu, mais qu'il nous est vraiment imposé; alors, derrière vous, nous serons unanimes.

Nous ne pouvons pas suivre ce raisonnement. Je suis monté bien des fois à cette tribune pour parler de l'Indochine. A chaque occasion, j'ai souligné la volonté de paix de la France. Cette volonté n'est pas douteuse, elle est éclatante et personne ne peut la mettre en question.

Cependant, j'affirme que si, aujourd'hui, nous faisions un appel solennel à Ho Chi Minh, et parce que je suis comme vous certain qu'il ne répondrait pas, nous aurions perdu sans doute le souvenir d'événements que mon prédécesseur à la rue Oudinot n'a pu, lui, oublier, à savoir le *modus vivendi* de septembre 1946 qui n'a servi qu'à une chose: permettre au Viet Minh, par sa duplicité et sa fourberie, d'organiser l'insécurité absolue de nos troupes, partout où elles avaient été engagées en vertu dudit *modus vivendi*. C'est à partir du mois de novembre 1946, jusqu'au coup du 19 décembre 1946, que cette guerre nous a été imposée par Ho Chi Minh. . . .

Je disais donc que si cette formule séduit beaucoup d'esprits généreux, si vous faisiez cet appel solennel, le seul et unique résultat que vous obtiendriez — car l'expérience a déjà été faite, précisément en 1946 — est que, d'une part, vous briseriez le moral du corps expéditionnaire et que, d'autre part, vous jetteriez d'un bout à l'autre de l'Indochine toutes les populations du Cambodge, du Laos et du Viet-Nam dans une panique effroyable, parce qu'elles sauraient, à partir de ce moment-là, que vous allez le lendemain les livrer à Ho Chi Minh.

Par conséquent, vous placeriez notre corps expéditionnaire dans une insécurite généralisée, du Nord au Sud et de l'Est à l'Ouest.

Autant je crois nécessaire, encore une fois, de rechercher tout moyen pour mettre fin à cette guerre, autant je dois vous demander de vous méfier terriblement de ce genre d'appel solennel, car il pourrait avoir des conséquences strictement opposées à celles que, en toute bonne foi et en toute honnêteté, vous recherchez. . . .

Que faut-il donc faire? Il faut faire ce qui est indiqué dans le rapport de la mission parlementaire, il faut tenir.

Mais, puisque nous savons que cet effort a une incidence grave sur les responsabilités que nous avons à assumer ailleurs, il faut tenir en faisant tout l'effort nécessaire pour que, peu à peu, nous soyons suppléés dans cet effort par les troupes nationales de ces États. . . .

Qu'on ne dise pas que cela est un rêve et que ce n'est pas logique. La logique veut que le Cambodge, le Laos et le Viet-Nam, qui sont les premiers intéressés à être protégés contre la tyrannie communiste, à ce que l'ordre et la liberté soient rétablis sur leurs territoires, y prennent une part majeure.

Et puisqu'ils sont indépendants — nous ne leur contestons pas cette indépendance, nous avons sur ce point la conscience pure, et cette politique n'est concevable en effet que si l'indépendance donnée à ces États n'est ni contestée, ni contestable — puisqu'ils sont indépendants, dis-je, leur premier devoir, que veut la logique, est d'accomplir leur propre effort pour préserver ce que, avec nous, ils estiment essentiel, l'indépendance de leur patrie et la liberté de leurs citoyens. . . .

Il faudra alors que nous restions, avec un effort singulièrement moindre, à leurs côtés, pour les aider dans cette défense si dure, mais les proportions seront à ce moment renversées.

Qu'on ne dise pas que c'est impossible, car le maréchal de Lattre de Tassigny a fait cette démonstration qu'un homme qui a la foi parvient vraiment à réaliser des choses auxquelles personne ne voulait croire avant lui. . . .

C'est ainsi qu'il a fait l'armée nationale vietnamienne parce qu'il a cru, et tous ceux qui, étant allés il y a quinze mois en Indochine, y sont retournés ces temps derniers, après son passage là-bas, sont unanimes à rendre ce témoignage que nous avons enfin vu sortir de terre quelque chose qui constitue vraiment une armée nationale.

Certes, tout n'est pas parfait, il reste encore beaucoup de difficultés. Mais il y a des bataillons, dont beaucoup sont entièrement encadrés par des Vietnamiens et qui, engagés seuls souvent contre le Viet-Minh dans des combats particulièrement difficiles, ont admirablement tenu, et c'est une preuve que rien n'est impossible, c'est la preuve qu'avec de la volonté et de la foi nous arriverons à faire cette armée nationale.

Quel est le problème qui nous préoccupe le plus? C'est le problème de nos cadres; ce n'est pas même celui de nos cadres supérieurs, c'est celui de nos cadres subalternes. Ces sous-officiers, ces aspirants, ces sous-lieutenants, ces lieutenants, ces jeunes capitaines, la démonstration a été faite tout au cours de l'année que l'armée vietnamienne est capable d'en avoir, et très rapidement.

Ainsi, je le répète, avec de la volonté, on peut obtenir à cet égard des résultats qui constitueront incontestablement pour nous l'allègement qui nous est indispensable.

Cela, il faut le faire, mais en affirmant cette volonté de la France de demeurer et en poursuivant cette politique d'allègement de notre propre effort. Alors nous découragerons le Viet-Minh lui-même, et ce n'est qu'à ce moment-là que vous aurez la chance de le voir peut-être venir vous demander comment l'on peut sortir de cette affaire.

Autrement, vous n'avez aucune espèce de chance, et vous n'en avez probablement même pas sur le plan international, car je crois aussi à la nécessité de rechercher sur le plan international, si les données nous en sont fournies, une solution à ce problème angoissant.

Et puis, on me dit: Mais si l'on veut alléger notre effort, pourquoi ne pas demander aux alliés, qui sont aussi intéressés que nous à la défense du monde libre, de prendre dès maintenant leur part effective dans le combat?

C'est parce que d'abord, dans l'immédiat, le problème se pose d'une manière telle que nous sommes à peu près assurés de la réponse qui nous sera faite, car vous savez fort bien qu'en particulier dans le cadre des Nations Unies le problème tel qu'il est posé en Indochine apparaîtra toujours à des hommes soucieux de formules comme un problème interne à l'Union française.

Cependant, nous n'avons pas cessé de parler avec nos alliés — et d'ailleurs d'arriver aux résultats dont je vous parlais tout à l'heure — pour obtenir d'eux que, dans tous les domaines où cela est aujourd'hui compatible avec la forme du conflit, où cela est compatible avec les responsabilités propres à la France, nous soyons assurés d'un appui qui tout de même nous apporte un soulagement non négligeable.

Ensuite et surtout, nous n'avons pas ménagé nos efforts pour essayer d'obtenir de nos amis et alliés des garanties et des engagements précis pour le cas où cette guerre se transformerait vraiment en une guerre internationale par l'envahissement du Tonkin par l'étranger. Nous n'avons pas eu de cesse et nous n'avons pas de cesse que nous n'obtenions sur ce plan des garanties extrêmement formelles.

Je ne puis rien dire, naturellement, à l'Assemblée sur l'état actuel de ces conversations. Ce que je puis dire, c'est qu'elles ont progressé d'une manière incontestablement favorable, en particulier depuis le voyage du maréchal de Lattre de Tassigny à Washington.[1]

[1] See *Documents* (R.I.I.A.) for 1951, p. 673.

к k

J'ajoute qu'il n'a tout de même pas été inutile d'entendre l'autre jour M. Eden déclarer avec tant de solennité que toute espèce d'agression qui pourrait être commise de nouveau dans le Sud-Est asiatique risquerait de comporter des conséquences redoutables pour l'agresseur éventuel.[1]

C'est là un engagement que nous avons noté, et nous espérons que nous obtiendrons dans les semaines qui vont venir tous les engagements que l'importance de la lutte que nous menons pour le monde libre nous autorise à demander.

Mais vis-à-vis des gouvernements des États associés, j'ai dit que nous pouvions et devions obtenir d'eux un effort, parce que les sacrifices que nous faisons nous permettent tout de même de parler avec quelque fermeté.

Ce n'est pas moi qui contesterai jamais l'indépendance qui a été donnée à ces pays, et je rassure M. Dronne en disant que c'est dans le cadre des accords signés que j'entends mener cette politique.

J'entends la mener avec le maximum de libéralisme, car il ne faut pas que cette indépendance soit contestable, mais nous demandons à ces pays simplement d'exercer cette indépendance à plein, par des mains intègres et par des gens soucieux du bien public. Nous leur demandons de bien vouloir constater et déclarer que ce n'est pas contre la France qu'ils défendront leur indépendance, mais avec la France, grâce à la présence de la France, grâce à l'amitié de la France, et que plus ils essayeront de délier les liens qui les unissent à la France, plus ils assureront la perte de leur indépendance.

Tout cela, nous avons le droit de le dire, comme nous avons le droit de rappeler avec suffisamment de clarté que les immenses efforts faits par la France depuis près d'un siècle dans ce pays nous donnent quelque droit d'y maintenir une action culturelle et de demander que le travail des Français y soit protégé.

Nous avons le droit de le dire, mais nous ne pouvons le dire que si nous sommes nous-mêmes intégralement fidèles à nos promesses et si nous ne gênons pas dans son action la jeune indépendance de ces États.

(ii) Statement at a press conference by Mr. Acheson regarding the French struggle in Indo-China, 18 June 1952[2]

As you are aware, M. Jean Letourneau, Minister of the Associated States for the French Government, has been spending the last few days in Washington exchanging views with representatives of various agencies of this Government. The Ambassadors of Cambodia and Vietnam have also participated in conversations with M. Letourneau and with our own representatives.

[1]   See above, p. 45.   [2] *Department of State Bulletin*, 30 June 1952, pp. 1009–10.

A communiqué covering the substance of the talks will be issued later today and I will therefore not go into details now. Yet I would like to share with you the feeling of encouragement and confidence which M. Letourneau inspires. His thorough grasp of the situation and his constructive approach to the problems involved—military, political, and economic—have impressed us all.

As you know, the Communist aggression in Indochina has been going on for 6 years. It has been greatly stepped up because of assistance received from Communist China during the past 2 years. Yet, under French leadership, the threat to this part of the free world has been met with great courage and admirable resourcefulness. The military situation appears to be developing favorably. It has been good to hear from M. Letourneau of the part played in achieving this result by the considerable quantities of American arms and matériel which the magnificent fighting qualities of the French Union forces, including those of the Associated States, have justified us in devoting to this area of the struggle against Communist aggression. The effort to make of Vietnam, Laos and Cambodia secure and prosperous members of the free world community has made great progress.

I have been particularly impressed by what M. Letourneau has told me of what is being done to enable the people of the three Associated States to play the constantly greater role in their own defense to which they rightly aspire. Much has been accomplished toward the creation, training, and equipping of the national armies. Units of these armies have distinguished themselves in battle and are performing vital security functions in many parts of the country. They look forward with confidence and determination to assuming an increasing share of the burden of carrying on the struggle. Their effectiveness fully justifies the program of expansion to which the governments concerned are committed and underlies, I believe, the soundness of our own decision, subject of course to the availability of congressional appropriations, to render increasing assistance in building these armies. M. Letourneau described these programs in the course of his address before the overseas writers yesterday.

Favourable developments have not been confined to the fighting fronts and to the national armies. There are increasing evidences of the growing vitality of the Associated States in handling their political, financial, and economic affairs. M. Letourneau's account of the manner in which these new member States of the French Union are envisaging and meeting their responsibilities was heartening. I do not think it is generally realized to what extent these new states in fact control their own affairs. Only a limited number of services related to the necessities of the war remain temporarily in French hands.

We in the United States are aware of the vital importance of the struggle in Indochina to the cause of the free world. We have earmarked for Indochina economic and matériel aid to a considerable amount during the past 2 years. We are doing our best to activate deliveries. As you are aware the 150th ship bearing American arms and munitions to Indochina arrived in Saigon within the last few weeks. We are now bearing a considerable portion of the total burden of the war in Indochina expressed in financial terms, although of course the entire combat burden is being carried by the French Union and the Associated States, with the latter assuming a constantly increasing share.

The Communists have made a most determined effort in Indochina. Their aggression has been checked and recent indications warrant the view that the tide is now moving in our favor. Once again the policy of meeting aggression with force is paying off, and we can I believe be confident that as we carry out the plans upon which we have agreed we can anticipate continued favourable developments in the maintenance and consolidation of the free world bulwark in Indochina.

(iii) COMMUNIQUÉ ISSUED AFTER THE TALKS BETWEEN M. LETOURNEAU AND MEMBERS OF THE UNITED STATES GOVERNMENT, WASHINGTON, 18 JUNE 1952[1]

Mr. Jean Letourneau, Minister in the French Cabinet for the Associated States in Indochina, has just concluded a series of conversations with U.S. Government officials from the Department of State, Department of Defense, the Office of Director for Mutual Security, the Mutual Security Agency, and Department of the Treasury. The Ambassadors of Cambodia and Viet-Nam have also participated in these talks.

The principle which governed this frank and detailed exchange of views and information was the common recognition that the struggle in which the forces of the French Union and the Associated States are engaged against the forces of Communist aggression in Indochina is an integral part of the world-wide resistance by the Free Nations to Communist attempts at conquest and subversion. There was unanimous satisfaction over the vigorous and successful course of military operations, in spite of the continuous comfort and aid received by the Communist forces of the Viet-Minh from Communist China. The excellent performance of the Associated States' forces in battle was found to be a source of particular encouragement. Special tribute was paid to the 52,000 officers and men of the French Union and Associated States' armies who have been lost in this six years' struggle for freedom in Southeast Asia and to the 75,000 other casualties.

---

[1] *Department of State Bulletin*, 30 June 1952, p. 1010.

In this common struggle, however, history, strategic factors, as well as local and general resources require that the free countries concerned each assume primary responsibility for resistance in the specific areas where Communism has resorted to force of arms. Thus the United States assumes a large share of the burden in Korea while France has the primary role in Indochina. The partners, however, recognize the obligation to help each other in their areas of primary responsibility to the extent of their capabilities and within the limitations imposed by their global obligations as well as by the requirements in their own areas of special responsibility. It was agreed that success in this continuing struggle would entail an increase in the common effort and that the United States for its part will, therefore, within the limitations set by Congress, take steps to expand its aid to the French Union. It was further agreed that this increased assistance over and above present U.S. aid for Indochina, which now approximates one third of the total cost of Indochina operations, would be especially devoted to assisting France in the building of the national armies of the Associated States.

Mr. Letourneau reviewed the facts which amply demonstrate the determination of the Associated States to pursue with increased energy the strengthening of their authority and integrity both against internal subversion and against external aggression.

In this connection Mr. Letourneau reminded the participants that the accords of 1949, which established the independence within the French Union of Cambodia, Laos and Viet-Nam,[1] have been liberally interpreted and supplemented by other agreements, thus consolidating this independence. Mr. Letourneau pointed out that the governments of the Associated States now exercise full authority except that a strictly limited number of services related to the necessities of the war now in progress remain temporarily in French hands. In the course of the examination of the Far Eastern economic and trade situation, it was noted that the Governments of the Associated States are free to negotiate trade treaties and agreements of all kinds with their neighbors subject only to whatever special arrangements may be agreed between members of the French Union.

It was noted that these states have been recognized by thirty-three foreign governments.

The conversations reaffirmed the common determination of the participants to prosecute the defense of Indochina and their confidence in a free, peaceful and prosperous future for Cambodia, Laos, and Viet-Nam.

Mr. Letourneau was received by the President, Mr. Acheson, and Mr. Foster, as Acting Secretary of Defense. Mr. John Allison, Assistant Secretary of State for Far Eastern Affairs, acted as Chairman of the U.S. Delegation participating in the conversations.

[1] *Documents* (R.I.I.A.) for 1949–50, p. 596.

(iv) Resolution on Indo-China adopted by the North Atlantic Council on 17 December 1952[1]

THE NORTH ATLANTIC COUNCIL

RECOGNISES that resistance to direct or indirect aggression in any part of the world is an essential contribution to the common security of the free world;

HAVING BEEN informed at its meeting in Paris on the 16th December of the latest developments in the military and political situation in Indo-China;

EXPRESSES its wholehearted admiration for the valiant and long continued struggle by the French forces and the armies of the Associated States against Communist aggression; and

ACKNOWLEDGES that the resistance of the free nations in South-East Asia as in Korea is in fullest harmony with the aims and ideals of the Atlantic Community;

AND THEREFORE AGREES that the campaign waged by the French Union forces in Indo-China deserves continuing support from the NATO governments.

3. Malaya

(i) Extracts from a speech to the Malayan Federal Legislative Council by the High Commissioner for Malaya, General Sir Gerald Templer, explaining his plans for ending the emergency and uniting the country, 19 March 1952[2]

Our task in this forthcoming session of Council will be to do all in our power to develop and give expression to this Malayan ideal.

We must make sure that what is done in this Council takes itself right down to the ground amongst all classes and communities.

The year 1952 will see determined efforts made not only to interpret the Government to these people but also to persuade them by tangible evidence that the Malayan way of life of which I have spoken has far more to offer than any imported social and political creeds under whose influence they may, through fear or ignorance, have fallen.

These determined efforts will be made on certain general lines.

These lines have been considered most deeply both by the Deputy High Commissioner and myself in the nine weeks during which we have been intensively studying this problem.

---

[1] Great Britain: Foreign Office: *Report of the North Atlantic Council Meeting, Paris, 15th/18th December, 1952* (Cmd. 8732) (London, H.M.S.O., 1953), Annex C, p. 8.
[2] *Straits Times*, 20 March 1952.

Critics may consider that this is insufficient even to reach certain general conclusions.

I disagree.

I believe the general conclusions to be sound, though the methods by which those conclusions will be brought into operation are in many cases fraught with difficulty.

It is obvious that the conclusions at which we have arrived are based on the directive which has been given to me by Her Majesty's Government.[1] It is a document sometimes referred to as 'my directive' or 'the High Commissioner's directive'.

It is not mine. I venture to suggest it is ours—yours and mine. . . .

The restoration of law and order was given to me as my—as our—first task.

To pretend that we can go as far or as fast as we should wish in certain directions unless and until the rule of law and order is restored throughout the land is merely to make a mockery of the ideals for which we are striving.

I said a moment ago that it was impossible to divorce the Emergency element of Government from the normal peace-time process. It is for this reason that the Federal War Council has been abolished.

We can only have one policy-making body in the Federation today. This change will place heavy and added responsibilities on the Executive Council as a body.

In the Federal Executive Council and in this Council must lie the responsibility for the evolution of Federal policy. . . .

There must one day be armed forces belonging to the Federation as a whole and of which all communities in the nation are proud.

All communities are unlikely to feel pride in their armed forces unless those forces contain elements at least of all those communities.

It will, therefore, be one of my main objectives to start off, even in a small way at the beginning, a Federation army containing, on the one hand and certainly as the elder brother, the Malay Regiment, of which we are so proud, and on the other hand, as the younger brother, an entity open to all communities, and which I suggest might be called the Federation Regiment.

Needless to say, this will not affect present plans for an increase in the strength of the Malay Regiment. . . .

Circumstances have forced upon us an experiment in the resettlement of some 400,000 people.

Perforce, the process has been a hurried one and without the opportunity for careful sociological and economic survey and planning which would normally precede so abrupt a disturbance of a long established pattern of rural life.

[1] *Documents* (R.I.I.A.) for 1951, p. 675.

Many social, economic and administrative problems demand our close and urgent attention if these new communities are to grow up as strong and healthy members of the corporate body of the Federation.

None of these problems is, I believe, of greater importance than that of land holding.

The tenure of land is, and always has been, a fundamental stabilising influence in the life of any country.

If these new agricultural communities are to be happy and enterprising they must have reasonable security in the tenure of their land.

It will be our aim to ensure this for every community in the country and that aim will be vigorously pursued. . . .

I firmly believe, from the bottom of my heart, in the principle of responsible local Government by local people.

I will do all in my power to foster this, and the quicker we can start on it the better. That is the firm foundation on which political progress must be based.

If it is not based on this principle, what is the future?

It is, therefore, proposed to lay on the table of this Council during the present session a statement showing the extent to which the development plans, as originally envisaged, have been retarded on account of the circumstances of the Emergency.

Now these principles which I have outlined are aimed at one thing and one thing only, the formation of a united Malayan nation in which the inhabitants are at peace with each other and in a common loyalty to the decent rules of law and order under which they live, or at least will live in the future.

It is my duty to guide the peoples of Malaya towards this object. To attain it, there will be a need for a considerable amount of give-and-take on all sides. It will require the energies and the support of all men of goodwill.

And above all, it must be achieved without any question of inter-community fear or mistrusts or dislike.

Perhaps some honourable Members will think that I am aiming high; that I am being unduly optimistic.

I will not take counsel of these fears.

Even after my short experience of this country and even in spite of the short time that the problem has been before me, there is one thing I am absolutely certain about; and that is that the only future of this country can lie in the direction of a common citizenship, and a common loyalty and a mutual respect and trust between the various communities.

Anyone who denies that, or works against it, is doing a deep disservice to the people of this land. . . .

I know of no way of ensuring that a proper agricultural and irrigation and forestry programme is developed in any country unless it be along the lines of a general pattern laid down for the country as a whole by the central government in consultation with the various states and settlements, and based on the advice of the best experts available.

The next requisite is that this general pattern is loyally accepted and carried out with sincerity throughout the land. If this is not accepted, real progress over a term of years cannot be made.

The fall of production occasioned by the resettlement of so-called 'squatters' has been serious. Production, however, is now beginning to increase again.

In the present session, I hope a Bill will be placed before the Council designed to deal with the suppression of crop diseases and another Federal Bill on the subject of irrigation areas. Both these are important measures. . . .

The gross surplus of the Government of the Federation on December 31, 1951, amounted to $433 million, out of which a reserve of $80 million has been set up to meet liabilities already incurred.

Customs revenue for the first two months of this year amounted to $86,940,969, which is $11,121,551 in excess of the estimate, but against this supplementary expenditure amounting to over $46,000,000, of which $18,500,000 is on account of defence and the Emergency, has already been approved by the standing committee on finance or has been recommended to this Council for approval since the beginning of the year.

It is clear that with the possibility before us of a sharp fall in the prices of our primary products and consequently in our revenue, all possible methods of economy that are consistent with our objectives in relation to the Emergency and the economic and social advancement of the people of this country should be examined.

I am making an urgent approach to the Colonial Office, in an endeavour to increase our organisation and methods staff, which although it has done very valuable work, is too small to tackle the enormous task of overhauling the administrative machinery of the whole Government which confronts it. . . .

(ii) EXTRACTS FROM A SPEECH IN THE HOUSE OF COMMONS BY THE COLONIAL SECRETARY, MR. OLIVER LYTTELTON, ON THE SITUATION IN MALAYA, 17 JULY 1952[1]

The last question was that of Malaya, and this is the last part of the subject with which I shall detain the Committee. I am glad the right hon. Gentleman[2] has raised it. When I succeeded the right hon. Gentleman

[1] H.C. Deb. 5th Ser. vol. 503, coll. 2378–82.
[2] Mr. James Griffiths, Colonial Secretary in the Labour Government.

at the Colonial Office, I regarded the Malayan problem as the most urgent and obdurate in the Colonial Territories; therefore I visited Malaya as soon as I could. I must say quite bluntly that few of the instruments of policy with which we were then attempting to handle this exceedingly complicated, delicate political and military problem were, in my opinion, adequate to the task, but the work of the British Army and British Commonwealth and colonial troops was of a high order and excited my admiration.

As in all human affairs, the political and social aspects of the problem over any long period are naturally of predominant importance, but at the same time we have to restore the country to a state of law and order, and in doing so we must never for a moment lose sight of our long-term political and social objectives. I shall come back to that subject.

When I had studied as intensively as I could the Malayan scene, I came to the conclusion that there were six matters, all involving major policy or major administrative matters, upon which we must concentrate, and I so reported to my colleagues. These are the recommendations upon which General Templer has, in the main, been working. In addition to my main six recommendations, there were 14 subsidiary matters of hardly less importance upon which I thought that urgent consideration and action must be taken. Clearly, I cannot go into them now, but I will pick out two at random to show the range of these subjects: the re-organisation of the intelligence, information and propaganda system and, in a widely different field, the prevention of tax evasion. These are two out of the 14 subjects.

The six points were these. First of all, the chain of command from the centre was imperfect. It was no good trying to deal with military and political matters in what was, in effect, two branches in Malaya as it was. Responsibility for both must be concentrated in one man, and now is. It is at the same time necessary that that man should be relieved of much of the civil administration, routine in particular, and should only have to consider civil matters—rather like a Cabinet—where they affect broad questions of policy and not detailed administration. It was for this reason that I persuaded the Rulers to agree to an alteration in the constitution, under which Mr. MacGillivray was appointed Deputy High Commissioner, and he has relieved the High Commissioner of much of the civil work.

Secondly, the Police Force was in need of urgent re-training and re-organisation. It had expanded to an almost unbelievable extent, far in advance of any measures designed to control it, co-ordinate it or train it. Moreover, it was all committed to the field—as we say in military parlance—and I have to say that it was largely in a haphazard manner. The Committee knows that the number of armed terrorists is somewhere between 3,500 and 5,000—a figure mentioned by the right hon. Gentleman.

MR. J. GRIFFITHS: Between 5,000 and 6,000.

MR. LYTTELTON: I think there were fewer than 5,000. I doubt whether there are as many as 6,000, but that is a matter of conjecture. Let us take the figure as 4,000 to 6,000. There were no fewer than 60,000 regular police, of which 38,000 were whole-time special constables, and about 250,000 part-time police, including the Home Guard. Why I emphasise that these were all committed is to give the Committee an idea of the difficulties involved in re-training and re-grouping such a large force. This matter has been tackled with the utmost energy and resolution and after four years there is some knitting together of these forces. Colonel Young of the City of London Police is in charge under the High Commissioner.

My third point is with regard to the organisation of a Home Guard. It is axiomatic that we must gain the support and help of the Chinese population and involve them much more deeply in the defence of a country in which they have so large a stake. Every hon. Member who is interested in the Malayan problem will know that one of the difficulties is that 95 per cent of the terrorists are Chinese and 95 per cent of the police were Malays. We are changing that. About one-third of the Home Guard is now Chinese and they are being encouraged to join the police. My latest reports are encouraging.

My fourth subject which was mentioned by the right hon. Gentleman concerns the protection of what were originally known as re-settlement areas, and which have, I think wisely, been re-christened 'new villages', because that is what they are. They have not only been re-christened, but altered. When I saw the state of the defences of these new villages it was deplorable. This matter, too, has been tackled with the greatest vigour, and although the defences are not yet complete, they are in an entirely different state from what they were at the end of last year. They are not completed yet, but when they have been completed the inhabitants can feel reasonably secure inside well-lighted and well-wired fences. This measure alone has obliged the enemy to split up into smaller groups, and he finds it increasingly difficult to get food at the point of the tommy gun by terrorising the inhabitants.

The next point is that of administration generally. I found that the conditions under which the Malayan Civil Service had to work could not be accepted. The housing shortage was acute. As an example, I heard of an officer, with his wife and two children, who, on returning from leave, had been posted to a new district. The only quarters they could find were over a Chinese shop, and I do not feel sure that the trade in that shop was entirely confined to inanimate commodities. One can think of the effect on the Service when those are the housing conditions.

The rapid rise in the cost of living had rendered the pay code, which was fairly rigid, unsuited to today's conditions, and exasperation among the Civil Service was mounting. I think their conditions are still hard, but they have been greatly improved. The Civil Service as a whole is very much over-strained, and while they were putting out super-human efforts during the emergency the machine had become clogged and paper-bound. I remember flying for 45 minutes in an Auster aircraft when going to Bantong in Pahang, and seeing some 20 or 30 planters and others, and being told that I was the only person from Kuala Lumpur, other than the High Commissioner himself, whom they had seen ever since the beginning of the emergency. . . .

It was obvious, under those circumstances, that a re-organisation of the duties of the administrative machine was long overdue. Further decentralisation, further recruitment and a quicker and more muscular organisation were as urgent as the other measures which I have outlined.

My last point, which is as important as all the others, is about education. If we are to win the war of ideas, and weld the widely conflicting interests and nationalities into a coherent whole, we can only hope to do it by pushing ahead as fast as we can with compulsory primary education; bringing the people together when they are children, and teaching them that they are citizens of Malaya first and foremost, owing their allegiance to the country of their birth and not the country of their parents' origin.

(iii) EXTRACTS FROM A STATEMENT TO THE PRESS BY SIR GERALD TEMPLER ON THE CAMPAIGN IN MALAYA, LONDON, 4 DECEMBER 1952[1]

There has been a marked decline recently in terrorist overt activity. And what is particularly encouraging is that the decline was not of their own choosing. We know now that as long ago as October 1951 the Communist Central Committee decided on a change of plan. As a result they instructed their branches to give up to a large extent indiscriminate terrorism and sabotage, and to concentrate instead on insidious subversion. Their main reasons were that the terrorist campaign had turned the masses of the people against them, and the improved security measures had rendered the whole business too dangerous. Like all changes in Communist party line it was a piece of purely cynical opportunism, forced upon them by our counter measures. These have been helped greatly by a growing confidence among the public generally. This growing confidence has had one very important result—we are getting higher grade voluntary information about the Communist terrorists from the public. That information is being more efficiently collated and can, therefore, be

---

[1] General Office of Information: Reference Division: *Progress of the Campaign in Malaya* (no. R. 2515), 4 December 1952.

used more effectively. Just how effectively is illustrated by the fact that during October our forces made 36 contacts with terrorists as a direct result of information supplied by the public. And on those 36 contacts 35 terrorists were killed.

The population's greater feeling of security is due in part to our steady successes against the enemy and in part to the many reforms the Government has introduced. Of these I shall speak later.

While there has been less sabotage of the country's industries and vital communications, our casualties—both among Security Forces and civilians—have been fewer, and those of the terrorists have increased in numbers and quality. By quality I mean that we are getting rid of more high-ranking Communist leaders.

In my report to the Legislative Council on November 19[1] I gave some figures that spoke for themselves. You will find these in the statistical note at Appendix A.[2] In every single instance the figures show an encouraging improvement and while the enemy casualties have gone up our own Security Forces casualties have been almost halved.

All of us in Malaya concerned with Operations against the Communist terrorists attach great importance to surrenders, because every one of the enemy who comes out of the jungle and gives himself up is not only a source of valuable information that may help the Security Forces, but he is also a potential ally in our campaign.

As you probably know, we have stepped up our psychological warfare directed towards the jungle. Recently, for instance, we have been using a 'voice plane' to broadcast messages from surrendered terrorists to their comrades in the jungle, and first results have been encouraging. It is, of course, difficult to assess accurately the state of the enemy's morale, but we have reason to believe that at least some of them are weakening and are ready to come over at the first opportunity. Time will tell. Meantime we are exploiting soft spots in their morale as they are exposed by our own intelligence sources and by surrendered terrorists.

There is, however, nothing to suggest that because of the hard knocks we have given them the Communist terrorist leaders intend to call off completely the shooting war. The evidence, indeed, is all to the contrary. We expect them to persist with their armed and more selective terrorism, and all our planning is based on that assumption. We cannot tell how long the battle will be, but we shall certainly go on until it is won beyond all shadow of doubt.

And now let me acknowledge the valuable help received in resources and funds not only from the peoples of the Federation, but also from the United Kingdom and from the British Commonwealth. These, I believe, are beginning to produce solid results, not only in the present battle

[1] *Straits Times*, 20 November 1952. [2] Not printed here.

against Communist terrorism, (which must continue to be our first objective) but also in the broader field of the welfare and unity of the Malayan peoples, which is our long-term objective. Not until the first objective is achieved beyond all doubt, can our full resources and energies be devoted to the long-range objective. I keep on emphasising that everywhere I go in Malaya, and I believe its truth is accepted by all except the terrorists, their Communist supporters and those whose thinking has been blunted by terrorist intimidation and threats. . . .

In the midst of what continues to be a grave Emergency, we are looking ahead to the time when Malaya is ready for self-government as laid down in several declarations made on behalf of Her Majesty's Government. We have, therefore, a broad concept for a Federation Army. We believe that an essential pre-requisite of eventual self-government is the training and equipping in sufficient numbers of Malaya's own forces so that they can be relied upon to maintain law and order internally and play a major part in deterring an external aggressor.

We made a practical start with the Federation Army concept in August this year, when recruiting began for the Federation Regiment in which Malays, Chinese, Indians and Eurasians can serve their country. Eight hundred and twenty-four men then applied to join. The first company is already in training. Within a few years we envisage three battalions, growing in strength and efficiency as finance, training facilities and man-power become available.

Side by side with the Federation Regiment, we have the Federation Armoured Corps. Whereas the Federation Regiment started from scratch, the Armoured Corps was able to draw on trained infantry soldiers from the Malay Regiment. The decision to raise an armoured corps was taken in the first week of August this year, and seven weeks later the first squadron was operational. Squadrons will form up as a regiment in 1954, and we envisage an early start in forming and training other technical units such as Engineers and Signallers.

None of these developments should be allowed to detract from the achievements and loyalty of the Malay Regiment. By the end of this year this Regiment will have six battalions, and within a few years three more battalions are to be raised.

I shall not attempt to conceal our disappointment at the unbalanced racial response to the appeal for recruits for the Federation Regiment.

I explained at my last news conference in London how essential it was to detain under the Emergency Regulations certain persons suspected of being dangerous to our sustained anti-terrorist campaign. The number in custody under detention orders at the end of last January was 7,365. In November of this year it was just over 4,300. These figures represent a 49% reduction in detainees. This very substantial reduction has been achieved partly by repatriation, partly by the continued success of our three major rehabilitation centres, and partly by a more liberal policy under which we have taken some calculated risks and released—some conditionally, others completely—a number whose histories showed they were probably more terrorised than terrorist. Broadly, our policy is, (keeping in mind that with the best will in the world liberalism can be overdone when innocent people are being murdered by terrorists) to keep in custody only those who, if they were allowed out, would be almost certain to give real help to the enemy.

You will agree, I think, that the picture I have just given you justifies the sober confidence which I suggested we were entitled to feel when I last spoke to you in June. But I want to warn you against anything which could possibly be called complacency either here or in Malaya.

Even if it were true (and there is not nearly enough evidence yet to suggest it) that we were in sight of the end of the 'shooting war' in Malaya, we should still be faced with very grave and difficult problems. Malaya, like so many South East Asian countries, is going through a period of extremely rapid development, both social and political. Such periods are inevitably times of tension and it is very easy for the Communist, whose aims are purely destructive, to exploit these strains and tensions. His hope, of course, is that they can be increased to breaking point, so as to bring the whole social structure down in ruins. We must be on our guard therefore against the next move in the Communist strategy; if they should ever decide that the present attempt at open rebellion has temporarily failed, we must expect from them a new and greatly increased campaign of underground subversion. And one feature of that campaign would certainly be what is normal Communist technique—an agitation against every precaution or regulation of Government which is burdensome to the public—and of course crippling to *them*. Don't think I don't realise how burdensome some of these regulations are. Of course I do. Nobody likes putting on curfews and sending out tappers without their lunch boxes. Above all I do not like imposing collective punishments such as Permatang Tinggi; but what evidence we can get on this very difficult question shows that on the rare occasions on which they have been used, they have been justified by their results. I hope that, as the present open Communist terrorist activity is brought to an end, it will be possible to relax gradually many of these controls, but it would be folly to imagine that in such a situation they could all be thrown overboard overnight. To disarm ourselves completely would merely be to invite the Communists to start their terrorist campaign afresh at the first opportunity. . . .

One point which I should like to stress, however, is the progress made towards building up a Malayan nation. Malaya is not only a plural society, but a plural society in which the two major communities have lived almost entirely separate lives. If we are to build successfully a Malayan nation we must give some proportion of the Chinese a peasant's stake in the land and encourage some proportion of the Malays to enter commerce and industry.

In the first respect we have made a good deal of progress. All State and Settlement Governments have formulated land policies under which Chinese settlers in New Villages know that they can get a secure title, usually on a 30 years lease, to the land they till. I think that security of tenure is doing a lot to build up a Chinese peasantry. I wish I could say that our efforts to get the Chinese to join the police and Federation Armed Services on an equal footing had been as successful—that is a matter which, in their own interests, the Chinese community must tackle in the very near future. We cannot build a united nation if 81 per cent. of applications for recruitment into the Federation Regiment continue to come from a single community, the Malays.

The other side of this problem, the economic advancement of the Malays is being tackled largely by R.I.D.A., the Rural and Industrial Development Authority. Since May 1951, R.I.D.A. has advanced just over a million-and-a-quarter dollars to projects which it is hoped will ultimately become self-supporting, and made grants of two million dollars for rural development. Larger schemes approved for next year include a ship-and-boat-building yard in Kuala Trengganu at a cost of a million dollars and a rubber factory at Muar in Johore at a cost of nearly half-a-million. These big schemes are not really so typical of R.I.D.A.'s work, however, as the large number of small improvements among the kampongs which never get any publicity but mean a lot to the man on the ground.

It is clear however that the work of R.I.D.A. is not going to be enough. This creation of some sort of a political and economic balance is not going to be an easy task. We are, therefore, considering plans to set up a Development Board to tackle some of the really long-term development plans. In the end, of course, the success or failure of the whole nation building policy must depend on the Malay, Chinese and Indian Communities themselves. . . .

One formal step in nation building has been taken. In September 1952 a new law of Citizenship came into force. Like any citizenship law it is extremely complicated but its general effect is to open citizenship automatically to all non-Malays born in Malaya provided one parent was also Malayan born. Through this and other provisos between 50 and 60 per cent. of the Chinese in Malaya have become citizens by operation of law. The reactions towards this step forward have been a good indication of the sort of difficulties we have to deal with. On the whole I think it is true to say that the Malays have accepted the new Citizenship Laws with some misgivings that they go too far; while the Chinese and Indians have accepted them with some misgivings that they do not go far enough. Which is a sign, to my mind, that they have been pretty fairly drafted. Anyhow, whatever their misgivings both Chinese and Indian leaders are urging their followers to acquire citizenship. As the new generation grows up the time when the vast majority of Malaya's inhabitants will be Federal citizens cannot be far distant.

INDEX

L l 2

PRINTED IN
GREAT BRITAIN
AT THE
UNIVERSITY PRESS
OXFORD
BY
CHARLES BATEY
PRINTER
TO THE
UNIVERSITY